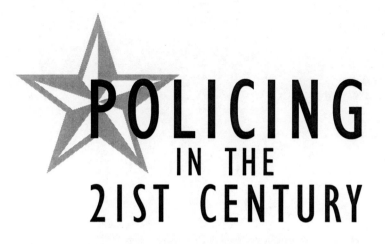

POLICING IN THE 21ST CENTURY

Community Policing

DR. LEE P. BROWN

AuthorHouse™
1663 Liberty Drive
Bloomington, IN 47403
www.authorhouse.com
Phone: 1-800-839-8640

© 2012 Dr. Lee P. Brown. All rights reserved.

No part of this book may be reproduced, stored in a retrieval system, or transmitted by any means without the written permission of the author.

Published by AuthorHouse 5/13/2013

ISBN: 978-1-4685-4097-0 (e)
ISBN: 978-1-4685-4098-7 (hc)
ISBN: 978-1-4685-4099-4 (sc)

Library of Congress Control Number: 2012900444

Any people depicted in stock imagery provided by Thinkstock are models, and such images are being used for illustrative purposes only. Certain stock imagery © Thinkstock.

This book is printed on acid-free paper.

Because of the dynamic nature of the Internet, any web addresses or links contained in this book may have changed since publication and may no longer be valid. The views expressed in this work are solely those of the author and do not necessarily reflect the views of the publisher, and the publisher hereby disclaims any responsibility for them.

DEDICATION AND ACKNOWLEDGEMENTS

Policing in the 21st Century: Community Policing is dedicated to the thousands of honorable men and women I worked with during the thirty plus years I spent as a senior law enforcement official.

They are the unsung heroes who went to work every day, often risking their lives to prevent crimes, arrest criminals, solve problems and maintain social order. They made our communities and business environments safe and livable.

The book is also dedicated to the legions of people who are presently members of the nation's law enforcement communities. It is my sincerest hope that they will embrace the philosophy of Community Policing, and continue to serve and protect the public with honor, dedication, integrity and respect.

I also want to express my appreciation to Joseph Green-Bishop for the many hours he put into editing the book. He was instrumental in getting the book completed and published. I would also like to thank Alan Bower at AuthorHouse, and his team for their numerous contributions.

Finally, special recognition goes to Ray Carrington III for taking the photograph that appears on the book's cover.

Lee P. Brown
Houston, Texas

TABLE OF CONTENTS

Preface   xvii

PART ONE

Chapter 1   Introduction   1
Changing Approaches to Policing   2
The Professional Policing Model   3
The Community Policing Model   4

Chapter 2   A Brief History of American Policing   9
Introduction   9
The British Police Experience   10
The Anglo-Saxon Era - A.D. 500 to 1066   10
The Era of the Middle Ages – A.D. 1066 to 1485   11
Tudor and Stuart Era - 1485 to 1714   11
The 18th Century   12
Henry and John Fielding   12
The 19th Century   13
Sir Robert Peel   14
The Introduction of Policing in America   18
Early American Police Patrols   19
The Initial Reform of the American Police   22
The Role of the FBI in Reforming American Policing   23
The Development of Police Professionalism   24
Summary   30

Chapter 3	The Development of Police Professionalism	35
	Introduction	35
	The President's Commission on Law Enforcement and Administration of Justice	36
	The National Commission on Civil Disorders	42
	National Advisory Commission On the Causes and Prevention of Violence	43
	National Advisory Commission on Criminal Justice Standards and Goals (1973)	45
	The American Bar Association Standards Committee	46
	The National Minority Advisory Council on Crime and Criminal Justice	46
	The National Commission on Higher Education for Police	48
	Mollen Commission to Investigate Allegations of Police Corruption and the Anti-corruption Procedures of the Police Department	52
	Independent Commission on the Los Angeles Police Department	53
	Special Advisor to the Board of Police Commissioners on Civil Disorder in Los Angeles	55
	The Professional Police Organizations	57
	International Association of Chiefs of Police	57
	The Police Executive Research Forum	57
	The National Sheriff's Association	57
	The National Organization of Black Law Enforcement Executives	57
	The Police Foundation	58
	The National Commission on Accreditation of Law Enforcement Agencies	59
	Summary	60
Chapter 4	The Era of Police Research	64
	Introduction	64
	The Law Enforcement Assistance Administration	64
	The Police Foundation	65
	The Early LEAA Studies	66
	Pilot Cities Program	66
	The New York City Patrol Initiative	67

	The Early Police Foundation Research Studies	67
	Kansas City Preventive Patrol	68
	Directed Patrol	69
	Other Police Foundation Research and Experimentation	70
	Field Interrogation Practices	71
	One Versus Two Officer Units	71
	Beat Profiling	71
	The Newark Foot Patrol Experiment	72
	Women in Policing	73
	The Rand Institute Experiments	73
	The National Institute of Justice	74
	Fear Reduction	74
	The Domestic Violence Experiment	75
	The Police Executive Research Forum	75
	Managing Calls-for-Service	75
	Problem Solving Policing	76
	Criminal Investigations	76
	Other Research	77
	The Flint Foot Patrol Experiment	77
	The Harvard Executive Session	78
	Summary	79
Chapter 5	Police and the Courts	83
	Introduction	83
	Background	84
	History of the Problem	86
	Fourth Amendment	87
	Landmark Decisions	87
	Mallory v. United States	87
	Mapp v. Ohio	89
	Gideon v. Wainwright	90
	Escobedo v. Illinois	91
	Miranda v. Arizona	93
	Terry v. Ohio	94
	Tennessee v. Garner	95
	Consent Decrees	97
	Summary	100

PART TWO
The New Policing Strategies

Chapter 6	The Evolution of Community Policing	107
	Introduction	107
	Development of Community Policing	109
	Police Community Relations Programs	110
	The San Jose Experience	119
	Crime Prevention Programs	126
	Program Example: Houston	127
	Crime Prevention Through Environmental Design	129
	Team Policing	130
	The Multnomah County Experience	133
	Problem-Oriented Policing	137
	Baltimore County	138
	Newport News	139
	Community Policing Programs	140
	Basic Car Radio Plan.	140
	Community Patrol Officer Program.	142
	Directed Area Responsibility Team.	142
	Intelligence-Led Policing	144
	Summary	145
Chapter 7	Community Policing: The Promise and the Challenge	149
	Introduction	149
	Differences Between Community Policing And Traditional Policing	150
	The Goals and Objectives of Community Policing	153
	The Principles of Community Policing	158
	Community Policing vs. Police-Community Relations	163
	Community Policing vs. Crime Prevention	163
	Community Policing vs. Problem-Solving Policing	164
	Community Policing vs. Team Policing	164
	Why Did Community Policing Develop?	165
	The Three Phases of Community Policing	166
	The Benefits of Community Policing	168
	Arguments Against Community Policing	169
	Evaluating Community Policing Successes and Effectiveness	171
	Summary	172

Chapter 8	Issues in Implementation	176
	Introduction	176
	Implementing Community Policing	176
	Program vs. Process	180
	Seven S Concept	182
	Community Policing and Values	
		187
	Staff	197
	Recruitment and Selection	198
	Recruiting in the Spirit of Service	200
	Life Themes	203
	Minority Recruiting	209
	Tips for Successful Minority Recruitment	214
	Training	217
	Definition of Training	218
	Recruit Training	221
	Supervisory Training	223
	Management training	223
	Role Changes	225
	Deployment	227
	Investigations	231
	Performance Evaluation	239
	Rewards	244
	Houston Case Study	245
	Evaluating Success and Effectiveness of Community Policing	254
	Summary	255

PART THREE
Leadership and the Development of the Profession

Chapter 9	Managing Change	263
	Introduction	263
	Understanding Change	263
	Effects of Organizational Change on the Police	267
	Defining Objectives	270
	Developing Action Plan	272
	Build new relationships	272

Discuss and Deliberate	273
Develop Shared Visions and Goals	274
Foster Social Capital	274
Ensure Broad Participation and Diversity	275
Determine Leadership Roles	275
Identify Outside Resources	276
Set Clear Boundaries	276
Draw on the Examples of Others	276
Adopt a Change Mindset	277
Summary	278

Chapter 10 Police Leadership — 281

Introduction	281
The Context of Police Leadership	282
Leadership versus Management	284
Leadership Development	289
Leadership and Vision	291
Leadership and Decision Making	292
Characteristics of Good Leadership	295
Case Study of Police Leadership: Lessons Learned	301
Summary	311

Chapter 11 Profiles in Leadership — 313

Introduction	313
August Vollmer	313
J. Edgar Hoover	315
Orlando Winfield Wilson	316
William H. Parker	318
Patrick Murphy	319
Herman Goldstein	320
Lee P. Brown	321
Summary	324

PART FOUR
Critical Issues in Policing

Chapter 12 Police Accountability — 329

Introduction	329
Political Accountability	329
Community Accountability	331

Departmental Accountability	332
Individual Accountability	332
Investigation of Citizen's Complaints.	335
Police Department Internal Affairs Unit	335
Civilian Review Boards	337
Hybrid System	338
The York City Civilian Complaint Review Board	339
Ombudsman	339
Community Control	342
Community Involvement	343
Principle	344
Tips	345
Police Integrity	346
Use of Deadly Force	355
Atlanta Case Study	360
Police and Politics	363
Chief and Mayoral Relations	364
Police and City Council Relations	367
Police and the Media	369
Summary	374
Chapter 13 Crime and Crime Control	**379**
Introduction	379
Understanding Crime	382
Fear of Crime	388
Drugs and Crime	390
Scope of the Problem	391
Coping with the Problem	391
Houston Case Study	393
Role of the Police in Controlling Crime	394
Effective Police Techniques	398
ComStat	398
Beat Profiling	400
Civil Enforcement Initiative	400
Role of the Federal Government	402
Summary	407
Chapter 14 Race Relations and Racial Profiling	**411**
Introduction	411
African Americans	411

Hispanics	416
Mexican Americans	417
Puerto Ricans	420
Cuban Americans	422
Asians	423
Chinese Americans	425
Japanese Americans	427
Filipino Americans	429
Korean Americans	430
Vietnamese Americans	431
Indian Americans	432
Racial Profiling	433
Definition	434
Racial Profiling: The Police View	435
Racial Profiling: The Minority View	436
Racial Profiling: The Solution	438
Summary	442

Chapter 15 Terrorism and Homeland Security 450

Introduction	450
Definition of Terrorism	452
Terrorist Groups	454
Domestic Terrorism	455
State Sponsored Terrorism	457
International Terrorism	457
Foreign Terrorist Organizations	457
Terrorism and the Role of Law Enforcement	466
Role of Local law Enforcement	468
Homeland Security and Community Policing	473
Houston Case Study	477
Role of Private Police	478
Intelligence	478
Role of the Media	479
Patriot Act	480
Department of Homeland Security	482
Background	483
Organization of the Department	484
State and Local Law Enforcement	487
Summary	487

Chapter 16	The Future of the Enterprise	496
	Introduction	496
	Criminal Justice System	497
	A Model Criminal Justice System: The Multnomah County Case Study	498
	Federal Law Enforcement	508
	State Law Enforcement	509
	Office of the Sheriff	510
	Local Law Enforcement	511
	Future of the Police Enterprise	512
	Community Justice	515
	Community Prosecution	516
	Case Study: Multnomah County (Portland, Oregon)	519
	Community Courts	520
	Case Study: Red Hook	522
	Community Defender Services	523
	Community Corrections	524
	Case Study: Project Safeway	526
	Community Government	528
	Case Study: Houston	528
	Summary	533
Appendix A		539
Bibliography		545
Index		573

PREFACE

Policing in the 21st Century: Community Policing is based on my three decades in law enforcement which began when I first walked a beat as a police officer in San Jose, California. I went on to serve as Sheriff of Multnomah County, Oregon; Public Safety Commissioner of Atlanta, Georgia; Police Chief of Houston, Texas; Police Commissioner of New York City; and later as a member of President Bill Clinton's Cabinet as Director of the White House Office of National Drug Control Policy. I ended my public service career by serving the maximum three terms as mayor of Houston, Texas. As mayor, I applied the concept of Community Policing to the entire government of the city, using the title Neighborhood Oriented Government.

With a Ph.D. in criminology from the University of California at Berkeley, graduating in 1970, I have throughout my career been simultaneously a student, a practitioner and an educator of law enforcement. I have, therefore, developed strong beliefs concerning how police agencies can best serve the public. These beliefs are incorporated in the concept of *Community Policing*.

For that I have been given the title of "Father of Community Policing." I have also been privileged to actively assist other police agencies as they have implemented similar efforts. For example, I introduced the concept in Portland, Oregon and have provided assistance to many other police departments throughout the United States. I introduced the concept of Community Policing in South Africa during the time of apartheid. After Nelson Mandela became President of a free South Africa, he implemented the concept. I also trained members of the Nigerian Police Force in Community Policing.

President George H. W. Bush's Administration acknowledged the importance of Community Policing by funding a consortium in 1990 which consisted of the National Sheriff's Association, the Police Executive Research Forum, the Police Foundation, and the International Association of Chiefs of Police to provide technical assistance to those law enforcement agencies throughout America that wanted to implement Community Policing. The idea of the consortium resulted from a meeting I convened as New York City's Police Commissioner. The National Organization of Black Police Executives was added to the consortium by President Bill Clinton in 1994.

Community Policing surfaced again during the 1992 presidential campaign. Presidential candidate Bill Clinton campaigned on a platform that pledged to put more police officers on the streets of America's cities. At the U.S Conference of Mayors' convention in Houston, Texas, I was scheduled to follow Mr. Clinton as a speaker. After being introduced to each other in the hallway while waiting to address the conference, Mr. Clinton told me about his plan to provide money to cities to hire 100,000 additional police officers. I emphasized to him that hiring officers was not as important as how they were used. I described what had been accomplished while I served as Police Chief in Houston and my current experiences with Community Policing in New York City.

After being elected, President Clinton was successful in getting Congress to pass legislation that provided funds for local police departments to hire 100,000 new police officers. I was especially pleased that the legislation passed by the Congress and signed by the President stipulated that the new police officers must be used to either implement or expand the concept of Community Policing. The President used the experiences of Houston, Texas and New York City as examples that should be emulated.

In addition to drawing on my own personal experiences, I have endeavored to include in **Policing in the 21st Century: Community Policing** that which has been learned from other organizations in the law enforcement and academic communities. **Policing in the 21st Century: Community Policing** incorporates useful and constructive examples of what many cities have done to implement Community Policing. I have included information that will help the reader understand not only the concept of Community Policing, but also how it should be implemented. Because **Community Policing is a concept and not a program**, it is applicable to small towns and metropolitan police departments as a style of policing.

Perhaps the paramount lesson to be learned from looking at the successes when Community Policing is implemented is the importance of support from the top levels of local government. In Portland, Oregon, the mayor and the city council mandated Community Policing. The Police Chief carried out the mandate and Portland became one of the leading cities in the nation in its implementation of the concept.

Over a short period of time, Community Policing has become the buzzword in police agencies throughout America. Many did not understand the concept when it was first introduced. Some still do not.

Fortunately, a number of Police Chiefs have taken it upon themselves to implement Community Policing. As a result, we now have a greater understanding of what Community Policing is, what it should be, and how it should be implemented. Today, hundreds of law enforcement agencies throughout America are at various stages in the process of implementing the concept.

This book is intended to provide the reader with a clear and comprehensive understanding of what Community Policing means and the advantages it offers to a police department and a community.

Policing in the 21st Century: Community Policing explores:
1. The reasons for implementing Community Policing.
2. What the ultimate goals should be.
3. The implementation steps.
4. How to evaluate the success of the implementation process.

Additionally, ***Policing in the 21st Century: Community Policing*** discusses in detail the need to change the structures that support police agencies as they execute or advance the implementation of Community Policing. This is necessary to ensure that it is institutionalized. Readers of this book will have a better understanding of the future of policing in America. They are given a clear picture of the final outcome of the movement towards Community Policing and the necessary steps that must be taken to get there. They will understand what Community Policing means for police departments and what it means for the public at large. They will understand it from an academic perspective and from the practical experiences of those who have been directly and actively involved in the development and execution of the concept.

When Community Policing reaches its final stages, many of the police practices that are held sacred today will be of lesser value. It may take a generation, if not longer, for the concept of Community Policing to become fully institutionalized throughout American police departments.

The book begins by providing a brief history of policing in both England and the United States. It then discusses important police research, police commissions and also some of the other critical issues in law enforcement today, specifically the courts, crime and its control, terrorism, homeland security, police accountability, race relations, racial profiling and leadership.

Policing in the 21st Century: Community Policing also examines the other components of the criminal justice system—prosecutors, courts and corrections—and predicts that they, too, will adopt the philosophies embedded in Community Policing. When that is accomplished, America will have a true system of justice where all components of the criminal justice system allow for community involvement and place major emphasis on crime prevention, not simply on arrests and punishment.

Policing in the 21st Century: Community Policing was written for police practitioners, students, policy makers and members of the public who have a vested interest in the performance of their local police.

The challenge for all of us is to keep focused on the role of the police in a free society and determine how all segments of society can play a role in keeping our neighborhoods safe and, in doing so, improve the quality of life for ourselves and our families. That is a responsibility that we all have. Community Policing provides the vehicle for that to occur.

This book differs from others on Community Policing because it is based on my personal experiences in law enforcement and not solely on secondary sources. Additionally, the reader has the advantage of my experience as the chief law enforcement officer in four American communities, including its largest, New York City.

Part One

Chapter One

INTRODUCTION

Community Policing is not a concept that someone thought up overnight. It has evolved from many years of law enforcement research and numerous demonstration projects, many of which have been the subject of careful and, quite often, rigorous evaluation.

Thoughtful and responsible police leaders endeavor to use resources available to them in the most effective ways. In order to do so, police administrators must approach the job of policing with fresh and open minds, not wedded exclusively to outdated concepts that they have used for long periods of time. Failure to adapt to changing circumstances and not having the advantage of ever-increasing knowledge about the non-effectiveness of traditional approaches will leave American cities under-protected and American police agencies under-utilized.

This book is about Community Policing, the strategy for law enforcement in the 21st century and beyond. It not only describes Community Policing as the future of policing in America, but also explains how the concept evolved, and how it is being implemented in various cities and smaller towns throughout the nation.

The purpose of this book is not only to discuss the concept and philosophy of Community Policing, but also to demonstrate how it should be implemented in police agencies. It is not "police-community relations," a *program* that was popular during the 1960s and 1970s. It is not a public relations *program*, nor is it a *program* that focuses exclusively on minority or special interest groups within the community.

Repeated observations reveal that the recognition of Community

Policing as a *concept*, as opposed to a specialized *program*, is widely misunderstood; and the distinction is critical. For years, many police departments have had specialized divisions assigned specifically to "community relations" or "police-community relations." That approach—which focuses cooperative community initiatives within a specialized division—is characteristic of the traditional policing model. Similarly, other agencies have implemented foot patrols, a *tactic* that harkens back to the old British "watch system," and have called the use of that tactic "Community Policing." While any division and many tactics may be used by departments which practice community oriented programs, use of any of those alone does not constitute much more than a specialized *program*, unless that agency bases its overall approach to policing on a philosophy that permeates all aspects of its operations.

This book discusses the successes that American communities have experienced in implementing Community Policing. Those successes have not come without some new understanding, often reinforcing the idea that Community Policing does not simply mean having just a specialized Community Policing unit, while the rest of the organization keeps doing business as usual. In fact, that approach led to the demise of many Police Community-Relations units in the 1970s. The same thing can happen to Community Policing if it is not institutionalized as the dominant style of policing for the entire organization.

Community Policing is not an idea that was imported from some other country, but it evolved from programs and experimental research conducted throughout the years. It is, however, in some respects similar to the Japanese Koban System in which officers are assigned to and work in specific geographical areas. In formulating ideas about how best to police a city, I had the opportunity to study the Japanese system. The idea of police "storefronts" or "boxes" was borrowed from the Koban system

CHANGING APPROACHES TO POLICING

Policing in America has undergone profound changes during the past two centuries. Prior to 1800, several American cities, including Boston and New York, adopted organized versions of the then extant British "watch system," which included paid "professionals" and volunteers. But during the first half of the nineteenth century, a major change in the way the police were organized and functioned brewed across the Atlantic.

Based on theories he proposed as early as 1809, which were codified in the Metropolitan Police Bill of 1828, Sir Robert Peel developed a new style of policing. The so-called "Peelian Reforms" created a blueprint for addressing the approach to policing throughout England. Peel's principles of policing included control by the government; a stable and efficient military-style organization; standards for selection and training; presence and accessibility to the community; and a focus on crime prevention rather than just apprehension of law violators.

As America began to develop more organized police "departments" during the first half of the nineteenth century, Peel's blueprint became the most common basis of operating. By the 1850s, Peel's ideas had reformed policing in most of the major cities of England and the United States. Indeed, his reforms set the standards that dominated American policing for the next one hundred years.

THE PROFESSIONAL POLICING MODEL

Although many of the principles of the Peelian Reforms are still applicable to American policing, the American police system underwent another major reform during the middle of the Twentieth Century. Rooted heavily in the approaches to policing that had been developed earlier by August Vollmer, this broader reform came about, in large measure, because corruption and political interference in police department operations had become commonplace.

O.W. Wilson, in his book entitled *Police Administration,* laid out the principles that police agencies would rely on for many years that followed. His book was used as a basic text, not only for colleges and universities but also for organizing police agencies, and as study material for police promotional examinations. It represented what was believed to be, at the time, the best way to organize and manage modern police departments. Wilson's concepts were the embodiment of the professional police reform movement.

Like August Vollmer, O.W. Wilson believed that police departments should be organized using the military model, but also should be structured according to specific functions performed. As a result, police department organizational charts reflected the different functions performed by the agencies. Separate boxes on the organizational charts represented patrol, investigative, administrative and support service functions.

Reflecting, in some respects, the reforms occurring in other aspects of city governments across the United States during that period, O. W. Wilson's model became known as the "professional" style of policing. The professional model—often referred to today as "traditional policing"

—became the new norm within the United States and has served America well for many decades.

THE COMMUNITY POLICING MODEL

During the 1970s and the 1980s, changing times and societal changes in general led many thoughtful police administrators to begin to question some of the tactics that had become commonplace and often taken at face value in their departments.

For many Americans, the image of the police as a protection force diminished significantly during the 1968 Democratic National Convention, when nation-wide television broadcasts showed members of the Chicago Police force brutally clubbing and using tear gas on young white Americans. For many, the scene was reminiscent of the days when police indiscriminately beat African Americans during peaceful protest marches in segregated southern states.

In the aftermath of the Chicago Democratic Convention there were a multitude of demands for police department reform. The police response was the creation and implementation of "Police-Community Relations Programs." The concept, however, did not bring about institutional changes within the police establishment. Police departments around the country created special entities called Police Community Relations Units. It became their task to create harmonious working relationships between police departments and the communities that they served, particularly in Black neighborhoods.

During the decade of the 1970s, Police-Community Relations Units frequently were replaced with Crime Prevention Units. Their objective was to prevent crime by implementing various tools such as neighborhood watch programs, burglar bars, and burglar alarms among others. Yet, the confidence of the American public in the police continued to wane.

The decade of the 1980s brought about significant questioning of the ability of the police to protect the American public. There was a tremendous increase in drug abuse, particularly the rise of crack cocaine. As a result, turf wars erupted among drug "entrepreneurs" who sold their wares on the streets of American cities. Each day, the evening news displayed the police arresting young African Americans accused of trafficking in drugs. Guns, especially high-powered automatic weapons, began to proliferate on the streets of American cities, often resulting in innocent people being killed, including small children. The problem was poignantly captured in a full-page ad that appeared in the *New York Post* in 1990, referencing then Mayor David Dinkins and the public's concern about young children being killed in that city. The ad begged, "Dave Do Something."

Notwithstanding the growth in crime during the '80s and early '90s, American police had not, in fact, performed badly. They performed their responsibilities in a more productive way than ever before when arrests were used as a means of measuring police productivity. Prisons were overcrowded, court dockets were jammed, and most of the public feared walking the streets of cities.

Actually the police were doing their jobs. Yet, the irony was that there was no way they could control the problems of crime, violence and drugs. In fact, police departments had long understood that they, alone, could not control the complex problem of crime, and faced with growing complaints, they admitted they could not. As a potential deterrent to crime, they knew that they were only one of several institutions that had to function effectively in the criminal justice system; but even then they knew that they could never eliminate crime because they did not control the factors that created the conditions that gave rise to it and allowed it to flourish.

Indeed, from a sociological standpoint, during the 1980s and the first part of the 1990s, crime flourished because several American institutions had started to crumble. There was a crisis in the family, where much of America experienced a 30-year period of single-parent households, frequently headed by impoverished females. There was a crisis in the secondary and elementary school systems, where children were not being trained to be globally competitive. And there was an economic crisis, which included a loss of jobs due to the advancing "information age" with large numbers of inner city youths ill prepared to participate in it. The gap between the haves and the have-nots grew significantly wider.

All of these events converged around the same time that America witnessed the unsightly emergence of crack cocaine. Some young people, particularly those in core cities, did not see a lawful way to escape the vicious cycles of poverty that confronted them.

Faced with these growing problems, Police Chiefs and other interested parties began to ask themselves a very provocative question: "Is there a better way of delivering police services to the community?" That question has led to more than twenty years of research conducted in police departments throughout the world, particularly in the United States. It produced a second major reform movement in American policing.

The fact that police administrators sought a better way to deliver their crucial services was not an indictment of traditional policing. The professional, then labeled the "traditional" policing model, had served many cities well for decades. But the societal changes and more than two decades of research made it clear to most police professionals that new approaches were needed to meet the challenges facing contemporary America.

Clearly, Community Policing is not a concept that someone "thought up overnight." It has evolved from many years of law enforcement research and numerous demonstration projects, many of which have been the subject of careful and, quite often, rigorous evaluation.

Perhaps the confusion concerning whether Community Policing is a philosophy or model of policing, rather than a program, derives from the fact that much of the research on which it is founded has been conducted on a variety of rather specialized programs, including Police-Community Relations, Crime Prevention, Team Policing, Crime Analysis, and Problem-Oriented Policing. All have been implemented by police departments over the years. In large measure, that research has taught us what works well and what does not, and has helped to define the new model of policing, a model which is still evolving.

What does the new era of Community Policing look like? First of all, it is important to understand that the Community Policing model does not reject all aspects of traditional policing. Rather it builds upon the positive aspects of the professional model of policing -- including various tactics that have proven successful -- but rejects those aspects that have no reliability.

For example, the Community Policing model builds on the concept inherent in Police-Community Relations Programs. The concept assumed that if police were effective in dealing with crime they needed the support and involvement of the people they served. The concept of Community Policing embraces that same principle.

Community Policing also builds on lessons learned from crime prevention programs. It recognizes that two elements must be present before a crime can be committed, desire and opportunity. Similar to crime prevention programs, Community Policing uses many of the techniques of crime prevention in an attempt to remove criminal opportunity. It also works with other community institutions to remove criminal intent.

Community Policing builds on the results of the Team Policing experience. It recognizes that problems can best be addressed if they are broken down into manageable geographic areas and specific responsibilities for those areas are assigned to specific groups of police officers on a permanent basis.

Community Policing also builds on the lessons learned from Problem-Oriented-Policing. Problem solving is incorporated into the philosophy by recognizing that criminal incidents might very well be the result of broader problems in the community. By analyzing and solving the broader problems, the crime problems can be reduced, if not eliminated.

Community Policing takes advantage of two decades of research that questioned some of the traditional wisdom about policing. Research conducted or underwritten by the Police Foundation, The Police Executive Research Forum, the Rand Corporation and the National Institute of Justice in cities like Newport News, Kansas City, Houston, San Diego and others has provided new insight into the benefits of random patrol, rapid response to crimes and the effectiveness of detective work.

This research served to dispel several myths of police work under which police departments labored:

Myth Number One: Random patrol prevents crime. Research revealed that the time-honored concept of random preventive patrol did not prevent crime. To the contrary, random patrol only produced random results.

Myth Number Two: Rapid response to calls-for-service. Research showed that unless it was an emergency, the time that it took a patrol car to arrive at the scene of a call did not make any difference in apprehending the offender.

Myth Number Three: Effectiveness of detectives. Most crimes were solved by information given to the police by citizens and not by evidence collected at the scene by detectives.

So, at the same time police departments around the country were faced with the crack cocaine epidemic and a proliferation of guns on their streets, they also had a plethora of research that had dispelled several myths about the effectiveness of traditional approaches to policing that provided fresh hope. Most cities such as Houston were also confronting serious budget problems; and with no prospect for additional resources, police administrators searched for alternative ways of using their people resources. This gave added impetus to the move towards Community Policing.

The concept has drawn heavily on the experiences of the Houston Police Department. Houston was the first city in the nation, considering how it wanted to police its city in the future, to implement a concept called Neighborhood Oriented Policing, which was the fore-runner of the Community Policing model.

The academic world, particularly the John F. Kennedy School of Government at Harvard University, has also contributed significantly to the development of the concept of Community Policing, in particular by sponsoring a four-year Executive Session that resulted in a series of papers entitled, "Perspectives on Policing." The papers provided additional insight into the problems of policing in America.

—Dr. Lee P. Brown
Houston, Texas
2012

Chapter Two

A BRIEF HISTORY OF AMERICAN POLICING

INTRODUCTION

Like other institutions that support the social, political and/or governmental fabric of this country, policing has continually evolved in response to the nation's dynamic social order. Some leading police professionals, to their credit, have recognized the necessity for such changes, raising provocative questions about the conventional wisdom regarding the most effective methods of performing their life's work - - methods that for most of the past century had been simply accepted as fact without any empirical basis. As a result, police in America are currently undergoing what can best be described as a quiet revolution.[1] It is revolutionary in that it represents a fundamental change in how police think about their work and, in some instances, how they go about delivering services. These changes in thinking and in service delivery are reflected in the philosophy commonly referred to as *Community Policing*.

To fully comprehend the rationale for changes in policing in recent years and their full significance requires an awareness of the various stages American policing has experienced since the first formal police groups were

> The ability of the police to perform their duties is dependent upon public approval of police existence, actions, behavior and the ability of the police to secure and maintain public respect.
>
> —Sir Robert Peel

organized during the 1830s and 1840s.² To that end, this chapter presents a brief historical overview of the evolution of policing. It begins with its development in England, continues with the establishment of the very first American police force in Boston and concludes with an examination of the system (Community Policing) that is currently evolving today.

THE BRITISH POLICE EXPERIENCE

Like many other American institutions, American policing was founded on the English policing experience. The development of policing in England, similar to the development of policing in America, can best be understood by reviewing both the socio-political conditions of the period and the contributions made by influential individuals. It should be noted, however, that the establishment of formal police agencies in England was hampered because of a general distrust of the idea of policing. During much of England's early history, policing remained reflective of its early Anglo-Saxon roots, a time when the community was responsible for policing itself. To many, even the word "police" was considered "un-English."³ It suggested centralized autocracy which alarmed many.⁴

THE ANGLO-SAXON ERA - A.D. 500 TO 1066⁵

The Anglo-Saxons were among the last of the invaders that settled in England. Settling in small villages, they implemented their own form of public safety. Law enforcement, based upon Anglo-Saxon customs, was the responsibility of the entire community. The people were responsible for keeping the peace. Violations were seen *as acts against the people's peace*, later translated into being *acts against the King's peace*.⁶

In practice, all males between the ages of 16 and 60 were *responsible for and obligated to* keeping the peace. To carry out their *responsibility*, they were duty-bound to catch law violators. They organized themselves into groups of ten families. Each was called a *tything*, headed by a *tythingman*. When a crime was committed by one member, each member of a tything was responsible for catching him. All members of a tything were required to pay a fine if they were unsuccessful. This insured their accountability.⁷

The title of sheriff was created during this era. Ten tythings were headed by a *reeve*. The court for a reeve was called the *shire* court. This gave rise to the title of *'shire reeve,'* which resulted in the position of sheriff. The sheriff was ultimately responsible for keeping the peace in the broader area and had the authority to recruit all able-bodied men in the shire. This authority was called *posse comitatus*.[8]

THE ERA OF THE MIDDLE AGES — A.D. 1066 TO 1485

This era is highlighted by the conquering of England by the Normans, who maintained the Anglo-Saxon system of law enforcement. During this time, the *constable* became the preeminent law enforcement official. It was an unpaid position responsible for sounding the *"hue and cry"*, arresting offenders, guarding them prior to trial, collecting and providing case related evidence to the courts.[9]

A new law was passed in 1285 that gave birth to the night watchmen concept. Called the *Statute of Winchester*, the law mandated that people be required to join the "*hue and cry*" and made everyone responsible for crimes committed in their districts. The *Statute of Winchester* also promulgated rules for the watchmen. It required citizens of walled towers to "watch" the town during the entire night and arrest any suspicious strangers. In the morning strangers were turned over to the constables. They were released if they were not law violators. It was the responsibility of the constable to develop schedules and make certain that the responsibilities of the watch were carried out by the people.[10]

In 1361, Parliament passed a bill creating the office of the *Justice of the Peace*. This office was charged with the responsibility of keeping order. Justices of the Peace were authorized to issue arrest warrants which were served by constables.[11]

TUDOR AND STUART ERA - 1485 TO 1714

During this period, constables were charged with the responsibility of assisting the Justices of the Peace in keeping the King's peace. The constable continued to be an unpaid position with regular duties; however, even greater responsibilities were placed on the position. They were still required to "catch wrong doers." But in addition to apprehending law violators, the constables were often charged with performing certain punishments.[12]

Wealthy people started the practice of paying others to perform their watchmen duties. As a result, some who served as watchmen were often ill equipped for the tasks. To avoid this growing problem, the City of London employed the first paid watchmen in 1663 during the rule of Charles II. Eventually, these men became known as *Charlies*.[13]

Although they were paid, the remuneration was very meager. So only the very old or those unable to perform other duties became watchmen. Despite the low quality of persons employed as Charlies, these first paid watchmen carried a lantern, a bell, a rattle and a staff, and served as the policing force of London until the start of the 18th century.[14]

THE 18TH CENTURY

During the 18th century England experienced the Industrial Revolution, transforming the nation's agrarian economy into an industrial one. This produced major population shifts as large numbers of people migrated from rural areas and traveled to cities in search of employment. Joblessness, homelessness, hunger and inadequate educational systems led to major social disorganization. The conditions exacerbated the problems of crime and disorder.[15]

This period also brought with it the beginning of additional reforms in the policing system. Two brothers pioneered the development.

HENRY AND JOHN FIELDING

Henry Fielding was appointed Chief Magistrate of Westminster in 1748 and served out of the Bow Street office.[16] In addition to being one of the first public officials to question the effectiveness of the English policing system; he is also recognized as a pioneer in crime prevention. Fielding assumed his position during a time of political corruption and a high level of lawlessness. Because of the population transitions created by the Industrial Revolution, towns like Manchester, Birmingham and London, in particular, had grown rapidly.[17]

Two years after assuming office, Fielding set out to improve law enforcement in London. With assistance from the government he was able to employ a full-time, non-uniformed force of constables. In addition, "Henry Fielding was the first person in Britain to suggest using the printed word to supplement the traditional "hue and cry". Pursuing robbers in the columns of the *Public Advertiser* and via handbills distributed to innkeepers, liverymen, and turnpike keepers…"[18] As a forerunner to what we know today as Crime Stoppers, John Fielding obtained funds from the government to offer a reward for a gang of burglars who before fleeing London, broke into a farm house, looted it and killed a servant. The reward was for information that led to the gang's arrest, not their capture and prosecution. The reward of L50 was announced in the *London Gazette*.

A man by the name of Isaacs betrayed his fellow gangsters. He identified them as the robbers and collected the money. [19]

In reporting his success to the Home Secretary, John Fielding wrote, "They were caught by the handbills. These were distributed so widely that they acted like a "hue and cry" throughout every parish in the Kingdom. This method of pursuit by paper is my favorite preventive machine. I wish to make it a regular occurrence." [20]

The small force of law enforcers, first labeled as "Mr. Fielding's People," ultimately became known as the "Bow Street Runners."[21]

Henry Fielding died in 1754 at the age of 47. His half brother, John, kept the Bow Street Runners in place and was able to advance the progress made by his brother. He expanded the practice of publicizing information about crime and the descriptions of criminals throughout London. For a short time, he was able to augment the Bow Street Runners with a horse patrol that covered the roads leading into the city. He also established a foot patrol of volunteer constables that policed the parks.[22]

In retrospect, Henry Fielding and his brother, John, have not received the recognition they deserve for their contributions to British policing. They laid the groundwork for future improvements by having a plan for policing the city of London. That plan envisioned a salaried professional police force with a full-time carefully selected staff with centralized authority. Their concept of policing included destroying the morale of criminals, apprehending law violators, involving the public by disseminating information about crime and criminals, the use of paid informants, and a rapid response by the Bow Street Runners, the first group of police detectives. [23]

After the death of John Fielding, who was knighted for his police work, London experienced riots and increased criminal disorder. Because of a pervasive sentiment against a strong police authority, only small advances were made in English policing during the latter part of the 18th century and the first part of the 19th century.

THE 19TH CENTURY

One of those advances was the creation of the River Police in 1800.[24] This salaried sixty member unit was responsible for securing the safety of the Port of London, and for reducing thefts and lawlessness on and around the River Thames.

The success of the River Police provided the impetus for an increase in the Bow Street Runners. In 1805, the Home Secretary augmented those policing initiatives by reviving the Bow Street Horse Patrol that had been established by John Fielding. The horse patrol was then staffed by former cavalrymen and given the responsibility of patrolling the roads outside of London. Members were equipped with pistols, cutlasses and truncheons. The horse patrol was later supplemented by an un-mounted police unit, which had become the training unit for the mounted patrol. The horse patrol and un-mounted police are now recognized as England's first uniformed police force. They were known as the "Robin Redbreasts" because they wore red waistcoats under blue uniforms."[25]

In 1822 a small daytime patrol was established to deal with robberies and other criminal problems that occurred during the day. The force was created by the Home Secretary, Sir Robert Peel, who has been credited with being the "father" of modern police work.[26]

SIR ROBERT PEEL

In 1822 Sir Robert Peel took office as Home Secretary.[27] He assumed office at the end of the war with France, a period of high unemployment. Disorder was high, yet popular distrust of a formal police force was still widespread. By 1828 London had a population of roughly 1.5 million people. There were only 450 police officers. They were assigned to the Bow Street Foot and Horse Patrols, the River Patrol and the city's nine police offices.[28]

Home Secretary Peel brought about substantive changes to policing in England. When Peel took office, the popular method of addressing the crime problem was the enactment of stricter laws and severe punishment.[29] Peel was a skilled and cautious politician who used popular sentiment to secure passage of laws that he deemed necessary. He used that tactic prior to addressing changes in the police system that might prove more difficult.

Because the penal system was an issue of great concern, he decided to start with it. In 1823 he was responsible for the passage of a bill that consolidated "laws relating to prisoners and improved prison discipline."[30] The measure set a precedent that enabled Peel to later address police issues. Prior to passing the police reform bill, Peel had obtained passage of: (1) the Juries Act of 1825; (2) the Criminal Justice Act of 1826; and (3) the Offenses Against the Person Act of 1828.[31]

In 1828 Peel began to focus his efforts on reforming the London Police Force. An inquiry committee was established that recommended a "general police office under the immediate direction of the Home Secretary, an exemption of the magistrates in charge of that office from ordinary judicial duties; payment of the cost of the establishment partly from public funds and partly from a rate to be levied on the parish within the area."[32]

As previously written, early policing in England was based on the concept that law enforcement was the responsibility of the entire community. The system of watchmen and constables grew from a sense that each individual was responsible for policing themselves and their neighbors. As the populations increased, the ability of individuals to police their peers became limited and more formal mechanisms evolved. The early constables and watchmen were most common. The focus of these early public order employees was to secure the safety of the public during the day and at night.

While these watchmen and constables had been created to bring some sense of order to the increasingly urban environment, they also assumed a broad range of other services defined by the populations they served, such as walking a beat, stopping fights, arresting drunks or beggars, observing crowds and taking reports.[33] But while the watchmen and constables brought a certain degree of order, they also introduced a growing amount of corruption as they became a benignant part of the political system.

The system of policing in place at that time still largely involved watchmen moving through the streets, checking on the city's welfare while a separate "mercenary" group of investigators sought those who committed crimes and received financial rewards for their captures. Peel envisioned a system free of such payments because the one in place was perceived as creating police officials driven by compensation rather than by a duty to solve crime and create civil order. Indeed, the reputation of these early detectives was such that reports of intimidation and fraud were common as they sought to maximize their incomes. [34]

One year after focusing his efforts on police reform, Sir Robert Peel introduced and obtained passage of "a bill for improving the police in and near the Metropolis," commonly called the *Metropolitan Police Act of 1829*.[35] Peel selected two men to serve as commissioners to implement the new police force. One was Colonel Charles Rowan, a military officer who fought at the Battle of Waterloo. The other was Richard Mayne, a distinguished lawyer. The two commissioners produced a manual for the implementation of the force."[36]The new Metropolitan Police Force was located in Westminster at Number 4 Whitehall Place, but it was the back entrance of the building that gave the force the name it has been known by in the years since its very inception: *Scotland Yard*.[37]

The first formal British police force resulted from the vision of Sir Robert Peel, who had recognized the necessity of creating a well-organized method of controlling disorder and crime in a rapidly growing society. Sir Robert Peel's vision reflected a number of elements far different from the informal policing arrangements of the day. Key elements of that vision included: a quasi-military organization; a command and control structure based on quasi-military orientation; the use of uniformed patrolling as the key policing tactic; a police perspective that was impersonal and professional; and authority flowing from the Crown, rather than from the political establishment. Sir Robert Peel's basic vision and principles for policing Britain became not only the cornerstone of policing in England, but also the basis for much of American policing for many years to come.[38]

In Peel's view, simply arresting law violators indicated police failure. He believed the police should focus their activities on prevention, with close contact between police and young people early in their lives. This was a broad social view of the police function, reflective of the perception that the prevention of crime was better than waiting until crime occurred. [39]

To control the activity of individual officers, the establishment of a quasi-military structure for command and control was coupled with uniformed patrolling as the key policing tactic. Keeping officers in clear public view was expected to reduce the illegal or unethical activity of the police, while the strong command structure provided police officers with the type of oversight needed to ensure consistency in action and purpose. Moving away from the rough and tumble orientation of the watchmen, the Peel policing vision required employees committed to dealing with people in a manner that would generate respect for their actions, and that would create a general sense of professionalism among the new policing force. [40]

To ensure the removal of the police from political control, Peel's vision provided that the Crown become the principal authority of the police, with the law setting forth the requirements for police action. Until the Peelian reforms were instituted, British police were known for their responsiveness to political whim or need. To guarantee that police were agents of the Crown, national control of the police was instituted, fully removing the police from local political influence. [41]

The Peelian reforms did not come about without difficulty. Public outrage over growing corruption and abuses by the watchmen and detectives had created sufficient public support for police reform. The basic elements of Peel's vision were incorporated in the *Metropolitan Police Act of 1829*.

Initially focused solely on the police of Metropolitan London, where the problems of crime control were most visible, by 1856 all British provinces were required to have a formal police force as experiences demonstrated the benefits of Peel's approach to dealing with the problem. [42]

By forming the police under a central authority, Britain was able to create widespread legitimacy for the police without the intervention of politics. While there was some citizen reluctance to forming a large-scale police force under national control, the perceived need for standardization, coupled with a need to remove police from local political control, convinced most citizens that central oversight of the police was desirable. By 1860 every British province had its own police, operating under the Crown's authority. [43]

Peel made an everlasting contribution to policing, not only in England but also throughout the free world. Not the least of his contributions was the establishment of a set of principles that provided an organized framework within which police services could be delivered. The *Peelian Principles of Law Enforcement*, written in the 19th century, continued to serve the police well into the 21st century: [44]

- The basic mission of police existence is to prevent crime and disorder as an alternative to the repression of crime and disorder by military forces and severe legal punishment.
- The ability of the police to perform their duties is dependent on public approval of police existence, actions, behavior and the ability of the police to secure and maintain public respect.
- The police must secure the willing cooperation of the public in voluntary observance of the law in order to secure and maintain public respect.
- The degree of cooperation of the public that can be secured proportionately diminishes the necessity of the use of physical force and compulsion in achieving police objectives.
- The police seek and preserve public favor, not by catering to public opinion, but by constantly demonstrating absolute impartial service to the law, in complete independence of policy, and without regard to the justice or injustice of the substance of individual laws; by readily offering individual service and friendship to all members of the society without regard to their race or social standing; by readily displaying courtesy and friendly humor; and by readily offering individual sacrifices in protecting and preserving life.
- The police should use physical force, to the extent necessary,

to secure observance of the law or to restore order only when the exercise of persuasion, advice, and warning is found to be insufficient to achieve police objectives; and the police should use only the minimum degree of physical force which is necessary on any particular occasion for achieving a police objective.
- The police must always maintain a relationship with the public that gives validity to the historic tradition that the police are the public and the public are the police; the police are members of the public who are paid to give full-time attention to duties which are incumbent on every citizen in the interest of the community's welfare.
- The police should always direct their actions toward their functions and never appear to usurp the powers of the judiciary by avenging individuals or the state, or authoritatively judging guilt or punishing the guilty.
- The test of police efficiency is the absence of crime and disorder, not the visible evidence of police action in dealing with them.

THE INTRODUCTION OF POLICING IN AMERICA

Contrary to popular belief, the very first policing system in America was not based on the English model. Rather, prior to Europeans arriving in America, Native Indians had their own systems of law and law enforcement. Not wholly unlike the concept of European policing, the objective of the original Native American model was to maintain order. Absent written codes, the law enforcement system of the Native Nation was oral, based on an understanding that each member of the tribe played an important role in its existence.

Because of the Native American's strong sense of community responsibility, reinforced by religion and culture, violations of tribal codes were uncommon. The nature of that community-oriented culture can be seen in the case of a man named Sticks Everything Under His Belt, a Cheyenne Indian, who had defied prevailing custom by declaring his independence and placing himself apart from the tribe. Under custom, tribal discipline was important for the overall survival of the group and Sticks Everything Under His Belt was permanently banned from the tribe for his behavior. [45] Banishment was considered the most severe form of punishment for a member of the Cheyenne nation.[46]

When the Europeans arrived in America, they operated under the mistaken assumption that Native Americans lacked systems of criminal justice.[47] This notion continued even after the adoption of the United States Constitution. For example, on August 7, 1789, the United States Congress established a War Department and assigned to it the responsibility of overseeing Indian affairs. The Indian Nations had effectively lost their independence and the Federal government had designated them as "domestic dependent nations." [48] As such, they were deprived of self-governance and placed under the jurisdiction of the Federal government, effectively destroying the tribal legal systems that had previously existed.[49]

By 1877, Native Americans had been deprived of their land and also their heritage. As a result, their customary means of maintaining order were destroyed.[50] In 1879 the United States Congress began appropriating funding for Indian police. By then, many Native Americans resided on government-created reservations and preferred control by Native police rather than control by Federal military forces.[51]

The European occupation of America had brought with it the displacement of Native Americans and the effective destruction of their pre-existing systems of law enforcement. Nevertheless, it is important to recognize that the first system of policing in America was not the European system; but rather, a well-entrenched system of community self-policing developed by Native Americans. The system created by the Federal government to replace the original Native American model continues to conflict, even today, with the traditional customs of tribal law enforcement.

EARLY AMERICAN POLICE PATROLS

Most historical accounts of policing in America begin with the establishment of police forces in northern cities such as Boston and New York. But America had a system of policing that most histories of American policing have virtually ignored. To develop a complete appreciation for the history of policing in America, it is important to delve even further into the nation's history.

It is generally accepted that the first Blacks arrived in America at Jamestown, Virginia in 1619. They arrived not as slaves but as indentured servants. The status of Blacks as indentured servants did not survive long in America; rather, Blacks became the victims of a deplorable system of human slavery that existed at least until the enactment of the Emancipation Proclamation in 1863.

Although a number of writers have focused on the "slave patrols" as the forerunner of policing in America,[52] the nature of that beginning can best be understood in words contained in the autobiography of a slave:

How it is in other dark places of slavery, I do not know but on Bayou Beef there is an organization of patrollers, as they are styled, whose business it is to seize and whip any slave they may find wandering from the plantation. They ride on horseback, headed by a captain, armed, and accompanied by dogs. They have the right, either by law or by general consent, to inflict discretionary chastisement upon a Black man caught beyond the boundaries of his master's estate without a pass, and even to shoot him if he attempts to escape. Each company has a certain distance to ride up and down the bayou. They are compensated by the planters, who contribute in proportion to the number of slaves they own. The clatter of their horses' hoofs dashing by can be heard at all hours of the night, and frequently they may be seen driving a slave before them or leading him by a rope fastened around his neck to his own plantation.[53]

Commonly called "paddy rollers," the primary role of the slave patrols was to protect the property of the slave owners. Physical abuse was routine and rather arbitrary. America's first police were slave patrols created to bring a sense of order to the American slave trade. They perpetuated the prevailing social order, an order that subjugated Blacks in an institution of brutality and inferiority. Policing in America had its beginnings in that context.

Hence, the evolution of policing in America must be partly viewed in the context of the nation's approach to its treatment of minorities; not only during that period when the practice of slavery had assigned much of humankind to property status, but also – as was noted earlier – at least throughout the Civil Rights Movement of the 20th Century.

Organized American police departments, as we know them today, were not birthed until sometime in the 19th century, established a few years after the initiation of the formal system of policing in Britain. In America, the homogeneity of early settlers had created little need for a formal police system among the early Dutch and British immigrants. Indeed, the earliest American policing systems, such as those established in colonial Williamsburg, Virginia were modeled after the older British systems with a Justice of the Peace and a Constable who reported to him. In fact, this traditional model was also adopted in Virginia's first state Constitution which was adopted in 1776.

However, as America rapidly became a melting pot of new citizens, the need for a more organized mechanism for policing larger cities quickly became apparent. Facing ever-increasing problems of crime and disorder, Boston organized its first formal police agency in 1838, followed by New York City in 1844.[54] These early forces were based on some of Sir Robert Peel's guiding principles, but they lacked his vision in setting the stage for future development. Thus, policing in the United States continued to develop as an entirely local affair and manifested a widespread mistrust of a nationally controlled enforcement capability.

In these earliest city forces, as with the Metropolitan London Police, only uniformed patrols were used. Having no responsibility for investigating crimes, this function had originally been the responsibility of private police organizations such as Pinkerton and other firms. As more serious crimes began to increase in major American cities, investigative units were added. Boston in 1846, New York in 1857 and Chicago in 1861 were among the first. [55]

By this time, policing in America had become a far different enterprise than it was in Britain. The American's fear of a national police force had created a greatly decentralized policing function throughout the nation's cities. But the inherently political environments within these cities during that period of the nation's history also created largely politicized police forces, with those forces frequently serving as little more than enforcers for local political groups. Indeed, in those years cities were frequently divided into smaller neighborhood governing groups with little relationship to a centralized city government. Political control of the police became a central issue of early 20th Century America. Local policing systems typically reflected an inherent involvement in local politics with the associated influences common in American cities during the industrial era. The police, at their best, reflected the most progressive political thought of the era. At their worse, they reflected the corruption that had become all too common in city government. [56]

The political legitimacy of early American police was far more limited than that of the British police, who were independent of local political influence and had the Crown as the basis for their authority. In contrast, police officers in American cities often had to achieve "legitimacy" through the use of tough enforcement tactics against those who challenged their authority.[57] Non-enforcement became as big an issue as enforcement. There were few guiding standards beyond the political tastes of those in power. Disputes were common over who should control the police, since the political activities in which the police were engaged were quite broad.

During a period in which the level of conflict and disorder in America's rapidly growing cities grew, the lawlessness of the police became one of the major issues in the country. [58]

THE INITIAL REFORM OF THE AMERICAN POLICE

Unlike Britain, which had Sir Robert Peel's vision to guide its development as early as 1860, the politically-driven and decentralized policing system in America lacked visionary leadership until years after the initial police forces were formed. It was not until the early 20th Century that America obtained its own much needed coherent plan for policing, introduced by August Vollmer, a thinker and visionary. [59]

Recognizing the need for major reforms in police practices, Vollmer became the primary author of the Federal Wickersham Commission Report which was created by President Herbert Hoover and named after its chairman, George Wickersham.[60] The Commission's Final Report was not completed until 1931 and was this country's first national review of police practices. It focused primarily on three major over-arching policing issues of the time: conduct, corruption and productivity.[61]

The Commission found that many prevalent police practices violated basic Constitutional standards and generated massive public mistrust. It also found rampant corruption in many cities and little cogency in the way police agencies approached problems in various communities. Influence over the police was controlled by those who paid the most money. The Commission found that police productivity, whether judged by a standard of apprehension or crime prevention, was nonexistent. American police were the tools of corrupt political establishments. A new vision for American policing was required. [62]

While an important part of the Commission's work was exposing corrupt practices in many major city police departments, it also provided a detailed set of principles which should be the basis of a professional police force. August Vollmer based those principles on his former experiences as Chief of Police in Berkeley, California and Wichita, Kansas, as well as his observations in other parts of the country. They included freedom from political influence, decent pay, adequate training and the utilization of modern technology to increase the effectiveness of limited resources. [63]

Vollmer believed that a chief of police should be independent from the political structure, a practice that allowed the police to operate without political constraints. But he also recognized the responsibilities that were consistent with police authority. He stressed the necessity for crime prevention. Vollmer viewed criminal apprehension as being one aspect of the police function while believing that activities aimed at preventing youth from engaging in lives of crime were equally important. Moreover, Vollmer proposed a broad public service role for the police, enhancing broad community confidence in them. [64]

THE ROLE OF THE FBI IN REFORMING AMERICAN POLICING

The role of the FBI in the reformation of American policing generally has often been understated. The Wickersham Commission Report did not emerge in a vacuum. While large American cities had continued to face growing problems, the first quarter of the century had also witnessed the beginnings of the so-called "Progressive Era," often associated with Theodore Roosevelt who was once a Police Commissioner in New York City. Other reformers of the time were recommending changes to reduce corruption and improve accountability in local police departments. The FBI was not formally created until 1910 when William Howard Taft was President. The first special agents who became members of the fledgling Federal agency had, in fact, been appointed in 1908 during the administration of President Theodore Roosevelt. [65]

In its formative years the FBI bore almost no resemblance, in mission or activity, to the institution it later became in. Its early concerns were national banking, bankruptcy, naturalization, antitrust, peonage, and land fraud. The Mann ("White Slave") Act and creation of field offices, several near border locations, greatly expanded the FBI's law enforcement activities into the areas of prostitution and smuggling when those offenses involved crossing state lines and/or the nation's borders. Unfortunately such crimes are highly susceptible to corruption. By 1917, the First World War resulted in the further expansion of the Bureau's role into espionage and sabotage. During the 1920s, prohibition resulted in increased violence and gang activity. The Bureau's focus shifted towards fighting illegal alcohol production and investigating organized crime.[66]

In 1924, when J. Edgar Hoover took over the still young crime fighting entity, he confronted a suspect and corrupt agency that needed a central focus. At the time, the 26-year-old Hoover, a graduate of George Washington University Law School, was a "poster-boy" for the Progressive Movement. The new focus he provided to the Bureau was to control serious crime. Such a focus allowed Hoover the ability to create an acceptable mission for his Federal officers in a manner that would greatly enhance their legitimacy in the eyes of the public. His aim was to avoid the potentially corrupting areas of vice and organized crime activity. [67]

Hoover was a master at creating a public image of importance and invulnerability for the agency. Following the Progressive tradition, and ensuring that its performance met his own narrow standards, he centralized control, increased the educational requirements for entry into the service and greatly limited the personal discretion of individual agents. Having done so, it was not necessary to implement a quasi-military model for control of officer behavior. His strategies provided the required degree of control that he felt necessary for success. [68]

The Hoover vision of law enforcement on the Federal level was far different from that held by August Vollmer. While the Vollmer vision pictured a police force with close professional ties to the community through crime prevention efforts, the Hoover vision was significantly narrower, with the Federal agency only accepting responsibility for crime control through criminal investigation. [69]

By selecting crimes that were relatively easy to solve, the public could be easily convinced of the success of an agency that had a narrow mandate. Hoover worked to ensure that modern scientific techniques were used in criminal investigations, supporting an image of a competent and highly effective organization.

The changes that Hoover made to the Federal Bureau of Investigation during his tenure as Director were critical to its success.

The FBI worked independently from the thousands of police organizations that were primarily responsible for working with local communities on problems associated with day-to-day crime. Often, the FBI supported the efforts of local agencies.

Director Hoover was not without his critics, particularly during the Civil Rights and Vietnam eras. While professionalism was present, the relationships between the FBI and local authorities were sometimes strained.

THE DEVELOPMENT OF POLICE PROFESSIONALISM

Hoover's vision for the Bureau when he took over might be viewed independently of the development of American policing except that Hoover's limited transformation was far easier to adopt than a total reform of the police function. Hoover's vision was attractive to a number of Vollmer's protégés, in particular O. W. Wilson, who believed that administrative and management improvements alone were sufficient to reform police practices throughout the country. If such management improvements were adopted, Wilson thought, it would be unnecessary to drastically re-structure the police or develop a new *raison-d'être* for them. There were serious conflicts between Vollmer's vision of college-educated police officers providing sensitive, professional service and the need to control police behavior. While Vollmer proposed that policing ought to become a profession by education, Sykes argued that policing only became a *quasi-profession* because it had improved the efficiency and effectiveness of internal management practices without re-orienting the nature of the function itself.[70]

The management reforms proposed and eventually implemented by reformers such as O. W. Wilson, V.A. Leonard and William Parker contributed greatly to improvements in American policing. The creation of a civil service system to isolate police employees from the vagaries of politics provided a sense of independence. To further the idea of a profession, police authority was narrowed from the law and community to the law itself, with the eventual addition of professional standards as a second source of authority.

With a narrowed police focus to the Hoover model of crime control, the police were spared the requirement of being responsible for all types of disorder and "dirty" crimes over which it was perceived they could have little impact, but which presented great potential for corruption.[71]

The Wilson approach, while a refinement of some of the basic Vollmer principles, reflected a substantial re-orientation for the police. The key elements of the Wilson reform era were:[72]

- Suppression of crime as the primary mission of the police
- Maximizing the efficiency of patrol coverage to provide an omnipresence police presence throughout the community
- Widespread use of the automobile to maximize total police presence
- Use of one-officer vehicles to increase police visibility, as opposed to the widespread practice of two-officer vehicles
- The ability to rapidly respond to service calls so that criminals could be apprehended at crime scenes
- Lessening the close contact between police and community so that potentially corruptive influences would decrease

Wilson's belief in the technocratic approach to police management was reflected in his widely read textbooks laying out the basic principles of modern policing. The major field test of the new principles was conducted in Los Angeles where William Parker, appointed Chief of Police in 1950, adopted all of the Wilson premises as the basis for re-structuring his department. Within several years the Los Angeles Police Department was known as a highly efficient agency with superior standards, excellent morale and effective service delivery. It was widely considered a highly successful example of the new theories. [73]

This movement towards police reform continued throughout the mid-20th Century, reaching its peak in the early 1960s. The second half of the decade saw the growth of an American counter-culture that gained strength from increasing resistance to the escalating war in Vietnam. Protests against the war expanded throughout the country and the police increasingly found themselves in the middle of conflicts as they attempted to maintain public order. [74]

During this same period, the United States Supreme Court moved towards a more liberal stance, and several close decisions greatly altered the view of what police could -- and could not -- do during criminal investigations. Following a series of particularly offensive police actions, the Court's decisions in cases such as Mapp v. Ohio (1960), Gideon v. Wainwright (1963), Escobedo v. Illinois (1966) and Miranda v. Arizona (1966), greatly restricted police search and seizure practices. A defendant's right to counsel was also expanded by the Court. [75]

Many police officials were outraged by these decisions, accusing the Court of "handcuffing the police" and preventing them from being effective. More thoughtful police managers, however, recognized that the restraints being place on them were a reaction to unnecessary police practices. Hard work and careful adherence to the law, they reasoned, would limit the impact of the new court decisions. Many past police practices were outrageous and there was little public confidence that the police would correct the questioned practices without guidance from the court.

The series of court decisions restricting police practices were only the beginning of a public focus on crime, and how the criminal justice system responded to it. Following a dramatic rise in crime in large American cities early in the 1960s, President Lyndon Johnson formed the 1967 President's Commission on Law Enforcement and Administration of Justice to determine how the criminal justice system could be more effective.[76]

The Commission did not question the basic assumptions made by Wilson and other reformers concerning police function, rather it focused on ways in which management, technology and procedures could be enhanced. While the Commission broke no new ground, it did provide strong support for the professional model of policing, advancing specifications about use of developing technology, enhancement of personnel systems and training and improvements in criminal justice system linkages between police, prosecution and courts. Without question, the Commission accepted the narrow crime control model for positioning the police function.

During this period, American society experienced rapid change in social orientation and utilization of technology. Government was focused on creating a "Great Society," using massive amounts of Federal money to solve perceived urban ills.[77] In an era of relative prosperity that began after World War II; nearly all homes had telephones, televisions and radios. With police radios in each mobile patrol vehicle, people could easily call the police for all sorts of problems which had received scant attention in prior years. This resulted in a major change in performance measures against which the police were judged. The creation of the 911 emergency number provided easy public access to police service. The police claimed that they could respond to each citizen request for service within minutes. And in some neighborhoods, they actually did.

But the changes in the center cities created a paradox for the police. Easy access to police response meant that police suddenly were overwhelmed as they attempted to meet the standard they had articulated for rapid response. In those neighborhoods where police service was important to the maintenance of order, police found themselves running from call to call. Simply improving the allocation of resources, or adopting the new 911 emergency numbers had done little to resolve the developing pressures on police agencies. Implementing the recommended changes appeared to have exacerbated the problem rather than solved it.

While conducting its research, the Commission on Law Enforcement and Administration of Justice found indications that there were developing strains between police and communities, especially in minority neighborhoods. To resolve these conflicts, the Commission suggested initiation of Community Relations Programs as an effective means of improving the relationship between the police and the community.[78] Thus began the era of formal Police-Community Relations programs which were widely adopted by police agencies throughout the country.

Creation of these initiatives did little to alter basic police practices; rather, in typical police practice, departments generally created a separate unit and assigned specially-trained officers to go into the community to develop relationships with residents and business people. But since those officers were a part of a special unit, routine activities by the remainder of the police officers in the agency continued as usual.[79]

One important result of the Commission was the formation of the Law Enforcement Assistance Administration (LEAA) which provided funding to state and local units of government for police improvement.[80] These monies were designed to fund increased technology, and provide greater educational opportunities for police departments. During its first ten years, $7.5 billion in Federal assistance was funneled to cities for equipment and training, mostly focused on bringing about police reforms reflected in the Wilson view of professionalism articulated 40 years earlier. [81]

The general theories of the Commission were quickly called into question, however, when rioting broke out in numerous American cities during the summers of 1967 and 1968. Responding to this rapid increase in urban violence, President Johnson created the *Advisory Commission on Civil Disorders*[82] which focused on determining the causes of escalating urban violence. The Commission's major disclosures sent shock waves across the country. It concluded that racism was the major reason for urban violence. Additionally, the Commission noted that many police practices in urban areas increased the potential for disorder. The Commission stated that simple police Community Relations Programs would not repair the fractured relationships between the police and the community. A basic re-structuring of the police and alteration of numerous police practices was necessary, it reported.[83]

The period around 1970 saw substantial questions raised concerning how to control police behavior. The actions of the police at several widely publicized events, such as the 1968 Democratic National Convention and the 1968 Newark, New Jersey race riots resulted in calls for drastic changes in the oversight of police departments and practices. A common suggestion was the creation of Civilian Review Boards, groups of citizens which would review police discipline and investigate official misconduct.

A number of these boards were established in several cities. Police executives argued against these bodies, arguing that discipline should be the responsibility solely of the Chief of Police. No clear-cut model for Civilian Review Boards evolved, but the debate raised public and police consciousness about the importance of high quality investigations of police misconduct.

In the early 1970s, partially in reaction to criticism of substantial LEAA funds for equipment and training, a number of innovative alternative strategies for policing were considered. Team Policing, which created units of officers assigned to neighborhoods, was one promising approach.[84] A large number of police agencies adopted this experimental policy which ultimately failed because the required support systems within police agencies were not created.[85]

An underlying weakness of all the new approaches experienced during this period was the failure to reconsider the basic tenets of the police relationship with the community. The professional model, first articulated by Vollmer and refined by O. W. Wilson and other reformers, created inside the profession a sense that in matters of crime control police were the experts. The community's only role was to be supportive as the eyes and ears of the police. Two problems were inherent with this approach. One, the community did not share responsibility with the police for crime prevention, crime control or maintenance of order in their neighborhoods. Two, the narrow scope of police responsibilities such as crime control, for which the police claimed expertise, left untouched the vast majority of problems that the community looked to the police to resolve.

Surveys of public attitudes taken in the 1970s indicated that citizen concern in urban neighborhoods was more focused on "incivilities" of congested urban living than on serious crime.[86] It became apparent to some observers that the police were out of touch with citizen expectations.[87] The professional model of policing had severe problems in urban environments.

It was during this period that the Black pride movement began to take hold. It was an expression by African Americans for full citizenship and recognition of the uniqueness of their history and their contributions to America. It included a demand that police threat people of color with dignity and respect.

Clearly, American policing was at a precipice. With increased public concern over the inability of the police to deal with either crime or disorder, the stage was set for a series of new initiatives which would eventually change some of the most important tenets of American policing. In 1970 the Ford Foundation, concerned with the perception of police practices, funded a new foundation with $30 million in seed money.[88]

The *Police Foundation* was charged with finding new solutions for dealing with policing problems in "America's major cities." The creation of this new foundation, and it early efforts at research into basic questions surrounding the police function, set the stage for a broad series of research initiatives that drastically altered the policing profession. It also spawned a series of new organizations focused on awareness about the impact of various police strategies and tactics.

SUMMARY

Borrowing from the British police experience, policing in America has emerged into a policing system that is now reflective of America's system of government. Unlike the British system, America opted for a system of policing with local control.

With the vision of pioneers such as August Vollmer, O.W. Wilson, V.A. Leonard and William Parker, major changes took place in American policing on management and operational levels.

With guidance from the Federal Bureau of Investigation, landmark court decisions and national commissions, policing in America moved towards a new era that has been labeled as the "professional era of policing". This style of policing served America well for decades. As other chapters in this book shall point out, policing in America has moved into another mode of operation that is called Community Policing.

NOTES: CHAPTER TWO

1. Kelling, George and Mark H. More, "The Evolving Strategy of Policing," Perspectives on Policing, Washington, D.C.: United States Department of Justice, National Institute of Justice and the Program in Criminal Justice Policy and Management, Cambridge, Mass.: Harvard University, November 1998, No. 4

2. Walker, Samuel and Charles M. Katz, Police in America: An Introduction, New York: McGraw-Hill, 2002, pp. 28-29

3. Gash, Norman, Peel, Longman: London, 1979, p.66

4. Ibid.

5. The Story of our Police: Preserving Law and Order from Earliest Times to the Making of the Modern Police Force, prepared by The Home Office and the Central Office of Information, 1976, Printed in England by the Soman-Wherry Press, Ltd., Norwich, pp. 1-2

6. Ibid. p.2
7. Ibid. p. 3
8. Ibid.
9. Ibid. p. 4
10. Ibid. p.5
11. Ibid.

12. Ibid. pp. 6-7
13. Ibid. pp.8-9
14. <u>Ibid</u>.
15. <u>Ibid</u>. p. 9
16. Ibid. p. 11
17. Ibid. pp. 8-9
18. Pringle, Patrick, <u>Henry and Sir John Fielding: The Thief-Catchers</u>, London: Dobson Books Ltd., 1968. p.123
19. Ibid. p.124
20. Ibid.
21. Op. Cit. Note 5, p. 12
22. <u>Ibid</u>.
23. Ibid. p. 26
24. Ibid. p. 13
25. <u>Ibid</u>.
26. <u>Ibid</u>. p.15
27. Ibid. pp.15-17
28. Ibid. p. 17
29. Op. Cit. Note 3. p. 65
30. Ibid. p.67
31. Ibid. p. 69
32. Ibid. p. 165
33. Op. Cit. Note 5, p.24
34. Op. Cit. Note 3, p. 105
35. Ibid. pp.105-106
36. Ibid.
37. Op. Cit. Note 5. p. 14
38. Peak, Kenneth J., <u>Policing America: Methods, Issues, Challenges</u>, Upper Saddle River, New Jersey: Prentice Hall, 1997. p. 13
39. Ibid. p. 133.
40. Ibid.
41. Op. Cit. Note 3, p.104
42. Op. Cit. Note 35
43, Op. Cit. Note 5, p. 22
44. Op. Cit. Note 5. p. 6 and op. Cit Note 38, p. 13
45. 37 Yale L.J. 351 (1928) Joseph J. Thompson, <u>Law Against the Aborigines of the Mississippi Valley</u>, 6 ILL. L.Q. 204 (1924)
46. Georgakas, Dan, <u>The Broken Hoop</u>, Garden City, New York: Doubleday and Company, Inc, 1973, p. 81

47. Young, Robert W. Comp., <u>Historical Backgrounds for Modern Indian Law and Order</u>, Washington D.C., Bureau of Indian Affairs, Department of Interior, Division of Law Enforcement Services, 1969

48. Worchester v. Georgia, 31 U.S. (6 Pct.) 515, 560-61 (1832)

49. <u>Ibid</u>. P. 10

50. <u>Indian Law Enforcement History</u>, Washington D.C.: Bureau of Indian Affairs, Department of Interior, Law Enforcement Services, 1975, p.6

51. Ibid. p. 44

52. Williams, Hubert and Patrick Murphy, "The Evolving Strategy of Police: A Minority View," <u>Perspectives on Policing</u>, Washington D.C. National Institute of Justice, United States Department of Justice and The Program in Criminal Justice Policy and Management, John F. Kennedy School of Government, Cambridge, Mass.: Harvard University, January 1988, No. 13

53. Northup, Solomon, "Twelve Years as a Slave," <u>Puttin' on Ole Massa</u>, G. Osofsky, (ED). New York: Harper Torch Books, 1969, p. 356

54. Sykes, Richard E. and Edward E. Brent, <u>Policing: A Social Behaviorist Perspective</u>, New Brunswick, New Jersey: Rutgers University Press, 1983, p.23 and Walker, Samuel, <u>A Critical History of Police Reform</u>, Lexington, Mass.: D.C. Heat and Company, 1977, p. 4

55. Patmeotto, Michael J., <u>Criminal Investigations</u>, 3rd Edition, Lanham, Md.: University Press of America, Inc., 2004 pp.3-4

56. Smith, Bruce, <u>Police Systems in the United States</u>, New York: Harper and Brothers Publisher, 1949, pp. 4-10

57. Op. Cit. Note 54

58. Op. Cit. Note 55, p.22

59. Goldstein, Herman, <u>Policing A Free Society,</u> Cambridge, Mass: Ballinger Publishing Company, 1977. pp. 228-229

60. National Commission on Law Observance and Enforcement, Washington, D.C: U.S. Government Printing Office, 1931, p. 140

61. Vollmer, August, "Abstract of the 'Wickersham' Police Report," <u>Journal of Criminal Law and Criminology</u>, V. 22, Jan., 1932, p.22

62. Ibid.

63. Op. Cit., Note 60, p. 140

64. Ibid.

65. See, http://www./fbi.gov/libref/historic/history/history/main.htm FBI History (4.6.09)

66. Ibid.

67. Hartman, Francis X, "Debating the Evolution of American Policing," <u>Perspectives on Policing</u>, Washington, D.C.: United States Department of Justice, National Institutes of Justice and The Program in Criminal Justice Policy and Management, John F. Kennedy School of Government, Cambridge, Mass.: Harvard University, November 1988, No. 5, p.4

68. Kelling, George L. and Mark H. Moore, "The Evolving Strategy of Policing," <u>Perspectives on Policing</u>, Washington, D.C.: U.S. Department of Justice, National Institute of Justice and The Program in Criminal Justice Policy and Management, John F. Kennedy School of Government, Cambridge, Mass.: Harvard University, November 1988, pp. 4-5 No.4

69. Ibid.

70. See, Wilson, O. W., <u>Police Administration</u>, New York: McGraw Hill Company, 1963; Carte, Gene E., <u>Police Reform in the United States: The Era of August Vollmer, 1905-1932</u>, Berkeley Calif.: University of California Press, 1975 and Sykes, Richard E. and Edward E. Brent, <u>Policing: A Social Behaviorist Perspective</u>, New Brunswick, New Jersey: Rutgers University Press, 1983

71. See Ibid. and Wilson, O. W. and Leonard, V.A., <u>Police Organization and Management</u>, Brooklyn, New York: The Foundation Press, Inc., 1951

72. Wilson, O.W., <u>Police Administration</u>, New York: McGraw Hill Company, 1963

73. Parker, William, <u>Parker on Police</u>, Springfield, Ill.: Charles C. Thomas, 1957

74, See, Barringer, Mark, <u>The Anti-War Movement in the United States</u>, http://www.english.illinois.edu/maps/vietnam/antiwar.html 4/21/09

75. See Chapter Five for a discussion of the landmark decisions that had an impact on American policing.

76. <u>Crime in a Free Society</u>, Report of the President's Commission on Law Enforcement and Administration of Justice, Washington, D.C.: U.S. Government Printing Office, 1966

77. The Great Society was a term used by President Lyndon Johnson in the 1960s to describe his vision for America. It included legislation, most passed by Congress, that featured the "War on Poverty," medical care for the elderly, Federal support for education and legal assistance to African Americans deprived of their voting rights by individual states. See http://www.answers.com/topic/great-societt (2/15/2009)

78. Op. Cit. Note 76, p. 100

79. Wasserman, Robert, Michael Paul Gardner and Alana S. Cohen, <u>Improving Police Community Relations</u>, Washington, D.C.: U.S. Department of Justice, National Institute of Law Enforcement and Criminal Justice, 1973, p. 21

80. Originally called the Office of Law Enforcement Assistance, an agency of the U.S. Department of Justice

81. http://lugar.senate.gov/services/pdf_crs/crime/crime_control.pdf

82. National Advisory Commission on Civil Disorders, <u>Report of the National AdvisoryCommission on Civil Disorders</u>, Washington, D.C.: United States Government Printing Office, 1968 (commonly called the Kerner Commission after it Chairman, Otto Kerner, then Governor of Illinois)

83. Ibid, pp. 167-168

84. Sherman, Lawrence W., Catherine H. Milton and Thomas. Kelly, <u>Team Policing: Seven Case Studies</u>, Washington, D.C.: Police Foundation, August 1973

85. Kelling, George L. "Neighborhood Cops," <u>City Journal</u>, New York, Winter, 1994

86. Lewis, Dan A, (Ed.), "Reactions to Crime," <u>Sage Criminal Justice System Annuals</u>, Vol. 16, Beverly Hills, Calif.: Sage Publications, 1981; also see Skogan, Wesley G., <u>Disorder and Decline: Crime and Spiral Decay in American Neighborhoods</u>, Berkeley, Calif.: University of California Press, 1991

87. Wilson, James Q. and George L. Kelling, "Broken Windows," <u>Atlantic Monthly</u>, March 1982, Vol. 249, No. 3, pp. 29-38

88. The Police Foundation was established in 1970 with initial funding from the Ford Foundation. Its stated purpose was to "foster improvement and innovation in American policing." See http://www.policefoundation.org/docs/history.html (3/15/09)

Chapter Three

THE DEVELOPMENT OF POLICE PROFESSIONALISM

INTRODUCTION

For many Americans the decade of the 1960s was chaotic and turbulent, yet it laid the groundwork for permanent changes in the American social and political landscape. Ushered in by the struggles of America's minority citizens, especially African Americans, to achieve equal rights and concluding with massive unrest and anti-war protests, the decade focused unprecedented public attention on the nation's police and their practices. Prior to this time relatively few Americans had personal experiences with the police, except for traffic stops and impressions gained from television personalities such as Joe Friday of *Dragnet* and Tooty and Muldoon of *Car 54*.[1] Suddenly, America's police were thrust into the national spotlight in ways that suggested to many citizens that crime and the police were out of control.

The 1960s also witnessed major increases in crime in many of America's large cities. The demographic of the nation's population was rapidly changing as large numbers of people born after the Second World War reached their teens, a population group that was severely engaged

> Profession: A vocation requiring specialized knowledge and often long and intensive academic preparation.
> —Webster's New Collegiate Dictionary, 1974, G. and C. Merriam Company, Springfield, Massachusetts

in criminal activity. A series of events drastically changed the national mood, including the 1963 assassination of President John F. Kennedy, the beginning of a long involvement in the confusing Vietnam War and massive white migration from the nation's major cities.

America's police found themselves ill prepared to deal with changes in the nation's population, increased crime and the disorder that was sweeping the country. Historically, the police had been viewed as defenders of the status quo. In this new environment, the public was uncertain as to which standards should guide police behavior.

The urban crisis, which resulted from the deterioration of many cities, increased the pressure on the police and other segments of the criminal justice system to keep urban blight and disorder from the public's view. Historically, the police believed that preventing the ills of the nation's cities from impacting the lives of middle class America was of more importance than the methods they utilized to handle these problems and the people who presented them.

Americans saw widespread civil protest and a police reaction, which many considered "unprofessional" at its best, and unnecessarily violent at its worst. With the nation consumed with the escalation of violence, televised reports of southern police officers violently handling civil rights marchers created a public demand for corrective action.

The stage was set for a major shift in police orientation. While police reformers of the early part of the century had laid the groundwork for a professional police orientation, the move towards that goal had not yet visited the country. A national push was needed. The mechanism to focus public and political attention on the problems of crime, disorder and police practices was a series of national commissions that brought together notable citizens from all walks of life, including academicians who could analyze the complex nature of the problems. This chapter will briefly discuss the major commissions and the contributions they made to policing and/or crime control in America. George Kelling has described this period as the time during which American policing made the transition from *politically oriented* policing to the era of *police reform*. [2]

THE PRESIDENT'S COMMISSION ON LAW ENFORCEMENT AND ADMINISTRATION OF JUSTICE[3]

The concerns about police practices and the escalation of crime in cities across the country led President Lyndon B. Johnson to form a national commission on crime and criminal justice in July of 1965. While no single event triggered the creation of the Commission, the growing concern over police practices and the increase in crime was so intense that the public believed something had to be done.

The Commission on Law Enforcement and Administration of Justice was the first major national review of policing practices since the Wickersham Commission Report in the 1930s. [4] While the focus of the Commission was the criminal justice system as a whole, the report focused heavily on the police, the institution that had the highest visibility and public apprehension.

The Commission held three national conferences, conducted five national surveys and held hundreds of interviews with criminal justice practitioners throughout the country. It commissioned a national survey on victimization which surveyed 10,000 representative households about their crime experiences. [5]

In its final report in 1966, the Commission observed that there was a "non-system" of criminal justice that involved the police, prosecution, courts and corrections. The Commission found that throughout the nation there was far more crime than what was reported to the police. Consequently, the authorities were aware of only a small percentage of criminal acts.

The Commission suggested that society must seek to prevent crime by assuring all Americans that they had a stake in the benefits and responsibilities of American life, by strengthening law enforcement and reducing the opportunities for criminal activity. While the Commission focused substantial attention on crime prevention, it offered a number of general recommendations designed to improve the operation of America's criminal justice system. These recommendations focused on strengthening coordination between elements of the system, which it found dysfunctional.

The Commission first reported that the criminal justice system needed to develop a broader range of techniques to deal with individual offenders. Second, acknowledging the often dual system of justice in America, the Commission concluded that the criminal justice system must eliminate unequal treatment if it was to achieve its goals and gain the respect and cooperation of all citizens. Third, the Commission reported that the criminal justice system needed to attract additional people with greater knowledge, expertise, initiative and integrity. Fourth, the Commission identified a need for more basic and operational research into the problems of crime and the administration of criminal justice. Finally, the Commission recommended far greater funding for the criminal justice system to support identified reforms.

In the area of police reform, the Commission identified the basic elements it believed necessary to support police professionalism. Those elements included improved and increased training on all levels, implementation of modern personnel and performance evaluation systems, and expanded use of the 911 emergency response systems.

It was within this context that the Commission believed that citizens, civic and business organizations, religious institutions and all levels of government must assume responsibility for planning and implementing necessary changes in the criminal justice system.

A number of specific operational changes were recommended for the entire criminal justice system. In the area of crime prevention, the recommendations included the need to strengthen the family, additional resources for schools located in poor neighborhoods, more job training and desegregation in education and housing. Indeed, the Commission's recommendations reflected the changing nature of the times as the country painfully moved to deal with a growing sense of unrest in its urban areas. It provided a clear message that poverty and joblessness were the results of social ills, not character.

To improve the criminal justice system's ability to deal with youthful offenders, the Commission recommended the establishment of youth services bureaus. Such institutions would serve as centralized community-based referral centers operating as a new type of correctional facility located close to communities and community services. The Commission also suggested that states implement work/study programs for inmates as a means of easing their transitions back into society.

The Commission noted that there was a need to eliminate unfairness in the administration of justice; that the criminal justice system had to move away from what it termed "assembly line justice" to an equitable, more humane means of dealing with societal offenders.

The recommendations for police reform were extensive and covered almost all aspects of police operations and management. The Commission agreed that the "professional model" of policing was best suited to improve police effectiveness. The highly structured military model, increased random patrol activities and implementation of new technical systems were all recommendations designed to improve police performance.

The Commission opined that an important part of the police

function was to maintain a positive relationship with the community. It recommended implementation of Community Relations Programs, different from the traditional public relations efforts which had traditionally been the mainstay of police relations with the public.

The underlying thesis of the Commission reflected the professional model at its best. Strengthened supervision would result in improved police performance through tighter control over police behavior. Increased training would provide better skilled and more knowledgeable officers. Increased educational requirements for police applicants produced a workforce of higher quality.

Some of the Commission's recommendations for police reform were quite innovative. A recommendation for multi-level lateral entry was aimed at increasing the flexibility of allowing officers to move from agency to agency, increasing promotional opportunities and infusing new perspectives into the organization with outside hires. Recommendations such as community service officer positions as an entry point for men and women first joining the police service, to requiring police to be college educated were proposals aimed at providing a career development framework designed to encourage officers to remain with the police force for longer time periods.

The Commission believed that quality education was an important determinant of police performance and structured many recommendations around that belief. At the time of the Commission, few police officers were college educated and few college educated men and women were willing to make policing their careers. Yet, the proportion of the national population that was college educated had risen steadily since the end of World War II. The police services received few college educated people, since career incentives for them were lacking in law enforcement.

The Commission also focused on the need for minimum standards for police training. It recommended that each state create a commission on training to develop and implement minimum training standards for new and in-service officers. In its research, the Commission found a lack of national training standards, with many new police officers receiving only a few weeks of training before being allowed to work alone in the field. This was unacceptable.

Finally, the Commission suggested a number of ways in which technology could be applied to the problems of policing as a means of increasing the efficiency of police operations. Key recommendations focused on ways to simplify and process citizen service calls. The recommendations included broadening public access to police services through expanding the use of 911 emergency numbers and increasing the use of computer-aided dispatching systems. This allowed for greater police control of police resources, the Commission stated.

Surveying the field of criminal justice, the Commission reported that far greater emphasis should be placed on basic research into improving methods of dealing with the problems of crime and disorder. It recommended increased funding for research in areas such as the economic impact of crime, effects of sanctions, improved strategies for police, courts, corrections and combating organized crime. A final recommendation called for the establishment of a national criminal justice research foundation with regional centers to stimulate and coordinate research and disseminate results. It also recommended the founding of a National Criminal Justice Statistics Center.

In retrospect, the Commission provided the first broad perspective on two important issues: the elements of police professionalism and the workings of the criminal justice system. While police professionalism had been discussed for years, a comprehensive picture of its elements and the inter-relationships between those elements had never been constructed. The Commission provided this linkage and set the stage for a decade of movement towards a professional model of policing.

Providing a new perspective on the criminal justice system was another major contribution that the Commission offered. Until the Commission carefully developed a picturesque flow chart detailing the numerous elements of the criminal justice system, few people truly understood the complex set of relationships between the elements in that system. Although the Commission characterized criminal justice as a "non-system," understanding the inter-relationships between the various parts was an important development because it placed the police and their procedures within an overall framework.

Many of the Commission's recommendations were implemented during the years that followed their being proposed. Many of those recommendations today form the basis of substantive thinking about the organizational requirements for effective policing. In this sense, the work of the Commission cannot be underestimated. With prodding by the Commission, the era of police reform took hold. Well-managed recruitment, high training standards, detailed policy making, programmatic community relations initiatives and application of technology to information processing assumed their roles as important characteristics of a well-run police agency.

Chart I: Sequence of events in the criminal justice system [2]

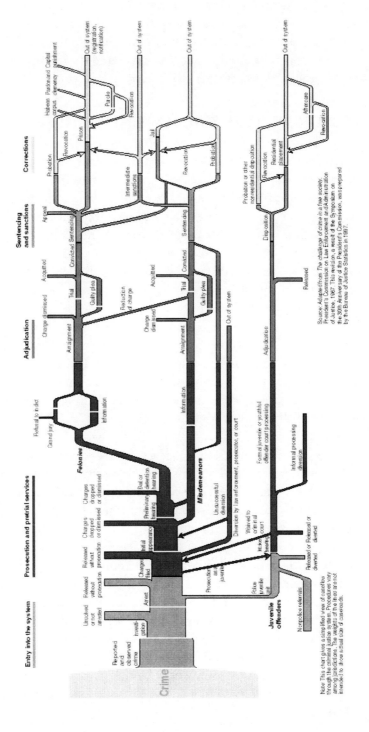

The recommendations are no less valid today than they were when they were made. What the Commission did not fully explore was the rapidly changing nature of the American urban landscape. Professional police, operating under the quasi-military model, found themselves unable to deal with the social upheavals that soon enveloped the country.

THE NATIONAL COMMISSION ON CIVIL DISORDERS[6]

In the summer of 1967, soon after the issuance of the President's Commission on Law Enforcement and Administration of Justice's report, widespread racial disorder erupted in many American cities.

Few large cities were immune from the violence. In community after community, as Black youth and adults rioted, the police were involved in incidents that were considered precursors of the violence. Additionally, once disorder began, the police were cast into a major role of trying to control the escalating violence. When the level of disorder spread from community to community, and the public became increasingly aroused about the charges that police actions created disorderly events, President Johnson formed a second Commission and charged it to study the causes of disorder. The body was also asked to recommend programs and policies that could help solve the growing problems that faced the nation's cities.

The charge to the National Commission on Civil Disorders, known as the Kerner Commission, named after its chairman, Otto Kerner, the Governor of Illinois, was straightforward: determine what occurred, why it occurred and devise a plan that would prevent future episodes from occurring. The Commission, made up of a distinguished panel of law enforcement, government officials and private citizens, visited cities where riots had taken place, heard witnesses, and interviewed numerous experts. The results of their assessment were startling. America, they said, was two societies, one Black and one white. The disparity between the two groups was severe and growing larger. The problems of the inner cities - hardened racial attitudes, discrimination and segregation in housing, lack of employment opportunity and a lack of access to quality education --were considered root causes of disorder, the Commission said.

It noted that in such a divided society, American police commonly reflected the attitudes of the white community, and thus were perceived to be insensitive to the needs and feelings of minorities. It observed that the aggressive tactics frequently used by the police to control crime often aggravated community tensions. The Commission also noted that there were inadequate complaint procedures that addressed citizen grievances about police practices.

The Kerner Commission recommended a number of ways in which police could reduce the tension in their relationship with the community, including a careful review of police operations in urban centers; increased police protection to inner city residents; the establishment of fair, responsive grievance procedures, and the development and adoption of policies designed to aid decision making by patrol officers who found themselves in difficult conflict situations. It also recommended increased minority recruitment and the establishment of community service officer programs designed to attract inner city youth to police work.

The Commission brought to the *professional model* of policing a set of new concerns that focused on the relationship between the police and the community. Cognizant of the divisive nature of race relations in America, the Commission suggested that the traditional model of professionalism was inadequate to deal with the problems faced by police working in inner city neighborhoods. The Commission called for the establishment of a relationship with community residents and an understanding that many urban residents wanted the police to protect them from crime, and that police tactics had to be acceptable to a majority of the community residents. In this sense, the Commission picked up where the Commission on Law Enforcement and Administration of Justice stopped. It recognized the nature of the relationship between urban citizens and the police and the importance of police tactics in defining community confidence in the police.

NATIONAL ADVISORY COMMISSION ON THE CAUSES AND PREVENTION OF VIOLENCE[7]

While the riots in America's inner cities declined and police became more sophisticated in dealing with urban violence, terror struck the heart of American society in other ways. The 1968 assassinations of Dr. Martin Luther King, Jr. and Robert Kennedy, on the heel of the assassination of President John F. Kennedy, created a nation-wide crisis of confidence. The violence that erupted during the 1968 Democratic Convention held in Chicago compounded that national sentiment and once again focused public attention on police reaction to civil unrest.

In response to the national outrage and queries as to why such violence appeared to be spreading, President Lyndon B. Johnson created another commission in June of 1968. Its charge was to determine the causes of violence in the United States and recommend strategies for preventing it in the future. After a comprehensive study of patterns of violence in American society, the Commission in its 1969 report noted that the pattern of violence fell largely within an American tradition of violence and that such violence normally subsided as political and social institutions gradually responded to the causation underlying social dislocations and injustices.

The Commission reported that to understand violence, there was a need to study the American society, past and present, and the traditions and institutions that accept or condemn, generate or reduce various forms of violence in the society. Enlisting the assistance of over 200 leading scholars in criminology, psychology, history, political sciences, sociology and law, the Commission suggested that the violence of the '60s - assassinations, group unrest and individual crime - was considerably more vicious than during preceding decades, ranking among the worse in American history. Indeed, the level of violence was so severe that it jeopardized all aspects of American society and was corroding the central political process of a democratic society. In this sense, violence had reached such a level that society was beginning to substitute force and fear for argument and accommodation.

The Commission concluded that no society could remain free, or deal effectively with its fundamental problems, if its people lived in fear of their fellow citizens. "A house divided against itself cannot stand," the Commission noted.[8] To deal with violence, the Commission recommended doubling the national investment in crime prevention and in the administration of criminal justice.

A number of the Commission's recommendations were novel, while others restated findings of the two previous Commissions of that decade. In commenting on police actions in handling disorders, the Commission reported that the police needed to develop more effective tactics in handling peaceful and violent demonstrations. It concluded that official behavior frequently determined whether protests remained peaceful or turned violent. To deal with the spread of violence involving firearms, the Commission recommended adoption of a national firearms policy to limit the availability of handguns.[9]

The Commission concluded that a society in which law was more feared than respected and where individual expression and movement were curtailed was violent by its nature. For America to survive as a healthy democratic institution, the Commission recommended that young people be given a greater role in determining their own destinies in shaping the future direction of society. It also suggested lowering the voting age, reformation of the national draft to increase fairness, and massive opportunities for youth to engage in public service.[10]

As was the case with previous appointed bodies, the Commission on Violence presented a series of recommendations focused on reforming police practices. It suggested increased foot patrols in congested neighborhoods, the establishment of interracial police teams, creation of neighborhood centers to house police and other human services, and more Police Community Relations programs in minority neighborhoods.

NATIONAL ADVISORY COMMISSION ON CRIMINAL JUSTICE STANDARDS AND GOALS (1973)[11]

As crime continued to increase during the decade of the 1970s, many observers suggested that a renewed national strategy for crime control was necessary. A national commission was formed by the Department of Justice in 1973 to develop an action-oriented strategy to guide the attack on crime by state and local agencies and the private sector.

Developments in criminal justice brought about a wide range of recommendations for reform and the landscape was littered with what were often divergent recommendations for improvements in the system. While the focus of the Standards and Goals Commission was on the increasing fear of violent crime and a perceived need to make the criminal justice system fair and effective, the underlying commitment was to provide local government with a single set of organizational and operational standards that built on the recommendations of previous national commissions.

The Commission on Standards and Goals was not created to provide mandatory standards for criminal justice agencies, but to provide them with flexible guidelines. In that context, it focused on four major areas:
- Dealing with juvenile delinquency
- Improving service to impoverished areas of the community
- Reducing delay in adjudication and disposition of cases, overcrowding of detention centers, and the use of plea bargaining
- Supporting community-based citizen groups in their crime prevention and control efforts

While many of the standards presented were expansions of the ideas set forth by the other national commissions, several key recommendations focused on important issues of crime and administration of the criminal justice system. Key among those recommendations were: (1) a reduction in the number of handguns in society through terminating the sale and manufacturing of such weapons, (2) the purchase of guns from citizens to get them off the streets, (3) making collected guns inoperative and (4) increased jail time for crimes committed with handguns.[12]

In the area of refining the criminal justice system, the standards proposed better coordination of the components of the criminal justice system, partial decriminalization of some vice crimes by eliminating incarceration and recognition of the burdens of social control placed on the criminal justice system when dealing with drunkenness, vagrancy and traffic violations.[13]

The American Bar Association Standards Committee was formed to further understand the dynamics of the police function in America and to propose standards for dealing with many of the difficult conflicts faced by the field. Written as policy statements accompanied by commentary, the standards provided lawyers, prosecutors and police executives with suggestions on how to deal with problems in policing.[14]

The ABA had a special interest in policing because of the important basis of its function in the law. Thus, the Committee's standards presented a picture of the nature of the function in a way that assisted other members of the criminal justice community to better understand their complexity.

The importance of the ABA work cannot be understated. Produced many years prior to the accreditation of law enforcement agencies, the reflective nature of the Committee's findings explored in detail the broad nature of police responsibilities and the need for police to utilize solutions to problems beyond those provided by the law. This broad perspective had not been presented prior to the committee's work and laid an important foundation for later re-conceptualization of the police function.

THE NATIONAL MINORITY ADVISORY COUNCIL ON CRIME AND CRIMINAL JUSTICE[15]

On June 18, 1976, the Administrator of the Law Enforcement Assistance Administration (LEAA) of the United States Department of Justice established the National Minority Advisory Council on Criminal Justice. The fifteen-member, multi-ethnic body released its final report four years later. It was charged with the responsibility of advising LEAA on crime and criminal justice policies and programs as they related to concerns of minority communities. The charge included the development of recommendations for Federal, state and local government regarding minority concerns.

The establishment of the Council was historic in that it represented the first time an agency of the Federal government had sponsored such a body to conduct research, hold hearings and give advice on critical issues of crime and criminal justice regarding the minority community. The members of the Council represented the four major minority groups: African American, Hispanic American, American Indian and Asian American.

In addressing the issue of crime, the Council concluded that minorities, with the exception of some Asians, were more likely than whites to be (1) suspected of criminal behavior; (2) arrested; (3) be held in custody rather than released on bail; (4) indicted; (5) convicted when tried; and (6) denied parole. In addition, the Council pointed out that minorities were more likely to be the victims of crime.

The Council reported that the disproportionate representation of minorities in the criminal justice system was not a result of race; rather it reflected the relative degree of socio-economic deprivation of minorities. It pointed out that minorities were more likely than whites to: (1) have lower incomes; (2) be unemployed; (3) have inadequate housing; (4) experience health care problems; and (5) be politically powerless.

In the first part of its two-part final report, the Council made its major contribution to the literature on crime and criminal justice by exploring the issues from the perspective of African Americans, Hispanic Americans, Asian Americans and American Indians. Part two of the final report addressed, from a minority perspective, five elements of the criminal justice system: police, courts, corrections, education and research and community anti-crime.

The work of the Council and its final report received only limited exposure, reflecting a general lack of concern during the period about minority criminal justice issues. Yet, the recommendations were significant and covered a number of important areas.

The recommendations were particularly important because they reflected the disorganized, often discriminatory, state of minority criminal justice application. Among the recommendations were the following:
- Give tribal law enforcement authorities - where they desired to do so - the authority to investigate Federal crimes that occurred on Indian reservations and the ability to present evidence to their prosecutors.

- Undertake policy analysis of the implications and probable impact of decriminalization of certain classes of behavior such as gambling.
- Make efforts to increase participation of Hispanics, especially professionals, at all levels of the court system and make every effort to select Hispanics who spoke English as jurors.
- Restructure state and local police agencies and mandate that they serve and work primarily under the control of local citizens to prevent crime.
- Strictly enforce a policy of disallowing police officer's use of deadly force, except where there was clear and present danger to the life or physical safety of an officer or third party.
- Require that police departments adopt mandatory record-keeping systems to document each instance of a firearm being discharged by an officer.
- Establish a minority scholar's research program, including minority scholars, that focuses on the causes of criminal behavior among minorities, the ways in which society might be protected from such behavior, and create methods aimed at reducing such behavior.
- Earmark a portion of each local jurisdiction's annual criminal justice budget to help organize community groups and operate effective community based criminal justice activities such as community based corrections, community dispute resolution centers and citizen anti-crime units. [16]

The final report of the Commission was never printed by the government's printing office. Rather, a limited number of copies were duplicated by LEAA and distributed mainly to members of the Commission.

THE NATIONAL COMMISSION ON HIGHER EDUCATION FOR POLICE[17]

In 1976 the Police Foundation, a Washington, D.C., based private organization, established the National Advisory Commission on Higher Education for Police Officers, which released its findings in 1978. This nine-member panel was charged with examining the following: "How can the quality of police education be improved to make it a more effective force for changing the police?"[18]

This examination of higher education for the police occurred one decade after the Congress passed legislation creating the Law Enforcement Education Program (LEEP).[19] The program, administered by the Law Enforcement Assistance Administration, awarded grants up to $400 a semester for employees of criminal justice agencies to attend college, and loans up to $2,200 a year for pre-service students. The loans to pre-service students were forgiven if a student was employed by a criminal justice agency for four years or more.

Because of the LEEP program, there was a significant increase in the number of students who pursued degrees in criminology and related areas. The increase included a large number of police officers who returned to school or enrolled in college.

In its final report, the Commission concluded that most existing college police science programs needed to implement fundamental changes if they were to assist the police in developing new methods to deliver their services in a more effective manner. The Commission concluded that even with a significant increase in the level of police education, a noticeable impact on police performance did not exist.

Because many police officers enrolled in college majored in police science, the Commission focused its attention on the nature and quality of the curriculum offered by that discipline. They concluded that the academic focus was too narrow and recommended that it be broadened, preparing students for a variety of career choices.

Furthermore, the Commission recommended that no more than one quarter of the courses taken by students majoring in criminal justice be in that field. The panel also recommended that police vocational training courses be replaced with academic subjects that dealt with concepts and theory in contravention to "how-to-do-it" training. The Commission stressed the importance of criminal justice students being exposed to disciplines that were not normally considered to be within the scope of the criminal justice system.

The Commission asked colleges and universities that offered police science programs to make major improvements in various areas. It recommended that institutions which offered such programs support them to the same degree they supported other areas of academic study. Such support should include full-time faculty, adequate library resources and requirements that criminal justice classes be held on campus, the Commission stated. In addition, the Commission recommended that college credit not be given to police officers for completing police department training. It also recommended that the police science faculty meet the same standards and requirements *required in other disciplines. The Commission felt that criminal justice* faculty members should not be selected solely on the basis of their criminal justice work experience.

Similar to previous panels, the Commission recommended the baccalaureate degree as the minimum entrance requirement for police department work. Recognizing that there would be a concern that such a requirement might have a disparate impact on minorities, they recommended that police departments conduct aggressive minority recruitment programs. The Commission also called on Congress to continue the LEEP Program with certain modifications that would allow greater opportunities for full-time residential education, including fellowships in a variety of disciplines. It also called for programs that would enable deserving police executives to secure degrees from top level management schools.

Charging that many police agencies had policies that hampered education from serving as an inducement to selecting police work as a career, the Commission recommended that police departments place a greater emphasis on recruiting pre-qualified persons as opposed to educating recruits. The Commission also called on police departments to experiment with different organizational designs and allow excused absences so officers could expand their educational training.

The Knapp Commission on Police Corruption in New York City was a different kind of commission driven by a series of events in a single police agency that greatly impacted the state of policing throughout the country.[20] Faced with a developing scandal of police corruption in New York City in May of 1970, Mayor John V. Lindsay established a citizen's commission to determine the extent and nature of police corruption. The commission examined existing procedures for dealing with corruption and recommended procedural improvements.

It found widespread corruption in the New York City Police Department. It uncovered the existence of standardized patterns of corruption, especially with regard to gambling investigations. Corruption in narcotics was less organized but often involved greater amounts of money. The commission characterized two types of police officers. They were "meat-eater" police officers who aggressively misused power for personal gain and "grass-eater" officers who merely accepted things as they were. It was the grass-eaters, the commission found, that made corruption respectable within the organization, encouraging a code of silence among officers.

The commission also noted that in every area where police corruption existed, it was always paralleled by corruption in other agencies of government, industry, labor, and other professions. Police, they noted, were singled out for public view because of their positions as keepers of the public good. This special attention seemed unfair to police officers, intensifying their sense of isolation and hostility. The commission also noted that group loyalty was an important element in corruption. Suspicion and hostility were directed at any outside interference in the department.

Officers on all levels refused to acknowledge serious problems within the agency. A key obstacle to meaningful reform was the prevalence in administrative circles of the "rotten apple" theory. The thought was that corruption was an isolated issue and that a single rotten apple spoiled an entire batch. In carrying out its investigation, the commission used testimony from corrupt police officers and employed undercover methods. Two drug addicts assisted the commission in its investigation by working in an undercover capacity, recording conversations and videotaping documented payoffs and other illegal activities.

The commission's recommendations were straightforward and strong. The key immediate recommendation was the appointment of an independent investigatory agency to serve as a police corruption watchdog. It was recommended that the agency be headed by a Special Deputy Attorney General for all five boroughs of York New City. Other recommendations included strengthening the police department's internal anti-corruption effort, increased command accountability and reorganizing the department's inspection services division, allowing it to function like the Inspector General of a Federal agency.

More important than these anti-corruption initiatives were recommendations that corrupt activity be curtailed by eliminating numerous situations that exposed officers to corruption and by controlling exposure to potentially corrupting situations. Additionally, the commission suggested that the temptation to engage in corrupt activity by the police and the public could only be reduced by subjecting both to significant risks of detection, apprehension, conviction, and penalty. Overall, the commission observed that police attitudes towards corruption had to change. The climate of reform had to be publically supported, it stated.

Police Commissioner Patrick V. Murphy took the commission's recommendations seriously. He made it the top priority of the agency and moved aggressively to change the culture that supported corruption in the department. Almost all of the key recommendations were implemented. Most importantly, no officer was promoted if there was any taint of corrupt activity in his or her background. New police recruits were subjected to indoctrination about corruption defenses, and the penalties for engaging in corruption were drastically increased.

The Mollen Commission to Investigate Allegations of Police Corruption and the Anti-Corruption Procedures of the Police Department was established some twenty years after the Knapp Commission by Mayor David Dinkins in 1992.[21]

It came about after Michael Dowd and five other New York City police officers were arrested in Suffolk County, Long Island for selling drugs that were purchased in Brooklyn's 75th police precinct. Retired Judge Milton Mollen was Mayor Dinkins' Deputy Mayor for Public Safety who also chaired the panel. The Mollen report was released on July 7, 1994.

The Commission concluded that corruption was a major problem in the New York City Police Department, but was not as systemic as it was when the Knapp Commission conducted its investigation a generation earlier.

It found that the Police Department had become more concerned that its image would be tarnished if corruption was publicized than it was about corruption itself. "As a result, its corruption controls minimized, ignored and, at times, concealed corruption rather that rooted it out."[22]

It found that over the past decade, the systems designed to control corruption were so weakened that the probabilities of discovering it were minimal. It also concluded that the department did not allocate sufficient equipment and resources to investigate corruption, placed a higher priority on petty misconduct than it did on corruption and closed corruption cases prematurely. Furthermore, the department did not provide adequate integrity training, assigned investigators to precincts with the fewest problems, did not hold commanders accountable for corruption, did not follow-up on information provided by field associates and did not adequately train officers responsible for detecting corruption.

In essence, the Commission concluded that command accountability in the New York Police Department had collapsed and commanders were not held accountable for breaches of integrity. Complacency set in as corruption raised its ugly head. Yet, the Commission expressed its confidence in the department's ability to address the problem.

The Commission concluded that to effectively address the corruption problem there had to be a two-prong approach. First improve the department's internal ability to carry out anti-corruption controls. That included: (1) improving the quality of recruits, (2) improving police training, (3) strengthening supervision, (4) upgrading prevention methods, (5) improving internal investigations, (6) enforcing command responsibility and (7) deterring and rooting out the causes of corruption.

A more far reaching recommendation was the creation of a permanent external Police Commission that would be independent of the Police Department to: "(i) perform continuous assessments and audits of the department's systems for preventing, detecting and investigating corruption; (ii) assist the department in implementing programs and policies to eliminate the values and attitudes that nurture corruption; (iii) ensure a successful system of command accountability; and (iv) conduct, when necessary, its own corruption investigations to examine the state of police corruption." [23]

The proposed body would have its own investigative staff and would submit its findings to the mayor and the Police Commissioner. Its investigations would center on assessing the state of corruption in the department, its controls and corruption hazards. It would not relieve the department of its own corruption control responsibilities.

The Report of the Independent Commission on the Los Angeles Police Department (Christopher Commission) that was established by Mayor Tom Bradley is another example of an independent body being formed to address a major problem in a single police department that had a widespread impact on law enforcement agencies. In this case, the problem was excessive use of force by members of the Los Angeles Police Department. [24]

On January 9, 1991, the Independent Commission on the Los Angeles Police Department released its report. It was commonly called the Christopher Commission, named after its chairman Warren Christopher. Mayor Bradley appointed the Commission after members of the Los Angeles Police Department brutally beat an African American male named Rodney King. The beating was caught on video tape by a photographer and resulted in four members of the LAPD being arrested and indicted.

The Christopher Commission was given the task of conducting a "... comprehensive investigation into the use of excessive force by the LAPD and related issues."[25] It was very blunt in its criticism of the LAPD. It stated that "... there are a significant number of officers in the LAPD who repeatedly use excessive force against the public and persistently ignore the written guidelines of the department regarding force."[26]

In looking at the cause of the problem, the Commission drew the following conclusions:

- The problem of excessive force was aggravated by racism and bias within the LAPD.[27]
- The LAPD had an organizational culture that emphasized crime control over crime-prevention and that isolated the police from the community and the people they served.[28]

The Commission offered a number of recommendations designed to address the problems identified in its investigation into the LAPD. First, it recommended that the leadership of the LAPD make ending extreme force its top priority, if the department was to progress. In addition, it stressed that command officers be held accountable for those officers working under them who used unnecessary or excessive force.

The Commission felt that lieutenants and sergeants should monitor the use of force by those they supervised. In pointing out that Los Angeles paid millions of dollars each year to settle lawsuits, the Commission stated that such litigation was, in reality, a reflection of the fundamental problems of excessive force. It also recommended the use of audio and video taping of police contacts with the public as a means of reducing excessive force. In addition, the Commission felt that "mid-level" techniques for dealing with suspects and combative suspects should be used by the LAPD.

One of the most far-reaching recommendations made by the Commission dealt with the position of Police Chief. Under the system that existed in Los Angeles at that time, the Police Chief was appointed by and reported to a civilian Police Commission. This unpaid, civilian, part-time body had the exclusive authority to appoint the Police Chief and set policy for the department. The Mayor and the City Council had little, if any, authority over the Chief. The Commission recommended changes to the system, with the Mayor, City Council and Police Board sharing responsibility for selecting and removing the Chief. Furthermore, it recommended that the Chief be given a five-year appointment limited to two terms, thus limiting the Chief's tenure to ten years. The Commission also recommended that the Police Board be given the authority to terminate the Chief, but only with the concurrence of the Mayor. The Police Chief would be allowed to appeal the termination to the City Council, which by a two-thirds vote could reverse the decision.

The Commission also challenged the Police Chief to "establish the principle that racism and ethnic and gender bias will not be tolerated within the Department." Other recommendations included minority recruitment, cultural awareness training, and equal opportunity in promotions for women and minorities and non-discrimination based on sexual orientation. The Commission also recommended that the LAPD modify its style of policing by adopting the concept of Community Policing as its dominant policing model.

The Special Advisor to the Board of Police Commissioners on Civil Disorder in Los Angeles released its report entitled *The City in Crisis* on October 21, 1992. [29]

When the jury in a Semi Valley courtroom announced its "not guilty" verdict in the case involving the four LAPD officers charged with beating Rodney King, polarization between the LAPD and the Black community moved to the forefront. The trial had been moved to Simi Valley, a predominately white suburb of Los Angeles. The jury found the officers not guilty on April 29, 1992. What followed was the worst rioting Los Angeles had experienced since the Watts riot of 1965. Forty-two people lost their lives, more than 700 buildings were burned down, and the amount of property destruction climbed to over $1 billion. [30]

On May 11, 1992 the Los Angeles Board of Police Commissioners voted to study how the LAPD responded to civil disorders that occurred following the King verdict. It also asked for a study of the police department's preparation for a possible disruptive verdict the previous month and a report on the disturbances that did occur. William Webster, a former Federal judge and past FBI Director, was selected to serve as a special adviser to the commissioners.

The Rodney King incident came to symbolize the "...deep-seated hostility, mistrust and suspicion," between the LAPD and the Black community," the report stated. It made major recommendations: (1) the department should place increased emphasis on patrol functions and minimize reliance on specialized units, (2) the department and the city as a whole should place greater attention on planning, training and responding to emergencies and (3) the department's communications system should be upgraded, allowing the city to respond to both routine and emergency situations. [31]

Consistent with the recommendations of the Christopher Commission, the Report of the Special Adviser also recommended a change in the philosophy of the LAPD by adopting Community Policing as its dominate style of delivering police services. [32] These two Commissions, created to study and make recommendations for improving the LAPD, are examples of local concern about a police department and how citizen and political involvement can lead to reform.

The Rodney King incident also turned out to be a watershed event for American policing. Many Police Chiefs throughout the nation were concerned about the impact the incident might have on law enforcement in general, and on their departments. In order to lessen the impact in other cities a group of eleven Police Chiefs convened in New York City on April 16, 1991 to discuss the use of deadly force. As a result of that meeting, they issued a position paper entitled "Police Chief's Position on Use of Excessive Force."[33]

The report read in part: "Police agencies across America are moving toward a community-based style of policing. This style of policing values partnerships, problem solving, accountability, and service orientation to our citizens. Our hope is for the Los Angeles tragedy to have a positive outcome by accelerating change for this new form of policing, in order to better serve our diverse communities." It further committed to:

- An open, thorough investigation of all citizen complaints of police abuse; and within the limits of the law, to share the results of those investigations with complainants and civilians in our communities.
- Eliminating the code of silence by furthering those values within the profession that clearly established the necessity for a personal commitment by every police professional to a reverence for the law.
- Accountability for the actions of our employees. Recognizing that most police officers are dedicated and hard working in very difficult situations, we will move decisively against those officers who violate the trust they have been given.
- Reinforce Robert Peel's admonition to "keep peace by peaceful means" as the dominant ethic of police work and search for metaphors that reflect lawfulness, constitutionality, justice and peace. We reject metaphors such as "war on drugs" and "war on crime," that imply violence. These metaphors present mixed messages.
- Enhance the training necessary to deal with difficult conflict situations, ensuring that officers do not use excessive force to solve problems.[34]

The fact that the Chiefs convened the meeting and issued the statement reflected a new breed of police leadership in America. Recognizing that they were criticizing a fellow Chief, they not only presented their position paper to the national media, they also sent copies to all of the major police organizations, the United States Congress, United States Conference of Mayors, the International City Managers Association and other policy makers.

THE PROFESSIONAL POLICE ORGANIZATIONS

Consistent with the experience in other professions, the movement towards police professionalism has fostered a number of organizations aimed at serving the needs of a variety of professional constituencies. The oldest of these organizations is the *International Association of Chiefs of Police* (IACP), formed in 1893 to serve the needs of Police Chiefs. The original founders of the IACP were Chiefs from medium- and larger sized cities. As the organization developed, it brought in large numbers of smaller-city Police Chiefs. Membership in 2009 was 20,000, representing 100 countries.

Over the years, the IACP has played an important role in developing standards for organization and management of police organizations. Indeed, few organizations have conducted more surveys of police departments than the IACP and the standards set forth in these surveys represented important criteria through which policing could be judged.

The Police Executive Research Forum (PERF) was formed with a grant from the Police Foundation in 1980 to serve the needs of larger city Chiefs. Its creation reflected a concern among some IACP members that the developing problems in larger communities required an approach to policing quite different than that required in smaller communities. Restricting its active membership to college educated Chiefs from police agencies serving communities over 100,000, PERF focused its energies on providing its members with research into important policing issues and providing a forum for discussion of important policing issues.

The National Sheriff's Association (NSA) was formed in 1940 to represent the interests of the nation's sheriffs. As political officers of the nation's counties, sheriffs believed that their needs were far different from those of Police Chiefs and wanted an organization that addressed their particular interests.

The National Organization of Black Law Enforcement Executives (NOBLE) was formed in 1976 to serve the growing constituency of African-American command officers. Initially, only officers at the rank of captain and above were eligible to join the organization. Membership requirements changed in the 1980s and any officer at the supervisory level could join the organization. The change opened NOBLE to high ranking sergeants and supervisors in Federal Law enforcement agencies.

While the professional orientation of the organization was much like that of the PERF and IACP, NOBLE provided a particular focus on issues of concern to its members, such as racism, career development and equal justice. Its stated mission was "to ensure equity in the administration of justice in the provision of public service to all communities of law enforcement by being committed to justice for all."

These four organizations, while the largest in membership, are not the only professional organizations in policing. Other organizations that have assisted in the professional development of law enforcement include the *United States Conference of Mayors, National League of Cities*, and the *International City Managers Association*. Members of these groups are elected officials who have regularly taken an interest in improving the police.

Police organizations have been an important catalyst in the professional development of its members. Annual conferences, which in some cases began as general membership meetings, have slowly evolved into important training and education events, serving as visible forums for discussion of emerging issues in law enforcement. As professional organizations, they have focused on the substance of policing more than the fraternal organizations, which focused on improving the working conditions of members. As such, the professional organizations are positioned to continue on their paths of providing professional development opportunities for their members and substantive direction to the field.

The organizations representing elected officials approached the issue of police development from a different perspective than that of the police officials. They were interested in the bigger picture, including quality of life in their cities. Crime was always a major quality of life issue and improvements in the police were seen as a way of reducing crime.

The Police Foundation is another organization that has contributed to the advancement of policing in America although it is not a membership organization. It was established in July of 1970 as the Police Development Fund with money from the Ford Foundation. Its name was changed almost immediately. It was organized to assist in the progression of policing in America and has made significant contributions. The Police Foundation sponsored the Kansas City Preventive Patrol Experiment, the Newark Foot

Patrol Project, the Houston and Newark Fear Reduction Projects, Women in Policing and other significant policing experiments and studies.

THE NATIONAL COMMISSION ON ACCREDITATION OF LAW ENFORCEMENT AGENCIES

By the end of the 1970s, executives of the Law Enforcement Assistance Administration believed that an effective means of getting police agencies to initiate improvement efforts was to adopt an accreditation model patterned after those used by other professions, such as hospitals and educational institutions. The challenge was to develop standards that law enforcement agencies would find acceptable.

The Commission on Accreditation was formed in 1978 to establish a body of standards designed to increase the capabilities of law enforcement agencies to prevent and control crime, increase agency effectiveness and efficiency in the delivery of law enforcement services, increase cooperation and coordination with other law enforcement agencies and, with other criminal justice agencies, increase citizen and employee confidence in the goals, objectives, policies, and practices of the agency. In addition, the Commission sought to develop an accreditation process that would provide state and local law enforcement agencies an opportunity to voluntarily demonstrate that they met an established set of law enforcement standards.

To ensure acceptance of the accreditation process by local law enforcement agencies, the four key policing professional organizations convened as partners in the accreditation enterprise. The *International Association of Chiefs of Police*, the *Police Executive Research Forum*, the *National Organization of Black Law Enforcement Executives* and the *National Sheriffs Association*, each with a particular constituency, became the conveners of the accreditation process. Each group was responsible for drafting a set of standards in areas where they had particular sensitivity or expertise. Commissioners were, and still are, appointed by the four sponsoring organizations and include eleven law enforcement professionals and ten representatives from the public and private sectors.

The Commission defined 48 topics that the standards addressed. Beginning in December of 1979, the Commission began considering standards developed by the four agencies. The standards covered almost every aspect of a law enforcement agency's administration and operations. Most required that an agency have a written directive governing the area that the standards covered. Size of agency was taken into account in determining whether a standard was required, optional, or not applicable. Agencies were required to comply with all required standards and a high percentage of the optional standards. A final draft of the standards was not approved until May of 1982. Field testing, with comments and reviews, resulted in the first set of 944 standards being adopted in April of 1983.

The resulting Standards for Law Enforcement Agencies represented a general consensus of the professional requirements for the model police organization. Acceptance of the accreditation process was slow. Not only was there substantial work for a police agency in providing the documentation required for accreditation, but the agency also had to undergo a peer assessment by law enforcement officials from other agencies selected by the Commission. Nine hundred forty-three agencies had been accredited by 2011, and approximately 90 percent of them re-accredited at least once. Not all police agencies receiving accreditation have been willing to go through the process again. The personnel commitment and expenses associated with the process were debilitating for some.

In 1993 the *Community Policing Consortium* was established by the United States Department of Justice's Bureau of Justice Assistance as a partnership between the International Association of Chiefs of Police, the Police Executive Research Forum, the Police Foundation and the National Sheriffs Association to provide training and technical assistance to police agencies and sheriff's departments in the area of Community Policing. Later, the National Organization of Black Law Enforcement Executives was added, and in 1994 it was shifted to the Office of Community Oriented Policing Services which now provides its funding.

SUMMARY

Blue-ribbon commissions have played an important role in advancing the professionalism of policing in America. During the decades of the 1960s and 1970s, no fewer than eight national panels were convened to examine the issues, the problems and concerns of the American public about crime, violence and the performance of the criminal justice system, especially the police. In addition, numerous local commissions or committees have been convened to address specific local problems.

Each commission was established to address a specific concern. Each conducted a comprehensive analysis of policing issues related to those concerns, resulting in recommendations designed to make improvements.

The President's Commission on Law Enforcement and Administration of Justice laid the foundation for the creation of the Law Enforcement Assistance Administration, which made large sums of money available to police agencies to develop and implement crime control programs. The National Advisory Commission on Civil Disorders and the National Commission on the Causes and Prevention of Violence and Unrest provided the public and the police valuable insight into the problems of crime and violence. They presented invaluably comprehensive recommendations for police reform.

The National Advisory Commission on Criminal Justice Standards and Goals and the American Bar Association reported on standards regarding the urban police function; and the work of the National Commission on Higher Education for the Police set forth standards designed to improve police services.

Finally, the work of the National Minority Advisory Council on Crime and Criminal Justice with its focus on crime and the police from the minority perspective, the Knapp Commission on Police Corruption in New York City, the Mollen Commission to Investigate Allegations of Police Corruption and Anti-Corruption Procedures of the Police Department, and the Independent Commission on the Los Angeles Police Department all had an impact on issues of integrity in policing throughout America. Each body addressed specific problems facing the police. Each offered straightforward recommendations for improvement.

Much of the work done by the commissions resulted in positive change. They have contributed to policing in America by providing the basis for increased professionalism as law enforcement prepared to enter the 21st century.

NOTES: CHAPTER THREE

1. *Car 54* "Where are you?" was a popular police television sitcom that was broadcast in the early 1950s. *Dragnet* was another popular police television show that appeared during the same time period.

2. Kelling, George L. and Mark H. Moore, "The Evolving Strategy of Policing," Perspectives on Policing, Washington, D.C.: U.S. Department of Justice, National Institute of Justice and the Program in Criminal Justice Policy and Management, John F. Kennedy School of Government, Cambridge, Mass.: Harvard University, November 1988, No. 4

3. President's Commission on Law Enforcement and Administration of Justice, The Challenge of Crime in a Free Society, Washington, D.C.: U.S. Government Printing Office, 1967

4. National Committee on Law Observance and Enforcement, commonly called the Wickersham Commission, named after its chairman, George W. Wickersham, January 1931

5. Op. Cit., Note 2 p.vi

6. National Advisory Commission on Civil Disorders, <u>Report of the National Advisory Commission on Civil Disorders</u>, Washington, D.C.: U.S. Government Printing Office, 1968

7. National Advisory Commission on the Causes and Prevention of Violence, <u>To Establish Justice, To Ensure Domestic Tranquility</u>, Washington, D.C.: U.S. Government Printing Office, 1969

8. Ibid. p. xxix

9. Ibid. pp. 155-156

10. Ibid. pp. 236-237

11. National Advisory Commission on Criminal Justice Standards and Goals, <u>A National Strategy to Reduce Crime</u>, Washington, D.C.: U.S. Government Printing Office, 1973

12. Ibid. p. 142-145

13. Ibid. p. 131-136

14. American Bar Association Project on Standards for Criminal Justice, <u>Standards Relating to the Urban Police Function,</u> 1972

15. National Minority Advisory Council on Criminal Justice, <u>The Inequality of Justice: A Report on Crime and The Administration of Justice in the Minority Community</u>, Washington, D.C.: United States Department of Justice, Law Enforcement Assistance Administration, 1982

16. Ibid. pp. 382-389

17. Sherman, Lawrence W. and The National Advisory Commission on Higher Education for Police Officers, <u>The Quality of Police Education,</u> Washington, D.C.: Jossey-Bass Publishers, 1978

18. Ibid. p. xi

19. Title I, Part D, section 406 (a –d), 42 U. S. C. Sec. 3701 and the following (Public Law 90 – 35) as amended by Public laws 91 – 644 and 93 – 81

20. The Knapp Commission, named after its Chairman, Whitman Knapp, was established in April 1970 by New York City Mayor John V. Lindsay. Its official name was the Commission to Investigate Alleged Police Corruption.

21. Commission to Investigate Allegations of Police Corruption and

Anti- Corruption Procedures of the Police Department, <u>Commission Report</u>, New York City, New York, 1972

22. Ibid. p. 2.

23. Ibid. p.152

24. Independent Commission on the Los Angeles Police Department, <u>Report of the Independent Commission on the Los Angeles Police Department</u>, Los Angeles, Calif., 1991

25. Ibid. Transmittal letter to Mayor Tom Bradley from Commission Chairman Warren Christopher.

26. Ibid., p.iii

27. Ibid. p. xii

28. Ibid., p. xiv

29. A Report by the Special Advisor to the Board of Police Commissioners on Civil Disorders in Los Angeles, <u>The City in Crisis</u>, Los Angeles, Calif., October, 1992

30. Ibid. p.23

31. Ibid. pp.176-177

32. Ibid. p.169

33. Police Chiefs' Position on Use of Excessive Force, New York City, unpublished, 1991

34. Ibid.

Chapter Four

THE ERA OF POLICE RESEARCH

INTRODUCTION

The problems that were highlighted by the commissions of the 1960s and 1970s created an environment in which there was substantial pressure for reform of the criminal justice system. There appeared to be dual concerns; one for ensuring that the police were trained and equipped to effectively deal with urban disorder and the "urban problem." The other was determining an effective strategy for reform of the criminal justice system.[1]

> The cumulative results of the policing research during the decade of the 1970s clearly concluded that the time honored practice of random preventive patrol was not productive.

Given the Federal government's movement towards a "Great Society," it was widely believed that criminal justice reform could only occur with pressure and support from it.

Local governments, it was reasoned, did not possess the tools, expertise or funding for serious reform of criminal justice practices. Police, with the greatest visibility, were widely viewed as requiring the largest amount of assistance.

THE LAW ENFORCEMENT ASSISTANCE ADMINISTRATION[2]

The Omnibus Crime Bill of 1968 established a Federal office for the support of law enforcement, including all aspects of the criminal justice system. As a part of this landmark legislation, the Office of Law Enforcement Assistance Administration (LEAA) was created in the Justice Department.

Initially funded with over $50 million, the new office initially focused on ways to reduce crime in urban areas. With the enactment of legislation in 1969, LEAA was formed to assume responsibility for Federal assistance to the national criminal justice establishment. In the early years, Federal assistance flowed through the states, which exercised great control over how the funds were spent. Each state established a planning agency to develop a master plan for criminal justice improvement. Based on state plans, Federal funds were allocated to state and local governments.[3]

Many state planning agencies allocated a majority of the resources to purchase equipment. Having been poorly funded for many years, local governments saw the expansive Federal funding as a means by which they could correct equipment deficiencies.

They would now be able to purchase necessary firearms, advanced weapons and, in some instances, riot control tanks. A few jurisdictions refused to accept Federal funds, believing that if funding was accepted they would come under more Federal scrutiny. Some believed that the Federal government's ultimate motive was to control local law enforcement.

This was a crucial time for American policing. Never before had such a large source of new funding been so widely available to local law enforcement. Initially, only a few critics complained that the equipment expenditures would ultimately have little impact unless basic systemic reform was undertaken. But concern over the massive equipment purchases grew and tighter guidelines were established. For the most part, however, these Federal funds were viewed by local law enforcement as a means for improving their technology, rather than seed money for important police reforms. The need for police improvement, so strongly mentioned in the Federal commission reports, had difficulty taking hold. One reason for the resistance was the lack of substantial knowledge about the impact of strategic and tactical approaches to policing so common throughout the country. Few people questioned the basic premises on which policing had developed.

THE POLICE FOUNDATION[4]

By late 1969, growing dissatisfaction with the ways that Federal money had been spent by local governments, and the failure to question important assumptions about the police function, led the Ford Foundation to establish the Police Foundation with $30 million in seed money. Having a fairly open agenda, the new foundation was charged with developing initiatives for improvement of the police through research, demonstration and education efforts.

The Police Foundation was clearly established in reaction to the failure of Federal efforts to adequately address important policy and reform issues in policing. The Foundation's mandate was the opposite of LEAA's. It sought to invest in strategic research and demonstration projects and did not fund so-called police improvements, unless they were a part of a research or demonstration effort. The initial president of the Foundation, Charles Rogovin, had previously been the Administrator of LEAA, where he was frustrated in his efforts to get the agency to assume a more focused role in criminal justice reform.

THE EARLY LEAA STUDIES

There were some early attempts by LEAA to try new approaches to the issue of police function. One of the earliest was the Pilot Cities Program, an effort to create a comprehensive approach to dealing with crime through reform of policing and criminal justice practices. By creating demonstration projects involving system-wide reforms, it was reasoned, the problems of crime and police-minority relations could be significantly improved.

Several cities with responsive, progressive police managers were selected and their police agencies were provided with relatively modest funding to engage in a variety of community activities intended to bring the police and community closer together, while also improving the operation of the criminal justice system.

The initial pilot cities were Dayton, Ohio; Charlotte, North Carolina; Albuquerque, New Mexico; Norfolk, Virginia; Omaha, Nebraska and Des Moines, Iowa, all medium-sized urban centers with histories of urban unrest and police departments with a sense of professionalism. Each city proposed a unique set of initiatives. In Dayton, for example, the focus was on implementing "team policing" in one section of the city and strengthening the police intelligence network to process criminal information. All of the cities were evaluated on two major standards, (1) building the capacity of local law enforcement and the criminal justice system and (2) contributing to national law enforcement and criminal justice theory and practice. While the individual strategies differed, the basic theory was generic. By implementing comprehensive improvements in the local police and criminal justice systems, the effectiveness of the entire criminal justice system could be impacted.[5]

THE NEW YORK CITY PATROL INITIATIVE

With LEAA support, a full-service-model policing program was designed in New York City, which provided a wide range of resources for policing the city's neighborhoods. Dr. Georgette Bennett and Dr. Ellen Mintz, both of whom started as consultants to the department and were later hired as employees, developed a demonstration program for the New York City Police Department which built on changes that had been implemented by Police Commissioner Patrick Murphy. The program's full-service orientation stressed the importance of the police "service function" and the need to recognize that role as part of the department's training program. The program also suggested improved relationships between the police and citizens as a means of preventing crime and apprehending offenders.[6]

THE EARLY POLICE FOUNDATION RESEARCH STUDIES

Social science research into American policing had been slight until the Police Foundation invested in a series of important research initiatives. While the problems of crime and delinquency had been the subject of numerous studies over the years, the police as an institution had rarely been observed; and the police generally had resisted researchers being present in their midst.

The few research efforts undertaken for the Commission on Law Enforcement and Administration of Justice created concern within policing circles because questionable policing field tactics were exposed. As part of a study of the Chicago Police Department by Albert Reiss, a Yale sociologist, researchers documented police activities while riding with officers.[7] The research exposed a variety of policing abuses and resulted in concern among numerous police executives. Their response was often to "close the doors" and refuse to allow researchers to observe the police while they worked.

The initial work of the Police Foundation laid the basis for the eventual reduction of this resistance. While the earliest Foundation work focused on trying to determine what strategies could be used to improve the quality of American policing, the Foundation eventually narrowed its efforts to researching the nature of police operations and assessing the impact of various strategies.

The initial research efforts concentrated on patrol activities in Kansas City, Missouri. Clarence Kelley, the Police Chief, was funded to hire a substantial number of additional police officers. Kelley had to think through the best use for this additional funding. While attending a number of Police Foundation meetings to discuss strategy, he suggested that his city was an excellent site to conduct significant research into police function.

Responding to his invitation, Police Foundation consultants worked with officers to identify important questions about policing strategies that needed to be answered. The first question raised by a task force became the basis of one of the most important research initiatives undertaken in policing. The question was relatively simple: "What was the impact of random preventive patrol?" It was an activity that consumed most of a patrol officer's time.

For years, patrol officers were taught that random car patrols throughout their assigned areas were the preferred means to prevent crime, apprehend criminals and develop citizen confidence in the police. Patrol officers were taught that the most effective patrol activity was to ensure that they maintain maximum visibility in all parts of their assigned areas. The randomness of this patrol strategy was expected to create a sense of police omnipresence throughout neighborhoods, developing citizen confidence, strengthen police job performance and create an apprehension among criminals that the police might appear at any time.

The Kansas City Preventive Patrol study tested these basic assumptions.[8] To determine the actual impact of preventive patrol, a section of Kansas City was divided into three types of areas. In one "control" area, nothing was changed. In the second "experimental" area, random preventive patrol was eliminated, with officers entering the area only in response to calls from citizens. In the third "experimental" area, the number of officers on random preventive patrol was doubled. Nothing else was changed. Even in the experimental areas, other policing activities continued as always. Only preventive random patrol was increased or eliminated.

Citizen perceptions of police visibility, citizen satisfaction and crime were then carefully measured for each area. The subsequent data analysis showed no difference in these factors between the three areas, regardless of whether there was preventive patrol. The research findings suggested that there might be more productive ways for police to spend their time rather than randomly driving around assigned neighborhoods, since that activity had little impact on perceived visibility, citizen satisfaction or criminal activity.

The Kansas City Preventive Patrol Experiment opened the door to additional police research that also questioned much of the traditional wisdom of American policing. Beginning as an exercise in participatory management, it altered the time-honored beliefs of the police world. Although some critics questioned the Kansas City results, the findings were so significant to policing that the research was replicated in four other cities, San Diego, California; Hartford, Connecticut; Peoria, Illinois; and Jacksonville, Florida. The findings in those cities mirrored those in the original Kansas City Preventive Patrol Experiment.

DIRECTED PATROL[9]

The thought that police officers, while not randomly patrolling, would direct their attention to other issues of concern to them, flowed from the Kansas City Experiment. Rather than being everywhere in the assigned "beat", it was suggested that the police devote the majority of their attention to areas with the highest incidents of crime. The concept was given the mantle of "directed patrol." It was widely adopted and provided police officers with a positive result, rather than a negative finding.

While widespread acceptance of the Kansas City Preventive Patrol study took years, the directed patrol concept, which was also developed in Kansas City, Missouri, was eagerly adopted. Variations reflected circumstances peculiar to various cities.

In New Haven, Connecticut, for example, the Police Department developed what they called "directed runs" (D-Runs) which permitted officers to call out of service and address specific problems at predetermined times of the day.[10] The department developed a D-Run book, which it updated every 28 days. The book was based on an analysis of crime and was basically statistical in its format. The program was ultimately abandoned, primarily because the officers felt that their discretion was taken away. Nevertheless, two lessons were learned from the experience. First, patrol officers did not want their activities directed by crime analysis, preferring the ability to determine their own courses of action based on information supplied by crime analysis. Second, it pointed out that if crime analysis was to be meaningful, it had to be current. Information about a crime committed thirty days earlier was useless. The Locator Patrol-Perpetrator Oriented Patrol (LOP-POP) in Kansas City, Missouri proved crime analysis data on crime *locations* had little value to patrol officers, compared to information on *perpetrators* who worked in a specific area. [11]

Wilmington, Delaware also experimented with the concept of directed patrol. Under a program called the Wilmington Split-Force, the department developed a three-pronged approach to patrol.[12] The first approach divided the patrol force into two groups: one group was called "basic" and the other "structured." The basic group was assigned 65 percent of patrol personnel with the remaining 35 percent going to the structured group. Officers assigned to the basic group did not have to patrol their beats; but they were required to respond to calls- for -service. The officers assigned to the structured group were required to perform both random and directed patrol, as well as respond to crime-in-progress calls and other non-emergency service calls.

Under the second component of the program, communications personnel handled service calls by taking reports over the phone, asking callers to come to police headquarters and make reports, and "stacking" calls that were non-emergencies. Third, the structure of the beats was rearranged for the basic group based on an analysis of the calls received. As a result, beat boundaries and shift hours were changed, resulting in officers reporting to duty at various times during the day.

Although the officers disliked the program, there were some positive results. First it showed that citizens were willing to accept having their reports taken over the phone or having to wait for an officer to respond. Second, it demonstrated that ninety-six percent of the workload could be handled by sixty-five percent of the patrol force.

OTHER POLICE FOUNDATION RESEARCH AND EXPERIMENTATION

The success of the Kansas City Preventive Patrol study led the Police Foundation to initiate a series of other research efforts, all aimed at better understanding the impact of policing tactics.[13] In San Diego, the Foundation undertook three important experiments: (1) measurement of the impact of field interrogation practices, (2) development of a beat profiling system and (3) measurement of the impact of one-officer versus two-officer patrol units.

FIELD INTERROGATION PRACTICES[14]

In an effort to determine the effect of field interrogations, San Diego undertook a study in which field interrogations were conducted as usual in one area. In a second area, officers were given special training on how to conduct field interrogations. In a third area, no field interrogations were conducted. The results showed that some field interrogations, rather than none, were associated with a reduction in crime. The study also showed that neither the frequency of the interrogations or the level of training influenced citizen attitudes or opinions. The researchers cautioned that the results should not be seen as applicable generally because of San Diego's training and traditional use of field interrogation techniques.

ONE VERSUS TWO OFFICER UNITS[15]

In reviewing the impact of one officer versus two-officer patrol units, the foundation discovered that two-officer units were no safer than single officer units. That finding contradicted conventional wisdom. When this research began in the mid-1970s, it was an important example of research focused on an important policing issue for which there had not been any prior empirical data available for decision makers.

BEAT PROFILING[16]

San Diego never received the recognition it deserved for its beat profiling project, a program designed by the department's Patrol Planning Unit. Under the program, patrol officers were required to learn the characteristics of their beats. As part of the beat profiling requirements, participating officers were required to contact citizens and ascertain their concerns and expectations from the department. In this manner, officers were accountable for the issues, problems and concerns of the people who lived in their areas of responsibility.

The program only involved a small number of police officers and when the department attempted to implement it city-wide, it did not survive because other members of the department were not prepared to participate in it. Nevertheless, three positive lessons were gathered from this program. First, the department benefited when its officers developed closer working relationships with members of the community. Second, assigning officers permanently to single beat assignments was preferable to rotating them among different beats. Permanent beat assignments allowed officers to develop a sense of ownership of the areas. In addition, officers could be held accountable for activities on their beats. Third, the failure to implement the program on a department-wide basis highlighted the importance of supervisors and managers in the change process. Failure to properly prepare and train those in ranks above patrol officer imperiled successful innovation in a police department.

THE NEWARK FOOT PATROL EXPERIMENT[17]

The Newark Foot Patrol Experiment focused on the impact of police officers walking beats in Newark, New Jersey. Carefully measuring the impact on public perception as well as reported crime, this experiment was the first attempt to measure the impact of a particular policing strategy aimed at replacing random preventive patrol. The Locator Patrol-Perpetrator Oriented Patrol undertaken in Kansas City, Missouri and evaluated by the Police Foundation preceded this. Unlike the foot patrol study it did not address citizen perceptions or fear of crime—only the probability of officers making arrests when provided with certain types of information.

To some the findings of the research were surprising. Officers who walked their beats gained far greater empathy and understanding of neighborhood concerns than those who rode in police vehicles. Likewise, citizens felt safer and believed the police were far more responsive to their concerns. But there was no demonstrable impact on crime. The impact of these findings went far beyond the utility of walking patrols as a policing strategy. It suggested that when police officers were in close contact with neighborhood residents and business people, they understood the culture of the neighborhoods and established relationships with residents, reducing public perceptions that neighborhoods were unsafe.

As an adjunct to the Newark Foot Patrol experiment, James Q. Wilson and George Kelling, in their important article titled Broken Windows, suggested that signs of crime created a perception of citizen fear, not actual victimization itself. Noting that when a neighborhood had a pattern of growing "signs of crime," it indicated to the public that the environment was out of control, attracted criminals, and was deteriorating. [18]

When indications of crime, such as rapidly repairing broken windows are quickly addressed, there is a belief that the neighborhood is under control and citizen fear is abated, according to the authors.

The supporting research by Dan A. Lewis at Northwestern University in the Reactions to Crime Project indicated that when people spoke of crime, they were actually referring to Wilson and Kellin's signs of crime such as noise, unclean streets, abandoned automobiles and gang activity.[19]

Giving favor to the Wilson and Kelling thesis, citizen fear was found to be directly related to neighborhood conditions and a community's sense as to whether or not police were in control of a neighborhood.

WOMEN IN POLICING[20]

The Police Foundation also conducted exploratory research into other important policing issues during its formative years. One of the important examples of that research was the work on Women in Policing. Although women had long been considered inappropriate candidates for most police work, this important Foundation study documented the substantial contributions women made to policing in a variety of environments and suggested ways in which police agencies could greatly expand the role of women as productive members of the agencies. Given the recruiting problems many police agencies faced, and the widespread acceptance among the public that women could be effective police officers, police agencies across the country expanded their recruiting and promotional efforts directed towards women. Before long, female officers performed nearly every function in a modern police agency.

THE RAND INSTITUTE EXPERIMENTS

As the idea of meaningful police research began to germinate, other research initiatives were undertaken. One of the more important focused on criminal investigation, a subject shrouded in mystique. Peter Greenwood and his associates at the Rand Institute observed criminal investigation work in a number of police departments and concluded that behind the detective mystique was a great inefficiency. With these observations, Greenwood published an article, suggesting that most police agencies could exist with far fewer detectives. The study also laid the foundation for research into what exactly solved crimes, suggesting that detectives produced little new information during their investigations. Based on the initial Rand work, LEAA supported a series of studies by the Urban Institute about the nature of the investigative function. Identifying "solvability factors" as the key elements on which crime solution was based, the research suggested that if specific types of information were not available or collected when the patrol officer responded to the initial crime scene, detectives were highly unlikely to solve crimes through follow-up investigations. [21]

As with the Kansas City Patrol Experiments, this research shook the foundation of American police thinking. The idea that detectives had little to do with solving most crimes ran counter to all police wisdom. As with the Kansas City research, the results and implications of the findings were greatly misinterpreted. Many police executives assumed that researchers were proposing that police agencies did not need detectives, when, in fact, what was being proposed was (1) the importance of information collection at the time of the initial response to a call and (2) the need to direct limited detective resources away from cases with small possibilities of being solved.

THE NATIONAL INSTITUTE OF JUSTICE

The emerging National Institute of Justice (NIJ) began to support the development of a model that increased investigative effectiveness, called the Managing Criminal Investigations Model. Field-tested in five cities, the model suggested strengthened patrol investigations, re-direction of investigative effort into solvable cases, prosecutor-police liaisons to improve prosecution effectiveness, and management of the continuing investigations. Yet, because the proposed reforms were again often misinterpreted, they were never widely adopted as discussed in later chapters of this book. [22]

FEAR REDUCTION[23]

Aware that quite often the fear of crime exceeded the actual incidences of crime itself, the National Institute of Justice funded the Fear Reduction Project. Two cities, Houston, Texas and Newark, New Jersey were selected to participate in the program. The Police Foundation evaluated the results in both cities.

The two cities had some common elements. Each published a newsletter for the community and offered storefront locations within the community where police conducted business and officers initiated contacts with residents. In Houston, the police also implemented a victims program where an officer telephoned crime victims, offering assistance and expressing the concern of the police department. Residents were also told about an effort by police officers to organize neighborhood resources.

Newark implemented a program designed to address the problem of incivility, or signs of crime, by focusing on physical and social problems. Newark also started a program to increase officer contact with citizens and provide them with information. The results of the evaluation revealed that the three most successful efforts were the police storefronts, citizen contacts and community organizing. The successful programs were the ones that empowered the officers to use their initiative to work with the community.

THE DOMESTIC VIOLENCE EXPERIMENT[24]

In 1981, NIJ funded the Police Foundation and the Minneapolis Police Department to conduct the Domestic Violence Experiment. In response to an ongoing debate about how best to respond to the problem of domestic violence, the police department tested and evaluated three police responses: (1) respond, quiet things down and leave, (2) attempt to assist by mediating the underlying cause of the dispute, but make no arrests, and (3) treat the violence like any other crime and if evidence of a violation was present, make an arrest. It was discovered that making an arrest was the most effective means of addressing domestic violence cases.

The National Institute of Justice sponsored considerably more research than covered in this chapter. Today it continues to contribute significantly to the body of knowledge in police work.

THE POLICE EXECUTIVE RESEARCH FORUM[25]

The Police Executive Research Forum (PERF) was founded in 1976 by a group of police executives from ten large cities who believed that other existing police organizations were resistant to evolving research.

With funding from the Police Foundation, PERF focused on a mission of supporting meaningful research and discussion among police executives in larger communities. By restricting membership to executives in communities with populations exceeding 100,000, the forum quickly became the focal point for research and discussion of important policing issues.

MANAGING CALLS-FOR-SERVICE[26]

One of the early research efforts undertaken by PERF focused on the nature of police calls-for-service. While a variety of research efforts on calls-for-service had been undertaken with Police Foundation and NIJ support, the research results had never been gathered into a cohesive model usable by interested police executives. A Kansas City Police Department study indicated that in only a small number of instances did criminals remain at the crime scene when a person called the police. Yet police response was frequently oriented solely at apprehending criminals. National Institute of Justice Research explored the true nature of calls-for-service and how the police, at the point of receipt, classified them.

PERF, in its monograph, "Calling the Police" established the basis for a model of managing the call-for-service function. [27] By better classification of calls at the point of intake, and determining the time of occurrence of each incident, the complaint operator could accurately determine which police response was most appropriate.

PROBLEM SOLVING POLICING

Some of the most important research undertaken in recent years has focused on problem solving. Beginning in 1978, a research team at the Northeastern University Center for Social Research analyzed data from calls-for-service from the Boston Police Department. Taking a sample of all calls between 1978 and 1982 the research team plotted these calls by city addresses obtained from the geo-base file. They found that over 50 percent of the calls-for-service were to addresses that the police had responded to at least ten times each year. [28]

During the four year period, Herman Goldstein of the University of Wisconsin Law School reflected on the nature of problems that the police were dealing with.

Noting that police were generally responding to problems rather than incidents, he provided a framework within which the Northeastern call-for-service analysis could be viewed. If most 911 calls to the police were actually ongoing long-term problems of a neighborhood, simply responding to those calls with a police unit and taking care of the immediate symptoms would have limited impact. This perspective led to formulation of the problem-solving model, recognizing that police respond to far more than isolated incidents and must develop a capacity for problem analysis to discover the true nature of a particular series of incidents and identify potential solutions. Two police departments, Madison, Wisconsin and Newport News, Virginia led the way in testing the concept of Problem Solving Policing. [29]

CRIMINAL INVESTIGATIONS

In **1978**, PERF also conducted research into the criminal investigation process, expanding on the managing criminal investigations model. Applying the principles of case screening and the use of solvability factors to burglaries, it determined that case closures increased with good screening methodology. [30]

In 1983, PERF published the results of another study on the investigation of burglary and robbery offenses. Unlike the RAND study on the investigative process, the PERF research found that both detectives and patrol officers played a significant role and contributed equally in the solution of burglary and robbery cases. The police more readily accepted this research because it did not state that the work of detectives was ineffective. The study recommended that investigations become proactive and focus on problem solving. By that, PERF suggested, "targeted investigations" as a means of improving the investigative process. Targeted investigations involved (1) defining the problem, (2) planning the approach, (3) conducting the investigation, and (4) evaluating the results. [31]

OTHER RESEARCH

THE FLINT FOOT PATROL EXPERIMENT[32]

In 1979, Flint, Michigan received a grant from the Charles Stewart Mott Foundation for an experimental foot patrol program. The program, which was evaluated by Michigan State University's Criminal Justice Department, started as a pilot project covering 20 percent of Flint. Later it expanded to include the entire city. This program was unique in that the community was instrumental in obtaining the funding that initiated it.

The evaluation revealed positive results. Overall crime declined, as did calls-for-service. Most importantly, when residents were polled they stated that they felt safer, especially when they knew that foot patrol officers were visible in the community.

The decade of the 1970s and, to a lesser extent, the 1980s, were the major periods for police research, helping to change policing in America. Cities such as Kansas City, Missouri; San Diego, California; Rochester, New York and New Haven, Connecticut helped to prove that operational research could be undertaken in police departments without disrupting the operations of the agency. Furthermore, the research provided new and valuable insights into police work, often challenging some of the notions held sacred by the police.

THE HARVARD EXECUTIVE SESSION[33]

Starting in 1985 and continuing for four years, the John F. Kennedy School of Government at Harvard University and the National Institute of Criminal Justice (NIJ) convened an executive session to discuss the institutional capacity of the police, including the problems that they were called on to resolve.

The work product of the sessions were reflected in several papers that were published by the NIJ and Harvard University titled *Perspectives on the Police*.[34] In summary, the executive sessions reached the conclusion that the police profession had learned a great deal from the research and experimentation during a twenty year period. The collection of papers, starting with one entitled "The Evolving Strategy of Policing "provided an intellectual basis that assisted the understanding of the Community Policing movement.[35]

The participants in the executive sessions also reached consensus in a number of areas. First, there was agreement that the police had come to realize that they could not by themselves solve the complex problems of crime, drugs, fear and urban decay. They realized that they had to work jointly with the community to control crime and that they had to create meaningful partnerships in the community.

Second, there was agreement that the police represented a significant investment of tax dollars and therefore their resources must be used in the most effective manner possible. Consequently, there was a consensus that the police could no longer afford to respond to "repeated incidents" from the same callers.

Resources must be used to solve problems and Problem Solving Policing differed significantly from the historical reliance on random patrol and rapid response, they concluded. The police must be concerned about results and finding solutions to the problems faced by people who lived in communities where they worked.

After having reached consensus in the above areas, the members of the executive sessions agreed that there must be fundamental changes in the organization and structure of police departments. Those changes centered on concepts such as decentralization, the creation and institutionalization of values, new roles for all members of the departments, and the implementation of different reward and evaluation systems.

The Harvard executive sessions were historic in two ways. First, they brought together police leaders, educators, researchers and the business community over a two-year period to concentrate exclusively on the future of policing in America. Second, it produced a series of well-written papers that occupy a lasting place in police literature.

SUMMARY

The cumulative results of the policing research during the decade of the 1970s clearly concluded that the time-honored practice of random preventive patrol was not productive. Rather, police departments should, based on an analysis of calls-for-service, direct their resources towards achieving predetermined goals. Additionally, the research revealed that rapid response to calls-for-service did not produce the desired results. Alternative ways of handling calls-for-service, such as taking reports over the telephone, proved satisfactory to citizens.

The research also concluded that given time and incentive, patrol officers could be trusted not only to identify the problems in the neighborhoods they served, but also to devise effective solutions. That responsibility was greatly enhanced by giving patrol officers timely information on crime as well as calls-for-service.

An important element that transcended most of the research was the need for citizen involvement in crime control activities. From an operational and managerial standpoint, this translated into permanent beat assignments and increased the officer's time to become acquainted with the people they served.

In the area of investigations, the research clearly suggested that both the patrol officers and the detectives have equally important roles in solving criminal cases.

The research of the 1980s led the police clearly in the direction of Community Policing. Directed patrol, problem solving, citizen involvement, managing calls-for-service and fear reduction provided police leaders with the necessary information to fundamentally change how police departments delivered their services.

In some instances, the research findings turned out to be uncomfortable for some because they challenged the conventional wisdom held by many police administrators. Yet, viewed as a whole, this era of police research provided a theoretical basis and rationale for fundamental changes in law-enforcement.

NOTES: CHAPTER FOUR

1. The Great Society was a term used to describe President Lyndon Johnson's programs to eliminate poverty, racial injustice and other social ills. http://en.wikipedia.org/wiki/Great_Society

2. Records of the Law Enforcement Assistance Administration (LEAA) http://archives.gov/rearch/guide-fed-records/group/423.html 11.3.10

3. Initially funded for $500 million, the new office began its focus on ways to reduce crime. See, Law Enforcement and Criminal Justice Assistance Act of 1967, 90th Congress, 1st Session, H.R. 5037, July 17, 1967

4. (http://www.policefoundation.org 11.3.10

5. Murray, Charles A. and Robert Krug, The National Evaluation of the Pilot Cities Program: Executive Summary, U.S. Department of Justice, National Institute of Law Enforcement and Criminal Justice, Washington, D.C.: U.S. Government Printing Office, November, 1975, p.6

6. Mintz, Ellen and Georgette Bennett Sandler, "Instituting a Full-Service Orientation to Policing," The Police Chief, Vol. 41, Issue 6, June 1974, PP. 41-50

7. Reiss, Albert J. Jr., The Police and the Public, New Haven, Conn.: Yale University Press, 1971

8. Kelling, George, Tony Pate, Duane Dieckman, Charles E. Brown, The Kansas City Preventive Patrol Experiment, Washington, D.C.: The Police Foundation, 1974

9. Kansas City Police Department, Kansas City Police Department Directed Patrol: A Concept in Community- Specific, Crime- Specific, and Service- Specific Policing, Kansas City, Missouri, 1974

10. New Haven Department of Police Services, Directed Deterrent Patrol, New Haven Department of Police Services, New Haven, Conn., 1976

11. Pate, Tony, Robert A. Bowers, Ron Parks, Three Approaches to Criminal Apprehension in Kansas City: An Evaluation Report. Washington, D.C.: Police Foundation, 1978

12. Tien, J.M, J.W. Simon and R.C. Larson, An Evaluation Report of an Alternative Approach to Police Patrol, The Wilmington Split Force Experiment, Cambridge, Mass.: Public Systems Evaluation, Inc., 1977

13. Kelling, George, Tony Pate, Duane Dieckman, Kansas City Preventive Patrol Experiment, Washington, D.C.: The Police Foundation, 1974

14. Boydstun, John E., <u>San Diego Field Interrogation – Final Report</u>, Washington, D.C.: Police Foundation, 1975

15. Boydstun, John E., Michael E. and Nicolas P. Moelter, <u>Patrol Staffing in San Diego: One or Two-Officer Units</u>, Washington, D.C.: Police Foundation, 1977

16. Boydsun, John, and Michael E. Sherry, <u>San Diego Community Profile: Final Report</u>, Washington, D.C.: Police Foundation, 1975

17. Police Foundation, <u>The Newark Foot Patrol Experiment</u>, Washington, D.C.: United States Department of Justice, 1981

18. Wilson, James Q. and George Kelling, "Broken Windows," <u>Atlantic Monthly</u>, March 1962, pp. 29-38

19. Lewis, Dan A. and Wesley G. Skogan, Aaron Podolefsky, Fredric DuBow and Margaret T. Gordon, <u>The Reactions to Crime Project</u>, Washington. D.C.: U.S. Department of Justice, National Institute of Justice, May 1982

20. Milton, Catherine, <u>Women in Policing</u>, Washington, D.C.: Police Foundation, 1972

21. Greenwood, Peter, Jan M. Chaiken, Joan Petersilia and Linda Prusoff, <u>The Criminal Investigation Process, Vol. III: Observation and Analysis</u>, Santa Monica, California: The Rand Corporation, 1975

22. Greenwood, Ilene and Robert Wasserman, <u>Managing Criminal Investigations</u>, Washington, D.C.: U.S. Department of Justice, Law Enforcement Assistance Administration, National Institute of Law Enforcement and Criminal Justice, 1979

23. Pate, Anthony M. Mary Ann Wycoff, Wesley G. Slogan and Lawrence E. Sherman, "<u>Reducing Fear of Crime in Houston and Newark</u>," Washington, D.C.: Police Foundation, 1986

24. Sherman, Lawrence E. and Richard A. Berk, <u>The Minneapolis Domestic Violence Experience</u>, Washington, D. C., Police Foundation, April, 1984

25. http://www.policeforum.org/ 6.25.11

26. Svindoff, Michele, <u>Calls for Service: Recent Research on Measuring and Managing Demand</u>, New York: Vera Institute of Justice, non-published, October 1982

27. Spelman, William and Dale K. Brown,<u> Calling the Police: Citizen Reporting of Serious Crime Police</u>, Washington, D.C.: Police Executive Research Forum, 1979

28. Pierce, G. S. Spaar and L. Briggs, "The Character of Police Work: Implications for Delivery of Police Services," Final Report to the

Department of Justice, National Institute of Justice, Washington, D.C.: National Institute of Justice, 1988

29. See Goldstein, Herman, <u>Problem Oriented Policing</u>, New York: McGraw Hill, 1990 and Eck, John and William Spelman, et al., <u>Problem Solving: Problem- Oriented Policing in Newport News, Virginia and Washington, D.C.</u>, Washington, D.C.: Police Executive Research Forum, 1987

30. Eck, John, <u>Solving Crimes: The Investigation of Burglary and Robbery</u>, Washington, D.C.: Police Executive Research Forum, 1983

31. Eck, J.E., <u>Managing Case Assignments: The Burglary Decision Model Replication</u>, Washington, D.C.: Police Executive Research Forum, 1979

32. Trojanowiez, Robert C., <u>An Evaluation of the Neighborhood Foot Patrol Program in Flint, Michigan</u>, The National Neighborhood Foot Patrol Center, East Lansing, Michigan: Michigan State University, 1985

33. An Executive Session is a formal working group composed of high-level practitioners and academics that come together periodically to redefine and propose solutions for a substantive police issue, and to reposition the organization whose mission might include responsibility for progress on that issue.) For additional information see Francis X Hartman, Mark H. Moore and Janet C. Gornick, Executive Session, Program in Criminal Justice Policy and Management of the Malcolm Wiener Center for Social Policy, John F. Kennedy School of Government, Harvard University, May 1989, Working Paper #89-07-01

34. The Program in Criminal Justice Policy and Management, John F. Kennedy School of Government, Cambridge, Mass.: Harvard University and the National Institute of Justice, U.S. Department of Justice sponsored an Executive Sessions on the Police and produced a series of publications titled <u>Perspectives on Policing</u>

35. Kelling, George L., Mark H. Moore, "The Evolving Strategy of Policy, <u>Perspectives on Policing</u>, U.S. Department of Justice, Office of Justice Programs, National Institute of Justice and Program in Criminal Justice Policy and Management of the John F. Kennedy School of Government, Cambridge, Mass.: Harvard University, November 1988, No.4

Chapter Five

POLICE AND THE COURTS

INTRODUCTION

To fully understand the police as a social institution, it is important to first recognize that just as the police impact other institutions in society, other institutions also have an impact on the police. One such institution is the court system.

This chapter will discuss how the courts, through landmark decisions, have contributed to the progress of police professionalism. It will explore precedent setting case law that impacted police procedures and practices, starting in the late 1950s.

> Over the years the courts have assisted in advancing the professionalism of American law enforcement.

In reviewing the cases discussed in this chapter, it is important to remember that the U.S. Supreme Court is the highest tribunal in the nation. It has the responsibility of interpreting the constitutionality of laws at the Federal, state, and local levels. Supreme Court rulings are based on the supreme law of the land.

The decisions handed down by the Court resulting in new laws or new police practices were predicated on police conduct or standards that were viewed as contravening the Constitution.

One of the sacred principles of Community Policing is that the police are responsible to protect the rights of every citizen, as guaranteed by the Constitution. That responsibility is no less important to the police than their responsibility to enforce the law.

Over the years, some police leaders criticized the Court and accused it of "handcuffing the police." During the 1960s, a polarization developed between the police and the Court.

Some police leaders, in response to what they believed were adverse Court decisions, raised a number of issues about the Court's interpretation of certain police actions. Those questions can best be summarized as follows:

- Should not a criminal, based on his confession or proof of guilt beyond a reasonable doubt, be held responsible for his act?
- Should not the Court give more weight to the fact that a criminal is guilty and hold him responsible by administering the prescribed punishment, regardless of legal technicalities that may arise during the course of as investigation or trial?
- Should more importance be placed on possible errors committed by the police in the area of search and seizure than on the fact that the person actually committed the crime?
- Isn't the guilty criminal responsible for his act, or should the concept of criminal responsibility, as applied to the insane, be applied to the collection of evidence and the guilty person freed on that basis, the same as an insane person who is not held responsible for his act on the basis of mental capacity....

On the other hand, there were those who firmly believed that in a Democracy it was better for a criminal to be set free than have his or her Constitutional rights violated. They argued that law enforcement was easier and more efficient in a totalitarian society than in a Democratic state because the police in a totalitarian society are not obliged to respect the rights of individuals or follow procedures based on Constitutional principles. Therefore, if they had to chose between a society with less crime, that did not respect individual rights, and a society with more crime, where the rights of the individual are guaranteed, they would chose the latter.

BACKGROUND

During the 1960s, the United States witnessed a rapid increase in its crime rate. For example, figures obtained from the Federal Bureau of Investigation showed that there were 1.6 million major crimes reported in 1958. In 1963, there were 2.2 million major crimes reported. Over that five-year period, there was a 40 percent increase in the number of major crimes reported in the United States. [1]

Figures from of the United States Census Bureau showed that in 1958 there were 174 million people in United States. In 1963, there were 189 million people, an eight percent increase. The crime rate increased five times faster than the population. The crime problem was a major concern to the majority of Americans and received widespread publicity. [2]

What was the reason for this rapid increase in the crime rate? When this question was asked during an Associate Press Poll of law enforcement officials from various parts of the nation, the answers clearly illustrated that the police resented the judicial system. John McCormack, Safety Director for Cleveland, Ohio had the following to say: "(The) apathy of citizenry, the period of unrest the country is going though, coupled with the civil-rights problem is a major cause, and leniency of the courts is a factor in some cases." [3]

Chief William H. T. Smith, of the Syracuse, New York Police Department replied: "There's no question about leniency having something to do with it. It seems to be getting more difficult to carry out police investigations because various laws hamper investigative work." [4]

Police Chief Paul Shaffer of Albuquerque, New Mexico answered: "I personally think we ought to take another look at our system as far as procedures and laws are concerned. It is getting increasingly harder to make a case against an individual..." [5]

Pennsylvania State Police Superintendent E. Wilson Purdy blamed the"... failure of the courts to support law enforcement." He went on to say, "We no longer try defendants on evidence. We try them on legality and technicality of obtaining evidence and arrest."[6]

The essence of the police position was summed up in a statement by United States Representative Burr P. Harrison, (Westchester, Virginia) when he said: "In the struggle between the forces of law and order and those of crime and treason, on which side are the men who are Judges of the Supreme Court of the United States? These nine men have opened the secret files of the FBI to the criminal; they have licensed the seller of filth and obscenity to the youth; they have assaulted the rights of the officers of the law to arrest for felonies committed in their presence; they have swept away the power of police to fight crime by reasonable interrogation of suspects and by introduction in evidence of volunteer and truthful confession..." [7]

HISTORY OF THE PROBLEM

The polarization of the Courts and the police was an important issue during the decade of the 1960s. In the opinion of many law enforcement practitioners, the United States Supreme Court was overly protecting criminals to the detriment of the larger society. They did not argue that individual freedom was not an important element of our democratic society; rather they argued that the protection of society as a whole was equally, if not more, important.

This was by no means a new issue. As far back as 1759, Dr. Samuel Johnson in his work, *Lives of the English Poets*, discussed some of Milton's ideas on liberty and made a statement that some believed applicable: "The danger of (such) unbounded liberty and the danger of bounding it has produced a problem in science of government which human understanding seems hitherto unable to solve."[8]

Professor Yale Kamisar, who took a strong stand in favor of the Court in the debate, commented on the background of the problem. According to him, in 1910 Curtis Lindley, President of the California Bar Association, declared the need for an "adjustment" in our criminal procedures "to meet the expanding social necessity." Mr. Lindsay said, "Many of the difficulties are due to an exaggerated respect for the individual..." He proposed, (1) that a suspect be interrogated by a magistrate and if he refused to answer the inquiries, the state should be permitted to comment on his refusal at trial; and (2) the requirement of a unanimous verdict for a guilty finding be reduced to two-thirds. [9]

In 1911, Charles Nott, a New York prosecutor, wrote an article for *The Atlantic Monthly*, entitled "Coddling the Criminal." Nott charged that, "The appalling amount of crime in the United States compared with other civilized countries is due to the fact that it is generally known that punishment for crime in America is uncertain and far from severe." According to Nott, the two law enforcement obstacles which had to be cleared were the protection against double jeopardy and the privilege against self-incrimination. [10]

Some critics went as far to say that American judges were following the path taken by England in 1912, when the original Judges' Rules were formulated. These rules were increased in 1915 and received an important interpretation in 1930. The rules were nine in number; but the gist of the rules can be stated in two propositions:[11]

1. When a police officer has made up his mind to charge a person with a crime, he should caution him in the usual words: Do

you wish to say anything in answer to the charge? You are not obligated to say anything unless you wish to do so, but whatever you say will be taken down in writing and may be given in evidence.
2. A person in custody must not be questioned.

Any violation of the Judge's Rules gives and confers judicial discretion to exclude from evidence any statement made by the arrested party.

Even though many police leaders of that period were extremely critical of the judicial system, the courts did facilitate major changes in American policing. Those changes were significant because the police take an oath to uphold the Constitution of the United States and the states where they work. The rights granted to all citizens are an important principle of the U.S Constitution.

Over the years, the Supreme Court has assisted in advancing the professionalism of American law enforcement. In order to fully understand the implications of the impact the Court has had on policing, it is important to review some of its landmark decisions. It is interesting to note that the facts of the cases clearly illustrate that the activities of the police precipitated judicial review.

FOURTH AMENDMENT

The Fourth Amendment to the United States Constitution was adopted in 1791 and provides that people have "the right to be secure in their persons, houses, papers, and effects, against unreasonable searches and seizures, shall not be violated, and no warrants shall issue, but upon probable cause, supported by oath or affirmation, and particularly describing the place to be searched, and the person or things to be seized."[12]

LANDMARK DECISIONS

MALLORY V. UNITED STATES[13]

One of the first landmark Court decisions that changed police practices was *Mallory v. United States*. This case involved Andrew Mallory, a 19 year-old African American, who was convicted in the United States District Court for the District of Columbia on a rape charge. The jury imposed the death sentence. There was a question concerning the interpretation of the Federal Rules of Criminal Procedure in this case, and for that reason the Supreme Court granted a petition for *certiorari*.[14]

The facts in this case showed that the rape occurred on April 7, 1954 in the basement of the victim's apartment. The victim had gone to the basement to do her laundry. Once there, she had trouble detaching a hose from the sink and went to seek assistance from the janitor. The janitor lived in the basement of the same apartment building with this wife, three sons, and Andrew, his half-brother. Andrew was the only person in the apartment at the time and he assisted the victim by removing the hose and then returned to his apartment.

A short time later a masked man, whom the victim said resembled Mallory and his two oldest nephews, attacked the victim. The victim stated that she did not hear anyone come down the wooden steps, which was the only way to enter the basement.

Immediately after the attack, Mallory and one of his nephews disappeared from the apartment house. Mallory was apprehended the next afternoon and taken to police headquarters, along with his two nephews. At least four officers questioned Mallory for 40 minutes in the presence of other officers. The police told Mallory that his two nephews said that he was the one who committed the rape. Mallory denied the charge. He spent the afternoon with his two nephews at police headquarters.

The next day, the three suspects were asked to take lie-detector tests and all three consented. The two nephews were examined first. Mallory was interrogated for one and a half hours and finally admitted that he *could* have committed the crime. He later stated that he did.

After he repeated his confession to other officers, the police attempted to contact a United States Commissioner for the purpose of conducting an arraignment. The attempt was unsuccessful and Mallory gave the officers permission to be examined by a deputy coroner who reported there was no evidence of physical or psychological coercion.

Mallory was later confronted by the victim, questioned by three officers and subsequently repeated his confession, which was typed. He appeared before a Federal Commissioner the next morning.

The trial was delayed for a year because there was some doubt whether Mallory had the capacity to understand the proceedings against him. At trial, the confession was submitted as evidence.

The Supreme Court reversed the conviction in the case, saying that under the law, the "...delay between arrest, and arraignment must not be of a nature to give for extraction of a confession."[15]

The opinion of the court was delivered by Justice Frankfurter, who pointed out that the case called for proper application of Rule 5 (a) of the Federal Rules of Criminal Procedure:

> The purpose of this impressively pervasive requirement of criminal procedure is plain…The lawful instructions of the criminal law cannot be entrusted to a single functionary. The complicated process of criminal justice is therefore divided into different parts, responsibility for which is separately vested in the various participants upon which the criminal law relies for its vindication. Legislation such as this, requiring that the people must with reasonable promptness show legal cause for detaining arrested persons, constitutes an important safeguard-- not only assuring protection for the innocent but also in securing conviction of the guilty by methods that command themselves to a progressive and self-confidence society. For this procedural requirement checks resort to those reprehensible practices known as the 'third degree' which, though universally rejected as indefensible, still find their way into use. It aims to avoid all the evil implications of secret interrogation of persons accused of crime.[16]

The decision in *Mallory v. U. S.* made the point that unnecessary detention could lead to the use of a prolonged interrogation and the possibility of use of the "third degree." Therefore, the Court found it necessary to exclude evidence obtained from the accused during the period of "unlawful detention."

MAPP V. OHIO[17]

The United States Supreme Court rendered Mapp on June 19, 1961. The facts in this case revealed that three Cleveland police officers, acting on a tip that a person involved in a bombing was hiding in the house of the petitioner where there was no hidden paraphernalia, requested permission to enter the residence to conduct a search. Mapp called her lawyer and refused to grant permission unless the police had secured a warrant. The police left the scene, but later returned and entered the house while claiming to have a search warrant.

Believing that the police were lying, Mapp asked to see the warrant. She snatched the paper from the officer's hand. There was a scuffle and the officer retrieved the paper. Mapp was handcuffed and the dwelling was searched. Her attorney arrived at the residence while the search was in progress, but was not allowed to enter. During the search obscene books and pictures were seized. Mapp claimed that the materials belonged to a former tenant.

Mapp was convicted for possessing obscene materials and the conviction was upheld by the Ohio Supreme Court.[18] Because of a rule limiting the power of the Ohio Court to invalidate state legislation, the affirmation occurred despite the fact that a majority of the State Supreme Court felt that the statute under which the petitioner was convicted was unconstitutional. Ohio had refused to adopt the exclusionary rule as a matter of local law; therefore, the theory of the "fruits of the unlawful search" did not provide grounds for reversal.

The U.S. Supreme Court ruled that states where required, by reason of the due process clause of the 14th Amendment, to exclude from state conducted trials evidence seized in violation of the U.S. Constitution. In doing so, the court overruled its 1949 decision in *Wolf v. Colorado,* as that case held that the state was free to accept or reject the exclusionary rule as a means to enforce the rights against unreasonable searches.[19]

Prior to Mapp the exclusionary rule only applied in Federal Court. In the Mapp case, there was no argument that the search was illegal and violated the constitutional rights of Mapp. The greatest impact of the decision was making Mapp retroactive.

GIDEON V. WAINWRIGHT[20]

The case of Gideon v. Wainwright established as law the right of any person charged with a felony to be represented by a court-appointed attorney.

The facts in this case showed that Gideon was arrested for breaking and entering a poolroom with the intent to commit a misdemeanor. Under Florida law, this offense was a felony. When he appeared in court, Gideon informed the judge that he did not have funds to retain an attorney and asked the court to appoint one for him. The judge told Gideon, "... I am sorry, but I cannot appoint counsel to represent you in this case. Under the laws of the state of Florida, the only time the court can appoint counsel to represent a defendant is when the person is charged with a capital offense."[21]

The case was tried before a jury, with Gideon acting as his own counsel. He was convicted and appealed to the Florida State Supreme Court, challenging the conviction on grounds that it was unconstitutional because the trial court refused to appoint legal counsel. He argued that his constitutional rights were violated.

The Supreme Court overruled the conviction. In writing the prevailing opinion, Justice Black wrote:

> The right of one charged with a crime to counsel may not be deemed fundamental and essential to fair trials in some countries, but it is in ours. From the very beginning our state and national constitutions, and laws have laid great emphasis on procedural and substantive safeguards designed to ensure fair trials before impartial tribunals in which every defendant stands equal before the law. This noble ideal cannot be realized if the poor man charged with a crime has to face his accuser without a lawyer to assist him.[22]

The Supreme Court based its decision on Section 1 of the 14th Amendment which was adopted in 1865 and held that "No state shall make or enforce any law which shall abridge the privileges or immunities of citizens of the United States of America; nor shall any state deprive any person of life, liberty, or property without due process of law; nor the equal protection of the laws." [23]

Gideon was subsequently retried, assisted by a court-appointed attorney. He was acquitted.

ESCOBEDO V. ILLINOIS[24]

The facts in this case were that on January 19th 1960, Escobedo's brother-in-law was fatally shot. Around 2:30 a.m. the following day Escobedo was arrested without a warrant and was interrogated by police. He did not, however, give the police a statement. He was released from custody at 5:00 p.m. after his attorney obtained a *writ of habeas corpus* from the state court. [25]

On January 30, Benedict DiGeraldo, who was in police custody, told the police that Escobedo fired the fatal shot. DiGeraldo was later indicted along with Escobedo. Later that evening, Escobedo and his sister (the widow of the deceased) were arrested and taken to police headquarters. He retained a lawyer who, upon reaching the police station and in spite of various requests to several officers, including the Chief, was not allowed to speak to Escobedo. He was, however, able to see his client briefly and waved at him. Escobedo believed that the gesture meant to remain silent. When Escobedo asked to see his lawyer, he was told that "his attorney didn't want to see him." Escobedo and his attorney were never given the opportunity to speak.[26]

Officer Montejano, who grew up in Escobedo's neighborhood and knew his family, allegedly told Escobedo (in Spanish)….. "you and your sister could go home if you pinned it on Benedict DiGerlando," and that he would see to it that "we would go home and only be held as witnesses, if anything, if we made a statement against DiGerlando …that we would be able to go home that night." Officer Montejano denied making such statements.

When the police brought Escobedo together with DiGerlando, he made several self-incriminating statements. Dr. Cooper, an attorney assigned to take statements, did not advise Escobedo of his constitutional rights, nor did anyone else during the course of the interrogation.

Escobedo moved before and during the trial to suppress the incriminating statement, but his motions were denied.

At trial, Escobedo was convicted and sentenced to 20 years. The Illinois Supreme Court upheld the conviction and he appealed to the Supreme Court, contending that he was not allowed to confer with his attorney and that his confession should not have been admitted at trial.

In a five to four decision, the Court reversed the lower court decisions. The majority stated:

> We hold, therefore, that where, as here, the investigation is no longer a general inquiry into an unsolved crime but has began to focus on a particular suspect, the suspect has been taken into police custody, the police carry on a process of interrogation that lends itself to eliciting incriminating statements, the suspect has requested and been denied an opportunity to consult with his lawyer, and the police have not effectively warned him of his absolute constitutional right to remain silent, the accused has been denied 'the Assistance of Counsel' in violation of the Sixth Amendment of the Constitution. As made obligatory upon the States by the 14th Amendment, *Gideon v. Wainwright, 372 U. S. at 342* and that no statement elicited by the police during the interrogation may be used against him in a criminal trial… We hold that when the process shifts from investigation to accusatory-- when its focus is on the accused and its purpose is to solicit a confession -- our adversary system begins to operate, and under the circumstances here, the accused must be permitted to consult with his lawyer. [27]

MIRANDA V. ARIZONA[28]

This case resulted in what is now known as the *"Miranda Warning"*, the routine notice given by the police to any person before they can conduct a custodial interrogation. As interpreted by the Supreme Court, a custodial interrogation means "... questioning initiated by law enforcement officers after a person has been taken into custody or otherwise deprived of his freedom of action in any significant way."[29]

The facts in this case showed that Ernesto Miranda, an indigent Mexican immigrant, who was "... a seriously disturbed individual with pronounced sexual fantasies... " was arrested on March 13, 1963 on charges of kidnapping and rape near Phoenix, Arizona.[30] He was taken to a police station where the victim identified him in a police lineup. He was then taken to an interrogation room. At the trial, two officers testified that they did not advise Miranda that he had the right to have an attorney present while being interrogated. After two hours, the police obtained a signed confession from Miranda. At the top of the form was a typed statement that said the confession was voluntary with no threats or promises of immunity. The statement also said "... knowledge of my legal rights, understanding any statement made may be used against me."[31]

Miranda was found guilty of kidnapping and rape. He appealed to the Arizona Supreme Court and it held that his rights were not violated, upholding his conviction.

In reversing the conviction, Supreme Court Justice Earl Warren wrote:

> From the testimony of the officers and the admission of respondent, it is clear that Miranda was not in any way appraised of his right to consult with an attorney and have one present during the interrogation, nor was his right not to be compelled to incriminate himself effectively protected in any other manner. Without these warnings the statements were inadmissible. The mere fact he signed a statement, which contained a typed- in clause stating he had "full knowledge" of his legal rights, does not approach the knowing and intelligent waiver required to relinquish constitutional rights.[32]

Because of the *Miranda decision* it is now an accepted requirement that the police read suspects their constitutional rights. The Miranda holding gives a suspect: (1) the right to remain silent, (2) the knowledge that anything said might be used against him or her and (3) the right to counsel and if indigent, appointed counsel.

As recent as 2000, the United States Supreme Court upheld the *Miranda Decision*, in the case of *Dickerson v. United States*.[33]

In Dickerson, the Court ruled that the Miranda decision was based on a Constitutional interpretation and therefore the Congress could not pass laws to supersede it. In writing the majority decision, Chief Justice Rehnquist wrote, Miranda has become embedded in routine police practice, a part of our natural culture. [34]

TERRY V. OHIO[35]

A second landmark Supreme Court Fourth Amendment case was decided in 1968 in *Terry v. Ohio*. The facts were as follows:

About 2:30 in the afternoon, Officer McFadden, a Cleveland plainclothes detective noticed two men standing on a street corner in downtown Cleveland. One of the suspects walked up the street, peeked into a store, walked on, started back, looked in the same store, and then joined his friend in conversation. The other suspect repeated his friend's actions. They repeated this activity. They also talked with a third man and later followed him up the street.

Officer McFadden thought the men were "casing" the store for a robbery and might be armed. He followed the suspects, confronted them and asked them to identify themselves. The men mumbled and officer McFadden spun Terry around and patted his breast pocket. McFadden felt a pistol and removed it. One of Terry's companions was also frisked, and a second pistol was discovered. A frisk of the third man did not disclose that he was armed.

Terry was charged with carrying a concealed weapon. He later moved to suppress the weapon as evidence. His motion was denied by the trial Judge and the Ohio Court of Appeals affirmed. The Ohio Supreme Court dismissed Terry's appeal.

In affirming the Ohio Supreme Court's decision, the Supreme Court concluded that the proper balance in a case of this nature was determined if the police officer had reason to believe that he was dealing with an armed and dangerous individual, regardless of whether or not he had probable cause to arrest the individual for a crime.

The Court further stated that the officer need not be absolutely certain that the individual was armed. The issue is whether a reasonably prudent person in the same circumstance would be warranted in believing that his safety or the safety of others was in danger. In determining whether the officer acted reasonably under the circumstances, the Court looked to the specific reasonable inferences which an officer is entitled to draw from the facts, given his experiences.

The Court found that Officer McFadden had reasonable grounds to believe that Terry was armed and dangerous. Also, necessity required that he take quick action to discover the true facts so that only minimal harm, if that, would come to him and others.

The Court determined that Officer McFadden had carefully restricted his search to what was appropriate and to only the particular item which he sought, in this case, a weapon. The Court also stated that cases such as Terry should be decided on their own facts.

The Court held that where a police officer observed unusual conduct which led him to reasonably conclude, in light of his experiences, that criminal activity might be possible and that the people he is dealing with may be armed and dangerous; and in the course of investigating their behavior he identifies himself as a police officer, makes reasonable inquiries; and where nothing in the initial encounter dispels his reasonable fear for his own or other's safety, he is entitled, for the protection of himself and others in the area, to conduct a carefully limited search of their outer clothing in an attempt to discover dangerous weapons. Such a search is reasonable under the Fourth Amendment, and any weapons discovered may be properly introduced as evidence.

Terry gave police officers greater authority to make a "*seizure*" and conduct a "*search*" when they have reasonable belief that their safety or the safety of others was at risk.

TENNESSEE V. GARNER[36]

Doing the decades of the 1960s, 1970s, and the early part of the 1980s, one of the most divisive issues between the police and the community, especially the African American community, was the police use of deadly force. In most cases, state law and police department policy allowed officers to shoot at "fleeing felonies." The Supreme Court, for the very first time, provided specific guidance on the issue in the case of *Tennessee v. Gardner*.

Two Memphis police officers responded to a "prowler inside call," late one evening according to the facts of the case. When they arrived at the location, they saw a women standing on her porch pointing towards a house next to her own.

She told the officers that she heard glass breaking and that she believed that someone had broken into the house. One officer radioed the dispatcher while the other walked behind the house. He heard a door slam and saw Edward Garner running through the back yard.

Garner reached a six foot high fence and stopped. Using his flashlight, the officer was able to see Garner's face and hands. He did not see a weapon and assumed that he was not armed. The officer approached Garner and called out to him. Garner attempted to climb the fence. The officer feared he would escape and shot him. The bullet hit Garner in the back of his head and he later died at a local hospital.

Under police department policy and then current Tennessee state law, the officer was justified in using deadly force to prevent Garner from escaping.

Garner's father took the case to Federal District Court, seeking damages and alleging that his son's Constitutional rights were violated. The District Court ruled that the action of the officer was Constitutional. The Court of Appeals reversed that decision and remanded the case to the District Court. The State of Tennessee intervened and appealed to the Supreme Court.

Justice White wrote the majority opinion:
The use of deadly force to prevent the escape of all felony suspects, whatever the circumstances, is constitutionally unreasonable. It is not better that all felony suspects die than escape. Where the suspect poses no immediate threat to the officer and no threat to others, the harm resulting from a failing to apprehend him does not justify the use of deadly force.

It is no doubt unfortunate when a suspect who is sight escapes, but the fact that the police arrive a little late or are a little slow does not justify killing the suspect. A police officer may not seize an unarmed and non-dangerous suspect by shooting him dead. The Tennessee statute is unconstitutional insofar as it authorizes the use of that force against such fleeing suspects.[37]

In reviewing the landmark court decisions involving police practices, two points are important. First, police practices or policies, themselves, precipitated the appeals to the Supreme Court. The Court, in its interpretation of the Constitution, determined that the actions of the police violated the rights of the individuals involved. Even though it might be clear to the Court that the accused actually committed the crime, the rights guaranteed to all citizens under the Constitution reigned supreme.

Second, the landmark Court decisions brought about fundamental changes in both the law and police practices. Although some, particularly police officials, expressed their frustration and disappointment with many of the decisions, history has proven that the decisions did not have a negative impact on the ability of the police to carry out their enforcement responsibilities. To the contrary, policing in America is better off because many of the practices of the past that were ruled unconstitutional by the Court forced the police to change. Those changes assisted in the police establishment's move towards professionalism and greater community respect. Most importantly, there has never been any convincing evidence to prove that the police were unable to properly do their jobs because of decisions by the Court.

Over all, the United States Supreme Court has had a positive impact on the police and the practice of law enforcement in the United States.

CONSENT DECREES

In recent years, *consent decrees* have been used by the United States Department of Justice as a tool to bring about changes in police departments. A consent decree is an agreement between two parties that is approved by the courts. In general, a city, town or state will enter into a consent decree with the United States government in order to avoid lengthy and potentially costly litigation because of allegations that there have been violations of law, "...that deprive persons of rights, privileges, or amenities secure and protected by the Constitution or laws of the United States." [38] The allegations are brought before a United States District Court by the Civil-Rights Division of the United States Department of Justice under authority of the *Violent Crime Control and Law Enforcement Act of 1994, 42 U.S.C. 14141.*[39]

When the judge approves an agreement it becomes binding on the defendant. The United States government is the complainant in such cases and both sides voluntarily enter into the decree in order avoid the risks and costs of litigation in the interest of supporting lawful and nondiscriminatory practices of police services.

In recent years the cities of Los Angeles, California; Pittsburgh, Pennsylvania; Steubenville, Ohio; Prince Georges County, Maryland and the State of New Jersey entered into consent decrees. Such decrees have been used since 2000. The Los Angeles and New Jersey cases are illustrative of revisions contained in consent decrees.

The city of Los Angeles entered into a consent decree because of a problem at its Rampart Station. The Department of Justice (DOJ) informed the city of its intent to a file civil suit alleging that the Los Angeles Police Department was "engaging in a pattern or practice of excessive force, false arrests and unreasonable searches and seizures." The city denied the allegations and entered into an agreement with the DOJ. The civil-rights consent decree lasted for a period of five years and the LAPD agreed that it would demonstrate that it made "substantial" progress in complying with the provisions contained in the decree. The LAPD agreed to improvements in nine areas. [40]

- *Management and Supervisory Measures to Promote Civil-Rights Integrity.* The LAPD agreed that it would establish a database containing relevant information about its officers, supervisors, and managers to promote professionalism and best policing practices, and to identify and modify at-risk behavior (also known as an early warning system).
- *Incident Procedures, Documentation, Investigation, and Review.* The department was required to establish a special unit to investigate all use of force cases.
- *Management of Gang Units.* The department was required to implement a protocol to manage and supervise all department units responsible for monitoring or reducing gang activity.
- *Confidential Informants.* The department was required to implement procedures for handling informants.
- *Training.* The department was required to address its training programs and place an emphasis on police integrity.
- *Integrity Audits.* The Police Chief was required to submit to the Police Commission all scheduled audits on an annual basis. An Audit Unit was established for the purpose of conducting audits.
- *Operations of the Police Commission and Inspector General.* The decree set forth certain obligations for the Police Commission, Inspector General, and Police Chief.
- *Community Outreach and Public Information.* The department was required to conduct a community outreach and public information program for each geographic area it covered.

The court approved the decree on June 15, 2001.

To ensure that the city carried out the provisions of the decree, an independent monitor was appointed. Both the city and DOJ selected the monitor based on a process which each side agreed to. If the two sides could not agree, each would submit two names to the court and the court would select the monitor from the list of candidates. The fees associated with the monitor, plus expenses, were paid by the city. The monitor served as an agent of the court and periodically reported to the court in writing on the department's progress in implementing the provisions of the decree.

A Federal judge ended oversight of the Los Angeles Police Department on July 17, 2009.[41]

The United States government, the state of New Jersey and the Division of State Police of the New Jersey Department of Law and Public Safety entered into a consent decree on December 30, 1999.

The consent decree was filed in the U.S. District Court for the District of New Jersey. It alleged that the New Jersey State Police had engaged in a pattern or practices "that deprives persons of rights, privileges, or immunities secured or protected by the Constitution and laws of the United States."

The state of New Jersey entered into a consent decree because of a public outcry alleging that state troopers engaged in racial profiling on freeways in the state. Although New Jersey denied any wrongdoing, it agreed to the following provisions and acknowledged the circumstances giving rise to them: [42]

- Required that state troopers "not rely to any degree" on race, national origin or ethnic origin when determining which motorists to stop, and when deciding the scope and substance of what actions are taken after the stops.
- Troopers must document the race, ethnic origin, and gender of all drivers stopped for traffic violations, and document reasons for each stop and actions taken.
- Supervisors must review the trooper's reports on stops, and videotapes of stops to ensure the appropriate practices and procedures were used.
- The state was required to develop and implement an early-warning system to identify and modify any problematic behavior by troopers.
- The state police must make complaint forms and information material available 24 hours each day at various locations and establish and publicize a 24-hour toll free telephone hotline to receive calls alleging misconduct and/ or discrimination.
- The state police were required to improve recruitment and in-service training to include communications skills, cultural

- diversity, and the non-discrimination requirements of the consent decree.
- The state police must issue semiannual statistical reports on law enforcement activities including traffic stops.
- An independent monitor, reporting to the court, was selected to monitor and report on the state's implementation of the elements of the decree.

The decree lasted for a five-year period, but could be changed if the monitor recommended a modification. The District Court judge dissolved the consent decree on September 21, 2009. [43]

The United States Department of Justice has used consent decrees as a tool to bring about reform of police agencies. Jurisdictions as diverse as Pittsburgh, Pennsylvania; Steubenville, Ohio; Los Angeles, California; Detroit, Michigan; Prince George's County, Maryland; the New Jersey State Police and The United States Virgin Islands have been placed under consent decrees.

In 2010, New Orleans, Louisiana's newly elected mayor, Mitchell J. Landrieu, requested that the U.S. Department of Justice investigate the New Orleans Police Department, an agency with a long history of problems.

Consent decrees have been effective tools to bring about necessary changes in police departments. Because an outside monitor is required to report to the court on a regular basis, departments are more likely to implement the requirements outlined in the decree. It is likely that consent decrees will be used more frequently in the future to address improper police procedures. In some cases the United States Justice Department will use its authority to review an agency as it did in the case of the New Orleans, Louisiana Police department.

SUMMARY

There is a public expectation that the police in a democratic society will perform their duties in a manner that is effective, fair and just. The police are expected to be the government's front line agency that protects the sacredness of the U.S. Constitution. To the extent that the police do not live up to that expectation, they will lose the respect and support of the community that they so desperately need to effectively perform their responsibilities. Such support is at the very foundation of the successful implementation and practice of Community Policing.

NOTES: CHAPTER FIVE

1. See Federal Bureau of Investigation, Uniform Crime Report, <u>Crime in America</u>, Washington, D.C.: 1959 and 1964

2. U.S. Bureau of the Census, Historical U.S. Population Growth: By Year 1900-1998, Current Population Reports, Series P-25, Nos. 311, 917, 1095, released on June 4, 1999, http://www.npg.org.facts/us_historical_pops.htm

3. <u>U.S. News and World Report</u>, August 3, 1964, p. 20

4. Ibid.

5. Ibid.

6. Ibid.

7. Harrison, Burr P., "Recent Court Decisions Hamper Effective Law Enforcement", <u>The Police Chief</u>, Vol. XXV, No. 4, April 1958, pp. 10-16

8. Johnson, Samuel, <u>Lives of the English Poets</u>, London: Jones and Company, 1825

9. Kamisar, Yale, "When the Cops Were Not Handcuffed," <u>The New York Times Magazine</u>, Nov. 7, 1965

10. Nott, Charles, "Coddling the Criminal," <u>The Atlantic Monthly</u>, 1911 (http://www.theatlantic.com/past/docs/unbound/flashbks/oj/nottf.htm) 11.9.10

11. "Police Interrogation and Limitations under Foreign Law." <u>Journal of Criminal Law, Criminology, and Police Science</u>, Vol. 53, No. 1 May, 1961, p. 50

12. Fourth Amendment of the U.S. Constitution

13. Mallory v. United States, 354 U.S. 449 (1957)

14. "A writ from a higher court to a lower one requesting a transcript of the proceedings of a case for review." http://www,answers.com/topics/certiorari (11.8.10)

15. Op. Cit. at note 13

16. Ibid.

17. Mapp v. Ohio, 367 U.S. 643, 81 S.Ct. 1684, 6 L.Ed. 2nd 1081 (1961)

18. Ibid.

19. Wolf v. Colorado, 338 U.S. 25 69 S.Ct. 1359, 93 L.Ed 1782 (1949)

20. Gideon v. Wainwright, 372 U.S. 335, 83 S.Ct. 792, 9 L.Ed.2d 799 (1963)

21. Ibid.

22. Ibid.

23. United States Constitution, Fourteenth Amendment.

24. Escobedo v. Illinois, 378 U.S. 478, 84 S.Ct. 1758, 12 L.Ed. 2d 977 (1964)

25. "A writ of habeas corpus is a judicial mandate to a prison official ordering that an inmate be brought to court so it can be determined whether or not that person is imprisoned lawfully, and whether or not he should be released from custody." http://www.leclaw.com/def/h001.htm 11.8.10

26. Op. Cit. at Note 24

27. Miranda v. Arizona, 384 U.S. 436, 86 S.Ct. 1602, 16 L.Ed. 2d 694 (1966)

28. Ibid.

29. Ibid.

30. Ibid.

31. Ibid.

32. Dickerson v. United States 530 U.S. 428, 120 S.Ct. 2326, 147 L.Ed. 2d 405 (2000)

33. Ibid.

34. Terry v. Ohio 392 U.S. 1, 88 S.Ct. 1868, 20 L. Ed. 2d 889 (1968)

35. Tennessee v. Garner, 471 U.S. 1, 105 S.Ct. 1694, 85 L.Ed. 2d 1, (1985)

36. Ibid.

37. Section 14141 of Title 42, United States Code, as adopted as part of the 1994 Crime Act

38. Ibid.

39. See United States v. City of Los Angeles Board of Police Commissioners of the City of Los Angeles, and the Los Angeles Police Department, http://www.lapdonline.org/assets/pdf/final_consent_decree,pdf (11.9.10)

40. Rubin, Joel, "U.S. Judge Ends Federal oversight of the LAPD," Los Angeles Times, July 18, 2009 http://articles.latimes.com/2009/jul/18/local/me-consent-decree 18 (11.7.10)

41. See United States v. State of New Jersey and Division of State Police of the New Jersey Department of Law and Public Safety, http://www.state.nj.us/oag/jointapp.htm 11.9.10

42. http://www.ng.gov/oag/newsreleases0931ahtml

43. For a review of the experiences of two agencies under a Federal consent decree, see Davis, Robert C., Nicole J. Henderson, Janet

Mandelstam, Christopher W. Ortiz and Joel Miller, *Federal Intervention in Local Policing: Pittsburgh's Experience with a Consent Decree*, U.S. Department of Justice, Office of Community Policing Services, undated; and Stone, Christopher, Todd Foglesong and Christine M. Cole, *Policing Los Angeles Under a Consent Decree: The Dynamics of Change at the LAPD*, Program in Criminal Justice Policy and Management, John F. Kennedy School of Government, Cambridge, Mass.: Harvard University, May 2009

Part Two

THE NEW POLICING STRATEGIES

Chapter Six

THE EVOLUTION OF COMMUNITY POLICING

INTRODUCTION

In the proceeding five chapters, we discussed the series of events and circumstances that precipitated changes in American policing. Reform minded police leaders, national and local commissions, and landmark court decisions have all paved the way for a new concept of policing that has been labeled *Community Policing*. This chapter will discuss how the concept has evolved.

The concept of Community Policing did not emerge overnight. And it was not the result of one person's imagination.

The decade of the 1990s presented American policing with its greatest opportunity for positive change since it experienced the transformation from a politically orientated system towards one of professionalism between the decades of the 1930s and 1970s.[1]

As America moved into the 1990s, it was poised to enter into a new era of policing; a period in which the police and law abiding citizens could learn to collaborate on initiatives that promised to have a significant impact on crime, violence and fear of crime. The catalyst for that transformation was the great perils that faced American cities at that time. Urban decay, characterized by an epidemic of drugs and the proliferation of guns caused violent crime, violence and the fear of crime to reach unacceptable levels. Many Americans were afraid and equated crime and violence to a destruction of law and order. In the minds of many, the police were viewed as incapable of stemming the tide.

It is in that context that the institution of policing in America experienced a fundamental change in its orientation to delivering its services to the American people. The change emerged because many thoughtful police leaders raised provocative and penetrating questions about their effectiveness to deliver police services. Enlightened police leaders asked the question, "Is there a better way to use police resources to serve the public?" The affirmative conclusion was yes! The new direction is called *Community Policing*. As a result, the once comfortable *traditional style* of policing, predicated upon random preventive patrol and rapid response to calls-for-service, was examined with an open mind, and with serious doubts about its effectiveness.

Community Policing emerged as both a managerial and operational philosophy that promised to greatly enhance the capacity of the police to meet the demands placed on them by the prevailing urban crisis. It viewed the police as a resource that could be combined with others, public and private, to make a difference in the quality of life lived in our nation's cities.

This challenge was not unlike that which was confronting other sectors of American society. The automobile industry, for example, was facing an enormous challenge from foreign manufacturers, requiring it to re-think many of its management and marketing practices in response to a rapidly dwindling market share.

Colleges and universities found that the traditional middle-class students who provided much of the financial support for schools could no longer afford to pay the costs, forcing major changes in recruitment and financial aid strategies in order to remain adequate levels of enrollment.

And the airline industry, responding to the intense pressures brought about by deregulation, had to adopt totally new cost structures and marketing strategies to remain competitive or risk going out of business.

The challenge that confronted American policing was no different. America was faced with rapid increases in crime, violence and citizen fear of crime in its cities. Private security was increasingly assuming a greater share of the responsibility for policing major parts of cities, challenging public police for market share. As a result, those with the greatest need for protection, who could least afford to pay, were left to rely solely on public policing. Indeed, this nation's police were slowly becoming the police of the poor, while financial support for public policing declined. After a decade of economic decline, the financial health of the nation's largest cities was increasingly bleak and funds available for new approaches to lingering problems were dwindling.

The police, from some perspectives, were far better prepared than previously to make the needed transformation. Many of the reforms of the previous 25 years had provided a sound infrastructure for a new paradigm of policing. Many technical systems were at the leading edge of science and technology. The educational level of police employees was far higher than in past years. The sophistication and sensitivity of police managers was greater than any time in the past. In addition, the knowledge base developed by police during the prior 25 years provided an important foundation on which the police could base their efforts.

A new philosophy to guide policing into the 21st century was clearly necessary if citizens were expected to continue their financial support of police activities. The challenge was clear. The police must reconsider the way in which they approached their work, and do so with a broadened perspective of their function. The traditional bureaucratic structure, aimed at controlling police behavior rather than ensuring a competent, effective level of service to the community, no longer met the current needs and expectations of the community.[2]

DEVELOPMENT OF COMMUNITY POLICING

The concept of Community Policing did not emerge overnight. And it was not the result of one person's imagination. Rather, it evolved over a 30 year period. It built on several major programmatic initiatives in American law enforcement. The first was Police Community Relations Programs, which peaked in the 1960s in response to the civil disorders that occurred in many American cities. The second was Crime Prevention Programs, which emerged at the same time that Police Community Relations were being abandoned by police agencies. The third was the short-lived experience with Team Policing conducted during the 1970s and 1980s. The fourth was Community-Oriented Programs; where the police reached out to the community through special programs.

And finally, Community Policing developed around the experiences of Problem Solving Policing which emerged around the same time that Community Policing was in its developmental stage and Community Oriented programs were being implemented. In recent years, some police agencies have embraced Intelligence LED Policing, a concept that merges some elements of Problem-Solving Policing with elements of ComStat.

POLICE COMMUNITY RELATIONS PROGRAMS

During the decade of the 1960s, Police Community Relations programs held the promise of assisting police agencies to address the many challenges that confronted them. Such programs were established in police departments throughout America as a means of bridging the gap between the police and the community, especially the African American community. Before that time, police departments did not consider collaboration with the public as a necessary priority. In fact, just the opposite was true. The general attitude was, "We are the experts - we can do the job alone."

Even though America was a much more violent country than most countries in Europe, police departments were not established in America until the 1840's. Even then, they were not looked upon with respect:

"The police in our past seemed like a foreign invention imported from abroad, un-American, and generally held in low status. The police force was frequently the scapegoat for all sorts of difficulties and it did not seem to be the agency through which the community could express its need for respected law enforcement." [3]

As discussed in Chapter Two, America's first police agencies were plagued with many problems. Many of those problems carried over into the Twentieth Century. Most significantly, the police were not paid sufficiently, which impacted their ability to recruit capable employees. The general public did not respect them. In most cases, the low esteem that the public had for the police was justified because they did not provide the community with effective protective services. In fact, "the aim of the police departments was merely to keep a city superficially clean and keep everyone quiet."[4]

The 1931 National Commission on Law Observance and Enforcement (the Wickersham Commission) conducted the most comprehensive study of law enforcement up to that time. Although the Commission did not recommend structured programs in Police Community Relations, it did discuss the crime problem as being influenced by immigrants and the foreign born. To address the problem, the report recommended that police departments hire minority police officers. The commissioners felt that having minority representation in law enforcement would be of great benefit because of their understanding of the culture, customs, language and habits of minorities. [5]

In his landmark 1940 study of police systems in America, Bruce Smith acknowledged the importance of police and community relationships when he stated:

> It is not courtesy, but civility that our uniform forces should cultivate, while the actual extent of civil rights violations and third degree practices is largely irrelevant so long as they do exist and are popularly believed to be both frequent and general. That belief will persist until the fully equal and lawful enforcement of the law is freely accepted by police as their standard of performance and is consistently applied, year in and year out, as a matter of core discipline and administrative routine [6]

Although he did not label it as such, Smith pointed out the importance of police and community relations. His principle is as valid today it as it was then. However, structured programs in Police Community Relations did not formally start until World War II. Then they were mainly efforts to train the police in human relations.

So was the state of police and community relations for decades to come. It was not until the 1960s that surveys showed positive changes in the public's opinion of the police. In a national survey conducted for the Presidents Commission on Law Enforcement and Administration Justice by the National Opinion Research Center, the vast majority of those surveyed felt the police were doing a good job of enforcing the law. Only eight percent said that they were doing a poor job. [7]

> Those results, however, did not reflect the total picture of police and community relations in America. For example, the same study revealed "... that nonwhites, particularly Negroes, are significantly more negative than whites in evaluating police effectiveness in law enforcement."[8]

In fact, whites reported that the police provided "very good protection to the citizens twice as often as non-whites."[9]

The relationship between the police and the minority community reached its boiling point during the decade of the 1960s. Starting with riots in the Watts community of Los Angeles, California in 1965, cities throughout America exploded. Often, the disorder was precipitated by a police encounter with a Black citizen.

The polarization between the police and the minority community did not go unnoticed by some police leaders. In 1968, George Edwards, a former Detroit Police Commissioner, warned his colleagues of the problem when he wrote, "The relationship between the police and minority groups in big city ghettos is one of the sorest spots in American life today."[10]

The National Advisory Commission on Civil Disorders established by President Lyndon B. Johnson, studied the factors that caused the riots of the 1960s and forcefully pointed out the problem of police and minority relations when it concluded, "The abrasive relationship between the police and minority communities has been a major - and explosive - source of grievance, tension and disorder."[11]

The Commission suggested that the police treat residents of central cities properly, provide proper security to central cities, establish mechanisms for handling citizen complaints against the police, develop proper guidelines for police behavior, and develop community support for the police.[12] The Commission said that the "...police cannot, and should not resist becoming involved in community service matters. There will be benefits for law enforcement no less than for public order," it said.[13]

The Report of the National Advisory Commission on Civil Disorders recommended that the police develop comprehensive Police Community Relations programs.[14]

It was against this backdrop that the programs were started. It should be noted that even though structured programs in police and community relations gained popularity in the 1960s, the concept of such programs date back to the English model of policing that was adopted by the United States.

The importance of developing an effective Police Community Relations program was pointed out by various sources. For example, a national survey jointly conducted by the International Association Chiefs of Police and the United States Conference of Mayors in 1967 entitled <u>Police Community Relations Policies and Practices</u>, reported:

> Perhaps the most important finding of this survey bearing on the state of Police Community Relations is the fact that less than one-third of the responding departments have established formal Community Relations Programs. While this number is disappointingly small, it is encouraging to note that those cities that do have such programs have established them on a basis that is well organized and comprehensive, providing for police-citizen communication at both the precinct and city-wide levels. Clearly,

the long term impact of these programs has been beneficial and their development poses a major question as to why more of the departments have not felt it necessary to establish similar programs of their own. [15]

The most significant commission report on crime and criminal justice since the 1931 Wickersham Report was released in 1967.[16] Called the President's Commission on Law Enforcement and Administration of Justice; its final report entitled The Challenge of Crime in a Free Society, focused extensively on the relationship between the police and the community. It recommended structured programs within police departments to improve the relationship between the police and the community, especially the minority community.[17] Specifically, it recommended the establishment of, (1) both headquarters and precinct Police-Community Relations units, (2) citizens advisory committees in minority neighborhoods, (3) recruitment of minority police officers and (4) effective citizen complaint procedures. [18] The Commission also pointed out "... a police-Community Relations program is one of the most important functions of any police department in any community with a substantial minority population. "[19]

Interest in Police-Community Relations programs was expressed at all levels of government. Several agencies took a leadership role in perpetuating that interest and an abundance of articles were published on the subject. Through the National Center on Police and Community Relations, located at Michigan State University, there was a reservoir of information on the subject. However, the resources of the Center were not utilized to its fullest extent.

The Office of Law Enforcement Assistance (OLEA) of the United States Department of Justice encouraged and assisted in the development of Police-Community Relations programs by providing a special grant program for metropolitan cities which enabled them to plan and develop programs in Police-Community Relations.

An additional effort to consolidate the knowledge regarding Police-Community Relations was made by OLEA via a conference it sponsored in Washington D.C. in June of 1967. It was designed for those police departments that participated in OLEA's special Police- Community Relations development program.

In addition, the International Association of Chiefs of Police, under a grant from OLEA, demonstrated their interest in Police-Community Relations by sponsoring a conference on the subject for police administrators which was held at the Indiana University Medical Center in Indianapolis from June 27th thru 29th, 1966. The annual Institute on Police and Community Relations, which was held at Michigan State University in conjunction with the National Conference of Christians and Jews, played an important role in sharing knowledge on the subject.

Starting in 1947, the National Conference of Christians and Jews (NCCJ) conducted a national program on Police-Community Relations. NCCJ was instrumental in establishing the previously mentioned National Institute on Police and Community Relations. The National Center on Police and Community Relations and NCCJ both provided consultative services on the subject.

The proceeding discussion represents only some of the services which were available to police agencies interested in Community Relations Programs. The early pioneers borrowed from the theoretical aspect of community involvement in an attempt to apply those principles to the practical application of police work. This was done in an effort to improve the diminishing image of the police and establish law enforcement as a vital part of the community.

Unlike other police functions, Police-Community Relations had the dual challenge of reconciling unproven theory with the practical need for functional programs. Through available literature, the police had at its disposal an adequate reservoir of theory, but little had been written on applying that theory to the actual implementation of Police Community Relations units.

Structured programs in Police-Community Relations began shortly after World War II in Chicago, Illinois. Joseph Lohman was a pioneer in the field. Lohman wrote the first book dealing with the subject entitled The Police and Minority Groups. [20] This was a manual prepared for the Chicago Park District Police Department's Training School. The manual, which was published in 1946, focused on the police relationship with minority groups. Its intent was spelled out in its preface:

> The problem of the relationship between various racial and national groups is one of major urgency throughout the world. The problem is especially critical in democratic countries. In a democracy like our own, the public agencies must be constantly alert to their responsibility in maintaining equal service for all groups, at all times. [21]

This training program was the first of its type in the nation and concerned itself with: [22]

- Worldwide, national, state, city and neighborhood aspects of human relations.
- The background and condition of racial, nationality, and religious tensions.
- Facts about race.
- Social situations in which tensions arise such as discrimination in employment, substandard housing and discrimination in recreation and social activities.
- Role of the police officer in dealing with tensions.
- Law and administrative controls as they impact human relations.

Two years prior to the publication of Lohman's book, the International Association of Chiefs of Police published a pamphlet entitled "The Police and Minority Groups."[23] J. E. Weckler, of the American Council on Race Relations of Chicago and Theo E. Hall, Chief of Police of Wilmette, Illinois, prepared the pamphlet. It was designed as "a program to prevent disorder and to improve relations between different racial, religious, and national groups."[24] It included a discussion of the 1943 Detroit riots in which 35 people were killed, the Harlem riots in New York City and the Pacheco riots in Los Angeles. The pamphlet focused primarily on:

- Methods of officer conduct to prevent riots.
- Police training in interracial relations.
- Police roles in preventing riots.[25]

In 1946 the California Department of Justice published a police training pamphlet entitled, "A Guide to Race Relations for Police Officers."[26] This document was prepared by Davis McIntire of the American Council on Race Relations. The forward stated it was designed to "... offer peace officers, for the first time, a concrete practical guide for training in the vitally important field of race relations or, more accurately, the racial aspects of human relations."[27] This training program was geared for an eight hour training course for police officers. It covered:[28]

- Police problems with minority group interaction
- Official attitudes of police towards race relations.
- Prejudice.
- Basic facts about minority groups.

- Minority group behavior.
- Practical police methods in race relations.

Also during that year a pamphlet was published by Joseph T. Kluchesky entitled, "Police Action on Minority Problems."[29]

During the Korean conflict in the 1950s, California Attorney General Edmund G. Brown published a pamphlet prepared by Davis McEntire and Robert Powers entitled, "Guide to Race Relations for Police Officers."[30] The primary concern of that pamphlet was attacks by whites on members of minority groups.

All the programs had one thing in common. They were directed to police officers, taught by police, tactically oriented and concerned exclusively with racial tension. None of the programs involved the community and none attempted to work on socio- economic problems confronting the community. These programs did not attempt to establish communication between the police and the people.

The National Conference of Christians and Jews (NCCJ) started its work in Police-Community Relations in 1947. NCCJ was established in 1928 by a group of religiously motivated laymen who were concerned about bigotry and hatred exhibited during the 1928 presidential campaign of Alfred E. Smith, a four term governor of New York. The group formed a civic organization to work through educational channels to combat bigotry, ignorance and misunderstanding. Their program centered on five basic areas, (1) inter-religious affairs, (2) education, (3) equal job opportunities, (4) parent-youth training programs, and (5) police and community relations.

In 1947, NCCJ established a nationwide program in Police-Community Relations which involved specialized workshops and institutes, publication of papers on basic issues in law enforcement, consultative services for police departments and human relations training for citizens and police. The programs were offered through 75 regional offices administered by NCCJ.

In 1955, NCCJ was instrumental in establishing the National Institute on Police and Community Relations that sponsored annual conferences at Michigan State University. The institute brought together citizens and police, for one week periods, to study problems related to police and community relations. Its graduates came from nearly every state in the nation.

In July of 1965, with a $100 million grant from the Field Foundation,

the National Center on Police and Community Relations was established at Michigan State University as a part of the School of Police Administration and Public Safety in the College of Social Sciences. The functions of the Center were listed as follows:
- Undertaking action-related research projects.
- Preparing, publishing and circulating reports, manuals, pamphlets, booklets, and other literature in the field of interest.
- Developing and coordinating educational training programs.
- Providing direct consultative service to interested police, community agencies and organizations.
- Training young professionals to work in the field of police and community relations.

The United States Department of Justice, through its Community Relations Services Division, was involved in promoting Police Community Relations programs by offering conciliatory and evaluation services to municipalities. This service was free of charge to local governmental agencies that requested it.

The proceeding has been a brief description of the development of Police-Community Relations. The St. Louis, Missouri police department was the first police agency in America to establish a structured police Community Relations Program. [31]

In May 1955, the National Conference of Christians and Jews, Missouri Region, convened a conference in St. Louis, to hear reports from the National Institute of Police Community Relations which was held earlier that month at Michigan State University.

The 60 participants in the conference, 30 police officers and 30 community officials, decided that constructive action was needed to improve the relationship between the St. Louis police and community. To implement such action, the conference established the St. Louis Committee for Better Police-Community Relations, consisting of representatives from community agencies and the St. Louis Police Department.

Between October 1955, and February 1956, Police-Community Relations committees were organized in those police districts where the crime rate was highest. These committees conducted various public education programs, and met regularly with police officials to discuss Police-Community Relations Programs.

In 1957, the Board of Police Commissioners voted to actively support the program by establishing a Police-Community Relations Division within the Police Department. Headed by a full-time civilian director, it was the first such division established by any police department. The Committee for Better Police-Community Relations voted in 1957 to become the St. Louis Council on Police- Community Relations.

So was the history of the establishment of the first Police and Community Relations Program within a municipal police agency. Subsequently, numerous cities implemented similar programs.

The country's first Police-Community Relations units were designed to include the entire community. That focus, however, changed during the latter part of the 1960s. The change came about because of major societal changes. Those social changes included the civil-rights movement, the Black Pride movement, and civil disorders which occurred in cities throughout the nation. Those events resulted in an increased polarization between Blacks and whites, especially between Blacks and the police. As a result, the focus of Police-Community Relations units and their programs changed from focusing on the entire community to primarily focusing on the Black community.

Police Community Relations programs were defined as the process utilized by the police to work in conjunction with the total community to identify problems that caused friction between the two groups. Programs were designed to solve the problems. The explicit goals of the programs were:
- Improving the relationship between the police and minority groups
- Developing community support for police programs
- Creating avenues of communications between the police and the public
- Gaining citizen support and participation in crime prevention efforts

I directed one of the nation's first Police-Community Relations programs and expanded on the definition when I discussed the San Jose, California Police Department's Police-Community Relations Unit during a speech that dealt with the topic:

> This would entail a *meaningful* relationship between the police and the total community. For example, a *meaningful* Police-Community Relations effort would be a case when the police

went into a neighborhood and openly met with the residents in an effort to determine what they saw as being the problems involving the police and that particular enclave. This does not mean that the police are going to tell the residents what the problems are; rather the police are going to listen to the residents tell them what the problems are. After identifying the problems, the police will take steps to solve them. For purposes of illustration, let us say that this particular neighborhood was concerned about a police practice such as field interviews. The police would then assess their field interview procedure to determine if they are, in fact, a source of irritation to residents.

If so, the police would not make excuses to justify this source of irritation, but would change their practices to eliminate the problem. The essence of this definition is a <u>meaningful</u> relationship between the police and the public designed to identify problems and then find viable solutions. [32]

During the latter part of the 1960s, the Office of Law Enforcement Assistance (OLEA) of the United States Department of Justice encouraged and assisted in the development of Police-Community Relations Programs by providing special grants to cities, allowing them to plan and develop Police Community Relations programs. Sergeant Brown obtained a grant for the San Jose Police Department. The following case study is typical of the reasons many Police-Community Relations Programs were established during the 1960s. It was not, however, atypical of the activities of most other programs.

THE SAN JOSE EXPERIENCE[33]

In 1966, I was a sergeant with the San Jose California Police Department. On August 18th of that year an incident occurred on the east side of town that had the potential of developing into a riot.

I was assigned by Police Chief J.R. Blackmore to develop a program for that part of San Jose. The specific charge was to develop a program to improve the relationship between the police and residents of the East side of town. Officer Daniel Campos and I conducted a study of the area and gave the Chief a series of recommendations aimed at improving the relationship between the residents and the police. Among others, we recommended the establishment of a Police-Community Relations Unit, a first for the city.

Chief Blackmore accepted the recommendations and appointed me to direct the entity. I knew that if it was to be effective, it was important that it have direct access to the Chief. For that reason, I requested that I report directly to him.

The objectives of the Police-Community Relations Unit, as I defined them, "... were to actively strive to obtain the highest degree of cooperation between citizens and the police department, and actively promote an understanding of the police function among the citizens. This can be done by building citizens' confidence in the police department, gaining support for the police department's programs and objectives, which would include compliance with laws, assistance in investigations and cooperation with special programs. "[34]

In order to accomplish the objectives, the Unit set out to work with all groups in the city to seek information from citizens about existing problems and assist in finding solutions. The Unit was also responsible for explaining to the community the role that police performed in the administration of criminal justice. The following groups were selected to cultivate relationships with:

- Civil Rights groups
- Community councils
- Parent-teacher associations
- Professional organizations
- Neighborhood action groups
- Religious groups
- Civic and social clubs
- Student groups

The Unit carried out its responsibility by assisting any organization that had problems related to the need for service or deficiencies of service by forwarding the concern to the proper agency for action.

The Unit also created *"Area Law enforcement Committees"* in various neighborhoods throughout the city. Those committees consisted of local residents who came together to exchange ideas and share information on problems they were having with the police in their neighborhoods. In addition, arrangements were made for area committees to meet and talk with the district sergeants and officers who worked in their areas. The Unit also developed in-service training programs in human relations for the police department, with a special emphasis placed on cultural differences and minority groups. We also applied for and received Federal funds to assist us in implementing the program.

The major challenge in developing a Police-Community Relations Unit was to develop a program that met the needs of the police department, while at the same time meeting the needs of the community. To be successful, I felt it was necessary for the unit to have continuous involvement with various communities in the city. To accomplish that objective, we developed Police Community Area Councils in conjunction with the Areas Service Centers of the Economic Opportunity Commission of Santa Clara County. The primary purpose of the councils was to serve as a liaison with the police department in order to develop an atmosphere conducive to greater police and community cooperation and in doing so, improve the effectiveness of the police in working with the community to solve problems.

The unit did things that were unprecedented, such as the development of an *Arrest Record Interpretation Program*. I was aware that there was a tendency on the part of employers, public and private, to automatically disqualify prospective employees because they had an arrest record. To address the problem, we devised a program to assist in mitigating this problem by allowing persons with police records to receive equitable consideration and not be automatically excluded from employment.

The *Arrest Record Interpretation Program* was based on the premise that our society operates on the principle that a person is innocent until proven guilty. I knew, however, that in practice this distinction was not always made. So, we designed a program to assist prospective employers make distinctions between an arrest followed by an acquittal and arrests followed by convictions.

To protect the potential employer, we conducted thorough evaluations of the circumstances surrounding each case and provided the results to prospective employers. The evaluations included the circumstances that led to the arrest and the circumstances that resulted in an acquittal, if that was the case.

In making our evaluations, we considered the frequency and severity of the offender's arrest record. For example, if an individual had a single conviction for a drunk-driving charge, we asked the question, "What impact would this have on his being employed as a janitor?" Recognizing the great variation in the severity of criminal offenses, we felt that proper interpretation could influence an individual's ability to find employment, and could determine if he would continue a life of crime.

Another important element of the *arrest interpretation program* was the age of the individual at the time that the illegal act was committed. For example, if an individual committed an offense while a teenager and reached adulthood without committing any additional violations of the law, that violation could be viewed as characteristic of his age at the time of the offense. I believed that as people grew older they developed a greater degree of maturity, including a greater knowledge of the law. The individual, therefore, should not be penalized for mistakes made when he was much younger.

The "whole individual" and the nature of work he was applying for was considered important. The term "whole individual " was used to refer to a person's family, educational level, abilities, and other relevant factors; rather than merely basing his capacity for employment on one single factor – an arrest.

In providing the arrest record interpretation, the Unit also took into consideration the social ideals and principles of the community. We reasoned that society operated under the principle that every individual could be successful. On other hand, it does not provide the means for every individual to achieve success. Because of that dilemma, some individuals developed low self-esteem resulting from a series of failures and disappointments. Some reacted to their circumstances by developing feelings of alienation, then seeking success through illegal means.

We also realized that the relationship between the police and the community could be improved if there were more minority police officers. To achieve that objective, we established a citizens committee for the purpose of raising funds to give scholarships to needy students who wanted to enter, or continue in a law enforcement program at one of the local colleges. The purpose of the program was to award scholarships to students and assist them with tuition, books, transportation, and living expenses. A citizens committee decided which applicants received a scholarship. The *Law Enforcement Scholarship Committee* received excellent support from the community. The fundraising drive netted $5,000 which was placed in a trust fund administered by San Jose City College.

The Police Community Relations Unit also published an information brochure designed to acquaint the community with programs offered by the San Jose Police Department. The brochures were distributed to numerous organizations and individuals throughout the city. After they were distributed, the department received numerous requests for speakers. To meet that demand, we established a speaker's bureau. Ten police officers were sent to a public speaking course sponsored by the Toastmasters Club. The Police Community Relations Unit subsequently formed the *San Jose Police Officers Speakers Bureau*.

In order to recognize citizens that assisted the police, we created a *citizens recognition program*. Under the program, when beat officers identified a citizen that assisted them in some manner, the case was referred to the Police-Community Relations Unit for screening and processing. The Unit designed a Certificate of Appreciation, which was awarded to the citizen by the Chief of Police. The awards were publicized in the newspaper and the presentation ceremony was featured on television.

In conjunction with the Independent Insurance Agents Association of San Jose, the Unit designed a program called the *Stamp Out Crime Crusade*. The program was designed to address the crime problem by eliminating public apathy and making the public aware of the problem, its seriousness and their responsibility to assist the police in overcoming the problem of increased crime. The goal was to energize citizens through a community wide program that encouraged people to cooperate with law enforcement. The program was very successful.

One of the objectives of the Police Community Relations Unit was to eliminate conflicts between the police and the community. To that end, the unit joined the Santa Clara Sheriff's Office, the National Conference of Christians and Jews, the San Jose Human Relations Commission and the San Jose Police Advisory Committee in sponsoring a seminar on Police and Community Relations.

The theme of the seminar was "Police and Community Relations in Our Changing Times." The seminar was based on the belief that crisis situations can be eliminated or tempered by the police and community working together in a continuous relationship to reduce suspicion, misunderstanding and hostility. And to discover their mutual interests and responsibilities. It was also designed to introduce citizens to police problems, the role of law enforcement agencies and the responsibility of the community to support law enforcement. Finally, it was designed to assist in the professional education of police officers, with an emphasis on the social, psychological and human dimensions of police work.

The unit designed and published the department's first monthly *Police-Community Relations News Bulletin*. It was widely distributed throughout the community and covered a variety of public interest items. One of its aims was to further the growth, communication, understanding and cooperation between the San Jose Police Department and citizens.

In addition, the Unit implemented the *Community Watch Program*. The purpose of the program was to encourage citizens, especially those with two-way radios, to support the police by calling in suspicious circumstances they observed. Citizens were also encouraged to use their telephones as well as their radios to report suspicious circumstances. Drivers with radio-equipped vehicles were especially targeted to serve as eyes and ears of the police department.

The Unit also created the *"Officer Dan"* program. This was a program named after Dan McTeague, a member of the Unit. It focused on elementary schools. The program was designed to convey to children that the police were their friends, and contacts with children were made at a very young and impressionable age. The officers who attended the schools talked with children in intimate classroom settings.

The Unit also assisted in establishing the department's *Police Athletic League*, a sports program for young people. It was designed to provide a regular and healthy outlet for young people and to promote a common platform for the police, young people and supportive citizens. The program consisted of an amateur athletic program that promoted good sportsmanship and orderly behavior. It operated under the sponsorship of business people who realized the importance of developing positive relationships between the police and community youth. The program offered football, baseball, soccer, basketball, boxing, judo, track and field and bowling programs. The program served close to 8,000 young people in a single year.

The Unit created a *Police Community Relations Aide Program*. That program was designed to have young people work as an arm of the police departments in areas where they lived. Initially, the program was designed to recruit young people who resided in areas where the Police Community Relations Unit had established *Police Community Relations Councils*. The program was also viewed as a recruitment vehicle for the department.

One of the major contributions that the Unit made was the creation of procedures for handling complaints against police officers. Much of the criticism about the San Jose Police Department involved the public's lack of confidence in the procedures used to handle complaints against officers in the department. Since part of the Police-Community Relations Unit's responsibility was to review departmental policies as they related to community relations, the Unit reviewed the department's complaint procedures in January of 1966 and found them inadequate. As a result, we recommended to the Police Chief that the department establish an internal Affairs Unit. He accepted our recommendation. The primary responsibility of the internal affairs unit was to receive and investigate complaints against members of the department. At my suggestion, the internal affairs Unit reported directly to the Police Chief.

The Unit also recognized that to be successful, Police-Community Relations must involve more than community relations officers participating in the affairs of the community. For that reason, the Unit arranged for a fifteen hour in-service training course in community and human relations at San Jose City College. The purpose of the class was to provide police officers with information to assist them in their daily work. Over 300 officers attended the class and received one college credit. Outside individuals were used as instructors. Because of the success of the class, the Police-Community Relations Unit was given the responsibility of preparing in service training bulletins on the subject. This provided the mechanism for continuous training.

In addition to devising programs for the department, the Police Community - Relations Unit also handled a variety of cases related to individual problems. It served as a problem-solving entity. If the Unit could not resolve a problem, the concern was referred to another agency in the community that offered the needed services. In that respect, Police-Community Relations officers acted as the discovery and referral agency for individual problems.

Some good examples of the types of cases handled by the Unit were those involving large numbers of people with complaints of unsafe living conditions. Among other things, they complained that the electrical wiring in their homes was hanging out from ceilings and created fire hazards. When the owner refused to correct the problems, I contacted the Legal Aid Society and they organized a rent strike. Once that was done, the owners of the apartments fixed the problems.

Police-Community Relations officers were quick to point out that they were not a part of a public relations operation. They saw public relations as a method of *selling* the police department, an attempt to project a good image to the public. Crime prevention, however, was viewed as the goal of Police-Community Relations.

In 1973 I was a professor at Howard University in Washington, D.C.

An educator succinctly summed up the demise of police Community Relations Programs when he wrote:

> In retrospect, Police-Community Relations programs were destined to fail from their inception. Many were hastily established because it was fashionable to have one. Some were created to "prevent riots." In both cases, the programs were given little, if any, direction and virtually no authority to deal with substantive community issues. In other cases, the existence of the unit was contingent on the condition that it did not do anything --- do not rock the boat. In some places, the unit became a dumping ground for officers who were misfits in other units. [35]

CRIME PREVENTION PROGRAMS

When Police-Community Relations lost favor during the latter part of the 1970s, police interest in the community did not end. Rather, there was a move towards *Crime Prevention Programs*. Police departments throughout the nation established Crime Prevention Units, in some cases using the same personnel that were previously assigned to the Police Community Relations units.

A lasting benefit from the Police-Community Relations era was the recognition that there was a role for the community to play in controlling crime. Thus, crime prevention, as an organized entity of police departments, had its beginning in the demise of Police-Community Relations Programs.

The idea of involving the community in crime control is not new to policing. In fact, crime-prevention is as old as policing in the western world. Going back as far as 1829, when Sir Robert Peel, the father of modern policing, established the London Metropolitan Police Department, the prevention of crime has always been a stated law enforcement goal. That can be seen in Peel's nine principles of policing as listed in chapter two.[36]

Crime prevention, as defined here, is different from *preventing crime*. Crime prevention is defined as a law enforcement program in which the police utilize a variety of techniques to keep crime from occurring. Crime prevention is the police anticipation of opportunities to commit crime and doing something to prevent it from occurring. The National Crime Prevention Institute developed the most acceptable definition of crime prevention: "The anticipation, recognition, and appraisal of a crime risk, and the initiation of some action to remove or to reduce it."[37]

Crime prevention represents formal programs offered by police departments that have the premise that certain criminal opportunities can be reduced by police and community action. As a result, most police departments have crime prevention programs that offer a variety of services to the community. An example of the types of programs offered can be seen in the list of programs offered by the Crime Prevention Unit of the Houston Police Department where I served as Commissioner from 1982 until 1990. [38]

- Auto Theft Prevention: This program discussed the precautions that could be taken to deter and prevent most auto thefts.
- Burglary Prevention: This program discussed all aspects surrounding the nation's fastest growing crime. Information was presented on the various lines of defense, including proper lighting, landscaping, locking hardware, and other preventive techniques.
- Citizens Assisting Police: This program encouraged the use of two-way radio communications by citizens to report suspicious activities.
- Crime Prevention for the Business People: The purpose of this program was to make business people aware of the impact crime prevention concepts have on the business community. Information was provided on office security, internal theft, shoplifting, burglary, and robbery prevention, with an emphasis on preventive measures that could deter the commission of these crimes.
- Crime Prevention for the Homeowner: This program discussed various crime prevention concepts focusing on burglary, credit-card abuse, auto theft, fraud and security measures, which were inexpensive and easily implemented.
- Crime Stoppers: This was a program that offered cash rewards for information that led to the arrest and grand jury indictments of felony crime offenders and fugitives.
- Drug Abuse: This program was designed to educate the public of the serious drug problem that existed in the city. Topics discussed included drug identification, symptoms of drug use,

and the legal, social and psychological impact of the drug problem.
- <u>Houstonians on Watch:</u> This was a program designed to organize neighborhoods into watch groups that encouraged its members to report suspicious circumstances to the police and to utilize crime prevention concepts designed to reduce criminal opportunity.
- <u>Operation Identification,</u> This was a citizens' participation program for residential and business communities. It involved the inventory and marking of property with an identifying number as a means of discouraging theft, as well as facilitating the return of stolen property to the rightful owners when recovered by the police.
- <u>Rape Prevention:</u> This program was entitled "Be Aware." It addressed the various theories and methods of rape prevention. Included were topics such as rape myths and statistical data on rape offenses, victims and offenders, police and hospital procedures, precautions and prevention.
- <u>Robbery Prevention:</u> This program discussed ways to discourage armed robbery and minimize the incidents of violence through sound business practices and proper employee training. Included were topics dealing with physical and procedural deterrents, as well as procedures to follow in the event of a robbery, which could be practiced as a minimum line of defense.
- <u>Security Surveys:</u> This was a service provided to the business and residential community. It consisted of an on-site examination of physical facilities and surrounding property, with the intent of recognizing, appraising and anticipating loss potential along with recommendations to minimize criminal activity.
- <u>Senior Citizens:</u> This program was called "Crime Prevention for the Golden Years " and addressed home security and other crimes commonly committed against the elderly, such as theft and con games.
- <u>Shoplifting:</u> This program was designed to assist the business community to create policies, procedures and physical deterrents to minimize shoplifting losses.

One of the nation's leading proponents of crime prevention is the

National Crime Prevention Council (NCPC).[39] This organization was formed in 1980 when the Crime Prevention Coalition developed a unified crime prevention message. Inherent in its mission was the knowledge that the individual, the community and law enforcement must work together to prevent crime. This organization founded the McGraw Crime Dog with its "Take a Bite out of Crime" public education campaign. NCPC was established to accomplish two main objectives: the McGraw campaign and to coordinate the activities of the Crime Prevention Coalition.

Preventing crime, on the other hand, refers to a broader effort on the part of all social institutions to address crime by not only preventing it, but also addressing its causes. Arresting offenders can be considered preventing crime because it removes the violators from circulation. Police patrol can be defined as preventing crime because the presence of a uniformed officer serves as a deterrent to potential offenders.

Preventing crime not only involves the police, it also involves a number of other relevant social institutions. The family plays an important role as the institution that has the primary responsibility for the socialization of children. It is in the family where children are molded to become responsible adults, to learn values and behavior that allows them to become productive members of society.

The educational system plays a role in preventing crime. Schools are charged with the responsibility of educating children; thereby enabling them to be contributing members of society. The schools also perform an important role in the socialization of children.

Religious institutions play a significant role in preventing crime. All religions provide believers with a set of values. Those values teach that we should help one another in society. All religions have a set of beliefs that teach against hurting others and causing them pain.

The marketplace plays a role in preventing crime. By providing constructive employment one can earn a living and be self-supportive. People need meaningful employment in order to provide for themselves and their families. Meaningful employment also enables them to educate their children.

CRIME PREVENTION THROUGH ENVIRONMENTAL DESIGN

A relatively new form of crime prevention is now being used throughout America called Crime Prevention Through Environmental Design (CPTED). It emerged during the past three decades. In concept, it goes beyond the traditional practices of locks, alarms and door bolts used by the police departments in their crime prevention programs. As defined by the National Crime Prevention Institute, "CPTED is the proper design and effective use of built environment which may lead to a reduction in the fear and reduction of crime, and to an improvement of quality of life."[40]

C P T E D developed a set of basic strategies that are generally accepted in the crime prevention field: (1) natural surveillance, (2) territorial reinforcement, and (3) natural access control.[41]

Natural Surveillance: By design, areas are modeled to lessen the opportunities for crime to occur. Examples include designing the area so potential offenders will not have a place to hide. This could include plantings shrubbery or trimming plants so no one can hide behind them. The objective under natural surveillance is two-fold. One, avoid opportunities for concealment. Two, make the environment so safe that those who use it can see and be seen.

Territorial Reinforcement: This refers to creating a sense of ownership, control, or influence over an area. The theory is that the potential offenders will not have secure feelings about their illegal activities and will acknowledge that others are in control of the area. Therefore, crimes are less likely to be committed.

Natural Access Control: Natural access control has as its goal the design of an area such that the opportunity to commit crime is diminished. It involves designing an area so that pedestrians or vehicle traffic follows certain natural paths that are under surveillance.

TEAM POLICING

As Police-Community Relations programs lost favor with police departments, *Team Policing* emerged as a new approach for providing police services to communities. Team Policing, as implemented in America, had its beginning in Aberdeen, Scotland in 1948. [42]. The concept received impetus from the 1967 President's Commission on Law Enforcement and Administration of Justice and the 1973 National Advisory Commission Criminal Justice Standards and Goals.[43] Both urged police departments to evaluate the concept and determine if it was applicable to their agencies. It received its greatest boost when the Law Enforcement Assistance Administration's Office of Technology Transfer offered grants to police agencies for its implementation. [44]

The original concept of Team Policing dates back to World War I.

It would not, however, catch on until the conclusion of World War II, when Aberdeen, Scotland implemented the concept. James McConnach, Aberdeen's Chief Constable, is credited with implementing Team Policing on April 4, 1948. He said of the concept:

In 1944, in anticipation of unsettled conditions in police service during the post-war period, I implemented a system of policing in the city of Aberdeen by teams equipped with transport and radio. Each team would be responsible for a part of the city and subject to certain directions, left to keep that part free from crime, complaints and accidents. [45]

McConnach's concept of Team Policing was based on his experience in the military. There, he saw small groups of people working together to achieve an objective. He observed that they had to depend on each other for survival and they did not have the luxury of waiting for directions from headquarters. The concept crystallized at that time out of necessity. In addition, the city was faced with the challenge of attracting qualified individuals into police service at a time when it was confronted with economic problems.

The goals of Team Policing as laid out by McConnach were as follows:[46]

- To utilize existing man power resources to their optimum potential
- To digress from routine, fixed or otherwise highly structured tactics [operational procedures]
- To expand the role of police constables' responsibility for conducting assignments
- To encourage initiative within the ranks
- To expand the opportunities for police experiences (emphasis on the position of constable)
- To expand the use of mechanical and/or technological aids to compensate pressures for increases in personnel (emphasis on vehicles and radios)
- To utilize to its maximum advantage the element of surprise in the apprehension of criminals, and the restriction of their activities

Chief Constable McConnach died at the age of 58 and Alexander John Matheson, Aberdeen's Deputy Chief Constable succeeded him.

Mathews modified the policing strategy for Aberdeen and Team Policing, as implemented by McConnach ultimately faded away. [47]

Team Policing was promoted as a system of improving police effectiveness by providing the means for the community, and the police to work together, identify neighborhood problems and find solutions. Some departments chose to implement the program because of inadequate resources and increased demands for their services. Others adopted the concept as a means of expanding police activity.

In general, Team Policing involved major changes in the way the police performed their duties. It included:
- Decentralization of decision making
- De-emphasis on specialization in favor of generalization
- Decentralization of services provided by the department
- Adoption of participatory management
- Community involvement in police operations

The goals of team policing were effective crime control and greater officer job satisfaction. The concept involved assigning to a team of officers the responsibility of providing police services to a specified geographic area. In addition to the patrol division, all other units of the department operated under the Team Policing model. For example the support division, which was responsible for staff functions such as administration, planning, research and inspections, also operated as a unit. The same was true for all other divisions in the department. Although the support functions operated as the team, they were responsible for coordinating their services for the entire department.

Team Policing placed a major emphasis on generalization by de-emphasizing specialization. As a result, patrol officers were given a greater responsibility for follow-up investigations on crimes against property and persons. The detectives were still expected to assist or conduct investigation of complex cases.

The basic principles of Team Policing can be summarized as follows:
- Teams of police officers, ranging from 14 to 15 members, were permanently assigned to a team that was responsible for specified neighborhoods on a 24-hour basis.
- Officers were assigned to neighborhoods for extended time periods.
- Manpower assigned to teams was based on workload.
- Specialists were given team assignments, making them

generalists and allowing them to play a role in team planning and decision-making.
- The role of the patrol officer was expanded.

Team Policing never caught on in America. When Federal funding ended so did the concept.

THE MULTNOMAH COUNTY EXPERIENCE[48]

I was appointed Sheriff for Multnomah County, Oregon in January of 1975. Similar to many other counties at the time, it was experiencing an increase in crime and increased demands for police services. This occurred during a time when the department experienced a decreased workforce cause by poor economic conditions. Officers in the department were highly educated. A college degree was a requirement for employment, having been added in the 1960s.

The department was a traditional paramilitary organization and highly specialized. Its members were highly motivated and morale was high. Prospects of increasing the size of the department did not exist.

A task force prepared a position paper to reorganize the department based on the concept of Neighborhood Team Policing. The rationale for doing so follows:

The role of the police in the community, and the participation of the community in the police function are constantly being examined and redefined. The thrust of the effort is to make police more responsive to the community and local government. There is considerable latitude left in the local government to set its own priorities and objectives.

Decisions regarding police resources, police personnel needs, police organization, and relations with other government agencies should be made in a manner consistent with the interests of the particular locality. [49]

Evidence at the time suggested that overall police effectiveness and productivity would be improved by changes designed to keep pace with the following social trends:
- High citizen power
- High citizen mobility
- High concern for minorities

- Personalize treatment for clients
- Democratically derived power within organizations
- Increased individual responsibility
- Decreased emphasis on hierarchies of authority and status
- Situational organizational structures
- Problem and consumer advocacy
- Increased employee discretion
- Increased tolerance of alternative lifestyles
- More dynamic goal definitions
- Increased opportunities for influencing priorities
- Employee and citizen participation in management decisions
- Service rather than crime orientation
- High openness and low secrecy

To assist in the implementation of the new concept, my office established 16 planning task forces and charged them with the responsibility of planning for the implementation of Neighborhood Team Policing. They were responsible for addressing issues such as case monitoring and priority systems, community involvement, physical facilities, grants, internal communications, public information, social area analysis and career patterns.

Actual implementation of the project started in April 1975 when five lieutenants were appointed to serve as managers of five teams. Members of the department were allowed to select their teams. All members of the department were required to go through a 40-hour training session at a live-in facility where they would be completely removed from their normal environments. Each team was trained at separate times using the services of persons with expertise in the areas of group dynamics and communication skills. Once the teams completed their training, they returned to the department and assumed responsibilities for policing their various neighborhoods.

The full-service model implemented by the Multnomah County Sheriff's Department involved, "… assigning a team of officers on a permanent basis to a designated geographical area and holding the team commander, and the team, accountable for police services in that area…"[50]

The full-service model of Team Policing also involved replacing the traditional authoritative model of management and supervision with a system of management by participation. The department revised its organizational chart to reflect the free flow of communications within the department. [51]

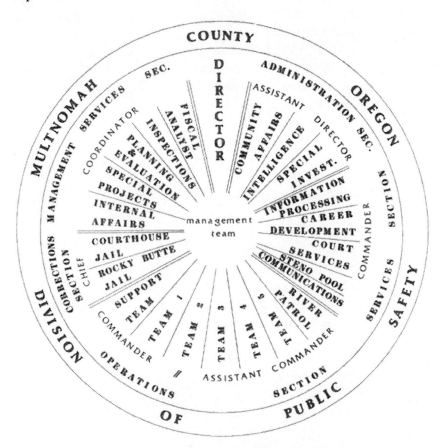

In redefining the responsibilities for each level in the department, it was decided that decisions should be made, when possible, at the level of execution. The responsibility for delivering police services was broken down into three components, administrative, team, and jointly. Those responsibilities were outlined as follows: [52]
1. Administrator responsibility
   - Departmental policy
   - Departmental goals and objectives
   - Team effectiveness evaluation
   - Philosophy and environment consistent with the full-service model of team policing

- Rewards based on the full-service model of team policing
- Intra team communications
- Management accountability
- Recruitment and selection
- Department-wide inspections
- Communications (dispatch)
- Records system
- Personnel unit
- Automated data processing

2. Team responsibility
   - Community involvement
   - Team activities
   - Resource allocation
   - Performance evaluation
   - Coordination of community resources
   - Community problem-solving
   - Delivery of police services, e.g., law enforcement, community relations, order maintenance

3. Joint responsibilities
   - Internal affairs
   - Planning
   - Evaluation
   - Communications (intra-departmental)
   - Budgeting (program)
   - Training
   - Management information systems
   - Organizational development

The implementation of the Full-Service Model of Neighborhood Team Policing involved a major reorganization of the Sheriff's office, including new reward systems, management by objectives, neighborhood storefronts, neighborhood profiles, and identification of neighborhood problems. The most important element was community involvement. [53]

I left Multnomah County in 1978 to assume the position of Commissioner of Public Safety in Atlanta, Georgia and shortly thereafter the department returned to its traditional style of policing.

PROBLEM-ORIENTED POLICING

Professor Herman Goldstein introduced the concept of *Problem-Oriented Policing* to American law enforcement in 1979. Today, Dr. Goldstein is considered the "Father of Problem Oriented Policing". The term has its origin in an article Goldstein wrote in 1979.[54] In that article he concluded that "Improvements in staffing, organization, and management remain important, but they should be achieved and may, in fact, be more achievable within the context of a more direct concern with the outcome of policing." [55]

In his article, Goldstein challenged the traditional wisdom of policing which allowed police departments to spend their time responding to calls-for -service without focusing on the problems that generated the calls. He argued that it would be more appropriate for the police not to focus exclusively on internal operations, e.g. staffing, management and organization. Rather, they should focus on the problems that require their response. He called that "the end product of policing." [56] Goldstein was influenced greatly by his work with police departments in Madison, Wisconsin; Baltimore County, Maryland; and Newport Beach, Virginia.

Problem-Oriented Policing emerged for a variety of reasons. One was the recognition that the traditional method of delivering police services was not effective. Under the traditional method, the police would receive a call from a citizen, dispatch an officer to the scene of the call, he/she would contact the complaint and make a report of the incident. Chances are the officer would be called on to go to that same location repeatedly. Why was this? Nothing was done to solve the problem. The police, in effect, were merely "*incident responders.*"

When officers were not responding to a call for assistance, they patrolled their assigned beats at random, waiting for the next call. Random patrols rarely resulted in police arriving while a crime was in progress. Rather, random patrol produced random results. On an average, an officer would spend up to 40 percent of his/her time on *random preventive patrol*.

Even when an officer was called to respond to a call, 80 percent of the time was spent dealing with non-criminal matters. In essence, American police officers spent their time dealing with what they considered urgent while neglecting to focus on what was important. As a result, police departments were not successful. One half of the crimes committed were never reported to the police. Eighty-five percent were never solved and the pressing problems of the community were not resolved.

That climate existed in police departments throughout America because they operated under a long-established system of traditional policing. Those beliefs formed not only the operations of the organization, but also its culture and value system. The police saw their role as a very narrow one, to fight crime. They never focused on the dismal success rate they had or the problems that were of concern to the community. In fact, under traditional policing, the police distanced themselves from the people they served. This created a mystique about police work in the mind of the average citizen.

To the credit of the police, many recognized that passive reliance on past traditions did not serve law enforcement or the public well. There were a number of police leaders that recognized that the traditional wisdom of American policing should be challenged.

They felt it was time to try new ideas, be creative, experiment, and take risks. They saw their role as not only delivering services to the community, but also voicing positive criticism of the past and questioning tradition in order to meet the demands of a rapidly changing future. They did not abandon tradition; rather they built upon the positive things that existed under traditional policing.

Herman Goldstein, who had studied the police for many years, led that group of thoughtful police leaders in formulating a new style of policing. He labeled it *"Problem Oriented Policing"*. Goldstein challenged police leadership to move beyond *"administrative competence"* and felt there were a number of pressures that would provide the impetus for them to do so, e.g. financial crisis, research findings, growth of consumer orientation, questioning of the effectiveness of the best managed agencies and increased resistance to organizational change. His remedy was *Problem-Oriented Policing*.

BALTIMORE COUNTY

One of the first jurisdictions in America to experiment with Problem Oriented Policing was Baltimore County, Maryland. In 1981, that agency implemented *the Citizens Oriented Police Emergency* (COPE) program. [57]

After two highly publicized murders, the fear of crime escalated in Baltimore County. As a result, the police department hired forty-five additional police officers. Rather than use the new officers in the traditional style of policing, they were assigned the responsibility of restoring public confidence in the ability of the police to protect the public. To accomplish that objective, COPE officers patrolled on small motorcycles and were encouraged to initiate contact with the public. In order to have time to achieve their objectives, they did not have to respond to calls for service. Rather, they were assigned to make contacts and provide crime prevention information to the community. The COPE program was one of the first problem oriented policing experiments in America. It was initiated to address a particular problem, the fear of crime.

NEWPORT NEWS

The second structured program where the program was implemented was in the Newport News, Virginia Police Department.[58] With the assistance of the Police Executive Research Forum and Herman Goldstein, the National Institute of Justice awarded the Newport News Police Department a grant to implement and evaluate Problem Oriented Policing. The Newport News Police Department was the first police agency to implement problem oriented policing agency wide.

The project started by requiring officers from all ranks to develop a problem analysis guide. The officers used the guide as a tool as they went through the problem solving process. A department-wide training program was offered so that all officers, not only knew how to use to the guide, but also knew the history of Problem Oriented Policing.

The Newport News problem-solving model consisted of four principles:[59]
- Viewing incidents in the broader context of problems
- Collecting information from sources other than the police
- Involving others in the problem solving process
- Evaluating results of the efforts

In reporting on the Newport News experiment, Eck and Spelman wrote: "The Problem-Oriented Policing approach is the outgrowth of twenty years of research into police operations that converged on two main themes: increased effectiveness by attacking underlying problems that gave rise to the individual incidents that consume patrol time, and closer involvement with the community." [60]

By definition, Problem-Solving Policing goes beyond the traditional style of policing. It requires the police to not only respond to incidents, but also to focus on the problems that created them.

S.A.R.A

Today, Problem Oriented Policing has evolved into a permanent part of American policing. Police agencies throughout America continue to use the concept in one form or another. Almost all have adopted a problem solving process called S.A.R.A., which is an acronym for scanning, analysis, response and assessment.[61]

SCANNING

This is the first step in the problem solving process. It involves grouping related incidents to determine if they constitute a bigger problem.

ANALYSIS

Here the problems are identified along with their causes and consequences.

RESPONSE

Using the combined resources of the police and the community to address the characteristics of a problem.

ASSESSMENT

An evaluation is made of the effectiveness of the responses to determine if the problems have been solved.

COMMUNITY POLICING PROGRAMS

Another step in the evolution of Community Policing was the various programs implemented by police departments throughout the nation that involved the community. Experience gained from those programs assisted in the formulation of the Community Policing concept. Three of the best-known pilot projects were the Los Angeles Police Department's *Basic Car Radio Plan*, the New York City Police Department's *Community Patrol Officer Program* and Houston Police Department's *Direct Area Responsibility Team*.

BASIC CAR RADIO PLAN.[62]

The Los Angeles Basic Car Radio Plan was designed to assist the Los Angeles Police Department to become more effective in delivering its services by establishing a closer relationship with the community. The objective of the plan was to assist the department address the crime problem by improving citizen attitudes toward the police, having a stable assignment of police officers in the neighborhoods, creating an environment where police officers had a proprietary interest in the neighborhoods and better knowledge of their roles as officers. The program operated as follows:

> Based on workload, a minimum radio car plan was established and became the *Basic Radio Car Plan*. The basic radio cars were called "A" units. A team of nine officers, consisting of one lead officer, five senior officers, and three probation officers were assigned to each Basic Radio Car District. Three of the officers were assigned to the radio district on each of the three shifts. Additional radio cars were deployed during periods of increased workload; these cars were "X" units superimposed on the *Basic Radio Car Plan*.
>
> The lead officer had the responsibility of coordinating the activities in his radio car district. Once a month the nine officers met at a local elementary school with representatives of the neighborhoods constituting that radio car's district. The purpose of the meeting was to hold discussions between the officers and community residents about police problems. The senior officer of each shift received additional pay and each of the lead officers received a category of pay above that of the senior officer. [63]

All officers assigned to this program were given leadership training. An important part of the program was the selection of community representatives to meet with the officers. This was done by having the division commander, with the assistance of community relations officers, contact key leaders in the community and request their assistance in selecting an advisory committee composed of residents who represented the basic car districts in that division. The objective was to select a representative from each block in the division. Each month, the nine members of the Basic Radio Car Team met with the district representatives. The objective of the meetings was to exchange information. After the general meeting, the attendees participated in discussion groups that were facilitated by the officers. After each meeting, there was a debriefing and an evaluation was completed. The team advisor reviewed the report and copies were forwarded to the division commander for distribution at his discretion.

COMMUNITY PATROL OFFICER PROGRAM.[64]

New York City's *Community Patrol Officers Program* was based on the concept that the success of the police in the community was contingent on the relationship between officers and the people they served. The objective of the program was to form a cohesive and functional partnership between the police, community and other organizations to work together to improve the quality of life in the community. The program was designed so that patrol officers served as a link between the police department and the neighborhoods they patrolled. The idea embodied the role of the traditional beat officer, community relations officers, problem analysis, strategic development and the tactical expertise of police planners.

Under the program, officers were permanently assigned to a beat. They were given the responsibility of identifying crime and other problems within their areas and to devise solutions to those problems. They were expected to meet regularly with residents and business persons in their areas to discuss issues that were important to the people. This was done in order to establish a partnership between police officers, residents and business people so they could address the issues that were identified.

It was also expected that the officers would engage in crime prevention activities. This involved conducting public education programs on crime prevention topics that were specifically geared to the neighborhood. They were also required to conduct residential and business premise inspections, and propose safety recommendations. Each patrol officer was given the latitude to develop their own plan for their daily activities. The goals were to control crime and solve problems in the areas where they patrolled. They were also required to review all of the crime analysis reports within their areas. When meeting with people who lived or worked in the area, they were expected to advise them of crime trends, and to suggest methods that were being utilized to address problems.

The Community Patrol Officers were required to confer with the precinct community patrol sergeant and coordinate approaches for dealing with problems and work with officers assigned to the radio patrol and anti-crime units. They also served as a resource to residents in their area regarding resources of both the community and the city that could be used to address problems in that area.

DIRECTED AREA RESPONSIBILITY TEAM.[65]

The Directed Area Responsibility Team (D.A.R.T.) represented a significant departure from the way the Houston Police Department traditionally delivered its services to citizens. One of the objectives of the DART program was to establish a closer and more positive relationship between patrol officers and the community. A second objective was to more efficiently utilize personnel assigned to field operations. A third objective was to institute a system of participatory management that focused on officers' job satisfaction.

The overall objective was to provide the Houston Police Department with a sound policing strategy which would reduce fear of crime, deliver improved services, and assist the department in meeting its future needs.

To meet the objectives, the Houston Police Department set out to alter their traditional methods of policing. The strategies included the following:

1. Deployment Strategies
   - Beat Integrity
   - One-officer Units
   - Tactical Assignments
   - Designated Report Units

2. Team Interaction Strategies
   - Communication among police officers
   - Investigative sergeants - decentralizes investigations

3. Job Diversification Strategies
   - Patrol officer follow-up investigations
   - Supportive response team
   - Structure patrol techniques
   - Participatory management techniques
   - Assistance squad leader appointments

4. Knowledge gaining / sharing strategies
   - Beat profiling
   - Crime analysis

5. Community Exchange Strategies
   - Community contacts
   - Neighborhood meetings
   - Police Community Relations Officer
   - Crime prevention/security surveys

The program was implemented in one Police District utilizing the officers already assigned to the district.

The above represents only three programs that were implemented throughout the nation that involved the police and the community. The overall objective of each of the programs was the same - to improve crime control by including the community in the policing process. The experiences from these programs also assisted in the formulation of the philosophy and concept of Community Policing.

INTELLIGENCE-LED POLICING

Intelligence-Led Policing had its origins in England during the early 1990s. It came about after a 1993 Report of the Audit Commission and her Majesty's Inspectorate of Constabulary "… advocated increased use of intelligence, surveillance and informants to target recidivist offenders so that police could be more effective in fighting crime…" Police forces in England, especially the Kent Constabulary, responded to the challenge to more efficiently manage their resources as a means of controlling crime.[66]

Intelligence Led-Policing gained significant notice in the United States in the aftermath of the terrorist attacks of September 11, 2001.

Intelligence-Led Policing can best be defined as "… a strategic future-oriented and targeted approach to crime controls focusing on the identification, analysis and 'management' of persisting and developing problems or risk." [67]

Intelligence-Led Policing does not replace Problem-Solving Policing or ComStat. Rather, it falls under the umbrella of Community Policing. In its truest form Intelligence Led Policing involves:[68]

- Information collection as part of the organizational culture
- Analysis is indispensable to tactical and strategic planning
- Enforcement tactics are an integral part of prevention activities and operations are focused on repeat violent offenders, serious organized crime groups, and specific attention is focused on dangerous roadways or intersections
- Problem solving principles are incorporated in community involvement techniques
- Privacy is practiced consistent with the principles of democracy

SUMMARY

As noted in this discussion, Community Policing emerged over a period of years. It built upon the successful aspects of *Police-Community Relations Units*, *Crime Prevention Programs*, *Team Policing*, *Problem-Oriented Policing* and *Community Oriented Programs*. It was not until the turn of the century that *Intelligence Led Policing* became popular in America.

Today, more than 80 percent of the police departments in America have implemented Community Policing in one form or another.

Community Policing is misunderstood, and many agencies still interpret the concept as a program. As written in the next chapter Community Policing is not a program, rather it is a philosophy of policing. It represents a new way of thinking about how to best utilize police resources.

NOTES: CHAPTER SIX

1. Kelling, George L. and Mark H. Moore, "The Evolving Strategy of the Police," in Perspective on Policing, Washington, D.C., U.S. Department of Justice, National Institute of Justice, and the Program in Criminal Justice Policy and Management, John F. Kennedy School of Government, Cambridge, Mass.: Harvard University, November 1988, No 4

2. Kelling, George L. "Police and Communities: the Quiet Revolution'" in Perspectives on Policing, Washington, D.C.: U.S. Department of Justice, National Institute of Justice, and the Program in Criminal Justice Policy and Management, John F. Kennedy School of Government, Cambridge, Mass.: Harvard University, June 1988, No. 1

3. Handlin, Oscar, "Community Organization as a Solution to Police-Community Problems," Police and the Changing Community: Selected Readings, Nelson A. Watson, (ED) Washington, D.C.: International Association of Chiefs of Police, 1965, p. 107

4. Schlesinger, Arthur M. Sr., The Rise of the City, 1878-1898, A History of American Life in 12 Volumes, Vol. X, Arthur M. Schlesinger, Jr. and Dixon Ryon Fox (EDS), New York: The McMillan Company, 1934, p. 115

5. U.S. National Commission on Law Observance and Enforcement, Reports, 14 Vol. 1931, George W. Wickersham, Chairman, Washington, D.C.: U.S. Government Printing Office, 1931

6. Smith, Bruce, Police Systems in the United States, New York: Harper Brothers Publishers, 1949, p. 344

7. National Opinion Research Center, <u>A National Sample Survey Approach to the Study of the Victims of Crime and Attitudes Towards Law Enforcement And Justice</u>, Chicago, Unpublished, 1966, p.1

8. President's Commission on Law Enforcement and Administration of Justice, <u>Task Force Report: The Police,</u> Washington, D.C.: U.S. Government Printing Office, 1967, p.146

9. Ibid.

10. Edwards, George, <u>The Police on the Urban Frontier – A Guide to Community Understanding</u>, New York: Institute of Human Relations Press, 1968, p. 2

11. National Advisory Commission on Civil Disorders, <u>Report of the National Advisory Commission on Civil Disorders</u>, Washington, D.C.: U.S. Government Printing Office, 1968, p.8

12. Ibid. 167

13. Ibid.

14. Ibid.

15. <u>Police-Community Relations and Practices – A National Survey</u>, jointly sponsored by the International Association of Chiefs of Police and the United States Conference of Mayors. Washington, D.C.: 1967, P.3

16. Op. Cit. Note 5

17. President's Commission on Crime and the Administration of Justice, <u>The Challenge of Crime in a Free Society</u>, Washington, D.C.: U.S. Government Printing Office, 1967

18. Ibid. p. 100

19. Ibid.

20. Lohman, Joseph D. <u>The Police and Minority Groups</u>, Chicago: Chicago Park District Police, 1947

21. Ibid.

22. Ibid.

23. Weckler, J. E. and Theo E. Hall, <u>The Police and Minority Groups</u>, Chicago: International Association of Chiefs of Police, 1947

24. Ibid.

25. Ibid.

26. McEntire, Davis and Robert B. Powers, <u>Guide to Race Relations for Police Officers</u>, State of California: Department of Justice, 1946

27. Ibid.

28. Ibid.

29. Kluchesky, Joseph T., <u>Police Action on Minority Problems</u>, New York: Freedom House, 1946

30. Daly, Emmet, Guide to Race Relations for Peace Officers, State of California, Department of Justice, 1952

31. St. Louis Metropolitan Police Department, History of Police-Community Relations, unpublished, undated

32. Brown, Lee P., Dynamic Police-Community Relations at Work, The Police Chief, 35 (4), 1968, p.47

33. For a more detailed discussion of the development of Police Community Relations Programs see Brown, Lee P., The Development of a Police Community Relations Program: An Assessment of the San Jose Project, Master's Thesis, School of Criminology, University of California, Berkley, 1964

34. Ibid.

35. Brown, Lee P., The Death of Police-Community Relations, Institute of Urban Affairs and Research, Howard University, Occasion Paper Vol.1, No. 1, 1973 Washington, D.C., p.18

36. New Westminster Police Service, Sir Robert Peel's Nine Principles of Policing, http: www.newwestpolice.org/peel.html February 1. 2009)

37. Http.//www.ncpi.org/. (February 1, 2009)

38. Houston Police Department, Community Service Division: Operational Profile," unpublished, 1982

39. http://www.ncpc.org/ (February 1, 2009)

40. For a comprehensive discussion of CPTED see Crowe, Timothy D., Crime Prevention Through Environmental Design, Boston, Mass.: Butterworth-Heinmann, 1991

41. Ibid. and Jeffery C. Ray, Crime Prevention Through Environmental Design, Beverly Hills, Calif.: Sage Publications, 1991

42. Gay, William G,, June P. Woodward, H. Talmadge Day, James P. O'Neil and Carl Tacher, Issues in Team Policing: A Review of the Literature, Washington, D.C.: National Sheriff's Association, 1975, p.1

43. Ibid.

44. Multnomah County Sheriff's Department received grant number 75-NI-10-0001

45. Hudiburg, David L. The Origin of Team Policing, copyright, David L. Hudiburg, 1975, p. 18

46. Ibid. P. 22

47. Ibid. p.45

48. Brown, Lee P. (ED.), Neighborhood Team Policing: The Multnomah County Experience, Portland, Oregon: Multnomah County Sheriff's Office, December 1976

49. Ibid. p. 48
50. Ibid. p. 16
51. Ibid. p.18
52. Ibid. pp. 16-17
53. Ibid. pp 94-100
54. Goldstein, Herman, "Improving Policing: A Problem-Oriented Approach," Beverly Hills, Calif.: Sage Publications: Crime and Delinquency, April 1979, vol 25, no. 2. pp. 236-258
55. Ibid. p.236
56. Ibid. p. 239
57. Taft, Phillip B., Jr., Fighting Fear in Baltimore County COPE Project, Washington, D.C.: Police Executive Research Forum, February 1986 and Cordner, Gary W. The Baltimore County Citizen Oriented Police Enforcement COPE Project: Final Evaluation, Final report to the Florence W. Burden Foundation: Crime and Justice Department, College, Park, Md.: University of Maryland
58. Eck, John and William Spelman, Problem – Oriented Policing in Newport News, Washington, D.C.: Police Executive Research Forum, 1987
59. Ibid. p. 2
60. Spelman, William and John E, Eck, Research In Brief: Problem-Oriented Policing, Washington, D.C.: Police Executive Research Forum, 1987
61. Op. Cite, Note 42
62. Los Angeles Police Department, The Los Angeles Police Department's Basic Car Plan, Los Angeles Police Department, April 1, 1972, unpublished paper
63. Ibid.
64. Brown, Lee P., Community Patrol Officer Program: Problem Solving Guide, Houston: Houston Police Department, 1982, unpublished paper
65. Houston Police Department, Directed Area Responsibility Team, Houston, 1982, unpublished paper
66. de Lint, Willem, "Intelligence in Policing and Security: Reflections in Scholarship:" Policing and Society, Vol. 16, No. 1 (March 2006), pp.1-6
67. http//jratcliffe.net/research/ilp.htm (10.2.11)
68. Justice Issues: Intelligence-Led Policing, US Department of Justice, Office of Justice Programs, Bureau of Justice Assistance http://www.ojp.u.s.doj.gov/BJA/topics/ilp.html (10.2.11)

Chapter Seven

COMMUNITY POLICING: THE PROMISE AND THE CHALLENGE

INTRODUCTION

The concept of Community Policing evolved over a three decade period. It built on previous programs such as Police-Community Relations, Crime Prevention, Team Policing, Community Oriented Policing Programs and Problem-Solving Policing.

> Community Policing is a collaborative partnership between the police and law-abiding citizens designed to prevent crime, arrest offenders, solve neighborhood problems and improve the quality of life in the community.

Proponents of Community Policing have always been asked to define it. This was expected since any new concept begs for a brief definition, a shortened way of defining and explaining what the new concept means. In the case of Community Policing, this was important for the police, policy makers and the general public. There was a desire for a short answer to the question, "What is Community Policing?"

Ironically, the same standard has not been applied to the concept of traditional policing. That is because the reforms that took place when the police moved from a politically corrupt policing system to the "professional model" (commonly called traditional policing) existed long enough to become institutionalized. Few, if any, police officers today serve under the politically corrupt system. Similarly, no police officer today serves in a police department that has fully institutionalized Community Policing.

If the question was asked, "What is *traditional policing*," there is no short answer that would adequately define it. Rather, *traditional policing would have to be defined as the system that police used to deliver their services.* That is to say, *traditional policing* would be defined by the activities performed by the police, how they organized themselves in performing activities such as random preventive patrols, rapid response to calls for service, centralization and specialization.

The same holds true for *Community Policing*. It is best defined as what the police do when they operate under the Community Policing concept. Conveniently, Community Policing has been given a descriptive definition:

> Community policing is a collaborative partnership between the police and law-abiding citizens designed to prevent crime, arrest offenders, solve neighborhood problems and improve the quality of life in the community.[1]

This partnership entails a four-stage process involving both the police and the community. It is designed to:
- Jointly identify crime and other problems that have a negative impact on the quality of neighborhood life
- Jointly determine the best strategies for solving those problems
- Using the combined resources of the police, various government agencies, residents and public and private organizations to address the problems
- Evaluating the results of the problem-solving efforts, making strategic adjustments as necessary.[2]

DIFFERENCES BETWEEN COMMUNITY POLICING AND TRADITIONAL POLICING

Under traditional policing, officers are driven by 911 calls, with little time for anything else. Police officers spend nearly ninety percent of their time responding to 911 calls.

Under Community Policing, the police should spend approximately sixty percent of their time responding to 911 calls. The objective is to allow officers ample time to get to know the people in their assigned areas,

POLICING IN THE 21ST CENTURY | 151

learning their problems and concerns while working with them to solve problems.

Random patrol is another defining feature of traditional policing. Historically, the police patrolled randomly in a defined area until a radio dispatcher sent them on an assignment. The officer then responded to the scene, handled the incident and returned to patrol until dispatched to another assignment. That process repeats itself 24 hours a day throughout America, because most cities operate under the traditional policing model. As a result, police officers are tied to their patrol cars and radios, isolated from the public. They are not encouraged to get to know residents and merchants on their beats. By design, the public is left out of the policing process.

By contrast, under *Community Policing*, officers are given permanent beat assignments with the expectation that they will get to know the people in their areas. Contact with the public is encouraged and expected. The public is included as an integral part of the policing process. Officers are expected to maintain high visibility in their areas as a means of deterring crime and reducing fear. Most importantly, officers are expected to get to know the problems in their assigned areas, seek support from other agencies, the community and the private sector in devising and implementing solutions to problems. The overall goal of the Community Policing model is to improve the quality of life in the neighborhoods where the police are assigned. In doing so, the city is made a safer and better place to live.

Community Policing represents a conceptual, managerial and operational philosophy for providing police service to cities. As a conceptual philosophy, Community Policing is not viewed as a program, but rather a style of policing that involves all aspects of the department. Unlike Police-Community Relations programs of the 1960s, police departments that implemented Community Policing as their dominant style of operation do not create separate Community-Policing units. Under Community Policing, every unit and every member of the department operates under the same concept of policing.

As a managerial philosophy, Community Policing represents a view of the police function that is anchored in *values*. Those values reflect a set of organizational commitments that guide how the police respond to community problems, deal with people and manage their activities. This view limits, if not rejects, the traditional paramilitary model of command and control by incorporating participatory management and supervision.

All members of the department, both sworn and civilians are viewed as essential members of the organization with a shared vision.

As an operational philosophy, Community Policing bases its activities on developing an understanding of the nature of the problems police are called on to handle. This new operational philosophy requires substantial bureaucratic reforms, collaboration between police and neighborhood residents, as well as direct linkages between police and other governmental and private organizations that provide a wide range of services to the community. The operational objective is to solve problems, rather than merely respond to incidents.

The overall philosophy of Community Policing acknowledged that police must be accountable not only to the law but also to law-abiding people. It is a basic democratic principle that citizens are empowered to authorize government actions in a variety of ways. To ensure effective policing, and have police actions accepted and supported by the community, the people must authorize police actions that deal with crime and disorder, and must generally approve of the strategies used. Absent such legitimacy, the police will be unsuccessful in their attempts to collaborate with the community in any meaningful way. Without a community partnership, police actions will not have the long-term imprint on changing neighborhood conditions which lead to the police being called to respond.

The Community Policing philosophy recognizes the need for community legitimacy, provides a mechanism for police accountability to neighborhood residents, and creates a framework within which the police can work in collaboration with residents to solve neighborhood problems that are related to crime, fear, violence and quality of life.

The basic tenets of Community Policing are community collaboration and problem solving. As such, police officers are assigned an area or "turf. They are expected to become "experts" on the conditions, issues and concerns of residents in those areas. In doing so, they must develop close linkages with residents and business people. Based on analyses of neighborhood crime and disorder problems, prioritized in collaboration with citizen, officers seek to identify police, government, business and citizen resources that can be mobilized to eliminate the conditions that give rise to community unrest.

Rapid response to emergencies, investigation of criminal acts and the apprehension of criminals are as important under Community Policing as they are under traditional policing. However, compared to officers using traditional approaches to policing, the daily tasks of Community

Policing officers are far less reactive and require police spending a greater percentage of time resolving problems and issues before they become major contributors to the cycle of crime, violence and disorder.

Under Community Policing, when a crime or quality-of-life problem is identified as a pattern, a solution is developed through collaborative discussions between residents and police. Under Community Policing, the police are no longer simply incident responders, nor do they position themselves as the sole experts in how to deal with criminal problems. The Community Policing collaboration is an intense and active affair, providing a true sharing of responsibility for the achievement of the desired goal of both the police and the community: safe and secure neighborhoods.

Simply stated, Community Policing can be viewed as a philosophy that governs how citizen expectations and demands for police services are integrated into the actions of the police to identify and address those conditions that have an adverse effect on the safety and welfare of neighborhood life. To that end, the very essence of Community Policing can be viewed from two important perspectives:

1. A realization that every community consists of neighborhoods that place different service demands on a police agency. The uniqueness of these demands requires police managers to devise "customized" service responses. Therefore, the term *community* is viewed from the perspective of "geographical locations." Given the diversity associated with these different locations, it becomes the department's responsibility to properly allocate, deploy and manage its resources so that services are adequately and consistently rendered from one location to the next.
2. Acknowledging the importance of knowing when to form interactive partnerships between the police and the public in order to identify and resolve neighborhood problems of crime and disorder. This perspective defines Community Policing in terms of citizen involvement. It becomes the responsibility of the department to determine when, where and how citizens can work with police officials.

THE GOALS AND OBJECTIVES OF COMMUNITY POLICING

Although one of the chief goals of Community Policing is to improve the quality of life in a community, its basic objectives are not particularly different from those of *traditional policing*. They include:

- Reducing crime and victimization
- Reducing the fear of crime
- Preventing crime
- Arresting criminals
- Promoting community security

Two other objectives, commonly considered insignificant under the traditional approach of police service delivery, greatly alter the nature of the police function under Community Policing. These are:
- Solving chronic neighborhood problems
- Developing a neighborhood's capacity to exist within a state of order and peace.

CRIME AND VICTIMIZATION

Few issues are as important to the citizen sense of well being as the absence of criminal victimization. Community Policing seeks to directly reduce the frequency of criminal victimization in a number of ways.

Being tough on crime and effective in dealing with it is the first objective of Community Policing. Through tactics, such as organizing communities to identifying those who victimize others by strengthening the quality of the criminal investigation process and by generating a community commitment to identify those who prey on other members of society, Community Policing provides a strong and highly effective approach to reducing criminal activity.

It, above all, is considered to be a smarter way of addressing crime problems. Rather than offering a simple bureaucratic response to individual incidents of crime, Community Policing requires the police to work collaboratively with neighborhood residents and merchants to identify law violators and bring them to justice. This joint commitment to justice reflects one of the most important commitments of Community Policing. In the interest of protecting the lives and property of the law-abiding citizens, it is a commitment to ensure that lawbreakers are dealt with quickly and fairly.

FEAR OF CRIME

Research has frequently shown that the fear of crime is out of proportion to the actual incidences of crime. Community Policing focuses not only on reducing the incidence of crime, but it also focuses on reducing the fear of crime. This is accomplished by a variety of means; chief among them being officers meeting with and getting to know people in the neighborhoods where they are assigned. While working with them to solve problems.

This process not only gives citizens a feeling that something is being done about their problems -- thereby reducing fear -- it also places the police in a better position to develop a full understanding of the problems, and be better equipped to address them.

Addressing the fear of crime also reduces crime. As citizens feel safer in their neighborhoods, they are more likely to walk their neighborhoods and, when necessary, leave their homes. Research has shown that the presence of people on the streets serves as a deterrent to crime.[3] Community Policing also facilitates residents getting to know one another while guarding one another's property, which, in turn, facilitates greater feelings of security.

CRIME PREVENTION

Community Policing also focuses on reducing the opportunities for crime to be committed and preventing crime through problem solving. Crime does not occur in a vacuum; it results from conditions that create environments that are conducive to illegal activities. In poorer neighborhoods, where there is substantial unemployment, poor education, and limited opportunities to participate in the American economic system, the opportunities for crime flourish. Of equal importance to the socio-economic conditions that create environments in which crime flourishes is the level of neighborhood cohesiveness. Highly organized neighborhoods -- areas in which there is full participation by residents and business people in the life of the neighborhood -- have far less fear than disorganized communities which are more susceptible to crime. [4]

Community Policing positions the police to establish a working partnership with neighborhood residents. Such partnerships support neighborhood organization, increasing its capacity to remain cohesive and reduce opportunities for crime to occur. Police officers, absent other organizing catalysts in the community, become the initiators of the police-community partnership. That partnership focuses on ensuring that there are limited opportunities for criminal victimization and supports an environment within which crime cannot flourish.

It is only when the economic and social conditions of poverty, poor education and other social ills are combined with neighborhood disorganization that crime becomes endemic to an area.[5] The working partnership between police and community provides a basis on which a strong, highly organized neighborhood can develop and flourish.

PROMOTING A COMMUNAL SENSE OF SECURITY

The working partnership between police and community places police officers in close, routine contact with neighborhood residents and merchants in a positive, problem-solving context. This creates a highly visible police presence in areas of the community where significant problems that concern residents exist. Rather than simply driving through a neighborhood in a marked police vehicle, the police officer in the Community Policing model uses the vehicle primarily as a means of transportation to get from one destination to another. A majority of an officer's time is spent interacting with residents, working on solving problems, and developing positive working relationships with agencies, businesses owners, young people and parents in the neighborhood. This type of initiative, a result of police presence in the community, is positive and personal. It results in a far greater impact on the public perception of safety than that realized utilizing the traditional random patrol of a neighborhood.

SOLVING CHRONIC PROBLEMS

The primary focus of Community Policing is solving problems. In that context, problem solving means intervening in an actual or potential pattern of incidents of concern to a neighborhood so that the underlying conditions which created the problem are eliminated. [6]

The problem-solving orientation of Community Policing is the antithesis of the traditional approach to policing, where the police are organized primarily to respond to incidents, each considered as an independent occurrence. The Community Policing problem-solving orientation recognizes neighborhood problems seldom just arise.

Furthermore, traditional police action in response to a 911 call often will make little difference in eliminating the on-going nature of the problem. Recognizing that the police are most often responding to repeat problems, Community Policing seeks to determine the nature of the problem and take actions that impact the underlying causes. It is because of this recognition that the problem-solving mode, discussed in the previous chapter, has become integrated into the broader model of Community Policing.

DEVELOPING A NEIGHBORHOOD'S CAPACITY TO EXIST IN A PEACEFUL AND ORDERLY STATE

By forming a partnership between police and citizens, Community Policing seeks to support the ability of neighborhoods to assume some responsibility for their sense of order and peace. As noted above, the degree to which a neighborhood is organized will impact its level of fear.

The degree of organization will also impact the neighborhood's ability to control its environment since it is primarily in disorganized neighborhoods that crime and disorder flourish. When neighborhoods rely on the police – who cannot be omnipresent – for maintenance of order, residents often keep their doors locked, and are unwilling to use their streets for recreation, seldom venturing outside of their four walls for fear of criminals who may roam the streets of the areas in which the live.

In a democracy the police authority, alone, cannot guarantee safe streets and order. Community Policing recognizes the role residents must play in maintaining safe and orderly environments. Traditionally, the police have tried to assume total responsibility for neighborhood safety and order, asking citizens to inform them whenever they observed criminal activity. The system has not worked.

Community policing recognizes that the police, at best, can only be co-producers of order in a neighborhood. It recognizes that the residents must commit themselves to maintaining an orderly environment. Community Policing seeks to maintain neighborhood order and stability through neighborhood involvement, with police providing assistance as needed and requested by residents.

It is in this context that Community Policing fosters a sense of trust, not only between the residents and the police, but also amongst residents. This interpersonal trust creates an atmosphere of reciprocity, which brings to bear resources of individuals and their organizations to work with the police and other agencies to address the issues of crime and quality of life in communities. This idea is consistent with the concept of *"social capital"* which was developed by political scientists and sociologists to describe the resources available to individuals via the organizations in which they were members. [7]

Social capital refers to those features of social relations -- such as interpersonal trust, norms of reciprocity, and membership in civic organizations — which act as resources for individuals to facilitate collective action for mutual benefit. [8]

Sampson applied the concept of social control to criminal behavior in Chicago and argued that, "In addition to encouraging communities to mobilize against violence through 'self-help' strategies of informal social control, perhaps reinforced by partnerships with agencies of formal control (community policing), strategies to address the social and ecological changes that beset many inner-city communities need be considered."[9] Properly implemented, Community Policing serves as the catalyst that facilitates the engagement, voluntarism and trust that enables the cooperation and coordination of all available resources to the benefit of the community.

THE PRINCIPLES OF COMMUNITY POLICING

There are six primary principles of Community Policing, all reflected in the definition of the philosophy.

PRINCIPLE ONE: COMMUNITY POLICING IS A PROACTIVE RATHER THAN REACTIVE RESPONSE TO COMMUNITY PROBLEMS.

Traditionally, the police have been a reactive service organization which responds to those problems and issues brought to its attention by the public, primarily through calls to 911. These requests for police service were viewed as individual incidents requiring some type of police response. They involved a wide variety of citizen requests, ranging from crime reports to concerns among neighbors about youth activities.

Inherent in the Community Policing philosophy is an understanding that the incidents to which the police are called frequently reflect a series of events that constitute a pattern. Under Community Policing, the police seek to understand the nature of both the problems underlying the pattern and the factors in the life of the neighborhood that gave rise to those problems. In doing so, Community Policing seeks to address the concerns of a neighborhood *before* they manifest themselves in incidents requiring a 911call or response.

The proactive nature of Community Policing can be seen in the fact that under traditional policing, officers were expected to engage in random preventive patrol when not occupied answering a citizen's call for service. This approach was based on conventional wisdom that random patrol prevented crime because potential violators would be deterred, since they did not know where or when an officer would appear. Important patrol experiments conducted in the 1970s raised serious questions about the effectiveness of random patrol.[10] Nevertheless, most police agencies today still require their officers to devote a large portion of their uncommitted time to randomly patrolling neighborhoods in order to provide a visible police presence. This presence is designed to assure the public that the police are available to respond to the next 911 call that is received. Community Policing advocates, on the other hand, argue that random patrol produces random results. They feel that the public deserves more for their tax dollars.

Under Community Policing, officers are trained to plan for the use of their uncommitted time in order to achieve a predetermined result. As such, officers under Community Policing devote all of their time providing some type of service to the community. Random patrol, for the sake of visibility, is not a priority under Community Policing. Visibility, however, is a by-product of the officer's activities in the community.

Proactive policing means the police assigned to the patrol function will focus their attention on learning about the neighborhoods they are responsible for, establish relationships with the people who live or work there and get to know the area's youth. It means working with law-abiding citizens to improve the quality of life in the areas. Although patrol officers are available to respond to citizen calls for assistance, the officers' preoccupation will be problem solving and not merely responding to incidents.

Proactive policing also involves other units of the police department in addition to patrol. Crime analysis is used to identify both crime and problem patterns, as well as to delve into the nature of these problems. Detectives and narcotics officers are assigned geographical areas of responsibility and, to a lesser degree than patrol officers, are required to get acquainted with the neighborhood, its people, conditions, problems and priorities. Thus, they become active components of the problem solving process. Support staff directs their efforts towards ensuring that line officers are successful in achieving their problem-solving objectives aimed at improving the quality of life in the community, including, but not limited to, crime prevention and arresting criminals.

PRINCIPLE TWO: COMMUNITY POLICING INVOLVES A PARTNERSHIP BETWEEN THE POLICE, PUBLIC AND PRIVATE AGENCIES.

If problem solving is the cornerstone of Community Policing, police-citizen partnerships are its foundation. Recognizing that there are a variety of public and private agencies and organizations that provide services to people, the interaction, communication and collaboration between the police and these agencies to solve problems is another key attribute of

Community Policing. Since the development of partnerships between the police and the community is a cornerstone of Community Policing, the police often work to organize neighborhood groups and link the needs of citizens with the services provided by law enforcement. The development and utilization of these agency resources enables the police to be more successful in preventing and solving crime. It has the added advantage of helping police better understand the concerns of the people and forge from that relationship a commitment to make crime fighting a total community effort and not simply a job for the police.

The importance of the partnership between the police and the community can be magnified in light of the fact that the police respond to a myriad of situations that have implications far greater and more complex than a single incident report might indicate.

Indeed, studies conducted in Boston and Minneapolis have shown that a large percentage of citizen calls to the police are to locations where the police have responded numerous times in the past.[11] This clearly illustrates that such incidents may represent on-going problems that continue to consume a large percentage of police time. Thus, a small percentage of the population ends up consuming the vast majority of police time and resources.

Resolving the underlying causes of problems that lead to calls for police service necessitates a careful analysis of the nature of the situation and a collaborative problem-solving effort by the police and other agencies of government, private organizations and the public. An added outcome of this partnership is that community members begin to realize that they have both the ability and responsibility to work with the police to improve the quality of life in their neighborhoods. The end result will make the job of the police more productive and rewarding.

Under traditional policing, officers take advantage of technology that allows them to respond quickly to citizen calls for service; but such a reactionary form of policing does not prevent or solve the repeat nature of the underlying problems. Furthermore, the underlying causes of the problems that produce calls for a police response do not necessarily surface in individual incidents, but they may have negative implications for quality of life in the community and have important implications for the police. Group or interpersonal conflict, signs of disorder, incivility and the fear of crime are issues that can be addressed through the problem-solving process. Under Community Policing, the police and the community collaboratively define the problems, set priorities as to which issues are to be addressed, determine the most appropriate tactics and/or strategies to be used and then utilize the combined resources of the police and the community to resolve issues.

Problem-Solving Policing requires careful analysis of the conditions and issues that give rise to problems. This is important because what may appear to be a single and isolated incident may in fact be part of a complex social condition that requires the intervention of agencies other than the police in order to achieve a resolution.

PRINCIPLE THREE: COMMUNITY POLICING IS BASED ON A SET OF VALUES.

Under Community Policing, the framework within which police services are delivered is set forth in a set of values, a clear and explicit articulation of what the organization believes in, and stands for. As such, values serve as the basis for setting policy, implementing programs, guiding behavior and ultimately delivering police services. It is within context of written values that members of the police department exercise their discretion and employ flexibility and creativity in carrying out their crime control and problem solving responsibilities.

Historically, police agencies have not taken the initiative to develop, reduce to writing and institutionalize matters of importance to them. This oversight is significant because values are an important element in developing the culture of an organization. Absent this initiative, which is characteristic of traditional policing, police department cultures have been allowed to develop based on often-unsupported beliefs concerning what worked, and did not work, in policing. This has resulted in a police cultural orientation deeply rooted in an autocratic managerial and operational philosophy of command and control. Internally, this meant that the actions, behavior and attitudes of the police were governed by a rigid set of rules and regulations. Externally, it was manifested in an authoritative control orientation in dealing with the public.

A value-driven department, an important attribute of Community Policing, creates a culture allowing the police to be judged based on criteria such as community power sharing, citizen involvement and a commitment to the rule of law inherent in principles of a democratic society. It has often been stated by Community Policing advocates that *it is democracy in action.*

PRINCIPLE FOUR: COMMUNITY POLICING FOCUSES THE DELIVERY OF POLICE SERVICES ON THE NEIGHBORHOOD LEVEL.

The philosophy of Community Policing recognizes city neighborhoods as the focal point for the delivery of police services. Inherent in this recognition is also a decrease on specialization in favor of a move towards generalization.

Under traditional policing, with its paramilitary command and control orientation, centralization of authority, planning and decision-making became the dominant orientation of the organization. At the same time, specialization was viewed as the most effective method of addressing specific problems. Consequently, police agencies operating under the traditional style did not formally recognize that the problems, concerns and priorities of one neighborhood might not be the same for all. Community Policing, in contrast, not only recognizes, but also organizes its planning and service delivery around small geographical areas of a city -- each with their own identity and distinctive characteristics. The residents of these neighborhoods generally have elements of commonality such as race, religion, culture, values, income and problems.

Under Community Policing, the officers are assigned to a neighborhood on a permanent basis and are expected to get to know the people who live or work there -- their problems, concerns and priorities -- but even more important, to engage them in a process of collaboration designed to solve problems and thereby improve the quality of life in neighborhoods of the city.

PRINCIPLE FIVE: COMMUNITY POLICING INVOLVES BEING ACCOUNTABLE TO RESIDENTS IN NEIGHBORHOODS.

This principle of Community Policing recognizes that the problems, issues, concerns and priorities differ from one neighborhood to another. In order to be responsive to the people, the police must know what is important to those who live in a given neighborhood. If the police are going to be able to obtain this understanding, they must have ongoing contact with the residents. Equally important, the police must keep the residents informed on what goes on in their community. It is this regular and ongoing contact with the people that enables the police to develop an atmosphere of cooperation and mutual respect. As the officers interact with the residents, they also become accountable to them. Under Community Policing, police officers are accountable not only to the department, but also to the people they serve.

PRINCIPLE SIX: COMMUNITY POLICING INVOLVES SHARING POWER WITH THE PEOPLE.

The nature of Community Policing is such that passive citizen involvement is not sufficient. There must be a sincere and legitimate partnership between the police and the people. The police must be willing to trust the law-abiding people in the community and involve them in the decisions that impact their lives. Both the police and the people benefit from this power sharing. The police benefit because quite often citizens have information that will be beneficial to them in both preventing crime and arresting offenders. The public benefits because they will ultimately have safer communities in which to live. Power sharing means that the police include the public in their decision making if legally permissible, and it does not jeopardize a legitimate police operation.

COMMUNITY POLICING VS. POLICE-COMMUNITY RELATIONS

During the 1960s and early 1970s, Police-Community relations programs were established as vehicles for bridging the gaps between the police and the community, particularly the minority community. The major focus of Police-Community Relations was the creation of special units that were given the responsibility of interacting with the community.

Although the concept of reaching out to the community was an appropriate strategy, Police Community Relations programs did not prevail for two major reasons. First, they were *programs* and only those officers assigned to the units had the responsibility of working with the community. For other members of the department, it was business as usual. Second, all of the systems that supported the police department remained the same. As a result, the programs were like radios: they could be plugged in, but they could also be unplugged.

COMMUNITY POLICING VS. CRIME PREVENTION

Crime-prevention, in contrast to Community Policing, is a set of programs designed by the police to involve the community in the process of preventing crime. It is mainly an educational program provided by the police to teach the public how best to protect themselves from becoming victims of crime.

Community Policing, however, incorporates the concepts of crime-prevention into its philosophy.

COMMUNITY POLICING VS. PROBLEM-SOLVING POLICING

Problem-Solving Policing continues to be an integral part of Community Policing. The technique of crime and problem analysis, the essence of Problem-Solving Policing, has been institutionalized in police departments throughout the country. Community Policing goes beyond problem-solving policing. Problem-Solving Policing is a technique used by the police to address problems in neighborhoods. Community Policing, on the other hand, is broader in scope and context. As pointed out above, Community Policing represents a managerial and operational philosophy supported by six principles. Rather than being a technique, it is a style for delivering police services.

COMMUNITY POLICING VS. TEAM POLICING

As pointed out in the previous chapter, in the early 1970s, a number of police agencies tried a new concept called "Team Policing" as a means for improving effectiveness in neighborhoods. The concept focused on three changes in the basic police strategy for crime control: (1) that a group of officers would be assigned responsibility for a specific neighborhood, not just individual officers on a shift; (2) supervision of policing in the defined area would be the responsibility of a single police supervisor; and (3) the officers assigned to the neighborhood would work closely with residents and business people on crime problems.

The key Team Policing strategy was the formation of the "Team." In contrast to assigning individual officers to "beats," the Team Policing concept provided stability of beat assignment for a group of officers. The same officers policed the same neighborhoods each day, creating a sense of neighborhood responsibility among the police.

While Team Policing was successful in a number of areas, it failed to become a widely accepted police strategy for a number of reasons. One, support systems linking Team Policing officers to others in the department were never established, resulting in Team Policing officers being considered as specialized and separate from the mainstream of policing. [12]

Two, the changes required for true community collaboration never developed. The police maintained a perspective of their role as being primarily that of law enforcement, which hindered meaningful problem solving activities in response to concerns brought to the police by the neighborhoods.

This is not to say that Community Policing does not substantially draw ideas from Team-Policing. It does. But Community Policing goes much further in building on some of the elements of the Team Policing strategy, adopting a far more sophisticated problem-analysis and problem-solving approach to policing, and providing the required organizational support for the initiative.

WHY DID COMMUNITY POLICING DEVELOP?

Historically, police administrators responded to crime, violence and citizen fear of crime by developing programs to "crack down on crime," making more arrests and seeking support for expansion of their police agencies. In the late 1970s and early 1980s, however, a number of police administrators recognized that more police, alone, would not solve the nation's crime problem. They came to recognize that the traditional method of responding to crime had woefully achieved its intended objectives. Although the traditional response to crime had been successful in bringing record numbers of people into the criminal justice system, crime and citizen fear had continued to increase while public confidence in the ability of the police to provide for their safety had eroded.

Historically, approaches to police improvement had focused on strengthening the operation of the police bureaucracy or adding additional resources. Neither had an impact on the deterioration of urban communities. Given the effectiveness of the police in arresting those who broke the law, the criminal justice system could not continue to successfully respond to greater police effectiveness in making arrests. An overburdened criminal justice system simply released criminals back to the streets, where many continued to engage in criminal activity. Neighborhood problems and criminals were not significantly impacted by that narrow approach.

Traditional policing strategy was unsuccessful for a number of reasons. One, there has never been a true collaboration between police and community, making it difficult for neighborhood residents to share responsibility with the police for crime control, order maintenance and fear reduction. To police traditionalists, community involvement had simply been a public relations requirement, undertaken to make police activities acceptable to an often skeptical citizens.[13] Thus, the type of citizen involvement encouraged by police had generally been benign and passive.

Two, the police were also out of sync with the values of large segments of the community, especially minorities. Without closely working with neighborhood residents, it was easy for police officers to develop their own sense of acceptable and unacceptable police practices. The opportunities to understand community expectations were limited as the police were, for the most part, relegated to driving through communities, responding to 911 calls. In extreme cases, police officers were known to have developed a sense of priority and probity that was far different from that which the community valued and accepted.

The centralized, control-oriented professional bureaucracy discouraged close police contact with members of the public, fearing the possibility of corruption if police spent significant time with residents.

These factors contributed to a somewhat alienated police force, present in, yet distant from the neighborhoods they served. The communities, themselves, were often undergoing a transformation in stability, faced with increasing pressures from crime, violence and drugs. Those conditions begged for a different way of delivering police services. Community Policing emerged as that different way.

THE THREE PHASES OF COMMUNITY POLICING

The inability of traditional policing to control the problem of crime not only concerned police administrators, but was also the underlying cause of public dissatisfaction.

The concern and dissatisfaction did not mean that all of the work that the police had performed was irrelevant or not appreciated and needed to be replaced by something totally different.

To the contrary, Community Policy is not a total rejection of all of the elements of Traditional Policing. It should be viewed as evolutionary and not revolutionary in American police work and history.

As an applicable theory it has built on the successful elements of past police work and has taken advantage of its victories. It builds on the successful elements of the past while at the same time taking advantage of the body of knowledge in policing that has developed. Historically, as police agencies adopted Community-Policing principles, there were three phases of development. While the stages are not necessarily inter-related, they can be considered on a continuum running from the *program phase* to the *style development phase,* to the *institutionalization phase.* [14]

The Program Phase of Community Policing exists when a police agency assigns a small group of police officers to engage in what are considered problem solving or Community Policing activities. The earliest Community Policing initiatives were programs, developed and tested by a small number of officers in a defined area of the community. [15]

The Los Angeles *Basic Car Plan* is an example of an early program of Community Policing.[16] Assigning a police officer in each patrol area responsibility for knowing that community and its problems, developing relationships with the residents of the area and working to problem-solve certainly fits the general criteria of Community Policing. So do the activities undertaken in Houston with the *Directed Area Response Team* (DART) program in which a group of officers assumed responsibility for all activities in a group of neighborhoods.[17] The DART Program was the forerunner of the neighborhood-policing model eventually adopted in Houston.

Early in the development of the problem-solving approach to policing, both Newport News, Virginia and Baltimore County, Maryland developed model problem analysis and problem-solving initiatives in their communities.[18] Undertaken by a small group of police officers specifically assigned as problem-solving officers, these initiatives provided important experiences with the problem-solving approach to policing.[19]

There is difficulty, of course, in getting programmatic activities institutionalized throughout a police agency. It has always been far easier to test new ideas under the umbrella of a program, where they are free of the pressures and demands brought to bear by the nature of the larger organization and its culture. Most programs remain just that: isolated efforts, which eventually become overwhelmed by traditional police institutions.

Developing a dominate style of policing is the second phase in the Community Policing continuum. Key to the development of that style is the creation of a set of values which define the standards for how the police respond to a variety of situations and conditions. With the development of values, the police organization begins to change its perspective and the complex process of institutionalizing the Community Policing philosophy throughout the agency.

In both Houston and New York City, the introduction of strong value systems provided those agencies with a vision for the future and a set of standards that allowed decisions to be made.

The second phase, then, moves the agency from one in which Community Policing is a program, into one where it becomes the dominate style that is used by the agency to deliver its services.

A police agency were Community Policing is the dominate style will have a majority of its officers in some sections of the city adhering to the Community Policing philosophy in all of their activities. While a large number of officers still may not be operating under the Community

Policing philosophy, over time, fewer officers will fail to adhere to its transcending principles.

Institutionalization: The third phase of the Community Policing philosophy occurs when all supporting systems are oriented to support it. Institutionalization involves changing the basic systems of the police agency, from recruitment and training to supervisory and management roles.

In the process of institutionalization of Community Policing, all systems are carefully reviewed and the impact that they have on the Community Policing philosophy are documented. The systems are then altered so that they support the Community Policing effort.

Recruitment and selection systems focus on identifying officers who have a desire to serve the community, rather than merely joining the police department for a sense of adventure. Training is directed at providing officers with the problem-solving and interpersonal skills necessary to effectively solve problems in the city's neighborhoods. Performance evaluation systems are developed that reinforce problem-solving skills and measure success of those important activities.

Under Community Policing, the demand for response to 911 calls are controlled and high priority calls are assigned to officers who are responsible for neighborhoods, not just to the next available police unit. New beat structures are designed that ensure that beat boundaries match neighborhood boundaries. Supervisory roles are changed -- and supervisors are trained -- in new problem-solving roles that are necessary to provide crucial support to patrol officers.

THE BENEFITS OF COMMUNITY POLICING

Community Policing has provided American cities with a number of benefits. It provides to the police the opportunity to leverage their abilities to deal with crime, while greatly increasing the potential for greater production from police employees. Under Community Policing, police officers develop a better understanding of neighborhood priorities and spend more time working to resolve issues and underlying problems. While police officers alone cannot resolve many of the problems afflicting city neighborhoods, they can certainly have a far greater impact than they have had in the past. They can also change those practices that alienate citizens. That alone is reason enough for police departments to adopt the Community Policing philosophy.

Community Policing enhances the creative capacities of police officers. The traditional police bureaucracy, with its command and control orientation, has severely limited positive police officer initiatives. Working in the heart of neighborhoods and given the opportunity to be creative about and pensive with neighborhood problems, officers have demonstrated a strong capacity to collaborate with residents and initiate activities that actually address the underlying causes of problems that concern residents.

Community Policing also provides neighborhood residents with a feeling that police officers are sensitive to their concerns. Citizen belief in order and organization dramatically increases when police officers learn to listen to neighborhood residents.

They are further emboldened when they recognize that the police are responsive to them, their ideas and their sensibilities.

The ability of neighborhoods -- and the police – to jointly deal with crime is greatly enhanced by the concept of Community Policing. Since crime prevention is largely related to a neighborhood's willingness to accept responsibility for control over its own environment, working closely with the police enhances the appetite of residents to identify criminals and unlawful behavior.

While the underlying conditions of poverty, poor education and joblessness may not be resolved, a highly organized neighborhood has the best chance to avoid falling prey to crime and the fear of crime. Residents have a vested interested in seeing this type of climate created.

ARGUMENTS AGAINST COMMUNITY POLICING

A number of observers have provided arguments against Community Policing. These arguments have fallen into three key areas: (1) a suggestion that Community Policing is not "real" police work; (2) the suggestion that there is insufficient time for the work required by Community policing; and (3) the suggestion that problem solving is the province of others, not the police.

The most vociferous arguments against Community Policing have focused on the belief that Community Policing is not "real police work;" that true policing is not engaging in activities beyond the narrow mandate of law enforcement. From this perspective, the police function is primarily to enforce the law and respond to 911 calls for service. Engaging in activities outside that scope, it is argued, take the police into areas that are properly the responsibility of other agencies.

No city agency encounters such a broad range of service demands than the police. Few requests for police service relate directly to crime control. Most calls-for-service relate to neighborhood conditions involving disorder and fear. If the police do not address these citizen concerns, they will not be addressed and a criminal environment will blossom. Since the police have a major responsibility to work with the community to relieve conditions that generate crime and disorder, a broadened focus for the police is easily justified.

A similar argument is made relative to the police not having sufficient time to properly conduct the work mandated by the Community Policing philosophy. Taking the view that the police have a responsibility to respond as quickly as possible to every call-for-service that comes from a citizen, these critics suggest that the increasing demands for police services limits the available time police have to engage in problem-solving activities.

What this view fails to consider is the fact that the number of calls-for-service received by the police directly relate to the success that the police have in solving neighborhood problems. When police officers view 911 calls as incidents, and simply respond to handle the "immediate" and underlying situations, the reality of what caused the incidents usually goes unresolved. More calls for service are generated.

Under Community *Policing*, officers focusing on the nature of the underlying problems which generate 911 service demands can resolve problems and thus limit the number of future calls-for-service that might otherwise might have been generated.

Careful management of call-for-service activity will screen out those calls for which the presence of the police is not necessary. Delaying response to such calls, or routing them directly to agencies that can more effectively impact the immediate problem, allows for additional police time that can be devoted to solving neighborhood problems.

Another argument against Community Policing focuses on the perception that the concept is little more than social work. Not unlike the perception that neighborhood problem-solving is beyond the purview of the police, critics suggest that there is a clear distinction between being a social worker and being a police officer. One enforces the law while the other provides counseling to people, critics argue.

Given the obvious difference in orientation and training, however, the work of a police officer under Community Policing has little to do with social work. Although both may deal with the community in a manner that is sensitive to the conditions of the neighborhood and to people in need, there is little overlap between police duties and those of a social worker. [20]

From this perspective, the Community Policing philosophy creates *an illusion* within neighborhoods that the police will have some direct impact on the quality of urban life. The critics suggest that the problems of urban areas are far more complex than those that could be addressed by the police.

Furthermore, critics say that any suggestion to residents that having police work closely with them on solving problems is beyond what can be delivered. They argue that any police department adopting the Community Policing philosophy is bargaining for more than it can handle. [21]

Community Policing is not a panacea and has never promised to solve the vast majority of urban ills. What Community Policing does promise to do, however, is to increase police effectiveness by working with neighborhoods, commencing the process of transformation. Bringing others into the problem solving process, Community Policing increases the collaboration of government agencies in dealing with issues that concern citizens such as crime, fear and violence. The chance that meaningful action will result is **greatly increased in communities where the philosophy is adopted.**

EVALUATING COMMUNITY POLICING SUCCESSES AND EFFECTIVENESS

When we look at evaluating the effectiveness of police agencies, a critical question is what constitutes a good police department? Another, what is it that makes one department outstanding when compared to others?

Community Policing presents the opportunity to establish new criteria for evaluating police departments. That evaluation is based on more than the ability of police to control the crime rate because many of the factors that cause crime are not controlled by the police.

While many of the traditional measures of police success are equally applicable to the Community Policing model, far more complex criteria are necessary if the true impact of Community Policing is determined. There are four primary categories used for evaluation: (1) crime reduction; (2) fear reduction; (3) community and government support for police initiatives; and (4) success at problem solving. [22]

Crime reduction has traditionally been the primary criteria used to evaluate the police. Based upon the Uniform Crime Reports, collected and published by the Federal Bureau of Investigation, crime statistics have become the hallmark of evaluating police effectiveness. However, increased community confidence in the police may result in increases in the number of crimes reported, even if the actual number of such incidents does not change, or is reduced. While the police can have a direct impact on crime and victimization, it is important to develop victimization base rates so that it is possible to measure whether there are actual changes in victimization. Reported crime, as measured by calls-for-service, is not an adequate measure of the level of crime.

Fear reduction is a second element of Community Policing evaluation. As expected, a neighborhood's fear of crime declines as police officers assist in developing the neighborhood's capacity to resist crime and enhance its level of order. Thus, the level of fear in a neighborhood is an important measure of police effectiveness.

Support for the police from both the community and the government is another important measure of policing effectiveness. In fact, community support of the police may be the most important criterion in evaluating the effectiveness of Community Policing. This is particularly true when considering the fact that the police do not control the factors that produce crime, nor do they control the decisions made by other components of the criminal justice system. Thus, how the public feels about the police is extremely important. Public perception of the police will, in large measure, determine their willingness to cooperate in areas of crime control, problem solving, and addressing quality of life issues.

SUMMARY

The concept of Community Policing did not emerge overnight. It has been an evolutionary process. The concept builds on successful policing efforts of the past, including many prominent police programs that required community involvement. Community Policing does not promise to solve all of the problems confronting the police and the community, but it does provide the vehicle for bringing all segments of the community together to work with the police to break the cycles of crime, fear and disorder.

It represents only the second major transformation in the history of American policing, the first being the move from the era of political policing to the professional model of policing that served America for decades.

NOTES: CHAPTER SEVEN

1. Brown, Lee P., Community Policing, speech delivered before the International Criminal Investigative Training Assistance Program, U.S. Department of Justice, Nassau, Bahamas, May 25, 1992

2. Ibid.

3. Brown, Lee P. and Mary Ann Wycoff, "Policing Houston: Reducing Fear and Improving Service," Crime and Delinquency, Vol. 33. No 1, January 1987, 71-89; Pate, Anthony, Mary Ann Wycoff, Wesley G. Skogan and Lawrence W. Sherman, Reducing Fear of Crime in Houston and Newark: A Summary Report, Washington,D.C.: Police Foundation, 1986: Williams, Hubert and Antony M. Pate, "Returning to First Principles: Reducing the Fear of Crime in Newark", Crime and Delinquency, Vol. 33 No. 1. January 1987, pp.55-70

4. Skogan, Wesley G., "Community Organizations and Crime," in Crime and Justice: A Review of Research, vol. 10, Michael Tonry and Norval Morris (Eds.), Chicago and London: University of Chicago Press, pp. 39-78

5. Lewis, Dan A., (ED), "Reactions to Crime," Sage Criminal Justice Systems Annuals, Vol. 16, Beverly Hills, Calif.: Sage Publications, 1981; Carvalho, Irene and Dan A, Lewis, "Service Beyond Community: Reactions to Crime and Disorder Among Inner-City Residents," Criminology, Vol. 41, Issue 3, August 2003

6. Skogan, Wesley G., Disorder and Decline: Crime and the Spiral of Decay in America Neighborhoods, Berkeley and Los Angeles: University of California Press, 1992, also see Goldstein, Herman, Problem-Oriented Policing, New York: McGraw-Hill, 1990 and Brown, Lee P., Problem-Solving Strategies for Community Policing: A Practical Guide, New York City Police Department, 1992

7. See Putnam, Robert, Bowling Alone, The Collapse and Revival of American Community, New York: Simon and Schuster, 2000

8. Berkman, Lisa F, and Kawachi, Ichiro, (Eds.), Social Epidemiology, New York: Oxford University Press, 2000; Fields, John, Social Capitol, New York: Rouledge, 2003; Putnam, Robert, "The Prosperous Community: Social Capitol and Social Life," The American Prospective, 13 (Spring 1993) pp.35-42

9. Sampson, Robert J., Stephen W. Raudenbush and Felton Earls, "Neighborhood and Violent Crime: A Multilevel Study of Collective Efficiency," Science, Vol. 277, August 1897, pp. 918-024

10. Kelling, George, Tony Pate, Duane Dieckman, Kansas City

Preventive Patrol Experiment, Washington, D.C.: The Police Foundation, 1974

11. Pierce, Glen, S.A, Spaar and L.R. Briggs, IV, The Character of Police Work: Implications for the Delivery of Police Services, Final Report to the National Institute of Justice, Boston: Northeastern University, 1988

12. Sherman, Lawrence W., Catherine H. Milton and Thomas V. Kelly, Team Policing: Seven Case Studies, Washington, D.C.: Police Foundation, August 1973

13. Green, Jack B. "Police and Community Relations: Where Have We Been and Where Are We Going," in Roger Dunham and Geoffrey P. Alpers' Critical Issues in Law Enforcement, Prospect Heights, Ill: Waveland Press Inc., 1987

14. Brown, Lee P., "Community Policing: A Practical Guide for Police Officials," Perspectives on Policing, Washington, D.C.: U.S. Department of Justice, National Institute of Justice, and the Program in Criminal Justice Policy and Management, John F. Kennedy School of Government, Cambridge, Mass.: Harvard University, September 1989. For an example of a plan to institutionalize Community Policing, see Brown, Lee P., Policing New York City in the 1990s. New York City Police Department, January, 1991

15. Ibid.

16. Los Angeles Police Department, The Los Angeles Police Department's Basic Car Plan, Los Angeles Police Department, April 1, 1972, unpublished

17. Brown, Lee P., Directed Area Responsibility Team, Houston, 1982, unpublished

18. Eck, John and William Spelman, Problem-Oriented Policing in New Port News, Virginia, Washington, D.C.: Police Executive Research Forum, 1987

19. Taft, Phillip B., Jr., Fighting Fear: The Baltimore County Project, Washington, D.C.: Police Executive Research Forum, February, 1986

20. Moore, Mark H., Robert C. Trojanowicz and George Kellings, "Crime and Policing," Perspectives on Policing, Washington,D.C.: U.S. Department of Justice, National Institute of Justice and the Program in Criminal Justice Policy and Management, John F. Kennedy School of Government, Cambridge. Mass.: Harvard University, June 1998, No 2

21. Ibid. Also see Manning, Peter K., <u>Police Work: The Social Organization of Policing</u>, Prospect Heights, Ill.: Waveland Press, 1997

22. Brown, Lee P., New York City Council Public Safety Hearing, <u>How to Evaluate the Effectiveness of the Police Department's Community Policing Program</u>, New York City, New York: November 14, 1991

Chapter Eight

ISSUES IN IMPLEMENTATION

INTRODUCTION

The trend in law enforcement throughout America, and many other parts of the free world, is toward adopting Community Policing as the dominant style for delivering police services.

Approximately 85 percent of the police departments in the United States had implemented Community Policing, in one form or another, by 2008.

> The real challenge confronting American policing is how to incorporate the principles of Community Policing, both its management and operational philosophy, into the day-to-day business of law enforcement.

In many instances, however, Community Policing, as a dominant style of delivering police services, has been misunderstood. In other cases, the implementation has been impeded by organizational problems.

This chapter discusses what organizational changes are necessary to successfully implement and institutionalize Community Policing as the dominate style of service delivery by a police agency.

IMPLEMENTING COMMUNITY POLICING

To successfully implement Community Policing, a police department must experience fundamental changes in how it conducts its business. The changes must touch, in one way or another, every aspect of the department. They involve redesigning how the department delivers its services to citizens. In effect, it means building a *new* police department that eventually will be more efficient and cost-effective.

As pointed out in chapter six, the transition from the traditional style of policing to Community Policing came about because of new information about the limitations of traditional policing, experiences with programs involving the community, commissions and court decisions, new technological advances and increases in crime and the fear of crime. The groundwork was laid many years earlier. The preparation for that change, however, started in earnest during the decade of the 1980s.

The first step in developing a new direction for any police agency is to conduct a thorough *assessment of the department.* This assessment should identify the strengths of the department as well as those areas where improvements are needed. The assessment should result in a *plan of action* that outlines a new vision for the department. That vision should call for the implementation or advancement of Community Policing and should be spelled out in both managerial and operational terms.

Two examples of this self assessment and action plan process were developed by the Houston Police Department in 1983, titled Plan of Action, and the New York City Police Department in 1990, titled Policing New York City in the 1990s.[1] They served as road maps for implementation of Community Policing in the two cities.[2]

Departmental assessments should result in a strategic framework that clearly outlines just what must be accomplished to ensure that the police department has the flexibility and direction to deal with an ever-changing environment. It should allow for building on the strengths of the agency and a mechanism for pursuing all opportunities for improvement. In effect, the assessment should serve as the blue print for the future of policing in the city.

The real challenge confronting American policing is how to incorporate the principles of Community Policing, its management and operational philosophy into the day-to-day business of the organization.

Under Community Policing, an important aspect of managerial thinking is to view their new role as being supportive of officers who are on the streets, engaged in problem solving with neighborhood residents. Critical to the officer's success is the ability of managers to create an environment in which they make it possible for the officer success. This means that they must work collectively and individually to remove roadblocks that serve as impediments to creativity. It means they must ensure that officers receive the support, internally and externally, that they need to achieve their objectives.

It also means they must take a close look at how they use their resources and authority, assuring that all police resources are invested in problem solving on the neighborhood level.

It means that current police managers must ensure that they use all of the resources at their disposal to improve the quality of life in city neighborhoods, continually emphasizing the idea of quality service in all of their operations by sworn and civilian personnel.

The move towards Community Policing and the implementation process necessary to achieve that objective means that the American police enterprise is undertaking a path that will serve the nation well into the future. This is important because during difficult times, the police should serve as a catalyst and as the very glue that holds a community together. This places a heavy burden on those who occupy leadership positions in law enforcement. It is their responsibility to ensure that their departments provide the best services possible with available resources.

There are major challenges that confront police departments as they implement Community Policing. The first is to ensure that as the department goes through the process of change, it continues to carry out its responsibility of addressing the problem of crime and the fear of crime throughout the city. The second is to prepare the department for the future. Inherent in its definition, Community Policing provides the framework to accomplish both objectives.

It is also important to recognize that Community Policing cannot be implemented or institutionalized quickly and hastily. There are numerous major tasks that must be completed before implementation. Every major system of the organization must be reviewed and, where appropriate, changed in order to support Community Policing.

It is insufficient for police leaders to have merely a vision about the direction they want their departments to pursue. They must work to ensure that their goal is achieved. Cities are constantly changing. That is the reason flexibility is a key element in implementing Community Policing.

Successful implementation requires both individual and collective efforts inside of the agency to ensure that the department achieves its vision of making the city a better place in which to live. That is done by preventing crime, arresting offenders and solving problems. That is the major goal of Community Policing.

To achieve that objective, American police leaders must rethink how they perform their jobs. They must empower officers and give them the support and authority they need to be successful in carrying out their functions. In the end, they will have a better police department that can serve as a paradigm of policing throughout the world. This chapter outlines the process for making that transition.

A police agency's ability to successfully move from traditional policing to Community Policing involves a number of important elements. One of the most important is to ensure that the change is systemic. That means the entire organization must work together towards achieving a common goal. It requires all members of the organization to have a clear understanding of that goal.

Beyond goal definition, the coordination of the various units within the police department becomes critical for goal achievement. This must be accomplished at various levels. From the organizational level, the executive corps has the responsibility to ensure that teamwork takes place. A corporate mind set then becomes critical for the success of the transition.

Teamwork is equally critical at the operational level. For that reason, the development of an effective management system is necessary to ensure that all units of the department work together in order to achieve a common objective.

It is also important that the management is committed to change. That commitment must be reflected in the attitudes of each team member. If, for example, only lip service is given to changes, that will hamper the believability of their commitment in the minds of subordinates. That is the reason that attitude becomes extremely important. Being knowledgeable about the concept of Community Policing, understanding what it means for the organization and what steps are necessary to implement it are concrete examples of that commitment.

Organizational change also generates skepticism among those who are at the operational level of the organization. They will naturally look for signs that tell them whether the organization is serious about change. In police agencies, policy is set through training, polices, rules, regulations, procedures and other written documents. Therefore, Community Policing must be reflected in the directive system and in training programs that comprise the policy making mechanisms of the agency.

This is important because under the command and control structure of police agencies and its paramilitary orientation, there are few incentives to work together and coordinate activities. Just the opposite is true under

Community Policing. Thus, the traditional structure of law enforcement agencies must be changed to reflect the philosophy of Community Policing. Inherent in that change is the recognition that police officers on the beat are the most important people in the organization. The task of everyone above the police officer level must be to assist officers in carrying out their responsibilities. This suggests that the command and control style of policing that served American policing well in the past must be modified. Most importantly, managers must trust their police officers. They must recognize that police officers are intelligent, creative and thoughtful individuals.

The future organizational structure of police agencies must be flexible. This flexibility must be based on the need to work together to achieve common objectives. All of the talent and skill in the organization, sworn and civilian personnel, must be used to help improve the quality of life of the people served by the agency. This involves different methods of communicating. Not only should there be vertical communications, there must also be horizontal communications. This is necessary to coordinate efforts by units to achieve a common goal.

On the precinct level, it is important that all units, (detectives, civilians, patrol, narcotics, vice etc.), have similar objectives. The challenge is to develop mechanisms to ensure that this is the case. Community Policing, with its emphasis on problem solving, provides that mechanism. Identification of problems, not only as seen by the police, but also by the community through the development of beat profiles, can provide the common objective for all units to work towards. This common problem identification process goes a long way in ensuring the coordination between detectives, patrol and other specialized units within the agency.

In summary, a major proposition of Community Policing is that the police department works to improve the quality of life in neighborhoods throughout the city. The police culture, therefore, must be centered on problem identification and coordination of all expertise in the department to solve problems. This is essential for the successful transition from *traditional* to *Community Policing*.

PROGRAM VS. PROCESS

The first step in institutionalizing Community Policing is to understand the difference between a program, such as *Police Community Relations* and a process such as *Community Policing*. Police Community Relations involved creating special units consisting of a few officers assigned the responsibility of working with the community. Community Policing, on the other hand, does not involve the creation of specialized units to work with the community while other members of the department carry on business as usual.

Community Policing involves all members of the police department. It represents a fundamental change in how police officers think about and carry out their responsibilities on a daily basis. This does not mean, however, that the police will stop responding to calls for service, a fundamental responsibility under Community Policing. What it does mean, however, is that police departments give officers time to engage in other activities, such as getting to know the people in the neighborhoods and working with them to identify, understand and cooperatively solve problems. This represents a fundamental change in how police officers have traditionally spent their time. Community Policing should not be viewed as simply a new program. Rather, it must be seen as a different model of policing where the police carry out their responsibilities in a manner different than they did under traditional policing. It represents a de-emphasis on specialization and gives patrol officers the responsibility for a greater variety of activities, allowing them to be creative in the pursuit of their objectives. This requires police officers to be more flexible in performing their duties. It also requires a different style of supervision, management and a new system of accountability.

Community Policing, in summary, is not a new program or even a set of programs. Rather, it represents a new set of realities. All members of the department must understand and support it. It requires the full mobilization of community resources to identify and resolve persistent neighborhood problems. In doing so, the department and the community reap numerous benefits by improving the quality of life in city neighborhoods.

There are distinct differences between a program and a process. *Programs* are specific to a given task or set of goals. They are discrete and comprised of distinct elements. Programs represent plans under which certain actions are taken.

A process, on the other hand, is broader in concept and anticipates a synthesis of operations. It represents a series of actions directed towards achieving ends of a higher plane. A process represents a synthesis of ideas and programs.

SEVEN S CONCEPT[3]

To fully implement Community Policing as a new style of policing, as distinguished from Community-Oriented Programs, it is necessary to change all the systems that support police agencies.

Police departments are more than structures on an organizational chart, although structure is important. Successful implementation of Community Policing involves more than developing strategies, although strategy is important.

Rather, successful implementation of Community Policing and its institutionalization as the dominate style of delivering services to the community requires an understanding of the relationship between (1) structure, (2) strategy, (3) systems, (4) style, (5) skills, (6) staff and (7) super ordinate goals.

In implementing Community Policing, it is necessary to understand that organizations are effective because of the interaction of several factors. Some of those factors are obvious while others are not. The McKinsey consulting firm developed the 7-S Model as a means of understanding organizational change.

Chart I: McKinsey 7 S Model [4]

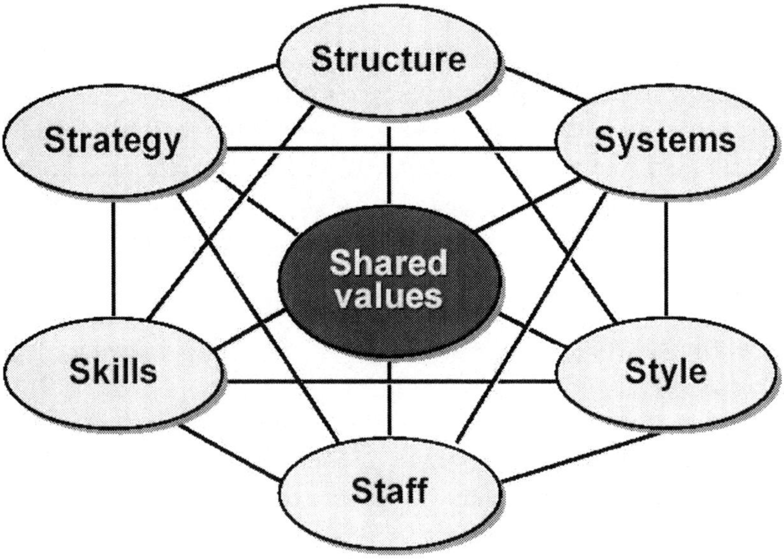

First, there is more than one factor that influences a police department's ability to change. In addition to its organizational structure and any strategies that are developed, there are at least five other elements. This suggests that substantive organizational change is not a simple undertaking. It is complex because of all of the elements involved.

Second, all of the variables included in the McKinsey change chart are interconnected. This suggests it is difficult to make substantive changes in one area without making changes in others. Therefore, if the different variables involved in the initiative, or their interrelatedness, is ignored it becomes substantially difficult to implement the desired changes.

Third, many organizations that have attempted to implement major changes have been unsuccessful. The failures were not in the planning process, but in the execution of the plans. Often, failure comes from not paying attention to all of the *Seven S concepts*. For example, it is generally understood that without adequate logistics, a military strategy is likely to fail. Similarly, inadequate staff, or incorrect systems can cripple the best plans of police organizational change.

Fourth, it should be noted that in the McKinsey diagram, there is no starting or ending point. It has no explicit or implicit hierarchy. As a result, it is impossible to determine, by looking at the chart, which of the seven factors will be more important in changing a particular organization at any given time. There may be instances in which the critical variable will be strategy, in others it may be systems, structure or style.

Institutionalizing Community Policing as the dominant style of delivering police services to a community can be understood by looking at the *Seven S Concept*.

STRUCTURE

Police agencies understand the traditional way of looking at structure. The basic theory of organizational structure is to divide tasks and allow for the coordination of those tasks. In the case of police departments, the organizational structure links similar tasks together. Police departments' organizational structures are basically functional organizations that deal with a chain of command, one person - one boss. They deal with span of control, grouping like activities or having commensurate authority and responsibility.

It is generally agreed that police departments' organizational structures are simplistic and understandable. Community policing suggests that there are least two things wrong with the current organizational structures of police departments. They are *size* and *complexity*.

As the population in our major cities continue to increase, the principles that are applicable in other organizations become important for police agencies. That is, when an organization reaches a certain size, it must decentralize a fundamental practice in the service delivery function of Community Policing. Because of the complexity of society and policing today, police departments must also follow what is occurring in other organizations. And be subject to change.

STRATEGY

It is generally understood in organizational theory that structure follows strategy. The term strategy, as used here, refers to how the organization intends to address problems that it is confronted with. For police agencies, it means the manner that they use to deliver their services.

Organizational theory states that structure follows strategy. That, however, does not hold true in all cases. There have been many organizations, including police departments, which have developed outstanding strategies that have been reduced to writing. Yet, they have been unable to execute them. In many instances, there was nothing wrong with their structure. The reason for the failure to successfully execute their strategies was due to other factors in their organizations. Strategy is a very important variable in any organizational design, but it is not all that counts. Other variables must also be taken into consideration.

SYSTEMS

Systems, as used here, refer to formal and informal procedures that allow the organization to continue to function. Procedures such as recruitment and selection, training, operations and budgeting systems are all examples of tasks that a police department must perform. One of the most important variables in the 7-S Model is systems, crucial to an agency that is implementing the concept of Community Policing.

To clearly understand how a police department works, it is necessary to look at it systems. Observe its operational procedures, its hiring procedures, its training programs and its rewards system.

You cannot change the orientation of a police department without first changing its systems. Organizational systems are very powerful and can enhance organizational change more so than if an agency merely changes its structure. For that reason this chapter focuses on those critical systems that must change if Community Policing is successfully implemented and institutionalized.

STYLE

The top managers of police departments set the style for their agencies. The way senior managers are perceived by members of their departments and communities, reflect departmental styles. The very nature of police organization is such that its members listen to what their leaders say. It would be incorrect to think that members of a police department do not believe what their top leaders articulate. The deeds of managers, as well as their words are important.

Style, while manageable, is a very important element. For example, under Community Policing, patrol officers are expected to interact with the community. They are more inclined to do so if they see their leaders providing an example. Managerial style is determined, to a large degree, by how managers choose to spend their time. If they want their officers to be involved with the community, they must attend community meetings. If the patrol division is considered the backbone of the police department, they must spend time with patrol officers.

The style of a police department is reflected in how top managers direct their attention. One way of determining if a department is serious about implementing Community Policing is to find out whether or not its managers are discussing it.

Style is not restricted to managers. Style is, however, reflective of a department's culture and has a great deal to do with the ability of an organization to bring about changes in performance. This is far more important than has been recognized historically. For example, when this writer became Chief of the Houston Police Department in April of 1982, it was a troubled entity.

There was very little positive interaction between the department and the community.

It is safe to say that the department saw itself as an entity unto itself. I, on the other hand, felt that the police must be a part of the people they served. One of several things I did to change the situation was to attend meetings, speak to groups and become visible in all segments of the community. I shared with all of my audiences my vision for the department and what needed to be done to achieve the stated goals. Before long, other members of the department became active in the community. I felt that I was successful when I attended a civic association meeting one evening and the beat officer for that area was the principal speaker. The officer, who had heard me speak on several occasions, said the same things I had been saying for months. He and many others came to share my vision. That evening I felt I had been successful in changing the style of the department.

STAFF

Staff, as used here, does not refer to the traditional distinction between line and staff relations as reflected on police organizational charts. Rather, in the context of implementing Community Policing, staff refers to things such as morale, attitude, motivation and behavior. Staff is extremely important, but is only one of several considerations.

SKILLS

This is an extremely important element because the transition from *traditional policing* to *Community Policing* requires officers to perform their duties in ways vastly different from how they operated prior to the evolution of the concept. They are required to develop new skills. Experience also tells us that it may be necessary to label the traditional skills in order to add new ones because the new skills may only come to fruition when the old ones are dismantled. Changing how officers conducted themselves under the traditional system of policing is a major challenge to police departments as they implement Community Policing. Therefore, care must be taken to create environments where new skills are viewed as necessary, primary and permanent.

SHARED VALUES

Here, we are referring to the values and aspirations of the organization. In the implementation of Community Policing, values serve as the fundamental ideal around which the department conducts its business. A basic premise of Community Policing is that everything a police department does is based on values. Those values must represent the future direction of the organization. They must serve to form the culture of the organization. Values also provide stability to the organization. Values are the foundation on which an organization is built. They serve as a basis of stability for the organization. In discussing values later in this chapter, it is noted that if they are to be meaningful, they must be short and easily understood. In addition, they must have meaning to all members of an organization.

As police departments implement Community Policing or move towards institutionalizing the practice, it is important for them to understand that traditional organizational theory that deals only with the structure or the combination of structure and strategy is not sufficient. That is because they do not explain why organizations do not change, or why it takes so long for changes to be implemented. The answers often depend on conditions such as outdated systems, management styles at odds with the stated strategy, the absence of values that hold organizations together, or the refusal to recognize and effectively deal with people problems. It is relative easy to bring about change in strategy and structure. It is much more difficult to bring about change in systems such as re-training of staff or creating enthusiasm for values necessary for good policing.

The *Seven S Framework* is only a conceptual tool used to assist while thinking and talking about what the organization needs to do to institutionalize Community Policing as its dominant style of delivering police services. It provides a basis for understanding the forces at work in efforts to bring about change and provides an opportunity for understanding the real levers of organizational change. Most importantly, it provides a framework to discuss what needs to be done to incorporate Community Policing as the dominant style for delivering police services, while at the same time understanding impediments to its implementation. Finally, it provides the basis for developing methods to avoid the pitfalls that are hazards to the successful institutionalization of Community Policing.

For all those reasons, it is important to recognize that all variables are important. The following section discusses some of the major systems that must be changed in order to institutionalize Community Policing.

COMMUNITY POLICING AND VALUES — A PRINCIPLE, STANDARD OR QUALITY REGARDED AS WORTHWHILE OR DESIRABLE[5]

One of the major principles of Community Policing is that the concept is based on a set of values. This is important for two reasons.

First, our society is continuously undergoing changes, some of revolutionary proportions. Those changes impact all of our social institutions, including law enforcement. They ultimately create a new social order, with new relationships between citizens and societal institutions. To be effective, police departments must be in sync with society as changes occur.

Second, values serve as a means of formally establishing a police department's culture. Historically, police leaders have not paid attention to the department's culture, even though every police department has one. It is important that police leaders focus their attention on developing the department's culture, and not allow the culture to develop without careful thought and leadership.

To be successful during periods of rapid change, police departments must define and articulate those beliefs that can be used to guide the department. Values serve that purpose.

The successful implementation and institutionalization of Community Policing must be predicated on a set of beliefs that the entire organization understands, believes in and uses to carry out their responsibilities. Values serve to guide the daily operations of police organizations, as well as individual police officers.

Police leaders must recognize that it is human nature for police officers to respond to situations using their own set of personal values in the absence of departmental guidelines. For that reason, it is important that police leaders develop a set of values that serve as the overarching framework for all members of the department. Otherwise, there is the possibility that each individual officer will carry out their duties using their own value system, with great potential of creating problems for the agency.

Once established, a police department's value system, if set forth in clear statements of beliefs and broad goals, will change as society changes. For that reason, values can serve as the parameter for flexibility in organization, operations and procedures. The value system, thereby, becomes the basis for developing plans for changing strategies of delivering police services.

A set of values serve a number of purposes for police departments:
- sets forth the department's philosophy of policing
- states in clear terms what the department believes in
- articulates in broad terms the overall goals of the department
- reflects the community's expectations of the department
- serves as the basis for developing policies and procedures
- serves as the parameter for organizational flexibility
- provides the basis for operational strategies
- provides a framework for officer performance
- serves as a framework from which the department can be evaluated

As Police Chief in Houston, Texas, I developed a set of values to guide the operations of the department. Those values set forth the philosophy of policing in Houston and the department's commitment to delivery of quality services to the community. Those values also reflected citizen expectations, which were ultimately manifested in the department's administrative policies and procedures. This was accomplished by ensuring that for each new procedure or rule issued by the department, a policy statement was issued setting forth the values inherent in the development of the procedure of the policy.

The Houston Police Department's values were as follows: [6]

VALUE ONE

Policing the community involves major responsibility and authority. The police cannot carry out their responsibilities alone. Consequently, they must be willing to involve the community in all aspects of policing which directly impacts the quality of community life.

Commentary: This value was written to convey the message that the police are public safety professionals who serve as the community's key resource in efforts to deal with problems of crime, safety and disorder control. But the police are not solely responsible for these efforts. The community must share equally with the police the responsibility of developing a safe and orderly environment. To achieve such collaboration and shared responsibility requires the police department to willingly permit the community to have access to decision-making, policy formation, and information about police operations.

VALUE TWO

The Police Department believes that it has a responsibility to react to criminal behavior in a way that emphasizes prevention that is marked by vigorous law enforcement.

Commentary: The purpose of this value was to convey the message that the primary focus of the Police Department was crime prevention - working to prevent crimes from occurring. When crimes do occur, the department must assertively react with vigorous law enforcement activity. Vigorous enforcement of law is an important deterrent to serious crime. The department must be committed to working with the community in efforts to prevent crime from occurring. The department must aggressively move towards arrest and prosecution of perpetrators when crime occurs. This value was also designed to address those who argued that Community Policing was soft on crime.

VALUE THREE

The Police Department adheres to the fundamental principle that it must deliver its services in a manner that preserves and advances democratic values.

Commentary: This value was developed to convey the message that as an agent of a law enforcement agency in a democratic society, a police officer must be the living expression of the values, meaning and potential of democracy. Police officers must not only know the most effective techniques for enforcing the law and maintaining order, they must do so in a manner that serves to preserve and extend the precious values of a democratic society. Thus, the police must not only respect, but also protect the rights of all citizens as guaranteed by the United States Constitution. In doing so, the police become the most important officials in the vast structure of government.

VALUE FOUR

The department is committed to delivering police services in a manner which will best reinforce the strengths of the city's neighborhoods.

Commentary: This value was designed to convey the message that as new and improved police operations were designed, the department was committed to working towards strengthening the quality of life in neighborhoods throughout the city. It was based on the knowledge that people live in neighborhoods and identify with localized areas. Beat boundaries, community service programs, crime prevention efforts, and related activities should be directed towards strengthening and improving neighborhood life.

VALUE FIVE

The Department is committed to allowing public input in the development of its policies which directly impact neighborhood life.

Commentary: This value was written to convey the message that if the police are to work collaboratively with the community in carrying out crime interception and prevention activities, the community must have input in the development of police policies which impact the quality of life in neighborhoods. It addressed the problem that for too long police agencies had isolated themselves from the community, often limiting community involvement to "Support Your Local Police" type activities. To add meaning to the department's belief that collaboration is important, the community must be allowed to assist the department in developing policies that are operationally sound and acceptable to citizens.

VALUE SIX

The department will collaboratively work with neighbors to understand the true nature of the neighborhood's crime problems and develop meaningful cooperative strategies which will best deal with those problems.

Commentary: This strategy was developed to convey the message that the police cannot effectively deal with the crime problem alone. For that reason, the police department must commit itself to a major effort of working at the neighborhood level, with residents and businesses jointly developing strategies to impact crime patterns. This cooperative relationship was based on joint planning, active police officer involvement in neighborhood activities and shared responsibility for carrying out crime interception and prevention strategies. As part of this effort, the department provided neighborhoods with accurate and meaningful descriptions of crime problem so residents and businesses could fully understand the nature and extent of the problems.

VALUE SEVEN

The department actively seeks the input and involvement of all employees in matters that impact job performance, and will manage the organization in a manner that will enhance employee job satisfaction and effectiveness.

Commentary: This value was developed to convey the message that effective management must include the active participation of employees in policy development, procedure, strategic design and program formulation. The involvement of officers in the design of the *Directed Area Responsibility Team* program, a pilot project that preceded *Neighborhood Oriented Policing* and operated in one

Police District, and the participation of officers in the design of *fear reduction strategies* under the Police Foundation/National Institute Justice program served as examples of how such involvement could pay substantial benefits. Policies, which directly impact employee job satisfaction, such as transfer policies, were addressed with active input from the employees potentially impacted.

VALUE EIGHT

The Department is committed to maintaining the highest levels of integrity and professionalism in all its operations.

Commentary: This value was designed to convey the message that integrity of the police department must not be compromised and that there should be neither questions nor suspicions among citizens regarding department ethics. It conveyed the message that it is imperative that the department maintain the highest levels of integrity and credibility; thereby ensuring that its standards are sufficiently high so there is not even a perception among citizens that questionable practices exist. Professionalism, in this sense, meant adherence to impeccable integrity and careful protection of all citizen rights. It also included the maintenance of equally high levels of accountability by those authorized to enforce the law.

VALUE NINE

The Department believes that the police function operates most effectively when the organization and its operations are marked by stability, continuity and consistency.

Commentary: This value was designed to convey the message that policing cannot be an arbitrary affair. Decisions must be made carefully and based on planning and research into alternatives, and their impact. Changes that were not meaningful were viewed as unacceptable. As police improvement progressed, it was important for the department to remain committed to ensuring that changes were only made when there was a substantial benefit. In order to increase consistency of operations, policies were designed to clearly state the department's position on the issue addressed and offices were provided guidance to carry out their duties. The value also conveyed the message that each individual officer could not operate under his/her own policies.

These values were established at a time when the Houston Police Department was a troubled organization. It had a negative reputation. It was seen by many as being out of control. It was an agency that was insular and not involved in the community. For all practical purposes, it existed for itself. The department had undergone several changes in leadership over the past few years and did not have a clearly defined and understood direction. Most troubling was the fact that the department had a bad reputation for its excessive use of force, and violations of citizen's rights.

It had just experienced a highly publicized case involving a Hispanic male who was thrown in the bayou by police officers with his hands cuffed, he drowned. There was also widespread dissension within the department. African Americans had filed lawsuits against the city alleging discrimination in hiring and promotions. Two unions were competing for membership and were extremely vocal in their criticisms of management.

Each of the values was designed to address a specific problem that existed in the Houston Police Department. Over a period of time, the department was reformed and its values were rewritten. The new value statement included (1) Department Mission, (2) Values and (3) Guiding Principles: [7]

DEPARTMENT MISSION

The mission of the Houston Police Department is to enhance the quality of life in the City of Houston by working cooperatively with the public within the framework of the U. S. Constitution to enforce laws, preserve the peace, reduce fear and provide a safe environment.

VALUES

Preserve and Advance Democratic Values

We will uphold the fundamental values of this democracy through belief in the Constitution and dedication to liberty and justice.

Improve Quality of Life

We are dedicated to improving the quality of life in our city through spirited and quality service.

Improve Quality of Work Life

We are dedicated to improving the quality of work life in our department through interaction and concern for each other.

Demonstrate Professionalism

We will demonstrate honor and integrity in all we do through our ethical behavior.

GUIDING PRINCIPLES

We believe that life and individual freedoms are sacred.

We believe in fair and equitable treatment of all individuals.

Our role is to resolve problems through the law, not to judge or punish.

We recognize the neighborhood as the basic segment of the community.

We cannot carry out our responsibilities alone; thus we must be willing to involve the community in all aspects of policing.

Our fundamental responsibility to the community is quality service.

We, as employees, are our department's most valuable assets.

We believe employee involvement is vital to a productive environment.

We are committed to the recognition of human dignity and enrichment of life through fair and equitable treatment of employees.

We demand of ourselves the utmost in honesty, integrity and professionalism.

We hold ourselves to a higher standard of social and professional conduct.

The above Mission Statement, Statement of Values, and Guiding Principles served the department well and continue to do so until this very day.

In 1990, I left the Houston Police Department and assumed the position of Police Commissioner for New York City. The New York City

Police Department did not have a written set of values. As part of the process of implementing Community Policing city-wide, the following values were developed for the York City Police Department.[8]

In partnership with the community we pledge to:
- Protect the lives and property of our fellow citizens and impartially enforce the law
- Fight crime both by preventing it and by aggressively pursuing violators of the law
- Maintain a higher standard of integrity than is generally expected of others because so much is expected of us
- Value human life, respect the dignity of each individual and render our services with courtesy and civility

The values developed for the York City Police Department differed from those developed for the Houston Police Department in a very significant way. They were more concise, yet still addressed the critical issues that were applicable to all law enforcement agencies.

That value statement was distributed to every member of the New York City Police Department, incorporated into every written policy, procedure or directive, and printed in all departmental internal publications. It was also prominently displayed behind the stage in the police department's auditorium so that everyone would be reminded of them each time they entered the facility.

Values for law enforcement are a major issue for police agencies in all parts of the free world. It was for that reason that on December 17, 1979 the United Nations General Assembly adopted the following Code of Conduct for Law Enforcement Officials: [9]

Article 1: Law enforcement officials shall at all times fulfill the duty imposed upon them by law, by serving the community and by protecting all persons against illegal acts, consistent with the high degree of responsibility required by their profession.

Article 2: In the performance of their duties, law enforcement officials shall respect and protect human dignity and maintain and uphold the human rights of all persons.

Article 3: Law enforcement officials may use force only when strictly necessary and to the extent required for the performance of their duty.

Article 4: Matters of a confidential nature in the possession of law enforcement officials shall be kept confidential, unless the performance of duty or the needs of justice strictly require otherwise.

Article 5: No law enforcement official may inflict, instigate or tolerate any act of torture or other cruel, inhuman or degrading treatment or punishment, nor may any law enforcement official invoke superior orders or exceptional circumstances such as a state of war or a threat of war, a threat to national security, internal political instability or any other public emergency as justification for torture or any other cruel, inhumane or degrading treatment or punishment.

Article 6: Law enforcement officials shall ensure the full protection of the health of persons in their custody and, in particular, shall take immediate action to secure medical attention whenever required.

Article 7: Law enforcement officials shall not commit any act of corruption. They shall also vigorously oppose and combat all such acts.

Article 8: Law enforcement officials shall respect the law and the penal code. They shall also, to the best of their capability, prevent and vigorously oppose any violations of them.

In developing a set of values for a police department, the ultimate goal is to create a framework that guides all activities of the department and its members. The values are also the framework in which the department's culture is developed.

Under Community Policing, the objective is to develop a culture in which the police department views itself as a service organization and each member of the department considers themselves as being representative of the department. The values serve to develop a police department that is people oriented, service oriented, problem-solving oriented and defenders of the rights of all people as guaranteed under the Constitution of the United States.

TIPS

- Every police department, large or small, should develop a set of written values.
- Values should be developed through an open process that involves members of the department, elected officials and the community.
- The values should be short, easily remembered and widely distributed throughout the department and included in all of its publications.
- The Police Chief and all managers must assume the responsibility of incorporating the values into all aspects of police operations.
- The Police Chief should designate a high-ranking member of the department to serve as value manager.
- The values should be used in the development of all police policies, rules, regulations and procedures.
- The values should be incorporated into all training programs.
- The values should be well publicized throughout the community.
- The mayor and other elected officials should be provided with a copy of the values and briefed on their usage.
- The values should be used as part of the performance evaluation system.
- The values should be used as part of the disciplinary process.
- The inspections unit should use the values when auditing the performance of units in the police department.

Because a value system is important for directing all members of the organization towards a common goal, carefully managing the incorporation of the value system into the organization is very important. A police agency is better served if it has more information than is needed, rather than not enough information. A common complaint among police officers is that there is a communications problem in their department. When it comes to values, it is better to over communicate than to under communicate.

STAFF

Since a police department's primary resource for providing services is people, staffing is the most important element for service delivery. It is also the most important element in implementing and institutionalizing Community Policing. For that reason the following section of this chapter will focus on staff.

RECRUITMENT AND SELECTION

The recruitment and selection of police officers is critical in determining the successful implementation and institutionalization of the community policing. It is critical because police departments are people organizations. Those who enter law enforcement will determine how police services to the community will be delivered. The importance of recruiting quality persons to serve as police officers has long been recognized. At least three presidential commissions have addressed the subject in their final reports.

In its <u>Task Force Report on the Police</u>, the President's Commission on Law Enforcement and Administration of Justice recognized that the successful accomplishment of the police mission was contingent on the quality of the personnel entering police service: [10]

> It is impossible to separate the performance of local government from the abilities of their personnel. Ordinances are not self-executing and no other service of local government has meaning except as it is planned, directed, and delivered by people. If these things are done well, communities may strive; if poorly, the future demand may outstrip all services, all facilities and all planning.[11]

The Commission recognized the complexities of the policing function and recommended that steps be taken to immediately require two-years of college, from accredited institutions, for all police officers. Recognizing that it was impossible to accomplish that objective immediately, the Commission recommended that no police officer be hired without a high-school diploma and demonstrated abilities to succeed in college level courses.

At that time, only twenty-two police departments in the nation had established some level of college education as a minimum entrance requirement. Twenty-one of those departments were in the State of California. The other was the Multnomah County, Oregon Sheriff's Department that required a four-year college degree. In 1957, the San Jose, California Police Department became the first agency in the nation to require two years of college, followed by the Berkeley Police Department in 1960. [12]

The Commission also recognized the need for diversity in law enforcement agencies. To that end, they recommended that all police agencies servicing large minority populations aggressively recruit minority officers. To accomplish that objective they recommended major improvements in the techniques used by police departments to recruit new officers. This was necessary because studies revealed that the majority of the police candidates hired were referred by active police officers. Since the number of minority police officers in police departments was very low, the referral of minority officers by active officers did not meet the hiring needs of law enforcement agencies. [13]

In its 1970 report on the police, the National Advisory Commission on Criminal Justice Standards and Goals developed three standards on police recruiting. [14]

General Police Recruiting (Standard 13.1) "Every police agency should ensure the availability of qualified applicants to fill police vacancies by aggressively recruiting applicants when qualified applicants are not readily available." [15]

The Commission recommended that every police department have its own recruiting program and utilize employees that were familiar with the "ideals and practices of professional law-enforcement."[16] They also recommended that police recruiting efforts focus on college educated applicants and candidates with varied ethnic backgrounds. [17]

To assist in the recruitment efforts, the Commission recommended that the residency requirement be eliminated, application and testing procedures decentralized, involvement of police in the recruitment and selection process, professional assistance in media and advertising, and continuous agency evaluation of recruiting efforts. [18]

College Recruiting (Standard 13.2) "Every police agency should immediately implement a specialized recruitment program to ensure that it had a sufficient number of college educated applicants to fill police vacancies as they occurred." [19]

In order to attract college educated police officers, the Commission recommended that police agencies establish permanent liaisons with placement officers, career counselors, and appropriate faculty members at nearby colleges and universities. It also recommended that police departments implement a "police to work program" to provide part-time employment to full-time students. The Commission also recommended that police agencies actively compete with other government and private sector employers on college and university campuses.

Minority Recruiting (Standard 13.3) Every police agency should immediately ensure that it did not present any arbitrary barriers -- cultural or institutional --that discouraged qualified individuals from seeking employment, or from being employed as police officers. [20]

The Commission strongly recommended that police agencies take affirmative steps to ensure that the ethnic representation of police agencies approximated the ethnic makeup of their jurisdictions. To accomplish that objective, the Commission recommended that police agencies undertake aggressive efforts to recruit minority applicants by implementing specialized minority recruitment programs.

Furthermore, the Commission recommended that every Police Chief executive personally ensure that the hiring, assignment, and promotional policies and practices of the agency were fair and did not discriminate against minority members. Finally, the Commission recommended that efforts to recruit minorities be evaluated on a regular basis and changed when and where appropriate. [21]

THE REPORT OF THE NATIONAL ADVISORY COMMISSION ON CIVIL DISORDERS [22]

This report focused its attention on the low representation of Blacks in police departments. In order to address the problem, the Commission recommended that the police recruit military men, and establish the Community Service Officer program that was recommended by the President's Crime Commission. [23]

RECRUITING IN THE SPIRIT OF SERVICE

Today, there is a consensus that because of the complexity and challenges of society, policing in America is more demanding than ever. It is for that reason that the recruitment and selection of qualified police officers must be designed to meet the challenges that officers will face on the streets of the cities where they will work. Equally important, the move towards Community Policing has changed the role of police officers in America, requiring them to engage in more complex activities.

Police officers working under Community Policing must be more than crime fighters. They must be problem solvers, planners, and community organizers. As a result, the criteria used for selecting candidates to serve as police officers under traditional policing are no longer sufficient.

The challenge of law enforcement today is to successfully compete with the private sector and other public agencies seeking the same caliber of employee. There is competition, not only among law enforcement agencies, but also with other agencies of government and colleges and universities for individuals that are mature, intelligent, articulate, and able to understand the social, economic and political dynamics of a changing society. Everything else being equal, a college education produces individuals better prepared for challenges in both the public and private sectors.

Many well-qualified individuals did not apply to become police officers. This was because police departments had not focused their recruitment efforts on them and the poor perception of the police that was generated by media reports on police behavior. This problem has been complicated in recent years by the large number of people in the employment pool sought after by the police who have had experiences with narcotics, especially marijuana and cocaine.

Historically, police departments have conducted their recruitment programs in the *spirit of adventure*. Their goal was to simply attract qualified individuals to carry out the mission of the department. That mission was narrowly defined as law enforcement and order maintenance. As a result, their recruitment programs focused on attracting individuals in the "*spirit of adventure.*" Such a focus can be seen in the recruiting material used by police agencies. For example, the Phoenix, Arizona Police Department's recruiting team posted on the world-wide web highlights of what they considered to be a listing of the "Popular Assignments." They were as follows:

- Undercover Detectives (drug enforcement, vice, organized crime)
- Investigations (homicide, robbery, assaults)
- Motorcycle Officer
- K-9 Handler
- Bomb Squad Special
- Helicopter Pilot
- Special Assignments Unit (SWAT)
- Field Training Officer
- Gang Squad Officer
- School Resource Officer
- Helicopter Pilot

The Recruitment bulletin went on to say, "The ability to secure any one of these assignments is obtainable by any Phoenix police officer with a desire to take on new challenges and who has completed 3 to 5 years of service as a patrol officer. There are also supervisory positions in each of these areas.[24]

What the bulletin does not do is emphasize the service aspects of police work. Rather, it focuses its attention on specialized units that are perceived as being exciting places to work.

Under Community Policing, police agencies should recruit and select new officers in the *spirit of service*.[25] That philosophy recognizes an expanded role for police officers. Rather than focusing exclusively on the officer's role of enforcing the law, recruitment and selection under Community Policing should also focus on an officer's interaction with the community, planning and problem-solving skills.

The idea of recruiting in the *spirit of service* is not new to government. The Peace Corps is a good example of recruiting in the *spirit of service*. The Peace Corps was created in 1961 following a challenge to students at the University of Michigan by then Senator John F. Kennedy to serve their country in the cause of peace by living and working in developing countries. This challenge resulted in the creation of a Federal agency, when Kennedy was President, devoted to helping people in developing countries meet their training needs and promote a better understanding of America and its people. Since its inception nearly 200,000 Americans have served as Peace Corps volunteers in one hundred and thirty-nine host countries working on issues such as AIDS education, information technology and natural preservation.[26]

The Peace Corps has been successful in carrying out its mission because it has been able to recruit people in the *spirit of service*. The same concept is applicable to police agencies. The objective of police recruiting should be to attract individuals who are committed to community service, as opposed to finding people who are interested in "action jobs." To that end, police departments must recruit in the spirit of community service.

Just as the Peace Corps was able to recruit large numbers of individuals who wanted to serve in other countries, so can police departments recruit individuals who want to serve their communities in the *spirit of service*.

The challenge for police departments today is to conduct recruiting campaigns that attract individuals that want to engage in the *spirit of service*. This can be accomplished by identifying life themes that are characteristic of those officers who have been successful operating under the concept of Community Policing.

LIFE THEMES

Life themes are the patterns of thought, feeling and behavior that correlate with the success of community officers working with residents. Life themes appear with predictability and can be measured. Most community officers have some measure of each of the themes. Those people stand out as community officers who have high measures of several of the themes. Few people have high measures of all the themes. [27]

While serving as Police Commissioner in New York City, my administration commissioned SRI Gallup to conduct a survey and analysis of successful community police officers and identify factors that could be used in the department's recruiting efforts as it implemented Community Policing. SRI responded by conducting a study that involved modeling the most successful community police officers within the New York City Police Department (NYPD). The objective was to identify those characteristics that enabled officers to perform their duties at a superior level. SRI Gallup had used that technique as a model for studying success in organizations for over 20 years

The purpose of the project was to develop a behavioral success model for the New York City Police Department as it implemented Community Policing. The model would then be used to serve as a basic guide for developing the department's image, marketing and recruiting strategies.

The overarching goal was to attract and recruit future members of the department with attitudinal and behavioral characteristics similar to those of the most efficient and effective community oriented police officers that were working in the department.

It was designed to increase the quality of applicants to the New York City Police Department by defining the life themes, (specific behavioral, attitudinal, and value-driven attitudes) of the best community policing officers in the NYPD.[28] It also had as its objective the development of a system for recruiting a diversified mix of quality candidates that reflected New York City's ethnic, racial and gender populations.

The researchers identified twelve Community Policing themes that were characteristic of successful community police officers in the NYPD. Those themes were: [29]

DEDICATION

The *dedication* theme referred to the predisposition for making a commitment to Community Policing. Those officers who were high on the dedication theme saw themselves as law-abiding individuals who believed in the law and wanted to obey it. They became police officers because of personal experiences. Some had been the victim of crimes, which served to strengthen their commitment to policing. Those who were high in the *dedication* theme had the ability to accept policing as a way of life, and not just as a job. They had developed an ownership of their neighborhoods and felt a responsibility for what happened in them.

Earlier in life, they were taught to respect the law and to do what was right. Since they believed in the law, they felt that it was their responsibility to teach others through action and explanation.

Those officers who were low on the *dedication* theme saw policing as just another job and were not committed to personally investing into the demands required of those who wanted to be New York City Police Officers.

ACHIEVER

Those officers that were high on the *achiever* theme had a drive to be active and productive. They had the stamina to push themselves in order to achieve more than others. Rather than seeing what needed to be done to just get by, they wanted to see how much they could accomplish. They were hard workers and spent more time on their beats interacting with members of the community than other officers. The achievers knew that it took a certain talent to be a successful police officer under the Community Policing concept.

They derived a level of satisfaction in helping others, solving problems and receiving recognition for their efforts. They were personally interested in the needs of their areas, and when problems were identified, they developed a strategy and implemented a course of action designed to solve them. They also stuck with the tasks until they achieved their objectives. The achievers had an appreciation for their relationships with their supervisors who allowed them to make even greater contributions.

Those officers that were weak on the *achiever* theme were also more likely to just do eight hours of work each day. They were disinterested and accomplished very little more than earning a paycheck for themselves and their families.

TEAM

The *team* theme refers to those officers who had the ability to get their fellow officers to work together in order to achieve a goal or complete a task. They were seen by their fellow officers as leaders and were capable of providing the energy needed to initiate activities. They built good relationships with their colleagues and were sought out by both officers and neighborhood leaders to discuss problems. They were good listeners and able to get people to work together to address problems in neighborhoods. Because they were good listeners, they were able to get others to confide in them, and feel free to discuss issues. These officers were able to individualize their efforts when correcting the behavior of others. They recognized that each situation was unique, requiring different responses.

They had the ability to understand the root causes of problems and not view them as individual incidents. They also had the ability to make themselves available and consistently focused on team-oriented events.

Those officers who were weak on the *team* theme had a tendency to isolate themselves and work independently.

CONCEPT

The *concept* theme refers to the capacity of officers to develop reasons for what they did. They would think through and develop a philosophy about their work, including the philosophy of Community Policing. Those officers that were strong on the *concept* theme wanted explanations for what they did. They developed a well thought out philosophy about their work. As a result, they were able to explain what they did and expected others to do the same. They were also able to get more out of conversations with other people.

Officers who were high on the *concept* theme had the need to see the full picture. They are thinkers and are concerned about what should be done. They were holistic in their viewpoints of history and believed that children were the future. They are practical and had the ability to see beyond punishing people and understood the value of education as a tool to get people to change. They did not accept the premise that some people are hopeless and therefore should be given up on.

Those officers who were weak in the *concept* theme tended to be reactive; rather than thoughtful and proactive in their behaviors.

GOODWILL

The *goodwill* theme refers to those officers that had a desire to build positive relationships with citizens in the neighborhood. Those who were high on the *goodwill* theme worked to achieve the approval of the people they worked with. They were quick to initiate conversations with people and were able to read and respond to the feelings of others.

Officers who were high on the *goodwill* theme were able to effectively deal with situations in which negative comments were directed towards them. They were also able to understand the needs of other people. They worked hard in their attempts to win over people and were seen as being generous and giving. Both adults and children in their neighborhoods liked them. Other people saw them as responsive and reciprocated.

Officers low on the *goodwill* theme were seen as unfriendly.

COMPASSION

The *compassion* theme refers to the ability of officers to "feel for" and to care about the people they serve, especially children. They have a passion for helping the poor and underprivileged. They are forgiving people and derive satisfaction from helping those in need.

Officers who are high in the *compassion* theme derive satisfaction from devoting themselves to making life better for the less fortunate. They love children and spent time supporting and doing things for them. They are champions of causes and seek out people who are down and out in order to help them save their dignity.

Officers who are weak on the *compassion* theme will treat people as things, rather than as human beings.

VIGILANCE

The *vigilance* theme refers to officers who are alert, observant and who have the tendency to anticipate events. They are more aware of what is going on around them than others. They had the ability to spot troublemakers on the streets. They were suspect of people on the streets, especially people they did not know. Those who were high in *vigilance were known to be* "street smart." As such, they had the ability to read body language.

Officers that were rated high in *vigilance* were more observant than others and were always looking out "for their backs". They regularly talked to children about the dangers of talking to strangers. They were seen as being very generous while at the same time able to identify liars more so than others.

Officers who were low on the *vigilance* theme were seen as gullible.

ACTIVIST

Officers high on the *Activist* theme were willing to speak for and act on behalf of people who they felt were in need of assistance.

They wanted to become police officers because of their desires to protect people. They did not dislike criminals, just their behavior.

The *activist felt that* people should pay for their criminal acts and derived satisfaction from the number of arrests they made. They enjoyed the concept of Community Policing because it gave them the opportunity to fulfill the lifestyle that they had imagined for themselves. They championed the cause of the less fortunate in the community.

Those officers that are weak on the *activist* theme do not derive satisfaction from the work they do protecting others.

COURAGE

Officers high on the *courage* theme possessed the strength to do what needed to be done, even when they faced resistance. They are able to enforce the laws necessary, and increase their determination when there is resistance. They had the ability to lay down the law, give orders to people, and be as tough as necessary. They exhibited "backbone".

Those who were high in *courage* were clear in their communication and others know where they stood. They exhibited a full range of emotions and were viewed as generous, kind, caring and approachable, while at the same time decisive and tough.

Those officers who were weak in the *courage* theme had the tendency to avoid some of the serious problems in their neighborhoods.

COMMAND

Officers who were high on the command theme had the ability to be "in charge" when the situation called for it. They were able to maintain their authority when confronted with aggressive behavior. Their mere presence communicated to others that they were in charge. As a result they could diffuse difficulty and emotional situations by just talking. They were firm in how they treated people and took the time to describe to others the consequences of their actions, and offered lawful options for their consideration. They made clear what lawful behavior was and did not allow police to be used as a "heavy," particularly to scare children.

Officers weak in the *command* theme did not generate respect from offenders who were likely not to pay attention to their orders.

ADAPTIVENESS

The *adaptiveness* theme referred to the ability to be flexible and meet the changing conditions within the police department, while engaging a wide range of communal expectations.

Officers who were high on the *adaptive* theme had the ability to arrange their behavior so that it fit into the world and the culture in which they lived. As children they concluded how to be safe and avoid accidents. As police officers, they worked hard to be the type of professional people in the neighborhoods admired. They adhered to tradition and believed that things should be done according to the law.

Officers high on the *adaptive* theme tended to be polite and considerate of others. They had a very strong family and home life and believed that it took time to achieve things of value.

Officers who were low on the *adaptive* them often found themselves in conflict with what the department expected of them.

ETHICS

Officers who were high on the ethics theme were honest, and would do what they said that they would do. They did not cut corners in their work and were honest in their relationships with others. They followed the rules, obeyed the laws and paid their bills in a timely manner.

They were seen by others as people of integrity and had the ability to foresee events and take the right actions when they were free to use their own initiative.

Officers who were low on the *ethics* theme were most likely to get into trouble.

SRI Gallup's survey identified patterns of behavior of successful New York City Community Policing Officers. The information derived from the survey was used to recruit officers who had life themes similar to those identified in the research. The characteristics could be incorporated into the recruiting literature and attract individuals to police departments who had not previously considered police work as an occupation.

Since people carry out the functions of police departments, it is important that police agencies attract individuals with the right disposition for serving the community under the Community Policing philosophy. The SRI Gallup survey represented the most important work ever undertaken in this area.

MINORITY RECRUITING

Over the past four decades, police administrators have come to recognize that every jurisdiction that has a substantial minority population can improve its services to the public by employing police officers who are from those minority groups.

Police administrators throughout the nation have searched for methods to increase minority representation in their departments. At least three presidential commissions have documented this need for minority police officers. The 1971 President's Commission on Law Enforcement and Administration of Justice went into great detail outlining the necessity for police departments to increase their minority representation. [30]

In addition, that report pointed out that those departments that police minority communities with white officers only leave themselves vulnerable to charges of being an occupying force.

Additionally, the report pointed out that the presence of minority officers can assist in destroying the racial stereotypes held by white officers; plus minority officers also do a better job of policing minority communities because of their familiarity with cultural differences and norms.

The 1968 report of the National Advisory Commission on Civil Disorders also strongly recommended that police departments increase their minority representation.[31] That Commission conducted a study of 28 police agencies and found gross inequities in their minority representation.

It revealed, for example, that while the median Black population for the cities surveyed was 24 percent, the median figure for Black sworn personnel was only six percent. The report pointed out that increased minority recruitment was a necessity if the police were going to be successful in performing their mission.

In addition, the report of the National Advisory Commission on Criminal Justice Standards and Goals contained a standard on minority recruiting. That standard read in part:

> Every police agency should adhere to the principle that the police are the people and the people are the police, and should immediately ensure that there existed within the agency no artificial or arbitrary barriers--cultural or institutional--that discourage qualified members of any ethnic minority from seeking employment or from being employed as police officers.[32]

The report called for every police agency to recognize the desirability of achieving a ratio of minority group employees in approximate proportion to their numbers in the population.

Although the need to employ minority police officers has been amply recognized and documented, even today minority representation in police departments does not meet the goal established by the Standards and Goals Commission. This can be seen by viewing the minority representation in the nation's ten largest cities as reported in the 2000 U.S. Census.

As can be seen in Table I, none of the ten largest cities in the United States achieved a minority representation of police officers that equaled the percentage of minorities residing in them. Yet, progress has been made. Philadelphia, Pennsylvania came closest with a minority population (African Americans and Hispanics) totaling 51.7 percent and 46.7 percent respectively, and a police department where 46.7 percent of the sworn personnel were African American and Hispanic. African Americans constituted the largest population with 43.2 percent in 2000, with African Americans comprising 46.7 percent of the police force's officers. [33]

Table I

City	Minority Representation In Ten Cities [34]					
	Percent Black	Percent Hispanic	Total Minority	Percent Black Police	Percent Hispanic Police	Total Minority Police
New York City	26.6	27.0	53.6	13.3	17.8	31.1
Los Angeles	11.2	46.5	57.7	13.6	33.1	46.7
Chicago	36.8	26.0	62.8	25.9	12.7	38.6
Houston	25.3	37.4	62.7	19.4	17.9	37.3
Philadelphia	43.2	8.5	51.7	41.1	5.6	46.7
Phoenix	5.1	34.1	39.2	3.9	12.0	15.9
San Diego	7.9	25.4	33.3	8.7	15.9	24.6
Dallas	25.9	33.6	59.5	21.4	13.5	34.9
San Antonio	6.8	58.7	65.5	5.8	41.7	47.5
Detroit	81.6	5.0	86.6	62.9	3.0	65.9

The issue of minority representation in American law enforcement agencies is equally important for state law enforcement agencies, sheriffs' offices, and small police departments. This fact alone should make minority recruitment a matter of great concern for every prudent police administrator.

To do otherwise leaves the department and its leadership vulnerable to charges of being insensitive to the police agency's responsibility to be representative of all people in the community.

As police departments address the issue of minority recruitment, it is important to recognize that the word minority is not an exact term. In its general context, it refers to racial minorities, those who speak a foreign language, and those of foreign ancestry (defined as ethnic groups). It is apparent that the determination of who is a minority must be given geographical consideration.

Historically, the problem of minority recruitment reflected a concern for the disproportionate low representation of African Americans in police service. This was because African Americans constituted the nation's largest racial minority population. For example, according to the 2000 U.S. Census, Blacks formed the majorities in Gary, Indiana (84.0); Detroit, Michigan (81.6); Birmingham, Alabama (73.5); Washington, D. C. (60.1); Newark, New Jersey (53.46); Atlanta, Georgia (61.39); Richmond, Virginia (57.19); Compton, California (40.31); *and* New Orleans, Louisiana (67.25). According to the 2000 U.S Census, there were 19 cities with a majority Black population.[35]

Over the last two decades, the racial composition of America has changed significantly. During that time, America has seen a large increase in its Hispanic population, and a significant increase in the Asian population.

In fact, the 2000 U.S. census revealed that Hispanics were then the largest minority group in America. In 2002, more than one out of every eight people living in the United States was Hispanic, representing 13.2 percent of the nation's population.[36] There were 18 American cities with a majority Hispanic population, most were in Texas or California: Laredo, Texas (94.1); Brownsville, Texas (91.3); Hialeah, Florida (90.3), McAllen, Texas (80.3); El Paso, Texas (78.6); Santa Ana, California (76.1); and El Monte, California (72.4). In addition, Miami, Florida's Hispanic population was 66.2 of the city's population; Los Angeles, California 46.8, Houston, Texas 37.6; Dallas, Texas 35.6 and San Antonia, Texas 58.9.[37]

The events of September 11 2001, when America experienced terrorist attacks in New York City, Washington D.C., and Shanksville, Pennsylvania created a new challenge for American policing. Previously, when the police focused their attention on religion, the concern was for the safety of the Jewish community. Today, they are also concerned with the Muslim community. As a result, police departments in cities with large Muslim populations are recruiting from that religious group.[38]

It is important for police administrators to understand that the problem of minority recruitment transcends moral considerations, although they are important. It transcends legal concerns, although the courts have increasingly addressed themselves to the problem. The issue is based on the basic and practical needs of the police, particularly in the context of Community Policing. Past experience has shown that the police are not going to be successful in carrying out their mission unless all segments of the community have their trust. Adequate representation of minorities in police departments serves as a vehicle to generate that.

In developing plans to increase minority participation, it is important to understand the reasons minorities have been reluctant to enter police service. Those reasons are directly related to the overall race relations situation that has historically existed in America.

When it comes to race, the recruitment of minorities, especially African Americans, is complicated by society's legacy of neglect and discrimination. Generations of young African Americans became sensitized to the inequities that affected the lives of their parents, and to a lesser degree, themselves today. As a result, they have developed a high level of awareness about pervasive discrimination and segregation that is present in the history of this country.

Older Americans witnessed the Black immigration and white exodus that created Black ghettos in many large American cities. Those that were old enough have read, and take seriously the report of 1970s National Advisory Commission on Civil Disorders when it reported that, "What white Americans have never fully understood-- but the Negro can never forget--is that white society is deeply implicated in the ghetto. White institutions created it. White institutions maintained it and white institutions condone it." [39]

The cause of their plight, as they viewed it, was confirmed in the same report that boldly reported that, "Race prejudice has shaped our history decisively; it now threatens to affect our future. White racism is essentially responsible for the explosive mixture, which has been accumulating in our cities since the end of World War II." [40]

The historical perspective of many Black Americans is that social institutions have not been responsive to African Americans. This basic distrust is also directed towards the entire criminal justice system - including the police. Too many African Americans, *Justia*, the goddess of

Justice, had removed her blindfold and reflected in her decisions all the biases inherent in those who make decisions in a racially bias society.

The systematic exclusion of Blacks from police departments continues to have an impact on minority recruitment. Many still view the selection process as one designed to screen them out, rather than as a sincere attempt to hire them.

In the past, Blacks have been screened out in one of two ways. First, by not being recruited by police departments and second by systematically eliminating those who did apply. As pointed out by the President's Crime Commission, "... There can be little doubt in both the North and South, discrimination in the selection of officers has occurred in the past and exists today. [41]

There is ample evidence to suggest that a number of police departments have had an unwritten quota for the number of Blacks they hire. As Fogelson pointed out, "The investigators rejected 41 percent of the Blacks as opposed to 29 percent of the whites in St. Louis in 1966, 68 percent of the Blacks as opposed to 56 percent of the whites in Cleveland in 1966, and 58 percent of the Blacks as opposed to 32 percent of the whites in Philadelphia in 1968. [42]

Historically, when many Blacks applied for police jobs there were several methods in the selection process that were used to screen them out. The first and most obvious mechanism was the written examination. Not unlike other civil service examinations, the written entrance examinations for the police were culturally biased against individuals who did not have a white middle-class background.

When individuals did pass the examination, they were subjected to an oral interview. This could take one of two forms: either appearance before an oral interview board comprised of police officers and representatives of the city's personnel department, or interviews in their homes conducted by police investigators. In the former case, Blacks were generally questioned on issues that had no bearing on their attributes for becoming police officers, but on matters such as their views on race. If the candidate did not answer the questions in a manner acceptable to the persons sitting on the interview board, they could be disqualified at that point and had no recourse to challenge the decision.

In the latter case, the police interviewer would go to the candidate's home to conduct the interview. There, they would make judgments about the character of the house after observing its cleanliness, the presence of pictures and books. The interviewer had the power to disqualify the candidate and again, there was no resource if a candidate was rejected.

One of the major eliminators of Black police candidates was the arrest record. In many large cities, young African Americans were arrested for very questionable reasons. For example, many were arrested for merely standing on street corners because there was no room in their crowded apartments. Or, failing to "move on" when ordered to do so by the police, and for catch all violations such as disorderly conduct, loitering (subsequently ruled unconstitutional) or violation of the curfew laws.

If the candidate successfully passed the background investigation, then they would have to pass a medical examination. At that point, many Blacks were disqualified because of ailments (often fictitious) such as heart murmurs, flat feet, asthma, and varicose veins among others.

A number of police agencies required their candidates to take a psychological examination after they had successfully passed all other hurdles. In many instances, that examination was also biased against African Americans. Illustrative of the point is the case of an Oregon Police Department that required a psychological examination of all police candidates. The psychologist who conducted the examination used as a baseline for comparing potential candidates the norms of policemen who entered the police service 15 years previously. This obviously worked to exclude African Americans.

The challenges of minority recruitment are not simple, but the task is possible. Many of the situations discussed above have been corrected. The challenge for today is to implement effective strategies to achieve the objectives of hiring minorities. There is no single magic formula for success in hiring minority police officers. However, a prerequisite to any successful program is to eliminate any artificial barriers that might exist and have a sincere desire to have a police force whose composition reflects our country's complexion.

TIPS FOR SUCCESSFUL MINORITY RECRUITMENT

Police recruiting can be improved by having a well thought out recruitment plan. That plan should address some of the flaws in the traditional methods of recruiting police applicants. There are several steps in the recruiting process that must be carefully thought out. They are:

MISSION STATEMENT

Similar to any other major undertaking, police recruiting should also have well-defined goals, short and long range, that are clearly understood by all members of the department. Those goals should become a part of the department's directive system and re-examined periodically. A clear definition of the characteristics of recruits sought by the department should be included in the mission statement. These characteristics should be developed based on the life themes discussed earlier in this chapter.

ADMINISTRATION OF PROGRAM

There should be one individual in the department that has the overall responsibility for managing the recruitment program. Care should be taken in selecting that person to ensure that he/she has the proper attitude and is committed to the goals of the process. All staff assigned to the recruiting unit must be properly trained and also must possess the characteristics needed to make the recruiting efforts successful.

ESTABLISH COMMUNITY SUPPORT.

One of the primary principles of Community Policing is the development of a partnership between the police and the community. The same principle applies to recruiting. The recruiting unit should develop a cadre of volunteers to assist in the recruiting efforts. Representatives from all segments of the community should be utilized in the endeavor. Particular emphasis should be placed on recruiting at the college level. Organizations that serve the minority community, such as the National Urban League, the NAACP, and the League of United Latin American Citizens should be called on for assistance.

DEVELOP RECRUITING MATERIALS.

Appropriate recruiting materials should be developed for use in the recruiting efforts. The materials should be developed for all elements of the media such as radio, television, newspapers and the internet. A CD should be produced and recruiters should make personal appearances whenever possible. They should be designed to attract people with characteristics desired for a Community Policing style of delivery.

RECRUITING STRATEGIES

A variety of strategies must be developed to ensure a successful recruiting effort. One such strategy should be to identify police officers that are representative of the type of person being recruited. For example, an African-American police officer should recruit in the African-American community, and a Hispanic American should be responsible for recruiting in Hispanic communities. Anyone recruiting on college and university campuses should have a college degree. Women police officers should be used to recruit potential women police officers. Different communities in the city should be targeted for special recruiting efforts. The utilization of community organizations, such as civic clubs, neighborhood associations, business groups, religious associations and special interest groups should be involved in the recruiting process. Uniformed police officers with good communication skills should be included as part of the recruiting strategy.

COMMUNICATIONS

A 24-hour hot line should be established. Targeted brochures should be created, along with recruiting videotapes.

FOLLOW UP

A member of the recruiting team should contact anyone who expresses an interest in the police department. They should receive, at a minimum, a telephone call and written correspondence.

Recruiting quality candidates to serve as officers is critical to the success of police departments. Under Community Policing, police candidates should be targeted who want to serve in the *spirit of service*, not the *spirit of adventure*.

It is also important to recognize that there are some risks in recruiting young people to become police officers. One major risk is that some who apply to become police officers have experimented with narcotics. The increase in the use of narcotics has forced law enforcement agencies to reconsider their policies about hiring persons who have used drugs.

This issue surfaced during the first part of the 1980s. For example, when I served as Public Safety Commissioner of Atlanta, Georgia we found that it was extremely difficult to hire recruits that had not experimented with marijuana sometime during their lives. As a result, we were compelled to change the policy for the Atlanta Police Bureau, and develop a more liberal policy relative to the use of marijuana. Even the Federal Bureau of Investigation has had to address this issue because of the prevalence of drug use in today's society.

TRAINING

Police training has evolved over the years. Only recently, however, have police departments taken a systematic look at their training and its importance to the delivery of police services. Much of the introspective examination came about because of the move towards Community Policing. The need for change was evident when you consider that under traditional policing, police departments trained their employees 85 percent of the time to do what they spent only15 percent of their time doing------enforcing the law.

In the late 1960s and early 1970s, brought about by recommendations of the President's Commission on the Administration of Justice, states started creating standards and training commissions that required all classified police personnel to have a minimum number of training hours.[43]

California was one of the first states to establish a standard and training commission. Created by the California State Legislature in 1959, the California Commission on Peace officers Standards and Training (POST) was given the responsibility of setting minimum standards for training of law enforcement agencies in the state. The State Penalty Assessment Fund was used to provide funds for the agency. That fund received its revenue from the penalties assessed on criminal and traffic violations. No tax money was used to support the Commission; rather it was supported by those who violated the law.

Today, nearly all states have a Peace Officers Standards and Training council that establishes minimum standards for the training and certification of police officers.

Community Policing forced police departments to rethink their training programs. Rather than just add additional hours to what was already being offered, police departments, adopting Community Policing, asked themselves what "knowledge, skills and abilities" are needed to work successfully in a Community Policing environment."

One of the first police departments to seriously look at training for Community Policing was the Houston, Texas Police Department. In 1989, it convened an executive session for the sole purpose of developing a training model to adopt as the department institutionalized Community Policing.

In 1992, as the New York City Police Department started the implementation of Community Policing city-wide, it also convened an executive session to address the training implications of the concept. The objective of examining training programs in both cities was to develop a systematic model of training that prepared both new officers and those already in police service to meet the needs of a police department that operated under the Community Policing model.

DEFINITION OF TRAINING

Training as defined here means "…..a learning process that involves the acquisition of knowledge, sharpening of skills, concepts, rules, changing attitudes and behavior to enhance the performance of employees."[44] The definition is used because it is clear that Community Policing will continue to be central to the future of policing during the Twenty First Century.

Training programs must be designed to give new recruits the knowledge and confidence that they need to function as police officers. Equally important, training must be continuous during an officer's career. Training must also provide supervisors and managers with adequate skills and knowledge, allowing them to be confident and competent in the performance their responsibilities as agents of change and societal leaders.

It has long been recognized that police department's main resource for delivering its services is people. Therefore, as the issue of training is addressed, careful consideration must be given to the skills that are necessary to carry out the policing function. Since police agencies do not control the educational system, they do not have the ability to impact the educational preparation of those they hire. They must, therefore, deal with those that come to them based on their previous educational backgrounds.

Although police training programs have improved significantly over the years, the elements of training are basically the same as they have been for decades. For that reason, there is a need to take a careful look at what this means for those who enter the field of police service, as it transforms to Community Policing.

First, the police training model must be restructured to provide police officers with a foundation that will allow them to utilize inherent intelligence. Police officers should be conditioned by their training to think. In fact, law enforcement would be better served if police officers were allowed to raise issues and suggest improved ways of doing things. Police officers should not be discouraged from thinking coherently about better ways to deliver police services and resolve neighborhood problems.

The ability to think coherently is something that can be taught in police academies. Lawyers, for example, are taught to think coherently when they are in law school. If police officers are trained in a manner that prepares them to use their intelligence and creativity, that would also broaden their perspectives on life and their views of society. Teaching police officers the skills to think creatively would also provide them with the skills that are necessary to function better as problem solvers.

Historically, police officers were not expected to use discretion. Rather, they were expected to follow the rules and regulations of the department and the directions of their supervisors. This was an issue that this writer raised as early as 1966 when he was a patrolman with the San Jose, California Police Department. He voiced his frustration by writing an article entitled "An Unforeseen Problem Resulting from College Educated Policemen." In the article, he wrote:

> Because of this dilemma between the old and the new, today's policemen find themselves in an unusual position. While in college, they are given a liberal education. They are trained to think for themselves. They are taught to be aware and to analyze what is going on around them. They are trained to form their own opinions based on their prior learning and objective evaluations. Their position is unusual because when they enter the field of law enforcement, they are told not to get themselves involved in community activities. They are told that they are policeman twenty four hours a day...It might be better for the public, as well as police administrators, to consider the possibility of loosening the restrictions that are placed on policemen. [45]

If the police training process is designed to improve the trainee's thought process, it should also serve to improve creativity. This in turn should better prepare officers to develop innovative ways to solve problems. By improving the thought process, police officers should also be more analytical in carrying out their responsibilities. This would give them the ability to analyze the issues they encounter and to develop creative solutions to problems that arise.

In effect, training should prepare police officers to become "*activists*" in the community, those who are involved in doing what is necessary to assist in improving the quality of life in the neighborhoods they serve.

The concept of police officers as "*activists*" in the community is something that some may consider revolutionary. Yet, if American law enforcement is to be successful, then *activism* on behalf of the people they serve must be a role that police of the Twenty First Century adopt. They should become, if you will, *ombudsmen* for communities. They should be community activists, knowledgeable and skilled in getting things done. For that to happen, policing in the Twenty First Century must include training on an ongoing basis as an integral part of career development. Effective training is critical not only on the entrance level, but also on the supervisory and management levels.

Secondly, the most important resource of police departments is its personnel. Police departments are *people organizations* and the vast majority of their budgets are for personnel costs. Since it is a people organization, training becomes critically important. It is important for police officers to continuously upgrade their knowledge, skills and abilities. Although there is little disagreement on this issue, there is a need for fresh ideas on training and the subject matter of training. The question is not whether there should be more training; the core question is what type of training police officers should receive to enable them to be successful in carrying out their Community Policing responsibilities.

Thirdly, there is a need to change the training police officers receive. The challenge is to make sure that the changes are consistent with current and future police functions. Police training should be changed in order to produce police officers that are leaders and not followers. Training programs should be designed to provide police officers with skills that will enable them to be leaders in the neighborhoods where they work.

Finally, as police departments develop new training programs, it is important for them to examine mechanisms to evaluate the performance of individuals in the class as well as the class as a team, or teams within the class. This is importance because it enables the department to take advantage of the fact that police departments are now multi- ethnic. As officers learn to appreciate cultural differences among their colleagues, they are better prepared to appreciate such differences in the broader community. One example of how this can be accomplished is by having members of the class compete in competitive team sports, where they are required to perform and be evaluated as a group.

RECRUIT TRAINING

Based on the role of the police under Community Policing, it is important to identify the skills required for police officers to effectively carry out their roles. That information can then be used to provide new police officers, supervisors and managers with the training they need to successfully perform their functions. While serving as Police Commissioner of New York City, I convened an executive session which resulted in identifying the following skill sets which were identified as necessities for policing in the 21st century. [46]

1. <u>Communication Skills</u>.

More so than ever, police officers are required to interact with people in the neighborhoods. Effective communication is necessary if people are to relate to and trust police officers. In addition to oral communications skills, police officers are required to have good writing skills. Both written and oral skills will become increasingly important as officers engage in problem-solving activities and are given greater responsibilities for investigations. They will be required to engage in more interviewing, interrogation and writing skills to properly record witness and victim information.

2. <u>Interpersonal Skills.</u>

As officers are given more time to interact with people in the areas they are assigned, attend community meetings and speak before various organizations, they will be called on to explain department procedures, policies and practices. They will also be required to explain what the department can and cannot do based on various constraints. To be successful in carrying out those responsibilities, officers must be able to speak tactfully and convincingly. Interpersonal skills are increasingly important as officers interact with members of the public under the concept of Community Policing.

3. <u>Public Speaking</u>.

Police officers will continue to be called on to attend meetings in areas where they are assigned. Depending on the area, such meetings may include business organizations, civic organizations, religious groups, block associations and tenant groups. Skillful public speaking becomes a valuable tool in helping officers connect with the community, share the department's concerns and participate in problem-solving activities.

4. <u>Crime Analysis</u>.

One of the major tenants of Community Policing is problem solving. In order to effectively engage in problem solving activities, police officers must be taught the skill of crime analysis. Crime analysis is the ability of police officers to identify crime patterns, link events to crimes and examine incidents to determine their cause in order to solve problems and prevent crimes.

5. <u>Problem Solving</u>.

Problem solving has emerged as an essential element of Community Policing. Certain techniques have proven to be effective in problem solving activities. Training must provide officers with both strategic and tactical analytical skills required to effectively engage in problem solving. They must be taught not only the strategies for solving problems but also how to identify the reasons for problems.

6. <u>Community Organizing</u>.

Organizing and working with neighborhood community groups is a major responsibility for officers under the Community Policing concept. They are called on to assist various community organizations to focus their attention on reducing crime and improving the quality of life in neighborhoods. In order to accomplish that objective, officers must be trained in the dynamics of communities and groups. They must understand what constitutes a community, and also the reasons that communities form and stay together. Officers must be trained in cultural, religious, and political differences. They must understand how they influence the structure of neighborhoods.

7. <u>Specialty Skills.</u>

The role of police officers is substantially enhanced under Community Policing. Therefore, it is necessary to provide them with skills that have historically been provided only to specialists. This includes skills in crime prevention, fingerprinting, investigative techniques, traffic investigations and computer usage.

SUPERVISORY TRAINING

As the role of police officers change, so must the role of supervisors. Both supervisory and management training should focus more on leadership skills in contrast to techniques of command and control. It will become their responsibility to provide officers with the assistance they need in order to accomplish their objectives. Those tasks will include assisting officers as they plan their work, helping them identify problems in their area, working with them to develop strategies to solve those problems and providing the assistance and guidance to obtain the resources necessary to address the problems identified. For this to occur, supervisory training for the future must include: [47]

1. <u>Basic Police Training</u>

For supervisors to be successful in carrying out their leadership and guidance responsibilities, they must be exposed to the same training that their police officers receive. In effect, police supervisors must also receive training in communications skills, interpersonal skills, public speaking, crime analysis, problem-solving and community organization.

2. <u>Values</u>

Police officers have always exercised a wide range of discretion. That discretion will be enhanced in the future. Police will be encouraged to make decisions using their judgment in the absence of close supervision. Values become extremely important in that environment. Police supervisors must be trained how to instill values in officers under their supervision. As leaders and role models, supervisors must reinforce the department's values in all activities.

3. <u>Coaching Skills.</u>

Under Community Policing, supervisors are responsible for providing both guidance and motivation to officers under their supervision. In effect, they are required to serve as coaches and mentors. They must assist their officers as they carry out their responsibilities by coordination, resources identification, and problem solving. In essence, supervisors must serve as facilitators while assisting officers to achieve their objectives.

MANAGEMENT TRAINING

Techniques of training police managers are changing throughout America. The traditional command and control style of management is rapidly changing. As a result, emphasis is now being placed on *innovation*; *entrepreneurship* and *delegation of responsibility* to the people who actually do the police work in the community. The manager of the future is expected to be creative, adaptive and more flexible than ever before.

Police managers are recognizing that there are limits on what the police alone can do to control the problem of crime. As a result, they are exploring new approaches to crime control. It is in that context that they are seeking new relationships with the community.

In their successful book, In Search of Excellence: Lessons for America's Best Run Companies, Peters and Waterman listed eight characteristics of successful organizations. Those characteristics are also applicable to police managers: [48]

1. A bias for action: This means wanting to get something done. Rather than referring problems or issues to committees, the successful manager takes action to accomplish objectives.
2. Staying close to customers: The successful manager knows the needs of the people in the community.
3. Autonomy and entrepreneurship: This means being creative in finding solutions to problems. It also refers to encouraging others in the department to think independently and creatively.
4. Productivity through people: The successful manager has the ability to instill in all of their people the understanding that they must contribute their best efforts to be successful and they will also share in the rewards of success.
5. Hands on and value driven: The successful manager understands that the department cannot be successful unless everyone contributes. The business of the department must be the business of every member.
6. Stick to the knitting: The department must do what it does best and that is working with the community to control crime, and improve the quality of neighborhood life.
7. Simple form: lean staff: Managers of the future will work to eliminate the excessive bureaucracies of police departments and create environments where decisions are made in timely and responsive manners.
8. Simultaneous lose-tight properties: Successful managers are required to create a climate in which the entire organization is dedicated to a core set of values.

The successful manager must be a leader. For that reason, chapter ten is dedicated to leadership.

ROLE CHANGES

Under traditional policing the role of all members of the department was well defined. They had developed over the years and were accepted. Under Community Policing, the role of every rank in the department must change. The implementation of Community Policing involves wholesale change. It represents a change in philosophy, a change in attitudes, a change in orientation and a change in operations.

POLICE OFFICERS

The role of police officers is significantly expanded under Community Policing. The role expansion is a result of the different functions officers are expected to perform. Under Community Policing, officers have overlapping responsibilities. Their duties are determined by the neighborhoods they patrol, their hours of duty and other factors.

Under Community Policing, the roles of police officers are trilateral. First, they must be *reactive* and respond to calls for service. The difference under Community Policing is they will take the time to develop the trust of citizens. This is done by not only conducting investigations, but also by using time to build citizen trust, provide crime prevention information, comfort victims, explain victim's assistance programs and prepare quality reports.

In order to perform their problem-solving responsibilities under Community Policing, they must be permanently assigned to their shifts and neighborhoods. This is necessary for them to become familiar with, and interact with, the citizens who live and work in their areas.

Second, police officers will be *proactive* under Community Policing. Rather than randomly patrolling and rapidly responding to calls for service, officers will engage in directed patrol, problem-solving and crime prevention activities. This could include conducting surveillance, security surveys, anti-crime, decoy activities and similar tasks. An officer's uncommitted time is used to engage in activities designed to prevent crime. This includes developing and implementing problem-solving strategies based on crime and other problems in their areas of responsibility.

Third, officers will be *co-active* under Community Policing. This involves self directed activities undertaken in partnership with the community.

Here, officers will develop and cultivate community resources to mutually identify problems that have a negative impact on the quality of life in the neighborhoods where they are assigned. This will require officers to develop the trust of the people in the areas where they work. In conjunction with the community, officers engage in problem-solving activities designed to solve the problems in the areas by utilizing all available police, city and community resources.

SUPERVISION

The roles of supervisors experience radical change under Community Policing. They must view themselves, their roles and the roles of police officers differently. The change is not superficial; rather it represents a fundamental change in philosophy. Supervisors will be required to direct officers under their supervision in a style of policing which is completely new to them.

Under Community Policing, the role of the supervisor moves from control to one of coaching, leadership, team-building and motivation. They must allow the officers under their command to be risk takers and facilitators. They must do what is necessary to make the officer's job easier and successful.

In their role as coaches, supervisors must ensure that officers spend their time working to identify problems in their areas and developing strategies to solve them. To accomplish that, they must allow time for officers to engage in problem identification and problem solving activities.

MANAGEMENT

The entire focus of management, under Community Policing, must be to support the supervisors and officers as they carry out their new roles. They will still be required to perform their traditional managerial responsibilities of planning, budgeting, inspection, policy development, discipline and establishing standards.

The major change for managers under Community Policing will be a new managerial philosophy and leadership style. They must do what is necessary to ensure that those under them are successful.

This involves a redefinition of the relationships between managers and the officers who serve under them. It necessitates treating officers in a different way. It includes mutual respect and empowering officers, demonstrating to them that they have a stake in the organization.

As pointed out by O'Keefe and Oettmeir, a different, more responsive attitude and managerial style will be required to stimulate, accommodate, and perpetuate the desired behavioral changes which will occur with redefining an officer's role. All managers must be encouraged that these transformations will become solid goals and objectives. [49]

Under Community Policing, managers are responsible for creating an atmosphere that encourages officers to be innovative. Officers must be allowed to use their talents to achieve the overall objective of improving the quality of life in city neighborhoods. To that end, managers must allow officers to have ownership of problems so they can have a sense of achievement once they are resolved.

DEPLOYMENT

Inherent in the philosophy of Community Policing is the acknowledgment that the police alone cannot successfully control crime and provide for the safety and security of the people they serve. Rather, members of the community are important shareholders in a community's effort of crime control, and must be engaged as partners with the police in their efforts to provide for the safety of the community. In addition, it is incumbent on the police to deploy their resources in the most effective manner possible. Equally important, police agencies must have an adequate number of employees to carry out their responsibilities. For example, if officers are expected to devote all of their time responding to calls for service, they will not have the time required to carry out the duties under Community Policing. Thus, the deployment of officers is an important undertaking for departments committed to operating under the philosophy of Community Policing.

Typically, officers are deployed to perform a variety of tasks. The majority of uniformed officers are deployed to beats where they spend their time patrolling areas, responding to calls for service, taking reports, investigating accidents, arresting offenders and providing other services.

Although there is no standard formula for determining the specific number of officers needed, typically, officers are deployed based on the number that are available to cover the beats in the city. There are, however, formulas that can be used to estimate the number of officers needed. At its simplest level, some estimates are based on the number of officers per 1,000 residents in the population.

That is not a very reliable measurement because even though the Uniform Crime Reports for 2009 reported that the average number of full-time officers per 1,000 residents was 2.3, there was a great variance depending on the geographical region of the country. The table below illustrates officers per region in various parts of the country. The northeastern cites had the highest, while the western cities had the lowest ratios. [50]

Table 2 [51]

Full-time Law Enforcement Officers by Region, Population Group and per 1,000 populations. 2009	
Average for Nation	2.3 per 1,000 population
Northeastern cities	2.7 per 1,000 population
Southern cities	2.6 per 1,000 population
Midwestern cities	2.2 per 1,000 population
Western Cities	1.7 per 1,000 population

Police departments can determine how many officers they need by conducting a resource allocation and staffing study. Organizations such as the International Association of Chiefs of Police, Police Executive Research Forum, National Organization of Black Law Enforcement Executives and private consulting firms provide that service on a contractual basis to police agencies.

In advertising its approach to conducting patrol staffing and deployment studies, the International Association of Chiefs of Police states: [52]

Ready-made, universally applicable police staffing standards do not exist. Ratios, such as officers per thousand residents, are totally inappropriate as a basis for staffing decisions. Accordingly, they have no place in the IACP methodology. Defining patrol staffing allocation and deployment requirements is a complex endeavor which requires consideration of an extensive series of factors and a sizable body of reliably current data.

In defining patrol staffing requirements, we consider the following factors, the mix of which is absolutely unique to each locality and agency:
- Policing philosophy
- Policing priorities
- Police policies and practices
- Number of calls for service

- Population size and density
- Composition of population, particularly age structure
- Stability and transiency of population
- Cultural conditions
- Climate, especially seasonality

In addition to the above, staffing and deployment studies should take into consideration additional factors such as desired visibility of police officers, response time to emergency and non-emergency calls, days off, sick time, vacations, court time and other times when officers are off duty. The methods used by patrol officers such as riding in cars, walking, riding motorcycles or scooters should also be considered.

Of supreme importance to Community Policing is the time available to officers to engage in activities such as problem solving and interaction with residents and business owners in areas they patrol.

CIVILIZATION

Many police departments use sworn officers to perform duties that a civilian employee could perform. In order to maximize the use of officers, departments should determine where they are using sworn officers to perform duties that do not require law enforcement authority. Examples of such functions or personnel are dispatchers, planning and research, crime analysis, budgeting, records, dispatching, vehicle maintenance, property control, equipment maintenance, communications and computer technology.

Generally, civilians who are specifically trained for certain tasks can be hired at salaries less than those of sworn officers. Salary, however, should not be the determining factor. Rather, the determining factor should be to free trained police officers so that they can perform law enforcement duties. In some instances, a position may require a salary higher than that paid to sworn personnel.

PRINCIPLES FOR DEPLOYMENT

Deployment of officers under Community Policing involves the following principles:
- Police activities should be decentralized unless there is a reason for maintaining a city-wide capability.
- 911 and all calls--for--service should be integrated into the

Community Policing philosophy. This should be done to enable officers to get to know the people and problems that exist in neighborhoods.
- Patrol officers should have ample time to engage in activities other than responding to calls-for-service. The maximum time devoted to responding to calls-for-service should not exceed 60 percent.
- Officers should be given permanent assignments and held accountable for activities in their assigned areas.
- Alternative means of handling calls for service should be utilized in order to allow offices time to engage in problem solving and other activities.
- Patrol officers should be empowered to enable them to get to know and advocate on behalf of residents and business people in their neighborhoods. Their objective is to enhance the neighborhood's ability to control their environment, and deal with the problems of crime, violence, disorder and fear of crime.
- Officers should enhance their visibility in neighborhoods by establishing contact and interacting with residents, including young people and business owners.
- Deploying officers to specialized units should only be done when it is clear that doing so will produce results that are far superior to those that would be achieved prior to the intervention.
- Officers should be assigned the appropriate mode of transportation that is best for their areas. They include car, foot, bicycle, scooter and horse.
- Civilians should be used to maximize the number of officers available for law enforcement or problem-solving activities in neighborhoods.
- Civilians with the required skills and education should perform duties that do not require law enforcement certification.
- To maximize the effectiveness of its personnel, departments should redesign their beat boundaries. This should be done by conducting an analysis to identify discrete neighborhoods. Neighborhoods are those areas where people have certain common characteristics such as housing divisions and shopping centers.

DEPLOYMENT OF DETECTIVES

Under traditional policing, detectives are assigned certain hours to work, and receive case assignments based on duty time. That proved to be ineffective because during the periods that the detectives were off duty their cases were not being handled.

Under Community Policing, detectives, similar to patrol officers, are assigned specific geographical areas. They receive their cases based on coverage area and not the time of day. This gives them the opportunity to get to know residents and business people in their areas.

Departments should maintain a centralized detective function in those areas that require special expertise, such as homicide and sexual assaults. They should also maintain a city-wide capability to follow up on those cases that are not isolated to a given geographical area of the city. Such cases include gang activities, those that show a geographical pattern, and organized crime.

In order to achieve the maximum effectiveness, police departments must constantly review how they deploy their resources. Under Community Policing, resources are deployed on a neighborhood level in order to enable officers to get to know the people who live or work in that area. In addition, the resources of the organization are enhanced by hiring civilians to perform duties that do not require a law enforcement officer. Similarly, detectives are assigned on a geographical basis, not based on time of day.

INVESTIGATIONS

Under traditional policing, patrol officers are limited in what they can do in criminal investigations. Typically, they respond to crime scenes to take reports. Because of the work process, detectives have historically been held in higher esteem than uniformed patrol officers.

The mystique that surrounded the role of detectives was greatly diminished by research conducted on the investigative process during the late 1970s and early 1980s. Herman Goldstein first raised the issue in 1977 when he wrote:

> Much of what detectives do consists of very routine and rather elementary chores, including much paper processing. A good deal of their paperwork is not exciting, it is downright boring; the situations they confront are often less challenging and less demanding than those confronted by patrol police officers; it is arguable whether special skills and knowledge are required for detective work; a considerable amount of detective work is actually

undertaken on a hit or miss basis; the capacity of detectives to solve crime is greatly exaggerated. [53]

The Institute of Defense Analysis, with the cooperation of the Los Angeles Police Department, conducted one of the first empirical studies on criminal investigations for the *President's Commission on Law Enforcement and Administration of Justice*. The study revealed that only 25 percent of all cases reported to the police were closed because of "arrests or other clearance." Of that number, 70 percent were cleared as a result of an arrest, and patrol officers made 90 percent of those arrests. Detectives who conducted the follow-up investigations, however, provided leads in 25 percent of those cases. The study concluded that the most important factor in determining whether a case would be cleared was whether the suspect was identified in the initial crime report. It pointed out that if the suspect was "... neither known to the victim nor arrested at the scene of the crime, the chances of ever arresting him are slim." [54]

In 1970, the New York City Rand Institute conducted a study of arrests made by the New York City Police Department. That study revealed that detectives investigating cases that they could not solve wasted a large amount of time. The study concluded that not all cases should be selected for follow-up investigations. Rather, only those cases with the probability of being solved should be followed up. [55]

In 1977, the Stanford Research Institute (SRI), with a grant from the National Institute of Law Enforcement and Criminal Justice, conducted a study in six cities located in Alameda County, California on the predictability of solving burglary cases.[56] The results revealed that if basic information was obtained from the victim or witnesses within an hour after the crime was committed, the probability that the case would be solved increased by 50 percent. The study concluded:

… all criminal cases do not have an equal potential for solution; "that a large number of cases essentially solve themselves" when particular investigative elements such as solvability factors are present; and that in the absence of these elements certain cases should be screened out of the investigative process. These conclusions are in direct contrast to traditional investigative strategy which supports active investigation, in varying degrees, of almost all criminal cases.[57]

In 1978, the Police Executive Research Forum conducted a replication study of the SRI burglary decision model. This study involved 26 police agencies and had as its goal the identification of burglary cases for follow-up that had the "greatest probability "of being solved. It found:

> ... It is the characteristics of burglary cases, not follow-up investigations that determine the overall success or failure rates of burglary investigations. These findings also mean that police management can use the screening device to select from the flood of burglary reports those cases that present the best chances of being solved. The screening model provides managers with a tested tool with which they can direct their investigators to be more productive, or, alternatively, less wasteful of increasingly scarce police resources. Managers thus have a tool with which they can control assignment of burglary investigations and impose a degree of order in an area -- police investigations --where attempts at management have traditionally been the exception rather than the rule. Currently, investigators make case assignment decisions based on their intuition or experimentally derived judgment. Collectively these individual decisions determine department practice in the absence of established management policy. Individuals, rather than management, are making important choices inherent in the investigative decision-making process, thus removing control of the process from management. [58]

The Rand Corporation conducted a landmark study on criminal investigations in 1975. The findings were reported in three volumes entitled The Criminal Investigation Process. The report found: [59]

- ... Differences in investigative training, staffing, workload, and procedures appear to have no appreciable impact on crime, arrest or clearance rates.
- The methods by which police investigators are organized (i.e., Team Policing, specialists vs. generalists, patrolman–investigators) cannot be related to variations in crime, arrest, and clearance rates.
- ... Substantially more than half of all serious offenses receive no more than superficial attention from investigators.
- ... An investigator's time is largely consumed in reviewing reports, documents and files, and attempting to locate and interview victims on cases that experience shows will not be solved. For cases that are solved (i.e., a suspect is identified),

an investigator spends more time in post-clearance processing than he does in identifying the criminals.
- … The single most important determinant of whether the case will be solved is the information that the victim supplies to the immediate responding patrol officer. If information that uniquely identifies the perpetrator is not presented at the time the crime is reported, the perpetrator, by and large, will not be identified.
- … Of those cases that are ultimately cleared but in which the perpetrator is not identified at the time of the initial police incident report, almost all are cleared as a result of routine police procedures … that is, required no imaginative exercise of investigative experience and skills… Investigative 'special action' made a perceptible difference in only three types of crimes: commercial burglary, robbery, and homicide. In these cases, we found that roughly ten percent of the cases were solved as a result of non-routine initiatives taken by investigators.
- … Most police departments collect more physical evidence than can be productively processed … allocating more resources to increasing the processing capabilities of the department can lead to more identifications than some other investigative actions.
- … Latent fingerprints rarely provide the only basis for identifying a suspect… [i.e.] fingerprint identification did not have a significant effect on overall arrest rates in any department.
- … In relatively few departments do investigators consistently and thoroughly document the key evidentiary facts that reasonably assure that the prosecutor can obtain a conviction on the most serious applicable charges.
- … Police failure to document a case investigation thoroughly may have contributed to a higher case dismissal rate and a weakening of the prosecutor's plea bargaining position in one of the jurisdictions studied.
- … victims desire to be notified officially as to whether or not the police have 'solved' their case…
- … investigative strike forces have significant potential to increase arrest rates for a few difficult target offenses, provided

they remained focused on activities for which they are uniquely qualified; in practice, however, they are frequently diverted elsewhere. [60]

The Rand research on criminal investigations raised serious questions about the efficacy of the traditional criminal investigative process. In order to make the process more productive, they made nine recommendations for improvement:

- Reduce follow-up investigations on all cases except those involving the most serious offenses
- Assign a generalist–investigator (who would handle the obvious leads in routine cases) to the local operations commander.
- Establish a Major Offenders Unit to investigate serious crimes.
- Assign serious-offense investigations to closely supervised teams, rather than to individual investigators.
- Strengthen evidence-processing capabilities.
- Increase the use of information processing systems in lieu of investigators.
- Employ strike forces selectively and judiciously.
- Place post arrest (i.e., suspect in custody) investigations under the authority of the prosecutor.
- Initiate programs designed to impress upon citizens the critical role they play in crime solution. [61]

In 1976 the National Institute of Criminal Justice and Law Enforcement implemented a national program that was based on results of the Rand and SRI research results. Called *Managing Criminal Investigations* (MCI), it incorporated five elements: (1) enhancing the role of patrol officers in the investigative process, (2) using case screening to determine solvability factors, (3) enhance management of investigations, (4) police liaisons with the prosecutor, and (5) continuation of the investigations. [62]

Case screening was the most significant component that came out of the MCI program. First, it provided management with a mechanism for controlling criminal investigations. Second, the concept could be tailored to any police agency. Finally, it provided empirical evidence that not all crimes reported to the police could be solved. In the latter context it was not unlike the research findings provided to police agencies about the merits of rapid response to calls service.

In 1983, the Police Executive Research Forum released the results of its study of the investigation of burglaries and robberies. Whereas earlier research such as the Rand study challenged the effectiveness of detectives in conducting follow-up investigations, it concluded that "... both patrol officers and detectives contribute equally important work toward the solution of cases." [63] In fact, "the single conclusion that unites all of the individual findings, as well as policy recommendations, is that sound management is required to ensure that investigations are effective, and that resources are not wasted," the study stated. [64]

Cohen conducted another important piece of research on investigations of the detective selection process. [65] Typically, officers are promoted to the rank of detective in one of two ways. First, there are those departments were officers are appointed to the position. The New York City Police Department is a good example of this procedure. There, promotion to the rank of detective is the sole prerogative of the Police Commissioner. Departments that use this system may have internal mechanisms for screening officers, but the final decision rests with the chief executive officer. Second are those agencies where the promotional process for detectives is spelled out by civil service rules. In those cases there is a structured process that consists of a written examination and, in some cases, an oral exam. Some jurisdictions also use performance evaluations as part of the process. In cities with civil service, the written examination carries the most weight, as much as 90 percent in some cases. Cohn offered the following suggestions for improving the detective selection process. [66]

> Two years of college education, exposing potential investigators to young adults and abstract thinking, and also demonstration that they are motivated to achieve the assignment of detectives;
>
> Screening procedures to identify officers with positive employment histories, thereby screening out officers with disciplinary problems;
>
> Testing for verbal and cognitive skills to include inductive and deductive reasoning;
>
> Assessing officers according to their rates of conviction instead of their number of arrests: "The conviction rate is a measure of responsibility for preparing cases against suspects so that they can be successfully prosecuted, and for not making unwarranted arrests." In this sense, it reflects the qualitative aspect of arrests;

Peer assessments, peer nominations, ranking, and rating, peer reviews ("a peer review and check of work output"), personal interviews, and assessment centers (a procedure that involves situational exercises, including, for example, leaderless group discussions, writing exercises, extemporaneous speaking, and role playing where participants pose as subordinates, peers and supervisors of the officers under evaluation.

Although research into the patrol function has been more extensive than research into the investigative function, there is ample information to reach some conclusions about what the role of investigation should be under Community Policing.

First, the information obtained when the patrol officer first arrives at the scene of a crime will generally determine if the case will be solved. If there are no leads that can be followed up on at that time, it considerably lessens the probability that the crime will ever be solved. This means that the role of both patrol officers and detectives are equally important in solving criminal cases. It also means the patrol officers should be given greater responsibility in the investigative process. This is not a new concept for police agencies in other countries. Canada is a good example of a system where patrol officers are given the responsibility for both initial and continuous investigations. No longer should criminal investigations be divided into two stages, preliminary and follow up. Rather, investigations should be seen as a continuous process, starting with the initial investigation and proceeding to continuing the investigation. Under Community Policing, either the patrol officer or detective will be responsible for continuing the investigation.

Second, if during the course of the initial investigation, no leads (solvability factors) are found, there is no need for the patrol officer or detective to continue to devote time to the case. For example, if the patrol officer conducts thorough interviews of the victim and all available witnesses, there is no benefit for the detective to re-interview them.

Third, cases should be assigned by area and not by time. Under the traditional Investigative system, cases are assigned to detectives by shifts, not geographical areas. For example, if a detective is working the evening shift and a crime occurs that calls for a continuation of the initial investigation, it is assigned to the officer and becomes that detective's case solely because he/she was working. Under Community Policing, detectives, similar to patrol officers, are assigned an area of the city and cases requiring continuing investigations are assigned to the detective responsible for that area.

Fourth, police agencies should develop a formal set of solvability factors. If a case does not meet the guidelines spelled out in those factors, the case should be closed. This will enable detectives to spend their time in a more profitable way, investigating cases that have the prospect of being solved.

The concept of Managing Criminal Investigations (MCI) is uniquely suited for criminal investigations under Community Policing. As pointed out previously, MCI involves, (1) assigning the patrol officer greater responsibility in the investigative process, (2) utilizing early case closure, (3) using solvability factors to determine if the case will continue to be investigated, and (4) focusing detective time on those cases with solvability factors.

Investigating under Community Policing involves more than handling cases, it also involves problem solving. It requires both patrol officers and detectives to focus on the nature of the crimes and what can be done to prevent them from reoccurring. A good example of this problem solving focus can be seen in what took place during the 1960s. At that time, municipal bus riders gave money to bus drivers when they boarded public transportation. The number of bus robberies increased significantly and often resulted in injuries to the drivers. After an analysis of the problem, municipal bus systems throughout America installed locked boxes. Riders had to have exact change or bus tokens. That one change all but eliminated the crime of robbing bus drivers. The problem, national in scope, was solved because the police focused on solving the root cause of the problem.

Community Policing requires police departments to have a sophisticated system of crime analysis capability. Such systems should provide information to all appropriate units of the department on crime patterns and repeat offenders. Crime analysis must serve as the cornerstone of the department's crime control efforts.

Community Policing, by definition, has the neighborhood as its focus. That also holds true for investigations. Detectives and patrol officers must become experts on a given neighborhood. Depending on the size of the city, detectives should be decentralized and become area specialists and crime generalists. This will enable them to focus on specific neighborhoods by getting to know the people who live and work there and, in doing so, involve the community in the crime prevention and crime control processes. The focus on neighborhoods is just as important to the investigative function as it is for the patrol function.

Community Policing empowers the patrol officer in the investigative process. Patrol officers must perceive their roles much broader than they did under the traditional policing system. They must also see themselves as investigators. Equally important, they must be given the responsibility to do more than respond to the scene of a crime, take a report and then return to patrol. They play an important role in the entire process by being the first to respond to the scene of a crime, solving it if they can. If not, following up on any available leads.

The successful implementation of Community Policing requires that the investigative function, similar to the patrol function, undergo fundamental changes. Most importantly, it requires that patrol officers and detectives work together to achieve the common objective of solving crimes and preventing crimes from occurring by utilizing proven problem-solving techniques.

PERFORMANCE EVALUATION

Most performance evaluation systems in use today were developed during periods when the traditional model of policing was being used. It was relatively easy to evaluate officers because the system relied heavily on easily measured activities such as absences, tardiness, citations, arrests, quality of reports, complaints and other quantifiable activities. Evaluating officer performance under Community Policing is much more challenging.

Under Community Policing, officer performance evaluation reflects the philosophy of the concept. As Wyckoff and Oettmeir wrote, officer performance evaluation focuses on "... the collection of activities or analysis that identify and evaluate purposive work. Purposive work assumes an objective. In the case of police work, that purpose might be to have an officer available to respond to calls in a specified area for a specified period time, to close a drug house, to reduce the probability that citizens will become victims and to increase community structure in a given neighborhood."[67]

To assist in designing a performance evaluation system for implementation of Community Policing, the New York City Police Department outlined several factors that were relevant to the process:
- Officers would be permanently assigned to specific neighborhoods or beats
- Officers would be required to develop and maintain a

knowledge base regarding problems, cultural characteristics and resources of neighborhoods
- Emphasis would be placed on the importance of officers reaching out to residents and business people to assure them of police presence and concern
- Officers would use formal and informal mechanisms to involve the community in identifying, analyzing and establishing priorities among local problems, and developing and implementing action plans to improve the community
- Officers would be given the responsibility of addressing both the crime and order maintenance problems in the neighborhood where they are assigned, including using their discretion to solve problems.
- Emphasis would be placed on increasing the flow of information from the community to the police and the usage of that information by all segments of the Police Department to make arrests and gather intelligence on illegal enterprises in the community
- Officers would be required to share accurate information with representatives of the community on local crime problems and the results of efforts to address the problems.[68]

Based on a representative sample of records kept by Houston Police officers during their tours of duty, Wyckoff and Oettmeir were able to identify a set of tasks and activities that officers performed in the neighborhoods that they were assigned:

Figure 1: Case/Activities [69]

Activities are listed below tasks that they are intended to accomplish.

Several activities could be used to accomplish a number of tasks:
1. Learn characteristics of area, residents, businesses
   a. Study beat books
   b. Analyze crime and calls-for-service data
   c. Drive, walk area and take notes
   d. Talk with community representatives
   e. Conduct area surveys
   f. Maintain area suspect logs
   g. Read area newspapers, including "shopper's guides"
   h. Discuss area with citizens when answering calls
   i. Talk with private security personnel in area
   j. Talk with area business owners and managers

2. Become acquainted with leaders in the area
   a. Attend community meetings, including service club meetings
   b. Ask questions in surveys about formal and informal area leaders
   c. Ask area leaders for names of other leaders

3. Identify officers to area residents. Share objectives with them
   a. Initiate citizen contacts
   b. Distribute business cards
   c. Discuss the purpose at community meetings
   d. Discuss the purpose when answering calls
   e. Write articles for local newspaper
   f. Contact home-bound elderly
   g. Encourage citizens to contact officers directly

4. Identify area problems
   a. Attend community meetings
   b. Analyze crime and calls-for-service data
   c. Contact citizens and businesses
   d. Conduct business and residential surveys
   e. Ask about other problems when answering calls

5. Discuss area problems with supervisors, other officers and citizens
   a. Maintain beat bulletin board in the station
   b. Leave notes in boxes of other officers
   c. Discuss area with supervisor

6. Investigate research to determine sources of problems
   a. Talk to people involved
   b. Analyze crime data
   c. Observe situation if possible (stakeouts)

7. Plan ways of dealing with problem
   a. Analyze resources
   b. Discuss with supervisor, other officers
   c. Write Patrol Management Plan, review with supervisor

8. Provide citizens with information on how to handle problems (educate/empower)
   a. Distribute crime prevention information
   b. Provide names and phone numbers of other responsible agencies; tell citizens how to approach these agencies

9. Help citizens develop appropriate expectations about what police can do and teach them how to effectively interact with police
   a. Attend community meetings/make presentations
   b. Be present at school programs
   c. Write articles for area newspaper
   d. Convene discussions with community leaders

10. Develop resources for responding to problem
    a. Talk with other officers, detectives, supervisors
    b. Talk with other agencies/individuals who can help

11. Implement problem solution
    a. Implement corrective action

> 12. Assess the effectiveness of solution
>   a. Use data, feedback from persons who experienced the problem, and/or personal observations to determine whether problem has been solved
>
> 13. Keep citizens informed
>   a. Officers inform citizens about what steps have been taken to address a problem and with what results
>   b. Detectives inform citizens about case status

The appraisal of officer performance under Community Policing must be results oriented. This is not to suggest that traditional knowledge, skills and abilities (K.S.A) are neglected. Rather it recognizes that K.S.A should be reflected in outcomes.

OBJECTIVES OF PERFORMANCE EVALUATION

No system of performance appraisal should be used merely to illustrate officer failures. Rather, they should provide officers with an assessment of where they are in meeting their predetermined job expectations. To that end, the objectives of performance evaluation under Community Policing should:

- Serve as a vehicle for constructive communication between officers and their supervisors
- Assist officers to enhance their performances
- Serve required legal requirements for promotions, etc.
- Serve as a tool for the institutionalization of Community Policing

PRINCIPLES FOR OFFICER PERFORMANCE EVALUATION SYSTEM

Recognizing that police agencies have historically struggled with developing good performance evaluation systems, they should use the transition from traditional policing to Community Policing as a vehicle for revising their system for appraising the performance of their officers.

The following are principles for an effective officer performance evaluation system:

1. Should not be complicated and must be easily understood by all involved

2. Should be based on the defined role of the officer
3. Must be fair and objective
4. Must be an ongoing process and not a single annual event
5. Must include successes as well as failures
6. Must reflect the principles of Community Policing
7. Must have a built-in process for monitoring the system
8. Must be consistently applied
9. Must reflect the objectives of the agency
10. Must allow officer awareness of the standards that will be used to evaluate them
11. Must include provisions for training the evaluators
12. Must provide for regular appraisal schedules
13. Must maintain adequate records
14. Must have a carefully designed grading system
15. Must meet all legal requirements
16. Must provide a linkage between officer performance and organizational goals
17. Must be based on mutual objectives agreed to by officers and their supervisors
18. Must have the full support of the Police Chief and management team

Just as the police must alter other systems as they transition to Community Policing, they must also modify their systems for assessing the performance of officers. Under Community Policing, this is extremely important because the appraisal of officer performance determines what the department feels is important. Thus, evaluation systems must reflect what the department expects their officers to do under Community Policing as the dominant philosophy for delivering services to the community.

REWARDS

Just as police performance systems must be revised under the principles of Community Policing, so must the reward system. Police reward systems are important mechanisms for motivating officers because recognition is a powerful motivational tool. It reinforces what the department considers to be important. Recognizing officer activity in both formal and informal ways reinforces behavior. Also, public recognition for officer activity is most effective.

Historically, officers have been rewarded for their law enforcement activities, such as felony arrests and the number of arrests made. Under Community Policing, officers are still recognized for their law enforcement activities, but other activities are considered as well.

Under Community Policing, officers are rewarded for solving individual and neighborhood problems, resolving disputes in the community and preventing crime, as well as arresting offenders. Ideally, mechanisms should be developed to reward officers for the reduction of neighborhood crime, reduction of disorderly activities, reduction of calls for service, knowledge of people in their assigned areas, and for the degree to which residents and business people know them personally.

Self-fulfillment for doing a good job comes from recognition by the police department for quality work. Officers who are rewarded for carrying out Community Policing activities are motivated to incorporate those activities as routine responsibilities of their jobs. It is human nature for people to want to be praised and recognized for doing a good job. What officers are rewarded for determines what they consider to be important. Therefore, it is extremely important to give officers positive recognition for accomplishing Community Policing activities.

HOUSTON CASE STUDY[70]

Houston, Texas is an example of one city's ability to successfully implement the concept of Community Policing. During the time this writer served as the Police Chief in Houston, it was the fourth largest city in United States and with over 600 square miles; the nation's largest in land area.

Houston was, and continues to be, very diverse. It had a population of 1.8 million residents. Twenty-eight percent of the total population was Black, 23 percent was Hispanic, and 6 percent was Asian. The police force had 4,200 uniformed officers and 1,000 civilian personnel.

When I assumed the position of Police Chief in 1982, my objective was to change the culture of the department. At the time, the institution was troubled, considered by some to be out of control.

The first step in achieving the goal of changing the culture of the department was to conduct a departmental assessment. That involved talking to both police officers and members of the community. Both groups were asked to share their concerns about the department and what they felt needed to be done to improve the delivery of services to all segments of the community. Based on the results of the assessment, the department prepared a plan of action which outlined the steps necessary for reform.

The first step in changing the culture of the department was the development of a set of values that would be used to change existing programs, policies, and procedures while formulating new ones. This proved to be extremely important and represented something that no other law enforcement agency in the United States had done. The values were consistent with the mission of the department, which was as follows: [71]

> The mission of the Houston Police Department is to enhance the quality of life in the city, working cooperatively with the public within the framework of the United States Constitution to enforce the law, preserve the peace, reduce fear and provide for a safe environment. [72]

A total of ten values were developed and they were incorporated into the plan of action. Each value represented what the department believed to be important as it carried out its responsibility of delivering quality police services to citizens of the city. Those values also served as the basis upon which the department would make decisions. Three of the values were indicative of the department's philosophy of policing and its commitment to Community Policing.

The first of those three values stated that the Police Department was committed to working with citizens in the interest of controlling crime. That value statement was designed to send a message to the citizens that crime is not solely a police problem; rather it is also a community problem and requires the involvement and cooperation of the police and the community. Most of all, it signaled to residents that all segments of the community had an extremely important role to play in addressing the problem of crime.

That position differed significantly from the traditional manner in which the police department delivered services. Historically, the department considered its operation a professional crime-fighting agency and did not see a need to involve citizens in its work. The change indicated the recognition that crime was both a community and police problem, and controlling it involved both police and community.

As a criminologist I also discussed with members of the police department and the community theories of crime causation. In doing so, I pointed out that there are a number of theories about why people commit crimes, e.g. sociological, psychological and economic factors. I stressed the point that the police and the public, acting alone, were not capable of successfully addressing the problem of crime. Rather, the problem must be addressed through a partnership between the police and the community.

The second of the three values dealt specifically with the need to set priorities. The value stated that crime prevention was the department's top priority. It was a priority because it was better to prevent crime than to wait until a citizen was victimized and wait for a police response. The value acknowledged that neither the police nor the community was able to prevent all crimes, yet the department pledged to maintain an aggressive law enforcement effort designed to apprehend those who committed crimes.

The third value also supported Community Policing by stating that the resources of the police department would be used to reinforce the concept of community and neighborhoods. This value was predicated on the position of social analysis which at the time reported that people were concerned about what goes on in their neighborhoods and therefore more willing than ever to get involved in initiatives to improve the quality of life on the neighbor level. The value clearly pointed out that the police department wanted to be a part of that self-help movement. [73]

PROGRAMS

The ten values developed by the Houston Police Department were used to develop new policies and procedures. They were also taught in the police academy and incorporated in all elements of the training curriculum. The next step, however, was to translate the values into action.

The overarching goal was to develop a new policing style for the delivery of services to citizens. The department implemented the number of programs to determine what worked and to allow the officers to get accustomed to the Community Policing concept. Some of the major programs implemented by the Houston Police Department are discussed below.

DECENTRALIZATION

As stated previously, Houston covered a large geographical area, over 600 square miles. As a result, one of the major initiatives of the department was to decentralize how it delivered its services. The overall decentralization plan called for dividing the city into four districts. A police station would be built in each of the four districts; thereby allowing the police to deliver its services out of regional facilities instead of having one central police headquarters. The plan also called for a deputy Police Chief of each station who was given the responsibility and authority for delivering police services to the area.

The department also redesigned its patrol beats. Following the tradition of most police departments in America, Houston's patrol beats were drawn up in a manner that separated natural neighborhoods. Major thoroughfares or other natural boundaries were used to design the beats. For example, the University of Houston's main campus was split in half by two police beats, even though the campus represented one community. Frequently, a major thoroughfare was used as the dividing lines between beats even though both sides were in the same neighborhood. The new beat design did not split up natural neighborhoods.

DIRECTED AREA RESPONSIBILITY TEAM PROGRAM (DART)[74]

The department started preparing for decentralization in 1983. The process started with the Directed Area Responsibility Team, which would be the first of several community-oriented projects undertaken. The DART program was a pilot project patterned after the Team Policing concept which had been attempted in several law enforcement agencies during the 1970s. The DART Program incorporated a number of strategies designed to address the concerns that were brought to the attention of the department by citizens during the departmental assessment. [75]

In order to address citizen concerns about crime and the fear of crime, DART represented the department's first attempt at decentralization of its services. DART consisted of a team of patrol officers, detectives, crime analysts and crime prevention specialists that was responsible for providing police services to a defined geographical area of the city. A lieutenant was placed in charge of the DART team and was given 24-hour responsibility for the area.

After three years, the DART project was evaluated and proved to be extremely effective in addressing concerns of citizens. Residents of the areas reported that they felt "more at ease" because of the DART project. This was due to the increase in police visibility because police used one officer patrol cars which created quicker response times. Equally significant, crime went down in the DART areas and clearance rates went up. This was attributed to the fact that officers had greater success in arresting law violators under the DART concept than they previously had.

The evaluation also revealed a significant improvement in how citizens rated the quality of life in their neighborhoods. Equally important, officers assigned to the DART pilot project reported an improvement in their attitudes towards their jobs because of their successes that reinforced the importance of their work.

When the DART project started, officers were very skeptical about change and new ways of doing things. After three years of operation, they saw the DART program as a superior way of delivering police services. [76]

FEAR REDUCTION PROJECT.[77]

The Fear Reduction Project was a response to an unusual phenomenon that occurred throughout America in 1983. During that year, the fear of crime was higher than ever before even though the actual crime rate was declining. This unusual dilemma attracted the interest of the Federal government's National Institute of Justice, which sponsored a research project designed to identify what police departments could do to reduce citizen fear of crime. Newark, New Jersey and Houston, Texas were selected as demonstration sites. Houston represented the western part of the nation and Newark represented the eastern.

Houston decided to try a variety of strategies to determine what would work in reducing citizen fear of crime. One strategy involved focusing on the victims of crime. The department wanted to know if fear would be reduced if the police worked with those who had been crime victims. This strategy was predicated upon the traditional response of the criminal justice system that focused almost exclusively on the offender to the neglect of the victim. To change that tradition, the department implemented a program called the Victim Re-contact Program which called for police officers phoning victims of crime and asking if the department could be of any assistance to them, and whether they had any additional information that would be helpful in solving the crime.

A second strategy that the Department utilized was the *Community Organizing Response Team* (CORT). Under this program, officers received special training on how to go into neighborhoods and organize the residents around quality of life issues. The officers were surprised at what they discovered. They found that residents were just as concerned about the "signs of crime," such as young people congregating on street corners, vacant buildings and unsightly lots, as they were with actual crimes such as burglaries. Once the concerns of citizens were determined, CORT officers assisted the residents by tapping into the resources of other agents of city government and the community to address them.

The third strategy was the *Direct Citizen Contact Program.*

Under this program, officers developed close relationships with residents of neighborhoods, meeting with them and business people. When they were not responding to calls for service, officers knocked on doors of residents or visited businesses, making statements such as "I am Officer Jones, your neighborhood police officer. What are some concerns I can help you address?"

The *Neighborhood Information Network* was the fourth strategy developed by the Fear Reduction Project. This strategy was designed to use the information network as a means of providing firsthand and accurate information about crime in the neighborhoods to residents. The strategy was based on the fact that most citizens were not crime victims; rather they heard about crime from a secondary source, especially the news media. As a result, the information they received was inaccurate or unbalanced. For example, if a sensational crime was committed any place in United States, it is usually reported on the news in almost all cities throughout the country. If the crime is solved, rarely is the result reported. Citizens are left with an incomplete picture of the process and are unaware of the steps that were taken to address problems. In an effort to reverse that situation, the department developed a newsletter and distributed it to 2,000 people that lived in a small designated area of the city. The newsletter contained information such as crime prevention tips and a monthly report on crime in specific neighborhoods.

The department's final strategy was *Neighborhood Storefronts.* Under this strategy, the department established community centers that served a geographical area where 2000-3000 people lived. A variety of police services were provided in the storefronts. They were strategically located to maximize accessibility for neighbors. The officers assigned to the storefront took citizen complaints, wrote reports and distributed crime-prevention tips. They also answered any questions that residents had about other services that the city offered. The beat officers assigned to that area served as support to the officers assigned to the storefront, assisting them if an arrest was made and transportation was needed to take an individual to a law enforcement facility.

The Police Foundation evaluated the Fear Reduction strategies and the results revealed that some of the strategies did in fact reduce citizen fear of crime. [78]

Of the four strategies tested, the *Direct Citizen Contact Program* was the most successful in reducing citizen fear of crime. This program was successful because it put the police in closer contact with citizens. The *Storefront Program* also turned out to be highly successful. Twenty years since its inception, the program is still in place and has expanded to more than thirty locations in the city.

POSITIVE INTERACTION PROGRAM (PIP).[79]

The *Positive Interaction Program* was also implemented in 1983. It was selected by the Police Foundation as one of 18 exemplary programs that served as outstanding examples of citizen involvement.

Under this program, the captains of each of the city's nine precincts were required to organize the people in their neighborhoods and meet with areas leaders on a monthly basis. The community leaders represented neighborhood civic associations, prominent business owners and religious leaders. During the monthly meetings, the citizens were given the opportunity to bring to the attention of the captain any problems that they were having in their neighborhoods. In turn, the captain was required to use his resources to address citizen concerns.

In between meetings, the beat officers were required to attend the meetings of the neighborhood associations and remain for as long as they could. This provided an opportunity for the people to get to know the officers who worked in their areas.

The program is still functioning today and celebrated its 25th anniversary in 2008.

The PIP program serves more than one purpose. In addition to allowing police officers to solve problems that are brought to their attention by residents, it also serves as an educational vehicle. During each meeting, community leaders learn more about police activities and that information is taken back to their organizations. As a result, the police are able to reach thousands of citizens that they would not have reached if they had to meet with each of them on an individual basis.

PROJECT OASIS[80]

Project Oasis was another program undertaken by the department as a prelude to the implementation of Community Policing. This project had as its objective a comprehensive approach for improving the living conditions and quality of life for residents in blighted neighborhoods characterized by vandalism, illegal drugs, burglary, theft, assault and other crimes.

Oasis was developed in Fort Lauderdale, Florida by the Oasis Institute.

The logic behind the technique was that if "good" things are introduced into blighted areas, they replace "bad" things, making areas better places in which to live.

The Houston Oasis Project was funded by the Federal government's Housing and Urban Development Department. A public housing development called Oxford Place was selected as a demonstration site. It had approximately 1000 residents, 90 per cent Black and seven percent Hispanic. More than 75 percent of the households were headed by single females. Oxford Place was a popular location for drug sales and was labeled "Drug Alley."

To address problems at Oxford Place, the department created a specialized Oasis Squad. The squad consisted of four full-time officers who volunteered for the assignment. They worked eight hours a day and focused on Monday through Friday. Scheduling was flexible in order to enable the officers to work special assignments when necessary.

An evaluation of the program showed that both crime and calls for service decreased at Oxford Place as a result of the Oasis Squad. [81]

CITIZENS POLICE ACADEMY[82]

In 1989, the department established a *Citizens' Police Academy*. This program was designed to acquaint citizens from all walks of life with the operations of the Police Department. Citizens who volunteered to attend the Academy were required to take 33 hours of training over a ten week period. The classes were conducted at the Houston Police Academy and taught by the same instructors who taught police cadets. The classes were held in the evenings and covered the same curriculum that was taught to cadets. As of March 3, 2011 there were 1,380 graduates. They formed the Houston Police Academy Association and are knowledgeable and strong supporters of the department.

POLICE ACTIVITIES LEAGUE[83]

In order to address the vast needs of young people, the Police Department in conjunction with the Exchange Club of Houston established the *Police Activities League* (PAL). This program was designed to meet the needs of young people who were not served by the traditional youth programs such as Boys and Girls Clubs, Boy and Girl Scouts and the YMCA. The program provided supervised recreation that stressed fair play and good sportsmanship. Houston police officers served as supervisors and promoted discipline and respect. Through sports, they also taught youth crime prevention techniques. They also were skills that aided them in becoming responsible and mature citizens. Funds for the program were raised by the Exchange Club from both public and private sources.

The program was unique because it used police officers to both train and supervise young boys and girls who participated in sporting activities. This helped establish a bond between police officers and the participants. Since its inception, a number of the PAL participants completed their educational requirements and have become members of the Houston Police Department.

BOND PROGRAM.[84]

The *Blocks Organizing Neighborhood Defense* (BOND) program was implemented in 1983 to involve the community in police activities that were designed to prevent and reduce crime. It was designed to supplement regular police activities in the neighborhoods. The program trained community residents to be extra sets of eyes in an effort to increase the amount of criminal activities that could be prevented or detected.

Residents were provided with training unique to their neighborhoods. After the training, they engaged in (1) informing other residents about improved home-security devices, (2) trimming hedges in order to improve visibility, and (3) engraving personal property so that items could be identified if stolen. In addition, the program served to reduce tensions between police officers and residents, and fostered a bond between community residents.

In its infancy, Community Policing evolved in two phases. Phase one was the experimentation with police programs oriented to the community such as those discussed in this chapter. Phase two was the actual implementation of Community Policing as the dominate style used by a police department to deliver its services. The actual institutionalization of Community Policing involves a change in the various systems that support the department as discussed earlier. To date, very few departments have surpassed phase one.

EVALUATING SUCCESS AND EFFECTIVENESS OF COMMUNITY POLICING

When we evaluate the effectiveness of police departments, the critical question is what constitutes a good department. What is it that makes one department outstanding when compared to others?

Community Policing gives us the opportunity to establish complete new criteria for evaluating police departments. That evaluation is based on more than the ability of the police to control the crime rate; many of the factors that cause crime are beyond the control of the police.

While many of the traditional measures of police success are equally applicable to the Community Policing model, far more complex criteria are necessary if the true impact of Community Policing activities is determined. There are four primary categories of evaluative criteria: (1) crime reduction; (2) fear reduction; (3) community and government support for police initiatives; and (4) success at problem solving. [85]

Crime reduction has traditionally been the primary criteria by which the police have been evaluated. Based on the Uniform Crime Reports, collected and published by the Federal Bureau of Investigation, crime statistics have become the hallmark of evaluating police effectiveness. However, increased community confidence in the police may result in increases in the number of crimes reported, even if the actual number of such incidents does not change, or is reduced. While the police can have a direct impact on crime and victimization, it is important to develop victimization base rates so that it is possible to measure whether there are actual changes in victimization. Reported crime, as measured by calls-for-service, is not an adequate measure of the level of crime.

Fear reduction is a second element of Community Policing evaluation. It can be expected that a neighborhood's fear of crime will decline as the Community Policing officer assists in developing the neighborhood's capacity to resist crime and enhance its level of organization. Thus, the level of fear in the neighborhood is an important measure of Community Policing success.

Support for the police from both the community and the government is another significant measure of policing success. In fact, community support of the police may be the most important criterion in evaluating the effectiveness of Community Policing. This is particularly true when considered in context of the fact that the police do not control the factors that produce crime, nor do they control the decisions made by other elements of the criminal justice system. Thus, how the public feels about the police is extremely important. Public perception of the police will, in great part, determine their willingness to cooperate in areas of crime control, problem solving and addressing quality of life issues.

SUMMARY

The successful implementation and institutionalization of Community Policing requires a new way of thinking about the delivery of police services.

It requires a change in all of the systems that support a police department. For that to occur, there must be recognition that Community Policing is not a program; rather it is a new way of delivering police services based on research and experimentation.

It is a new style of policing that has as its major tenets, partnerships and problem solving. It is value driven and represents true policing in a democracy. It is more than the wave of the future. It is the very ocean itself.

NOTES: CHAPTER EIGHT

1. Brown, Lee P, Plan of Action, Houston Police Department, April 1983

2. Brown, Lee P, Policing New York City in the 1990s, New York City Police Department, January 1991

3. The 7-S Model was by developed by Tom Peters and Robert Waterman when they served as consultants with McKinsey and Company. For additional information see Waterman, Robert Jr. and Tom Peters, "Structure is not Organization," Business Horizons, 23, 3, June 1980, pp. 14-26; Also see Recklies, Dagmar, "The 7-S- Model," http:/www.themanager.org./Model/&S%20Model.htm. (Searched 2.4.09) Also see Peters, Tom and Robert Waterman, Jr., In Search of Excellence, New York and London: Harper, 1982

4. Peters, Thomas J. and Robert H. Waterman, Jr., In Search of Excellence: Lessons from America's Best-Run Companies, New York: Warner Books, 1982, pp. 9-11

5. Webster's New Riverside University Dictionary, Boston, Mass: Houghton Mifflin, 1988, p.1275

6. Brown, Lee P. "A Police Department and its Values," The Police Chief, Vol. LI, No. 11, November, 1984, also see Op. Cit. Note 1. pp. 7-13

7. Hurtt, Harold L., "Department Mission, Values, and Guiding Principles", General Orders, Houston Police Department No. 100-06, April 22, 2008

8. Op. Cit. Note 2, pp 17-18

9. Code of Conduct for Law Enforcement Officials, Adopted by the United Nation's General Assembly, Resolution 34/169 on December 17, 1979

10. President's Commission on Law Enforcement and Administration of Justice, Task Force: The Police, Washington, D.C.: United States Government Printing Office, 1967

11. Ibid. p. 120

12. Ibid. p 126.

13. Ibid. 169.

14. National Advisory Commission on Criminal Justice Standards and Goals, Police, Washington, D.C.: U.S. Government Printing Office, 1973

15. Ibid. p.321

16. Ibid.

17. Ibid.

18. Ibid. p.321

19. Ibid. 326

20, Ibid. 329

21. Ibid.

22. Report of the National Advisory Commission on Civil Disorder, Washington, D.C.: U.S. Government Printing Office, 1968

23. Ibid. p. 166

24. Phoenix Police Department - Police Officer Recruitment, http://www.Phoenix.gov/joinphxpd (11.16.10)

25. Recruiting in the *spirit of service* is a term coined by this author while serving as Police Chief in Houston.

26. Peace Corps, http://www.peacecorps.gov/index.cfm?shell=leanr, whatispc

27. SRI Gallup, New York City Police Department: Community-Oriented Police Officers, Lincoln, Nebraska, September 1992, p.38

28. At that time, the New York City Police Department had Community Policing Officers serving as specialists assigned to precincts.

29. Op. Cit. Note 27, pp. 39-51

30. Op. Cit. Note 9 p. 167

31. Op. Cit. Note 22, p.166

32. Op. Cit. Note 14, p. 329

33. Population data on U.S. cities taken from U.S. Census Bureau, American Fact Finder, at http://factfinder.cencus.gov/servlet/basicFastsServiet and U.S. Information on Minority Representation in Police Departments taken from U.S. Department of Justice, Bureau of Justice Statistics, Police Departments in Large Cities, 1990- 2000, Special Report NCJ 177775703, Washington D.C. U.S. Department of Justice, May 1996, p. 11

34. Ibid.

35. U.S. Census Bureau's County and City Data Book: 2000, Table C-2

36. Ramirez, Robert R. and G. Patricia de la Cruz, <u>The Hispanic Population in the United States</u>: March 2002, Current Population Reports, P250-545. U.S. Census Bureau, Washington, D.C.

37. U.S. Census Bureau's County and City Data Book 2000, Table C-1

38. On September 11, 2001 Al-Qaeda, an Islamic terrorist organization, carried out coordinated attacks on the United States, destroying the Twin Towers at the World Trade Center in New York City, New York; crashing a plane into the Pentagon in Washington D.C. and crashing another plane in Somerset County, Pennsylvania. See <u>The 9/11 Commission Report: Final Report of the National Commission on Terrorist Attacks on the United States,</u> Washington, D.C.: United States Government Printing Office, 2004

39. Op. Cit. Note 21, p.1

40. Ibid. P.5

41. The President's Commission on Law Enforcement and Administration of Justice, <u>Task Force Report: The Police</u>, Washington D.C., U.S. Government Printing Office, 1967, p.168

42. Fogelson, Robert M., <u>Big-City Police</u>, Cambridge, Mass.: Harvard University Press, 1977, p. 251

43. The President's Commission on Law Enforcement and Administration of Justice, <u>The Challenge of Crime in a Free Society</u>, Washington, D.C.: U.S. Government Printing Office, 1967

44. What is Training: Definition of Training, Introduction to Training http://trainganddevelopmnet.naukrihud.com/traing.html (5.2.09)

45. Brown Lee P. "An Unforeseen Problem Resulting From College Educated Policemen," <u>Police,</u> Vol. 10, No. 3, January-February, 1965

46. Brown, Lee P., <u>Police Department City of New York: Executive</u>

Session Training Implications of Community Policing, New York City Police Department, 1992, p.19

47. Ibid. p. 39

48. Op. Cit. Note 4

49. O'Keefe, James and Timothy N. Oettmeir, Neighborhood Oriented Policing – Role Expectations, Concept Paper No. 2, Houston Police Department, unpublished, 1988, p. 3

50. Uniform Crime Report, Crime in the United States, 2009, U.S. Department of Justice, Federal Bureau of investigation, Sept. 2009

51. Uniform Crime Report, Crime in the United States, 2009, U.S. Department of Justice, Federal Bureau of Investigation, September 2010, Table 71

52. Patrol Staffing and Deployment Study, Washington, D.C.: International Association of Chiefs of Police, unpublished, undated

53. Goldstein, Herman, Policing a Free Society, Cambridge, Mass.: Ballinger, 1977, p. 55

54. Silver, Isidore, The Challenge of Crime in a Free Society, New York: Avon, 1968

55. Greenwood, Peter W., An Analysis of the Apprehension Activities of the New York City Police Police Department, New York: The New York Rand Institute, R-529 NYC, September

56. Renamed National Institute of Justice (NIJ)

57. Greenberg, Ilene and Robert Wasserman, Managing Criminal Investigations, Washington, D.C.: U.S. Department of Justice, National Institute of Law Enforcement and Criminal Justice Law Enforcement, 1979

58. Eck, John E., Managing Case Assignments: The Burglary Investigation Decision Model Replication, Washington, D.C.: Police Executive Research Forum, 1979

59. Chaiken, Jan M., Peter W. Greenwood and Joan A. Petersillia, The Criminal Investigation Process: A Summary Report, Santa Monica, Calif.: The Rand Corporation, June, 1976

60. Ibid.

61. Op. Cit. Note 59

62. Miron, H.J., et. al. Managing Criminal Investigations, A Handbook, U.S. Department of Justice, Law Enforcement Assistance Administration, Washington, D.C.: U.S. Government Printing Office, 1979, see also Bloch, Peter B., Donald R. Weldman, Managing Criminal

Investigations, National Institute of Law Enforcement and Criminal Justice, Washington, D.C.: U.S. Government Printing Office, 1975

63. Eck, John, E., Solving Crimes: The Investigation of Burglary and Robbery, Washington, D.C.: Police Executive Research Forum, 1983

64. Ibid. p. xvi

65. Cohen, Bernard and Jan Chaiken, Investigators Who Perform Well, Washington, D.C.: U.S. Department of Justice, National Institute of Justice, U.S. Government Printing Office, 1987

66. Ibid.

67. Oettmeir, Timothy N. and Mary Ann Wyckoff, "Personnel Performance Evaluations in the Community Policing Context," in Police and Policing: Contemporary Issues, edited by Kenney, Jay and Robert P. McNamara (EDS), Westport, Conn.: Prager Publishers, 1999, pp. 361-362

68. Brown, Lee P., "New York City Police Department Proposal: Development of a Performance Measurement System for Community Policing," a proposal submitted to the National Institute of Justice by the New York City Police Department, June 2, 1992, p. 5

69. Op. Cit. note 67, pp. 183-185

70. Also see Tumin, Zachary, Community Based Policing: The Houston Experience, Case Study, Program in Criminal Justice Policy and Management, John F. Kennedy School of Government, Cambridge, Mass.: Harvard University

71. Op. Cit. Note 6

72. Brown, Lee P. Plan of Action, Houston Police Department, April 1983, pp.7-13

73. Op. Cit. Note 6

74. Bales, John P. and Timothy N. Oettmeir, "Houston's D.A.R.T. Program: A Transition to the Future," Houston Police Department, unpublished, no date

75. Houston Police Department, "An Evaluation of the Houston Police Department's D.A.R.T. Program," unpublished, 1984

76. Ibid.

77. Brown, Lee P., "Fear Reduction Project," Management Report 2, Houston Police Department, unpublished, no date

78. Pate, Antony M., Mary Ann Wycoff, Wesley G. Skogan and Lawrence W. Sherman, Reducing Fear in Houston and Newark, Washington, D.C.: Police Foundation, 1986

79. Thielepape, Joyce, Positive Interaction Program: Community

<u>Involvement in Crime Prevention</u>, Houston Police Department, unpublished brochure, no date.

80. The Oasis Technique was developed by the Oasis Institute, Fort Lauderdale, Florida. One of its major functions was to assist local police departments and housing authorities resolve problems related to slum areas and urban blight.

81. (NIJ Quick Response Evaluability of Oasis Projects Final Report), prepared for the National Institute of Justice, U.S. Department of Justice, Washington D.C.: by Research Management Associates, Inc., Alexandria, Va., August 1986, p.23

82. See http://www.houstontx.gov/police/vip/vip/_hcpa.htm (1.18.11)

83. Brown, Lee P., "Police Activities League," <u>Management Report 14</u>, Houston Police Department, unpublished, no date

84. Brown, Lee P., "Bond Program," <u>Management Report 23</u>, Houston Police Department, unpublished, no date

85. Brown, Lee P., Testimony before the New York City Council Committee on Public Safety, Public Hearing on "How to Evaluate the Effectiveness of the Police Department's Community Policing Program, New York City Hall, November 14, 1991

Part Three

LEADERSHIP AND THE DEVELOPMENT OF THE PROFESSION

Chapter Nine

MANAGING CHANGE

INTRODUCTION

UNDERSTANDING CHANGE

In his book <u>The Prince</u>, Nicola Machiavelli stated, "It must be considered that there's nothing more difficult to carry out, nor more doubtful of success, nor more dangerous to handle than to initiate a new order of

> The definition of insanity is doing the same thing over and over again, and expecting different results.
>
> —Albert Einstein

things. For the reformer has enemies in all those who would profit by the old order and only lukewarm defenders in all of those who would profit by the new order" [1]

The implications of his quote are applicable to police agencies today. As America entered into the Twenty-First Century one thing was readily obvious, the nation and the world were experiencing monumental change.

This transformation results in a major restructuring of our social institutions. Recognizing that these changes are taking place, police leaders must focus on their role, so that the police enterprise does not lag behind society, clinging to old ideas, old methodologies, old assumptions and old measures. This is particularly important when we are told by futurists that societal changes will continue to occur, and have fundamental impact on the social order.

The magnitude of the changes that are taking place in America and throughout the world are of such a nature that risk takers are not those who advocate and implement change, but are those who attempt to maintain the status quo by conducting business as usual. Managing change is probably the most difficult aspect of directing police departments today. It requires a different way of thinking about how police services are delivered to the community. It is not an easy undertaking.

In the past, many police administrators did not embrace change. They believed they were in their positions because of their ability to fit into and maintain the status quo. As a result, they did not take risks by trying to implement major changes in their organizations.

Today, most police administrators recognize that major changes are occurring throughout society. They understand that the greatest risk of failure does not come from change, but from not recognizing that change is taking place.

The ability of police leaders in the Twenty-First Century to manage change will, in many respects, determine their success. A classical example is People's Express Airlines.[2] It began as a very successful company that was innovative and was viewed as an excellent company. It did not, however, change its business model when other airlines did and, as a result, is no longer in existence.

Police leaders must understand that societal realities are such that they require departments to be innovative in the delivery of services. It would be a grievous error for police leadership to assume that changes occurring in the broader society will not impact them.

One of the realities of contemporary American society is that the country is no longer an industrial nation. For example, in 1959 sixty-five percent of American workers were employed in manufacturing jobs. Today, less than 20 percent of American employees work in manufacturing.

At the beginning of 2000, more than sixty-five percent of American workers were working with information and knowledge. This is just one example of the fundamental changes that are taking place in American society. It tells us that the major resources of our contemporary society are knowledge and information. America is now in what the social analysts call the information society in which computers reign supreme. It also tells us that police leadership cannot afford to lag behind, and must take advantage of technological advances as well as adjust to other societal changes.

It is clear that technology is having a great impact on society, and is changing many of the outdated ways of doing things. Police leadership must understand how technology will influence the future of law enforcement.

Modern technology is having an impact on all aspects of contemporary living. We now hear about developments such as optical storage discs, super chips, artificial intelligence, parallel processing, optical computers, nano technology, etc. For most Americans, these developments are difficult to understand, let alone comprehend their future meaning. If law enforcement is to be successful in carrying out its responsibilities, it must understand the potential of technological advances and utilize them to improve service delivery. Rather than resisting change, police leaders must view this as an exciting time to be in law enforcement. It is exciting because it offers law enforcement an opportunity to participate in the rapidly developing era of information technology, which can be used to improve its service to the community.

Another change taking place in America that impacts law enforcement is the trend towards decentralization. In the past, America was a centralized nation. This came about during World War II, the depression and times of rapid industrialization. During those periods, the conventional wisdom suggested that the best organizational model was one that was hierarchical, centralized and worked best from the top down. That model worked well in the past, but has now been replaced with one that is decentralized.

The composition of the nation's population has also changed. The United States Census Bureau reported that in recent years, the Hispanic population grew faster than any other minority group. In March of 2010 the Hispanic population was 50 million, making it the largest minority group in America.[3] Hispanics surpassed African Americans who numbered 39 million.[4] In third place were Asian Americans who numbered 14.6 million.[5]

In 2010, 58.5 percent of the Hispanics in the United States were of Mexican origin; 8.4 percent were from Central and South America, 9.6 percent were from Puerto Rico, and 3.5 percent were Cuban.[6]

The distribution of both Hispanics and African Americans has changed. The U.S. Census Bureau reported in 2010 that the Hispanic population was more likely to live in the western United States. Forty one percent of the nation's Hispanic population resided in the west, while thirty-six percent of the Hispanic population lived in the south.[7]

On the other hand, fifty-five percent of the nation's African American population lived in the south, while 18 percent of the group's total resided in the western portion of the country.[8]

The fact that Hispanics are currently 16.3 percent of the population,[9] Blacks 12.6 percent,[10] and Asians 4.8 percent[11] has significant implications for policing in America. The population shifts present fundamental challenges for American law enforcement. America is no longer a Black and white society; it is now Black, Brown and white.

The realization that America was changing became even more acute after September 11, 2001 when America experienced terrorist attacks on the World Trade Center in New York City, the Pentagon in Washington D.C and a plane crash in Shanksville, Pennsylvania.[12] The attacks resulted in a major reorganization of the Federal government, and also added new responsibilities to local police departments in every part of the country.[13]

Understanding change is important for the continuous progress of law enforcement. Police leaders must understand that progress will not occur if they only imitate what already exists. Such thinking does not serve their departments or communities well. Just as society is continuously changing, so must the law enforcement enterprise. This is challenging because it will be easier to manage the status quo than to manage change in Twenty-First century.

Managing change requires police leaders to have different strengths than their predecessors. They must understand that business as usual is risky for police management in the Twenty-First century. Just because things worked in the past, does not mean they will work today, or in the future. Police leaders must not only accept those things that they have known or done throughout their history; rather they must question the traditional ways of doing things, and determine if there are better ways to accomplish their objectives.

In addition to changes in society, the law enforcement enterprise itself is also changing. The change that is taking place in law enforcement is only the second institutional change that has occurred since police departments were established in America. The first was the transition from a politically corrupt system of policing to a professional system that is generally called *Traditional* or *Professional* policing. The second change is the current move towards Community Policing as a dominant style of delivering police services.

In reality, change has been difficult for some police officials because it challenges their long-standing practices and beliefs about law enforcement. Nevertheless, resistance to change, the traditional response of some police leaders, will not suffice for the present or the future. The future of American policing rests on the ability of police leadership to clearly understand change; know which questions to ask and how to respond appropriately.

Change within police organizations *must* begin with an understanding of the needs, concerns and priorities of the community. The interest of the community must guide the direction of police agencies.

Law enforcement must understand what it means for police to deliver services, and provide the necessary leadership to chart the future course. If police leaders are unable to accomplish this objective, law enforcement will find itself lagging behind and delivering services in a manner that does not satisfy the public's demand for security or its sense of justice. The worst thing that can happen to law enforcement at this stage in its history is to be out of step with the communities it serves.

The changes that occur in society should be viewed as an opportunity for the police to change, and provide services consistent with the expectations of those they serve. Changes provide the opportunity to transcend from a crisis oriented institution to one that is in tune with contemporary conditions of the community, providing necessary leadership that assists neighborhoods in their quests for better qualities of life.

Such changes cannot be merely cosmetic. They cannot be mere extensions of how things have always been done. Rather, they must challenge traditional wisdom about the role of law enforcement in a democratic society.

EFFECTS OF ORGANIZATIONAL CHANGE ON THE POLICE

As America entered the new century, rapid changes presented unique challenges to police leaders. Among the challenges was how to provide the requisite leadership to deal with the dynamic social, economic and political changes that were occurring.

The problems brought about by rapid change presented unique challenges for law enforcement due to community demands for increased services brought about by crime, fear of crime, drugs and guns.

Change would not just be a byword of the twenty-first century; rather, perpetual change would be the expectation. The status quo would not be the norm. It would be the exception.

In addition, there would be greater demands for accountability of the police. Both the public and elected officials would continue to ask, "What are we getting for our money?" The police could also expect tighter fiscal controls to be placed on them. There would be more questions from those who made budget decisions about police department proposed spending needs.

During the 1980s, there were also important redeeming factors in favor of the police. A greater emphasis on self-help among the American people emerged. Citizens were more inclined to get involved in making their neighborhoods less dangerous and safer.

Police managers of the twenty-first century must have talents that were not previously required. They must be innovative. New ideas and new techniques must be built into the culture of the organization. Similarly, a spirit of inspiration and enthusiasm about the job must become a part of the organization's culture. The acceptable question for policing in the Twenty-First century must be "Is there a better way?"

Police management has been criticized in the past, but it is important to remember that past management techniques were appropriate for the time periods in which they were employed. Managers of the twenty first century, however, must understand that times are different, requiring varied techniques and styles of management.

For example, police chiefs, historically, were promoted from within the ranks of their departments. Now, most cities conduct national searches when selecting their most senior law enforcement officers. As a result, today's police managers are better educated and equipped to deal with the complexities of modern day society than were those who came before them.

In the past, law enforcement agencies were slow to change. Not only did they resist change, there was an inbred adherence to the status quo. This was true, in large part, because of the culture of police departments. A good example of how change can occur in a police agency is the Houston Police Department where I served as chief for eight years, having been appointed in 1982.[14] During that time we were able to plant a new culture in the organization. Today the foundation of what was started in 1982 remains in place.

The first objective in reforming the Houston Police Department was to change the culture of the organization. We began the process by developing a set of values that addressed identifiable problems. We also announced to members of the department and the community that substantial changes would be made to improve the department's delivery of services to the community.

Rather than hiring an outside consultant to conduct an assessment of the department, we chose to do it through the department's planning division that worked under the direct supervision of the Police Chief. That gave ownership of the final product to the department, not to an outside entity.

The final assessment report was given to every member of the department and they were asked to share their observations about it and make suggestions on what should be done to correct problems that were identified. Next, the command staff was taken on a retreat away from the department and asked to provide solutions to the problems. This process resulted in the development of a <u>Plan of Action</u> for the department.[15] The <u>Plan of Action</u> served as a road map for the transformation of the Police Department.

Before implementing Community Policing in the Houston, we convened an *executive session* consisting of members from all ranks of the department, and members of the community. We met on a regular basis to answer the question, "What should be the future of the Houston Police Department?" This process resulted in the production of a document entitled "*Implementing Neighborhood Oriented Policing in the Houston Police Department.*"[16] It served as a guide for the department as it became the first police department in the United States to implement the concept that is now known world-wide as Community Policing.

The same model that was used in Houston was also used, with some modification, to implement Community Policing in New York City. The process served to reduce the anxiety associated with major changes in the philosophy and operations in each of the departments.[17]

When efforts are made to bring about major organizational changes in police agencies, it is important not to lose sight of the fact that police officers are the ones who must carry out the changes. They play an important role in establishing, maintaining or changing the culture of the organization. Therefore, it is important for police leaders to understand the reasons that officers might resist change.

Some resist because they do not have complete and accurate information about the changes or the reasons for them. Some resist because they believe that change would be detrimental to the organization. Others resist for personal reasons. They believe that the change will deprive them of something that they believe to be of personal benefit. Finally, changes are resisted because of fear of the unknown. It is natural for people to cling to that which they know and are familiar with.

Police leaders must recognize and address the impediments to change. They can do so by providing accurate and complete information about the changes, why they are necessary and the implications they have for both the agency and its member.

It is important that they involve members of the organization in both the planning and implementation of change. Change is more readily accepted if the agency experiments by developing pilot projects to show positive benefits before proceeding with department-wide implementation. That is the reason the Houston Police Department implemented a variety of community-oriented programs as discussed in chapter eight.[18]

DEFINING OBJECTIVES

Chief among the desired characteristics of Twenty-First Century leadership is a commitment to long-term planning. The police leader cannot be a mere crisis manager, responding from one crisis to another. Rather, they must be able to think ahead and anticipate future issues.

They must lead their departments into the future, consistent with the changes that are occurring in the larger society. Police leaders must not only be concerned with the daily operations of their agencies, but must also develop long range plans. Such plans should not be viewed as substitutes for short-range planning.

The police leader of the Twenty-First Century must be able to develop a multi-level perspective for delivering police services. The multilevel perspective represents the future direction by which people will identify with government and indeed their own experiences. This should occur at the neighborhood level, and will necessarily involve special interest groups. Thus, police leaders must be flexible in order to deal with the different perspectives brought to bear on their departments.

Managing change will be the key element to determine the success of police leader-managers in the Twenty-First Century. In many respects, police leaders of the future must be like college presidents. They must manage their organizations, and also secure the necessary funding to achieve their objectives.

Considering the ongoing emphasis that is being placed on Homeland Security, police leaders must be skillful in tapping available Federal resources to prevent terrorist attacks against their cities, and have plans and resources available if an attack does occur.

Recognizing that the fiscal conditions of municipalities will be restricted in the future, they must also tap into resources that exist in the community. They must be convinced that the corporate community fully understands their civic responsibilities. The resources of corporate America are generally available to support the police. Such support does not have to financial. Rather, businesses can provide in-kind services, such as printing of brochures and pamphlets, use of loaned executives, and sponsorships of special projects.

Because of the tremendous challenges confronting police leadership in the Twenty-First Century, they have to be different managers than their predecessors. They must be willing to take risks, chart new courses, be pathfinders, introduce new ideas, manage change, and perform tasks that were unheard of in previous decades. Although the prospect of doing so represents a real challenge, it can and is being done as law enforcement provides quality service to communities throughout America.

The true measure of an effective police leader is not the degree that they are able to maintain and adhere to the status quo during times of rapid social change. Rather, it is the degree they understand that the society is undergoing massive social change, and that change touches all of our social institutions and creates a new order of things. They must provide the leadership needed to ensure that the police enterprise is in tune with the new social order. In summary, police leaders must be able to:

1. Understand what needs to be changed

Changes made only for the sake of change can be counter-productive. For that reason, it is important for all members of a police department to have a clear understanding of what needs to be changed and the purpose of the changes. This must be articulated with a great degree of specificity.

2. Understand the impediments to change

As police departments undergo change, they must clearly understand the issues that will hamper their ability to accomplish their goals. They must understand the constraints, internal or external. It is important for them to understand who has control over the issues, e.g., the police department, city council, mayor, etc. It is also important for the police to know whether the community is supportive or opposed to change.

3. Understand the difficulty of change

After addressing the impediments to change, it is necessary to determine the difficulties associated with implementing change or reform. The question must be answered, "Can the change/reform logically be accomplished." If the answer to the question is yes, then the next step should be to develop a *plan of action*.

DEVELOPING ACTION PLAN

In order to effectively prepare for the future, police managers must plan for the future. They must ensure that their long-range plans are consistent with the changes that are occurring in the broader society. It would be inappropriate to establish goals without taking into consideration whether or not those goals are compatible with societal needs.

Every police leader should understand the principles of organizational change. Most importantly, they must develop adequate plans for any new undertaking. Even though it is not possible to plan for all the eventualities, it is possible to develop a framework within which to work. That framework should include a system to evaluate activities undertaken by the department. It should offer rewards for success. The plan should consider the future and allow for flexibility within the organizational structure. Effective internal communications is essential for any change strategy.

In his article entitled "Understanding Change: The Dynamics of Social Transformation," Scott London conducted an extensive review of the phenomenon of change. In his conclusion, he outlined a strategy for change.[19] That strategy is appropriate for police leaders as they look for practical solutions to assist them in addressing the uncertainties associated with change. The elements of that strategy, as applied to the police enterprise, are discussed below:

BUILD NEW RELATIONSHIPS

Successful police managers must be capable of winning the confidence of the community. No police agency can be successful in achieving its mission without the understanding, support and cooperation of the people they serve. The role of police leaders is critical in generating that support. They must be able to effectively communicate with the community and generate public confidence in the police department. They must be able to inspire support, understand and cooperate with people. No police department can be successful if the public loses confidence in its ability to deliver quality services in a fair and impartial manner.

It is also important to include members of the department in the change process because they play a major role in implementing it. As leaders look at the role of the individual officer, they must understand the officers' perspective. It is not uncommon for individuals to think that their activities are not important or that their contributions are insignificant. That, however, is not the case. Change, even on a small scale, can be multiplied into significant consequences. If each officer buys into the goals of the department and carries out their responsibilities in a way that is consistent with the vision of change, transformation will be easier to achieve.

DISCUSS AND DELIBERATE

Police leaders must include the community as a partner in its delivery of services. No longer can police leaders say that they are the experts in law enforcement and, therefore, the only ones who know what services should be provided to the community. Rather, police leaders must involve the community in deciding what services are needed. The public should be included as partners, not just consumers. This requires involving the community in policy development, problem identification, strategy development and implementation, and evaluation of results. Police leaders must marshal the skills and resources of the community in order to address the needs of the community. In effect, they must become community leaders. They must become change agents and use their resources to improve the quality of life in the neighborhoods.

The successful police leader of the Twenty-First century must also be a leader within their organizations. This involves looking at leadership in a different context. Traditionally, many police leaders have operated under a belief that all knowledge resided at the top of the organization. As a result, a great wealth of knowledge and creative possibilities went untapped. Twenty first century police leadership must tap those resources by creating an environment which encourages creativity and innovation which taps into the special skills, abilities, and knowledge of all members in the organization.

Police leaders must be flexible and allow the organization to experiment with new ideas. Experience has shown that little things can make a difference. If someone comes up with an idea, rather than squashing it, police leaders should be willing to evaluate it to determine if it can make a positive contribution.

During the course of discussion and deliberation, patrol officers should be involved in the process because they have ideas about how to improve the quality of services that they provide to the citizens. It is important for police departments to have a mechanism which allows those ideas to be presented, tried and evaluated. This also encourages officers to buy into the goals of the department because they develop a sense of ownership.

Not all projects will be successful. Some ideas will be tried and determined to be of no value after they are evaluated. Police leaders must be prepared to accept failure of some ideas presented by police officers.

DEVELOP SHARED VISIONS AND GOALS

As police leaders manage change in the Twenty-First Century, they must develop both a vision and goals for their organizations. This will enable all members to understand the department's direction and help facilitate teamwork. Vision refers to the broad picture shared by all members of the department. It is more than just a strategy; yet strategies may be part of the vision.

A good example of vision was when President John F. Kennedy shared his dream of landing a man on the moon, and returning him to earth. That vision was clear and was ultimately achieved because those who worked in the space industry shared it.

Another example where vision has assisted an organization achieve a major objective occurred when Theodore A. Vail was President of AT&T. He developed an idea of universal telephone service where everyone would have a telephone. When he articulated that vision, less than one percent of the people in the country had a telephone. The entire AT&T organization participated in achieving his vision, and their commitment greatly increased the number of telephones in use.

Finally, the successful manager in the twenty-first century cannot be an autocratic leader. In many respects, modern Police Chiefs must be similar to the chairmen of corporate boards. It is their responsibility to develop a management team. They are responsible for organizing and motivating all members of the team, and must draw on their individual and collective talents to achieve the objectives of the organization.

FOSTER SOCIAL CAPITAL

Social capital means developing public trust in the agency. Again, it is worth repeating, the police cannot do the job alone. They need the understanding and cooperation of the people they serve. That cannot be achieved unless the public has confidence in their police.

The essence of Community Policing is the development of a partnership between the police and the public. Police leaders in the twenty-first century must have the capacity to see their roles as leaders within the broader context of the community. They must understand that past events cannot be changed, and that they must direct their efforts toward the future, with community members as their partners.

ENSURE BROAD PARTICIPATION AND DIVERSITY

Everyone has a stake in the success of the police mission. Therefore, every law-abiding citizen must be given the opportunity to assist the police as they undergo change. No single group has all the information necessary to ensure that the appropriate strategies are developed to achieve the goals of a police department.

For that reason, the police must reach out to all segments of the community. They should take advantage of technological advancements, economic changes, demographic changes; their impact on society as a whole, as well as their impact on their organizations.

Police leaders should be aware of information about the future and its impact on their organization. Such information can be obtained from individuals and organizations in the community. If police leaders focus only on their agency, they will become insulated from the public.

A major principle of Community Policing is that police departments involve the public in nearly all of its activities. In order to be all-inclusive, the police must embrace the ethnic, racial, religious, economic, political and sexual diversity of society. The police cannot afford to lose touch with the people in the communities they serve.

DETERMINE LEADERSHIP ROLES

Just as the communities are diverse, so is their leadership. There are many forms of leadership. In some cases, constituents elect their leaders, e.g. political and organizational leaders. In other cases, people become leaders because of their positions, e.g. appointed officials, religious leaders, business leaders, and educational leaders.

Some are leaders because of their personalities, e.g. community activists and indigenous leaders. Police leaders must be able to identify community leadership and allow it to assist them in understanding the needs of their constituents.

Police managers must also accept their role as leaders. They must understand that when change occurs, there is a natural tendency for some to resist it. History has shown that ultimately the attitude of resistance evolves forward. Police leaders can facilitate that.

IDENTIFY OUTSIDE RESOURCES

Fundamental change in police organizations is not an easy task to achieve. For that reason, the police should not be hesitant to tapping into the resources of the community. Those resources could be philanthropic foundations, outside consultants, governmental agencies, or any other legitimate resource that can assist the department in achieving its goals.

For example, when the New York City Police Department started the process of implementing Community Policing throughout the entire city, it called upon a variety of resources for assistance. First, the New York City Police Foundation and the Guggenheim Foundation provided funds to hire consultants. Second, the Bank of Manhattan provided meeting rooms for retreats. Third, representatives of several civic associations worked with the department to develop strategies for change. Fourth, the McKinsey consulting firm provided assistance in change management.

SET CLEAR BOUNDARIES

For the sake of the entire organization, there must be a clear direction and well-defined boundaries for the implementation of the proposed changes. In New York City, the goal was to implement Community Policing in the entire city. That was made clear so that everyone in the department could understand the direction that was being pursued.

In order to reach that objective, the department developed fifty-seven major tasks that had to be accomplished. Those tasks gave focus to the overall goal of the department. It also provided a framework by which the department could measure the progress made toward achieving the overall goal. Although the undertaking was a monumental one, by establishing the fifty-seven tasks, it became apparent to the entire organization that the implementation of Community Policing was both practical and achievable.

DRAW ON THE EXAMPLES OF OTHERS

No one agency has a monopoly on knowledge. For that reason, police leaders must be willing to take advantage of the experiences of other police agencies. There are countless examples of how police departments have handled change or solved problems. In fact, the United States Congress of Mayors has published a series of pamphlets on best police practices.

The Major City Police Chiefs, a division of the International Association Chiefs of Police, meets twice a year. During those meetings, each Chief is given the opportunity to share with their colleagues the major issues that their agencies have dealt with since the last meeting. Some of the Chiefs discuss a problem and seek input from colleagues. In most instances they share problems that they have successfully handled. Many also bring printed material that describes successful programs in their departments.

ADOPT A CHANGE MINDSET

Police Chiefs must develop a mentality that change is going to continue to occur. Change is a given in our society. Accordingly, they must assist the agency by developing a mind-set of perpetual change. Police Chiefs do not have to wait for a crisis to occur in order to implement change. As they develop their strategic plans, one of the major components should be *continuous management improvement*. This presents the opportunity to regularly look at what they are doing, in the context of the contemporary environment, and to plan accordingly.

Police managers must recognize that they live in a society where the individual is unique. Consequently, society purports to give the individual opportunity to develop and achieve on personal merit and potential. In order to develop the mindset for change, the following must be considered: do police agencies follow the same line of thinking and do police agencies allow members of their departments to contribute and achieve in their own individual manner, and to their own potential? Unfortunately, law enforcement has not maintained pace with the broader society.

Developing a mindset for change requires a concerted effort on the part of police leaders. If police departments are to remain relevant to the broader society, they must change the culture of their organizations. They must understand the values of society. They must understand that their employees want to be a part of the organization, and have some sense of achievement in their work.

Failing to recognize this has far reaching implications for change in law enforcement. Traditionally, "good management" has been perceived as having written directives to guide each individual member of the department as they carry out their responsibilities. Unfortunately, such a system does not encourage members of the organization to be creative and use their initiative and creativity to solve problems. Such a system does not encourage innovation. Such a system does not facilitate individual officers and other employees to fulfill their potential. Such a system, however, does allow management to control members of their departments.

The new mindset for the police must deviate from tradition. Police leaders must understand that being preoccupied with control inhibits the ability of the organization to change. Moreover, when change does occur, it usually arrives too late.

Even the concept of organizational change has historically been one that has not been fully understood, and certainly not one that has been embraced by law enforcement agencies. As a result, change in law enforcement has not matched that which has occurred in the larger society. Consequently, when police agencies did experience change, it was in small increments, usually involving one unit or one program designed to address a specific problem inside the police department.

SUMMARY

Leaders of police organizations, particularly during times of societal change, must be able to determine what programs and policies make a difference. It is important for the organization to maintain a focus and not be deterred by negative outside influences. In the end, the single most important characteristic of a successful police leader is the ability to make his subordinates feel successful, and capable of achieving success. This involves an ongoing process of organizational development, and the continuous evaluation of the results.

The ultimate objective of change in police departments must be to improve the delivery of service to the community. Changes in institutions such as police agencies are necessary. They are welcomed by members of the public, elected officials and enlightened members of the law enforcement community.

NOTES: CHAPTER NINE

1. Written in the Forward of <u>The Prince</u> in 1513 by Nicola Machiavelli, an Italian Statesman and author

2. Peoples' Express Airline was started on February 1, 1987 as a very successful, no frills low fare airline. Because it failed to change its business model as conditions dictated, it went out of business in February of 1987. See http://www.britannica.com/Ebchecked/topic/450532/ Peoples'-Express-Airlines (2/8/2009)

3. Humes, Karen, R., <u>Overview of Race and Hispanic Origin: 2010</u>, United States Census Bureau, U.S. Department of Commerce, Economics and Statistic Administration, Washington, D.C.: U.S. Government Printing Office, March 2011, p. 4

4. Ibid.

5. Ibid.

6. Ennis, Sharon R., Merarys Rios-Vargas and Nora G. Albert, <u>The Hispanic Population: 2010</u>, United States Census Bureau, U.S. Department of Commerce, Economic, and Statistics Administration, Washington, D.C., May 2011, p.3

7. Ibid. p. 4

8. Rastogi, Sonya, Tallese D. Johnson, Elizabeth M. Hoeffel and Malcolm P. Drewery, Jr., <u>The Black Population: 2010</u>, 2010 Briefs, U.S. Department of Commerce, Economic and Statistics Administration, U.S. Census Bureau, Washington, D.C., September 2011, p.7

9. Humes. Karen R, Nicolas A. Jones and Roberto R. Ramirez, <u>Overview of Race and Hispanic Origin: 2010</u>, U.S. Department of Commerce, U.S. Census Bureau, Economic and Statistics Administration, Washington, D.C.: March 2011, p.4

10. Ibid.

11. Ibid.

12. <u>The National Commission on Terrorist Attacks on the United States, 9/11 Commission Report,</u> Washington, D.C.: U.S. Government Printing Office, July 2004

13. The Federal Government underwent a major reorganization pursuant to the Homeland Security act of 2002, Public Law 107-296, passed on November 25, 2002 by the 107th Congress of the United States

14. Lee P. Brown, the author of this book was the Chief of Police

15, Brown, Lee P., <u>Plan of Action</u>, Houston Police Department, unpublished, April 1992

16. Oettmeir, T. N. and W. H. Beck, <u>Developing a Policing Style for Neighborhood Oriented Policing: Executive Session No. One</u>, Houston Police Department, unpublished, 1986

17. See Brown, Lee P., <u>Policing New York City in the 1990s</u>, New York City Police Department, unpublished, 1991

18. See, for example, Brown, Lee P., "Community Policing: A Practical Guide for Police Officials," <u>Perspectives on Policing</u>, Washington, D.C.: U.S. Department of Justice, National Institute of Justice and the Program in Criminal Justice Policy Management; John F. Kennedy School of

Government, Cambridge, Mass.: Harvard University, September 1989, No 12

19. London, Scott, <u>Understanding Change: The Dynamics of Social Transformation</u>, http://www.scottlondon.com/reports/change.html (2/8/2009

Chapter Ten:

POLICE LEADERSHIP

INTRODUCTION

The decade of the 1980s was significant to policing in America for a number of reasons. An atmosphere existed that gave those who wanted to make a difference in American policing the opportunity to implement innovative practices and procedures. Three dominant factors contributed to the changes in American policing.

> Leadership in a police organization is the process of influencing human behavior to achieve organizational goals that serve the public, while developing individuals, teams and the organization for future service.[1]

First, large numbers of police officers and members of the community recognized that there was a climate for the implementation of significant changes in law enforcement. Many police officers readily accepted change because of the prospect of getting support and recognition from the community for solving problems. Thus, a climate existed that embraced the concept of Community Policing.

Second, precipitated by over two decades of research the 1980s was a time when police leaders began to question some of the traditions that they held sacred throughout their careers.

Lastly, it was a time when both the public and police were interested in having real meaning in their lives. They were willing to participate in activities designed to improve their quality of life. It was the era of the self-help movement.

During the 1980s, fundamental changes swept police departments in the United States and in other parts of the free world. The most significant of these changes occurred under the philosophy of Community Policing that resulted in new ways of thinking about policing, new techniques for delivering police services and new relationships between the police and the people they served. Equally important, as America witnessed this new direction in policing, there was an unprecedented interest in police leadership.

This chapter focuses specifically on police leadership. It does so recognizing that leadership is a subject of major scope. The chapter does not attempt to provide an in-depth analysis of leadership theory that can be found in other texts. Nor does it offer a leadership-training curriculum. Rather, it stresses the importance of leadership on all levels of police work from the officer on the street to the Police Chief. It views leadership in context of the past, present and future; and it points out how leadership is of utmost importance during times of rapid social change.

Leadership must be viewed at different levels in police organizations: first, at the management level (lieutenants and above); second, among first line supervisors (sergeants); and third, at the officer level. Although the principles of leadership are applicable to all three levels, leadership training and development programs must be designed to meet the specific needs of each level. For example, in addition to being leaders, police managers have the responsibility of carrying out management tasks. The training provided to them, therefore, must be designed to reflect those responsibilities. The same is true for supervisors and officers. For those reasons, this chapter will focus on leadership in general with specific emphasis on the manager level. The term leader-manager will be used throughout the chapter to reflect that emphasis.

THE CONTEXT OF POLICE LEADERSHIP

It is important to view police leadership in the context of how police departments are organized in America. Because police departments are organized along military lines, they are more structured to maintain the status quo than to have the flexibility that would allow them to effectively deal with the changes that take place in a dynamic society. Furthermore, police leaders have traditionally learned, by training and example, to act authoritatively in the management of their organizations. Such a management style is not conducive to the leadership needs required by Community Policing.

To capitalize on the developments that have occurred during the Community-Policing era requires a new type of leader. It requires that a police leader create an environment in which officers have opportunities to identify problems, define solutions and work with the community in solving those problems. Police leadership for the Twenty-First Century must redefine the mission for police officers who daily patrol the streets of cities throughout the nation. That new environment must provide personal satisfaction to officers and a sense of security to the public.

In the past, when the issue of leadership was examined within police agencies, it was surrounded by an aura that tended to cloud the discussion. Consequently, it was difficult to obtain a clear picture of what was meant by the terms "police management" and "police leadership." It was generally assumed that all police managers were, by virtue of their position, leaders.

For that reason, it is important to recognize that the position of police manager or any other position of authority does not necessarily make one a leader. This is not to suggest, however, that there is no relationship between position and leadership. It does mean that the mere fact that a person occupies a high level position with a police department does not guarantee that the person will be an effective leader. Certainly, a management-level position in a police department carries with it symbolic values and traditions that often characterize leadership. There is an expectation in the public and in the police department that police managers will be leaders. This expectation is, in itself, an advantage because it increases the possibility that those who occupy such positions will perform as leaders. It may also help subordinates to perceive them in such a manner.

Any discussion of police leadership must begin by recognizing that police managers have a great deal of authority. It would be a mistake, however, to confuse authority with leadership. Authority is power legitimized by a position. For example, a Police Chief has certain powers by virtue of position. That power, however, does not necessarily translate into leadership.

Similarly, all police officers legally possess and may exercise certain power by virtue of position. However, the exercise of that power does not automatically constitute leadership. One of the goals of Community Policing is to recognize every police officer as a leader in the area in which he or she patrols.

Successful police leaders in the Twenty-First Century must be able to recognize the broad context in which their departments operate. They must be able to understand the relationship between their departments and the people they serve. Such recognition is critical to the success of police leaders. They must view themselves as leaders not only within their police departments, but also within their communities. Such a mind-set requires a transformation in how police administrators have traditionally viewed themselves. They can no longer consider themselves as police administrators or managers in a narrow meaning. Rather, they must see themselves as "leader-managers."

The responsibilities, expectations and political environments of the police have changed. As a result, police leaders have raised questions about the traditional way in which they have delivered their services. They are re-thinking the wisdom of the assumptions, which guided them in the past. They have recognized the rapid rate of change and innovations that are occurring in the broader society. They now know that they have to perform their responsibilities in an environment of complexity and uncertainty. They know that many of the decisions they must make carry a certain amount of risk. They also know that the environment for policing is dynamic and they must be attuned to the associated changes.

LEADERSHIP VERSUS MANAGEMENT

Frequently when we talk about leadership, we also talk about management. In a generic sense, managers are those who have a responsibility in an organization for directing activities. They direct functions, allocate resources and rely upon others to achieve objectives.

Leaders and managers differ in a number of ways:
1. Police leaders have a vision. They do not allow themselves to be overburdened with the daily administrative duties of their agency.
2. Police leaders have perspectives that go beyond their agencies. They not only understand law enforcement and its role in society, they also understand the communities they serve. In effect, they have the ability to see the police in the broader context of the broader society.
3. The influence of police leaders extends beyond their departments. They are also community leaders and their presence and decisions impact people in the community as well as the departments.
4. Police leaders place priority on matters other than the day-to-day activities of their departments. They have, as mentioned

above, a vision based on values and are motivated toward achieving a vision.
5. Police leaders understand that they have competing constituents with whom they must interact. Police leaders have the conflict resolution skills that are necessary to engage all segments of society.
6. Police leaders constantly look for ways to make improvements. They are not content with accepting the status quo. They recognize there is a need for a continuously evolving organization.
7. Police leaders understand they cannot accomplish the job alone. For that reason they involve others in both planning and implementation through a team approach.
8. Police leaders recognize that they are not the sole possessors of knowledge. They strive to attract people who are provocative and thoughtful to assist them in carrying out their visions.
9. Police leaders develop effective means of communication. They understand the importance of keeping their constituents and members of the department informed.
10. Police leaders do not expect everything to flow from the top down; rather they allow communications to also flow from the bottom up.

It is possible to distinguish between a leader and a manager because the manager is more closely tied to the organization than the leader. Managers of the Twenty-First Century must clearly understand that managing is not the same as leading. Managers are tied to a process that ensures, to the extent possible, predictability in performance and conduct. Police agencies have traditionally adhered to the philosophy that by following certain methods they would achieve the necessary results. Thus, policies, rules, regulations, and procedures were designed to reach the preferred goals.

The human aspect of the organization was controlled, ignoring the fact that individuals have both weaknesses and strengths that often determine not only what is done, but also why things are done in a certain way. Historically, police agencies felt that if employees were provided with a clear set of objectives, they would automatically perform their tasks as instructed. In many instances, that has not proven to be true.

On the other hand, leaders recognize the value of creativity and imagination in carrying out the responsibilities of the organization. Leaders care about creativity; they encourage and develop new ideas. Beyond that, they have the ability to motivate others to assist them in achieving their objectives. They create the culture within the organization that fosters creativity and innovation.

Leaders are creative in achieving their objectives and are not tied to a standard procedure. To the contrary, they are innovative in developing programs, ideas, and concepts in order to achieve goals. Oftentimes, leaders find themselves stepping out ahead of organizations. This is called risk-taking. If an idea or concept is strong enough, it will be adopted by the formal organization and carried through until completion.

A leader does not adhere to the traditional concepts of management. That is, leaders understand that they do not necessarily have to adhere to a standard processes in order to be successful. Rather, they are creative and prepared to take the road "previously not traveled" in order to achieve an objective. This does not suggest that leaders should negate all of the previously followed concepts of management. Rather, they borrow from management theory in order to achieve their objectives.

A good way to determine the difference between managers and leaders is to look at how critical decisions are made. A manager focuses attention on "how" decisions are made as opposed to the leader who is as concerned with "what" decisions are made during the decision making process.

Similarly, managers are involved with how communication takes place, whereas leaders are concerned with what is communicated, as well as how the communication takes place. The manager is one who is interested in process and style, compared to a leader who concentrates on substance.

In contemporary society, being a police manager also means being a police leader. The use of the term management may have been appropriate in the past, but it is impossible to talk about management in the contemporary era without talking about leadership; thus the term *leader-manager*.

In law enforcement, as in other organizations, managers are generally solid people; hence, any criticism directed toward police managers does not mean that their intelligence, dedication, and professionalism are being questioned. To the contrary, they are professionals who have been taught and rewarded for working in particular ways. Unfortunately, they often are not conditioned to take the risks that are necessary to achieve innovative objectives. Their convictions are often tied to command and control, and not to innovation and creativity.

Leaders, on the other hand, may sometimes appear to be unpredictable because they do take risks. They are committed to certain concepts, ideas, or values. That conviction is what creates the passion for carrying out their responsibilities, and generates the support in the organization to follow them. Contrast that with police managers who are generally content with pursuing the traditional goals of law enforcement. Such goals have been institutionalized within law enforcement establishment over generations.

Police leaders are entrepreneurial in character. They create new goals, new ideas, and new visions for the organization. They do not dutifully adhere to doing things just because that was the way they were always done. Rather, they look at what should be done. They experiment with new concepts, new ideas and new ways of doing things.

Managers tend to compromise. Rather than holding on to a conviction with passion, when conflict occurs, they often try to reach a middle ground so that all people are comfortable with the final decision. Oftentimes, the compromise occurs within the context of the organizational structure e.g., rules, regulations, policies, and procedures and not because of the substantive issues that are being addressed. As a result, those who are not on the winning side are inclined to blame the procedures, rules and regulations and not the person who made the decision.

Leaders, on the other hand, are comfortable with conflict. They are capable of managing what is called "organizational chaos." They are prepared to take risks because they have a vision of what should exist. They stimulate thinking in others

Managers feel that they must belong to the organization, whose members they envy. The manager's concept of self is inwardly directed toward the organization and not externally directed. Leaders are not afraid of being labeled an outsider, an outsider in context of where he/she stands. They are prepared to make decisions because they believe in them and they feel that they are correct. As a result, leaders are more likely to formulate change.

A manager relates to others according to the role one plays in the organization or in the process; whereas leaders are more concerned with one's knowledge, one's ideas and one's ability to conceptualize.

Managers are more interested with how things are done. Leaders are involved with what things are being done and what those things mean to the people who are doing them or the clients of the organization.

In police organizations, the unity of command is a strong principal of organizational theory that is adhered to by managers. Managers are reluctant to give up that principle in order to facilitate change. Leaders believe that they may want to look at the organizational structure and flatten it out. They have a more systematic view of the organization than managers. If there are conflicts within an agency, leaders want to resolve them in the best interest of the organization and not in the best interests of a particular unit. Leaders attempt to avoid political infighting in the interests of getting something done in the best interest of the organization.

Although this discussion may seem somewhat critical in distinguishing managers and leaders, it is important to understand that the principles of management utilized by police departments emerged with the evolution of police agencies in America. It was necessary for police managers to operate under a control and command style in order to address the corruption that existed in previous eras of political policing.

The reform police managers also learned from the private sector. They adopted the principles of management that were adhered to in the private enterprise, including command and control. Today, we find that some of those principles have outlived their usefulness. In retrospect, they placed too much of an emphasis on structures in order to control the behavior of officers. They placed too much emphasis on the processes that controlled people. They placed a premium on those skills that facilitated adherence to the status quo and productivity that resulted from the officers' activities.

Without a doubt, managing a police department is a very challenging and extremely important function. Those who do so must be skilled and talented. Leadership is one of the most important talents that one must have in order to be a successful police manager. Too often, people are appointed to the position of police manager because they were a good police officer or a good investigator. It does not necessarily follow that because one was a good police officer or investigator that they will make a good police manager. Many police managers have failed because of that misconception.

Leadership skills, on the other hand, do not necessarily ensure success, but they help. A good leader is one who can contribute to the organization through systematically thinking about what needs to be done and how it should be done. They deal with getting others to follow them in achieving the predefined mission of the organization. Subordinates respect good leaders and follow them because of that respect. Good leaders are able to deal with the human relations aspect of the organization and in doing so encourage creativity and innovation. Ideas are important to police leaders because good ideas create excitement within the organization.

In summary, it is important to realize that police management evolved over time and police leadership, similar to Community Policing, is still evolving today. Leadership stresses ideas and focuses on the "what", as compared to the "how." Leadership involves having a vision about what the organization should be and how to get there. Leaders take risks as a means of bringing about change.

The key to challenges that confront police organizations in the Twenty-First Century is leadership. For that reason it is a very important to review leadership differently than management. Even though there may be certain similarities between the two, there are some very distinct differences.

Leadership versus Management[2]

Leadership	Management
1. A quality	1. An art and science
2. Provides vision	2. Deals with realistic perspectives
3. Deals with concepts	3. Relates to functions
4. Exercises faith	4. Deals with facts
5. Seeks effectiveness	5. Strives for efficiency
6. Influences good with potential resources	6. Coordinates available resources for maximum results
7. Provides direction	7. Concerned with control
8. Seeks opportunity	8. Succeeds on accomplishments

LEADERSHIP DEVELOPMENT

Any discussion of leadership development must begin with the understanding that leadership in the police enterprise is not only critical but also very difficult. As a result, there is no one set of guidelines about what makes a good leader. Leadership differs from one situation to another. The reason leadership is so difficult is because our contemporary society is constantly undergoing changes. Police leaders must always be cognizant of those changes. The changes that are taking place in our society have a profound impact on the role of police leadership. Not only has contemporary police management changed, but the responsibilities, societal complexities and expectations have as well.

Consequently, police leaders have raised questions about the traditional ways in which they have delivered their services. Police leaders are rethinking the wisdom of the assumptions which guided them in the past. Successful police leaders recognize that changes and innovations are occurring at a high rate. As a result, they have to function in an environment of complexity, uncertainty and make decisions that are at best risky. This is important because, as futurists have told us, change will be the by-word for the foreseeable future.

Leadership development must be an ongoing process. Additionally, it is the responsibility of those in leadership positions to prepare future leaders. There are a number of steps that can be taken to achieve that objective:

1. Exposure to the Literature.

Police leaders must continuously upgrade their knowledge. In order to do that, they should continuously be exposed to the literature inside and outside of law enforcement. They should read books that are written for leadership and management in the private sector. Every police leader should read journals such as the Harvard Business Review. In addition, ideas from leadership publications outside of the police field should be placed on promotional examinations.

2. Exposure to Other Environments.

Police leaders must expand their horizons beyond the policing environment. There are a number of ways of accomplishing this objective. First, continued education at the college or university level allows them the opportunity to increase their knowledge base. It also exposes them to professors, students and their ideas. Second, by attending outside training programs sponsored by both law enforcement and non-law enforcement organizations. Third, exchange programs. Police leaders can benefit by working with other departments as part of an exchange program. Similar programs can also be implemented with the private sector utilizing private sector managers who are assigned to the police department to share their expertise.

3. Field Training for Managers.

Most police departments have, in addition to academy classroom training, field-training programs for new officers. The concept of field-training is also applicable for new managers. It should involve classroom training for newly appointed managers, then assigning them to seasoned managers for practical experiences on how to function as effective leaders.

4. <u>Management Development Program</u>.

A management development program should be designed to determine the knowledge, skills, and abilities needed to become a successful leader at each level in the organization. After that determination is made, standards should be set for various levels. Then an assessment should be made of each incumbent, based upon those standards. That would give the organization the information to develop the third step, which would be an individualized training program ensuring that everyone meets established standards.

5. <u>Excellence in Policing</u>.

Police departments should develop a program which calls for regular visitations to fellow police agencies and to businesses that have reputations for excellence in order to learn from them. Also, the study of foreign police agencies provides an opportunity to learn about their operations and how they relate to their constituencies. These foreign agencies should also be visited. It is a good investment and something that departments in other countries do on a regular basis.

6. <u>Networking</u>.

Police organizations should develop ongoing opportunities to interact with others, inside and outside of the police profession. The computer can be of great value in creating networking opportunities.

LEADERSHIP AND VISION

Successful police leaders are those who have a vision for what needs to be done to improve their organizations. They are also dedicated to ensuring that the vision is realized. Successful police leaders are also good planners and set goals for the organization. They are the ones who have a personal commitment to excellence. In addition, it is the role of police leaders to ensure that the expectations of the organization are ahead of reality. That is an important part of vision. Every police agency should have a vision statement that is clear and concise. Such statements should present a realistic challenge that is conveyed throughout the organization. It should present a mandate that all members of the department can realistically achieve.

LEADERSHIP AND DECISION MAKING

It is generally agreed that managing police agencies is more difficult today than in the past. This is true primarily because of the complexity of our society and the changes that have occurred in the recent past. In his book Megatrends, John Naisbitt states that "in today's Baskin-Robbins society, everything comes in at least 31 flavors."[3]

Police leaders are decision-makers. The successful leaders are the ones who make decisions based on research and facts. They are also the ones who are willing to change a decision if they conclude that their facts are incorrect.

Successful police leaders also develop mechanisms for including their superiors, e.g. mayors, city managers, etc., in the decision-making process. This is important because they need support from the political leadership for a variety of reasons; not the least of which is their budget. This does not mean, however, that political leadership should be allowed to be involved with the operations of the agency.

Equally important, good leaders also solicit input from their management teams. One successful technique that has proven beneficial is to circulate a decision making memorandum that will ultimately be approved or rejected by the chief administrator. By doing that, other people in the department are given the opportunity to make comments. As a result, better decisions are reached, and generally with a consensus. Thus, part of the leader-manager role is to ensure that subordinates are prepared for increased levels of responsibility within the agency.

All too often, decisions are made in police organizations without the benefit of careful analysis. Increasingly, considering the complexity of our society and the complexity of the decisions that police managers have to make, it is imperative that police managers use careful analysis as a means of making decisions. In doing so, they will have adequate information to serve as the basis for the decisions.

To be effective, the police leader-manager must be willing to make difficult, sometimes unpopular, decisions. This does not mean, however, that the successful police leader-manager must be autocratic in the decision making process. Experience has clearly shown that the best decisions are obtained when the leader-managers are able to obtain a consensus. This necessarily requires others to contribute to the decision-making process and to have an understanding of the issues that are being decided. It is in this context, again, that careful and rational analysis is a necessity.

In making decisions, it is important for police leader-managers to have input from those who have something to contribute in determining solutions to problems.

Police leader-managers must take every opportunity to advance the goals of the organization. This should be done in making decisions; this should be done when appearing before the legislative body; this should be done when making appearances in the community; and, this should be done when addressing problems.

In summary, to be successful in the Twenty-First Century, police leader-managers must focus on the following areas:

- <u>Awareness</u>: It is critical that police leader-managers be aware of what is going on in the community. In order to accomplish this objective, police leader-managers should get input from community stakeholders prior to making major decisions.
- <u>Rethink success:</u> Police leader-managers must re-define what determines success. Do they continue to use crime as an exclusive measurement of success? The answer should be no! They should look at other things such as peace and security in the neighborhoods, and solving community problems when making determinations about successful departments.
- <u>Collaborate</u>: Police departments cannot depend solely on their resources to achieve their mission. They must involve all segments of the community, including religious, civic, business, and government. Strategies must be developed to accomplish these objectives.
- <u>Value based</u>: Police leader-managers must focus on those things that make a difference; e.g., preventing crime and solving problems in the neighborhoods throughout the city.
- <u>Technology:</u> Police leader-managers must take advantage of modern technology. They must develop information systems that link service delivery systems.
- <u>Flexibility:</u> Police organizations must be flexible enough to change as society changes. They must also be able to allow

members of the organization to use their creativity in solving problems.

In their article entitled "How to Choose a Leadership Pattern," Robert Tannenbaum and Warren H. Schmidt assert that it is important to understand the concept of authority.[4] Equally important, subordinates must understand how authority is exercised. One method of doing that is for leader-managers to ensure that there is an explicit understanding between themselves and those who report to them about the decisions they make and the decisions they delegate to their subordinates. The decisions should be based on a number of variables such as:

1. What are your real feelings about allowing others to participate in the decision-making process?
2. Do you have confidence in the abilities of your subordinate to make appropriate decisions?
3. What is your leadership style? Do you feel it necessary to make all decisions?
4. Are you prepared to accept mistakes when they occur?

In delegating decision making authority, police leader-managers must understand their subordinates. In doing so, they should determine whether or not subordinates:

1. Have a personal need for independent decision making.
2. Are adequately prepared by background and training to take the responsibilities that come with decision making.
3. Can be held accountable for decision making.
4. Have an interest in problem solving.
5. Understand the culture of the organization, its goals and its missions.
6. Have the expertise for making decisions.
7. Expect to share in the decision-making process.

In answering these questions, police leader-managers must realize that both individuals and organizations have a culture. Anyone who is a manager in an organization must understand the culture of the organization in order to be successful.

The essence of decision-making is that the leader-managers must understand themselves and the context of the organization in which they operate. They must also understand the individuals within the organization and what they are capable of doing. They must understand themselves and others in context of the total organization, and the broader society in which they all operate. Leaders must understand the limitations and capabilities of those under them.

In addition to developing the understanding listed above, leader-managers must also be able to act appropriately for the situation. If the situation calls for an immediate decision, they must be able to make it. If the occasion calls for others to make the decision, they must be allowed to do so. If the situation calls for participatory management, they must be able to create the environment in which that occurs. In essence, the successful leader-manager is one who is able to operate both as a strong manager and at the same time be a capable leader. It is not one way or the other. They must be flexible and do what is necessary based on the situation at the time.

One of the critical responsibilities of police leadership is to create an environment within the agency which allows all members to feel that they have a stake in the success of the department. Inherent in such an environment must be a feeling among the members that encourages them to use their initiative, talents, time and skills to assist the department in serving the community.

CHARACTERISTICS OF GOOD LEADERSHIP

Joseph Jaworski felt that there was a lack of strong leadership in America and founded the American Leadership Forum to groom leaders to fill that void. Jaworski outlined five characteristics of a good leader.[5]

1. <u>A successful leader must have a compelling vision.</u>

A review of the literature makes it quite clear that vision is a very important aspect of leadership. In addition, it is also quite clear that it is not sufficient to just have a "compelling vision," leaders must also be able to translate that vision into reality. It is in that context that police leaders of the Twenty-First Century must be concerned about the basic reason for the existence and mission of their agency. The mission must be developed in concert with the community. Police leaders cannot afford to be preoccupied with a "how to do it mentality." The successful police leaders of today must have a clear understanding of the entire agency, and be capable of coordinating all components to meet their vision. That vision must be something that all members of the department can understand and work towards achieving. The vision must provide the police department with an identity that is clear, sensible, challenging and achievable. It must have "organizational integrity."

2. <u>The successful leader must be powerful</u>.
The term powerful as used here refers to getting people to do what needs to be done to achieve the objectives of the organization. Successful police leader-managers have the characteristics of being powerful but not autocratic in providing direction to the organization. They are concerned about people, sensitive to the community, respectful of the organization, compassionate and are not afraid to empower both employees and community to assist in achieving the police mission. The successful police leader-managers are the ones who can get their organizations to share in their vision and cooperate in making the vision a reality. In essence, the successful police leaders are the ones who are powerful because they allow members of the organization to participate in a meaningful way in the decision-making process. Such participation facilitates risk-taking, dedication, and working diligently to achieve the vision that the leader-manager has for the department.

3. <u>The effective leader-manager must exemplify the highest values of the organization</u>.
The successful leader-manager must be someone who is respected by members of his department and residents in the community. In order to obtain and retain that respect, they must personify the highest standards of policing and concern for the community they represent. In order to be trusted, police leader-managers must be sincere in their actions, both internally and externally. They must not say one thing to members of the police department and something different to the community.

4. <u>The new police leader-manager must provide breath and risk-taking entrepreneurial imagination for their organization</u>.
The successful police leader-manager of the Twenty-First Century cannot afford to rely solely on the past. Rather, they must be forward-looking in their vision and view situations in a context that may be different from that to which they are accustomed. They must not look at issues as just problems, but also see them as challenges. They must confront these challenges by developing

new ways to solve problems. They must be problem solvers. They must be creative, able to anticipate and integrate thoughts of others. They must be risk takers. The police leader-manager of the Twenty-First Century must be capable of bringing about change. They are obligated to try new ways of delivering their services to the community. They must promote a "can-do" attitude throughout the organization. They must be able to identify resistance to change wherever it exists and resolve the resistance in order to achieve the objectives of the organization. They cannot merely accept past techniques as fact. They must ask why things cannot be done differently.

5. <u>The truly effective leader-manager is a transforming leader</u>.
The successful police leader-managers of the Twenty-First Century must be someone capable of providing guidance to their organization as change takes place. This translates into coping with people as well as the organizational structure. Transforming leaders must be constantly involved in the process of change and growth. In many respects, the successful police leader-managers of the Twenty-First Century must be a counselor, teacher, and in many respects, a philosopher. They must have the ability to convince members of the organization and community that what they are doing is "the right thing". In effect, they must be able to bring their people along with them. The major resource of any police organization is its people. The employees of the organization are the ones who deliver the services. They are the ones who the public call upon daily to make decisions. It is through them that the police organization achieves its vision.

In summary, Jaworski felt that a good leader-manager was the person who: "......With wholeness of purpose and a compelling vision, with almost a spiritual quality to it. One who is empowering, sensitive, empathetic, and compassionate. A person with high intensity and authenticity, earning the trust of his followers. A renewed and creative person, encouraging his followers to assume risks, and remain independent. And finally, a teacher, a transformer, capable of directing his followers through fundamental personal growth and change.[6]"

He concluded by saying, "Good leadership is an art - and transforming leadership is the highest form of that art.[7]"

The essence of Jaworski's comments are that the successful police leader-manager of the Twenty-First Century must be someone with self-discipline and a willingness to master those characteristics that he outlined as the basis of good leadership. American policing in the Twenty-First Century requires no less.

The literature on leadership is replete with theories on what makes a good leader. Those characteristics can be summarized as follows:

- <u>Flexibility</u>.

Leaders of the Twenty-First Century must maintain flexibility in how they think. That means they will consider alternative means of achieving their objectives. It also means being tolerant when others make honest mistakes. This is particularly important when departments are implementing a new style of policing such as Community Policing.

- <u>Self- Confidence</u>.

Leadership in the Twenty-First Century is sufficiently confident in one's ability to take into consideration different viewpoints. One of the most significant things that successful leaders do is create, within the organization, an atmosphere in which everyone believes that they are there to serve the needs of the people, and perform their responsibilities in that vein. They recognize that the citizens are, indeed, the clients and customers of the police department.

- <u>Change</u>.

One of the major responsibilities of successful leaders of the Twenty-First Century is the management of change. Not only must they be able to anticipate what is going to occur, but they must be able to maintain flexibility and do that which is necessary to ensure that changes take place in an orderly manner.

- <u>Work Environment.</u>

The successful police leaders must also be able to make life, through work, meaningful for all members of the organization. They must be able to create an environment where officers are committed to their jobs. Leadership is successful when members of the department develop a personal feeling for what they are doing, a passion for what they are doing, a desire to continue doing what they are doing and more than anything else, a commitment to do what they are doing. They must be public servants in the truest sense of the term.

- Democratic Principles.

Successful police leaders are the ones that understand the role of the police in a democratic society. They understand that police departments get into trouble when they operate outside the boundaries of a set of values that reflect the principles of our democratic form of government. Successful police leaders are the ones with a vision of good policing in context of our democracy. They develop a set of principles that enables them to make the right decisions, even in times of crisis. They are able to express those values so others can understand them. Their principles represent the totality of their leadership. It is within the framework of democratic principles that they make decisions. By having principles based on the Constitution, the decision-making process becomes easier because principles provide the framework within which decisions are made. They also provide everyone with the opportunity to see that the decisions are not made for personal reasons, but for the good of the organization and the community.

- Consistency.

Consistency is an important characteristic of leadership. Police leader-managers must not say one thing in one setting and something different in another. Members of the department should not see their leaders merely reacting to events as they occur. Rather, they must be organized and project an image of being in charge of whatever situations that may occur.

- Visibility.

Good leaders are visible in both the organization and the community. Experience has shown that one cannot be a good leader and be invisible to those who are led.

- Trust.

Police leaders receive a tremendous level of public trust. They control an organization that has the right to deprive people of their liberty and their lives. As a result, there is no acceptable reason for a police leader to betray that trust. Even if it may seem to be in the best interest of the community, violation of the public trust is never acceptable. Violating it has a negative impact on the community and the department.

- Diversity.

Police leaders celebrate diversity. They see it as strength and not a weakness. They recognize that America is made up of people of all colors, religions, nationalities and ethnic background and sexual orientations. They recognize that the nation was founded upon the principle that "all men are created equal" and that national value is captured in the Declaration of Independence. Successful police leaders have the ability to feel comfortable with all segments of the community. They do not limit their involvement to just other police officers. Doing so would restrict their exposure to a very narrow sub-culture. Police leaders are better served, and serve better when they associate, professionally and socially, with a broad range of people that represents various cultures.

- Ethics

The most important characteristic of a police leader is ethics. The character of police leaders must be beyond approach. This applies to their professional and personal lives. Police leaders and police officers must never compromise their ethics. They must be beyond suspicion at all times because so much is expected of them. They represent not only the legal but also the moral authority of society. That is the reason the New York City Police Department adopted as one of its values, "Maintain a higher standard of integrity than is generally expected of others because so much is expected of us."[8] The police, as a profession, live or die on its honor.

- Delegation

Successful leadership requires the ability to delegate. Delegation involves trusting others. It is impossible for any one individual to know everything that goes on in an organization. Equally true, it is impossible for only one person to perform all the tasks and make all the decisions in an organization. Leadership involves focusing on the broader picture and making sure that all elements of the agency are working together to achieve the overall mission. There may be tasks that the leader can perform better than subordinates, but leadership dictates that subordinates be allowed to perform the tasks. That is how they grow and develop the organization. The role of the leader is to teach their subordinates when the opportunity presents itself. In the end, there are certain things that only the leader can do.

CASE STUDY OF POLICE LEADERSHIP: LESSONS LEARNED[9]

Based on this author's career as a police leader who served as chief executive of four different law enforcement agencies, this case study summarizes some of my impressions about the qualities that make police leaders successful.

OFFICER-LEADER

I commenced my law enforcement career with the San Jose, California Police Department as a patrol officer. I did not enter civil service because of a childhood dream to be a police officer. I joined because I desperately needed a job to feed my family. In fact, I did not even respect the police at that time because I had experienced extremely negative personal encounters with them. That perspective changed shortly after I became an officer. It changed because people in the neighborhood where I lived looked up to police officers. I received a level of respect that I never thought possible. People would stop and speak to me as I walked my beat. Neighbors even came to my home to seek my advice on a variety of subjects. I was often the principal speaker at churches and civic clubs.

From the public's perspective, I was a leader in the community even though I was only a patrol officer. The community considered patrol officers as leaders simply because we were uniformed police officers.

LESSONS LEARNED:

When we talk speak leadership, we are not just referring to police managers. We are referring to every member of the department. Leadership skills are put into effect on all levels of the organization; not just at the top. Police officers on the street, investigators, and civilian employees all exercise leadership in their respective areas of responsibility.

Being a *leader-manager* is not the same as being an *officer-leader*. There are certain aspects of leadership that require a different way of thinking through, and viewing situations. For example, while police officers focus on their own well-being and their careers, leader-managers focus on the well-being of the entire organization, the community, and members of the department.

In my case, even though I was only a patrol officer in rank, I was considered a leader by the public. I did not consider myself a leader, nor did anyone else in the police department. Yet, by virtue of being a uniformed police officer, I was viewed and treated by the community as a person of high respectability.

Without labeling it as such, I exercised leadership traits as I carried out my responsibilities as a patrol officer. For example, when I patrolled my beat, I would stop and talk to the people that lived in the neighborhood. They would share with me their concerns and I would attempt to do something about them. I tried to solve their problems. In effect, I communicated with the people. Communication is a very important function of leadership. I solved problems. Problem solving is a very important function of leadership. When I responded to disturbances, I instinctively took control of the situation. That was an exercise of leadership. Even though I never thought about it as such, I was performing as a leader.

When I interacted with young people, they listened to me because they perceived me as a leader, someone to be admired and respected.

The lesson learned from that experience is that patrol officers, by virtue of their positions, are leaders. Historically, and to a large degree today, police departments do not view officers as leaders. Rather, patrol officers are expected to follow the rules and regulations of the department and not use their creativity. If the problem is complex, they are expected to call their supervisors.

Community Policing deviates from that method of thinking. Under the concept, police officers are expected to engage the community and work with the people to identify and solve problems. In reality, they are recognized as leaders in the community.

Accepting that premise, it is incumbent on leader-managers to assist their officers to be successful as they carry out their responsibilities as the "back bone" of the department. Community Policing entails, among other things, providing officers with leadership training.

Leadership means being both engaged and engaging. Patrol officers do that every day. Leadership, especially under Community Policing, means solving problems. Patrol officers do that every day, too. One of the best ways leader-managers can assist patrol officers to be successful in carrying out their duties is to provide them with leadership training.

Leadership training should be an integral part of educating recruits at the police academy.

LEADER-SUPERVISOR

When promoted to sergeant, I was a leader because I supervised other officers. Although I had a recognized position of leadership and was responsible for providing direction, I had never received any formal leadership training.

LESSONS LEARNED:

The one important lesson to learn from that experience is that the first line supervisors are more significant to officers on the street than anyone else in the department; including the Police Chief. That is true because first line supervisors can impact the lives of the officers they supervise on a day-to-day basis. They are the ones that determine working hours, days off, vacation time, and other matters that are important to officers. The first line supervisors are called when patrol officers encounter complex problems or difficult situations.

Sergeants should receive leadership training because of the importance of their responsibilities. The first line supervisor is an important leadership position in police departments. For example, during the decade of 1960s, several American cities had urban riots, with the loss of property and lives.

San Jose, California did not experience civil disorder due, in part, to the nature of the relationship between the police department and the community.

I had recommended to the Police Chief that a Department of Community Relations be established. The Chief accepted the recommendation and charged me with the task of managing the unit.

As a result of our reaching out to the community and working with them, we were able to avoid the sad experiences of other cities. And even though I had never received any leadership training, I was able exercise traits of leaderships that made a difference in our city.

I also recommended that the department organize an internal affairs unit that could receive and investigate complaints made against members of the department.

Again, the Chief liked the idea and a unit was created. For the first time, anyone with a grievance against the police could file a complaint in a central location and be assured that it would be properly investigated.

The major lesson that can be learned from my experience is that every member of the department has something to offer; especially the first-line supervisor. Leader-managers must create a culture in their departments in which every member feels comfortable being creative. All members of the department, especially leader-supervisors, must be trained and allowed to exercise their leadership skills. That is vitally importance under the philosophy of Community Policing.

LEADER-MANAGER

In addition to serving with the San Jose Police Department, I also served as the head of several other law-enforcement agencies. The first was The Multnomah County, Oregon Sheriff's Department. There I reorganized the department under the concept of Team Policing. The department adopted the concept after a task force, representing all ranks in the department, explored the best methods of delivering services to the county. The result of that initiative was the Full Service Model of Team Policing, a concept similar in many ways to Community Policing.

The experience taught me that leader-managers must trust members of their departments and use their talents for the improvement of their agencies. They, too, have a stake in the department and want to contribute. They also take pride in being part of an organization that is well respected by the community.

My next position was as Public Safety Commissioner for Atlanta, Georgia. I served in that position during a period when Atlanta experienced the case of the missing and murdered children, an event that terrorized the people of that city for nearly two years.

I was responsible for leading the investigation. In addition to the investigation, I also initiated a massive prevention program designed to protect the children in Atlanta. I also instituted a city-wide mental health program to assist families cope with the uncertainty generated by the prolonged investigation.

LESSONS LEARNED

The major lesson learned from the Atlanta experience was the importance of public trust in police departments. That trust cannot be developed by the leader-managers alone. The men and women that interact with the public each day must earn it. They are the ones that inspire public trust in the department. That is not to say that the Chief's role is not important. It is.

The Chief is the spokesperson for the department. Considering the fact that most people will not have personal contact with the police, but will get their information from the media in times of crisis, the Chief plays an extremely important role. His demeanor, alone, can reassure the public that the police department has things under control during times of crisis.

A second lesson I learned during the Atlanta crisis was the importance of the Chief as a community leader. In my case, not only was I able to undertake programs to prevent children from being abducted, I also exercised leadership by recognizing the mental health consequences of the climate that was created in the city, and in organizing the local medical community to design and implement programs to address the problem.

My next position was Police Chief of Houston, Texas. It was in that position that I implemented the concept of Community Policing, now being used in some form by over 85 percent of the police agencies in America.

The concept was developed when I convened an executive session comprised of representatives from the department and members of the community to consider the future of policing in Houston. Participants in the session recommended that the department implement a new style of policing that they called Neighborhood Oriented Policing, Today, the concept is known as Community Policing.

LESSON LEARNED:

There were several lessons learned from that experience. First, every rank of the department, as well as the public, has something to offer if given the opportunity to do so. Second, by developing a vision for policing and sticking with it, not only can leader-managers change their departments, they can also contribute to changes in the police enterprise.

Third, police departments can provide leadership to the entire city by systematically engaging in the process of improving the quality of life in neighborhoods. Fourth, during the implementation of the concept patrol officers, if properly trained, can provide the leadership that makes a difference in their assigned neighborhoods.

Fifth, the implementation of Neighborhood Oriented Policing also reinforces the importance of the rank of first-line supervisors as leaders in carrying out a new concept of policing. Sixth, there is a rapid turnover of Police Chiefs in America for political and performance reasons.

Those Chiefs who serve the longest are those who are able to establish good relationships with the community. They are the ones that earn the trust and respect of the community. They are the ones who involved the community in the policing mission. They are the ones who have the trust of the political leadership.

The Houston Police Department was a very troubled agency at the time I assumed the position of Police Chief. During my eight years of service I experienced success because I refused to dwell on the past.

I did seek to understand the past so that I could implement innovative and practical policing procedures that had an impact on what I was facing and the future of policing in the city of Houston. The Houston experience demonstrated to me that it was sufficient to simply have a vision. Success required the implementation of the vision. It requires putting a plan together and working towards it. It also requires the implementation of the vision. I found that a vision without proper means of implementation was worthless.

I next accepted the position as Police Commissioner of New York City. There I implemented Community Policing on a city-wide basis.

After one year of implementation, the crime rate decreased. That was the beginning of the most drastic reduction of crime in New York City's history.

LESSONS LEARNED

Much of what was achieved in New York was based on techniques that had been tested and proven while I served in previous positions in other jurisdictions.

A major lesson learned was the importance of training all members of the department to become leaders. In addition to the skills that were traditionally taught at the training academy, I added leadership training for all ranks.

I also advanced the concept of management accountability. Each of the seventy-five NYPD precinct commanders was required to conduct an assessment of their precincts and, in conjunction with the community, identify the major problems. Also, they were required to prioritize the problems and implement programs to solve them. Once a month, they were required to meet with the command staff and give a report on the progress they were making in addressing the problems in the precincts.

That, along with computer crime mapping that was piloted in precinct 72, was the beginning of what is now known as ComStat.

Another lesson learned was that leadership is not about just being popular, it is about service. It is about doing things that at the time might be unpopular. Effective police leaders are not motivated by glory but by making things better for their communities.

Equally important, the effective police leader must serve as a model for others in the department. If the Police Chief declares himself "the toughest Chief in America," it follows that the officers will want to be the "toughest cops in America." That attitude results in abuse of authority and of citizens. The late Maynard Jackson, former mayor of Atlanta, was fond of saying, "The speed of the boss is the speed of the crew."

Policing New York City is probably one of the toughest policing jobs in the world. There is always a crisis and mistakes are made. Another lesson learned from that experience is that effective police leaders do not avoid bad news. Rather, they actively seek out problems before they become major public issues. They understand that it is better to know about a problem as soon as possible and do something about it. Otherwise, small problems grow into big problems and become both political and media issues. Effective police leaders work to create a culture in which their subordinates are not afraid to bring bad news to them. The "don't shoot the messenger" attitude, where people are fearful of retaliation if they bring bad news to the leader, is not conducive to addressing problems before they explode beyond control. Effective police leaders encourage feedback.

While in New York, I was asked by the African National Congress, the South African Police and others to join a sixteen member international team of criminal justice experts to develop a program to prepare the South African Police Force for the transition to Democracy.

The South African Police Force was responsible for enforcing the system of apartheid. Every police officer had that responsibility. To white South Africans, the police were the protectors. To Black South Africans, the police were the oppressors.

I introduced the concept of Community Policing to the South African Police and other leaders during the numerous workshops and forums that were held. (In fact, the South Africans adopted Community Policy when drafting their new Constitution.)

In doing so, I shared with them that Democracy demands that police are guided by principles that are pronounced in a Constitution.

For that very reason alone, I said, the police are the most important people in the entire structure of government. They are the ones responsible for protecting the foundational principles of Democracy.

For that reason, the police are the most important people in the entire structure of government because they are the ones responsible for protecting the principles of democracy, I told the South Africans.

Based on more than four decades of direct or indirect involvement in law enforcement, the following is a summary of the leadership lessons I have learned.

First, the individual's background before becoming a police leader will play a major role in determining if he or she will be successful. Experience has shown that the more varied the experience, the more likely the leader-manager will be successful. That background includes being exposed to various components of the police department, as well as being exposed to many segments of the community. That combination of experiences is invaluable to the police leader.

Police leaders must have good analytical skills. They should know what is going on in the police department as well as in the community. They must have, or develop, the ability to absorb volumes of information and quickly determine priorities. That role is made easier if they develop networks within and outside the department. It is not realistic to expect information to automatically come to the leader as the leader must actively seek it. This can be accomplished in a variety of ways such as riding along with officers on patrol, attending roll calls, walking around the department and having an open door policy.

Leaders should attend community meetings in order to obtain feedback from the community. They should not shy away from bad news. Rather, it is important for police leaders to know that problems exist and then formulate solutions before the problems become major dilemmas. If leaders wait until there is a crisis, they are reacting rather than being proactive.

Third, successful police leaders are not autocratic. They recognize that not all knowledge resides in the minds of managers. The successful police leader is one who assembles a knowledgeable, talented and supportive management team. The skills of team building, coalition building and consensus building are important to the police leader. Leaders must have the ability to assess their top-level personnel and build team cohesiveness.

Furthermore, they are not afraid to make tough decisions such as removing someone from the management team who is not performing properly.

Fourth, successful police leaders are good at networking and developing relationships with others. They must be able to make quick decisions about people and determine what they have to contribute to the organization. They are able to communicate the department's vision to both the police force and the community. They welcome input from others. Open communications is a trademark of successful police leaders. The successful police leader plays a dual role. On one occasion he or she is a member of a management team. On another, he or she is the leader of the team. It is of great importance that a leader has the ability to see that team members develop to their full potential. They are not egotistical, but have the ability to ensure that all members of the team continuously develop their knowledge, skills and abilities.

A major responsibility of police leadership is decision-making. The successful police leaders are the ones who are decisive and willing to make decisions, whether they are easy or difficult. They are also able to determine which decisions require careful analysis and which ones do not.

They also recognize that many decisions, if wrongly decided, can be reversed with no measurable harm. Some decisions, however, can do irreparable harm to the organization and therefore require careful analysis. The police leader must be able to make a determination as to which category the decisions fall.

Equally important, police leaders are confident in their ability to make decisions and are willing to accept responsibility for them, right or wrong. In addressing the issue of decision making, President Eisenhower said, ". . . The ability to decide what is to be done, and then to get others to want to do it," is a definition of leadership. However, President Richard Nixon wrote, "What lifts great leaders above the second raters is that they are more forceful, more resourceful, and have a shrewdness of judgment that spares them the fatal error and enables them to identify a fleeting opportunity."

Experience has shown that successful police leaders are the ones who are creative and innovative. They are always searching for ways to do things better. Those police leaders who are set on maintaining the status quo are those who are constantly reacting to problems, and not forging ahead to explore new approaches. Successful police leaders have a vision that allows their organizations to find new and better ways to deliver services. It is the role of the police leader to create the vision that enables an organization to strive for improvement. It is also his role to create a culture where people feel comfortable being innovative and creative.

Experience has also shown that when a Chief takes over the leadership of a police agency, it is helpful if he or she does an analysis of that department. This should be done to provide a picture of where the agency stands, compared with the direction in which the department should be headed. It also reveals any problems and allows time for the development of a plan to address them.

The analysis also gives the new Chief a mantle from which to articulate a vision, empower members of the organization and present a plan of action for improving the department.

Experience also shows that successful police leaders are good at "innovative transfer." That is, they are able to stop doing things that are not successful or productive and focus on things that are. This may involve massive and extensive change within the organization. It is the role of the police leader to develop and articulate a vision to both the department and the community that may be new to them.

The Chief must promote the new vision in civic and professional speeches, in meetings; on television, radio, in newspaper interviews, during staff meetings and through any other means of communication. It is important because the vision must be stated repeatedly so that people will comprehend it.

The successful police leader is one who is capable of developing a clear picture of the organization, assembling a good management team, making decisions, and articulating a vision for the department. The successful police leaders are those who are able to bring their vision to fruition and be persistent in their efforts to implement change and improvements.

Changing the culture of the police department is a major undertaking and requires years of work. Police leaders who have been successful in doing so are those who did not give up because of adversity. Rather, they are those who continue to maintain their vision regardless of any difficulties they experience. They are able to overcome setbacks and deal effectively with adversities. They are ones who can continue to project a positive attitude about their vision even when problems occur. For example, when I implemented Community Policing for the first time in Houston, there were many skeptics. However, I understood that the department was headed in the right direction and I did not allow the criticism to detour the mission. As a result, Houston was the first police agency in America to implement the concept of Community Policing.

It is also important to point out that successful police leaders enjoy what they do. They are not eight-to-five people, but rather they put in the amount of time necessary to carry out their responsibilities. In every department where I served as chief executive officer, I worked seven days a week, both day and night.

It is understood that successful police leaders also have unquestionable integrity. There must not be a single question about the integrity of the Chief or those he or she leads. Probably one of the most important aspects of being a police leader is moral integrity. Their moral standards and their values must be beyond reproach. These characteristics must be demonstrated every day; not only through their communication, but also through their actions. There should never be allegations about their integrity. Their peers and the community must consider them to be highly moral people with values that are exemplary.

They must adhere to the law enforcement code of ethics. They must have a strong sense of personal ethics that will allow them to make proper decisions. Their personal ethics should be incorporated into the values of the organization, the mission of the department and its overall policies and procedures. If the organization is to have the respect of the public, police leaders must be beyond suspicion. No one should ever have a reason to question his or her integrity.

Successful police leaders also have consistency. As they carry out their responsibilities, people do not have to guess what they stand for. Rather, their vision, programs and objectives are well understood and are consistent.

SUMMARY

Experience has shown that preparation, decisiveness, team building, analytical abilities and integrity are key characteristics of successful police leaders.[10] Fundamental change in police organizations cannot occur without effective leadership. As police agencies move to implement Community Policing as the dominate style for delivering services to the community, transformational leadership becomes a necessity.

The institutionalization of Community Policing represents a monumental undertaking that cannot be accomplished without effective leadership. Although every member of the organization has an important role to play, institutional change cannot be accomplished from the bottom up. Fortunately, many of the contemporary police leaders are well prepared to fill that role.

They have prepared themselves with training and education. Compared to past generations, America today is in a good position because its police leaders are capable of rising to the occasion to provide the services and needs demanded by people in a democratic society.

NOTES: CHAPTER TEN

1. International Association of Chiefs of Police, <u>Leadership in Police Organizations</u>, Vol. 1, Area1-2, New York: McGraw-Hill Custom Publishing, 2004. p. xi

2. Hesser, Larry, (former Police Chief of Georgetown, Texas) "Leadership Verses Management," unpublished, no date.

3. Naisbitt, John, <u>Megatrends,</u> New York: Warner Books, 1982, p. 232

4. Tannerbaum, Robert and Warren H. Schmidt, "How to Choose a Leadership Pattern," <u>Harvard Business Review</u>, May-June, 1973

5. Jaworski, Joseph, "The Attitude and Capabilities Required of the Successful Leader," <u>Vital Speeches</u>, November 14, 1982. His five concepts on leadership are applied to police leadership.

6. <u>Ibid</u>.

7. <u>Ibid</u>.

8. See, Brown, Lee P., <u>Policing New York City in the 1990s</u>, New York City Police Department, January 1991, pp.17-18

9. This is a case study on the career of the author, Dr. Lee P. Brown

10. The topical outline for this case study was taken from Harton, Thomas R. "Qualities of Successful CEO", <u>Hyatt Magazine</u>, Fall, 1987, pp. 22-27

Chapter Eleven:

PROFILES IN LEADERSHIP

INTRODUCTION

Throughout the years, countless numbers of people have made significant contributions to American law enforcement. Certainly, recognition must be given to our English predecessors as discussed in Chapter two.

> "If your actions inspire others to dream more, learn more, do more and become more, you are a leader."
>
> —John Quincy Adams

This chapter focuses on American law enforcement pioneers who have spearheaded major institutional changes in American policing. This does not diminish, in any way, the multitude of contributions that others have made. There have been many, but due to space contributions they are not included in this chapter.

AUGUST VOLLMER (1876-1955)[1]

Just as Sir Robert Peel is recognized as the father of modern policing in England, August Vollmer is the acknowledged father of policing in America.[2]

Born in New Orleans, Louisiana in 1876, Vollmer moved to Berkeley, California in 1891. In 1905, at the age of 29, he was elected City Marshal for the City of Berkeley. Four years later, the position was changed to Chief of Police. Vollmer served in that position until 1932. During that year, at the age of 79, he took his own life.

His contributions to American policing were many and varied. His officers used both bicycles and motorcycles for patrol. Under his leadership, Berkeley was the first city to use radios in patrol cars.

To assist in criminal investigations, he developed a handwriting and fingerprint system, modus operandi file, supported the development of the polygraph and established a scientific crime laboratory.

A strong believer in education, Vollmer recruited and hired college graduates to become police officers. In 1908, he established the Berkeley Police School and taught many of the classes himself.

Although he only had six years of formal education, Vollmer urged colleges to offer police science courses and assisted in the creation of a Police Science Program at the University of California at Berkeley. This was the first time criminal justice was viewed as a field of academic study.

In addition to developing a model police department in Berkeley, he also assisted other cities to reform their police departments – Kansas City, Missouri; Chicago, Illinois; Dallas, Texas and Havana, Cuba. He was selected to serve on the National Commission on Law Enforcement (Wickersham Commission). [3]

Vollmer maintained very strong positions on the role of the police in society. He felt that the role of the police was to help people and wrote an article entitled "The Police as a Social Worker," which was published in the Police Journal in 1919.

He opposed the use of force by police to secure confessions and was a strong advocate of delinquency prevention programs. Vollmer believed that all people should be treated fairly and forcefully opposed racial and gender discrimination. Berkeley was one of the first cities to hire women as police officers.

Not only was Vollmer an innovative police administrator, he was also a scholar, having served as a faculty member at the University of Illinois and the University of California at Berkeley. In 1936, he wrote the book titled The Police and Modern Society. [4] In 1949, he wrote another book entitled The Criminal. [5]

It can be said that today's police officers who patrol cities in cars, on bicycles and motorcycles with radios for communication, fingerprint suspects, use the polygraph or process evidence in the crime lab, receive training in a police academy or attend college classes in criminal justice, work with children to prevent crime, and much more, owe it all to August Vollmer, known as the "Father of American Policing."

J. EDGAR HOOVER (1895-1972)[6]

J. Edgar Hoover was born in Washington, D.C. on January 1, 1895. He is best known for his 48 years of service as Director of the Federal Bureau of Investigation.

He started his career with the government in 1913 as an employee of the Library of Congress. Three years later, he obtained his law degree from the George Washington University Law School. His next position was with the Justice Department, and in 1924 he was appointed Acting Director of the Bureau of Investigation, the forerunner of the FBI. He was appointed permanent director the following year.

Hoover was in that position until his death in 1972. He served eight Presidents, a longer tenure than any other Federal executive in the history of the nation.

Hoover is both praised and cursed for his role as FBI director. He is praised for taking a fledging, scandal-ridden group of Federal investigators and turning them into what is arguably the most professional law enforcement agency in the nation, if not the world.

Similar to other reform law enforcement pioneers, one of his first efforts was to de-politicize the agency. He approached the task by improving the quality of personnel recruited and employed. In addition to terminating a large number of unqualified employees, he required all new agents to be between 25 and 34 years of age. He gave preference to applicants with legal or accounting backgrounds. He changed the promotional system that was based upon politics and seniority in favor of a system of performance evaluations. He established a formal training program and implemented a system of regular inspections in all field offices.

Hoover established an identification division that ultimately became the central depository of fingerprints for Federal, state and local law enforcement agencies. He also developed a scientific crime laboratory and a system for collecting crime statistics, now known as the Uniform Crime Report. In an effort to serve local police agencies, the Bureau created the *National Academy* to provide training to state and local law enforcement personnel.

Hoover was excellent at public relations and in a relatively short period of time, the FBI gained the reputation of being a highly effective, professional and incorruptible law enforcement agency.

Hoover became one of the most powerful men in America. He obtained his status by what is now known to have been an abuse of power. He acquired it by collecting information, and keeping secret files on the personal lives of politicians and their associates, including their family members. Those files were not a part of the agency's official records and were destroyed immediately after his death.

Hoover was obsessed with what he described as subversive activities. In 1936, the FBI was given the responsibility of investigating espionage and sabotage. He was strongly anti-communist. Some say that in his zeal to fight communism, he grossly abused the power of the agency.

Through a program called CointelPro (Counter Intelligence Program), the FBI regularly exceeded its authority in efforts to disrupt groups that Hoover deemed dangerous to America. During that period of its history, the FBI engaged in illegal break-ins, wiretaps and bugging. It also distributed negative information on the personal lives of people that Hoover considered subversive. Individuals and groups such as civil rights leaders, suspected communists, radicals and the Black Panthers were targeted. Hoover was also criticized for his investigation of Dr. Martin Luther King, Jr.

Under Hoover, the FBI became an autonomous, powerful agency with no oversight. For that reason, in 1968, the Congress passed legislation that limited the tenure of the FBI director to ten years.

Hoover's legacy lives on. In 1966, he received the Distinguished Achievement Award from President Johnson. The new FBI Headquarters in Washington, D.C. was named after him, and when he died he was given a full state funeral. He authored three popular books, Persons in Hiding, [7] Matters of Deceit, [8] and A Study of Communism. [9]

ORLANDO WINFIELD WILSON (1900-1972)[10]

O. W. Wilson was born in South Dakota and graduated from the University of California at Berkeley. He was recruited by August Vollmer to join the Berkeley Police Department while at the University of California.

During the decade of the 1960s, Wilson was the foremost authority on police administration. To many police officers who served during the decade of the 1960s and early 70s, Wilson was best known for two books he wrote. One was entitled Police Administration.[11] The second was Police Planning.[12] Both were standard texts in college police science programs and were on the reading lists for promotional examinations of police departments throughout the nation.

Wilson also had a distinguished career as a Police Chief. In 1925, he was appointed Police Chief of the Fullerton, California Police Department. Three years later, he was appointed Chief of Police of the Wichita, Kansas Police Department. While serving as Police Chief in Wichita, Wilson implemented many of the innovations that Vollmer had pioneered as Police Chief in Berkeley, California, including crime laboratories and use of the polygraph.

In 1939, Wilson was named a professor in the political science department at the University of California, Berkeley.

In 1950, the University of California, Berkeley established the School of Criminology and Wilson was appointed as its first dean. He was responsible for developing the school from its inception. That included both recruiting a faculty and developing a curriculum.

Wilson's approach to criminal justice education was revolutionary for his time. His philosophical approach included not only the traditional classes in police science, but also courses in the etiology and prevention of crime, as well as the elements and operations of the criminal justice and legal systems. The curriculum was interdisciplinary, drawing from the fields of law and the social sciences and, to a lesser degree, the natural sciences. His philosophy of what should constitute criminology as a discipline shaped many of the programs that are currently taught at colleges and universities throughout America.

In addition to his contributions to the literature in the field of criminal justice, Wilson is best known for his service as Superintendent of Police for the City of Chicago.

In 1960, Wilson was selected to chair a committee to select a new Police Superintendent for Chicago. This followed a major scandal in the Chicago Police Department that involved a case where police officers were engaged in a burglary ring. After interviewing several candidates, other members of the blue ribbon selection committee concluded that Wilson was the best person for the position. After careful consideration, Wilson accepted the challenge and was appointed Superintendent of the Chicago Police Department, then the second largest police agency in America.

Wilson inherited a troubled department where politics influenced decisions and graft was widespread. He set out to reform the department by removing politics. He moved police headquarters out of City Hall and redesigned the beat boundaries beyond political considerations. In another effort to take politics out of the police department, he established a civil service system and administered promotional examinations.

Wilson cracked down on graft by establishing an Internal Investigation Division. His reorganization included new standards of recruitment and training and the implementation of professional administrative procedures.

Operationally, Wilson purchased new patrol cars, reduced foot patrols, reformed the department's crime laboratory, computerized record keeping and improved the communications system. He also improved the department's relationship with the Black community by hiring and promoting minorities.

Wilson retired from the Chicago Police Department in 1967. A protégé of August Vollmer, he is best remembered as a police reformer. His two books served as manuals for police departments throughout the nation.

He felt that police administrators could address the problem of corruption by employing effective management techniques. Those techniques included attracting qualified people to police service, properly training them, establishing appropriate organizational structures, and adhering to proven management principles. He was a strong advocate of planning.

Similar to Vollmer, Wilson understood that the police did not control the factors that caused crime; but they could reduce the opportunities for criminals to commit crime through a visible police presence. It was this belief that led to the concept of preventative police patrol. Wilson will be always be recalled as one of America's most significant police reformers.

WILLIAM H. PARKER (1950-1966)[13]

William H. Parker is best known as a reform Chief who served longer than any other in the Los Angeles Police Department (LAPD). He joined the force in 1927. After 15 years, he took a leave of absence to serve in the military during the World War II. At the conclusion of the war, he returned to the department and was appointed Chief in 1950. He served in that position until his death on July 16, 1966.

Under his leadership, the LAPD became the most recognized police agency in America. Parker is credited with reforming a troubled and understaffed police force.

Parker is recognized for his advancement of professionalism in the LAPD. A man of the high integrity, he was a strong disciplinarian who stressed honesty among his officers. He streamlined the department, ended waste and implemented total reorganization. In an effort to take politics out of the department, he enforced civil service rules.

He promoted efforts to keep the community informed of department activities and introduced the LAPD motto, "To Protect and Serve."

The image of the LAPD was challenged in 1965 when the city experienced the Watts Riots. The riots resulted in 20 deaths and hundreds more injured. The National Guard was called in to restore order. Because of the riots, many people who previously viewed the militaristic LAPD as their protectors raised questions about its ability to prevent, if not control, disorders.

Under Parker's leadership, the LAPD set the standard for professional law enforcement. It was the model for television programs and movies that further served to advance the LAPD as the model by which other police agencies were judged. *Dragnet* and *Adam-12* were two of the first television programs modeled on the LAPD.

If O.W. Wilson wrote the definitive book on police administration, Parker implemented its principles. When he died, the LAPD headquarters building was named after him. He wrote the book Parker on Police. [14]

PATRICK MURPHY (1920-2011)[15]

Patrick Murphy is best known for implementing anti-corruption reform in the New York City Police Department. In addition, he was the first Director of the Law Enforcement Assistance Administration and President of the Police Foundation.

Murphy started his police career in 1945 with the New York City Police Department (NYPD) and was promoted up the ranks. From 1963 to 1964 he served as chief of the Syracuse, New York Police Department. He took over at a time when the Syracuse Police Department was rocked with scandal and was able to implement major reforms during a brief time period.

In 1967, he was appointed Public Safety Director in Washington, D.C and in 1970 he was appointed Police Chief in Detroit.

Murphy served as Police Commissioner of the NYPD from 1970 to 1973. He was appointed at a time that the Knapp Commission was looking into the problem of widespread corruption in the department. He was credited with implementing far-reaching reforms to curtail corruption.

In addition to heading four police departments, Murphy also served as Director of the Police Policy Board of the United States Conference of Mayors. From 1973 to 1985 he was President of the Police Foundation. Under his leadership, the organization conducted ground breaking research that helped shape the future of policing in America.

Born in 1920, Murphy received his bachelor's degree from St. John's University in New York City and a Master's Degree in public administration from the City College of New York. He was a graduate of the Federal Bureau of Investigation's National Academy.

HERMAN GOLDSTEIN (1931 --)[16]

Herman Goldstein is best known for his pioneering work in the concept of solving police problems. Although he never served as a police officer, his works have contributed greatly to the professionalism of American policing.

Goldstein's interest in policing started when he served as a member of the American Bar Association's Foundation Survey of the Administration of Justice. He conducted his police research in Wisconsin and Michigan. He was the major author of parts of the final report that dealt with the police.

From 1960 to 1964, Goldstein served as the executive assistant to O.W. Wilson, the reformer Superintendent of the Chicago Police Department. In 1964, he joined the faculty of the University of Wisconsin.

Goldstein has contributed extensively to police literature. His first book, published in 1977, was *Policing a Free Society*.[17] The other, *Problem-Oriented Policing, was published in 1990*.[18]

He has served as a consultant to a variety of commissions and organizations such as the President's Commission on Law Enforcement and Administration of Justice, the National Advisory Commission on Civil Disorders, the United States Department of Justice's National Institute of Justice, New York City's Knapp Commission, the Police Foundation, the Police Executive Research Forum and numerous police agencies throughout the world.

He is credited with developing the problem solving techniques known as S.A.R.A. (solving -- analysis -- response -- assessment), which is the essence of his Police Problem-Solving model.

In recognition of his scholarly contributions to policing, the Police Executive Research Forum established the Herman Goldstein Award which is given annually to a police agency for its innovative work in Problem Solving-Policing. Goldstein is currently a Professor of Law emeritus at the University of Wisconsin's Law School.

LEE P. BROWN (1937 --)[19]

Lee P. Brown is known as the father of Community Policing. He began his police career as a patrol officer with the San Jose, California Police Department in 1960. Shortly after the Watts riots in 1965, he developed a Police-Community Relations program, one of the first in the nation. His work in Police-Community Relations was credited with preventing riots in San Jose, California and became a model for other police departments across the country.

Brown earned a bachelor's degree in criminology from Fresno State University, a Master's degree in sociology from San Jose State University, and both a Master's and Doctorate in criminology from the University of California, Berkeley. He was the first Black person in the world to earn a Doctorate in criminology.

Brown also achieved a number of other firsts. In 1975 he was appointed the first African American Sheriff of Multnomah County, Oregon. There he pioneered the concept of Team Policing. In 1977 he was appointed Director of Justice Services for the county. Justice Services consisted of all of the county's criminal justice agencies (sheriff, district attorney, courts, corrections, juvenile probation and detention, and legal aid services.)

In 1978, he was appointed Public Safety Commissioner for Atlanta, Georgia. There, he was responsible for police, fire, corrections and civil defense. He gained the nation's attention for leading the investigation of the missing and murdered children's case. This episode involved young Black children being killed during a two-year period. In Atlanta he developed a state-of-the-art computerized investigative system and pioneered the *investigative consultant* concept. Brown is credited with "holding the city together" doing a very difficult time in its history.

In 1982, Brown was appointed the first African American Police Chief of Houston, Texas. He was recruited to reform the department which had a national reputation for being brutal and racist. In Houston, Brown marshaled all of his past experiences in Police-Community Relations, Team Policing and Problem Solving into a concept called *Neighborhood Oriented Policing*, known today as *Community Policing*. Under his leadership, the Houston Police Department pioneered the concept of Community Policing and ultimately became one of the most respected police departments in the nation.

In 1990, Brown was appointed Police Commissioner of New York City. There he implemented Community Policing, and one year later crime decreased in all categories. That was the beginning of the most drastic reduction of crime in the history of the city.

Brown developed Precinct 72 into a model entity to pilot a variety of innovative concepts. One of those concepts was *Crime Mapping* which serves as one of the elements of what is known today as ComStat.

He also required each precinct commander to conduct an assessment of their precincts, identify problems, devise and prioritize solutions to the problems, and personally report to the command staff on a regular basis. That process was later incorporated into a different format and is also an element of ComStat.

In 1994, President William Clinton recruited Brown to serve in his cabinet as Director of the White House Office of National Drug Control Policy. He was the first law enforcement officer to serve in a president's cabinet. He changed the nation's drug control strategy by placing a greater emphasis on drug education, prevention and treatment.

In 1998, Brown became the first African American mayor of Houston and served the maximum three two-year terms. As mayor, he applied the concept of Community Policing to the entire city and called it *Neighborhood Oriented Government*. Under that concept, he divided the city of Houston into 88 super neighborhoods and each neighborhood formed a Council. Each Council developed a Neighborhood Action Plan that identified problems in their areas. The city then used its resources, combined with other resources of other governments and the private sector to address the problems that were identified by the 88 Neighborhood Councils. Brown was successful in applying the concept of Community Policing to the governance of the entire city of Houston.

In addition to his work as a police practitioner, Brown also had an extensive career in academia. In 1967, he served as an adjunct professor at San Jose State University's School of Police Science. There, he developed and taught the university's first course in Police Community Relations.

From 1968 through 1972, Brown served as Chairman of the Department of Administration of Justice at Portland State University. He developed a grant funded certificate program into one that offered advanced degrees, including a doctorate.

In 1972 Brown joined the faculty of Howard University in Washington, D.C. as a professor of public administration and associate director of the Institute for Urban Affairs and Research. While at Howard, he developed the University's first criminal justice program, which included a doctorate in criminology.

During the 1980s, Brown served as a Research Fellow in the Kennedy School of Government's Criminal Justice Program at Harvard University. He was a member of the University's Executive Session that examined the future of policing in America and produced a series of publications entitled *"Perspectives on Policing."*

Brown served on the faculty of Rice University from 1996 until 1997 as a professor in the Department of Sociology, and was the first Senior Scholar at the James A. Baker III Institute for Public Policy. After leaving the mayor's office he returned to Rice in 2004 as a scholar in the School of Social Sciences.

Brown has contributed extensively to police literature, particularly on the subject of Community Policing. [20]

He not only pioneered the concept, but also introduced it to other countries such as South Africa and Nigeria. Prior to South Africa becoming a free nation, he introduced Community Policing to the African National Congress and other representatives of the South African government as they prepared to transform their country from apartheid to democracy.

Once it became a truly free society, under the leadership of President Nelson Mandela, South Africa adopted the concept and made it a formal part of their country's written constitution.

Brown also conducted training programs on Community Policing and provided consultation to the Nigerian Police Force as it transitioned from a military oriented police agency to one where Community Policing would become its dominate philosophy.

He has been involved in many of the progressive movements in American Policing over the past four decades. He represented the United States as a National Correspondent to the United Nations Program for the Prevention of Crime and Treatment of Offenders.

He was a member of the National Commission on Criminal Justice Standards and Goals and chaired its Education and Training Committee. He chaired the National Minority Advisory Council on Criminal Justice, was a founding member and chairman of the Commission on Accreditation of Law Enforcement Agencies. Brown was also a member of the National Commission on Higher Education for the Police.

Additionally, he was a founding member of the Police Executive Research Forum, a founding member of the National Organization of Black Law Enforcement Executives and was elected as the first African American President of the International Association of Police Chiefs.

Brown is currently Chairman and CEO of Brown Group International, a full-service consulting company that provides services to police agencies in the United States and around the world

SUMMARY

Throughout the history of policing in America, many individuals have contributed to the development of the enterprise. The contributions have taken many forms. An untold number have contributed by providing professional and ethical leadership to their departments and to the communities where they served. They are the unsung heroes of American policing.

Only a few of the pioneers of American Policing have been highlighted in this chapter. They were selected because of their unique contributions to policing, and their abundant influence on the practice, and theories of law enforcement. They are among the real pioneers of American policing.

NOTES: CHAPTER ELEVEN

1. For popular biographies on Vollmer see, Parker, Alfred E., Crime Fighter: August Vollmer, New York: McMillan, 1961; Carte, Gene E. and Elaine, N. Carte, Police Reform in the United States, The Era of August Vollmer, Berkeley, Calif.: University of California Press, 1975. Also see Morris, Albert, "The American Society of Criminology: A History: 1941-1974," Criminology, August 1975; August Vollmer, Regents of the University of California, Bancroft Library, Berkeley, CA, 2 Vols.; http://www.ci.berkeley.ca.us/police/History/history.html (10.05.11)

2. Gash, Norman, Peel. London: Longman, 1979

3. National Commission on Law Observance and Enforcement, Washington, D.C.: U.S. Government Printing Office, 1931

4. Vollmer, August, The Police and Modern Society, Berkeley, Calif.: University of California Press, 1936

5. Vollmer, August, The Criminal, Berkeley and New York: Foundation Press, 1949

6. For definitive biographies on Hoover see, Powers, Richard G., Secrecy and Power: The Life of J. Edgar Hoover, New York: The Free Press, 1987; Gentry, Curt, J. Edgar Hoover: The Man and the Secrets, New York: Norton and Company, 1991; Demaris, Ovid, J. Edgar Hoover: As They Knew Him, New York: Carroll and Graf Publishers, 1975; Theoharis, Athan, From the Secret Files of J, Edgar Hoover, Chicago: Ivan R, Dee Publishers, 1993; Whitehead, Don, The FBI Story: A Report to the

People, New York: Random House, 1956; Federal Bureau of Investigation, "History of the FBI," http://www.fbi.gov/libref/historic/history/text/htm (2/11/09);

7. Hoover, J. Edgar, Persons in Hiding, New York: Little Brown. 1938

8. Hoover, J. Edgar, Masters of Deceit: The Story of The Communist Party in America and How to Fight It, New York: Henry Holt and Company, 1958

9. Hoover, J. Edgar, A Study of Communism, New York: Holt, Rinehart and Winston, 1962

10. For a complete and concise chronology of Wilson's life see, "Orlando Winfield Wilson, Criminology: Berkley," in University of California In Memoriam, July 1975 at http:/cdn.calisphere.org/data/1303/sO/tF3v19n6s0/files/tf3v 19n6s0.pdf 10.5.11

11. Wilson, O.W., Police Administration, New York: McGraw-Hill Company, 1963

12. Wilson, O.W., Police Planning, Springfield, Ill.: C.C. Thomas, 1957

13. For a brief sketch of Parker's biography see "Chief William H. Parker's Biography," http://www.lapdfoundation.com/bio.htm (2/11/09) and History of the LAPD – Chief Parker, http://www.lapdonline.org/history of the LAPD (10.5.11)

14. Parker, William H. Parker on Police, Springfield, Illinois: Charles C. Thomas, 1957

15. No definitive biography has been written on Patrick Murphy who has made many contributions to police literature, including Murphy, Patrick and Thomas Plate, Police Commissioner, New York: Simon and Schuster, 1977

16. Although no definitive biography has been written on Herman Goldstein, see "Herman Goldstein: Biography," http://www.law.wisc.edu/profiles/hgold@wisc.edu (10.5.11) Goldstein has made significant contributions to police literature

17. Goldstein, Herman, Policing A Free Society, Cambridge, Mass: Ballinger Publishing Company, 1977

18. Goldstein, Herman, Problem-Oriented Policing, New York: McGraw- Hill, 1990

19. No definitive biography has been written on Lee Brown; Brown has made significant contributions to police literature, including Johnson, Thomas A., Gordon Misner and Lee P. Brown, The Police and Society:

An Environment for Collaboration and Confrontation, Prentice Hall, 1981; Brown, Lee P. (Ed.), Neighborhood Team Policing: The Multnomah County Experience, Multnomah County, Oregon, 1976; and Brown, Lee P., (Ed.), Developing Neighborhood Oriented Policing, Washington, D.C.: International Association of Chiefs of Police, 1988

Part Four

CRITICAL ISSUES IN POLICING

Chapter Twelve:

POLICE ACCOUNTABILITY

INTRODUCTION

A quiet yet powerful debate is taking place in America about the accountability of the police. This debate views police accountability in a variety of ways. The debate is focused to guarantee that the police in America perform their duties in a manner that is consistent with the principles of a democratic society, based on Constitutional principles.

> Community Policing represents the most promising vehicle for ensuring that the police are accountable to the community.

There are few subjects as important in a democratic society as the role of the police. The powers given to the police - the power to arrest, detain, and to use physical and deadly force - are all extraordinary.

They are all the more so in a democratic society where the role of the police includes maintaining a degree of public order, which makes the continuous functioning of a free society possible. In fact, we call a society "a police state" when the authority of the state is used so extensively that it stifles freedom of all types, including political dissent. To deprive someone of their liberty, if only for a few hours, is a serious matter in a democratic society. Yet the police are given that authority.

Political accountability of the police surfaced as an issue because the professional *police reform* model, which previously existed in America, resulted from negative political interference in the operation of police agencies. During the *"political era"* the police were controlled by local politics and politicians. The powers and resources of the police were used to maintain the political status quo. [1]

Some police observers have described the police of that period as "adjuncts of the political machine." Not only did the politicians employ police officers, they also determined their assignments, supported and protected them. The police, in turn, helped politicians by campaigning during elections.. They often rigged elections. A community's ability to receive police services was directly tied to its organized political power.

The early history of policing in America, when political control manipulated and corrupted the police, became unacceptable to the American people. The reform model, called *Professional Policing,* freed the police from political manipulation, and a new model emerged that was based on a management system characterized by professionalism and internal controls. [2]

Today the adequacy of this autonomous model is being questioned by some veteran police observers and elected officials. It is being questioned because there is a sense that an autonomous closed system germinates in police departments that are insulated, self-serving, inflexible and non-responsive to legitimate political interests.

Under the Professional model, a large gap emerged between the popularly elected officials and the police. This was problematic because our democratic system of government requires all public agencies to be open and accountable. Police cannot be entities unto themselves.

Political accountability can take a variety of forms. One is budgetary. Now, more than ever, elected officials are asking police managers to justify their budget requests on more than increasing crime rates. Now political leaders are asking questions about the results of police activities. They want to know what the taxpayers are getting for their money. For that reason, the police must now show quantifiable results.

The authority to appoint the Chief of Police is another form of political accountability. Today the average tenure of a Chief is approximately three years. This is true, partly, because of the political process. When new mayors are elected, they often want to appoint their "own" Police Chiefs. In many instances, this does not have anything to do with the capability of the existing Chief. Newly elected mayors often prefer their own appointees who are dependent on them for employment.

No longer are police departments left to their own devices to define and perform their activities. It is recognized and accepted that the police in a democratic society are accountable to elected officials. Furthermore, they are part of the executive branch of government. On the national level, law enforcement agencies are responsible to the President. On the state level, they are responsible to the governor. On the local level, they are responsible to the mayor, or city manager. One notable exception is at the county level where the sheriff, with few exceptions, is an elected official.

COMMUNITY ACCOUNTABILITY

The movement toward accountability has not been restricted to police. Rather, there are increasing demands being placed upon all governmental agencies to be more responsive to the public. Questioning the "legitimacy" of public institutions, however, is more pronounced in policing than in other public institutions, mainly because of the nature of police service.

Moreover, during the decade of the 1990s events unfolded such as the Rodney King incident in Los Angeles, which raised questions about police accountability and questioned whether or not they should retain the autonomy that they have historically enjoyed.[3]

Two age-old questions surfaced. They were "who controls the police and how can the community hold the police accountable?" The establishment of the Christopher Commission by Los Angeles Mayor Tom Bradley on the heels of the Rodney King incident is a classical example of a city searching for answers to those questions.[4] The ultimate objective, from the community's perspective, was to make the police more responsive and accountable to the all the people they served.

A variety of efforts have been undertaken over the years to address the issue of police accountability. Some efforts included police boards or commissions such as those in Los Angeles, California; Chicago, Illinois; and Detroit, Michigan. Other cities, such as Houston, Texas, established a police advisory committee.

Those bodies should not be confused with *civilian review boards* which exist for the purpose of receiving and investigating citizen complaints alleging misconduct by police. Rather, the boards and commissions were created to deal with, in one way or another, the selection of the Police Chief, the establishment of police department policies and procedures, or the improvement of police relations with the community.

Community Policing represents the most promising vehicle for ensuring that the police are accountable to the community. It is predicated on a partnership between the police and community, one that allows the community to be involved in most aspects of police policy and activity.

It is not an adverse relationship, but one that benefits both the police and the community.

DEPARTMENTAL ACCOUNTABILITY

The move on the part of political leaders and the public to hold the police accountable for their actions, and quality of their services, prompted police leaders to focus on the issue of how they should be held accountable. That recognition has had far reaching implications for Community Policing, which has as its cornerstone a partnership between the police and the community.

Police leaders are recognizing that if they do not respond to the rapid changing dynamics of society, they can expect to see external forces exert influence in their organizations.

Self imposed accountability should allow police leaders to involve others in their decision making processes. Such involvement is totally consistent with the concept of Community Policing. The challenge for police leadership, is to determine how best to allow others to have input in the decision making processes without compromising the operational integrity of the organization, their management prerogatives, or violate the values that are so important for police agencies in a democratic society. Community Policing provides a mechanism for police leaders to be responsive to the accountability movement, while at the same time avoiding any potentially negative pitfalls from the pressures exerted for external input into their operations.

INDIVIDUAL ACCOUNTABILITY

It is generally recognized that Police Chiefs are ultimately accountable for the overall operations of their departments. The challenge is to determine the appropriate criteria by which their performance can be judged by both elected leaders and the public.

Historically, the evaluation of police departments has been based upon the crime rate. When crime goes down, it is commonly assumed that the police department and, by inference, the Chief are doing a good job. If crime goes up, the common judgment is that the police department and the Chief are ineffective.

That combined with the political decisions by newly elected mayors to bring in "their own" Chiefs account measurably for the brief tenures of Police Chiefs in America.

Realistically, Police Chiefs should not be judged solely on the crime rate because they do not control the factors that produce crime. They should, however, be held accountable for what they do to address both the problem of crime and citizen's fear of it. Also, Police Chiefs can and should be held accountable for the organization and management of their departments. For example, if the crime rate goes up, the Police Chief should be judged on the department's efforts to address the problem.

Such an evaluation should include whether or not the department has a crime analysis capability, and if the information derived from that process is used to design and implement activities to address the problem. If there is widespread citizens' fear of crime, Police Chiefs should be judged by what they do to address both the problem of crime and citizen's fear of it.

In respect to actual crime, the efforts of the police department should be crime specific, area specific, and/or general in their approach. For example, if there is an increase in robberies, the police should design programs specifically for the reduction of that specific crime. If there is a general increase in crime, the police should have an overall plan to address the problem. By the same token, if crime is increasing in specific areas of the city, the police should design a plan to address the problem in those particular locations.[5]

Furthermore, Police Chiefs can be judged on the management of their departments. The following elements can be used to evaluate and hold them accountable for their management responsibilities:

- <u>Values</u>: Does the department have a set of written values and are all members of the agency familiar with them?
- <u>Mission statement:</u> Does the department have a mission statement that is clearly understood by all members of the organization?
- <u>Plan:</u> Does the department have a departmental plan that outlines its direction by establishing goals, objectives and productivity standards?
- <u>Performance Evaluation</u>: Does the department have a performance evaluation system that measures the tasks and goal achievements of both the organization and its members?
- <u>Training:</u> Does the Department have a human resource system that enables it to (1) recruit quality personnel, (2) train new recruits adequately for the job under the philosophy of Community Policing and (3) keep all members of the agency up-to-date on all aspects of police operations?

- **Personnel assignments**: Does the Department have a system for the allocation of its resources to meet the demands placed on it?
- **Problem Solving**: Does the department have a system for identifying and resolving neighborhood problems?
- **Community Relations**: Does the department have mechanisms for assessing its relationship with the community?

Just as Police Chiefs should be held accountable for the overall operation of their departments, each member of the department should also be held accountable for their area of responsibility. This is relatively easy to do because police departments are organized along functional lines and someone under the Chief is responsible for each function, e.g., patrol services, investigative services, support services, administrative services, etc. However, a system of accountability must take into consideration a variety of elements, the most important being the resources required to carry out the responsibilities.

Criteria for accountability should be designed for each level in the organization - managers, supervisors and officers. Every member of a police department should be responsible for certain activities and answerable to someone for those activities.

Each manager should be held accountable for the functions under their command. Each supervisor should be held accountable for the personnel and activities under their command. Most importantly, each officer should be held accountable for the activities they are assigned to perform.

Another important element of accountability is the process for identifying those officers who constantly find themselves in trouble. Commonly called a *Personnel Concerns Program*, such a system should be designed to identify those officers with problems and/or who regularly have complaints filed against them. Those complaints could be an indication of personal problems greater than the departmental violations for which they have been charged. An effective *Personnel Concerns Program* should be positive in nature, and provide an opportunity for the department to refer the employee to appropriate counseling or other support services.

Since one of the most important elements of a manager's responsibility is that of accountability, it is essential that they communicate their expectations to others in the organization and develop mechanisms to determine whether those expectations are being met. It is also the responsibility of each member of the organization to know exactly what is expected and know that they will be held accountable for the results of those expectations.

INVESTIGATION OF CITIZEN'S COMPLAINTS.

Trust in all aspects of police operations is a prerequisite for citizen support. Other than the use of deadly force, no other aspect of police activities have divided the police from the community more so than the investigation of complaints against police officers, and/or policies, practices or procedures of the department.

Handling complaints against the police, similar to other aspects of police work, must be based upon principles of good policing. In this case, the principle should be that in a democratic society, the police derive their authority from the people.

Therefore, it is important that police departments develop mechanisms that allow them to receive and investigate citizen complaints in a fair and objective manner.

This aspect of police management should receive no less attention, and be viewed as no less importance than the investigation of crime. Anyone who feels that they have been aggrieved by actions of a police officer or the police department through its rules, regulations, policies or practices has a right to have their complaints fairly investigated. When appropriate, corrective measure should be taken.

Over the years there have been a variety of methods designed to receive and investigate allegations of police misconduct. Those efforts can be broken down into three models: (1) Police Department Internal Affairs Units, (2) Civilian Review Boards, and (3) Hybrid Systems of Investigations.

POLICE DEPARTMENT INTERNAL AFFAIRS UNIT

Under this model, the police department is responsible for receiving complaints alleging misconduct by police officers or complaints about police policies, practices or procedures. Typically, police departments will establish an internal affairs unit to handle citizen complaints. Exceptions to this would be small departments that have very few complaints lodged, and no need for a specialized unit. In those cases, when a complaint is received, they are generally investigated by a supervising officer.

- There are three standard stages in the process for investigating complaints made by citizens. The first stage is *intake*. Here, the complainant contacts the police department to register the complaint. In most departments, this can be done in person, by telephone, or mail. Typically, police departments have developed forms to record complaints and forward them to the appropriate unit or person for investigation. As a convenience to the public, some departments have distributed their citizen complaint forms to community groups, and to other departments of city government. Almost all departments will take a complaint 24 hours a day, seven days a week.

The second stage of the process is to conduct an *investigation* into the allegations contained in the complaint. This is usually done by the internal affairs units, although some departments will assign minor complaints to the employee's supervisor for investigation. The first phase of the investigation is to determine the facts in the case. This is not unlike any other investigation conducted by a police department. It involves taking statements from all available witnesses, collecting evidence and interrogating the parties involved. If the complaint alleges possible criminal conduct on behalf of an officer, the district attorney's office is usually contacted and gets involved.

After the fact-finding phase of the investigation, the internal affairs unit makes a determination as to whether or not there were violations of the law, departmental policies or procedures.

The final phase of the process is *disposition* of the case. As a general rule, the Police Chief has the authority to make the final disposition of all disciplinary cases. In addition to any procedures established by civil service or, in some instances, state law, the Chief retains discretion on how to dispose of cases.[6] Some cities use an administrative review board or a departmental trial committee to review the cases, making recommendations to the Chief for disposition. The final decisions, however, are nearly always left to the Police Chief.

Police departments across the nation use basically the same terminology to determine the disposition of complaints:
- Sustained - investigation revealed that the facts supported the charge (guilty)
- Not sustained - insufficient evidence to prove or disprove the allegation
- Exonerated - the act alleged in the complaint did occur, but was lawful and proper

- Unfounded - the act did not occur (not guilty)

In reaching the final disposition, Police Chiefs are increasingly using the practice of progressive discipline. The standard levels of final disposition are as follows:
- Oral reprimand
- Written reprimand
- Suspension
- Demotion
- Dismissal

CIVILIAN REVIEW BOARDS

Historically, the police have been accused of not objectively investigating their own. It is for that reason that demands for the creation of Civil Review Boards have come from various segments of the community.

Such boards receive and investigate misconduct complaints against the police. Calls for Civilian Police Review Boards were most pronounced during times when there was massive distrust between the community and the police. Questionable shootings and highly publicized cases involving excessive force often led to such calls.

During the 1960s and 1970s minority groups, particularly African Americans, were the major advocates for Civilian Review Boards. In the 1980s and 1990s, others joined the demand which usually followed a police action that was considered unwarranted.

Almost without exception, when demands were made for the creation of Civilian Review Boards, the Police Chief and police unions opposed them. The opposition was based on the argument that civilians did not understand police work and were therefore not qualified to judge the actions of the police.

Review boards function independently from the police. They employ their own staff of civilian investigators and membership on the panels generally consists of five to nine members, appointed by the mayor, the city manager or city council.

The stages of the investigation for the external boards are very similar to those of internal affairs units. At the *intake* stage, most boards require that the complaint be submitted in writing and signed by the complainant. As a general rule, they do not accept anonymous complaints. Unlike internal affairs units, the external boards generally operate only during normal business hours, but do distribute their forms to other agencies for greater accessibility.

Investigations conducted by the external review boards are very similar to those conducted by police internal affairs units. In most instances, the boards do not have subpoena power. As a result, the Civilian Review Boards do not receive the same level of cooperation from police officers as do the police internal affairs units' investigators. The boards may also conduct public hearings. Such hearings are informal and the rules of evidence are not strictly applied. Testimony, however, can be taken under oath.

Disposition of the case is a responsibility of the board. If there is disagreement the case is resolved by a majority vote. With some exceptions, final dispositions use the same standards as the police internal affairs units.

In some instances the disposition of cases are binding and forwarded to the mayor or city manager. In some jurisdictions, the board's decisions are only advisory. They recommend to the Police Chief the disposition of the case, and a level of discipline, if necessary.

Cities such as Honolulu, Hawaii; Minneapolis Minnesota; New Orleans, Louisiana; Oakland, California; San Diego, California; San Francisco, California; Washington D.C. and several other major cities have external Civilian Review Boards.

HYBRID SYSTEM

Increasingly, jurisdictions are adopting the hybrid system for handling complaints against the police. Although there are a variety of models, the most common is a combination of civilian and police personnel. Under this system, the police department conducts its own internal investigations and the results are reviewed by the civilian board. The results of the civilian review are submitted to the Police Chief with recommendations that are non-binding.

There are other models where the police and civilians staffs work together during the investigative stage, through either the police department or the review board. In other cases only civilian boards participate in the review or disposition stage.

THE YORK CITY CIVILIAN COMPLAINT REVIEW BOARD

The New York City Civilian Complaint Review Board was established in its current form in 1993 as an all-civilian agency with subpoena power. The board has 13 members, five who are designated by the York City Council, with one representing each of the five boroughs. The Police Commissioner designates three and the mayor designates five. The Mayor, however, must appoint all members.

Prior to 1993, the board consisted of 12 members, six which were private citizens appointed by the mayor with consent of the City Council and six executive level members of the Police Department appointed by the Police Commissioner. At that time, the board had a mixture of police and civilian investigators.

The current board has an all-civilian staff that conducts investigations on its behalf. Upon completion of the investigations, the board recommends disciplinary action against New York City police officers based on findings that they were guilty of (1) use of excessive or unnecessary force, (2) abuse of authority, (3) discourtesy or (4) the use of offensive language. Dispositions of the board, which may also include recommendations on appropriate disciplinary action, are made to the Police Commissioner,

Anyone may file a complaint may also be filed by mail. A self-mailer complaint form provided by the Civilian Complaint Review Board can be obtained at the office of the Complaint Review Board or in person at any New York City Police Department Precinct. Complaints can be made at anytime during the day, seven days a week.

OMBUDSMAN

During the decade of the 1960s, the concept of an ombudsman was explored as a means of addressing citizen's grievances against the police. The office of the ombudsmen was first established in 1809 in Sweden. [7] It was created to "...ensure that judges and other officials act according to existing law."[8]

To perform those duties, the Swedish Ombudsmen was given the following powers:

> ...the Ombudsman has the authority to investigate any fault of neglect and to express his opinion about what has happened. He has, however, no power to amend decisions made by courts or administrative agencies. On the other hand, he is free to give

non-binding recommendations to competent legislative and executive bodies. [9]

The Swedish Ombudsman, however, cannot interfere in cases which have been decided, nor can he change a decision once it has been rendered by the court or by other public agencies. However, if he feels that the decision was wrongly decided, he can contact the proper authority and present his argument for changing the decision.

The Ombudsman does, however, have a powerful tool at his disposal -- his annual report. Each year the Ombudsman has to submit a report to the Parliament on the activities of his office. The report must also provide details on the most important cases handled that year. The fact that the Ombudsman's report is seen as a "Who's Who" in reverse, government officials take great care to see that their names do not appear in the report. As a result, the mere existence of Office of the Ombudsman has the effect of preventing the abuse of power. [10]

The Ombudsman concept is rather simple. It merely provides an office where a citizen aggrieved by official governmental action, or inaction, can take their grievance to a person with the power to investigate and draw conclusions which are acted upon. As stated by Professor Stanley B. Anderson:

> The ombudsman is a grievance commissioner appointed by parliament to investigate citizen's complaints of administrative abuse. Anyone may complain, but the ombudsman has complete discretion in deciding which cases to probe, including those which he initiates spontaneously. At the investigation, the ombudsmen may express an opinion, privately or publicly, as to the propriety of the governmental action. Following exposure, agents may change the challenged decision, revise the pertinent regulations, or bring disciplinary action against the erring official. The ombudsman has no power, normally, to compel such a response. For the effectiveness of its recommendations, he must rely on the persuasiveness of his views and the pressure of public opinion. [11]

On May 31st, 1966, Nassau County, New York City created a public protector, or ombudsmen. This was the first position of its kind in the United States and the first in local government anywhere in the world. The law creating the Office of Public Protector gave it the authority to receive and investigate complaints from the public concerning any department, agency of the county or it towns, cities, incorporated villages or special districts.

In addition, the law created a six member Public Protector Advisory Council. They were charged with the responsibility of undertaking investigations and studies in cooperation with the Public Protector. The County Executive, with the approval of the Board of Supervisors, appointed the Public Protector.

Nassau County's Public Protector had broad powers to investigate and study, but had no enforcement power. The powers of the office were in its ability to demonstrate that a complaint was valid, and corrective action was necessary.

There were many arguments in support of the creation of an Ombudsman in Nassau country. Basically, the concept appealed to the average citizen because it provided a place where an aggrieved person could go when he felt he had been mistreated by a government agency or employee. In such cases, the police were not singled out for special attention.

All government agencies, including the police, were under the scrutiny of the "People's Protector." It was argued that a system which had jurisdiction over all government agencies had more to offer than a special Police Review Board.

This was important when considering that there were reasons to complain about other governmental agencies and employees, for example, poor housing, inadequate medical care and substandard schools.

Those who supported the Ombudsman concept argued that it was a "savior" for the "little people," providing them with a place to complain about maladministration without going through the usual expenses, and spending the time that generally accompanied an attempt for redress against the bureaucracy.

Some believed that the office helped restore the public's confidence in government by providing the means that allowed an individual citizen to make public his or her grievances.

The complaints that were received in a sympathetic environment were properly investigated at no costs to citizens who were pleased with the dispatch with which the Ombudsman conducted his duties.

Some argued that the existence of the Ombudsman served to improve public administration by allowing for the centralized collection of complaints, leading to improvement in the general society.

Just as there were proponents for the Ombudsmen in the United States, there were also those who opposed the concept. The major argument against the Ombudsman was its inconsistency with the "American form of government."

Countries that had implemented the Ombudsman practice had a parliamentary form of government, and government ministers served at the pleasure of the existing government. In the United States, members of the legislative and executive branches of government are elected to office for a specified period of time. The argument recognized the strong separation of powers between the legislative and executive branches of government.

Other arguments against the Ombudsman concept were based on the premise that our government is both legal and political. It was argued that many decisions were made for political reasons. There was partisan political pressure, and would not be effective.

It was also argued that the Ombudsman concept would not work in the United States because there was distrust towards government. It was pointed out that in countries where the Ombudsman concept had been in practice, it was not adopted to "clean up a mess," and there was not the level of distrust of government that existed in the U.S.

While the concept was debated and considered in a number of cities, it never took hold in the United States. It simply never "caught on," as they say.

COMMUNITY CONTROL

Another more radical approach to addressing citizen grievances against the police was the idea of creating citizen control of the police department. This idea also surfaced in the 1960s but did not enjoy widespread support.

According to a report of a conference on community control of the police, co-sponsored by the Institute for Public Policy and the Center for the Study of Law and Society of the University of California at Berkeley, three models for establishing community control of the police were discussed:

1. Neighborhood political control over beat policemen through elections of neighborhood commissions with full or considerable power over the police as considered as was the creation of new neighborhood based police.
2. Creation of counter-culture organizations ("unions" of those policed) with a political base and the ability to hear grievances and force changes.
3. Transformation of the police profession and role to end the isolation of the police from the rest of the community and

establish de facto community control by informal, rather than formal means.

The most serious attempt to implement community control over the police was developed by the Black Panther Party.[12] Petitions to place their model on the ballot were circulated throughout cities in America. They were only successful in getting the issue before voters in Berkeley, California where it was soundly defeated .

The Berkeley model called for establishing three separate police departments - one for the Black community, one for the white community and one for the university community.

Under the proposal, the departments were separate and autonomous. They were to use the same facilities, with full-time Police Chiefs administering each department.

It was proposed that the Chiefs be selected by Neighborhood Police Control Councils composed of fifteen community residents who were selected by their neighbors.

Each department had five community council divisions. The Councils had the authority to discipline officers for breaches of department policy or violations of the law. They could direct their Police Commissions to make changes in departmental policy by a majority vote of the five department Commissioners. The Council could recall the Commissioners it appointed anytime it found that they were no longer responsive to the wishes of the community. The community could recall the council members when they were considered to be non- responsive. Finally, all police officers were required to live in the areas where they worked.

The major criticism of the Berkeley model was that it created three separate and autonomous police departments that never came together at any level. Opponents called the concept a pyramid without an apex. On a more practical basis, the referendum did not pass because it would have removed control of the police from elected officials.

COMMUNITY INVOLVEMENT

Two other models addressing the issue of citizen control of the police are worthy of mention. The first was the *Citizen's Alert Program*, which was established in San Francisco in 1966 by a group of citizens. That program was proposed as an alternative to Police Review Boards. The *Citizen's Alert Program* brought together people who had an interest in police work. Its objective was to give citizens a vehicle to communicate and file complaints against the police. One of its goals was to establish police standards that the people wanted to see established.

The basic activities of *Citizen's Alert* were to collect, analyze and report on police misconduct. This was accomplished by having someone on call daily to respond to allegations of police misconduct. The organization had the services of doctors and lawyers. Their report, if the findings warranted, was taken to the San Francisco Police Department's Community Relations Unit or Complaint Bureau for action against the police.

An operation similar to the *Citizen's Alert Program* was formed in 1966 in the Los Angeles area of Watts, shortly after the widely publicized Deadwyler case.[13] This was an organization composed of residents who went to the streets to "protect and serve." The participants used *Community Alert Patrol* cars and carried flash cameras, tape recorders and two-way radios. Their mission was to observe and document police activities.

The *Community Alert Patrol* provided security for the 1966 Watts Festival and later provided security for the area when Stockley Carmichael, a Civil Rights activist who headed the Student Nonviolent Coordinating Committee (SNCC) and popularized the phase "Black Power," appeared in Los Angeles.

The *Community Alert Patrol* felt that their activity in the Watts area helped to avoid rioting. Their main goal was to negotiate with the police over police activities in the community.

In order to have the confidence of the public in this very sensitive area, the community should have input into determining what procedures the police use in handling citizen complaints made against them. Equally important, that decision should be based on a principle for good policing.

PRINCIPLE

Discipline is an important function of governance. Police leaders have a responsibility to ensure that complaints from citizens are courteously received, thoroughly and fairly investigated and when appropriate, handled with disciplinary action. The public should be involved in establishing the mechanism for carrying out this responsibility.

Citizen involvement in the complaint process is consistent with Community Policing. There are models for that to happen that still retain the principles stated above.

TIPS

The following are tips for police managers to follow in carrying out their responsibility for controlling the actions of those under their command:
- Establish a process where internal affairs investigators are held accountable for the quality of their work product.
- Read every major investigative report to determine its accuracy, fairness, and completeness.
- Be consistent in discipline. Develop a range of disposition for each category of offense and follow that guideline.
- Ensure that the complainant is notified of the outcome of the investigation of their complaint, including the action taken if it is determined that the officer committed the violation.
- Ensure that the complainant understands the reason an officer is found not guilty, if that is the case. Do not use police terms in giving explanations.
- Where legal, allow citizens to review the investigate files of all major incidents.
- On a regular basis, provide the public with reports on the activities of the internal affairs unit.

Over the years, a variety of methods have been proposed for handling citizen complaints against the police. Experience has shown that there is no single answer to the issue. Rather, police departments should develop a process that is consistent with the culture of their community.

Citizen involvement in making that decision is imperative under the philosophy of Community Policing. Furthermore, the experiences of several American large cities have shown that a process that involves citizens in all aspects of the complaint investigation process is helpful in establishing public confidence in the process.

Since discipline is a function of management, the Police Chief should ultimately be responsible for determining the appropriate actions taken against his/her officers. If citizens are involved in conducting the investigations, they should be allowed to make recommendations to the chief.

An open and transparent system for handling citizens' complaints goes a long ways in developing an atmosphere of trust between the police and the community. That trust is necessary if Community Policing is to be successful.

Kessler conducted one of the first studies on the effects of Community

Policing on complaints against police officers. He found that officers in the Houston Police Department, who worked in areas where Community Policing had been implemented, "...received significantly fewer complaints than other officers." He concluded that Community Policing had the potential of reducing tension between the police and the public. [14]

He also concluded that the interaction between police and citizens, which is the foundation of Community Policing, diminishes ugliness towards the police. Kessler attributed this to the fact that under Community Policing officers were trained to be responsive to the concerns of citizen, avoiding abrasiveness.[15]

His findings also refuted the beliefs held by some advocates of the *professional model* of policing that close contact between the police and the community would result in increased corruption. [16]

POLICE INTEGRITY

"Integrity is that honest matching of words and feelings with thoughts and actions with no desire other than for the good of others, without malice or desire to deceive, take advantage, manipulate, or control, constantly receiving your intent as you strive for congruence." (Stephen Corey in Principle Centered Leadership)[17]

No police agency can be successful unless they have the trust of the people they serve. Police departments cannot expect, nor will they receive that trust if they engage in unethical activities.

The basic foundation of police integrity is built upon police ethics. Ethics represent the core of the police enterprise. Simply stated, ethics means doing the *right thing*.

The challenge for police leaders is twofold. First, to determine for the department what is the *right thing*. Second, to establish and maintain a culture whereby all members of the department will know what is *right* and conduct themselves accordingly at all times.

In a democratic society, it is assumed that those who are given the responsibility of enforcing the law will not violate it in the process of performing their duties. Ethics is the framework within which that occurs.

Integrity is more important in the police enterprise than any other institution in society. That is because the police are empowered by society to uphold and enforce the law. Any violation of that trust not only diminishes the image of the police, it also diminishes public respect for the system of law that is essential for order in a democratic society.

Police ethics is a multidisciplinary subject that represents a set of principles and/or values which are designed to prescribe the proper conduct of police officers. Ethics relate to both individuals and the agency for which individuals work. Ethics represent principles and standards of conduct designed to guide the behavior of police officers.

Police leaders recognized the need for ethical standards as far back as 1957 when the first Law Enforcement Code of Ethics was developed. The challenge for police leaders today is to link the values, codes and principles to daily police operations.

Police ethics start with the principles that are spelled out in the Declaration of Independence, United States Constitution and the Bill of Rights. Those documents mandate that the police are obligated to ensure that everyone is afforded due progress.

Additionally, the police have the obligation to carry out their activities in context of the principal "…that all men are created equal, that they are endowed by their Creator with certain inalienable Rights, that among these are Life, Liberty and the pursuit of Happiness." [18]

The Declaration of Independence goes on to say, "…governments are instituted among men, deriving their just powers *from the consent of the governed…*" [19]

Second, both state law and the laws of the jurisdiction that employ the police govern their obligation to uphold the law. As a condition of employment, they take a pledge to uphold those laws, as well as the Constitution of the United States.

Third, the Law Enforcement Code of Ethics and Cannon of Conduct as discussed in chapter eight shapes police ethics. These documents further serve as guides that officers are expected to use to govern themselves.

Fourth, police ethics are influenced by a police department's values. Those values are also discussed in chapter eight and are instrumental in establishing the police culture.

Fifth, police department rules and regulations that provide guidance to officers as they carry out their duties also serve to shape police ethics. They should be based on the law Enforcement Code of Ethics, Cannons of Conduct and departmental values. They serve as guidelines for proper police behavior.

Sixth, police training programs, both recruit and in-service, play a major role in preparing officers to do *what is right.*

Finally, the communities in which police officers grow up, and the communities they serve help shape police ethics.

In effect, police integrity is influenced by a variety of factors. First and foremost are family values. Psychologists report that a child's basic personality is formed during the first six years of life (some say the first three years). It is within the family that children first learn right from wrong and good from bad. That will influence them for years in the future.

Ethics not only regulates the conduct of police officers, they also imply certain consequences for not adhering to ethical standards.

Public trust in the police begins with the actions of individual officers. Every member of the department, sworn and civilian, must understand that they occupy a position of public trust. As such, they must carry out their responsibilities in a manner that will always uphold that trust. Most of all, they must be honest and ethical in all of their activities.

Under Community Policing, the police assume a greatly expanded role, far beyond that of rapidly responding to calls for service and randomly patrolling their beats. They are expected to use their initiative and discretion to solve problems. In doing so, they must work cooperatively with the community. That partnership is essential to control crime and the fear of crime.

Because the public has bestowed authority upon the police that is not given to the general public, e.g., to deprive one of their freedoms and use deadly force, they are held to a higher level of ethical standards. Betrayal of that trust diminishes the willingness of the public to work with the police which lessens their ability to be successful in carrying out their responsibilities.

The role of the police in society is different from that of the general public because the police take an oath of office and in doing so pledge to uphold the law. Although such an oath may be required of other public employees, such a pledge is not required by those employed in the private sector. The police play a special role in our society. And holding them to higher standards than others is justified.

Therefore, it is incumbent upon police officers to recognize that they represent an institution that survives on trust. On or off duty, they are required to conduct themselves in a manner that does not result in disrespect for themselves, their agency or law enforcement.

Police officers must view themselves as public servants. They must be fair and impartial as they carry out their responsibilities. They must never allow their personal feelings, attitudes, prejudices or biases to influence their ability to exhibit the highest standards of the police enterprise. They must never forget that "all men are created equal, that they are endowed by their creator with certain inalienable rights, among them are life, liberty and the pursuit of happiness."[20]

Ethical policing includes equitable policing. That means police officers must not discriminate against anyone based on their race, religion, ethnicity, socio-economic background or sexual orientation.

Police officers must always recognize that their authority is derived from the people and that its practice must never be used for personal reasons. They must also recognize that their actions have an impact on their agency as a whole. Therefore, police officers must always conduct themselves in a manner that is beyond reproach. They must always remember that integrity means honesty. Honesty means that police officers will not accept gratuities.

Even though it has been a long standing practice in some agencies to allow eating establishments to give police officers free or discounted meals, free cleaning of uniforms and a variety of other gratuities, it is incumbent on each individual officer not to accept such gratuities. It is also incumbent on police leaders to ensure that such practices are not tolerated. If the "freebies" are not given to the general public, the police also should not accept them.

Some might argue, "What's wrong with accepting a free cup of coffee?" The answer is everything. Even though the motive of offering free things to police officers may appear to be a noble and innocent gesture, the acceptance is not. This is one case where "there is no such thing as a free lunch" has real meaning. Ethics dictates that police departments have a zero tolerance when it involves police officers accepting gratuities.

There are still many eating establishments that insist on giving free food to officers in uniform. For some it is a tradition. When such offers are made, it is appropriate for officers to say, "Thank you very much, but I am not allowed to accept your kind offer." If the proprietor insists and says, "I am not going to take your money," officers should leave the cost of the meal on the table and tell the owner, "If I can't pay, I cannot come here again."

In some states, such as Texas, there are state laws making both the offer and the acceptance of anything of value to police officers illegal. If such laws exist, officers should share that information with those who offer them gratuities. Clearly, every police department should have and enforce policies prohibiting police officers from accepting gratuities.

A reliable guideline for police decision making is the following set of questions:

Is it legal? Is it ethical? Is it in the best interest of the community? Would it bring discredit on the department? Will it bring discredit on me?

Police officer conduct should be guided by the appropriate answer to all of those questions

Zero tolerance must apply to every member of the department, including the Chief. It would be hypocritical for police leaders to accept gifts from the public when their officers are not allowed to do so.

Why should the police be concerned about ethics? Morality is fundamental to social interaction in all societies. Rules that govern right and wrong are necessary in order to have an orderly society. Yet, not everyone has been socialized in the same manner. We have police departments because there are those in society who will violate the law. Similarly, the police must assume that not all of the people they employ will adhere to the same principles of right and wrong. The responsibility of police leadership is to create a culture within their organizations which is based on values, and to provide the support systems to ensure that all members of the department operate within the boundaries of expectations.

Each recruit enters police work with at least two decades of life experience. During that time, their basic personalities have been developed. As a result, they have views of people, ethics and the role of the police in society.

For that reason, police departments cannot assume that the attitudes, perceptions, and any bias they bring into the police service are consistent with the culture of the department and the expectations of its officers. Police training programs play a key role in preparing new recruits for what is expected of them as they enter law enforcement. Just as members of the legal and medical communities are taught the ethics of their professions, the police must be similarly educated.

Police leaders must be aware that in addition to the formal organizational culture and its inherent expectations, there is also an informal culture in police departments. The informal culture is sometimes stronger than the formal culture. For that reason, police leaders must not only understand the informal culture, but also implement systems to ensure that the formal culture is the dominant one for members of the department.

The formal training of new recruits represents the expectations of the formal organization. The informal system manifests itself when trainers say things such as, "This is what we are supposed to do, but when you are on the streets, you need to take care of yourself. It's a jungle out there."

Today, it is common for police departments to have field training officers who supervise and evaluate the activities of new officers when they leave the academy. Field training officers have a profound impact on both the attitudes and behavior of new officers. It is not uncommon for field training officers to tell their trainees, "Forget what you learned in the academy. This in how we do things on the street." New recruits are taught that the sooner they conform to "how things are done", the sooner they will be accepted. It is also said that "The key to being a successful cop is don't stand out." [21]

Such coaching is being replaced by more insightful guidance to new officers by highly professional field trainers. Under Community Policing, field training officers are carefully selected so that new officers are indoctrinated into police work under the philosophy of Community Policing. Yet, the challenge to police leaders is to ensure that the first field orientation given to new officers reflects the values and ethics of the formal organization.

Under Community Policing: [22]
- Decisions to enforce the law are based on illegal actions of the suspect and not who the suspect happens to be.
- It is not the role of the police to punish suspects or use unnecessary force.
- Physical or deadly force should only be used as a last resort. Deadly force should only be used to protect life.
- Due process is a constitutionally guaranteed right and should not be violated under any circumstances.
- Police officers must be truthful at all times. Perjury is illegal and police cannot break the law to enforce it.
- When not responding to calls for service, police officers should use their time in a productive way to solve problems in the community.
- It is illegal for the police to take gratuities of any type.

The paramount duty of the police is to protect the public, never breaking the law under any circumstances. They should be viewed as the primary government institution that the public can depend on. Violations of the law by police undermine public confidence.

Police integrity is at its lowest when the police engage in organized crime and vice activities. During the Political era of policing in America it was not uncommon for the police to do as the politicians asked. Police integrity is also compromised when the hiring, assigning and promotion of police officers is influenced by the political process. That, too, was the practice during the political era of policing.

There will always be questions about their ethics due to the wide latitude that police have when it comes to making crucial decisions in society. This is true even though guidance is provided by the Federal Constitution, local and state laws, code of ethics, cannons of conduct, police department values and its rules and regulations. The challenge for all police officials is to live up to those lofty expectations in everything they do.

To maintain the integrity of the police, departments cannot allow individuals to perform their duties based solely on their individual sense of what is right and wrong.

Ethical behavior is unique to each individual who enters the department. Those principles are established long before they become police officers. Each individual brings with them their own sense of right and wrong based on their life experiences.

For example, many have grown up in segregated neighborhoods, attended segregated schools and have segregated social and personal relationships. They enter police services with distinct attitudes about people who are difference from their families, friends and themselves. Those attitudes have the potential of establishing beliefs that their culture is good and others are bad.

That is the reason why training is so important. It is reasonable for the public to expect all police officers to treat everyone the same. The police are obligated to prepare all officers with an understanding of their responsibilities to policing in a democratic society.

Police decision-making is not absolute. For that reason, the police are given a great degree of discretion in how they make decisions. If an officer stops a car for speeding, he can either issue the driver a citation or give a verbal warning. Would their decisions differ based on the race of the driver?

If a young person is caught shoplifting candy from a store, the officer has the discretion to release him or take him into custody. Does the economic status of the youth's parents influence his treatment? What should a police officer do if a homeless person steals food from a grocery store? What should an officer do if a wealthy socialite is caught shoplifting in an upscale boutique?

While officers are empowered to use their judgment in making decisions, police leaders are responsible for establishing the boundaries in which they exercise that discretion. That framework is based on the culture of the police department and its value. Those values must be reinforced through training and reflected in all of the department's policies and procedures.

It is generally agreed on today that police officers cannot engage in illegal activities. There are however, some departments that continue to allow their officers to accept gratuities. Consider the following situation:

> During the Christmas season, certain officers were told by their supervisors to go by a certain law firm and pick up their Christmas gifts. The gifts were bottles of liquor. The officers that are selected were detectives and accident investigators.

A senior officer and his new recruit stopped a homeless man with a clothing iron in his possession. When the officers asked the man where he got the iron, he told them he found it. The senior officer accused the homeless man of stealing it, took the iron and told him he was going to give him a break. Later, he gives the iron to the recruit and tells him, "You can take this home with you. It will save us some paperwork."

A young officer working the evening shift stops to check on a liquor store just before closing time. As he was leaving, the clerk takes a bottle of whiskey off the shelf and gives it to the officer saying, "Take this. The other officers who work this beat come in and pick up their bottles, you should do the same".

A restaurant offers free meals to all police officers in uniform. Two officers came in, eat dinner and the waitress yells, "No charge, we don't charge officers."

If it is acceptable to take a free cup of coffee, is it acceptable to take a free meal? If it is acceptable to take a free meal, is it acceptable to accept a free dinner for your family.

If is okay to take a free dinner for the family, is it okay to accept free services from the cleaners? If it is okay to accept free services from the cleaners, is it okay to accept a discount on a car?

The point is where should police officers draw the line? Should they accept anything free? Ethical policing tells us that the answer to that question is no. The police must be the standard bearers of integrity. They must serve as an example for the rest of society. Over time, the line between a free cup of coffee and things of greater value become blurred. Again, the old adage, "There is no such thing as a free lunch" has real meaning here.

Police leadership plays an important role in curbing corruption. Both managers and supervisors have the responsibility to serve as positive role models and aggressively pursue those who violate their sworn oaths of office. They must be vigilant in their commitment to rid all elements of corruption from police departments.

Officers must not allow themselves to be corrupted, even if the corruption is viewed as minor. The results will be the same. What is the difference between officers accepting small gifts from a citizen and accepting larger gifts? Is it okay to accept a free cup of coffee, a half-priced meal, a free dinner, tickets to a ball game, or a turkey at Thanksgiving or Christmas?

What is the role of police leadership in maintaining police integrity? First, they must establish and maintain a culture that promotes integrity. That climate must be based on a set of values. Police leaders must lead by example. They must not violate the ethical values of the department. They must continuously send out the right message about ethical standards that are mandated for all members of the department.

In those instances where institutionalized corruption exists, it is likely to also be tolerated by other institutions in the community. For widespread corruption to exist, other elements of the criminal justice system, e.g. prosecutors, and courts, are likely to be involved. Equally significant, the community must be willing participants. Those communities that have zero tolerance for corruption will be relatively free of institutionalized corruption. That is not to suggest that individuals will not engage in illegal activities, but it would be an exception and not the rule.

Integrity policing is not only important; it is essential to everything that the police do. Under Community Policing, where police officers are obligated to work with the community in order to identify and solve problems, their integrity cannot be questioned. It is, therefore, critically important for police leaders to develop and implement policies prohibiting both gratuities and corrupt practices. Since most departments have such policies, they must ensure that they have mechanisms for monitoring the integrity of their officers. There is no compromising on matters of police integrity.

USE OF DEADLY FORCE

Deadly Force: An amount of force that is likely to cause serious bodily injury or the death of another person. [23]

There is no aspect of police work that creates more tension between the police and the community than the police use of deadly force. Although most police shootings do not result in civil disorder, they generally generate significant concern from the public.

That concern has manifested itself in civil unrest, demonstrations, political activism or lawsuits against the police department and the city. Shootings that take a citizen's life frequently result in serious consequences such as community protests, political inquiries, civil lawsuits, termination of officers and even criminal prosecution. Most damaging is the distrust they generate between the police and the public.

This is particularly true in the African American community and increasingly so in the Hispanic community, where such shootings are likely to not only trigger public concern and demonstrations, but also political mobilization. Bittner pointed out as early as the 1970s that police use of deadly force was at the core of policing in America and was related to the elusive issue of police discretion.[24]

What happens before a crisis often determines what will happen during and after. For that reason, it is important for police departments to cultivate and maintain good relationships with the community, especially the minority community. If there is a climate of trust between the community and the police, there is less likelihood of community unrest when an unfortunate shooting incident occurs. If communities have confidence in its police departments, they are more likely to patiently await the outcome of the investigation, rather than jump to conclusions that the police were wrong.

The Community Relations Services (CRS) of the United States Department of Justice has handled numerous cases of police shootings of minorities. Based on that experience, CRS concluded:

> There are certain flashpoints that commonly occur after a police use of force incident occurs. Whenever an incident involves a police shooting or use of force, officers must be aware that their actions are not viewed in a vacuum. There are usually witnesses to an incident. How the incident is perceived will be subject to many

interpretations. When distrust between police and community is present, any police action will be subject to suspicion and scrutiny.[25]

From the perspective of the police, it is not only the number of police shootings; it is also the consequences. From the perspective of the community, it is both the number of shootings and the injuries and grief of the family members. From both perspectives, there is the concern that police shootings can escalate into community-wide issues often based on the victim's race.

BACKGROUND

Only with a historical perspective of such incidents can anyone fully understand the community tensions that generally result when the police use deadly force, particularly when a citizen loses his or her life. Second, it must be viewed from the perspective of the contemporary status of policing in American society.

From a historical perspective, as pointed out in chapter two, America policing was adopted from the English policing system. The use of deadly force in America was derived from English common law. When this country was first founded, it adopted the same policing system that was used in England. That included the same ideas about the use of firearms. As a result, when policing was first started in America, like in England, the police were not armed. It did not take long, however, for that to change.

It was around the middle of the 18th century when the idea to arm American police emerged. Change resulted from a case in which a police officer used his privately owned gun while performing his duties.

The matter was taken to court and the authority of the police to use firearms was upheld. Subsequently, the police were allowed to carry firearms. Today, they are a normal part of the police officer's working equipment.

Until recently, police officers had broad discretion on when they could use deadly force. State law allowed the police to shoot fleeing felons, and many crimes that did not carry the death penalty upon conviction were classified as felonies.[26]

Any discussion of police use of deadly force should occur in the context of several factors. First, American society, similar to all societies, must have a system for maintaining order. That system must be consistent with the democratic principles spelled out in the Constitution. That means

American police officers must not only know the best way of maintaining order, they must also be able to do so consistent with the principles of our democratic society. It is the role of the police to enforce the law and to advance the precious principles of democracy that are so cherished in this country. Adhering to this philosophy ascribes to the police the role of protecting the individual rights of citizens.

Second, the police cannot consider themselves an entity unto themselves. Rather, they must realize that they are an integral part of government. The role of the police in a democratic society is to serve the people. To that end, it is imperative that the police are responsive and responsible to civilian control.

This point is significant because police policy should not be developed in isolation. Rather, it should be reflective of the positions and policies backed by publically elected officials. The policy regarding when the police are allowed to use deadly force is a matter of high public concern.

For that reason, the public should have input into that decision. Such input is consistent with the philosophy of Community Policing. In fact, a major tenet of the philosophy is that officers get to know the people in the neighborhoods where they work. To the extent they know the people, the less likely their encounters with them will result in the use of force. Furthermore, "Community Policing allows citizens to hold police officers immediately and personally accountable for their actions, unlike the traditional system, which inadvertently promotes anonymity on both sides of a law."[27]

Third, the police are the only agency in government authorized to use force to compel people to obey the law. They are the only persons who, in the course of carrying out their duties, have the legal authority to use deadly force against citizens. The police are the only institution that can use force to compel citizens to obey their orders. This is an awesome power and responsibility that has been delegated to the police - one that has the potential of abuse, and must be controlled by a variety of means.

Fourth, the United States Supreme Court, the nation's highest tribunal, has addressed the issue of police use of deadly force. One of the primary reasons this issue was brought before the Court was the disproportionate number of minorities shot by the police. Because of that disparity and the fact that state law gave the police broad discretion over the use of deadly force, the Court in Tennessee v. Garner ruled that deadly force could only be used by the police in cases when their lives or the lives of others were in danger.[28]

The Court ruled that the use of deadly force was subject to protections of the Fourth Amendment. The ruling struck down the broad use of the "fleeing felon" doctrine that was prevalent in most states. The Court's majority wrote:

> Apprehension by the use of deadly force is a seizure subject to the Fourth Amendment's reasonableness requirement. To determine whether such a seizure is reasonable, the extent of the intrusion on the subject's rights under that amendment must be balanced against governmental interests in effective law enforcement. This balancing process demonstrates that, notwithstanding probable cause to seize a suspect, an officer may not always do so by killing him. The use of deadly force to prevent the escape of felony suspects, whatever the circumstances, is constitutionally unreasonable.[29]

Fifth, the police have great discretion in carrying out their responsibilities. This discretion includes the use of deadly force. This broad police discretion is given to every officer whether they are professionally trained or not.

Finally, police leaders have the responsibility for developing guidelines to assist officers in carrying out their responsibilities, including the exercise of their discretion. Historically, the decision to use deadly force was an individual one, usually made under conditions that were perceived as threatening to an officer. The point is important when we consider developing policies to guide the use of deadly force. The guidelines should not hamper police in the performance of their duties.

As police administrators develop standards to control the use of discretion by their officers, particularly the use of deadly force, they should do so based upon philosophies and principles that are consistent with our form of government. In fact, "police administrators have the legal and moral obligation to ensure that officers understand and adhere to their policies concerning the use of deadly force. This understanding is vital to the continuing growth and development of our society, where each individual is guaranteed life, liberty and the pursuit of happiness."[30]

Robert Lamb, who worked for the Atlantic City, New Jersey Police Department, and who served as a Regional Director of Community Relations Services (CRS) for the U.S. Department of Justice, is credited with undertaking a personal and selfless crusade that elevated the issue of police use of deadly force to the level of national debate, and ultimately to the United States Supreme Court. Lamb's efforts started in the early 1970s when he worked while a Federal official with the Sheriff of Multnomah County, Oregon to develop a firearms use policy which later became a model for other law enforcement agencies throughout the nation.

The essence of that policy was that sheriff deputies could only use deadly force in defense of life. Lamb then persuaded the National Organization of Black Law Enforcement Executives (NOBLE) to pursue the issue. NOBLE made the issue its top priority because a disproportionate number of Americans shot by police were Black. [31]

As a result of Lamb's effort, NOBLE adopted and promoted a "defense of life" policy. By working through the CRS and with other Police Chiefs, the issue was examined as part of the national discourse during the late 1970s. Ultimately, in 1985, the Supreme Court set a national standard on the deadly force matter in the case of Tennessee v. Garner.

The majority opinion declared unconstitutional those state laws that allowed police officers to use deadly force to apprehend non-violent suspects who were unarmed.

Prior to the *Tennessee v. Garner* case, the prevailing standard used by police departments in America was the "fleeing felon" standard. That standard gave police officers the right, by law and departmental policy, to shoot at a suspect who was believed to have committed a felony, and who was going to escape. [32]

The use of deadly force policies, similar to other police policies, should be predicated upon principles and values for good policing. To begin with, the police must realize that every time they use their weapons there is a potential that they will take someone's life. Thus, any policy developed to control the use of deadly force must be based on the premise that human life is sacred, and is our most precious resource.

Also, any police firearms policy must recognize that the use of lethal force "…must not only be legally authorized, but it also must be socially and morally warranted in keeping with the ideal of rational and humane social control in a democratic society." [33]

In effect, policies developed to control the use of deadly force must be structured to ensure the safety of both the police and the public. Such policies must not be complicated, must be easily understood by all police officers, must be easy to enforce and must hold officers who use deadly force accountable for their decisions.

Police use of deadly force is not just an issue for local law enforcement agencies. It is also a matter of grave concern to state and Federal law enforcement agencies. For example, on October 18, 1995, the United States

Department of Justice (DOJ) issued a new deadly force policy for all DOJ law enforcement agencies.

The policy was developed as a result of a 1992 incident at Ruby Ridge, Idaho when FBI agents ended a day-long standoff with a white separatist named Randy Weaver. The incident resulted in the death of Weaver's wife and son, both killed by FBI agents. The new policy stated:

> Law enforcement officers of the Department of Justice may use deadly force only when necessary, that is, when the officers have a reasonable belief that the subject of such force poses an imminent danger of death or serious physical injury to the officers or to another person. [34]

POLICY MAKES THE DIFFERENCE

Research has shown that policies restricting the use of deadly force can reduce the number of police shootings. Uleman, in his research on police agencies in Los Angeles County, found that fewer shootings occurred when deadly force policies were strictly enforced.[35] Fyfe reached the same conclusion in his research of shootings in the York City Police Department.[36] Sherman, in his studies of Atlanta, Georgia and Kansas City, Missouri reached similar conclusions. [37]

Unfortunately, research has also shown that accurate information on the use of deadly force is limited because "... law enforcement agencies themselves do not universally and systematically collect information about the use of various types of force."[38] This problem could be corrected by the creation of a National Deadly Force Reporting System.[39] Such a system would serve as a central repository of all deaths that are caused by police action. [40]

ATLANTA CASE STUDY

The Atlanta, Georgia experience is a good example of how one city reduced its number of police shootings by changing policies and enforcement practices.

Atlanta, similar to many other cities, did not keep deadly force records prior to the 1970s. In 1971 there were 12 citizens killed by the Atlanta police; eight in 1972, 17 in 1973, 12 in 1974, seven in 1975, five in 1976, and six in 1977. [41]

Maynard H. Jackson was elected Mayor in 1974. He immediately set out to reduce the number of shootings by Atlanta police officers by changing the city's firearms policy.

Prior to 1974, there were only three regulations which governed the police use of force and firearms. One stated that a detailed report must be written whenever an officer discharged his revolver or firearm in the line of duty. The second required a detailed report whenever a prisoner required medical attention when deadly force was used. The third rule prohibited officers from carrying an automatic weapon, or any handgun other than regulation revolvers, while on duty. There were no other regulations governing the use of deadly force. [42]

Mayor Jackson believed that elected officials were responsible for controlling the use of deadly force by police. He said:

> The speed of the boss is the speed of the crew. Get a mayor who allows police brutality and police abuse happens. Get a mayor who presumes that the police officer has done no wrong, and can do no wrong, or get a mayor who is afraid to say that a police officer may have done wrong; or get a mayor who does not set up a system to find out whether a police officer has done wrong. Then, you're going to have police abuse.
>
> Citizens manifest their roles through elected officials. If there is police brutality, it means that the mayor and the city council members are not cutting it; they're not taking care of business. They ought to be un-elected. It is as simple as that. [43]

Mayor Jackson ensured that his philosophy was carried out through police policies that were based on the principle that police use of deadly force must be reflective of society's sacred value of human life. Mayor Jackson's action is an example of how one engaged person can make a difference.

In summary, the issue of police use of deadly force is of paramount concern to the nation, and of greater concern to minority communities. It must also be of great concern to police leadership. Police leaders have a moral and professional obligation to develop policies that provide officers with guidance as they exercise their awesome authority.

All police agencies should adopt a firearms use policy that is designed to guarantee the safety of police officers and the public. Such a policy should state, in no uncertain terms, that no officer shall discharge a firearm except to defend his life or the life of another person. The shooting should take place only after all other means of arrest have been explored and exhausted. The policy should leave no room for questioning, there should be no need for interpretation and it should be followed without difficulty.

In addition to being easily understood, it must be enforceable and hold officers accountable. Because the use of deadly force is a complex issue, no single approach is sufficient for addressing the issue. Rather, there must be a multi-faceted approach. The elements of an effective police firearms control policy should include at least the following:

- Community input:

Political leadership and community members should be allowed to have input into the development of the deadly force policy.

- Values:

Police use of deadly force policy should be based on police values. The most important value is that human life is sacred.

- Unambiguous:

Police use of deadly force policies should be clear on when it is appropriate to use deadly force.

- Culture:

Police leaders should develop a culture in which police officers view community residents as "their people". They must view themselves as protectors.

- Retreat and conceal:

Police officers should be taught that it is proper procedure to retreat and even take cover behind barriers, a standard technique used by the highly trained police Special Weapons and Tactics (SWAT) teams.

- Warning shots.

Officers should not be allowed to discharge warning shots.

- Fleeing vehicles.

Officers should not be allowed to shoot at vehicles that are fleeing.

- **Moving vehicles.**

Officers should not be allowed to shoot from moving vehicles.

- **Training.**

Officers should be trained on how and when to use their firearms. Training should also be designed to acquaint the officers with the legal and moral issues concerning their use of firearms.

- **Non-lethal alternatives.**

The law enforcement enterprise should develop non-lethal techniques as alternatives to the use of deadly force.

- **Review.**

Every discharge of firearms by officers should be reviewed and a final report should be prepared.

- **Educate.**

The police should educate the community on the use of deadly force issues. Allowing community leaders and the media to experience the "shoot-no-shoot" program helps them to understand decisions that police make on a regular basis.

POLICE AND POLITICS

The term politics has a different meaning for the police than it does for elected officials. For elected officials it means campaigning to get elected to office and then performing the duties of the office.

It also means getting votes from their colleagues in order to promote their legislative agendas. It means handling constituent complaints. In effect, it is the art of compromise. Often politicians make decisions based on what is politically expedient rather than what is in the best interests of the community.

The police, on the other hand, try to avoid politics. They view politics negatively. They are still influenced in their thinking by the reform era of policing, which sought to remove politics from police work. Police are oriented, especially under Community Policing, to do what is in the best interests of the community.

It is important for the police to avoid partisan politics. It is the responsibility of police leaders to protect the police department from political interference. Political interference means allowing politicians to be involved in the: (1) hiring, (2) assigning, (3) promoting, or (4) disciplining of police officers. This must be done with the understanding that police departments are not entities unto themselves. In the hierarchy of city government, the police department is subordinate to a civilian authority, mayor or city manager. It is important for police leadership to always be cognizant of the fact that they are part of city government, while at the same time protecting the operational integrity of the police department.

The average tenure of Police Chiefs in America is approximately two years. This is due to politics. Mayors often run on campaigns of "fighting crime" and that often translates into promises to appoint a new Police Chief. Also, many Chiefs are appointed when they are close to retirement, a fact that explains the brief tenures. In addition to the Chief's immediate supervisor (mayor or city manager) there is also a body of elected officials that are responsible for setting policy and approving the police department's budget. The police department's relationship with the city council is a very important and delicate issue.

Ultimately it is the Police Chiefs' responsibility to protect the department from improper political interference. Adhering to the principal of chain of command can accomplish that. Just as members of the police department are not required to report to more than one person, neither should a Chief.

Police Chiefs should report to the appointing authority of the city and not take orders from others. The relationships should be made clear when the Chief is appointed. The CEO of the city has a responsibility to keep politics out of the police department.

CHIEF AND MAYORAL RELATIONS

A mayor or city manager serves as the chief executive officer of a city. As chief executive officer, they are responsible for managing the executive branch of city government that includes the police department.

Police departments cannot be successful without the support of the chief executive officer. To ensure that support, the Police Chief should establish guidelines for the working relationships between the department and the mayor, or city manager. The most important element of that relationship is an open line of communication.

The Chief should request regularly scheduled meetings with the mayor or city manager. The day and time for those meetings should be established at their initial meeting. Ideally, the Chief should meet weekly with the city's chief executive. That weekly meeting should be in addition to the Chief's regular meetings as a member of the chief executive officer's cabinet.

Some cities with strong mayoral forms of government will also have a chief administrative officer (CAO) who is responsible for handling the day-to-day administrative duties on behalf of the mayor. Because of the nature and sensitivity of police work, the Police Chief should still report to and work directly under the mayor even if there is a CAO.

In addition to establishing a regular meeting time, there are other basic issues that should be agreed to by the Police Chief and the mayor/city manager. First, they should determine what events the mayor/city manager should be routinely notified about. For example, does the mayor/city manager want to be notified about every officer involved shooting, major arrests, officer injured or killed, and other major incidents?

Furthermore, the Chief should determine the times that the mayor/city manager wishes to receive a telephone call regarding police matters. As a matter of practice, the Chief should not routinely call the mayor in the middle of the night unless it is a very unusual occurrence. Rather, events that occur then should be relayed to the mayor early the next morning by email or telephone. One exception is when an officer is shot, or seriously injured.

Also, as a matter of practice, the mayor/city manager should be briefed on any matter that is possibly newsworthy, enough to demand a mayoral response. To the extent possible, the Chief should see that the mayor is not caught by surprise on matters related to the police department.

Second, there should be an exchange of telephone numbers: private, car, cell and home between the mayor/city manager and the Police Chief. Since the Chief should be available to the mayor at all times, procedures should be established so the mayor/city manager can contact him at anytime.

Third, the Chief should determine how the mayor/city manager wishes to deal with the media. Some chief executive officers choose to be actively involved in most police department press conferences, whether the news is good or bad. Others only want to be involved in press coverage involving the police if the news is favorable. They prefer that the Police Chief handle all negative news.

Ideally, the Chief, and not the chief executive officer, should be the spokesperson for the police department. The Chief should, however, offer the mayor/city manager the option of participating in public announcements of all major new programs or positive events involving the police department. The Chief should be prepared to handle all negative media coverage without the presence of the chief executive officer, but the mayor/city manager should be given the choice of whether or not they want to be present.

Fourth, in clarifying working relationships, the Police Chief should determine how to handle those situations in which he disagrees with the mayor/city manager. The Chief should have the prerogative of being able to argue his position with the chief executive officer.

Once a decision is made, however, it is the Chief's obligation to support the mayor/city manager's position. This is no different than what occurs within police departments. Most Police Chiefs allow their subordinates to argue their positions. However, once a decision is made, the Chief expects total compliance and support.

The concept is applicable to the Police Chief's relationship with the mayor/city manager. The chain of command does not stop at police headquarters; rather it extends to City Hall. For that reason, Police Chiefs should not publicly disagree with mayors/city managers. If a professional or personal decision is made that the Chief cannot live with as a matter of principle, he is obligated to resign.

It is important to remember that the mayor, not the Police Chief, was elected to make final decisions regarding the total administration of the city, including the police department. Similarly, a city manager is hired for the same reason. This does not apply to operational matters because the Chief is best qualified to make those decisions, but it does apply to police policy.

Finally, the Chief should determine how the mayor/city manager wants the police department to interact with members of the city council and other elected officials. This is extremely important because the mayor/city manager is ultimately responsible for managing the politics of the city. The Chief, on the other hand, is responsible for protecting the operational integrity of the police department, not allowing political interference.

In summary, the following is a checklist of what the Police Chief should accomplish regarding the police department's relationship with the mayor/city manager:

- Agreement on the goals and objectives of the police department.
- Establish a regular day and time to meet.
- Determine what matters, and when, the mayor/city manager wishes to be notified and briefed on.
- Exchange phone numbers; home, office, cell, car and private.

- Establish ground rules for debating the issues with the mayor/city manager.
- Determine how to deal with the media on police related matters.
- Establish ground rules for dealing with members of the city council.
- Establish ground rules for dealing with other elected officials.

POLICE AND CITY COUNCIL RELATIONS

Members of the city council are also critical to the success of police departments. For that reason, Police Chiefs should meet with each council member individually. The purpose of those meetings should be to get acquainted, establish relationships, and to determine mutual interests. It is important to remember that council members are part of the team elected to set policy for the city, including the police department. Therefore it is important for the Police Chief to know their priorities.

The Police Chief must understand the role of the city council, its responsibilities, powers and authority. Chiefs who do not understand the system often get into trouble.

In dealing with the city council, the Chief must remember that it is the ultimate policy making body for the city. The Chief is appointed to carry out the policies they promulgate. The city council represents, theoretically, the will of the people and it is important for the Chief to have their support. In order to do so, there are a number of things Police Chiefs should do.

- <u>Get acquainted</u>

Get to know council members personally. Find out what is important to them regarding the police department. Learn about their philosophies. Be proactive and ask them for advice. It is the responsibility of the Police Chief, with the mayor's approval, to reach out to council members. They should not wait for council members to take the first step.

- <u>Educate</u>

It is the Police Chief's responsibility to educate members of the city council on police matters. The Chief should not expect council members to know much about police work. That is the responsibility of the Police Chief. Therefore, as the Chief briefs council members on policing issues, they should assume that members do not know much about police matters. Be basic. Understand that they have other civic issues to deal with.

- Respect

The Police Chief should remember that council members are elected to represent the will of the people. Chiefs should never embarrass an elected official, even if the Chief is publically embarrassed by a council member. It must always be remembered that they are elected officials who have to run for re-election. Most importantly, they have the power to assist or harm the police department.

- Be responsive

All members of the police department should be responsive to elected officials, individually and collectively, without violating any professional principles. The Police Chief is responsible for protecting the operational integrity of the department.

Whenever a councilmember calls and asks the department to do something legal for a constituent, it should be done. Remember, they are elected officials and it helps if they are able to do things on behalf of their constituents. Chances are, if the constituent called the department and made the request, it would be granted. There is nothing wrong with assigning top priority to the calls of council members. In fact, it is good for the department and the city. It is not considered political interference.

- Keep the mayor/city manager informed

The mayor/city manager should be kept informed about the police department's relationship with members of council and other elected officials. When communicating with other elected officials in writing, the mayor/city manager should be copied. It is important not allow the police department or its members to become "political footballs".

The police do not operate in a vacuum. They are a social and political institution. They are political because they are a part of a subdivision of government and accountable to elected officials. Police departments should not be involved in partisan politics. Although police officers have the right to exercise their constitutional right to vote and support the candidates of their choice, they must do so as private individuals and not as police officers.

POLICE AND THE MEDIA

We are now living in what social analysts refer to as the information society. An important characteristic of the information society is the rapidity of information transmission. An event can occur in one part of the world and be televised in other parts instantaneously.

The information society also has had a profound impact on law enforcement. Today, most Americans learn about police departments from secondary sources, mainly the news media. Therefore, police departments are not necessarily what they think they are. They are actually what the media depicts them to be. How the media presents the police determines, to a large degree, is how the public perceives the police.

Most members of the general public do not have the opportunity to obtain firsthand information about police activities. In fact, most police officers do not have the ability to obtain firsthand information about most events that occur in their own departments, if they are not personally involved in the events.

More so than ever, the media determines what citizens know about their police departments. In that respect, the media has a tremendous amount of power. They not only determine what is possibly newsworthy, they also determine the context in which the news is presented to the public.

The power of the media is awesome. That power is derived from the Constitution, Article I, which states, "Congress shall make no law... abridging the freedom of the press." It is from that constitutional guarantee that the media derives its power, but it has little accountability.

Police officials have frequently criticized the media for being insensitive, and sometimes getting their facts incorrect. Nevertheless, freedom of the press represents a symbol that the police sometimes may not like, but is something that they, and almost all Americans, support. Although the police may periodically criticize the media, it would be naive to conceive of the idea that the press will simply go away. Freedom of the press is a principal that is embedded in both history and the Constitution.

The actions of the police sometimes generate negative media coverage. Each time the police are charged with engaging in activities that result in allegations of criminal conduct or violations of a citizen's civil rights, they rightfully receive unfavorable media coverage. Under those circumstances, the police are hesitant to openly discuss the incidents. The media, in turn, accuses the police of being deceitful, secretive and uncooperative.

There is a long history of antagonism between the police and the media. As a result, an "us" versus "them" relationship has developed. Under Community Policing, police leaders understand the need for public support. That support, to a large degree, is determined by the image that the public has of the police. The media, more than any other institution, shapes the image of the police.

Many police agencies have undertaken practical steps to develop better relationships between the police and the media. Enlightened police leaders recognize that the media plays an important role in determining how the public views the police.

Since Community Policing relies on the public to participate in the crime control and problem solving processes, it behooves police leaders to cultivate positive relationships with the media. In doing so, they are more likely to receive fair, accurate and balanced coverage. The following are things police leaders can do to cultivate positive police/media relations:

CREATE POLICE/MEDIA ADVISORY COMMITTEES

Police Chiefs should create media advisory committees that meet on a regular basis to discuss and resolve any problems that might occur between their departments and the media. The media should be allowed to select their representatives who serve on the committee. The committee should meet on a regular basis and quickly resolve problems that emerge that threaten to harm the relationship between the two groups.

MEET ON A REGULAR BASIS WITH EDITORIAL BOARDS

Newspapers have editorial boards comprised of senior managers. They are the group, not unlike police departments' command staff, which sets policy and direction for the paper. Regular meetings with editorial boards benefit police leaders in two important ways. One, they provide an opportunity to educate members of the editorial boards on issues of importance to the police department. Absent such information, members of the editorial boards must rely on their reporter's account of the facts, just as their readers do. Second, such meetings often result in favorable news articles and/or editorials. Similar meetings should also be held with other media outlets such as radio and television stations.

MAINTAIN PERSONAL CONTACT WITH THE MINORITY MEDIA

Often the minority media does not have the resources to cover the police. Often they are not able to send reporters to press conferences. Holding regular meetings with minority media provides an opportunity to answer questions, educate and correct misconceptions about the police.

MAINTAIN PERSONAL CONTACT WITH NEIGHBORHOOD NEWSPAPERS

Many cities have community newspapers that cover items of interest to specific neighborhoods. Similar to the minority press, these newspapers do not have the resources to cover the police as do major media outlets.

Quite often, they must rely on press releases for their stories. Ensuring that they receive press releases and other appropriate correspondence from the police department assists them in publishing accurate stories about the police. It also allows the department to receive coverage in areas that otherwise might have been neglected by the major media.

MEET REGULARLY WITH THE POLICE PRESS CORPS

Large media outlets assign reporters to cover the police beat. Police leaders should establish and maintain ongoing personal relationships with the police press corps. Holding regular press briefings with them can accomplish the goal.

Police leaders should not make the mistake of only meeting with major media outlets. Every news outlet is important. It is important to understand that reporters are required to write articles, and police can provide them information for those articles.

LEARN HOW THE NEWS MEDIA OPERATES

The news media is a business that has an organizational structure. Within that structure is a division of labor. For example, reporters have a specific job to do, write stories.

Police leaders should understand what the police department should do to assist reporters in carrying out their responsibilities. They should know what information reporters are looking for, and their deadline schedule. They should understand that there are different deadlines for print media, radio and television. They should understand the roles played by copy editors, assignment editors, rewrite editors, headline editors and editorial page editors.

Just as the police ask that the news media understand them, the police must also understand the inner operations of the news media.

CULTIVATE TRUST WITH THE NEWS MEDIA

A cardinal rule in dealing with the news media is not to lie to them or intentionally mislead them. Doing so will destroy any possibility of establishing future trust. There is nothing wrong with saying "I do not know." Better yet, if you do not have the answer to a question, consider saying something such as, "I consider this issue far too important to make an instant analysis. I will get briefed, and get back to you as soon as possible."

BE PREPARED BEFORE MEETING WITH THE MEDIA

Always be prepared when meeting with the media. Remember, reporters are seeking information that they can use to write stories. They are dependent on you to provide them with foundational information.

Take advantage of the opportunity to educate reporters any time it presents itself. Get briefed before hand, and also brainstorm with your staff prior to meeting with the press. Anticipate questions that reporters might have, and the appropriate responses. This will assist in assuring that you are not surprised by questions.

BE PROACTIVE AND MARKET THE DEPARTMENT

Police leaders must be practical and, similar to the private sector, market their departments. Remember, it is not sufficient to just do a good job. The public must constantly be reminded of the good job you are doing.

THINK TELEVISION

Increasingly, the public relies on television as a main source of news. If you prepare your press presentations for television, you will also meet the needs of print and radio media.

USE PRESS KITS

A press kit provides the media with background material that can be used to prepare stories. Press kits are beneficial because you cannot rely on reporters having the necessary information for their stories.

A press kit provides reporters with thorough information. It is essential that information provided in the kits be accurate, answering questions such as who, what, when, how and how much. Because you are preparing for television, include charts, photos or other visual materials. It is important for television to be able to show something other than "talking heads." The private sector has successfully used press kits in dealing with the media.

DO NOT BE PRESSED INTO SAYING WHAT YOU DO NOT KNOW

Police leaders frequently get into trouble by responding to questions too quickly. For example, if an officer is involved in a shooting there is always a request for an immediate response from the department. Many police leaders, trying to be supportive of their officers, will tell the press that, "the shooting appears to be within the guidelines of the department" prior to an investigation.

It would be more appropriate to say, "This matter is currently under investigation and I will give you a response once I receive additional information." By the same token, when it is determined that an officer has done something wrong, do not hesitate to say so. Honesty and transparency in policing is always the best policy.

Police and media relations have historically been tense. Yet, each has the same constituents - the public. It is important that the police and the media work together to develop a positive approach to service. There are many examples of how working together can produce positive results. The ultimate goal must be increased professionalism by all parties.

Recognizing that there has been a long history of distrust between the two groups, the police must no longer consider themselves solely responsible for controlling crime, because the public also has responsibility. Police should no longer work in isolation and must be transparent in all of their operations. They need the support of the public in order to achieve their objectives. How the public relates to them will largely determine the support they receive.

Police departments with good reputations are more likely to receive cooperation and support from citizens. The reputation of the police is determined mainly by how they are treated by the media. The police should recognize that the media can be of great assistance to them in the areas of educating the public about crime and crime prevention. Programs such as Crime Stoppers have proven to be of great benefit to those cities that have implemented them.

The police should not view the media as adversaries. Rather, they should have a policy of transparency, one that allows the media access to all information, consistent with the law, departmental integrity, personnel concerns and the investigative process.

Just as the police have the responsibility of being open and transparent, the media has a responsibility to be objective and truthful in their reporting. They are obligated to be balanced in their reporting and recognize that they also have a responsibility to the community. Criticism of the police, when warranted, is part of that responsibility. But, they also have a responsibility to the public to get the facts right, be objective in their reporting and be critical when necessary.

The ultimate goal must be increased professionalism by the police and the media. For too long there has been animosity between them that has resulted in a disservice to the public. The police and the media must work together to establish and maintain a positive relationship, one conducive to serving the public positively.

SUMMARY

Much of the literature on police accountability focuses on the accountability of individual police officers.[44] Although of extreme importance, it does not go far enough under the philosophy of Community Policing. Indeed, it is important that individual officers be held accountable for their actions.

Under Community Policing, however, the concept of police accountability must expand to include all segments of the community, including elected officials. Indeed, it includes the accountability of the Police Chief and other managers of the police department.

In essence, police accountability under Community Policing includes all elements of a police department's operations that have any influence on how it relates to, and interacts with all segments of the community. Thus, an important function of police leadership under Community Policing is to ensure that there are mechanisms in place that support a culture of accountability.

This enhanced culture must focus on accountability to the community, accountability to elected officials, accountability to the media, and vitally important inter*nal* systems to ensure that every member of the police department understands that they derive their power from those they serve.

In order to achieve success in carrying out their responsibilities to the community, they must earn the respect and support of all the people who live and do business where they work and serve.

NOTES: CHAPTER TWELVE

1. Kelling, George L. and Mark H. Moore, "The Evolving Strategy of Policing," Perspectives on Policing, Washington, D.C.: United States Department of Justice, National Institute of Justice and the Program in Criminal Justice Policy and Management, John F. Kennedy School of Government, Cambridge, Mass.: Harvard University, November 1988, No. 4

2. Ibid.

3. For a review of the Rodney King incident, see "The L.A. Riots: 15 years After Rodney King," Time Magazine, April 27, 2007

4. Christopher, Warren, "Report of the Independent Commission of the Los Angeles Police Department," Los Angeles, California, July 1991

5. For examples of such plans, see Brown, Lee P., Crime Control Plan: A Citizen/Police Partnership, New York City Police Department, 1991 or the series of Police Strategies developed by Raymond Kelley and William Bratton while serving as Commissioners of the New York City Police Department

6. Texas is a state where police civil service rules are established by the state legislature, and administered by local police departments.

7. Bexelius, Alfred, "The Origin, Nature, and Functions of the Civil and Military Ombudsman in Sweden," The Annals of the American Academy of Political and Social Science, Vol. 377, May 1968, p.11

8. Ibid. 13

9. Ibid.

10. Ibid. p.17

11. Anderson, Staley V., "The Ombudsman: Public Defender Against Maladministration," Public Affairs Report, Bulletin of the Institute of Government Studies, Berkeley: University of California, Vol. 6, April 1965, No. 2, p.1

12. "Berkeley Petition for Community Control of the Police: Summary of Berkeley Police Control Amendment," Black Panther Party and Peace and Freedom Movement, unpublished petition, Berkeley, 1970. Also see, Waskow, Arthur I., Community Control of the Police: Report of a conference co-sponsored by the Institute for Police Studies and the Center for the Study of Law and Society, University of California, unpublished, no date

13. In 1966, Leonard Deadwyler, an African American, was driving his pregnant wife to the hospital when he was stopped and shot to death by a Los Angeles police officer. The jury ruled the death an accidental

homicide. This was the first trial of its type in California history that was televised.

14. Kessler, David A., "The Effects of Community Policing on Complaints against Officers," Washington, D.C.: Justice Research and Statistics Association, unpublished and undated article.

15. Ibid. p. 37

16. Ibid. p. 33

17. Covey, Stephen R., <u>Principle Centered Leadership</u>, New York: Free Press, 1992.

18. United States Declaration of Independence

19. Ibid.

20. Op Cit. Note 18

21. Webber, Alan M., "Four Hours on the West Side: Listening to the Rank and File", Cambridge, Mass: <u>Harvard Business Review</u>, May/June, 1991, pp. 114-115

22. Radelet, Louis A. "<u>The Police and the Community</u>", New York: Macmillan Company, 1973, p.110

23. Lehman, Jeffrey, Sherelle Phelps and Thompson Gale (EDS), "Deadly Force", West's Encyclopedia of Law. 2nd Ed. 2005 eNotes.com. 2006. 7 Jan., 2006 http://Law.enotes.com/wests-law-encycopedia/deadly-force

24. Bittner, Egon, <u>The Functions of Police in Modern Society</u>, Washington, D.C.: United States Government Printing Office, 1971

25. <u>Police Use of Force: Addressing Community Racial Tensions.</u> Washington, D.C.: United States Department of Justice, Community Relations Service, p. 2 http: www.usdoj.gov/crs/pubs/pubbullpoliceuseofforcedraftrevision7202.htm

26. For a good review of the Constitutional issues concerning police use of deadly force see Sherman, Lawrence W., "Execution Without Trail: Police Homicide and the Constitution," <u>Vanderbilt Law Review</u>, Vol. 33, No. 1, January 1980, pp. 71-100

27. Trojanowicz, Robert, "Community Policing Curbs Police Brutality," <u>Footprints: The Community Policing Newsletter</u>, The National Center for Community Policing, East Lansing, Michigan: Michigan State University, Vol. III, No. 1&2, Spring/Summer, (Double Issue), 1991, p. 3

28. Tennessee v. Garner, 471 U.S. 1, 1985

29. Ibid.

30. Brown, Lee P., Remarks made at a seminar on police Use of

Excessive and Deadly Force, National Organization of Black Law Enforcement Executives, St. Louis, Missouri, June 22 , 1978

31. See Goldkamp, John S., "Minorities as Victims of Police Shootings: Interpretations of Racial Disproportionality and Police use of Deadly Force," <u>Readings on Police Use of Deadly Force</u>, James J. Fyfe, (Ed.), Washington, D.C.: Police Foundation, 1982, pp.128-151

32. Op. Cit., Note 27

33. Op. Cit., Note 30

34. Hall, John C., <u>FBI Training on the New Federal Deadly Force Policy</u>, April, 1996, http//www.fbi/publications/leb/1996/april1996.xxx

35. Uelman, Gerald F., "Varieties of Public Policy: A Study of Policy Regarding the Use of Deadly Force in Los Angeles County," <u>University of Loyola at Los Angeles Law Review</u> 6: 1973, pp.1-65

36. Fyfe, James, <u>Shots Fired: Examination of New York City Police Department Firearms Discharge</u>, unpublished dissertation, Albany State of New York: 1978

37. Sherman, Lawrence W., " Reducing Police Gun Use: Critical Events, Administrative Policy and Organizational Change," Maurice Punch, (ED), <u>The Management and Control of Police Organizations</u>, Cambridge, Mass.: MIT Press, pp. 98-125

38. Pate, Anthony M. and Lorie A., Fridwell, <u>Police Use of Force: Official Reports, Citizen Complaints and Legal Consequences</u>, Washington, D.C.: Police Foundation, 1993, p.63

39. Geller, William A. and Michael S. Scott, <u>Deadly Force, What We Know - A Practitioner's Desk Reference on Police-Involved Shootings</u>, Washington, D.C.: Police Executive Research Forum, 1992, P. 44

40. Ibid.

41. Brown, Lee P.,<u> Police Use of Deadly Force: What Police and Community Can Do About It:</u> A Workshop Conducted by the Community Relations Services at the 1978 Annual Conference of the National Association of Human Rights Workers, United States Department Justice, Community Relations Services, United States Department of Justice, Washington, D.C.: United States Government Printing Office, Nashville, Tennessee, October 1978, pp.20-27

42. Ibid.

43. National Minority Advisor Council on Criminal Justice, <u>The Inequality of Justice: A Report on Crime and the Administration of Justice in the Minority Community</u>, U.S. Department Justice, Law Enforcement Assistance and Administration, unpublished, 1982, p.244

44. Kelling, George L. Robert Wasserman and Hubert Williams, "Police Accountability," <u>Perspectives on Policing</u>, Washington, D.C.: U.S. Department of Justice, and The Program in Criminal Justice Policy and Management, John F. Kennedy School of Government, Cambridge, Mass.: Harvard University, November 1998, No. 7. Also see United States Commission on Civil Rights, <u>Who is Guarding the Guardians?: A Report on Police Practices</u>, Washington, D.C.: and The Program in Criminal Justice Policy and Management, John F. Kennedy School of Government, Cambridge, Mass.: Harvard University, November 1998, No.7

Chapter Thirteen:

CRIME AND CRIME CONTROL

INTRODUCTION

Long before the emergence of modern society, crime plagued people of the world. The first American settlers faced crime, as did their family members who remained behind in the Old World.

As long as human beings have lived on this planet, there has been murder, rape, assault and theft. Only the volume and types of crimes committed, and the degree with which the public views crimes as a threat to its well-being, have changed over the years.

> There is much crime in America, more than is ever reported, far more than is ever solved, too much for the health of the nation.
> —President's Commission on Law Enforcement and Administration

Now crime is one of the major problems confronting large cities and small towns throughout the country. Crime results in fear, despair and hardship. It is a serious societal problem.

Crime diminishes the quality of life in communities. Its impact varies from one community to another, but all Americans pay the price of crime in one form or another. Many Americans live impelled by the prospect that they will become victims of a criminal act. As a result, many have drastically changed how they live.

The crime problem in America is not limited to what is generally referred to as street crime. Americans are also concerned about corporate crime, political corruption, white-collar crime and organized crime, even while they generate less fear of personal harm.

The consequences of crime can be seen in society's expenditures for its control. Tax dollars invested in the police, prosecutors, courts and corrections represent major government expenditures on all levels. Billions of dollars are spent each year in the effort to control the crime problem.

It has been the subject of academic studies, legislative actions and national inquiries. Today many colleges and universities offer courses in criminology or criminal justice.

In 1994 the United States Congress passed President Clinton's Comprehensive Crime Control bill.[1] The most recent comprehensive inquiry into crime as a national problem occurred in 1967 when the *President's Commission on Law Enforcement and Administration of Justice* recommended far reaching reform of the criminal justice system. [2]

Any discussion of crime should begin with the recognition that crime is a complex subject. For that reason, there are no simplistic solutions. However, Community Policing holds the greatest promise for addressing crime in America. Yet, despite all the promises, neither the police nor the criminal justice system can accomplish the job alone. Many of America's social issues must also be addressed if America is to effectively control its crime problem.

There must be an understanding of crime before any effective solutions can be developed. This was recognized by Fyoder Dostoeveski, the Russian writer, who wrote in his novel, The House of the Dead, "With readymade opinions one cannot judge of crime. Its philosophy is a little more complicated than people think." The writer's warming is alarming and should give pause to anyone who gives any thought to the issue of crime.[3]

The police have historically viewed crime in a strictly legal context. Crime is viewed in context of the penal code and its definition of illegal acts. Seldom have the police approached the crime problem from a sociological, economic, cultural or psychological context.

Because of their narrow understanding of crime, the police have historically viewed their role in crime control from the perspective of enforcement. Such a narrow viewpoint has hampered the police in their efforts to effectively deal with the problem.

Both the police and the community must understand that there are limitations on what the police alone can do to reduce crime. Their functions must be placed in their proper perspectives.

For example, the police do not have the means to prevent the majority of crimes committed because they occur when an individual or groups seizes upon an opportunity to do wrong in the absence of an officer.

In fact, the police will never have the ability to address all crimes of opportunity that occur, for instance, when the driver of a car leaves the door of a parked vehicle unlocked.

Community Policing instructs police to view crime within a much broader context. To do otherwise only perpetuates the historical manner in which the police have handled crime, and the results will be equally limited. Because the police do not control the factors that produce crime, they should not be held exclusively accountable to resolve it.

Crime and the police are not unlike doctors and sickness. Neither the medical professionals nor the general public hold doctors accountable when a patient gets sick. They do, however, expect the doctor to take the necessary steps to treat the illness, and prescribe a course of action that will prevent it from spreading or returning.

The police should be treated the same way that doctors are perceived. They should not be blamed for the crime problem, but should be expected to develop and implement initiatives to apprehend offenders, and develop programs that deter or prevent crime.

The basic premise that must be understood when examining the crime problem is that it is not just a police problem. Indeed, the police are limited in what they can do to maintain public safety without the involvement of citizens. This is true even though society places the primary responsibility for controlling crime on the backs of the police.

The police can address this dilemma by understanding, and educating the general public that crime is caused by a variety of societal problems that they do not control. For that reason, the entire community must assume responsibility for addressing crime. Effective crime control calls for a cooperative relationship between the police and the community. Such a relationship is at the very heart of *Community Policing*.

To properly carry out their role, the police must develop a philosophical context in which they undertake their role of crime control. Community Policing provides that philosophical context.

As the principal agency responsible for protecting the public, it behooves the police to develop an understanding of the complexity of crime. This chapter will provide the reader with an exploration of that issue.

UNDERSTANDING CRIME

In order to effectively control crime, it is necessary to understand its causes. Historically, America has dealt with the crime problem through the criminal justice system with little regard for the underlying factors that contribute to criminal behavior. Such an approach has limited results.

Increasingly, it is being recognized that the crime problem in America stems from the failure of many of society's social institutions. "Crime has its roots in many social ills which the criminal justice system is neither equipped nor designed to solve."[4] This point was clearly made by Currie when he wrote:

If we wanted to sketch a hypothetical portrait of an especially violent society, it would surely contain these elements: it would separate large numbers of people, especially the young, from the kind of work that could include them securely in community life. It would encourage policies of economic development and income distribution that sharply increased inequities between sectors of the population. It would rapidly shift vast amounts of capital from place to place without regard for the impact on local communities, causing massive movements of population away from family and neighborhood support in search of livelihood. It would avoid providing new mechanisms of care and support for those uprooted, perhaps in the name of preserving incentives to work and paring government spending. It would promote a culture of intense interpersonal competition and spur its citizens to a level of material consumption that many cannot lawfully sustain.[5]

The crime problem will not be resolved by a major breakthrough in policing. The crime problem will not be resolved by a major breakthrough in prosecution. The crime will not be resolved by a major breakthrough in the courts. The crime problem will not be resolved by a major breakthrough in corrections. Only by dealing thoroughly with the socio-economic problems that cause crime can the problem be effectively addressed.

In the United States, there are several serious social problems that contribute to the crime problem.

1. <u>Education</u>.
The vast majority of people in our jails and prisons were unable to complete their high school educations. In the United States, 40 to 50 percent of those who start school never graduate. Of those who

do graduate, up to 25 percent are functionally illiterate, unable to read or write.

The educational demands of the workplace have changed. Today, the majority of Americans do not make a living using their hands. Over 80 percent of Americans earn their living in a service industry that is often closely tied to advanced technology. In fact, America is experiencing what the social analysts call the information society, where knowledge is important. Yet, the educational system is not producing people with the knowledge necessary to participate in today's marketplace. As a result, all too many chose crime as a means of survival.

2. <u>Family</u>.
There is no institution more important than the family when child development is considered. Public policies that strengthen the family also serve to reduce the problems of crime in America. But today, America is witnessing a breakdown in the institution called family.

Over 50 percent of all marriages end in divorce, often leaving a female head of the household who lives in poverty. Experience has shown that a large percentage of children who live in such situations also end up getting into trouble with the law. Furthermore, each year thousands of teenagers become parents without the benefit of adequate income, parenting skills or other support needed for a family to function as a unit. Nor is there sufficient effort to prevent repeat pregnancies.

3. <u>Narcotics</u>.
The illegal use and sale of drugs has changed the landscape of crime in America. During the crack epidemic of the late 1980s and early 1990s, America witnessed the development of a culture of violence, unlike anything the country had ever experienced.

Coupled with the ready availability of guns on the streets of American cities, violence exploded in urban America unlike any other time in history. Although open market drug selling has substantially subsided, crimes of violence are still a product of the drug industry. In some segments of society, there exists a culture that tolerates violence in low-income minority communities, especially those with open drug markets.

4. <u>Underclass</u>.
An underclass has merged in America. This underclass consists of poor people, mainly people of color, who reside in parts of cities that are separated from economically viable neighborhoods. Poor housing, inadequate health care, failing schools, drugs, gangs, crime and violence characterize such neighborhoods. They consume a disproportionate share of police time, yet crime continues to soar.

5. <u>Policy Failure</u>.
At the end of 2008, America had over 1,610,446 persons incarcerated in its jails and prisons.[6] The incarceration of large numbers of people or the imposition of severe sentences does not serve to reduce the level of crime. The national crime rate reached its peak when the incarceration rate was increasing the quickest. Those who advocated stiffer sentences during the 1970s and early 1980s find it difficult to explain why the "get-tough" policy adopted by the system failed.

The more liberal penal policies practiced in the 1960s were not successful, and are not a viable alternative. Certainly, incarceration does have some impact on crime, but it has proven to be minor. Some argue that it is counterproductive to invest large amounts of public funds into prison construction and operation given the results we see.

6. <u>Employment.</u>
Unemployment and underemployment contribute to the crime problem. Research has consistently shown a direct link between unemployment and crime. "In a society where work is the indispensable key to most things material that our culture considers worth having, it's easy to see why unemployed people try other, less legitimate ways to achieve success.

And since work is also one of the most important ways for individuals to become integrated into a larger community, it is not surprising that those excluded from working will be held less tightly by the bonds that keep a society together."[7]

Furthermore, "the relationship between unemployment and crime is real; we won't be able even to begin an attack on crime that is both humane and effective if we do not confront them." [8]

7. <u>Community Dysfunction.</u>
There are societies that have a higher level of poverty than the United States and their unequal distribution of wealth exceeds that of the U. S., yet the level of crime remains low. India is such an example. In that country, there is a low rate of youth crime because young people are involved in a network of relationships that involve a variety of obligations among family, sub-cast groups and the community.

Unlike America, those relationships provide a fundamental sense of belonging to a supporting community where informal sanctions against crime are embraced. Such a sense of community is lacking in America.

To be effective in addressing the crime problem, America must stop relying exclusively on the criminal justice system. Rather, it must realize that education, jobs, family stability and other socio-economic issues must also be addressed. Equally important, the gap between those who are materially blessed, and those who suffer must be addressed. Poverty is a contributing factor to crime. For the most part, the criminal justice system is reactive, going into motion when a crime has been committed.

In order to see how the above described conditions contribute to the crime problem, one only has to compare America with other industrialized nations. Take, for example, Japan where there is a very low unemployment rate. This is attributed to the fact that the private sector provides a cushion for the callous marketplace.

Or consider the Scandinavian countries where government provides a safety net for its people. Also consider Canada and Germany, where more advanced educational systems and means of controlling the proliferation of guns allow governments to avoid the crime problem that envelops America. The following facts help place America's crime problem in its proper perspective:
- "In recent years, Americans have faced roughly seven to

ten times the risk of death by homicide as the residents of most European countries and Japan. Our closest European competitor in homicide rates is Finland, and Americans murder one another more than three times the rate than Fins." [9]

- "With similar frontier traditions, Australia and Canada have murder rates that are, respectively, less than a fourth and less than a third of ours."[10]

"But careful research reveals that Americans are more than three times as likely to be raped than West Germans, and six times as likely to be robbed."[11]

- "In the severity of its crime rates, the United States more closely resembles some of the most volatile countries of the third world, than other developed Western societies..."[12]

Examining the characteristics of different neighborhoods in the same American city also reveal the factors that either contribute to, or cause crime. Crime is lower in those neighborhoods where the educational level is high, schools are functional, unemployment is low, income is high, and housing is decent.

On the other end of this spectrum, crime is high in those neighborhoods that are characterized by poor housing stock, high rates of unemployment, poor performing schools, high dropout rates, broken families and high drug use.

One does not have to conduct statistical analysis, or be a criminologist to recognize that there is a direct or indirect correlation between crime and the socio-economic factors of a city or country. Clearly, for crime to be controlled, those factors that produce or contribute to illegal behavior must be addressed. The police alone cannot do that.

Community Policing, however, provides the police with the capacity to engage others in the crime control role. America can no longer afford to address its crime problem by producing stricter law enforcement that results in significant increases in rates of incarceration, but no lasting reduction in crime.

This was pointed out in 1981 when the Attorney General's Task Force on Violent Crime reported, "Though violent crime can strike anyone, most frequently it affects the poor, the young, the very old, and residents of the inner cities - precisely those persons who are least able to protect themselves. And even those who can afford a suburban residence or a privately guarded city apartment often find themselves defenseless on the streets."[13]

It went on to say, "The causes of crime are variously said to be found in the weakening of familial will and communal bonds, the persistence of unacceptable social disadvantages among some segments of society, and the easy spread of attitudes that favor immediate over deferred gratification."[14]

Arrests, prosecution, corrections and incarceration are important crime control mechanisms, but by themselves they will not effectively resolve the crime problem and result in a sustained reduction of crime in America. Rather, there must be a realization of the comprehensive efforts needed to make a lasting impact on crime. It is not realistic to expect the criminal justice system alone to have a significant impact on crime without addressing the social and economic issues that contribute to the cause of criminal behavior. Consider the following:

> The paucity of affordable housing, the failure of primary and secondary schools adequate enough to educate or provide our youth with marketable job skills, unemployment and institutional poverty, inadequate health care and mental health care, and a host of other indicia of social collapse are hardly within the immediate purview of the local police.
>
> Police can achieve their potential effectiveness only when government acts to reform these institutions, and when it provides each component of the criminal justice system - the police, the courts, corrections, prosecution, and probation and parole - with the legislation, resources and support they require.[15]

In the long run, if crime is to be controlled in America, there must be a national commitment to address those social and economic problems that lead to crime and, equally important, allow them to flourish.

Arguably, if the most important function of government is to provide for the safety of its people, then the government of America has been a failure.

Unless America addresses its social and economic problems, it can expect to continue to be deeply troubled by problems of crime and violence. "If we're serious about rethinking the problem of crime, we need to engage the issues on the higher level of moral and political values."[16] Furthermore, "we have the level of criminal violence we do because we have arranged our social and economic life in certain ways rather than others. The brutality and violence of American life are a signal - and a particularly compelling one - that there are profound social costs to maintaining those arrangements." [17]

"The general nature of the remedy is implicit in the diagnosis. If we are serious about attacking the roots of this American affliction, we must build a society that is less unequal, less depriving, less insecure, less disruptive of family and community ties and less corrosive of cooperative values. In short, we must begin to take on the enormous task of creating the conditions of community life in which individuals can live together in compassionate and cooperative ways. "[18]

FEAR OF CRIME

Victimization is an obvious result of criminal behavior. Less obvious, but equally prevalent is the fear of crime. Fear of crime is a major problem in America. This is true even though research has shown that fear may not be reflective of the actual likelihood of being a victim of crime.

Many citizens are afraid of crime and the prospect that they will be crime victims. Researchers have revealed that the fear of crime is greater than the actual incidence of crime. Part of this incongruity seems to result from the fact that fear derives from concern about various "signs of crime" and other sources, as well as from direct or indirect experiences with crime. For example, neighbors suffering from vandalism, loitering, public drinking or gambling convey the feeling of having been abandoned. Other factors, including personal relationships between citizens and police, and lack of information about crime and crime prevention techniques may create a sense of powerlessness, leading to higher levels of fear.[19]

As a result, many Americans have changed their way of life to accommodate their fear. Many refrain from walking out of their homes at night. They buy defensive devices, purchase weapons and guard dogs. They alter their social habits and limit the number of times they venture out at night.

When there is a strong fear of crime, there is correspondingly less loyalty to a neighborhood. The fear of crime can result in a breakdown of a community.

Under a program funded by the National Institute Justice of the United States Department of Justice, Houston, Texas and Newark, New Jersey participated in a demonstration project to determine what could be done to reduce the fear of crime. The Police Foundation evaluated the programs implemented by the two cities. An important element of the project was to implement programs that did not require an increase in the budgets of the departments.

The results of the evaluations supported the philosophy of *Community Policing*, by revealing that close contact with the community not only served to reduce fear; it also encouraged citizen support of the police in its efforts to reduce crime. The following are the activities that, based on the evaluations, had the greatest impact of reducing citizen fear of crime. [20]

- Officers should take advantage of every available opportunity to increase the quantity and improve the quality of contacts between police officers and the citizens they serve. They should use their "out of service" time to initiate contact with citizens.
- When officers are in contact with citizens, they should use the opportunities to determine what residents of particular neighborhoods believe are their biggest problems, the causes of those problems and what they think the remedies are.
- Officers should make conscious efforts to reach out to all people, not just those who contact the police or who are easiest to reach.
- Police departments should implement programs designed to address the problems identified by citizens and not rely only on their own beliefs.
- Citizen involvement in addressing the problems that they identify.
- A process should be implemented to determine when problems have been resolved.
- Officers should be given the respect, trust and latitude to determine the nature of the problems they should address and how best to do so.
- Officers who are creative, enthusiastic and self-motivated are the best performers.
- Supervisors should give officers the latitude to experiment in problem solving and, occasionally, to fail.
- Officers who perform well and carry out their responsibilities to Community Policing should be given proper recognition.
- Supervisors should provide enough oversight to demonstrate concern, but not so much that individual officer initiative is stifled.

The guidelines listed above are consistent with what is expected of all officers under the concept of Community Policing. As concluded by the evaluators, "the most significant implication of all is that there is , based on these results, reason to believe that the police, if they follow the suggestions provided above, can interrupt the cycle of fear of crime that has been destroying our urban communities".[21]

DRUGS AND CRIME

The sale and use of illicit drugs continue to be a major problem for both urban and rural America. It is a major problem, not only because of the culture of violence associated with drug trafficking, but also for the human misery it generates. Drug use places a heavy burden on the nation's health care system. Its ramifications include the spread of HIV and AIDS.

The crimes associated with drug abuse include the sale or possession of drugs; property crimes or prostitution to support drug habits; and violent crimes, reflecting aberrant behavior. In fact, offender drug use is involved in more than half of all violent crimes and in 60 to 80 percent of child abuse and neglect cases. It is estimated that 70 percent of the people in state prisons and in local jails have regularly abused drugs, compared with approximately nine percent of the general population.[22]

In 2000 about sixty percent of all male juvenile detainees and 46 percent of the females tested positive for drug use. The estimated cost to society of drug abuse in 2002 was $181 billion. Of that amount, $107 billion was associated with drug-related crime.[23]

Studies have consistently shown that comprehensive drug treatment works. It not only reduces drug use but also curtails criminal behavior and recidivism. Moreover, for drug- abusing and offenders, treatment facilitates successful reentry into the community. This is true even for people who enter treatment under legal mandates.[24]

Illicit drug use is a significant factor in crime. The sale and use of drugs constitute a major problem confronting America, and this country continues to be the world's largest consumer of illegal drugs.

The consequences of drug use are severe. It diminishes the quality of life of families and neighborhoods, increases the fear of crime, results in accidents, poor workmanship, theft in the business place, and thousands of hours of non-productivity. It also results in increased health-insurance premiums, workman's compensation and unemployment costs.

Drug use has a significant impact on crime. Many of the robberies, burglaries and thefts are motivated by people dependence on drugs. For many Americans, drugs have a disquieting impact on their lives.

SCOPE OF THE PROBLEM

The United Nations has estimated that the global illicit drug trafficking industry is in excess of $381 billion annually. [25] The cost to the United States is estimated at $110 billion each year. [26]

COPING WITH THE PROBLEM

Consistent with the philosophy of Community Policing, the entire community must work together to address the drug problem. The police should serve as a catalyst that generates and coordinates community involvement. There is a role for all segments of the community:

FAMILY

The family has the first and primary responsibility for keeping their children drug free. It is stated that the basic personality of a child is developed by the age of three. Parents, as care keepers, should start educating their children about drug as early as that age. Adults in the family must serve as positive role models by being drug-free.

SCHOOLS

Schools play an important role in drug prevention. Children spend a significant amount of time in school and the school has the second greatest influence on children. Schools should incorporate drug prevention into their curricula. They should also assist young people to deal with the problems of growing up in today's society where they are exposed to many conflicting opportunities, including drug use.

RELIGIOUS INSTITUTIONS

Religious institutions play a significant role in reinforcing values. They have an equally important role to go beyond spiritual teaching, and focus on issues that impact the lives of their congregations, including drug education. Religious figures can also help by using their roles as leaders to work with the police and others to reduce the use of drugs.

BUSINESS COMMUNITY

A large number of those who use drugs also hold down a job and go to work every day. Companies should ensure that they maintain a drug free workplace by implementing policies and programs, and when appropriate, drug-testing. Drug-free workplace programs are important because what is learned in the workplace can also be carried over into the home. The importance of the workplace in addressing the drug problem cannot be overly emphasized as an integral part of the communities' overall drug control efforts.

COMMUNITY GROUPS

All communities have a variety of community groups such as civic clubs, neighborhood associations, fraternal organizations, religious and professional clubs. They should be engaged in a community-wide drug control effort. Individually and collectively, they should engage sponsor programs to control the drug problem in their communities. They can also assist by educating themselves on the Community Policing concept and insist that their police departments adopt it as their dominant operating philosophy.

Experience has shown that the police are not the only agency responsible for controlling drugs in the community. To be successful in controlling drugs requires the collective efforts of the police, other agencies of local government, state and Federal agencies, the private sector and other social institutions and organizations. Cooperation and coordination is the essence of Community Policing, and can be effective in reducing drug use more than the traditional drug control efforts of enforcement alone.

HOUSTON CASE STUDY

In 1988 the City of Houston recognized that its fragmented approach to drug control was not successful in addressing its drug problem. Under the leadership of Mayor Kathy Whitmire, the city created an agency of government called Houston Crackdown. All segments of the community participated in the program - city and county government, law enforcement agencies, office of the prosecutor, courts, drug treatment agencies, religious leaders, educators, volunteer organizations, alcohol and other drug programs, treatment and rehabilitation programs and drug prevention organizations.

Its stated vision was, "Working together, everyone in the Greater Houston Community has the knowledge, skills and sense of self-responsibility to create a society free of fear, crime and the negative impact of drugs, including alcohol and tobacco." It served as:[27]

- A catalyst for community mobilization, neighborhood enrichment and collaborative strategic planning.
- A source of funding for prevention and treatment programs through the Houston Crackdown Bright Ideas Community Grant Fund.
- A public policy organization monitoring alcohol and other drug-related legislation and regulations, and it advised the mayor and Houston Crackdown members on the potential effects of these issues at the local level.
- A volunteer coalition of individuals and organizations dedicated to reducing drug use in Houston and Harris County.
- A 24-hour bilingual drug Information line providing access to treatment and recovery resources; specific drug information for families and youth; information on how to report illegal activity; and how to get involved in neighborhood prevention activities.
- A community awareness campaign about the negative effects of drug use and ways to deal with them, individually and collectively.
- An information and referral network for substance abuse programs and events.

The Houston crackdown has survived the test of time and still operates today.

ROLE OF THE POLICE IN CONTROLLING CRIME

The legislative branch of government determines what constitutes a crime. The executive branch of government is given the responsibility of enforcing the laws. The judicial branch interprets the law and makes critical decisions of guilt or innocence. As pointed out by Currie, "We take for granted that it is the business of the criminal justice system to deal with crime, but someone else's to deal with the social, economic, or family problems that foster it. As a result, the more important causes of crime are nearly always regarded as someone else's problem."[28]

The American criminal justice system is composed of several components: (1) police, (2) judicial and (3) corrections. All play an important role in crime control. The police, however, play a pivotal role because of their responsibility to arrest offenders. They also use their resources to prevent crime.

The police are in a unique position because they are the only agency of government that has a presence on the streets of cities. Furthermore, as they patrol the streets they receive the grievances of the people and deal with neighborhood problems; many which have the potential of becoming illegal activities. In addition, the police, through the 911 telephone system, receive citizen complaints.

The importance of the police can also be seen in their role as gatekeeper to the criminal justice system. It is mainly through their actions that the other components of the criminal justice system receive their clients. "Unlike the courts and prisons, the police have the supreme advantage, in terms of efficiency, of being able to stop crime before it happens, rather than merely dealing with offenders after the fact."[29]

Yet, it is a generally recognized that neither the police nor the criminal justice system alone can effectively address the crime problem. There are even questions about the ability of the courts and corrections to effectively deal with those the police bring into the system. Police leaders who have adopted Community Policing as their dominate style for delivering police services have no illusions that their work alone will result in the resolution of the deeper problems that result in criminal behavior. They understand that Community Policing involves educating the public that they also have an obligation to participate in crime control efforts. The police are the engine of the crime control train.

Police leadership should recognize that if society is to be successful in addressing the crime problem, it must go beyond the system of arrest, prosecution and incarceration. It must also focus on the conditions that generate criminal behavior.

In order to do that the police must work in partnership with other agencies of governments, and all segments of the community. Such a collaborative effort is necessary to maintain order, reduce crime, the fear of crime and ensure an acceptable level of stability in neighborhoods throughout American cities.

Community Policing provides the philosophical and operational framework for moving the police beyond the short-term, after-the-fact style of policing to a more proactive and collaborative style that has proven to improve quality of life in neighborhoods.

Historically, only police departments have been held accountable for crime. In the past, the *Uniform Crime Reports* were seen as a noose around the necks of the police. When reported crime went up, the police were viewed as ineffective in carrying out their crime control responsibilities. Many police leaders added to the problem by taking credit when reported crime went down, giving the false impression that they, alone, controlled crime.

Thoughtful police leaders have come to understand that they are not solely responsible for the crime problem, and it is their responsibility to educate the general public and elected officials about the complexities of crime. Governments should ensure that the responsibility for crime control is shared with other components of the criminal justice system by publicizing their statistics so that all elements of the criminal justice system can be held accountable.

For example, they should publish statistics of prosecution in cases where there is plea bargaining, and when a case is lost in a court. They should publicize court decisions so that the public knows when offenders are found guilty or innocent, and what punishment they received if any. They should publish the statistics of the corrections system so the public is aware about early release, and recidivism rates.

Police agencies throughout America have consistently defined their roles as crime fighters. They measure their success on the status of the crime rate, up or down. Yet, they have historically paid very little attention to what causes crime.

A recent survey revealed that 92 percent of the Police Chiefs in America felt that the country could sharply reduce crime if government invested additional funding in programs such as Head Start. The survey found that

Chiefs believed that crime would be reduced if there were more child abuse prevention programs, and after school mentoring programs. [30]

Under Community Policing, police departments no longer respond to crimes as mere incidents. Rather, they take steps to determine the reasons for delinquency among children and crime among adults. That information is then used to work with the community to develop programs designed to solve the underlying problems that required police involvement.

As the police analyze the circumstances surrounding acts of crime, they are discovering that there are problems in other institutions of society. For example, the family does not exist as it did in the past. Large numbers of people do not actively participate in religious activities. There are some families that do attend a church, mosque or synagogue, where concepts of right and wrong are reinforced.

In the past it was commonplace to hear "Thou shall not…" You heard it in families, the religious institutions and in the schools. But because of societal changes, the family has given over many of its responsibilities of child rearing to other institutions.

Community Policing returns police work to earlier days when law enforcement was considered the responsibility of the people. As pointed out in chapter two, before there was full-time law enforcement officers, citizens were required to raise the "hue and cry" and it was the responsibility of citizens to apprehend the law violator.

Over the years, full-time police officers were employed to serve as protectors of the community and the role of the public diminished. Yet, the public still has an extremely important role in crime control. No longer are they expected to apprehend the violators, but they are expected to work with the police to prevent crime and provide information to apprehend offenders when a crime occurs. Over the years the police have developed numerous programs designed to involve the public in crime control. Chapter six discusses the development and evolution of those efforts.

Under Community Policing, the role of the community in crime control is threefold: (1) compliance with the law, (2) crime prevention, and (3) assistance in the apprehension of offenders.

Crime control in a democratic society is extremely complex. It is complex because of the inter-relationships between the nature of the problems that the police must address and the divergence of the solutions. It is complex because social control in a democratic society cannot be imposed upon the society; rather, it must be accepted by the people. There is an implied contract between the people and government that the people will comply with the law. And that the police will protect them under the law. Otherwise, there would be social chaos. Because the social contract is the norm, the vast majority of Americans are law abiding.

The police in America have a dual mission. As viewed by the public, their core mission is to control crime. Based on actual activities, they spend much of their time maintaining order. Historically, the police have organized themselves around their crime control mission. As a result, they have been reactive in both their organization and operation. This has resulted in a reactive response to crime with little emphasis placed on proactive activities that might prevent crime from occurring in the first place. Community policing reinforces both the organization and operation of the police. Moore and Trojanowicz pointed out that the police can improve their crime control role by:[31]

1. Diagnosing and managing problems in the community that produce serious crime
2. Fostering closer relations with the community to facilitate crime solving
3. Building self defense capabilities in the community

Community policing is designed to achieve those three objectives. Thoughtful police leaders no longer feel that the criminal justice system is capable of controlling the crime problem. There is a strong belief that unless the social institutions, e.g. family, school, church, business, etc. do their job, the corrosive consequences will continue to result in criminal activities.

One of the most significant articles dealing with how the police should focus their efforts to control crime was Wilson and Kellin's <u>Atlantic Monthly</u> article entitled "Broken Windows." This article pointed out that when neighborhoods are allowed to physically deteriorate or crime is left unaddressed, residents do not take pride in their neighborhoods and allow physical deterioration while crime flourishes.[32]

It concluded by stating, "Above all, we must return to our long-abandoned view that the police ought to protect communities as well as individuals. Our crime statistics and victimization surveys measure individual losses, but they do not measure communal losses. Just as physicians recognize the importance of fostering health rather than simply treating illness, so the police---and the rest of us---- ought to recognize the importance of maintaining intact communities without broken windows."[33]

EFFECTIVE POLICE TECHNIQUES

ComStat:

Over the past two decades a number of crime control techniques have emerged in American law enforcement. One of the most popular is ComStat (Computer Statistics). *ComStat* was developed in the York City Police Department. It is a system for managing police operations designed to address crime and quality of life issues and hold managers accountable for what goes on in their areas of responsibility. It was designed to provide the department with snapshots of preliminary crime statistics; thereby allowing the departments to conduct tactical planning for the deployment of departmental resources to fight crime. The ComStat unit is responsible for compiling and analyzing Crime Data and generating electronic maps of crime locations throughout the city. It prepares briefing presentations for the police commissioner and the information is used to evaluate the effectiveness of field commanders in addressing the crime problems in their areas of responsibility.[34] There are a variety of versions of ComStat, but the basic goal is to identify crime trends and deploy resources of the department to focus on the problems.

The following are the four basic principles of ComStat:[35]

ACCURATE AND TIMELY INTELLIGENCE

If the police are to respond effectively to crime and to criminal events, officers at all levels of the organization must have accurate knowledge of when particular types of crimes are occurring, how and where the crimes are being committed, and who the criminals are. The likelihood of an effective police response to crime increases proportionally as the accuracy of this criminal intelligence increases.

EFFECTIVE TACTICS:

Effective tactics are prudently designed to bring about the desired result of crime reduction, and are developed after studying and analyzing the information gleaned from accurate and timely crime intelligence.

In order to merely avoid displacing crime and quality of life problems, and in order to bring about permanent change, these tactics must be comprehensive, flexible, and adaptable to the shifting crime trends that are identified and watched.

RAPID DEPLOYMENT OF PERSONNEL AND RESOURCES
Once a tactical plan has been developed, an array of personnel and other necessary resources are promptly deployed. Although some tactical plans might involve only patrol personnel, experience has proven that the most effective plans require that personnel from several units and enforcement functions work together to address the problem.

A viable and comprehensive response to crime or quality of life problems generally demand that patrol personnel, investigators and support personnel align their expertise and resources in a coordinated fashion to address problems.

RELENTLESS FOLLOW-UP AND ASSESSMENT
As in any problem-solving endeavor, an ongoing process of rigorous follow-up and assessment is absolutely essential to ensure that the desired results are actually being achieved.

This evaluation component also allows law enforcement the time to assess the viability of particular tactical responses and to incorporate knowledge gained in subsequent tactics and development efforts.

With evidence of how well a specific tactic worked on a particular crime or quality of life problem, and by knowing which specific elements of the tactical response were most effective, law enforcement is better able to construct and implement appropriate responses for similar problems in the future. The follow-up and assessment process also allows re-deployment of resources to meet newly identified challenges once a problem has abated.

The process involves regular meetings with police commanders where they are questioned about the actions they have taken to address the problems identified by ComStat. Commanders are asked questions about specific problems and are expected to be prepared to respond to all questions. The initial New York City model was often embarrassing to the high-ranking officers, and most cities have changed the nature of the meetings, making them more professional and respectful of the rank of the participants.

BEAT PROFILING

Beat Profiling did not catch on, as did ComStat. Nevertheless, it is a very effective police technique and consistent with the principles of Community Policing. Beat Profiling was pioneered in Houston, Texas as a process by which police officers are assigned to a given beat and required to learn about the characteristics of that beat in order to develop plans to deliver quality police services to residents and business people in that area. Officers were required to develop a written description of the beat, its characteristics, key issues of concern to the residents and business people, and crime and disorder issues. Each patrol officer, upon being assigned to a neighborhood, was required to spend several days collecting information about the beat for the Beat Profile Book. If a *Beat Profile* book for the neighborhood already existed, the officer was required to update the information. The *Beat Profile* was kept in a master book at the police station and it was available to any officer assigned to that area. Under community policing, Beat Profiling serves as a key ingredient in the police department's strategy to bring patrol officers, neighborhood residents and businesspersons together in a partnership to develop a safer city. [36]

CIVIL ENFORCEMENT INITIATIVE

The *Civil Enforcement Initiative* was developed by The New York City Police Department as part of its transformation to Community Policing. It reflected the department's mandate that all elements of the department were required to develop strategies to address the problems facing the communities in New York City. The approach recognized that police departments cannot rely solely on arrests to address the quality of life concerns in neighborhoods. For example, rather than making numerous prostitution arrests at the house of prostitution, under the civil enforcement initiative, the Police Department attempts to close the location through the appropriate civil remedy and thereby stop the illegal activity by providing an incentive for the landlord to seek a legitimate tenet. The following are examples of civil enforcement actions were taken by the New York City Police Department:[37]

NUISANCE ABATEMENT
The Nuisance Abatement Law of the New York City Administrative Code enabled the Police Department to close a location for violations of the Penal Law, the Vehicle and Traffic Law and the Alcohol Beverage Control Law.

PADLOCK ACTIONS
The Police Commissioner is authorized to close a location for one year or order the discontinuance of the illegal activity in any location where there was two arrests resulting in one conviction within the past year. A third arrest at that location serves as the triggering arrest needed for the Padlock Unit of the Legal Bureau to commence an action against the owner of the location to discontinue the illegal activity.

NEW YORK CITY FORFEITURE ACTIONS
The Police Department may commence actions for forfeiture in New York State Supreme Court against people claiming the return of property seized by the police at the time of arrest. Pursuant to the New York City Administrative Code property seized as the instrumentality of crime, or property that is the proceeds of crime may be forfeited to the City if the Police Department can demonstrate by a preponderance of the evidence that the owner of the property had knowledge of the underlying criminal act.

NEW YORK STATE FORFEITURE ACTIONS
The District Attorney may commence forfeiture actions, before a conviction, if the underlying criminal action is against the owners of property used as the instrumentality of crime or property that was the proceeds of felony crime. The law also empowers the District Attorney to commence actions against real property. Forfeited property is divided between the District Attorney's Office, the Police Department, the City, and the State Substance Abuse Fund.

FEDERAL FORFEITURE ACTIONS
The Federal government may forfeit property seized by the Police Department, which cannot be forfeited under local or state law.

In these cases, the government must demonstrate that there is probable cause to believe the property was the instrumentality or proceeds of crime. The burden of proof then shifts to the defendant to show by a preponderance of the evidence that there was no knowledge of the underlying criminal activity. Property forfeited under this statute may be transferred to law enforcement agencies to be used for law enforcement purposes.

NEW YORK STATE REAL PROPERTY EVICTION ACTIONS

Under this law, a government agency may commence an action against the landlord to compel the eviction of tenants who are conducting illegal activities from the location. If the landlord fails to commence the action, the government can command it, naming a landlord as a defendant and seek fines for the landlord's failure to act.

ROLE OF THE FEDERAL GOVERNMENT

As early as 1974, Attorney General William B. Saxbe warned that, "The Nation is in deep trouble in its effort to reduce crime."[38] He went on to say, "The Federal government must shoulder part of the blame for the crime problem. There been too many grandiose promises and too much patch-work performance in Washington. After the years of struggle, after spending billions of dollars, it should be clear to everyone that there is no touchstone to be invoked in crime control."[39]

Similar to education, labor, health and human services, transportation and other issues that in the past mandated the creation of a Federal department, crime also mandates a coordinated Federal response.

A number of past efforts have been initiated at the Federal level to address crime as a national problem. As a result of the 1967 Presidential Crime Commission, the Law Enforcement Assistance Administration (LEAA) was created in the Department Justice. LEAA was designed to provide funds to state and local government to assist them in addressing the crime problem.

In 1967, the last Federal commission to study crime, the President's Commission on Law Enforcement Administration of Justice noted that, "There is much crime in America, more than ever is reported, far more than is ever solved, far too much for the health of the nation."[40]

Over four decades later, crime continues to be a pervasive problem for the American people. In one way or another, crime impacts every American. Crime is costly to the American society. The Federal government, through its resources, must provide local government with information on how best to address the crime problem. At the end of the first Bush administration in the early 1990s, a number of crime control initiatives were initiated.

WEED AND SEED

This program was designed to go into select high crime neighborhoods and eliminate (weed) crime and then address the social problems believed to be the cause of crime (seed). In order to assure Federal cooperation, the United States Attorney was placed in charge of the program. Although the program placed a greater emphasis on "weeding", it did provide a mechanism for coordinating various components of the Department of Justice.

VIOLENCE PREVENTION

The Center for Communicable Disease Control in the Department of Health and Human Services (HHS) implemented an initiative to prevent violence. This program was based on the premise that violence is not only a crime problem; it is also a public health problem. In fact, murder was identified as the leading cause of death among young African-American males. Viewing crime as a public health problem led to the conclusion that techniques used by the public health discipline should also be used to address the problem of violence in the community. This approach brought a new focus to violence. It involved a multi-agency approach, an epidemiologist's focus on prevention, and the criminal justice system's approach to violence with disciplines that focused on prevention.

PUBLIC HOUSING INITIATIVE

The Department of Housing and Urban Development (HUD) got involved in the crime control effort out of necessity. Public housing Projects had the highest

THE COMMUNITY POLICING CONSORTIUM

The Bureau of Justice Assistance (BJA) and the National Institute Justice (NIJ) provided Federal funds to create a Community

Policing Consortium initially comprised of three major police organizations, the International Association of Chiefs of Police, the Police Executive Research Forum and the Police Foundation. Subsequently, the National Organization of Black Law Enforcement Executives was added to the consortium. The Consortium was designed to promote Community Policing by providing police departments with technical assistance, surveys, training, program evaluation and support for demonstration projects.

COMMUNITY ORIENTED POLICING SERVICES.

Under the Clinton administration, Congress passed a comprehensive crime control bill. A major component of that bill was the creation of the Community Oriented Policing Services (COPS) with funds to place 100,000 additional police officers on the streets to start or expand the Community Policing philosophy in police departments. The COPS office funds were dramatically reduced by the second Bush administration.

It is important to recognize that there is no single or simple solution to the crime problem. Similarly, no one program can provide the answer to the social problems that often lead to crime. For that reason, the Federal government must take the lead in controlling crime in America. The following are recommendations for crime control efforts on the Federal level:

1. Presidential Leadership

The President of the United States should take a leadership role in addressing crime. There are two major things that the President can do. First, he can articulate the nation's concern about the crime problem. In doing so, the President should point out that to effectively address crime in America, it is necessary to address those factors that cause crime. In that context, the President should state that the Federal government will focus its resources on economic issues such as unemployment, underemployment, poor housing, poverty, inadequate education, inadequate health care and other problems that the Federal government is best equipped to address. It has been more than four decades since the last President's Crime Commission released a report on crime in America. It is time for a new Presidential Commission on Crime. The commission should be interdisciplinary and bring to bear expertise from all relevant disciplines; criminal justice, social sciences, public health and more to develop a comprehensive approach to the problem of crime. It should look at crime in context of today's society and be charged with determining what must be done to reduce crime in America, There should also be a commitment to focus Federal resources from all segments of the Federal government to wage a comprehensive, long-range assault on crime.

2. <u>Economic Opportunity</u>

A key component of the Federal government's response to crime should be an understanding of the relationships between poverty, unemployment, underemployment and crime. To address that issue, the Federal government should establish policies that provide a job for each American who is willing and able to work.

3. <u>Safe and Decent Housing</u>

It is possible to plot crime on a map of any large city in America by determining those areas where overcrowded and inadequate housing conditions exists. There is a relationship between the quality of housing, social problems and crime. The Federal government should address this issue by developing a policy to provide decent housing for all citizens.

4. <u>Revitalization of Cities</u>

Over the years, many large cities have deteriorated. As a result, they are experiencing a high rate of crime. The deterioration has occurred for a variety of reasons, mainly the loss of job opportunities. Cities such as Camden, New Jersey; Detroit and Flint, Michigan and Newark, New Jersey are clear examples of where the Federal government should undertake a massive rebuilding effort. The nation should do no less for American cities than what was done at the end of World War II when billions of dollars were spent on the Marshall Plan to rebuild war-torn Western Europe.

5. <u>Adequate Health Care</u>

The total needs of individuals must be considered in developing a comprehensive national crime control initiative. Today, many Americans do not have and cannot afford adequate health care. To correct that problem, the policy of the United States should be that healthcare is a right and not a privilege. Health-care should be made available to all Americans, including preventive services, health maintenance and health education.

6. <u>Drug Treatment and Enforcement</u>

There is a clear relationship between drug trafficking, drug use and crime. Historically, America has focused its drug control efforts on enforcement and interdiction. In order to address the crime problem, precipitated by illicit use of drugs, America drug control strategy must place a greater emphasis on reducing the demand for drugs. This means putting more funds into prevention, education and treatment programs.

7. <u>Television Violence</u>

Because research has shown that there is a correlation between watching violence on television and aggressive behavior in young people, the Federal government should take aggressive steps to control the high levels of violence shown on television in American homes.

8. <u>Education</u>

Because of the lack of adequate education, an underclass has emerged in America that is characterized by unemployment, drug use, idleness, despair and crime. The policy of the Federal government should be to improve the public educational system so all students can receive a meaningful education. It should be designed to reverse the trend of millions of children dropping out of school each year. It is important that adequate funding be provided to ensure success in this endeavor.

9. <u>Corporate Crime</u>

In recent years America has witnessed widespread corruption in the business community. Cases such as Enron and World Com have clearly demonstrated that crime is not a one-dimensional phenomenon. Corporate crime and white-collar crime also have a detrimental impact on the community. They are no less serious than other crimes that routinely receive the attention of the criminal justice system.

10. Federal Funding to State and Local Government
Unlike the 1960s when there was a rapid increase in the crime rate, we now have better information based on research about what can be done to reduce crime. Federal funding should be made available to state and local government to assist them in their crime control efforts. The Community Oriented Policing Service Program (COPS) that was implemented under the Clinton administration provided assistance to police agencies to either expand or implement the concept of Community Policing. Based on the findings of the previously recommended President's Crime Commission, Federal funding should be made available to state and local governments to address the crime problem in America.

11. Family and Community Policy
All departments of the Federal government should develop policies that are supportive of families and communities. The policies should be geared to recognize and reinforce the strengths of these two institutions. Income maintenance, family counseling and social services should be the cornerstone of these policies and should involve all of the communities' resources; including businesses, schools, and religious institutions. Special emphasis should be placed on employing members of minority groups and teenagers who are parents.

SUMMARY

Crime will continue to be a problem for America in years to come. There are no quick or simple solutions. The problem, however, can be effectively addressed. To do so will require a bold new focus that involves the combined efforts of Federal, state and local governments; the corporate community and all segments of the civic community. The solution requires a new way of looking at crime and no longer relying solely on the criminal justice system. It will require a total commitment to address the societal problems that result in criminal behavior, while at the same time reforming the criminal justice system. Police departments must adopt Community Policing as their dominant style for delivering police services.

In the long run, there will only be significant and lasting reductions in crime when there are fundamental changes made in the social and economic conditions that create and maintain a system of those who have abundance and those who have very little.

There must be a two-pronged approach to crime. Community Policing provides the umbrella for both approaches. First, the police must continue to carry out their traditional responsibilities of law enforcement. They must also provide the catalyst for engaging other institutions of society in addressing underlining causes of criminal behavior. The latter approach involves developing a coalition of community institutions, both public and private, that work together to resolve the circumstances in society that, if left unattended, have a high probability of resulting in criminal behavior. In the long run, there will not be a significant reduction in crime unless there are fundamental changes in the social and economic conditions of society.

NOTES: CHAPTER THIRTEEN

1. Violent Crime Control and Law Enforcement Act of 1994, H.R. 3355, Pub. L 103-322

2. President's Commission on Law Enforcement and Administration of Justice, <u>The Challenge of Crime in a Free Society</u>. Washington, D.C.: U.S Government Printing Office, 1967

3. Dostoyevsky, Fyodor, <u>The House of the Dead</u>, London: Penguin Books, 1862

4. Department of Justice Study Group, <u>Report to the Attorney General: Restructuring the Justice Department's Program of Assistance to State and Local Governments for Crime Control and Criminal Justice System Improvement</u>, Washington, D.C.: U. S. Department of Justice, June 23, 1967, p. 5

5. Currie, Elliot, <u>Confronting Crime: An American Challenge</u>, New York: Pantheon Books, 1988, p. 278

6. Sabol, William L. , Heather C. West and Mathew Cooper, <u>Prisoners in 2008</u>, Washington,D.C.: Bureau of Justice Statistics, Department of Justice, December, 2009

7. Op. Cit., Note 5, p. 105
8. Ibid. p. 105
9. Ibid. p. 5
10. Ibid.
11. Ibid.
12. Ibid. p. 6

13. U.S. Department of Justice, "Attorney General's Task Force on Violent Crime," Final Report, August 17, 1981, p.1

14. Ibid.

15. Brown, Lee P., "Crime," in Changing America: Blueprints for the New Administration, Mark Green, (ED.), New York: New Market Press, 1992, p. 309

16. Op. Cit., Note 5, p.16

17. Ibid. p. 58

18. Ibid. p. 226

19. Pate, Antony M. and Mary Ann Wycoff, Wesley Skogan and Lawrence W. Sherman, Reducing Fear of Crime in Houston and Newark: A Summary Report, Washington, D.C.: Police Foundation, 1986, p.1

20. Ibid. pp. 37-38

21. Ibid. p.38

22. Volkow, Nora D., "Threat the Addict, Cut the Crime Rate," The Washington Post, August 19, 2005, p. A17

23. Ibid.

24. Ibid.

25. Pollard, Niklas, "U.N. Report Puts World's Illicit Drug Trade at Estimated $321B," The Boston Globe, June 30, 2005 (http://boston.com/news/world/articles/2005/06/30/un_report_puts_worlds_illicit_dr. 10/20/2010)

26. National Institute on Drug Abuse and National Institute on Alcohol Abuse and Alcoholism, The Economic Costs of Alcohol and Drug Abuse in the United States 1992, Rockville, Md.: U.S. Department of Health and Human Services, 1998, pp.1-10

27. http: www.houstontx.gov/publicsafety/cracdown.html

28. Op. Cit., Currie, p. 18

29. Op. Cit., Currie, p.232

30. Kerlikowske, Gill, "Invest in Kids Now, Prevent Crime Later," Subject to Debate, a newsletter of the Police Executive Research Forum, vol. 10, No. 10, October 1996, p.2

31. Moore, Mark H. and Robert C. Trojanowicz, "Crime and Policing," Perspectives on Policing, United States Department of Justice and the Program in Criminal Justice Policy and Management; John F. Kennedy School of Government, Cambridge, Mass.: Harvard University, June 1988, No. 2

32. Wilson, James Q. and George Kelling, "Broken Windows," Atlantic Monthly, March, 1982, pp.29-38

33. Ibid., p. 12

34. http://www.nyc.gov/html/nypd/html/chfdept/comstat.html

35. http://www.nyc.gov/htmlnypd/html/chfdept/reduction.tml

36. Brown, Lee P., <u>Management Report 9, Houston Police Department: Beat Profiling</u>, unpublished, no date

37. Brown, Lee P., <u>Civil Enforcement Initiative</u>, New York City Police Department, June 1992

38. Address by William B. Saxbe, Attorney General of the United States at the Major Cities Chief Associations' Conference on Urban Crime, August, 1974, Chicago, Illinois

39. Ibid.

40. The President's Commission on Law Enforcement and Administration of Justice, <u>The Challenge of Crime in a Free Society</u>, Washington, D.C.: U.S. Government Printing Office, 1967, p. 1

Chapter Fourteen:

RACE RELATIONS AND RACIAL PROFILING

INTRODUCTION

To fully comprehend police and race relations in America today, it is important to understand the history of the various minority groups in the United States. Historically, when police and race relations were discussed, the conversation centered primarily on the police relationship with African Americans.

> "There is perhaps no greater challenge facing our country than increasing understanding and cooperation among people of different racial backgrounds."
> —The Princeton Prize in Race Relations

In recent years that has changed, and today any discussion of the police and race relations encompasses the relationships between the police and three major ethnic groups: (1) African Americans, (2) Hispanic Americans and (3) Asian Americans. This chapter briefly discusses all three of the major minority groups and their experiences in America. In doing so, it points out both similarities and differences in their issues and problems.

AFRICAN AMERICANS

The uniqueness of the Black experience in America demands special attention in any discussion of race relations. That discussion must begin by looking at the institution of slavery, which was one of the saddest periods in the history of America. Slavery was an institution that exploited one group of humans for the benefit of another. The ramifications of slavery are still present today. As Higginbotham pointed out, slavery was supported by, "... a legal process that assured blacks a uniquely degraded status-- one in which the cruelties of slavery and pervasive racial injustices were guaranteed by laws."[1]

Blacks first came to America in the year 1619 and landed at Jamestown, Virginia. They arrived in what was then the British Colonies as indentured servants. At the time, indentured servitude was not restricted to Blacks, whites were also indentured servants. Indentured servitude was a means used by the colonists to obtain workers to help build the colonies. The indentured servants were given contracts to work for specific time periods in exchange for transportation from England to America where they were provided with food, lodging and other simple necessities.

Servitude differed from slavery in that it was voluntary and at the end of the contract period, the servant was free. Also, during the period of service, unlike slaves, they retained certain rights.

Slavery, on the other hand, was an economic institution upheld by law. By 1640 the majority of Africans involuntarily brought to the colonies no longer had the status of indentured servants, and had no prospects for freedom. The general view of the slave holder was:

... slaves were not persons but property; and laws should protect the ownership of such property, and should protect whites against any dangers which were likely to arise from the presence of large numbers of Negroes. Laws should keep Negroes subordinate, so that discipline and a maximum amount of work could be achieved[2]

In 1787, when the United States Constitution was signed, Blacks were again subjected to unequal treatment. Although the Declaration of Independence said, "all men are created equal," Article I, Section 2, Paragraph 3 of the United States Constitution read: "Representation and direct taxes shall be apportioned among the several states which may be included within this union, according to their respective numbers, which shall be determined by adding to the whole number of free persons, including those bound to service for a term of years, and excluding Indians not taxed, *three fifths of all other persons.*"

What relevance does this background have on the police today? In their paper, "The Evolving Strategy of Police: A Minority View," Williams and Murphy pointed out:

The fact that the legal order not only countenanced slavery, segregation and discrimination for most of our nation's history - and the fact that the police were bound to uphold that order - set a pattern for police behavior and attitudes toward minorities that has persisted until the present day. That pattern includes the idea that minorities have fewer civil rights, that the task of the police is to keep them under control and that the police have little responsibility for protecting them from crime within their own communities.[3]

Starting three decades prior to the Civil War, both free Blacks and runaway slaves left the south and settled in the north and west in search of better opportunities.[4] This influx of Blacks was not well received and states enacted laws commonly called "Black Codes " that made blacks second-class citizens.

Even the United States Supreme Court, in the infamous 1887 *Dred Scott* decision, ruled that " a free Negro of the African race, whose ancestors were brought to this country and sold as slaves, was not a 'citizen' within the meaning of the Constitution of the United States."[5]

In 1863, President Abraham Lincoln issued the *Emancipation Proclamation* that abolished slavery. Yet, it took a Civil War and three amendments to the Constitution to correct the legal disenfranchisement of Blacks. In addition to the Thirteenth, Fourteenth and Fifteenth Amendments to the Constitution, which removed the legal basis of discrimination, the United States Congress passed additional legislation, including the Civil Rights Act of 1875 to supplement and reinforce the amendments to the Constitution.[6]

But America remained a divided nation. Blacks were regulated to segregated neighborhoods, schools and jobs. America was, the Kerner Commission said, "Two societies, one Black, one white - separate and unequal."[7]

In defiance to the laws of the land, several Southern states enacted racist laws that prohibited Blacks from "voting, serving in the military, serving on juries and assembling without white law enforcement officers present"[8]

In response to the *Black Codes*, Congress enacted the *Reconstruction Act of 1867*. In addition to dividing the southern states into five military zones, it also set up as a condition for reinstatement into the Union that states ratify the *Fourteenth Amendment*. That amendment gave equal protection under the law to Black Americans.[9]

Reconstruction saw the emergence of groups such as the Ku Klux Klan that used intimidation and violence to prevent Blacks from exercising rights that were guaranteed to them by the United States Constitution.

In 1896, the U.S. Supreme Court reinforced legal segregation in the landmark case of *Plessy v. Ferguson*.[10] In that case the Court upheld the rights of states to have segregated public accommodations. This had a dramatic impact on the progress that had been made since the passage of the *Reconstruction Amendments* (Adoption of the Thirteenth, Fourteenth and Fifteenth Amendments to the United States Constitution between 1866-1870).

One of the most disturbing aspects of the Twentieth Century was the violence against Blacks. That violence manifested itself in the form of race riots and hangings. Blacks were lynched for such crimes as threatening to sue a white man, attempting to register to vote, enticing a white man's servant to leave his job, engaging in union activities, being disrespectful to or 'disputing with' a white man, or sometimes for no discoverable reason at all."[11]

In an objective study of race relations in America, the Swedish scholar Gunnar Myrdal described the treatment of Blacks in the criminal justice system as follows:

> "… In criminal cases where only Negroes are involved there is sometimes a disposition on the part of the prosecutors, judges and juries to treat offenses with relative lightness. In matters involving offenses by Negroes against Whites, Negroes will often find the presumptions of the court against them, and there is a tendency to sentence them to a higher penalty than if they had committed the same offense against Negroes. Negro witnesses have been made the butt of jest and horseplay. Negroes are more likely than whites to be arrested under suspicious circumstances. They are more likely to be accorded discourteous or brutal treatment at the hands of the police than are whites. The rate of killing of Negroes by the police is high in many Northern cities…"[12]

The decade of the 1950s gave birth to the Civil Rights movement. Blacks won a major victory in 1954 when the U.S. Supreme Court ruled in the case of Brown v. Topeka Board of Education that "separate education facilities are inherently unequal."[13] In 1957, the U.S. Congress passed a

Civil Rights Bill, the first such legislation since 1875. The law established the United States Commission on Civil Rights. [14]

The Civil Rights Movement was highlighted in 1955 when Dr. Martin Luther King Jr. led the Montgomery bus boycott which was precipitated by Mrs. Rosa Parks, a seamstress, when she refused to give up her bus seat to a white man, and was arrested. This act of defiance was the spark that ignited the fuse of years of discrimination, intimidation and violence against Blacks.

During that period of American history, Eugene "Bull" Connor, Commissioner of Public Safety for Birmingham, Alabama and a die-hard segregationist, was the personification of police in the south. Through the actions of his officers, the nation witnessed law enforcement at its worst when the police and firemen used dogs, water hoses and cattle prods against peaceful African American demonstrators, many small children among them.

Starting in 1961, Black and white activists called Freedom Riders tested the Supreme Court decision of *Boynton v. Virginia* that held it unconstitutional to have segregation in interstate bus and rail stations.[15] The *Freedom Riders* were met with intense hostility and excessively rabid violence. They were beaten, killed and jailed. Their busses were burned and the police did nothing to protect them.[16]

In 1963, Dr. Martin Luther King Jr. organized the largest demonstration in the history of the nation with the March on Washington where he delivered his famous "I have a Dream" speech. That march gave impetus to the far-reaching Civil Rights Act of 1964 that was passed by the Congress and signed by President Lyndon B. Johnson on July 2, 1964. Among other things, the legislation:

"... gave the Attorney General additional power to protect citizens against discrimination and segregation in voting, education, and the use of public facilities. It forbade discrimination in most places of public accommodation and established a Federal Community Relations Service to help individuals and communities solve civil rights problems. It established a Federal Equal Employment Opportunity Commission and extended the life of the Commission on Civil Rights... One of its most controversial provisions required the elimination of discrimination in federally assisted programs authorizing termination of programs or withdrawal of Federal funds upon failure to comply."[17]

The 1960s was also the decade of riots, but unlike riots in which whites attacked Blacks, the riots of the 60s involved Blacks lashing out against symbols of white influence in their neighborhoods. In response to the unprecedented level of civil disorder, President Lyndon Johnson established the National Commission on Civil Disorders to determine, "What happened? – Why did it happen? -- and what can be done to prevent it from happening again?"[18]

The Kerner Commission's basic conclusion was that "Our nation is moving toward two societies, one black, and one white - separate and unequal."[19] It went on to conclude:

> What white America has never fully understood - but what the Negro can never forget - is that white society is deeply implicated in the ghetto. White institutions created it, white institutions maintain it, and white society condones it."[20]

Since the turbulent sixties, African Americans have made major gains. Blacks are now members of Congress, mayors, city council members, Police Chiefs of major cities, chief executive officers of large companies, educators, doctors, lawyers and even President of the country. Yet the African American community is still confronted with many problems, including a highly disproportionate representation in jails and prisons, high school dropout rates and high levels of unemployment. Although significant progress has been made, many Blacks still suffer from problems of discrimination, even though the nation elected Barack Obama, as its first African American President in 2008.

HISPANICS

Hispanics are now the largest minority group in America. They surpassed African Americans as the largest ethnic groups in the 2000 census count. They are also the fastest growing minority group.

The term Hispanic is a relative new term and is used to describe anyone of Puerto Rican, Cuban, Mexican or Central and South America heritage, regardless of race.[21] The term is also used to describe a number of ethnic groups who speak a language other than Spanish; for example, Brazilians who speak Portuguese, French Guineans who speak French and Surinamians who speak Dutch.

Because of the diversity of the people who are called Hispanic, it is impossible to discuss them as a group. They have both different and similar experiences in America. For that reason this chapter only focuses on the three major Hispanic groups.

MEXICAN AMERICANS[22]

Because of the United States' proximity to Mexico, the largest number of Hispanics in America comes from that country. This is due, in large part, to the fact that almost half of the territory which previously belonged to the Republic of Mexico, including "... all or part of Arizona, California, Colorado, Nevada, New Mexico, Texas, Utah and Wyoming, is now part of the United States."[23] In addition, the Mexican population grew rapidly during the twentieth century because of increased immigration and a high birthrate.

Mexican Americans are not a race. Rather they are a multi-racial group primarily of Spanish and Indian descent. To a much lesser degree they have an African heritage.[24]

The colonization of Mexico started during the latter part of the 16th century. The state of New Mexico was the very first target. That was followed by the states of Arizona, California and Texas. The history of Mexico's territorial relations with America is long and varied, starting in 1821 when Mexico defeated Spain and won its independence. The United States and Mexico have had both good and bad relations.[25]

In 1829, the establishment of the Old Spanish Trail from Santa Fe, New Mexico to Los Angeles, California greatly increased communication between the two neighbors. Between the years 1821 and 1846, two distinct Anglo-American and Mexican relationships developed. First were the Anglo trappers who settled in Mexico who married Mexican women, became Mexican citizens and were given land grants by the Mexican government. The second group was the pioneers who settled in California, brought their families with them and did not integrate into Mexican society. This latter group rebelled against the Mexican government and became, for a short of time, secessionists. The revolt lasted less than a month and created animosity between Spanish-speaking Californians and Anglo Americans.[26]

The settlement of Texas differed from that of California and New Mexico where Anglo Americans remained a minority. In Texas, Mexicans constituted a majority by a ratio of six to one. Initially the Anglo settlers received land grants from the New Spanish government under the conditions that they: (1) become Mexican citizens, (2) obey the laws of Mexico, (3) become Catholics, (4) learn Spanish, and (5) assimilate into the Mexican society. When they did not comply with the conditions set out for them, the Mexican government imposed restrictions that represented greater central control by the government. That ultimately led to the 1835 Texas revolution which the settlers won and created the Republic of Texas. The Republic of Texas joined the American nation in 1845. [27]

Mexico did not accept the annexation of Texas and between April 25, 1846 and September 14, 1847 the United States and Mexico were at war. A peace treaty was signed on February 2, 1848 with Mexico recognizing the United State's annexation of Texas and conceding California and New Mexico.[28]

The immigration of Mexicans to the United States during the latter part of the 19th century was modest and centered on the Gold Rush in California and farm worker migration to Texas. The number of Mexican immigrants increased significantly during the twentieth century. With the development of the railroads, Mexicans were able to travel throughout United States.[29]

Initially, Mexican migration to the United States was not a major issue. In fact, the agricultural and industrial industries supported it because Mexicans were a source of inexpensive labor. It was not until the 1920s that opposition to Mexican immigration grew, coming from labor unions, business communities and welfare agencies. The issue ultimately generated a national debate that led to the creation of the U.S. Bureau of Immigration in 1924. Because of World War II, there was a great demand for manual labor in the United States. As a result, the U.S and Mexican governments established the *Bracero Program*, which allowed Mexican farm workers to enter into the United States to work in the farming industry.[30] The El Paso Herald Post wrote:

> More than 80,000 Braceros passed through the El Paso center annually. They're part of an army of 350,000 or more that marches across the border each year to help plant, cultivate and harvest cotton and other crops throughout the United States.[31]

The program ended in 1947, but was re-established by the U.S. Congress in 1951 and lasted until 1964. It was re-established mainly because of the Korean War. At its peak in 1959, some 450,000 Braceros came to work in the United States. [32]

Although the Bracero Program provided a valuable service for the United States, its participants were not always treated fairly:

> Generally speaking, the Latin-American migratory workers going into

West Texas were regarded as a necessary evil, nothing more or less than an unavoidable adjunct to the harvesting season. Judging by the treatment that met them in that section of the state, one might assume that they were not human beings at all, but a species of farming equipment that came mysteriously and spontaneously into being, consistent with the maturing of the cotton crop that required no upkeep or special consideration during the period of its usefulness, needed no protection from the elements, and when the crop had been harvested, they vanished into the limbo of forgotten things until the next season rolled round. They had no past, no future, and only a brief and anonymous present.[33]

Green cards, which allowed Mexican workers to enter the United States, on a temporary basis, succeeded the Bracero program. [34]

The decade of the 1940s saw serious conflicts between the police and Mexican Americans, with the most publicized incident being the Sleepy Lagoon case, which occurred in Los Angeles. Sleepy Lagoon was a reservoir on the east side of Los Angeles that served as a swimming hole used mainly by Mexican American youths. On August 1, 1942, a young man by the name of Jose Diaz was beaten and stabbed to death on a nearby ranch. The police conducted a sweep and rounded up over 100 young Mexican American men. A grand jury indicted 24 of them on charges ranging from assault to first-degree murder.[35]

During the trial, the judge allowed the prosecutor to introduce the issue of race and he exhibited blatantly bias attitudes toward the young Mexicans. The news media helped fan the flames of prejudice against the defendants and they were convicted. The California District Court of Appeals subsequently overturned the convictions, but the case had already created an atmosphere of prejudice against Mexican Americans.[36]

Similar to African Americans, Mexican Americans have historically experienced both good and bad times in America. The good times are evident by the fact they continue to migrate to America in search of a better life. They have benefited from social programs, such as the G.I. Bill, which educated those who served in the military. Yet, that did not allow Mexican Americans to gain full equality. They continue to work in jobs such as unskilled laborers, farm and agricultural workers, construction and many low paying positions. They continue to be drastically under-represented in the professions and in business. The disparity is also reflected in income for Hispanic workers.

Equally significant, educational achievement for Mexican Americans is lower than whites. Historically, they have attended schools with lower expenditures per student. Mexican American students have been disproportionately assigned to special education classes.

Mexican Americans have also been the victims of discriminatory treatment from law enforcement agencies. The conclusions reached by the U.S. Commission on Civil Rights, Mexican Americans and the Administration of Justice in the Southwest hold true today as they did in the beginning of their migration. The Commission found that Mexican Americans were the victims of "...excessive patrolling of Mexican American communities; anti-Mexican prejudice among police and judicial officials and wrongful use of law enforcement agencies in the search for undocumented aliens."[37]

Yet, similar to African Americans, Mexican Americans have made some progress. There are Mexican Americans in the United States Congress, mayors of large cities such as Los Angeles, California; Police Chiefs, educators, owners of successful businesses and they serve as directors on corporate boards. There is even a Hispanic justice on the United States Supreme Court, appointed by President Obama.

PUERTO RICANS[38]

Puerto Rico is a Caribbean island located east of the Dominican Republic. It is slightly less than three times the size of Rhode Island, measuring 100 miles long and 35 miles wide. It is one of the most densely populated communities in the world. It was discovered by Columbus and claimed on behalf of the Spanish Crown on his second voyage to the Americas in 1493. Indians, whose indigenous population was almost exterminated after 400 years of colonization, originally inhabited the island. Around that time, African slave labor was introduced to the island. As a result of intermarriage between Puerto Ricans and Africans, the skin complexion of Puerto Ricans ranges from very light to very dark. Puerto Ricans retained the Spanish language and are predominately Catholic. English is taught in schools as a second language.[39]

The United States has a very special relationship with Puerto Rico. In 1898, as a result of the Spanish American War, Puerto Rico was ceded to the United States. In 1917, Puerto Ricans were granted U.S. citizenship. As such, they have many of the same rights as U.S citizens. They serve in the military but they do not pay Federal income taxes and do not have the right to vote in American Presidential or Congressional elections. On three separate occasions, 1967, 1993, and 1998, plebiscites were held and the citizens of Puerto Rico voted to retain their status as a commonwealth.[40]

According to the U.S. Census Bureau, in 2000 there were 35 million Hispanics in United States. The vast majority, 58.5 percent were of Mexican descent. Border regions accounted for 9.6 percent or 3,406,178. That number almost equals the population of the Commonwealth of Puerto Rico.[41]

The Puerto Rican migration to the United States started around the turn of the twentieth century, with the majority of the immigrants settling in New York City. Today, Puerto Ricans live in every state in the nation.

Like other immigrants, Puerto Ricans came to the United States for job opportunities. Contrary to what some have said, they did not come to America because of better "welfare benefits."[42] Rather, companies seeking workers recruited many of them to come to America. Over the years, depending on the state of the U.S economy, the number of Puerto Rican immigrants has fluctuated. They followed in the steps of other minorities and filled low paying jobs that were once held by other immigrants. In New York City they worked in the hotel, restaurant and garment industries.[43]

Similar to African Americans and Mexican Americans, Puerto Ricans also experienced discrimination. They came from a country where color had little meaning, to this country where skin color was very relevant. In their home country discrimination existed, but it was based on economics and not color. Also similar to other immigrants, they found themselves in low paying jobs. As a result they were the least educated and poorest of the minority immigrants. [44]

The Puerto Rican experience in New York City was described by Rivera as follows: "Young immigrants kept coming from Puerto Rico full of high hopes and plans, only to find themselves facing a very hard reality. Their will power shattered and embittered by circumstances, they easily fell into crime."[45] As could be expected under those circumstances, many soon found themselves getting into difficulty with the law and entered the illegal drug trade. It did not take long for the media to start depicting Puerto Ricans as a problem.

Although many Puerto Ricans have obtained success in America and have white-collar jobs and high levels of education, many others suffer from economic problems and are the most economically disadvantaged of all Hispanic groups in America. Many also hold on to their ties with Puerto Rico. Similar to other groups, Puerto Rican communities in large urban areas are plagued by problems of crime, drugs and unemployment. Because many are a mixture of African and Spanish peoples, they have often suffered from the same problems that African Americans experienced.

They are becoming increasing active in the political process, especially in New York City.

CUBAN AMERICANS[46]

According to the 2000 U.S. Census, an estimated 1.2 million Cubans live in the United States. Cuban immigration to the United States dates back to the 1800s. Most, however, came during the past 40 years. Their immigration to America, under the dictatorship of Fugencio Batista, was estimated to be between 10,000 and 15,000 annually. They were "... a heterogeneous group, including members of the ruling classes who were out of favor at the time, other politically or socially alienated persons and unemployed persons seeking employment."[47]

After the 1959 revolution, when Fidel Castro and his forces defeated the Batista government, and announced that they would restructure the government of Cuba, the number of Cubans migrating to the United States increased significantly. It is estimated that about 155,000 Cubans fled to the United States between 1959 and 1962.

The United States government, because of its hostility towards the Castro regime, facilitated that immigration by not placing a quota on the number of Cubans who could legally enter the country. In fact, they granted some Cubans refugee status, which meant despite Cuba's immigration quota, there was no limit on the number of Cubans who could migrate. Americans embraced Cuban immigrants with open arms and a government celebration that was not given to other immigrant groups, particularly those of darker skins.

They were generally successful prior to leaving Cuba, as business owners, government officials and managers. They brought their families with them and expected to be able to return to Cuba in the future. Today, they are still in the United States and have been successful. Cuban Americans have a strong pride in their culture and are generally anti-Castro.[48]

The second wave of Cuban migration to the United States occurred between the mid-1960s and the mid-1980s. They came for both economic and political reasons. They were generally disenchanted with the Castro government and the direction the country was taking, contrasted to the first group that left because they were against the revolution. This group tended to be less educated and economically and educationally fragile. The group included criminals, both political and convicted law violators, the mentally ill and other "undesirables."[49]

About 125,000 of those coming to the United States during that period were Marielitos, people the Cuban government wanted out of the country. This included groups of criminals released from the prisons, and mentally ill persons.

They were placed on boats at Mariel Port in Cuba and sent to Miami. The United States government allowed them to enter the country while unaware that some were criminals and mental patients. Some were placed in U.S. prisons, released or allowed to return to Cuba.

Subsequent accounts questioned the number of criminals and mentally ill persons allowed to enter the United States, and it turned out that a smaller number had migrated to the U.S. [50]

Media reports in Cuba and the United States were generally negative towards the new immigrants. This created an attitude of resentment and animosity towards the Marilitos among Cubans in America.

In 1994, because of poverty and a lack of opportunities, thousands of Cubans set out for Florida on rafts and small boats. That influx was cut short when President Bill Clinton decided that the United States would not allow additional Cuban refugees into the country. Many of those attempting to make it to Florida were stopped at sea by the United States military and returned to the U.S. naval base at Guantanamo Bay, Cuba.

Today, the vast majority of Cuban-Americans reside in Florida. Miami is the home of more Cuban Americans than any other city in the United States. Cubans have also established themselves in New York, California and New Jersey. [51]

Cuban Americans have suffered from the same problems as other minority groups, but to a lesser degree. During the 1990s, Cuban Americans were the oldest of the Hispanic groups and among the highest educated. They also had the lowest level of poverty among the Hispanic groups, as well as the lowest level of unemployment.[52]

Cuban Americans have made substantial achievements in America. They have established themselves in all aspects of American life. In Florida, they have been extremely successful in politics.

ASIANS

Asians represent the smallest minority group in the United States. Initially, the term Asian was used to apply to those of Chinese, Japanese, Korean and Filipino dissent. Subsequently, the term was used to include Pacific islanders (Samoans, Hawaiians, Guamanians and Malaysians) as well as new arrivals - Vietnamese, Laotians, Cambodians and Thais. Indians and Pakistanis are referred to as South Asians.[53]

The 2000 U.S. Census reported that 11.9 million Asians or 4.2% of the American population was Asian.[54] The U.S. Census defined Asians as follows:

The term "Asian" refers to people having origins in any of the countries of the Far East; Southeast Asia or the Indian subcontinent (for example, Cambodia, China, India, Japan, Korea, Malaysia, Pakistan, the Philippine Islands, Thailand and Vietnam). Asian groups are not limited to nationality, but include ethnic terms as well.[55]

Asians, similar to African Americans and Hispanics, have been the victims of racial discrimination in America. The following reflects some of the difficulties Asians experienced when they arrived in the United States.

After its investigation into the civil rights issues confronting Asian Americans, the United States Commission on Civil Rights concluded that Asian Americans still faced widespread prejudice, discrimination and denial of equal opportunity.

Equally significant, the Commission concluded that Asian Americans were deprived of equal access to police protection, education, healthcare and the judicial systems. The commission identified three major factors that contributed to their plight:[56]

- The general public continues to have stereotypes that Asian Americans have overcome all negatives and is now a successful minority group.
- Cultural and linguistic barriers prevent Asian Americans from equal access to public services, including participation in the political process.
- Asian Americans suffer from a lack of political representation.

The Commission made 44 recommendations to address the problems of Asian Americans.[57]

The growth of the Asian American population after 1965 was attributed to refugees from Asia and, to a lesser degree, the Pacific islands.[58]

Collectively, Asian Americans as a group exceed the general population in education, employment and income.[59]

In 1990, the United States Commission on Civil Rights identified several reasons for intimidation and violence against Asian Americans.[60]

They included the ever changing racial characters of neighborhoods, racial hatred by organized hate groups and economic competition based on racial and ethnic lines. Insensitive media coverage was also cited.

Today, it would be a mistake to view the Asian American community as monolithic. Until the 1960s, the Asian Americans were mainly Chinese and Japanese. It is now a very diverse population, consisting of almost 30 ethnic groups, each with its own distinct culture.[61]

After September 11, 2001, following the terrorist attacks on the World Trade Center, the Pentagon and the forced crash of a plane in Pennsylvania, the United States waged a "war on terror." As a result, many South Asian Americans (Arab Americans and Muslim Americans) and individuals who "looked like" Muslims were targeted by American law enforcement.

They were subjected to questioning, surveillance, detention and deportation by the government. That was a clear case of official racial profiling.

CHINESE AMERICANS

The Chinese were the first Asians to arrive in the United States. Starting in the 1840s they came to work on plantations in Hawaii. In the early 1850s, they settled on the west coast to work in gold mines. Later they provided the labor to build the cross-country railroad.[62]

Chinese immigration to the United States began in 1848. Because of political turmoil in China and the promise of employment on the west coast, Chinese immigration to the United States increased significantly in the mid 1850s. For example, some 20,026 Chinese migrated to San Francisco in 1852. The Chinese population in the United States grew to 105,465 by 1880.[63]

The Gold Rush was the major economic reason for Chinese immigration to the United States. But, by 1854 gold mining by hand was replaced by mining that required the use of heavy hydraulic equipment. That reduced the number of claims that were worked by individuals and white miners came to see the Chinese as competitors, and forcibly took over their most productive claims.

In the 1850s California responded to the concerns of the white miners by passing a "foreign miner tax." Over the next few years additional legislation was passed that readjusted the tax rate.[64] Consequently, the ability of the Chinese to work in mines all but ended.

Discrimination against the Chinese was most evident by the fact they were not allowed to testify against whites in court cases.[65] This deprived them of due process when they were charged with a crime or when they were the victim of crimes committed by whites. It has been speculated that this was the reason for such a large number of Chinese imprisoned during the 1800s.

In 1882, the United States passed "The Chinese Exclusion Act." [66] The legislation restricted an entire nationality from immigrating to the United States. It was renewed every ten years until 1902.

The Chinese exclusion Act of 1882 "… was a watershed event in American history. Besides identifying for the first time a specific group of people by name as undesirable for immigrating to the United States, the Act also marked a fateful departure from the traditional American policy of unrestricted immigration."[67]

It is interesting to note that the Chinese government actually agreed with the legislation. They did so with the understanding that the United States would also enact legislation prohibiting American citizens from trafficking opium into China. As a result, in 1886 the United States enacted its first international drug trafficking law.[68]

The legislation had an unintended consequence for Chinese living in America. Not only did it restrict Chinese immigration, it also diminished the concept of family for Chinese men who came to United States to work. Male dominated societies emerged in the Chinese community because wives and children were forced to remain in China. This resulted in what we know today as "Chinatown," initially a community consisting of only Chinese males.[69]

Even before the Chinese Exclusion Act, many of the unions and political parties in the west embraced anti-Chinese platforms.[70] By 1871 both the Democratic and Republican parties in California adopted platforms opposing Chinese immigration and both national parties passed anti-Chinese resolutions in their platforms in 1876, 1880, 1888 and 1904.[71]

As, reported by Zhigham, "No variety of anti-European sentiment has ever approached the violent extremes to which anti-Chinese agitation reached in the 1870s and 1880s. Hangings, boycotts and mass expulsions harassed the Chinese."[72]

The media sparked much of the sentiment against the Chinese. The New York Times, for example, printed the following:

> We have four million degraded Negroes in the south. We have political passion and religious prejudice everywhere. The strain upon the Constitution is about as great as it can bear. And if, in addition, to all the adverse elements we now have, there were a tidal wave of Chinese population - a population befouled with all

social vices, with no knowledge or appreciation of free institutions or constitutional liberty, with heathenism souls and heathenism propensities, whose character, and habits, and modes of thought are firmly fixed by the consolidating influence of ages upon ages - we should be prepared to bid farewell to Republicanism and Democracy.[73]

Chinese workers were subjected to violence. Some twenty Chinese were massacred in Los Angeles in 1871 by a mob. Their homes and businesses were looted and burned.[74]

During World War II, China and the United States became allies. Subsequently the United States passed the *Magnuson Act* in 1943, also known as the *Chinese Exclusion Repeal Act of 1943*. Under that legislation, Chinese were able to migrate to the United States and become naturalized citizens. They were given a quota of only 105 immigrants annually.[75]

Today, Chinese Americans are a permanent part of the America landscape. Although *Chinatowns* still exist in many large cities such as San Francisco, New York, Los Angles and Chicago, Chinese Americans participate in all aspects of American life.

They are elected officials; they serve in the military and are entertainers. They are educators, professionals and athletes. Yao Ming, the former center for the Houston Rockets professional basketball team, is not only well known in China, but was also a recognized star in the United States before his retirement in 2011. Even outside of Chinatowns, Chinese restaurants are popular eating places. Some of this nation's leading academics are of Chinese descent.

JAPANESE AMERICANS

According to the 2000 U.S. Census, there were 796,700 Japanese Americans in the United States, making them the sixth largest Asian American group in the nation. The vast majority of Japanese immigrants settled on the west coast, mainly California. Even today, California is the home of more Japanese Americans than any other state, with Los Angeles having the largest concentration.[76]

Although there were similarities between Japanese immigrants and Chinese immigrants, there were major differences. The Japanese arrived in the United States later than the Chinese. Unlike the Chinese, Japanese women migrated to the United States sooner and in larger numbers than

Chinese women. Also, unlike China, Japan was a nation rapidly merging toward modernity.

Similar to the Chinese who immigrated to the United States, Japanese immigrants were also the victims of racial discrimination. It is a truth that "they inherited much of the resentment and prejudice that had been directed against the Chinese."[77]

One of the saddest chapters in the history of the United States was the internment of the Japanese during World War II. After Japan attacked Pearl Harbor, President Franklin D. Roosevelt signed *Executive Order 9066* on February 19, 1942, which authorized the Army to evacuate, and intern persons from "sensitive areas" for reasons of "national defense."[78]

Pursuant to that authority, on March 2, 1942, General John L. DeWitt announced the evacuation of persons of Japanese descent from an area that boarded the Pacific Ocean. This included all of California and most of Oregon and Washington. At the beginning, they were relocated to other parts of the country, but later were placed in relocation camps mainly on the west coast. Sadly, Japanese families were given less than one week's notice, and were only allowed to take with them things they could carry.[79]

Over 100,000 Japanese were interned in relocation camps and were not released until after the war was over.[80]

In retrospect, most Americans now acknowledge that the internment of the Japanese was a huge public policy mistake. There was no intelligence information that supported the executive order or General policies.[81] Actually, the Japanese did not pose any threat to the national security of the United States.

In 1980, the United States Congress established the *Commission on Wartime Relocation and Internment of Civilians* (CWRIC) to investigate the internment of the Japanese. It concluded:

The propagation of *Executive Order 9066* was not justified by military necessity and the decisions that followed it - detention, ending detention, and ending exclusion -were not driven by analysis of military conditions. The broad historical causes which shaped these decisions were racial prejudice, war hysteria and a failure of political leadership. Widespread ignorance of Japanese Americans contributed to a policy conceived in haste and executed in an atmosphere of fear and anger at Japan. A grave injustice was done to American citizens and resident aliens of Japanese ancestry who, without individual review or any probative evidence against them, were excluded, removed and detained by the United States during World War II.[82]

In 1976 President Ford issued *Executive Order 4417*, which rescinded Executive Order 9066. He also offered apologies to those who had been interned. In addition, prompted by the CWRIC report, the United States Congress passed the *Civil Liberties Act of 1988*. This legislation authorized reparations in the amount of $20,000 for each living survivor of the internment camps.[83]

Today, Japanese Americans are an integral part of American society and participate in all aspects of American life.

FILIPINO AMERICANS

According to the 2000 U.S. Census there were 1.8 million Filipino Americans in the United States, making it the second largest Asian American group in the nation.[84] Their migration to the United States can be attributed to two factors. Initially, the Philippines were a territory of the United States and its people were designated as "American Nationals."

Because of that designation, the laws that applied to other Asians did not apply to them. As a result, they were aggressively recruited to enter the country to serve as agricultural workers on the west coast. Because of the nature of the work, the majority of Filipino immigrants were males.[85] Also, they were one of the largest immigrant populations because of United States military activities in the Philippines.[86]

The earliest Filipino Americans arrived in the United States in 1763 and settled in Saint Malo, Louisiana. During the 1970s, a large number of Filipino immigrants settled in California, and in the southern part of the country. The majority came to the United States in search of employment, while a smaller number came seeking political freedom. Many had Spanish surnames because prior to becoming an American colony in 1898, the Philippines were a Spanish colony.

Similar to other Asian immigrants, Filipino Americans were also the victims of racial discrimination. "They were often called half civilized (or half savage), uneducated, worthless and unscrupulous. Racism against Filipinos was rampant since they were viewed as taking jobs from white workers.

Filipinos were also accused of luring white women; hence an anti-miscegenation law was passed. They were also called wasteful for their alleged ostentatious display of lifestyle, mainly clothing. Filipinos were denounced as being prone to crime and violence. In reality these statements were based on prejudice."[87]

Since the 1970s, the Philippines have been the largest supplier of health care professionals to the United States, sending nearly 25,000 nurses to this country between 1966 and 1985, and another 10,000 between 1989 and 1991. In 1989, Filipino nurses constituted close to 75 percent of the United States' foreign born nurses. In 2002, this figure rose to 85 percent.[88]

Filipino Americans generally came to the United States well educated. They were able to obtain white-collar jobs and fit rather easily into American society. According to Bankston... "At the close of the 20th century, Filipino Americans were more likely than others in the United States to work in management and professional jobs, showed rates in English proficiency similar to the rest of the population, and had higher percentages of high school and college graduates than other Americans did. While only 43 percent of traditional college-aged young adults in the United States were enrolled in an institution of higher education, the majority of the Filipinos in this age group were attending such institutions."[89]

KOREAN AMERICANS

According to the 2000 United States Census, there were 1,076,872 Korean Americans in the United States, making it the fifth largest Asian American subgroup. The largest Korean American population resided in Los Angeles, California.[90]

Koreans first came to the United States in 1903 as laborers. Between the years 1904 and 1907, some 1,000 Koreans moved to San Francisco, California. The Immigration and Nationality Act of 1965 ended the quota systems that restricted the number of Koreans that could enter the United States. At the end of the Korean War, a number of Korean wives of American servicemen came to the United States, as well as some 150,000 adopted children.[91]

When the first Koreans came to the United States they were targets of discrimination that included being accused of stealing jobs from Americans because they worked for lower wages.[92]

Korean Americans received national attention when they were targeted during the 1992 Los Angeles riots. The riots were precipitated by the acquittal of four white Los Angeles police officers who had been indicted for beating Rodney King, a Black man. Rioting erupted in the South Central Area of Los Angeles, an area known as Korea Town. South Central is predominantly Black, but Korean owned businesses were prominent.

Over the years, tensions had grown in the area between Black residents and Korean merchants because of cultural and language differences. A widely publicized shooting of a young black girl by a Korean grocer exacerbated the problems.

The riots destroyed over 2,000 Korean businesses that resulted in damages exceeding $400 million. A significant number of Koreans moved out of the area, many relocating to neighboring Orange County.[93]

Koreans are the highest self-employed ethnic group in the United States. They own fruit and vegetable markets, fresh fish stores, dry cleaners and nail salons. Approximately a third of the Korean immigrant families operate small businesses.[94]

VIETNAMESE AMERICANS

Vietnamese Americans are defined as residents of the United States who are of Vietnamese heritage.[95] They are relatively new arrivals to the United States, who started their immigration after the end of the Vietnam War in 1975. About 700,000 Vietnamese became refugees in the United States, making them the largest refugee group in the history of the country.[96]

When South Vietnam fell to the Communists on April 30, 1975, the United States immediately made emergency arrangements to bring thousands of Vietnamese to America.[97] The initial refugees were those who had served either the United States or Vietnam governments, either in official or quasi-official capacities. They were both military and civilians. Others were people of prominence, such as those of financial or social status (doctors, educators, journalists, entertainers and businessmen).[98]

The first Vietnamese refugees consisted of families or extended families. There was an average of four children per family, which accounted for the fact that 42 percent were under the age of 17 and 18.3 percent were between 18 and 24 years of age.[99]

Prior to 1975, there were virtually no Vietnamese people in the United States.[100] According to the 2000 United States Census, there were 1.2 million Vietnamese Americans in the United States, one-third living in California.[101] San Jose, California has the largest Vietnamese population in the United States.

Unlike other Asian Americans who came to the United States for economic reasons, the Vietnamese came as political refugees. Similar to other ethnic groups, Vietnamese Americans also had their problems with mainstream Americans. The Vietnamese refugees arrived in the United States at a time when American sentiment against them was high. It had been an unpopular war and many Americans wanted to put that experience behind them. That sentiment led to some resentment against the new arrivals.

One major example was the conflict between Vietnamese and white fishermen on the Gulf Coast of the United States during the 1980s. Because of this and the intervention of the Ku Klux Klan, the Community Relations Service of the United States Department of Justice interceded as mediator and helped negotiate a resolution.

Vietnamese gangs also became a significant problem. They engaged in home invasion robberies of other Vietnamese. The victims were reluctant to report the crimes to the police because of their distrust of government in their homeland. In an effort to bridge that gap, Houston, Texas was the first police department in America to hire a Vietnamese police officer.

The Vietnamese arrived when the United States was experiencing a recession. Because of high unemployment rates, it was difficult for many to find employment. As a result, many were forced to take jobs below their levels of education and prior experiences. They established small businesses, such as restaurants, grocery stores, beauty shops and nail salons.

President Jimmy Carter signed the *Refugee Act of 1980* which: (1) defined a refugee, (2) created the Office of Refugee Resettlement, (3) set 50,000 as the number of refugee admissions allowed by the United States (could be changed in event of an emergency) and (4) allowed refugees to change their refugee status after one year and begin the citizen process after the appropriate number of years.[102]

Today, Vietnamese American students have excelled academically. Members of the Vietnamese community have distinguished themselves in business, the professions and are increasingly becoming a part of all aspects of American life.

INDIAN AMERICANS

The term Indian American should not be confused with American Indians, who are the Native Americans. Indian Americans are people who immigrated to America from the country of India.

According to the 2000 United States Census, there were 1,679,000 Indian Americans in the United States.[103] That number grew to 2,570,000 in 2007, which represented a 53 percent increase.[104] Indian Americans have the highest rate of growth of any Asian American group. Indian Americans now constitute the third largest Asian American ethnic group in the United States.[105]

"While Indians have migrated to the United States for a variety of reasons since the late 19th century, changes in U.S. immigration policy in 1965 created the social conditions for a more rapid influx of professionals."[106]

Indian American's educational attainment is higher than any other ethnic group in the United States. Twenty four percent of all Americans have obtained bachelor's degrees or higher while nearly sixty four percent of Indian Americans have earned bachelors or advanced degrees.[107] A large number of Indian Americans have earned Master's degrees, doctorate degrees and other professional degrees.

Discrimination against Indian Americans has centered primarily on the issue of American companies relocating jobs to that country.

Indians are currently one of the most affluent U.S. minority populations. They have emerged as a 'model minority' whose public profile fits neatly into the logic of American multiculturalism.

They are hard-working, businesses owners and subscribe to a political conservatism that supports their material interests. Most importantly, they have attempted to define themselves in cultural terms and have avoided any obvious racial references.[108]

RACIAL PROFILING

Race and religious relations in America are threatened when the police single out people for a law enforcement action based solely on their race, religion or national origin. The problem of racial profiling reached the level of national debate during the past two decades.

The issue, however, has been a reality in American policing ever since there has been public law enforcement. Recognition of the problem has resulted in fundamental changes. Laws have been enacted prohibiting racial profiling and requiring police departments to capture information and report on their activities associated with citizen contact. Police departments have developed policies that prohibit racial profiling and implemented training programs that support those policies.

Racial Profiling represents a continuation of the issue of race relations that has long been an issue in American policing. Progress has been made over the years as evident by the number of minorities that now serve as police officers - including heads of police departments. Additionally, police officers are better educated today than ever before. Police departments have better training that includes diversity training. Nevertheless, racial profiling involves complex issues, and those issues are addressed in this chapter.

DEFINITION

Racial Profiling is a new phrase in the American language. Previously known as "*driving while black*," racial profiling describes incidents in which officers target minorities for a law enforcement action because of their race, religion, color or national origin.

It is the practice of officers stopping or investigating individuals or a group of individuals when nothing else links them to a crime. It impacts minorities of all social and economic levels.

Initially, racial profiling was practiced primarily against African Americans and to a lesser degree against Hispanics. After the terrorist attacks of September 11, 2001, Muslims, South Asians, Arabs and Middle Easterners became the subjects of profiling by law enforcement officials.

The Police Executive Research Forum (PERF), in its publication entitled Racially Based Policing: A Principled Response, discussed the "... accounts of people who have been stopped by police on questionable grounds and subjected to disrespectful behavior, intrusive questioning and a disregard for their Civil Rights. The storytellers came from all walks of life: they are young men and women, the elderly, people from the middle and upper classes, professional athletes, lawyers, doctors and police officers of every rank. "[109] The following are real examples of racial profiling:

- A young woman, in desperation, finally trades her new sports car for an older model because police have repeatedly stopped her on suspicion of possessing a stolen vehicle.
- An elderly African American couple returning from a social event in formal dress are stopped and questioned at length, allegedly because their car resembles one identified in a robbery.
- A prominent Black lawyer driving a luxury car is frequently stopped on various pretexts.
- A Hispanic deputy Police Chief is stopped numerous times in neighboring jurisdictions, apparently on "suspicion."
- A young Hispanic man working evening shift drives home on the same route five nights a week after midnight, and is stopped for suspicious behavior nearly every night.
- A Black judge far removed from her home jurisdiction is

stopped, handcuffed and laid face down on the pavement while police search her car. No citations are issued.

RACIAL PROFILING: THE POLICE VIEW

Police officers, similar to everyone else in society, are a product of their social environments. In effect, they are the products of the same social machinery that produces everyone else in society. Police officers have similar mental images of minorities, as do members of the general population. To a large degree, the face of the criminal, in the eyes of many, is a Black person.

Racial profiling is not an irrational response, rather it is a reaction to the mental image that some police officers have that Blacks are the personification of a criminal.

Consequently, there is an automatic response to an entire group of people without consideration of individual characteristics or distinctions. In other words, racial profiling is a consequence of minorities being stereotyped by police officers who mentally view blacks as criminals. They feel justified in stopping them without any evidence to support their actions.

The singling out of certain groups by the police is a natural consequence of the status of minorities in America. For example, if the police have an image of criminals as being Black or Hispanic, or the terrorists as being Muslim or Arab, in their minds they are properly performing their duties. They think they're preventing crime or preventing a possible terrorist act.

This problem is complicated because police officers are trained to be suspicious. They look for the normal so they can recognize the abnormal. In the minds of some, Blacks driving expensive cars or seen in predominately white neighborhoods is abnormal. Thus, the drivers are stopped, even though there is no evidence to suggest that they have committed a crime.

Although prejudice is an individual trait, it becomes a problem for the police because officers have the power to deprive others of their constitutionally guaranteed rights and their freedom.

The fact cannot be overlooked that there are some police officers that harbor racial feelings towards minorities and are inclined to inject their personal attitudes into the performance of their official duties. In doing so, they violate their oaths of office and cast abhorrent shadows on all police officers. The person who harbors prejudicial feelings may not recognize that they have them. Consequently, they carry out their duties and may allow their personal attitudes to influence their professional responsibilities. They see people who are different from them in a negative light. Thus, stopping a black man because he drives an expensive car is not considered as something wrong or unacceptable.

Racial profiling is also the consequence of the police constituting an occupational subculture. They work together and often socialize together. As a result, there is an environment for reinforcing the activities they engage in. Rarely will officers speak out against each other, even if they know an officer has done something wrong. This is known as the "blue code of silence."

To say that the vast majority of police officers are professionals is true, but that does not get to the root of the problem. Almost everyone would agree with that premise. It does, however, explain why racial profiling has been so prevalent in American policing.

Ultimately, racial profiling will be resolved when America resolves its race problem. In the meanwhile, the police have the unique opportunity to lead that change. Their success is critical because the minority segment of society has increased significantly in recent years and will continue to do so. A number of cities throughout America already have a minority population that is more than 50 percent.

As the police implement Community Policing, it is essential that they have the cooperation of all segments of the communities they serve. If large segments of the community believe the police discriminate against them, they are less likely to cooperate with officers. Even though the vast majority of police officers are fair and do not engage in wrongful conduct, those that do create a perception that all police officers are unfair and biased.

RACIAL PROFILING: THE MINORITY VIEW

Members of minority communities view racial *p*rofiling as a discriminatory and prejudicial police practice. That perception, in great part, is viewed as a continuation of their historical experience with policing in America. African Americans, for example, have always been a minority in the United States "…and until relatively recently have been systematically excluded by prejudicial laws and discriminatory policies from fully enjoying or participating in the cultural and economic promises of the American dream."[110]

The experiences of segregation have been passed down through the generations. The history of the police servicing as agents of the prevailing power structure to subjugate Blacks to an inferior status has not been forgotten. The struggles of the civil rights movement are still told to today's generation of African Americans.

The March on Birmingham, Alabama in May of 1963 represented a watershed day in the civil rights movement. The actions of the police are still remembered as an example of how the police were used to maintain the status quo. Birmingham Police Chief Eugene "Bull" Connor was the personification of racist police in the south. He ordered the use of high-powered fire hoses, police dogs and cattle prods against peaceful marchers; some as young as seven years of age.[111]

Selma, Alabama's segregationist Sheriff Jim Clark's actions were equally reprehensible when he ordered the police to use tear gas, nightsticks and whips to enforce Governor George Wallace's policies of segregation.[112]

Although the examples are extreme, many Blacks view racial profiling as a continuation of the racist practices of the police against them, although much less brutal. It took the intervention of the Federal government to allow those who were protesting on behalf of the rights of African Americans to engage in peaceful demonstrations, a right guaranteed by the Constitution.

The success of the Civil Rights movement brought about major changes in American society and brought with it changes in American policing. Yet, memories of the police as enforces of the status quo carry over even today. Celebrated cases such as the beating of Rodney King by Los Angeles police officers are incidents that serve to perpetuate racial disharmony.

Racial Profiling has a negative impact on those who are subjected to it. First, it has a psychological impact. Almost everyone, regardless of race, has a sense of anxiety when stopped by the police. This emotion is enhanced when minority persons are stopped and know that they have not done anything wrong. The problem is further exacerbated when the officers cannot give a legitimate reason for making the stop. This ultimately results in anger and a feeling of powerlessness because there is nothing they can do about the officer's actions. Even if they file a complaint at a later date, it is not likely that the officer will be found guilty of any wrongdoing. In most instances, it is the officer's word against the complainant's.

Second, it reinforces a belief held by many minorities that the police are racially biased. Being unjustly stopped is seen as a manifestation of the history of Blacks and law enforcement in United States. It generates a feeling of degradation and resentment towards the police in general.

Racial profiling is particularly troubling to minority men when they are stopped while their children are riding with them. They find themselves in a position of powerlessness, having to give deference to another adult in the presence of their children. To them it is a demeaning and humiliating experience that creates lasting resentment and bitterness.

I have personally experienced racial profiling. As a student at Fresno State College during the 1950s, I lived in the college dormitory on the east side of Fresno, which was predominantly white. On regular occasions I would be stopped at night on my way to my dormitory by white police officers and asked the same question, "What are you doing on this side of town?" I was always released after telling the officers that I was criminology major at Fresno State College.

As Sheriff of Multnomah County, Oregon I drove an unmarked county vehicle. One day while attending a meeting in Salem, the state capitol, I received a message asking me to call my office. When I called my secretary she told me that a Salem police officer, after checking the license plate of my vehicle, called to ask why a Black man was driving a sheriff's department vehicle.

While serving in the Cabinet of the President of the United States I was provided personal security by the U.S. Marshal's office. On one occasion I boarded a plane and was sitting in an exit row when a flight attendant informed my security detail that "prisoners cannot sit in the exit row."

While serving as Police Chief in Houston, Texas, I attended a meeting in Los Angeles, California. While standing in the lobby of the hotel wearing a suit and tie, I was approached by a well dressed white man who said rudely, "Get my bags and bring them in."

RACIAL PROFILING: THE SOLUTION

In addressing racial profiling, it is imperative that everyone understands that in a democracy every person is equal. It is also important to understand that the police are given a large amount of discretion in how they carry out their responsibilities:

Discretion allows tremendous flexibility of police response in any given situation, and allows for a tremendous amount of law enforcement and social policy making at the point of police-citizen contact. Discretionary choices - whether and how to enforce a particular law or policy - are inevitably impacted by the individual officer's biases and prejudices, by a cultural bias and prejudice ingrained in the law, and by the prescribed policies and practices of the police agency.[113]

The police can move beyond their current state of affairs by adhering to the principles of policing in a democratic society.[114]
1. Accountability
2. Integrity Beyond Reproach
3. Equal Enforcement of the Law
4. Value for Human Life
5. Respect for Others

Accountability in a democratic society means that the police are accountable to the law and the community. The people have the right to expect that all police activities will conform to the spirit as well as to the letter of the Constitution. Racial profiling is a violation of the basic public trust invested in the police by society. Accountability includes all aspects of the agency - hiring, training, evaluations, rewards, promotions, but most importantly it covers the responsibility for the conduct of all employees and how officers exercise their authority and individual integrity.[115]

Integrity beyond Reproach: Police officers in a democracy adhere to the limitations that are placed on their discretion and lawfully prescribed use of police authority in order to maintain and protect the civil liberties of every person. Because the police are granted awesome powers in a democracy and have a great deal of discretion; the potential for abuse of authority is always present. Racial profiling is an abuse of authority, police powers and discretion and is a distinct violation of integrity that strikes at the very heart of the fundamental principles on which a democracy is based – liberty and equality before the law, fairness and human dignity. Police departments must develop policies that clearly prohibit racial profiling and have a mechanism to receive and investigate alleged violations. They must also educate the public on how to register complaints charging officer misconduct.

Equal enforcement of the law means the police must apply the same standards of justice to every member of society. Equal enforcement requires all police officers to adhere to the guidelines and dictates of the Constitution, especially the 14th Amendment that declares that all men and women are to have equal protection under the law. To complement and reinforce the principles of the Constitution, police departments should develop a set of values stating that it is the responsibility of the police to not only enforce the law but also to protect the rights of all individuals. Recognizing the vast discretion granted to the police, Goldstein offered steps that can be taken to control that discretion and ensure credibility:

If discretion is to be exercised in an equitable manner, it must be structured; discretionary areas must be defined; policies must be developed and articulated; the official responsibility for setting policies must be designated; opportunities must be afforded to citizens to react to policies before they are promulgated; systems of accountability must be established; forms of control must be instituted; and ample provision must be made to enable persons affected by decisions to review the bases on which they were made.[116]

Values for human dignity are an attribute given to all members of a democratic society. Racial profiling is contrary to that principle. How officers treat people, especially minorities, is of utmost importance. Thus, the conduct of officers has great legal, social and moral implications.

Stopping or investigating individuals or groups based on race, religion or ethnicity is contrary to the principles of a democratic society and serves to polarize the police and minority communities. Demands of a democratic society dictate that the police do not discriminate against any person in the performance of their duties. It is essential that police departments establish clear guidelines and directives prohibiting racial profiling. Additionally, police applicants must be carefully screened and psychologically tested. Training must be devoted to address the moral, ethical and legal ramifications of racial profiling. Appropriate and objective reviews must be made when allegations of racial profiling are made.

Respect for the individual dignity of others is a value that every police officer must adhere to as he or she performs their duties. In a democratic society, especially under Community Policing, the police must be respectful of all communities and each individual in the community. It must never be forgotten that the police derive their powers from the community - all segments of the community - and can expect to maintain it only as long as the community has positive regard for their exercise of it. For the police to diminish their esteem through a disregard of individual and human rights is to diminish their capacity to regulate social behavior through persuasive, rather than proactive means. Under Community Policing, the police can only be effective if they have the admiration, esteem and respect of all segments of the community. In doing so, the difficult role of the police is far less difficult.

Racial Profiling demonstrates a lack of respect for individuals in all members of the minority community and is an affront to democracy and the principles it cherishes. The disparagement of any individual cannot be tolerated by policing in a democratic society. [117] Police agencies must ensure through hiring, training, discipline and, most importantly, by example of police leadership that no officer engages in racial profiling.

To complement the above principles, the police must establish relationships with minority communities.[118] Under Community Policing, the police must establish ongoing positive relationships with all segments of the community - including all minority communities. Absent such relationships, the police are less likely to accomplish its mission. It is important for the police to understand that what they do to involve the community in their efforts is essential to their success. It is incumbent upon the police to initiate and establish those relationships. To the extent the police know the people they serve, there is less likelihood to engage in the practice of racial profiling. [119]

Recognizing that racial profiling does exist (called Racially Biased Policing) the Police Executive Research Forum (PERF), reached the following conclusion:

"If prejudice, and arbitrary decisions, treatment disparity and disrespect are to be replaced by universal respect and equitable use of police powers, then we must begin a process of bringing all policing into accord with democratic principles. We must insist that protection of human rights is a fundamental responsibility of police. We must assure at all costs the primacy of the rule of law, and scrupulously monitor the use of police authority for compliance. We must carefully examine our beliefs regarding the role of the police, and eradicate from the police culture the mentality that leads to the use of bias in dealing with citizens. We must do this everywhere, and all of the time."[120]

DATA COLLECTION AND ANALYSIS:

PERF also determined that it is not sufficient to just collect anecdotal evidence on racial profiling. It is also essential that police agencies collect data as a means of self-assessment. Indeed, some police departments and some states have mandated data collection as a means of addressing the concerns of the community.[121] The Houston Police department was the first police agency in the nation to establish a racial profiling policy and implemented a system for collecting data on police officer self-initiated stops.

SUMMARY

Racial profiling has been acknowledged as a problem in American policing by police leaders, mayors, the U.S. Attorney General and the President of the United States. The challenge to American policing now is to ensure that the practice is abolished. This is important because racial profiling is illegal and unconstitutional. Equally important, it results in a humiliation that has a long-term negative impact. *Community Policing*, when properly implemented, enables the police to establish relationships with all segments of the community. That coupled with training in race relations, religion and cultural diversity should help bridge the historical gaps of mistrust that have long been a part of America policing.

NOTES: CHAPTER FOURTEEN

1. Higginbotham, A. Leon Jr., In the Matter of Color: Race and the American Legal Process, The Colonial Period, New York: Oxford University Press, 1978, p. 10

2. Franklin, John Hope, From Slavery to Freedom: A History of American Negroes, New York: Alfred A. Knopf, 1948, p. 186

3. Williams, Herbert and Patrick V. Murphy, "The Evolving Strategy of Police, The Minority View," Washington, D.C.: U.S. Department of Justice, National Institute of Justice and the Program in Criminal Justice Policy and Management, John F. Kennedy School of Government; Cambridge, Mass.: Harvard University, No. 13, January 1990, P.2

4. National Minority Advisory Council on Criminal Justice, The Inequality of Justice: A Report on Crime and the Administration of Justice in the Minority Community, Law Enforcement Assistance Administration, U.S. Department of Justice, Washington D.C: 1982, p.5

5. Dred Scott v. Stanford 60 U.S. 393 (1856)

6. See Bell, Derrick, Race, Racism and America, Boston: Little Brown and Co., 1980

7. National Advisory Commission on Civil Disorders, Report of the National Advisory Commission on Civil Disorders, Washington, D.C.: Government Printing Office, 1968, p. 1

8. Gossett, Thomas F., Race: The History of an Idea in America, New York: Schocken Books, 1965, pp. 261-262

9. Ibid. p. 258

10. Plessy v. Ferguson, 163 U.S. 537 (1896)

11. Op. Cit. Note 8, p. 279, also see National Association for the

Advancement of Colored People, <u>Thirty Years of Lynching in the United States,</u> New York: Arno Press, 1969

12. Myrdal, Gunnar, <u>American Dilemma: The Negro Problem and Modern Democracy</u>, New York: Harper and Brothers Publishers, 1944, pp.526-527

13. Brown v. Board of Education of Topeka, 347 U.S. 483 (1954)

14. Civil Rights Act of 1957, Public Law 85-3-15, September 9, 1957

15. Freedom Riders were Black and white Civil Rights activists who rode interstate transportation through the segregated south to challenge the opinion rendered by the United States Supreme Court in the case of Boynton v. Virginia

16. Boynton v. Virginia 364 U.S. 454 (1960)

17. Franklin, John Hope, <u>From Slavery to Freedom</u>, 5th ed., New York: Alfred A. Knopf, 1980, pp. 473

18. Op. Cit. Note 7

19. Ibid. p.1

20. Ibid.

21. Orlov, Ann and Reed Ueda, "Central and South Americas," <u>The Harvard Encyclopedia of</u> <u>American Ethic Groups</u>, Therstrom, Stephan, Ann Orlov and Oscar Handlin, (EDS), Cambridge, Mass.: The Belknap Press of the Harvard University Press, 1980, pp. 210-217

22. Cortes, Carlos E., "Mexican Americans," <u>The Harvard Encyclopedia of American Ethic Groups</u>, Thernstrom, Stephan, Ann Orlov and Oscar Handlin, (EDS), Cambridge, Mass.: The Belknap Press of the Harvard University Press, 1980, pp. 697-867

23. Op. Cit., Note 4, p. 59

24. Ibid.

25. Ibid.

26. Ibid. pp. 59-60

27. Ibid. p. 60

28. The Mexican War. http:// www.lone-star.net/mall//texasinfo/mexicow.htm

29. Op. Cit. Note 4, p.61

30. http://www.farmworkers.org/bracerop.html

31. <u>El Paso Herald Post</u>, April 28, 1956

32. Op. Cit. Note 4, p. 62

33. Kibbe, Pauline R., <u>Latin Americans in Texas</u>, Albuquerque, New Mexico: University of New Mexico Press, 2000

34. Op. Cit. Note 4, p. 62

35. Endore, S.Guy and Orson Wells, The Sleepy Lagoon Case, Los Angeles, Calif.: The Committee, 1943

36. Ibid.

37. U.S. Commission on Civil Rights, Mexican Americans and the Administration of Justice in the Southwest, Washington, D.C.: U.S. Government Printing Office, 1970

38. See, Fitzpatrick, Joseph P., Ann Orlov and Oscar Handlin (EDS), "Puerto Ricans," The Harvard Encyclopedia of American Ethnic Groups, Thernstrom, (EDS), Cambridge, Mass: The Belknap Press of the Harvard University Press, 1980, pp. 859-867

39. Op. Cit. Note 4, pp.65-66

40. The World Fact Book, Central Intelligence Agency https://www.gov/library/publications/the-world- factbook/geo/rq.htmlcia.gov/cia/publications/factbook/geos/rq.htm 1 (10-7-11)

41. Grieco, Elizabeth and Rachel C. Cassidy, "Overview of Race and Hispanic Origin, Census 2000 Brief, Washington, D.C.: U.S. Census Bureau, March 2001, p.3

42. Rodriguez, Clara E., Puerto Ricans: Immigrants and Migrants, a Historical Perspective, Americans All, a National Education Program, no date, http://www.americansall.comPDFs/02-americanc.all/9.9pdf (10-7-11)

43. Op. Cit. Note 4, pp. 67-68

44. Ibid. p. 69

45. Rivera, Cesar Iglesias, Memoirs of Bernardo Vega; A Contribution to the History of the Puerto Rican Community in New York City, New York: Monthly Press, 1984

46. Perez, Lisandro, "Cubans," The Harvard Encyclopedia of American Ethic Groups," Thernstrom, Stephan, Ann Orlov and Oscar Handlin, (EDS), Cambridge, Mass.: The Belknap Press of the Harvard University Press, 1980, pp. 256-261

47. Sessions, Peter L., The Hispanic Experience of Criminal Justice, New York: Hispanic Research Center: Fordham University, 1979, p.34

48. Op. Cit. Note 4, pp. 71-72

49. Op. Cit. Note 4, p. 76

50. Aguirre, B.E, Rogelino Saenz and Brian Sinclair James, "Marielites Ten Years Later: The Scar Face Legacy," Social Science Quarterly, Vol. 78, No.2, June 1997

51. "Cubans in the United States," Pew Hispanic Center, August 25, 2006 http://pewhispanic.org/files/factsheets/23.pdf (10-7-11) Also see

Giuseppe, R.A., (ED), The Story of Hispanics in America, http://www.history-world.org/hispanics.htm (10-8-11)

52. Ibid.

53. Chin, Laura (Ed.), <u>Civil Rights Issues of Asians and Pacific Americans: Myths and Realities</u>, A Consultation Sponsored by the United States Commission on Civil Rights, May 8-9, 1979, Washington, D.C.: U.S. Department of Health, Education and Welfare, National Institute of Education, 1980

54. Barnes, Jessica S. and Claudette E. Bennett, "The Asian Population: 2000," Washington, D.C.: U.S. Department of Commerce, Economics and Statistics Administration, United States Census Bureau, February 2002, p.1

55. Ibid.

56. Op. Cit. Note 4, p. 190

57. Ibid. PP. 190-206

58. Ibid. p. 13

59. Ibid. p.16

60. United States Commission on Civil Rights, "<u>Intimidation and Violence: Racial and Religious Bigotry in America</u>," Washington,D.C.: A Statement of the United States Commission on Civil Rights, Clearinghouse Publication 77, January 1983

61. Omatsu, Glen, "The Four Prisons and the Movement of Liberation: Asian American Liberation: Asian American Activism From the 1960's to the 1990's," in Zhou, Min and J.V. Gatewood, (EDS), <u>Contemporary Asian America: A Multidisciplinary Reader</u>, New York: New York University Press, 2007, p. 76

62. <u>Civil Rights Issues Facing Asian Americans in the 1990s,</u> A Report of the United States Commission on Civil Rights, Washington, D.C.: February 1992, p.2

63. Thomas, Chin, (EDS), <u>A History of Chinese in America</u>, San Francisco, CA: Chinese Historical Society of America 1969, p. 9

64. Ibid. p. 24

65. Ibid.

66. Chinese Exclusion Act, Forty-Seventh Congress, Section 1.1882, Chapter 126. This Act was the first significant legislation restricting an ethic group from immigrating to the United States. Also see, United States Commission on Civil Rights, <u>The Tarnished Golden Door: Civil Rights in Immigration</u>, Washington, D.C.: U.S. Government Printing Office, 1980

67. United States Commission on Civil Rights, <u>The Tarnished Golden Door: Civil Rights in Immigration,</u> September 1990, p.2

68. Forty Ninth Congress. Sess. H. Chas. 209, 210 1887, February 23, 1887. http://Constitution/uslaw/sal/024-Statutes-at-large.pdf pp.409-410 (10.31.11)

69. Daniel, Roger, <u>Asian America: Chinese and Japanese in the United States Since 1850</u>, Seattle: University of Washington Press, 1988, pp. 18-19

70. Ibid. p. 36

71. Op. Cit. Note 4, p. 6

72. Zhigham, John, <u>Strangers in the Land: Patterns of American Nativism: 1860-1925,</u> New York: Athenaeum, 1963, p.1

73. "Growth of the United States Through Immigration – The Chinese," <u>The New York Times</u>, September 3, 1865, p.4

74. Hata, Don Teruo, Jr., and Nadine Ishitani Hata, "Run Out and Ripped Off: A Legacy of Discrimination" <u>Civil Rights Digest</u>, Vol. 9, No.1 (Fall 1976), p. 10

75. Wei, William, <u>The Chinese American Experience: An Introduction</u> http://immigrants.harpweek.com/ChineseAmericans/.1Introduction/BillweiIntro.htm (10.17.2011)

76. Barnes, Jessica S. and Claudette E. Bennett, "The Asian Population: 2000, Census 2000 Brief, U.S. Census Bureau, February, 2002, p. 10

77. Takaki, Ronald, A History of Asian Americans: Strangers From a Different Shore, New York: Little Brown and Company, 1982, p.181

78. Op. Cit. Note 74, p.8

79. Op. Cit. Note 69, p .214

80. Commission on Wartime Relocation and Internment of Civilians, <u>Personal Justice Denied</u>, Washington, D.C.: U.S. Government Printing Office, 1983, pp. 101-107

81. Ibid. pp. 51-60

82. Op. Cit. Note 69, p. 331

83. Op. Cit. Note 69 p.33

84. Barnes, Jessica S. and Claudette E. Bennett, <u>The Asian Population: 2000, United States, February 2002,</u> Washington, D.C.: Department of Commerce, Economics and Statistics Administration, United States Census Bureau, p.9

85. Melendy, H. Brett, <u>Asians in America: Filipino, Korean and East Asians</u>, Boston: Twayne Publishers, 1977, p.46

86. Ibid. p. 33

87. Banston, Carl L. III and Danielle Antoinette Hidalgo, "The Waves of War: Immigrants, Refugees, and New Americans from Southeast Asia," in Zhou, Min and J.V. Gatewood (EDS), <u>Contemporary Asian America: A Multidisciplinary Reader</u>, New York: New York University Press, 2007, P. 150

88. The Philippine History Site, "Racial Discrimination," http://opmanong.ssc.hawaii.edu/fillipino/discrimination.html/ (5.8.09)

89. Espiritu Yen Le, "Gender, Migration. and Work: Filipino Heath Care Professionals in the United States," in Zhou, Min and J.V. Gatewood, (EDS), <u>Contemporary Asian America: A Multidisciplinary Reader</u>, New York: New York University Press, 2007, P. 259

90. Banston, Carl L. III, and Danielle Antoinette Hidalgo, "The Waves of War: Immigrants, Refugees and New Americans from Southeast Asia," in Zhou, Min and J.V. Gatewood, (EDS), <u>Contemporary Asian America: A Multidisciplinary Reader</u>, New York: New York University Press, 2007, P. 150

91. United States Census Bureau, <u>American Fact Finder, QT-P3. Race and Hispanic or Latino: 200</u>

92. Korean American, http://en.Wikipedia.org/wiki/KoreaAmerican (4.10.09)

93. Nash, Amy, "Korean Americans: Overview," http://everyculture.com/multi/Ha-La/Korean-Americans.html (4.10.09)

94. "Special Report: The Impact of the Los Angeles Riots on the Korean American Community," <u>Asia Today</u>, April 12, 2009 http://AsiaSource.org/news/At_mp_02_efm?newsid-7941 (4.21.09)

95. Lee, Jennifer, "Striving for the American Dream: Struggle, Success, Intergroup Conflict among Korean Entrepreneurs," in Zhou, Min and J.V. Gatewood, (EDS), <u>Contemporary Asian America: A Multidisciplinary Reader</u>, New York: New York University Press, 2007, P. 243

96. Wikipedia, The Free Encyclopedia, <u>Vietnamese American</u>, http://wikipedia.org/wiki/Vietnamese_America (4.10.09)

97. "The Vietnamese American Community," <u>Asian Nation</u>, p. 1. http://www.asian-nation.org/vietnamese_community.shtml (4.21.09)

98. Montero, Darrell, "Vietnamese Refugees in America", <u>International Migration Review</u>, 13, winter 1979, pp.16-17

99. Cassidy, William L., Observations on the Investigation of Crime Involving Vietnamese Suspects, Oakland, Calif.: Intelligence Studies Foundation, Inc., 1984, p. 1

100. Op. Cit. Note 98

101. Bankston, Carl L. III, "Vietnamese American: Overview," http://www.everyculture.com/multi/Sr-Z/Vietnamese-Americans. Html (4.21.09)

102. Op. Cit. Note 91

103. Vietnamese Americans: Lessons in American History, Vietnam and Vietnamese Americans After 1975 www.teachingtolerance/vietnamese (4.10.09)

104. Op. Cit. Note 91

105. United States Census Bureau, <u>American Fact Finder</u>, "United States – ACS Demographic and Housing Estimates: 2007"

106. Ibid.

107. Subramanian, Ajantha, "Indians in North Carolina: Race, Class, and Culture in the Making of Immigrant Identity," in Zhou, Min and J.V. Gatewood,(EDS), <u>Contemporary Asian America: A Multidisciplinary Reader</u>, New York: New York University Press, 2007, P. 162

108. Reeves, Terrance J. and Claudette E. Bennett, <u>We the People: Asians in the United States</u>, Census 2000 Special Report, U.S. Census Bureau, December 2004, p. 12

109. Subramanian, Ajantha, "Indians in North Carolina: Race, Class, and Culture in the Making of Immigrant Identity," in Zhou, Min and J.V. Gatewood, (EDS), Contemporary Asian America: A Multidisciplinary Reader, New York: New York University Press, 2007, p. 162

110. Fridell, Lorie, Robert Lunney, Drew Diamond and Bruce Kuby, <u>Racially Based Policing: A Principled Response</u>, Washington, D.C.: Police Executive Research Forum, 2001

111. Brown, Lee P., "Role of the Police in a Democratic South Africa – The Problem of Police Partisanship in Divided Communities: Lessons Learned from the American South," a paper presented at the Conference on Policing in the New South Africa; The Center for Justice, Natal: University of Natal Law School, June 5, 1991

112. Sitton, Claude, "Rioting Negroes Routed by Police in Birmingham, <u>New York Times</u>, May 8, 1963, p.1

113. Reed, Ray "25,000 go to Alabama's Capitol: Wallace Rebuffs Petitioners: White Rights Worker is Slain, <u>New York Times</u>, March 26, 1965, p. 1.

114. Op. Cit, Note 111. p. 5

115. The elements discussed here revised from Ibid.

116. Goldstein, Herman, <u>Policing a Free Society</u>, Cambridge, Mass.: 1977, Ballinger, p.131

117. Ibid. p.110
118. Ibid.
119. Op. Cit. Note. 110, p. 9
120. Ibid.
121. Op. Cit. Note 109, p. 10

Chapter Fifteen:

TERRORISM AND HOMELAND SECURITY

INTRODUCTION

September 11, 2001 was a watershed day for America, especially American law enforcement. What is now referred to as 9/11 was a coordinated attack on the United States that involved the hijacking of four American commercial airliners. The events that transpired that day changed not only America, but also the entire world forever.

> Law enforcement must continually seek to strengthen democratic institutions as the best defense against terrorism

Terrorist attacks struck New York City, Washington D.C. and Shanksville, Pennsylvania. The attack in New York destroyed the twin towers at the World Trade Center, a visible symbol of America's economic might. An airplane was flown into each of the two towers. Both towers crashed to the ground.

The Pentagon, headquarters for the United States military and a symbol of America's military might, was a target of the Washington, D.C. attack. A third plane was flown into the Pentagon which is located in Arlington, Virginia, just outside of Washington, D.C.

A fourth plane was forced to the ground by its passengers in the rural area of Somerset County, Pennsylvania, about 80 miles east of Pittsburgh. It is believed that the plane had as its intended target either the United

States Capitol or the White House, both symbolic of America's democratic form of government.

The attacks resulted in 2,986 people losing their lives and billions of dollars in damages.[1]

According to *The National Commission on Terrorist Attacks on the United States*, 19 of the hijackers were members of *al-Qaeda*, an Islamic terrorist organization. The head of the group was Osama bin Laden, a Saudi. Khalid Sheikh Mohammad is credited with planning the attacks.[2]

Prior to September 11, 2001, the United States did not have an earnest fear that terrorism would occur on American soil. As a result, it was caught off-guard by the attacks. Other than the Japanese attack on Pearl Harbor on December 7, 1941, the September 11th attacks were the first time America had been attacked on its own soil. The attacks brought home one of America's greatest fears. Although America had been the target of terrorist activities before, the country had been fortunate not to have those attacks occur on American soil; rather they occurred mainly overseas, with American facilities being the targets.

The attacks of September 11, 2001 ultimately resulted in a major change in the structure of the Federal government and its relationship with state and local governments. That day also added a new term to the vocabulary of the nation - *"Homeland Security."* Homeland Security, by definition, means protecting America from additional terrorist attacks. The events also changed law enforcement's understanding and response to the problem of terrorism.

In response to the attacks, the United States and its allies launched a massive attack in Afghanistan against the Taliban and its leader Osama Bin Laden.

Announcing that Saddam Hussein, the dictator of Iraq, posed an imminent threat to the United States because he possessed Weapons of Mass Destruction (WMD), the United States and its allies launched a massive attack against that country. After an extensive search, Hussein was captured by American troops and turned over to the Iraqi government to stand trial for war crimes. His government was tumbled and a new government was installed. American troops remain in Iraq; yet no WMDs were ever discovered. Hussein was convicted for crimes against humanity on November 5, 2006, sentenced to death by hanging and publicly executed on December 30, 2006.

DEFINITION OF TERRORISM

Terrorism is a word loaded with connotations that people use to refer to a variety of violent activities. However, upon close inspection of the etymology of "terrorism," it can be seen that in the beginning, the word was used in a loose manner to describe many activities.

The Jacobins first used the word in 1796, to describe their violent, but unorganized revolutionary actions in a commendatory way.[3] The 1798 supplement to the Dictionnarie of the Academy Francaise defined terrorism as "...*systeme, regime de la terreur.*"[4] From its inception, the definition of terrorism remained loose, alluding to chaotic, violent acts connected to the ambiguous political goals of the Jacobins. This loose definition of group supported and politically inspired violence can be used to examine some of the incidents of terrorism throughout history. [5]

The Jacobins were not the first terrorists. One of the earliest instances of terrorist activities was that of the Sicarii, a religious sect that existed during the first century A.D. that fought against the Roman rule of Palestine by using subversive methods such as attacking crowds with concealed weapons and sabotaging Jerusalem's water supplies. [6]

During colonial times, secret societies' murders in India and China took on mystical and political overtones, while their aims were never clearly political or religious.[7]

It is apparent that while terrorism is not a new concept, it has developed into something broader in scope than those early historical examples of small groups fighting for political or more obscure reasons.

Modern examples of terrorism began with the rise of nationalism in the 18th and 19th Centuries. These are distinguished from previous examples by the scope of their activities. During this period, terrorist movements galvanized support from believers in democracy and nationalism. They had long been oppressed by monarchies or authoritarian governments and perpetuated systematic waves of terror against their oppressors. Russia weathered several waves of politically motivated violence that targeted Tsar Alexander II and later the Communist Party. Struggles for independence increasingly characterized terrorist movements, as seen in Ireland in the 1860s, Armenia in the 1890s, and Macedonia in the early 20th Century.[8]

Nationalist-independence movements continued to dominate the realm of terrorism preceding World War I and continuing into post World War II, becoming more right wing and urban in nature. Assassinations in Egypt and the rise of the Muslim Brotherhood signified the ominous beginning of Middle Eastern terrorist movements. Modern terrorism had left the realm of historical obscurity and become intertwined with notions of freedom fighting and nationalism. [9]

Modern scholars struggle to define terrorism because they face the difficulty of oversimplifying the term and therefore rendering it indistinguishable from other types of violence or by contrast, making the definition overly complex or verbose in order to cover all examples of terrorism. [10] Grant Wardlaw, senior criminologist from the Australian Institute of Criminology, avoids both pitfalls by neither paring down the term to a general and uninformative concept nor encompassing too many examples of terrorist activity:

> Political terrorism is the use, or threatened use, of violence by an individual or group, whether acting for or in opposition to established authority, when such action is designed to create extreme anxiety and/or fear-inducing effects in a target group larger than the immediate victims with the purpose of coercing that group into acceding to the political demands of the perpetrators. [11]

While comparing different explanations of terrorism, several definitive characteristics emerge: (1) unlawful use of force, (2) intentional intimidation and coercion of victims, and (3) a target group larger than the immediate victims. Keeping these three characteristics of terrorism in mind is useful when determining whether an act or group can be described as "terrorist."[12]

Following are examples of the variety of ways terrorism has been defined:

- Terrorism is an action, usually involving the placement of a bomb or fire explosive of great destructive power, which is capable of delivering irreparable loss to the enemy. [13]
- The calculated use of violence such as fear, intimidation or coercion, or the threat of such violence to reach goals that is political, religious or ideological. Terrorism involves a criminal act that is often symbolic in nature, intended to influence an audience beyond the immediate victims.[14]
- Title 22 the United States code, section 2656f (d) defines terrorism as, "…premeditated, politically motivated violence perpetrated against noncombatant targets by sub-national groups or clandestine agents, usually intended to influence an audience."[15]

- The Code of Federal Regulations, (28 CFR 0.85 (L) defines terrorism as "… the unlawful use of force and violence against persons or property to intimidate or coerce a government, the civilian population, or any segment thereof, in furtherance of political or social objectives." [16]

<u>Terrorists</u> are defined as those "…individuals who plan, participate in, and execute acts of terrorism."[17]

<u>Supporters of terrorists</u> are defined as "… individuals, loose knit groups, tightly knit groups, political factions, agencies of governments and even governments themselves." [18]

<u>Victims of terrorism</u> are "… individuals, family members, a community, or a whole race, ethnic group, or nation."[19]

<u>Counter-terrorist operatives</u> are "Anyone actively engaged in the battle against terrorism…" [20]

TERRORIST GROUPS

Terrorists groups, by definition, exist for a wide range of reasons. The following are examples of well-known terrorist organizations.

Minority Nationalist Groups

Organizations that fall in this category are formed to oppose the dominant political authority, culture or community. Examples of those who fit into this category are the *Official and Provincial Wing of the Irish Republic Army* (IRA), the *Spanish Basque National Movement* (ETA), the *Corsican Separatist Movement* (Ein Tiro) in North Eastern Italy and the *Fuerzas Armadas de Liberation Nacional* (FALN) in Puerto Rico.[21]

Marxist Revolutionary Groups

These groups have as their goal socialist revolution. They include such groups as the *Weather Underground* in the United States, the *Red Brigade* in Italy, *Direct Action* in France and the *Communist Combatant Cells* in Belgium. [22]

Anarchist Groups

These groups are characterized as anti-establishment, mainly of European origin. They represent such organizations as the *Baader-Meinhof Gang* in West Germany and the *MIL* in Spain. [23]

Neo-Fascist-Right Wing Extremists
Groups that fall into this category are mainly an American phenomenon. These groups are white supremacists that identify with Nazi symbolism. The *Aryan Nation*, *Posse Comitatus* and the *Ku Klux Klan* are examples of such groups. [24]

Pathological Group/Individuals
Individuals such as *Charles Manson* and groups such as the *Symbionese Liberation Army* fall into this category. [25]

Ideological Mercenaries
This category represents groups that believe in worldwide revolution. Groups such as the *Japanese Red Army* fall into this category. [26]

The following characteristics are present in the vast majority of terrorist acts:
- The use of violence as a method of systematic persuasion
- The selection of targets and victims with maximum propaganda value
- The use of unprovoked attacks
- The act is designed to gain maximum publicity with minimum consequences to the terrorist
- The use of surprise to overcome countermeasures
- The use of threats, harassment and violence to create an atmosphere of fear
- The lack of recognition of civilians or women and children as "noncombatants"
- The use of propaganda to maximize the effect of violence and to achieve political or economic goals
- The perpetuation of terrorist attacks by groups whose only loyalty is to each other

DOMESTIC TERRORISM

The Federal Bureau of Investigation (FBI) defines domestic terrorism as "... unlawful use, or threatened use, of force or violence by a group or individuals based and operating entirely within the United States (or its territories) without foreign direction, committed against persons or property to intimidate or coerce a government, the civilian population, or any segment thereof, in furtherance of political or social objectives." [27]

In its 1999 report, the FBI reported on the following domestic terrorist organizations:

Animal Liberation Front (ALF) does not have a formal organization. Its stated goal is to reduce animal suffering in the world through direct action and inflict economic damage on the abusers. [28]

Earth Liberation Front (ELF) describes itself as: "... an international underground movement consisting of autonomous groups of people who carry out direct action in defense of the planet." [29]

World Church of the Creator (WCOTC) has as one of its 16 commandments to, "...populate the lands of this earth with white people exclusively," [30]

Aryan Nation, is an all-white, racist, anti-Semitic, white supremacy group that has the goal of establishing, "... a white Aryan homestead on the North American continent..." [31]

Posse Comitatus is a loose organization of people who believe the county is the only government, the sheriff is the highest governmental official and that the Federal government has no authority. It is an anti-government, anti-Semitic, anti-tax and anti-Black extremist group. [32]

Special interest terrorism consists of those groups that "... seek to influence specific issues, rather than effect widespread political change. Special interest extremists conduct acts of politically motivated violence to force segments of society, including the general public, to change attitudes about issues considered important to their causes. These groups occupy the extreme fringe of animal rights, pro-life, environmental, anti-nuclear and other movements." [33]

Right Wing Terrorists "...often adhere to the principles of racial supremacy and embrace anti-government, anti-regulatory beliefs. Generally, extremist right-wing groups engage in activity that is protected by constitutional guarantees of free speech and assembly." The World Church of the Creator and the Aryan Nations fit this category. [34]

Left Wing Terrorists "... generally profess a revolutionary socialist doctrine and view themselves as protectors of the people against the dehumanizing results of capitalism and imperialism. They aim to bring about change in the United States and believe this change can be realized through revolution rather than through an established political process." Groups such as the Popular Puerto Rican Army and the Los Macheteros fit into this category. They have as their goal full independence of Puerto Rico from the United States through violence.[35]

STATE SPONSORED TERRORISM

The U.S. Department of State is required by law to designate those countries that repeatedly provide support for international terrorism. Such a designation has four major consequences: (1) restrictions on U.S. foreign assistance, (2) a ban on defense exports and sales, (3) certain controls over exports of dual items and (4) miscellaneous financial and other restrictions.[36] There are also sanctions against individuals and countries who engage in certain trade with countries that have been designated as state sponsors of terrorism. As of 2009, there were four countries designated as state sponsors of terrorism: (1) Cuba designated on March 1, 1982, (2) Iran, designated on January 19, 1984, (3) Sudan, designated on August 12, 1993 and (4) Syria, designated on December 29, 1979.[37]

INTERNATIONAL TERRORISM

The FBI defines *International Terrorism* as "violent acts or acts dangerous to human life that are a violation of criminal laws of the United States or any state, or that would be a criminal violation within the jurisdiction of the United States or any state. These acts appear to be intended to intimidate or coerce a civilian population, influence the policy of a government by intimidation or coercion, or affect the conduct of the government by assassination or kidnapping. International terrorist acts occur outside the United States or transcend national boundaries in terms of the means by which they are accomplished, the persons they appear intended to coerce, or intimidate, or the location in which the perpetrators operate or seek asylum."[38]

FOREIGN TERRORIST ORGANIZATIONS

The United States Department of State has the responsibility of designating foreign organizations as *Foreign Terrorist Organizations* (FTO). Such a designation is used as a means of curtailing support for terrorist activities with the intent of getting the organizations out of the terrorist business.[39]

For an organization to be designated a foreign terrorist organization, it must be a "foreign organization" that engages in terrorist activities as defined by the laws of the United States, or have the capacity and intent to engage in terrorist activities or terrorism.[40] The activities of the organization must threaten the security of United States citizen or the national security of the nation.

Once an organization is designated as a FTO, it becomes illegal for "a person in the United States, or subject to the jurisdiction of the United States, to knowingly provide 'material support or resources' to it. In addition, any member or representative of a FTO, if they are not U.S citizens, are not allowed to enter into the United States, and under certain circumstances may be removed from the country. Furthermore, any U.S. financial institution that becomes aware that it has control over funds of a designated FTO must freeze the funds and notify the Office of Foreign Assets Control in the Treasury Department."[41]

As of September 2011, there were 49 organizations on the United States Foreign Terrorist Organizations list: [42]

1. *Abu Nidal Organization (ANO)* was founded in 1974 and its goal is the destruction of the state of Israel and the establishment of a Palestinian state. It has a few hundred members.

2. *Abu Sayyaf Group (ASG)* was founded in 1991 and its goal is the establishment of a separate Islamic state for the minority Muslim population of the Philippines. It has been reported that since the late 1990s, the organization has evolved into a violent gang of bandits seeking financial gain. It is estimated that its membership ranges between 200 and 500.

3. *Al-Aqsa Martyrs Brigade (AAMS)* was founded in 2000 and its goal is to expel Israeli soldiers and settlers from the West Bank and Garza, and establish a Palestinian state.

4. *Al Shabaab (The Youth in Arabic)* was founded in 2004 as an Islamic militant group that has as its goal the creation of an Islamic state in Somalia. It has approximately 3,000 to 7,000 members.

5. *Ansaar al-Islam (AAI)* was founded in Somalia in 2001 with the goal of establishing an independent Islamic state in Iraq. It is a Sunni extremist group consisting of Iraqi Kurds and Arabs. Its membership is about 700 to 1,000.

6. *Asbat al-Ansar* was founded in the 1990s and has approximately 300 members, mostly Palestinian refugees in Lebanon. Its stated goal is to establish an Islamic state in Lebanon, and to eliminate anti-Islamic and U.S. influence in that country.

7. *Aum Shinrikyo (AUM))* was established in 1987 and its goal is the control of Japan and the world, and the creation of a global utopian society. It is estimated that the organization has between 1,500 and 2,000 members.

8. *Basque Fatherland and Liberty (ETA)* was established in 1959 and has as its goal the establishment of a Basque homeland focused on Marxist principles in the ethically Basque areas of Spain and southwestern France. It is estimated that there are several hundred members or supporters of the organization.

9. *Communist Party of Philippines/New People's Army (CPP/NPA)* was established in 1969 and has as its goal the creation of a Marxist state in the Philippines through a violent uprising against the Philippine government. It is estimated that there are between 5,000 and 11,000 members.

10. *Continuity Irish Republican Army (CIRA)* was founded in 1986 and has as its goal the removal of British forces from Ireland and unification of the country. It is estimated to have fewer than 50 hard core activists.

11. *Gama'a al-Islamiyya (Islamic Group)* was established in the late 1970s and its goal is the overthrow of the secular Egyptian government and replacing it with an Islamic state, which would be governed by Shari' law, and void of "un-Islamic" influences. At its peak, the organization had several thousand followers but the number of followers at this time is unknown.

12. *Hamas (Islamic Resistance Movement)* is a radical Islamic Palestinian organization whose initial goal was to expel Jews and Israel from Palestine in order to create an Islamic Palestinian state. The group recently modified its goals, giving an indication that they would likely accept a favorable Israeli -Palestinian agreement. The exact number of members

and/or sympathizers is unknown. There are some estimates that suggest there are tens of thousands of members and sympathizers that are uncompromising in their "anti-Israel position, attacks against Israel and opposition to corruption in the Palestinian Authority."

13. *Harakat ul-Ji-Island/Bangladesh (HUJI-B)* was founded by a group of Bangladeshi veterans with the goal of establishing Islamic rule in Bangladesh. It is reported that Osama bin Laden's International Islamic Front assisted them. They operate primarily in Bangladesh and India. It is estimated to have 1,500 members.

14. *Harakat ul Mujahidin (HUM)* was started in the 1980s and is a Palestine-based militant organization whose goal is to take Jammu and Kashmir from India and create an Islamic state comprised of Pakistan and certain territories. It is estimated that the group has several thousand armed supporters.

15. *Hizballah (Party of God)* was established in 1982 and its goal is the liberation of Jerusalem, the destruction of Israel and ultimately the establishment of an Islamic state in Lebanon. It is estimated that the group has between 2,000-5,000 supporters and several hundred terrorist operatives

16. *Islamic Jihad Union (IJU)* is an Islamic terrorist group that split from the Islamic movement of Uzbekistan. It advocates holy war. Aligned with the Taliban and al-Qaeda, its membership is estimated to be between 100 and 200.

17. *Islamic Movement of Uzbekistan (IMU)* started in 1991 has as its goal the overthrow of secular rule in Uzbekistan. It also wants to establish Islamic rule in other Central Asian countries. It is dedicated to fighting declared enemies of Islam. It is estimated that the group has less than 1,000 members.

18. *Jaish-e-Mohammed, (JEM) or (Army of Mohammed) was* established in 2000. Its goal is Indian rule in Jammu and Kashmir. Ultimately it seeks to unite Jammu and Kashmir with

Pakistan by expelling Indian security forces from the region. The organization has several hundred armed supporters.

19. *Jemaaah Islamlya (JI)* dates back to the 1940s but the name did not emerge until the 1970s. It is a radical Islamic group whose goal is the creation of a strict Islamic state to replace Indonesia, Malaysia, Singapore, the southern Philippine Islands and southern Thailand. The number of members is unknown. Estimates range from several hundred to 5,000.

20. *Kahane Chai (Kach)* was established in 1971 as a radical Jewish group that has the goal of restoring the biblical state of Israel by annexing the West Bank, Gaza as well as parts of Jordan. It also strives to expel all Arabs from that territory and establish a strict implementation of Jewish law. The exact membership of the organization is unknown.

21. *Kata 'ib Hezbollah (KH)* is a radical Shia Islamist group with a jihadist ideology. It is against the western establishment and has conducted strikes against the United States and Iraq. It was established a few months before the Iraq war. Its goal is to end U.S and other foreign intervention in Iraq and establish a Shiite Islamic government. It is estimated that they number about 200 fighters and supporters.

22. *Kongra-Gel (formerly Kurdistan Workers Party (PKK, Kadek)* was established in 1978 with the original aim of establishing an independent Kurdish homeland in the ethically Kurdish regions of the Middle East which overlaps the borders of Turkey, Iran, Iraq and Syria. More recently, the organization's goal was to establish greater political and cultural rights for Kurds within Turkey. It is estimated that there are between 4,000 and 5,000 fighters in the organization.

23. *Lashkar-e-Tayyiba (LTO or Army of the Righteous)* was established in 1990 as a radical Islamic group in Pakistan with the goal of establishing Islamic rule throughout South Asia. India blamed the organization for the Mumbai attack in December 2008 that killed 174 people, including nine gunmen. The group also aims to establish Islamic rule over

all of India. It is estimated that there are several hundred members in the organization.

24. *Lashkar I Jhangvi (LJ)* was established in 1996 with the goal of making Pakistan a Sunni Islamic state based on Islamic law. The group has close ties with Al Qaeda and adheres to an anti western and anti U.S. ideology. It is estimated that they have less than 100 followers.

25. *Liberation Tigers of Tamil Eelam (LTTE)* was established in the 1970s as a separatist group in Sri Lanka with the goal of establishing an independent state to include the ethically Tamil region of the island. Recently, the group has changed its goal and now states that they will accept, "a solution that respects the principal of self-determination, possibly an autonomous area for Tamil-speaking peoples within a Federal structure." It is estimated that the group has between 7,000 and 10,000 armed combatants and a substantial number of supporters both in Sir Lanka and overseas.

26. *Libyan Islamic Fighting Group (LIFG)* was founded in the early 1990s and is a radical Islamic group that is committed to overthrowing the Libyan government. It is estimated to have between 100 and 2,000 members and sympathizers.

27. *Moroccan Islamic Combatant Group (GICM)* is a Sunni Islamic terrorist organization affiliated with al-Qaeda. It was formed in the 1990s. Its goal is the creation of an Islamic state in Morocco. The size of its membership is unknown.

28. *Mujahedin-e Khalq Organization (MEK)* was founded in the 1960s and opposed the regime of the Shah of Iran in the 1970s. It is in favor of a secular government in Iran. It has voiced its support for the Arab-Israeli peace process and the rights of Iran's minorities. Its membership is made up of Iranian dissidents who are opposed to Islamic rule in Iran. It is estimated that there are several thousand fighters in Iran, and other members operating overseas.

29. *National liberation Army (ELN)* was established in 1964 with

the goal of overthrowing the government of Colombia and replacing it with a socialist system. It modeled itself after Cuba's Marxist revolution. It claims to represent the oppressed poor in Colombia against the wealthy and opposes privatization and the influence of the United States in Colombia. It is estimated that there are between 3,000 and 5,000 armed militants with an unknown number of supporters.

30. *Palestine Liberation Front (PLF)* was established in 1959 with the goal of destroying Israel and establishing a Palestinian state on its territory. It is estimated that it has between 300 and 500 members.

31. *Palestinian Islamic Jihad (PIJ)* was established in 1979 by Palestinian students in Egypt. Its goal was the establishment of an Islamic Palestinian state and the abolishment of the state of Israel. The exact number of members of the organization is unknown but in the past it was reported to have as few as 250 militants.

32. *Popular Front for the Liberation of Palestine (PFLP)* was established in 1967. Its goal is the destruction of the state of Israel and the establishment of a socialist Palestinian state. It also seeks to end American influence in the region. It is reported to have between 800 to 1,000 members.

33. *PFLP-General. Command (PFLP-GC)* was founded in 1968 in a split from the Popular Front for the Liberation of Palestine, claiming that it wanted to focus on a military solution rather than a political one to resolve the Israeli conflict. It has close ties to Syria and Iran. It has a membership of several hundred.

34. *Qaeda in Iraq Al-(AQI)* is a Sunni Muslim extremist group that was founded in 2003 as a division of Osama bin Laden's al-Qaeda organization. Its goal is to force the United States and its allies out of Iraq and to help govern the country. It is estimated that membership exceeds 10,000.

35. *Al Qaeda (AQ)* had its beginning with the invasion of Afghanistan by the Soviets in 1979. Its goal is to destroy

the regimes of the Muslim countries that it deems to be "non-Islamic" and establish a world-wide Islamic religious government using the ancient Caliphates as its model.

The United States and its allies are viewed as the major roadblocks to their goals and the group has called on all Muslims to kill Americans, military or civilian, in order to end Western influence in the Muslim world. Al Qaeda was responsible for the attacks in America on September 11, 2001 in New York, Virginia and Pennsylvania. Its founder, now deceased, was Osama bin Laden. Although the size of the organization is not known, it is believed that they have several thousand fighters.

36. *Al Qaeda in the Arabian Peninsula (AGAP)* was formed in 2009 by merging Al Qaeda's Yemeni and Saudi Arabian branches. It is based in Yemen. Its American-born cleric leader, Anwar al-Awlaki was killed on September 30, 2011 in an American drone attack. It is believed that the organization has several hundred members.

37. *Al Qaeda in the Islamic Maghreb (formerly GSPC)* was known as the Salafist Group. It was founded in 1998 and has as its goal replacing the current government with an Islamic state. It is estimated to have between 300 and 800 members.

38. *Real IRA (RIRA)* was established in 1997 with the goal of expelling British troops from Northern Ireland. Its objective is to unify the island of Ireland. It is estimated that there are between 100 and 200 active members of the organization.

39. *Revolutionary Armed Forces of Colombia (FARC)* was established in 1964 and its goal is to establish a Marxist state in Colombia. It is estimated that there are between 9,000 and 12,000 armed members of the organization.

40. *Revolutionary Organization 17 November (17N)* was established in 1975 with the goal of removing U.S. bases from Greece. It also opposes the Greek establishment, Greek ties to the United States, the European Union and the Turkish presence

in Cyprus. The exact number of members in the organization is unknown. Some estimate that its membership is between 20 and 100 supporters.

41. *Revolutionary People's Liberation Party/Front (DHKP/C)* was established in 1978 as an anti-western Marxist group with a goal of removing Western influence from Turkey and turning it into a socialist state. Its membership is unknown.

42. *Revolutionary Struggle (RS)* is a far left Greek paramilitary group known for its attacks on Greek government building and the American embassy. It emerged in 2003 with the bombing of the Athens courthouse complex. It has between 300 and 800 members.

43. *Shining Path (Sendero Luminoso SL)* was established in the late 1960s in Peru. Its goal was to over throw the government and social structure of Peru and neighboring countries, and replace them with a Marxist socialist system controlled by the indigenous people of the region. The group opposes any foreign influence in Peru. It is estimated that the group has between 400 and 500 members.

44. *United Self-Defense Forces of Colombia (AUC)* was established in 1997 with the goal of protecting the economic interests of the wealthy landowners in Colombia and combating the Revolutionary Armed Forces of that country and the National Liberation Army. It is estimated that there are between 6,000 and 15,000 fighters in the organization.

45. *Harakat-ul Jihad Islami (HUJI)* is an Islamic fundamentalist group based in Pakistan with an affiliate in Bangladesh. It was founded in 1980 in Afghanistan during the Jihad fight against the Soviets. It has carried out several terrorists attacks. Its membership is believed to consist of several hundred people in Cashmere.

46. *Tehrik-e Taliban Pakistan (TTP)* was formed in 2007 to fight the "infidel," Pakistan. It forged ties with other terrorist networks and engaged in bombing and suicide attacks. Its

stated goals are to force Shari, united against coalition forces in Afghanistan and engage in defensive jihad against the Pakistani Army. The group was responsible for the attempted bombing in New York's Time Square in May of 2010. Its membership is unknown.

47. *Jundallah, also known as the Peoples Resistance Movement of Iran,* was founded in 2003 and is known for its high profile attacks on Iranian targets. It operates primarily in the Islamic provinces of Sistan and Baluchistan. It claims to be fighting for the same rights as the Iranian Shiite people. According to the United States State Department, the group is responsible for the deaths and maiming of scores of civilians and government officials.

48. *Army of Islam (AOI)* was founded in 2005 and is a Palestinian organization based in the Gaza Strip. In addition to supporting armed Palestinian resistance it also subscribes to a Salafist ideology global jihad. The organization has been responsible for attacks against American, British, New Zealander, Israeli and Egyptian citizens. In 2006, it launched rocket attacks on Israel. In 2007, it kidnapped British journalists. Its estimated membership is several dozen.

49. *Indian Mujahideen (IM)* is a loose network of Islamic organizations that have been responsible for killing hundreds of innocent citizens since 2005. Its overall goal is an Islamic Caliphate across South Asia. Its method of achieving that goal is to carry out terrorist attacks against non-Muslims. It must establish itself as an Indian based terrorist group, and is believed to have links to Pakistan. Its membership is not known.

TERRORISM AND THE ROLE OF LAW ENFORCEMENT

Even though the issue of terrorism has a long history, combating it remains an extremely complex and complicated subject for American law enforcement agencies. It is complicated because unlike many other nations that have national police systems, America has a system of policing that includes thousands of Federal, state and local law enforcement agencies that range in size from one officer departments to departments with thousands of officers.

The complexity stems from the fact that such a decentralized system hampers the ability of the nation to undertake a comprehensive planning effort capable of preventing and combating terrorism. This is particularly problematic when law enforcement agencies have the primary responsibility of protecting America from terrorist attacks and, until recently, were not totally clear which level of government was responsible for dealing with terrorism in America.

It is now generally accepted that Federal law enforcement agencies, along with national security agencies, have the lead role in anti-terrorism activities. That includes intelligence gathering, prevention, arrest and prosecution.

Only the Federal government has the ability to conduct widespread intelligence activities within the United States and in other countries. Only the Federal government has the responsibility for conducting investigations that are interstate or international in scope.[43] This is true because the Federal government has the resources, legal mandate, technology and overall ability to serve in these capacities.

It is also recognized that the Federal Bureau of Investigation (FBI) is the lead law enforcement agency in the fight against terrorism. However, if the terrorist act does not occur on an army base or a nuclear site, local police will be the first to respond.

Because local law enforcement agencies are the first and primary responders to a terrorist attack, they must be included in the national plans designed to prevent and respond to such attacks. That involvement includes intelligence gathering and sharing; planning, strategy development and decision-making.

The threat of terrorism resulted in the Federal Bureau of Investigation redirecting its core efforts. It assigned about 15 percent of its agents to the fight against terrorism.

In doing so, it drastically reduced its efforts in traditional enforcement areas such as narcotics which were left to other Federal agencies to handle. Contrary to its traditional role, the agency is focused on preventing crime and terrorism. Intelligence gathering now plays a much greater role for the Bureau. [44]

ROLE OF LOCAL LAW ENFORCEMENT

September 11, 2001 resulted in local law enforcement agencies throughout America reviewing and improving upon their emergency response capabilities. The events of that day also forced law enforcement agencies to examine their relationships with other agencies at all levels of government, as well as their relationships with the communities they served.

In his article in the Police Chief Magazine, Chief Dennis Rees of the Loveland, Ohio Police Department pointed out that September 11th required police agencies of all sizes to focus on five areas of responsibility.[45]

- Business infrastructure
- Business, schools and manufacturing
- Training
- Inter-operability and sharing
- Information overload

INFRASTRUCTURE[46]

After September 11, all law enforcement jurisdictions undertook a comprehensive assessment of the vulnerable infrastructures in their communities. That inventory included water and power plants, all utilities, bridges and other potential terrorist attack targets.

A variety of techniques were used to enhance security at those locations such as extra patrols, fixed post assignments and video surveillance. Patrol officers, more so than ever, were required to know their beats so they would be aware when anything was out of the ordinary.

SCHOOLS, BUSINESS AND MANUFACTURING[47]

Historically, the police and schools have had a good working relationship. After September 11, 2001 the police enhanced that relationship by ensuring that schools had appropriate policies and procedures in place in case of a disaster. They established closer ties with school security personnel.

Also, the police forged closer ties with manufacturing plants and other businesses. They took it upon themselves to know that a manufacturing plant existed in an area and also became familiar with what was being produced. Of utmost importance were those plants that regularly used chemicals that were shipped. The police also recognized malls and large office buildings as potential targets. They enhanced their relationships with those locations; especially forging closer ties with private security that also had responsibilities for those areas.

PATROL STRATEGIES[48]

Agencies that had adopted *Community Policing* were well suited to better protect their communities from attacks. This was true because *Community Policing* requires officers to know the people in their areas, and work with them to solve community problems. After September 11, 2001, patrol officers focused on identifying those areas on their beats that were potential terrorist targets and worked with the community to mitigate that potential.

TRAINING[49]

In addition to enhancing local training, many jurisdictions took advantage of training opportunities provided by the Federal government. For example, the United States Department of Homeland Security's Center for Domestic Preparedness located in Anniston, Alabama provided free training opportunities for first responders in: (1) weapons of mass destruction, (2) critical incident response, (3) hazardous materials and (4) managing civil action during threats.

Additionally, the Federal government offered free training, including paid travel expenses, in (1) bomb response, (2) radiological and nuclear awareness and (3) chemical and biological integrated response in Nevada, New Mexico and Texas. The training taught officers techniques of directed patrol with Homeland Security as the major concern.

SHARING AND[50]

Information sharing and interagency cooperation historically, have not been the hallmark of the American law enforcement community. September 11, 2001, however, forged relationships between law enforcement agencies. The terrorist *Early Warning Group,* which is a regional effort supported by the Federal government, provides local governments with intelligence and investigative information upon request. The Department of Homeland Security now provides information on specific suspects in an unprecedented manner.

The *Joint Terrorism Task Forces,* consisting of local, county, state and Federal agencies, have been very successful in sharing information and conducting investigations. Subsequent to September 11th, American law enforcement agencies at all levels of government are working together to share information to protect America from terrorist attacks.

INFORMATION OVERLOAD[51]

Historically, there has been a lack of information sharing between law enforcement agencies. This was especially true between local law enforcement agencies and Federal law enforcement agencies, especially the Federal Bureau of Investigation.

Post September 11th, law enforcement agencies at the local level received an extensive amount of information related to homeland security. In an area as important as Homeland Security, all information is important. For that reason, police agencies sometime felt overloaded with information, most of which led to negative results. Yet, all information must be examined to determine its relevance. This put a strain on already scarce law enforcement resources.

Although Federal agencies have the lead role in combating terrorism in America, local government has an equally important role. In the event of a terrorist attack, local police, fire and emergency medical services will be the first to respond. Local governments will be required to contain the damage, care for victims, rescue people and prepare for recovery.

For example, when the World Trade Center in New York City was attacked, it was the police department, the fire department and the emergency medical services units that were the first to respond.

The threat of terrorism has added new responsibilities to local law enforcement. Those responsibilities are in areas such as security for airports, seaports, transit systems, water plants, target buildings and chemical plants.

In preparation for a response to those threats, local law enforcement agencies have enhanced their bomb squads, increased training, purchased additional equipment and involved the community in looking for suspicious activities and people.

Local law enforcement's major challenge is to balance the protection of American cities against criminal activities and to perform their national security responsibilities, brought about by the threat of terrorist activities.

Special events now present special concerns to local jurisdictions. Some major events are now designated *National Special Security Events*. In such cases, the United States Secret Service is assigned the responsibility for coordinating the security operations of local, state, and Federal agencies.

The Salt Lake City, Utah Winter Olympics Games and recent Super Bowl football games are examples of such special events.

By necessity, local police agencies have changed their priorities and are now placing a greater emphasis on preparing for any type of disaster, natural or manmade, with a special concern on nuclear, biological or chemical attacks. This has created new expenses for local governments. In response, additional funds were budgeted for new emergency equipment, computers, communications equipment and additional training.

One of the goals of terrorism is to create fear in the general public. Therefore when a terrorist act does occur, government reacts. Because of widespread public fear, government has the tendency to pass new laws and implement new initiatives. For example, immediately after the 9/11 attacks, military air patrols were carried out over Washington D.C. and New York City and troops were assigned to provide security at the Salt Lake City Winter Olympic Games.

The role of local law enforcement in combating terrorism is two-fold: (1) preventing terrorist acts from occurring and (2) responding when a terrorist act does occur. The primary task is to prevent terrorist acts from occurring. Gathering intelligence information, which must be a coordinated effort between all other levels of government, is the basic tool used to accomplish this objective.

Local law enforcement agencies must recognize that terrorism can strike at any time and for any reason. Terrorism is not just the work of outsiders. It can be generated from local communities and serve as a "weather vane" to assess the potential for impending acts of violence. No police agency can wait for terrorists to commit their acts, nor should they be lulled into believing that an act of violence will only come from foreign groups. A major concern today is terrorists who legally reside in the United States and who want to harm the nation.

Recognizing the importance of community involvement, local police agencies have urged citizens to be vigilant as they carry out their day-to-day activities. Local law enforcement agencies also have the challenge of maintaining relations with religious and ethnic groups in the Muslim and Arab American communities. They have to address such issues as racial profiling which came to the forefront when former Attorney General John D. Ashcroft requested local law enforcement agency assistance in questioning thousands of people with passports from countries believed to have terrorist cells. Many Police Chiefs refused to do so, citing violations of the Constitution and police relations with their ethnic and religious communities. By refusing to cooperate, the Chiefs forced better relations between the anti-terrorist task forces, and the sharing of information between local police departments, and Federal law enforcement agencies.

The issue was not unlike that which police leaders have faced over the years, a balance between controlling crime and preserving the rights of citizens. With the guidance of the courts, the police have accepted the position that it is better for a criminal to go free than to erode the precious freedoms that make America the envy of other countries. That belief prevailed after September 11, 2001 when American police leaders took a stand, refusing to engage in what they believed were practices that would deprive people of their rights guaranteed by the U.S. Constitution. In doing so, many refused to honor Attorney General Ashcroft's request.

Considering that the goal of terrorism is to create fear among the general public, America must not over react to the threat of terrorism by curtailing the national sense of morality, the nation's longstanding values, individual constitutional rights and other cherished freedoms. If that was allowed to happen, terrorists would accomplish goals that they could not achieve by violent means.

The threats of terrorist attacks have had many ramifications for local governments. They have had to spend additional funds for police and fire departments and emergency medical services. Those funds have been used for additional emergency equipment, communications equipment, planning and training.

Local communities have also had to address the issue of what should be the role of the military in America relative to civilian government. For example, immediately after 9/11 armed members of the National Guard were placed in airports, on the streets of Washington, D.C., and around New York City to provide extra security.

It is important for law enforcement organizations to have a thorough understanding of the terrorist mind. From studying accounts of terrorist actions in other parts of the world, particularly the Middle East, it is clear that Americans have a limited understanding of the religious and social backgrounds of cultures that produce terrorists. Thus, many of the assumptions previously held by American law enforcement are not valid. The irrational mind of the terrorist may be quite rational in that individual's culture. Understanding the mind of the terrorist is an important prerequisite for a sufficiently effective response.

As law enforcement addresses the problem of terrorism in America they must address an overriding strategic challenge. That strategic challenge goes beyond operational response and preparation or intelligence gathering. It strikes at the very heart of America's commitment to democracy and provides policing with one of the greatest pressures it has faced in modern times.

That challenge is to ensure that basic human rights are protected. Law enforcement must continually seek to strengthen democratic institutions as the best defense against terrorism.

One of the first responses to the threat of terrorism is to limit personal freedoms. The strength of America's democratic society is built upon those freedoms and any attempt to limit them will only weaken the very fabric of the country's best defense against terrorism and violence.

Prior to the attacks of September 11 2001, the level of fear about terrorism in America was low. The level of tolerance for violence resulting from terrorist attacks was even lower. The major challenge at that time was to maintain a commitment within the population that violence would not be tolerated; that those who engaged in terrorist acts would be severely dealt with.

While local law enforcement agencies' internal intelligence systems can help to identify early signs of potential danger, assistance from outside agencies can strengthen that detection even further. Maintaining a good liaison between local police departments, state and Federal agencies will go a long way toward early detection. The sharing of information will increase local law enforcement's anti-terrorist capabilities. Recognizing the threat of terrorism as it is today, no law enforcement agency can afford to stand separately, letting personal or petty jealousies overshadow the mission at hand.

HOMELAND SECURITY AND COMMUNITY POLICING

The basic premise upon which Community Policing was developed provides an ideal framework for police agencies to plan for homeland security. This is true because the prevailing tenet of Community Policing is involvement of the community in the policing function. Similarly, the community should be involved in homeland security efforts.

Consistent with the priorities of Community Policing, the police must share information with the community. They must keep the community, business and civic leaders, informed about the threats of terrorism and about what actions are being taken to prevent them. Just as the police involve the community in efforts to control crime and the fear of crime, they must also engage the community as partners in the fight against terrorism. This goes beyond asking the public to be vigilant; they must be told how to be vigilant.

Community Policing provides a framework for policing under the threat of terrorism. The main elements of Community Policing include citizen involvement, a partnership between the police and community, joint problem identification, collaboration between the police and the community to solve problems and evaluation of the results. Inherent in this model is open sharing of information.

All cities should develop their homeland security plans based upon the principles that a threat to America's infrastructure is always present and no community can afford to be unprotected. It is incumbent upon every jurisdiction to develop plans to prevent attacks on their facilities and infrastructure and to be prepared to respond if an attack occurs. Such plans to involve the community, both public and private entities, must be a collaborative effort designed to protect both public and private assets. The following is a framework for developing a Homeland Security Strategy at the local level.

PLAN DEVELOPMENT

Each jurisdiction should develop a comprehensive plan that involves public and private entities in a coordinated effort. Community input is essential to the planning process. The plan should identify all foreseeable threats and develop a strategy to address them. The plan should build on the existing infrastructure and recognize the funding necessary to implementing the strategies. This comprehensive plan should serve as the jurisdiction's framework for preventing and responding to all disasters, natural or man-made. [52]

In addition to identifying potential targets of attack such as airports, buildings, water and power plants and seaports the plan should include a detailed operational response strategy that outlines how Federal, state, local, private entities and the community will work together to prevent and/or respond to critical incidents. This strategy should include both an immediate and long-term action plans. It should also identify key components of the response system and establish key systems and systems interfaces that are needed to support the response to such critical incidents.

LINK INFORMATION SYSTEMS

The various independent information systems within a region should be linked to assure the rapid flow of information between the various components of the criminal justice system, e.g. police, prosecutors, courts and corrections, to identify where crime occurs and its offenders. Through analysis, this information should be used to identify suspicious trends and target those involved in criminal activity. This is an essential element of Community Policing, and the same systems are essential components of any strategy to prevent and respond to critical incidents and terrorist attacks.

USE OF TECHNOLOGY

Each jurisdiction should ensure that all available technology is used to prevent a terrorist attack. This involves the inter-operability of communications systems. This entails coordinating the various independent voice and data systems that are maintained by all levels of government to allow for the flow of information among the various entities that comprise the criminal justice system. Such exchanges of information are important for the control of crime and disorder, and especially for preventing and responding to acts of terrorism.

Connecting the fixed sites and mobile radio "patches" is necessary to have an effective communications system among regional law enforcement agencies and other governmental entities.

The vehicles for involving the community in homeland security efforts already exist in most police departments. Those programs that were developed to prevent crime or arrest offenders can easily be applied to homeland security. Programs such as neighborhood watch, citizens on patrol, cabs on patrol, crime stoppers and citizens' academies are a few examples.

Post 9/11 training of police officers must include training in terror prevention. This includes training police officers to identify signs of terrorism, e.g., indications of persons making bombs, evidence of radical religious movements and other activities that should raise suspicion.

In effect, police officers must be trained to identify indications of potential terrorist acts. They should work with the community to enable neighborhoods to identify any abnormality conducive to terrorist acts. In addition to being first responders, the police under Community Policing can become "first preventers."

Most cities have developed the capacity to conduct crime analysis. Such efforts are geographically focused and include crime mapping. Through use of computers, crime can be mapped and analyzed on a geographic basis. That could include neighborhoods, a city or an entire region. The information obtained in the combined resources of global positioning systems (GPS) technology, 911 calls, 311 information, police reports and other data sources can be used to analyze potential terrorist threats.

When a terrorist attack occurs, local law enforcement is the first to respond. The Community Policing philosophy of working with the community and the various programs that fall under the umbrella of the concept are uniquely suited to address the issue of terrorism.

SOURCES OF INFORMATION

Community Policing encourages the exchange of information between the police and the community. A focus group convened by the Massachusetts Law Enforcement Technology and Training Center identified the following sources of important information that can assist the police in their efforts to prevent terrorism:[53]

- Neighborhood Watch – a law enforcement sponsored program that trains citizens to look for suspicious activities in their neighborhoods, and report them to the police
- Hotels and motels employees are in a good position to provide the police with information on suspicious guests
- Real estate agents are constantly in the community and can provide information on suspicious circumstances
- Storage facilities can be on the lookout for any suspicious materials that are stored that might be used in terrorist activities
- Religious groups can provide information on suspicious visitors or speakers
- Fraternal, social and civic clubs are good sources for information on planned gatherings
- Colleges and universities – are a good source of information on suspicious activities on campus
- Printing shops – can provide information on requests to print illegal documents or literature of a suspicious nature
- Business managers – can provide information on purchases of dangerous materials
- Transportation centers and tourist attractions – can provide information on suspicious persons or activities

- Major industrial enterprises – are a source of information on suspicious activities
- Schools – can report on suspicious activities or individuals
- School and office building custodians – are a source of information on suspicious or illegal activities in or around the school
- Health-care providers - can report on unusual injuries or illnesses
- Bars and liquor stores – are a source of information on suspicious conversations or activities
- Inspectors and code enforcers – travel throughout the community and can report suspicious circumstances
- Facility licenses – can provide information on activities such as the storage of chemicals
- Licenses and permits – are a source of information about suspicious persons applying for licenses, e.g., firearms.
- Delivery services – can provide information about suspicious packages or persons
- Department of public works – work in the community every day and can provide information on suspicious circumstances
- Housing managers – can provide information on suspicious activities or unusual rentals
- Meter readers – are in the community everyday and can provide information on unusual circumstances
- Automobile and truck rental companies – can report on suspicious items left in vehicles
- Taxi and delivery drivers - drive the streets everyday and can provide information on unusual circumstances

All segments of the community can play a role by knowing what to look for, yet not burden the police with unnecessary work, or provide information that is irrelevant.

HOUSTON CASE STUDY

Houston, Texas implemented a new model of city services based on the Community Policing model. The program was called Neighborhood Oriented Government (NOG). Under it, the city was divided into 88 super neighborhoods. Each created councils comprised of existing leaders from community organizations, businesses and religious groups.

In one super neighborhood, the council volunteers, with the assistance of the city's planning department, developed an instrument to survey the neighborhoods that made up their Super Neighborhood area. The volunteers went to each house in the area and obtained information on who lived in the house and asked if any responsible adult would be willing to volunteer their services in the event of a disaster. The survey also identified any disabled persons who resided in the house. That information was to be used to notify emergency services and utility providers so that location would receive priority services in the event of a disaster.

After the survey, those who indicated that they were willing to serve as volunteers if a disaster occurred were invited to a Saturday training program. The training program was organized by the Super Neighborhood Council, utilizing the services of all relevant city agencies such as police, fire, emergency medical services, health, public works, solid waste and private utilities. The participants were briefed on the role of each agency and what role they would play if a disaster occurred. They were also told what they should be looking for and how to contact the police to report suspicious circumstances.

ROLE OF PRIVATE POLICE

Although public law enforcement has the legal responsibility for protecting the public from terrorist attacks, there is also an important role for private security. This becomes increasingly clear when the following facts are considered:

- The private sector owns and operates 85 percent of the nation's infrastructure
- There are more private than public police in America. The ratio is three to one
- Americans are spending more of their time in places where private security protects them--- gated communities, work places, means of transportation, and educational institutions.
- Community Policing calls for fundamental changes in how police resources are used, to include using the resources of all segments of the community.

INTELLIGENCE

The collection of raw intelligence is the foundation for combating terrorism. It is important that information is shared. The FBI Anti- Terrorist

Task Forces (JTTF) have proven to be a valuable mechanism for the exchange of information.

The FBI's Joint Task Forces includes representatives of local, state and Federal law enforcement agencies. Their objective is to prevent and respond to acts of terrorism by:
1. Providing real-time information exchanges on terrorist indicators/ threats
2. Making Federal counter- terrorism information available to local police agencies
3. Bolstering cooperation between local, state and Federal law enforcement agencies
4. Enhancing training for state and local agencies
5. Sharing timely and relevant counter-terrorism information between law enforcement on all levels of government

The establishment of the JTTFs recognized that effective responses to terrorism required a coordinated effort between Federal, state and local governments, as well as the private sector.

In the event of a terrorist attack, local agencies will be the first to respond. When the problem exceeds the capacity of local governments, state resources will be utilized. If the problem exceeds the capacity of local and state governments, the Federal government gets involved.

According to Tully, there are four major steps in dealing with the terrorist threat:[54]

- <u>Intelligence gathering</u>: Here, raw intelligence is gathered by intelligence organizations. This includes information on their membership and whether or not they intend to use violence.
- <u>Prevent activity:</u> Based upon intelligence, the next step is to prevent the activities planned by terrorists.
- <u>Contain damages:</u> If a terrorist act occurs, law enforcement is responsible for minimizing and containing the damage.
- <u>Apprehend and convict</u>: The final step is to apprehend, prosecute and convict the terrorists. This includes dismantling terrorist organizations.

ROLE OF THE MEDIA

The media plays an important role in educating the public about the problem of terrorism. Media should be utilized to provide the community with timely information that will help them thwart terrorism. Most importantly, the media must be used to educate the public when a terrorist act occurs.

It is important for law enforcement to keep the media informed as events unfold. By the same token, the media must not sensationalize the events. Doing so confuses the public and plays into the hands of terrorists, making the jobs of law enforcement even more difficult. It is the role of the media to educate the public on the nature and extent of a disaster. The media must look to law enforcement for information to inform their readers, listeners or viewers.

It is natural to expect terrorism or the threat of terrorism to create "behavior, attitudinal, and emotional responses"[55] among the general population. Effective communications can lessen those responses. In that context, media has an important role to play as part of the overall disaster plan. It can best assist government by providing the public with information about terrorism, the threat of terrorism, how the public can assist in preventing terrorism and what to do if a terrorist act occurs. That role can only be carried out if they are given adequate information. The police should be the primary government organization to brief the media.

It is important for the police to establish good relationships with the media prior to a disaster. To accomplish that, they should involve the media in the planning process.

By the same token, the media has a civic responsibility to the public. When a community is under attack, the media should report the facts and take care not to create panic by overly sensationalizing the events. That only plays into the hands of the terrorists.

PATRIOT ACT

After the September 11, 2001 attacks, America reacted in an aggressive manner. One such response was the passage of the *Uniting and Strengthening America by Providing Appropriate Tools Required to Intercept and Obstruct Terrorism Act*, called the *U.S. Patriot Act.*[56] The Act was passed by Congress and signed into law by President George W. Bush on October 26, 2001.

The Patriot Act made some sweeping changes in existing United States law. The changes occurred in the following areas:[57]
- Wire Tap Statute (Title III)
- Electronic Communications Privacy Act
- Computer Fraud and Abuse Act
- Foreign Intelligence Surveillance Act

- Family Education Rights and Privacy Act
- Pen Register, Trap and Trace Statute
- Money Laundering Act
- Bank Secrecy Act
- Right to Financial Secrecy Act
- Fair Credit Reporting

The political climate in America at the time was such that few members of Congress opposed the legislation.

Senator Russell Feingold was the only member of the Senate to vote against the law. He voiced his concerns about the possible discriminatory use of the new powers granted to the government as follows:

> To the extent that the expansive new immigration powers that the bill grants to the Attorney General are subject to abuse, who do we think that is most likely to bear the brunt of the abuse? It won't be immigrants from Ireland. It won't be immigrants from El Salvador or Nicaragua. It won't even be immigrants from Haiti or Africa. It will be immigrants from Arab, Muslim and South Asian countries. In the wake of these terrible events our government has been given vast new powers and they fall most heavily on a minority of our population that already acutely feels the pain of this disaster. [58]

Although the Act won widespread support from the United States Congress, it was immediately attacked by constitutional rights organizations and civil libertarians.[59]

The Act contained ten titles, each of which contained a number of sections: [60]

- Title I: Enhancing Domestic Security Against Terrorism
- Title II: Enhancing Surveillance Procedures
- Title III: International Money Laundering Abatement and Anti-Terrorist Financing Act of 2001
- Title IV. Protecting the Borders
- Title V: Removing Obstacles to Investigating Terrorism
- Title VI: Providing for Victims of Terrorism
- Title VII: Increased Information Sharing for Critical Infrastructure Protection
- Title VIII: Strengthening the Criminal Laws Against Terrorism
- Title IX: Improved Intelligence
- Title X: Miscellaneous

The 2001 Patriot Act, which was hastily approved by Congress in the wake of the September 11, 2001 attacks, came under heavy criticism because it granted expanded authority to the government to, (1) engage in searches, (2) conduct surveillance, (3) conduct wiretaps, (4) seize business records, and (5) detain and /or deport suspects that are in terrorism investigations.

Section 215 was one of the most controversial sections of the Act. That provision allowed the Federal government…"to obtain a warrant in camera from the United States Foreign Intelligence Surveillance Court for library or bookstore records of anyone connected to an investigation of international terrorism or spying."[61]

The American Library Association was very critical of that section and advised its members to address this concern by developing an understanding of their states' confidentiality laws and work with their legal counsels in order to respond to law enforcement's requests for information under the section.[62]

The American Library Association's concerns centered on their belief that the Act infringed upon the rights of individuals that are guaranteed by the *United States Constitution* and *The Bill of Rights*. Specifically, they were concerned that both citizens and non-citizens, who used the facilities of libraries to browse the web or obtain e-mails, would be under surveillance by the Federal government without their knowledge.[63]

Criticism of the *Patriot Act* also came from those who felt that parts of it were not needed and in fact infringed on rights to privacy, freedom of speech and freedom of the press. For example, *Section 215* of the Act provided for the judiciary to allow *ex parte* permission for the government to examine personal records, e.g. financial, medical, phone, Internet, student or library records.[64] Judges were allowed to issue such orders on the basis that the information was "relevant for an ongoing investigation concerning international terrorism or clandestine intelligence activities."[65]

The Act was set to expire on December 31, 2005 but was extended on February 3, 2006 and later to March 10, 2006. After several changes, President George W. Bush signed it into law on March 9, 2006.

DEPARTMENT OF HOMELAND SECURITY

Creation of the Department of Homeland Security (DHS) was another consequence of the September 11, 2001 attacks.[66] This represented the most extensive restructure of the Federal government in recent history. Using a three- pronged approach to terrorism: (1) prevention, (2) protection and (3) recovery – the Bush administration set out to combine 22 different Federal agencies under one command. The stated objective was better coordination of Federal disaster services. The task met with considerable skepticism and, in fact, was not accomplished in a timely and effective manner.[67]

BACKGROUND

Patricia A. Dalton, in a Government Accounting Office (GAO) report published in August of 2003, pointed out that the Federal approach to counter terrorism started as early as the 1990s. [68]

The response resulted from events such as the Tokyo subway attacks which were carried out in that country by terrorists.[69] And the Oklahoma City bombing incident, carried out by domestic terrorists. Both attacks occurred in 1995.[70]

In June of 1995 *Decision Directive 39* was issued which gave Federal agencies the responsibility for combating terrorism. In 1996, Congress passed *the Defense against Weapons of Mass Destruction Act*, which mandated training and equipping local and state emergency services, recognizing that they would be the first to respond to a domestic terrorist attack. Over 40 Federal agencies were given some responsibility for counter terrorism activities, with 20 having specific responsibility for dealing with bio-terrorism. At the time, the nation did not have a central directive, comprehensive oversight or specific measures for accountably. As a result, America's counter terrorism efforts were weak.

The structure of the Federal government posed major problems for state and local agencies as they attempted to obtain funds to carry out their counter terrorism obligations. Because there was no department or agency that handled all Federal counter terrorism programs, state and local government were required to seek funding from different Federal agencies, a cumbersome and often confusing process.

Just as September 11th, 2001 proved to be the catalyst for many changes in Federal policy, it also precipitated a major change in America's approach to counter terrorism. In October of 2001, President Bush established the *Office of Homeland Security* and in June of 2002, he proposed the creation of a *Department of Homeland Security* (DHS) and issued a National Homeland Security Strategy.

THE NATIONAL STRATEGY

The national strategy was designed to address six major mission areas and key government roles: (1) intelligence and warning, (2) border and transportation security, (3) domestic counterintelligence, (4) protect critical infrastructures and key assets, (5) defense against catastrophic threats and (6) emergency preparedness and response. [71]

It was felt that this…"definition should help the government more efficiently administrator funds, and coordinate activities both inside and outside the proposed new department and ensure that all parties were focused on the same goals and objectives." [72]

Furthermore, the strategy outlined the foundation of the DHS. "These foundations -- law; science and technology; information sharing and systems; and international corporation" were intended to prove a "basis for evaluating homeland security investments across the Federal government." [73]

ORGANIZATION OF THE DEPARTMENT[74]

The plan for the creation of the DHS identified the agencies slated to be housed in one of the four directorates: Border and Transportation Security, Emergency Preparedness and Response, Science and Technology, Information Analysis and Infrastructure Protection.

The *Border and Transportation Directorate* was designed to bring the major border security and transportation operations under one roof and included:

- U.S. Customs (Department of Treasury)
- Immigration and Naturalization Service [part] (Department of Justice)
- Federal Protective Service Transportation Security Administration (Department of Transportation)
- Federal Law Enforcement Training Center (Department of Treasury)
- Animal and Plant Inspection Service [part] (Department of Agriculture)
- Office of Domestic Preparedness (Department of Justice)

The *Emergency Preparedness and Response Directorate* would oversee domestic disaster preparedness training and coordination of government response to disaster. It included:

- Federal Emergency Management Agency (Federal Emergency Management Agency)
- Strategic National Stockpile and National Disaster Medical System (Department of Health and Human Services)
- Nuclear Incident Support Teams (Department of Energy)
- Domestic Emergency Support Teams (Department of Justice)
- National Domestic Preparedness Office (Federal Bureau of Investigation)

The Science and Technology Directorate would work to utilize all scientific and technology advantages to secure the homeland:
- Chemical, Biological, Radiological and Nuclear Countermeasures Programs (Department of Energy)
- Environmental Measurements Laboratory (Department of Energy)
- National Biological Warfare Defense Analysis Center (Department of Defense)
- Plum Island Animal Disease Center (Department of Agriculture)

The Information Analysis and Infrastructure Protection Directorate would analyze intelligence information from other agencies, including the CIA, FBI, DIA and NSA concerning threats to homeland security and evaluate vulnerabilities in the nation's infrastructure. It would bring together:
- Critical Infrastructure Assurance Office (Department of Commerce)
- Federal Computer Incident Response Center (Government Service Administration)
- National Communications System (Department of Defense)
- National Infrastructure Protection Center (Federal Bureau of Investigation)
- Emergency Security and Assurance Program (Department of Energy)

Because they are exempt by statute, the Secret Service and Coast Guard would also be relocated to the DHS, but remain intact and report directly to the Secretary. In addition, Immigration and Naturalization Service's Adjudication and Benefits Programs would report directly to the Deputy Secretary, as would the U.S. Citizenship and Immigration Services. [75]

On March 3, 2002 President Bush signed the *Homeland Presidential Directive 3*, which established the Homeland Security Advisory System (HSAS). [76] The system was designed to advise all levels of government and the American people on the potential threat of terrorist attacks. The color-coded system was designed to advise the level of threat as follows:

- Red — Severe risk
- Orange — High risk
- Yellow — Elevated risk
- Blue — Guarded risk
- Green — Low risk

The system was criticized for not providing information that would clearly let governmental agencies and the public know the nature of the threat or what to do about it. It was also criticized because it did not advise the public of the criteria used for establishing the threat levels. In addition, it did not have a method of determining the accuracy of the threat level because the green (low risk) and blue (guarded risk) were never used. The system was also subject to political manipulation and there was often disagreement within the administration on threat levels.

In response to those criticisms, on January 27, 2011 the Department of Homeland Security discontinued the color-coded alarm system and implemented the new National Terrorist Advisory System (NTAS) designed to be more effective by communicating "... information about terrorist threats by providing timely, detailed information to the public, government agencies, first responders, airports and other transportation hubs, and the private sector." [77]

In announcing the new National Terrorism Advisory System, Homeland Security Secretary Janet Napolitano stated, "security is a shared responsibility, and we must work together to keep our nation safe from threats. This new system is built on a clear and simple premise: when a credible threat develops that could impact the public, we would tell you and provide whatever information we can so you know how to keep yourself, your families and your community safe." [78]

Under the new system, DHS will coordinate with other Federal entities to issue formal, detailed alerts when the Federal government receives information about a specific or credible terrorist threat. These alerts will include a clear statement that there is an "imminent threat" or "elevated threat." The alerts will also provide a concise summary of the potential threat, information about actions being taken to ensure public safety, and recommended steps that individuals and communities, businesses and governments can take." [79]

STATE AND LOCAL LAW ENFORCEMENT

The strategy also pointed out the importance of intergovernmental cooperation by placing an emphasis on the participation of state and local governments.

Posner identified the benefits of integrating state and local agencies into the DHS. He pointed out that by working collectively with state and local governments; the Federal government gains the resources and expertise of the people closest to the challenge. For example, protecting infrastructure such as water and transit systems is first and foremost the responsibility of non-Federal levels of government. [80]

This was especially true in the area of law enforcement. For example, after the events of September 11, 2001 a task force comprised of mayors and Police Chiefs came together and called for a new protocol to govern how local law enforcement agencies developed a closer working partnership between Federal and local law enforcement agencies, especially the FBI. The U.S. Conference of Mayors noted that a close partnership between Federal and local law enforcement agencies, which included the sharing of information, would expand and strengthen the nation's overall ability to prevent and respond to domestic terrorism.

SUMMARY

The challenge to America and its allies throughout the world is to recognize that the focus of terrorist attacks is changing. Unlike the 9/11 attacks, countries are now seeing a move away from large style attacks to smaller events.

The London attacks are such an example. [81] The 2003 bomb attacks in Turkey represented a second example of such attacks. [82] One year later, the attacks on trains in Madrid reminded the world that local groups were responsible for such attacks. The acts did not appear to be the work of Al-Qaeda.[83]

The threat of terrorism is not only changing, it is largely unknown. That presents a real challenge to the government's intelligence efforts. This is true because terrorists are becoming increasingly more sophisticated,

"… with members linked to new technology and loosely linked groups of cells, allowing them to operate in environments whose borders are viral, and detection is difficult." [84]

Illustrative of the concern about terrorist attacks being committed by people living in the United States is the following list of recent attempted attacks on the United States as reported by Reuters. [85]

> September 2009: Najibullah Zazi, an Afghan born man and a permanent U.S. resident living in Colorado, plotted a suicide bomb attack on the New York subway system. He received training from Al Qaeda in the remote Waziristan region of Pakistan, which borders Afghanistan. He chose New York in preparation for the attack but discarded bomb-making materials after learning, from a local Imam, that he was under surveillance. He was arrested in Colorado and pleaded guilty to the plot. He later cooperated with the authorities.

> October 2009: U.S. authorities arrested a Pennsylvania woman, Colleen LaRose, who used the nickname 'Jihad Jane' on charges of being engaged in a plot to kill a Swedish cartoonist who had depicted the prophet Mohammed in a way that some Muslims found offensive. She said in 2008 that she was desperate to do something to help end the suffering of Muslim people. LaRose also told her co-conspirators that her appearance as a white woman with blonde hair would allow her to avoid detection by authorities. She pleaded guilty and faces a possible life sentence if convicted.

> November 2009: U.S Army Major Nidal Hassan, a Muslim born in the United States, was accused of killing 13 people and wounding 32 others during a shooting rampage at the U.S Army installation in Fort Hood, Texas. Officials learned later he had been communicating with Muslim cleric Anwar Al-Awlaki who was killed by a U.S. drone attack in 2011. Hassan is awaiting trial.

> December 2009: Omar Farouk Abdulmutallab, originally from Nigeria, was arrested Christmas day on a Northwest Airlines flight from Amsterdam to Detroit, for allegedly attempting to detonate a bomb that was in his underwear. Explosives, identified as PETN, failed to detonate fully and passengers and crew subdued Abdulmutallab. He began cooperating with U.S authorities who

said he confessed to receiving the bomb from and being trained by an Al Qaeda affiliate in the Arabian Peninsula. At a court hearing he confessed to some of the pending charges.

May 2010: A U.S. citizen, born in Pakistan, Faisal Shahzad, drove a sports utility vehicle, packed with a crude bomb, into the heart of Times Square in New York on a crowded Saturday evening. The bomb failed to go off and was discovered by a passerby. Shahzad was caught days later as he tried to flee to Dubai. He admitted receiving bomb–making training and funding from the Tehrik-e-Taliban Pakistan, a terrorist group. He pleaded guilty and was sentenced to life in a U. S. prison

October 2010: After U.S officials received a tip from Saudi Arabia; two packages containing explosive materials destined for Jewish centers in Chicago were intercepted by authorities in England and Dubai. The explosives were tentatively identified as PETN, a strong explosive used in the past by Al Qaeda in the Arabian Peninsula. The packages were carried by UPS and FedEx, but were intercepted overseas before they could arrive in the United States.

February 2011: A Saudi -born student, Khalid Aldawsari, was arrested in Texas after FBI agents were tipped off by a chemical supplier and a freight company that he was trying to purchase materials that could manufacture bombs.

He had also composed a list of possible targets that he mailed to himself. The list included New York City, the Dallas home of former president George W. Bush, hydroelectric dams, nuclear power plants and a nightclub, according to an FBI affidavit.
The United States has had its successes in dealing with terrorists. On Sunday night, May 1, 2011, President Barack Obama held a press conference to announce that the U.S. military had killed Osama Bin Laden who was hiding in a compound in Abbottabad, Pakistan
The operation took place in the early morning of May 2nd, 2011, Pakistani standard time, nearly ten years after Al Qaeda successfully carried out the most deadly attacks ever on American soil.
Although it was often reported that Bin Laden was hiding in caves in a remote area on the Afghanistan-Pakistan border, he was killed in a

million dollar compound, a short distance from Islamabad, the capitol of Pakistan.

Highly trained Navy Seals, acting on the President's orders, carried out the attack which was based on information developed by the Central Intelligence Agency and U.S. intelligence sources.

In addition to the 9/11 attacks at the World Trade Center, the Pentagon and the airplane crash in the Pennsylvania field, Al Qaeda was also responsible for the bombing of the United States Embassies in Dar es Salaam, Tanzania and Nairobi, Kenya. Bin Laden was listed number one on the FBI's most wanted list.

When the President announced that he had been killed, spontaneous celebrations erupted outside the White House, in Times Square and at the site of the World Trade Center. Americans of all colors and ages excitedly waved American flags and sang the national anthem.

Bin Laden, born in a family of privilege in Saudi Arabia, had used his money to finance Al Qaeda and its deadly acts around the world. At his death, he reportedly had six wives and more than 20 children. Following Islamic tradition, his body was given a burial at sea by the American authorities, with an Imam presiding.

Government officials were quick to point out that the death of Bin Laden did not kill Al Qaeda, but it did weaken the organization. After his death, American law enforcement agencies were placed on high alert in anticipation of reprisals from his sympathizers.

Establishing a response to terrorism does not mean starting from scratch. Rather plans that have been developed for other disasters, for example, natural disasters, should be used and improved to deal with the issue of terrorism. To that end, strategies prepared for traditional disasters such as hurricanes or tornadoes should be utilized to respond to terrorist attacks.

Those departments that have adopted Community Policing as their dominate style for delivering police services are well suited to address terrorism. Community Policing, by definition, involves the community in the policing effort. Because of their role in the community, the police should take the lead in guiding the civil energy of the community as part of the government's overall homeland security strategy.

Community Policing has proven that citizens are more than willing to assist the police in addressing issues that threaten them or have a negative impact on their quality of life. The challenge of government is to engage that resource by organizing and training citizens as an integral part of the counter-terrorism effort.

NOTES: CHAPTER FIFTEEN

1. The 9/11 Commission Report, Final Report of the National Commission on Terrorist Attacks Upon the United States, Executive Summary, http://govinfo.library.unt.edu/911/report/911report Exc.pdf pp 1-2 (10-9-11)

2. Ibid., p.2

3. Laqueur, Walter, A History of Terrorism, New Brunswick: Transaction Publishers, 2001

4. Ibid, Also see Laqueur, Walter, "Terrorism: a Brief History," http://www.laqueur.net/index2.php?r=2&id=71 (10-9-11)

5. Op. Cit., Note 3

6. Ibid.

7. Ibid.

8. Ibid.

9. Ibid.

10. Hoffman, Bruce, Inside Terrorism, New York: Columbia University Press, p.15

11. Wardlaw, Grant, Political Terrorism: Theory, Tactics, and Countermeasures, New York: Cambridge University Press, 1989

12. Op. Cit., Note 10

13. Marighella, Carlos, Minimanual of the Guerrilla, June 1969, http://www.usma.edu/dmi/IWmsgs/LoweProfile=InsideOut.pdf (10.12.2011)

14. Jenkins, Brian, "On Emergency Terrorism," Emergency Preparedness Project, Center for Policy Research, Washington, D.C.: National Governors' Association, May, 1979

15. United States Law Code Title 22, Chapter 38 Paragraph 2656 (d)

16. United States Code of Federal Regulations, Title 28 C.F.R. section 0.85 (1)

17. Bolz, Frank Jr., Kenneth J. Dudonis and David P. Shultz, The Terrorism Handbook: Tactics, Procedures and Techniques, New York: Elsevier Science Publishing Company, 1990, p.74

18. Ibid.

19. Ibid.

20. Ibid.

21. Ibid. p. 78

22. Ibid. pp.78-79
23. Ibid.
24. Ibid.
25. Ibid.
26. Ibid.
27. Terrorism: 2002-2005, U.S. Department of Justice, Federal Bureau of Investigation, Washington, D.C., p.v http://www.fbi.gov/stata-services/publication/terrorism-2002-2005, p.v (10-9-11)
28. http://www.animalliberationfront.com/ALFront/ALPrime3.htm (5.1.09)
29. http://www.elfpressoffice.org/theelf.html (5.1.09)
30. Southern Law Poverty Center, Intelligence Report, Church of the Creator: A History," http:www.spicenter.org/intel/intelreport/article.jsp?sid=219 (5.1.09)
31. http://www.aryan-nation.org/about.htm (5.1.09)
32. Geldard, Ian, The Posse Comitatus, http://www.boogieonline.com/revolution/commerce/taxes/posse.html
33. U.S. Department of Justice, Federal Bureau of Investigation, Terrorism In the United States: 1999, p. 20
34. Ibid. p. 18
35. Ibid. p. 19
36. U.S. Department of State, State Sponsors of Terrorism, http://www.boogieonline.com/revolution/commerce/taxes/posse. Html
37. Ibid.
38. Op. Cit, Note 27, p.v
39. U.S. Department of State, Foreign Terrorist Organizations FTOs), p.1 http://www.state.gov/s/ct/rls/fs/37191.htm (10.1.11)
40. Ibid. p. 2
41. Ibid.
42. U.S. Department of State, Foreign Terrorist Organizations http://www.state.gov/s/ct/rls/other/des/123085.htm *(10.12.11)*
43. Tully, Edward J., "Terrorism: The Impact on State and Local Law Enforcement," Major Cities Chief's Association Intelligence Commanders Conference Report, unpublished, June 2002
44. "Terrorism Pushes FBI into Unknown Territory, Houston Chronicle, August 20, 2006, p. A16
45. Rees, Dennis M., "Post September 11: Policing in Suburban America," The Police Chief, Vol. 73, No 2, February 2006, pp. 72-77
46. Ibid. p.73

47. Ibid. p.74
48. Ibid.
49. Ibid. p.75
50. Ibid. p 76
51. Ibid.
52. See for example, the Houston, Texas All Hazard Emergency Operation Plan
53. Doherty, Stephen and Bradley G. Hibbard, "Community Policing and Homeland Security," The Police Chief, Vol. 73, No. 2, February 2006, pp.78-80
54. Op. Cit. Note, 43, p. 2
55. Committee on Science and Technology for Countering Terrorism, Division of Engineering and Physical Sciences, National Research Council, "Making the Nation Safer: The Role of Science and Technology in Countering Terrorism," Washington, D.C.: National Academy Press, 2002, p.270, http://www.nup.edu/html/stel/index.html
56. H.R. 3162 , 107th Congress, "Uniting and Strengthening America by Providing Appropriate Tools Required to Intercept and Obstruct Terrorism," (Patriot Act) October 24, 2001
57. Ibid.
58. Senator Russell Feingold, "Statement on Terrorist Bill" made from the U.S. Senate floor, October 24, 2001
59. For a quick overview of the Patriot Act, see Doyle, Charles, "The USA Patriot Act: A Sketch," CRS Report for Congress, Congressional Research Services—Library of Congress, Order Code R521203, April 18, 2002
60. Steinzor, Ruth, "Democracy Dies Behind Closed Doors, "The Homeland Security Act and Corporate Accountability," Washington, D.C.: Center for Progressive Regulation, March 12, 2003
61. Op. Cit., Note 56, Section 15, also see, American Civil Liberties Union, "Surveillance under the USA Patriot Act," December 10, 2001, http://www.aclu.org/national-security-under-usa patriot-act. (10.14.11)
62. Op. Cit. note 56, Section 215 "Access to Records and Other Items Under the Foreign Intelligence Act." Also see, http://www.ala.org/Template.cfm?Section=ifissues&Template=/ContentManagement/ContentDisplay.cfm&ContentID=51866 (10.15.11)
63. American Library Association, "Resolutions on the USA Patriot Act and Related Measures that Infringe on the Rights of Library Users," adopted by the ALA Council, January29, 2003 hhttp://www.ala.org/

Template.cfm?Section=ifresolutions&Template=ContentManagement/ContentDisplay.cfm&ContentID=11891 (10.13.11)

64. Op. Cit. Note 56

65. Op. Cit. Note 62

66. For the legislation that established the Department of Homeland Security, see 107th Congress, Public Law 107-296; November 24, 2002

67. Dalton, Patricia A., "Homeland Security: Effective Intergovernmental Coordination is Key to Success," testimony before the Subcommittee on Government Efficiency, Financial Management, and Intergovernmental Relations, Committee on Government Reform, U.S. House of Representatives, August 20, 2002

68. On March 25, 1995, members from Aum Shinrikyo, a Japanese religious cult, released lethal gas in three Tokyo subway stations, killing eight people and injuring hundreds. The group's leader, Aum Shinrikyo, was arrested in May, 1995

69. On April 19, 1995 a bombing attack occurred at the Alfred P. Murrah Federal building in Oklahoma City, Oklahoma. The attack killed 168 people and injured more than 680. Timothy McVeigh and Terry Nichols were arrested. They were both anti-Federal government activists. Both were convicted. McVeigh was executed in 2001. Nichols was sentenced to life in prison without parole.

70. Op. Cit, Note 68, p. 8

71. Ibid. p.7

72. Ibid.

74. Department of Homeland Security, "Department Components," http://www.dhs.gov/dhspublic/display?theme=13&contents=3345

75. Department of Homeland Security, Management Directive System, MD Number: 0003 "Acquisition Line of Business Integration and Management," October 28, 2004, p.2

76. Homeland Security Presidential Directive 3: Homeland Security Advisory System March 11, 2002, http://www.dhs.gov/xabout/lws/gc/1214508631313.shtm

77. Homeland Security, "Secretary Napolitano Announces Implementation of National Terrorist Advisory System, Press Release dated April 20th, 2001, http://www.dhs.gov/ynews/releases/pr 1303296515462.shtm (10.13.11)

78. Ibid.

79. Ibid.

80. Posner, Op.Cit, Note 68, p.11

81. On July 7, 2005, 37 people were killed and over 700 injured in four bomb attacks on London's public transit system

82. On November 15, 2003 and November 20, 2003 four truck bomb attacks killed 57 people and injured 700 in Istanbul, Turkey. Seventy-four people with ties to Al Qaeda were arrested and charged with the attacks.

83. On March 11, 2004, 191 people were killed and 1,800 wounded by a series of bombs in Madrid, Spain. Twenty-eight people were tried and 21 were found guilty of charges that ranged from forgery to murder. Eighteen were Islamic fundamentalists, and there were also Spanish accomplishes.

84. "Strategic Priority: Terrorism," Royal Canadian Mounted Police, htt://www.rcmp-gre.ge.ca/terrorism/index_e.htm

85. Reuters, FACTBOX – Recent attempted attacks on the United States. May 9, 2011 http://in.reuters.com/articlt/2011/03/09/idINIndia-55446520110309 3/21/2011

Chapter Sixteen:

THE FUTURE OF THE ENTERPRISE

INTRODUCTION

The United States entered the 21st century faced with many of the same problems that it confronted during the 20th century.

American cities faced crime, fear of crime, violence, drugs, homelessness, unemployment, under-employment and a struggling educational system.

Many of the problems were spreading to areas other than large cities. Workers in other countries were performing jobs once performed by Americans, as U.S. businesses increasingly relocated their operations abroad. Immigration was heatedly debated as both a social and economic problem.

Those issues were affecting all Americans, regardless of their social standing. The system for the administration of criminal justice remains fragmented. Yet there is a reason for optimism. The concept of *Community Policing* offered hope not only for the police, but also served as a model for other components of the criminal justice system.

> "It lacks any effective mechanism for coordination, and it lacks any permanent agencies for evaluation and long-range planning. No reasonable person should ever deliberately design such a system; much less put it into operation without such controls."
>
> —Judge John Beatty, Multnomah County, Oregon

CRIMINAL JUSTICE SYSTEM

The process for the administration of criminal justice in America is extremely complex. It starts with the arrest of a suspect and ends with correctional supervision of the convicted offender. It involves several entities: (1) the police, (2) the prosecutors, (3) the courts and (4) corrections.

Because of its complexity, different funding sources, different government jurisdictions, and different goals and objectives, the American system for the administration of criminal justice is dysfunctional. Not only is the so-called system divided into four separate components, it is also divided by levels of government—Federal, state, county and city.

It was not until the 1967 *President's Commission on Law Enforcement and Administration of Justice that* the process was carefully examined. In its report, The Challenge of Crime in a Free Society, the Commission published the first comprehensive flow chart depicting the various steps in the criminal justice process.[1] The two- chart vividly depicted the various steps and decision points an offender experiences.[2]

The negative consequences of such a fragmented system were summed up by the Commission when it reported:

> The system of criminal justice America uses to deal with those crimes it cannot prevent and those criminals it cannot deter is not monolithic, or even consistent. It was not designed or built one piece at one time.[3]

The National Advisory Commission on Criminal Justice Standards and Goals also addressed the issue when it reported:

> "Fragmented," "divided," "splintered," and "decentralized" are the adjectives most commonly used to describe the American system of criminal justice. [4]

In reality, what is labeled as the criminal justice system is not a system, rather it is a process comprised of four components, each with its own goals, objectives and procedures and all centered on crime and offenders. Within that context, the police are responsible for preventing crime and apprehending offenders. The prosecutor is responsible, as a representative of the state, for prosecuting those charged with committing crimes.

The courts have the role of determining guilt or innocence and sentencing those who are found guilty. Corrections have the dual role of incarcerating those who have been convicted and preparing them for their return to society or supervision under a community-based sentence.

Corrections can be broken down into subcategories. *Jails and prisons* are used to incarcerate offenders who are sentenced to incarceration by the courts. *Probation* is a sentence that allows offenders to remain in the community under the supervision of a probation officer in lieu of serving time in jail or prison.

Parole, on the other hand, involves convicted offenders serving a portion of their sentences in prison, and the remainder in the community under the supervision of a parole officer.

The inherent problem of the criminal justice system was best articulated by Multnomah County, Oregon Circuit Court Judge John Beatty when he said:

> It lacks any effective mechanism for coordination, and it lacks any permanent agencies for evaluation and long range planning. No reasonable person would ever deliberately design such a system; much less put it into operation without such controls.[5]

Patrick Murphy, a pioneer in American law enforcement, challenged the nation to address the problem when he noted:

> The most readily observed characteristic of the American criminal justice process is its disarray. What is supposed to be a system of criminal justice is really a poorly coordinated collection of independent fiefdoms, some ridiculously small, which are labeled police, courts, corrections and the like. This diagnosis was true in 1967 when the President's Commission on Law Enforcement and Administration of Justice discerned the outline of what should be a workable productive system of criminal justice. That diagnosis, equally true today, is easy to make; the challenge is to discover and chart useful routes toward coordination of criminal justice, whose hallmarks are harmony, effectiveness and, indeed, justice.[6]

A MODEL CRIMINAL JUSTICE SYSTEM: THE MULTNOMAH COUNTY CASE STUDY[7]

Multnomah County, Oregon attempted to rectify the inherent problems of a fragmented criminal justice system by creating a *Department of Justice Services* that included all of the county's criminal justice functions.

CRIMINAL JUSTICE SYSTEM OVERVIEW

The criminal justice system that operated in Multnomah County, Oregon prior to the establishment of the Department of Justice Services involved a large number of agencies, authorities, institutions and services. They were as follows:

- *Law Enforcement*: The two major law enforcement agencies in the county were the Portland Police Bureau and the Multnomah County Sheriff's Office. In addition, the cities of Gresham, Wood Village and Troutdale operated police departments. Law enforcement services were also provided by the state police, Federal law enforcement agencies and the port of Portland.
- *Courts*: The two-state court system handled all criminal cases that originated in Multnomah County. The Circuit Courts were responsible for the more serious offenses such as felonies, as well as cases of dissolution, equity and law. The District Courts handled the less serious offenses (misdemeanors) as well as civil, small claims and traffic matters.
- *Prosecutor and Defense*: The Office of the District Attorney served as the prosecuting arm of the county's justice system. That office was responsible for filling charges against those alleged to have committed illegal acts. Private attorneys handled the defense of persons charged with violations of the law. Persons who were unable to pay for the services of a private attorney and who qualified as indigents were assigned an attorney from the *Office of the Metropolitan Public Defender*. That office also represented indigents that were subject to involuntary commitments to mental institutions.
- *Local Corrections*: The County's Division of Corrections operated four correctional facilities: (1) Central booking center, (2) a major jail for men, (3) a jail for females and (4) a work-release center. In addition, the division administered the county's probation services.
- *Inebriate Detoxification:* The County's Department of Human Resources administered a detoxification program for sobering drunks. Since 1992, drunkenness in the State of Oregon had not been a criminal offense.
- *The Juvenile Justice System:* Four judges elected to the Domestic Relations Bench of the Circuit Court rotated as Juvenile Court

Judges. In addition, the county operated a Juvenile Detention Center and Juvenile Probation services. Under contract with the county, Legal Aid Services provided defense counsel for indigents in Juvenile Court.

- *Civil Process:* Civil Process was a separate division of county government and was responsible for the execution of all legal papers.

THE PROBLEM

It was generally recognized by all students of criminal justice that the county's criminal justice system was, in reality, a series of separate components that comprised a complex process. It was further recognized that the effective functioning of that process depended on the degree to which the various components related to one another. If a process for relating did not exist, the end result would be fragmentation and ineffectiveness. It was clear that when the workings of the various components were not coordinated, the public suffered.

Clearly, the problems of a non-coordinated criminal justice system were well recognized. So was the solution to that problem, as can be seen in the following recommendation from the President's Commission on Law Enforcement and Administration of Justice:

...officials of the criminal justice system itself must stop operating, as all too many do, by tradition or by rote. They must reexamine what they do. They must be honest about the system's shortcomings with the public and themselves. They must be willing to take risks in order to make advances. They must be bold. [8]

Multnomah County, unlike most other jurisdictions throughout the nation, implemented a structure for addressing the problem, and followed the recommendation of the President's Crime Commission.[9]

HISTORY OF THE DEPARTMENT OF JUSTICE SERVICES

On December 21 1972, Multnomah County's Board of Commissioners enacted Ordinance No. 64, prescribing the restructuring of county departments and assigned functions to the departments. The purpose of restructuring the departments was spelled out in *Section 3* as follows:

To maximize citizen participation, increase communication and cooperation of persons performing similar services; coordinate and synchronize group services addressing the same or related needs of the county; centralize administration and provide for vertical responsibility; provide a method of evaluation in accomplishing county goals and objectives; encourage individual responsibility and reduce duplication of effort and to provide for budgeting on a systems basis to efficiently allocate limited resources. [10]

The ordinance spelled out the board's commitment to a system of checks and balances and the distinction between the administrative, legislative and judicial branches of county government. It made clear that the ordinance should not be interpreted as interfering or abrogating any duties and responsibilities given by the Oregon Constitution relating to the duties and responsibilities of the three branches of government.

In creating the Department of Justice Services, the ordinance outlined its specific responsibility as follows:

> The Department of Justice Services shall consist of the following functions and such other functions relating to the protection and the safety of the people of Multnomah County which may on occasion be assigned to it by the board
> 1. Provide services to perform duties imposed by state law and county ordinances relating to the county clerk, district court clerk and sheriff, with reference to administration of the courts and court processes, and the recording and custody of public records
> 2. Provide law enforcement services and perform duties required by state law and the county sheriff
> 3. Provide for the protection of the public against disaster or calamity
> 4. Provide and operate facilities for detention of prisoners, maximum and otherwise
> 5. Perform those county services required by the judicial branch of government including the courts and offices of the district attorney

The Board of County Commissioners' affirmation of the doctrine of separation of powers made it clear that they did not intend, nor imply that the Director of the Department of Justice Services would administer the courts or the office of the district attorney. Rather, the explicit intent was to place those functions organizationally under the Department of Justice Services for the purpose of creating a discreet departmental budget unit and facilitate systematic coordination of like functions.

It was clearly understood that the district attorney, an official elected by the public, was responsible for the administration of that office. The same was true for the district and circuit courts. The sheriff in Multnomah County, however, was an appointed official. Therefore the Director of the Department of Justice Services had direct line authority over that office as well as corrections and the civil process divisions.

The ordinance specifically addressed the duties of all county department directors, but it was clear that the Department of Justice Services was unlike any other department within Multnomah County's governmental structure.

Its uniqueness was based primarily on the fact that the functions of the courts, district attorney, medical examiner and Juvenile Court and Home were assigned to the department, even though they were headed by elected and/or appointed state and county officials with statutory responsibilities. As a result, the director of the Department of Justice Services did not have direct vertical authority and responsibility over all departmental functions, as was the case with other county departments.

On June 1, 1976 I was appointed to serve as the Director of the Department of Justice Services. Upon assuming office, it became immediately obvious that no definitive statement had been made relative to the relationship between the director's office and the heads of the various departments and units. As a result, there had been a continuous debate over what authority and responsibilities rest with the Director of Justice Services and the other departments.

The enabling legislation that created the Department of Justice Services gave the Office of Director broad responsibility in several areas. Those areas were budget, coordination and planning. It did not outline the relationships between elected officials and the Director, nor did it give clear direction to the relationship over those agencies as to where a direct line of authority existed. It appeared as if this was done intentionally, in order to give the Director the latitude necessary to develop such relationships outside of the legislative process.

DEFINING RELATIONSHIPS

In March of 1977, I submitted a memorandum to the Board of County Commissioners requesting a definitive statement on the role of the Director of the Department of Justice Services. In response to that request, the board issued an *Order* on March 24, 1977, formally stating that the Office of the Director, on behalf of the Board and its Chairman, was responsible for the following: [11]

1. Provide administrative and planning guidance, support and coordination in the area of criminal justice to the various components of the criminal justice system, consistent with the legal responsibilities of elected officials and the separation of branches of government.
2. Provide coordination and liaison among criminal justice agencies to assist in the improvement of the components and intra-agency operations.
3. Provide budgetary overview, guidance, support, and approval to criminal justice agencies, consistent with legal responsibilities of elected officials.
4. Serve as the coordinator of the activities of elected officials and appointed division heads in order to achieve planning and coordination of criminal justice activities.
5. Work with heads of the criminal justice agencies in developing a coordinated approach to establishing system-wide goals and objectives.
6. Provide guidance and assistance to criminal justice agencies to prepare proposals and recommendations designed to facilitate agency and system effectiveness.
7. Provide support in government proposal development and coordinate all county requests for outside funding obtained by one agency to determine if the funding negatively impacted others.
8. Represent the Board of County Commissioners before the public in legislative and criminal justice policy and concerns.
9. Serve as the Chairman's representative in all matters regarding criminal justice and public safety.

Based on the board order, the Director of Justice Services explicitly had responsibility for four areas: (1) personnel, (2) planning, (3) budget and (4) policy formation and execution.

As previously stated, the Department of Justice Services was comprised of four distinct types of agencies:
1. Elected officials with clear statutory relationships between the agency and the county. The office of the District Attorney and the two court systems fell into that category.
2. Elected and appointed state and county officials where indistinct relationships existed. The medical examiner and the Juvenile Court and Home made up that group.

3. Appointed county officials, where direct line authority existed. The divisions of Public Safety (Sheriff), Corrections and the Civil Process Section were agencies in that category, as were certain functions delegated to the courts such as clerking and processing.
4. Agencies which the county contracted for services such as the public defender and legal aid were in that group. The law library was also included.

Because of the differences that existed, the Office of the Director of Justice Services had to relate to each group in a different manner. The following is a discussion of that relationship by category.

1. Elected officials with clear statutory authority
   a. *Personnel:* A county ordinance placed the administration of the personnel matters for all court employees in the Personnel Division of the Office of County Management and in the Merit System Civil Service Council. The two Court Administrators, acting as agents of the Presiding Judges, and the District Attorney, as an elected official, had the authority to develop personnel and compensation plans and present them to the board for approval. The Office of the Director of Justice Services was responsible for ensuring that the plans and actions were consistent with the county administrative and budgetary policies, and recommend to the board approval or rejection of such plans and actions.
   b. *Planning:* Initially, most planning was done either internally or in an insular manner. The district attorney, for example, had a planning staff and continued internal planning. The courts, on the other hand, had no planning staff. The role of the Office of the Director was to assist the internal planning only as requested, and direct primary efforts toward engaging agencies into system-wide planning. An important part of that process was the examination and coordination of all Federal grant applications. It was important that one agency not be allowed to place others in operational jeopardy. This planning process resulted in greater coordination between agencies. The Office of the

Director of Justice Services served as the vehicle for such coordination.

   c. *Budget*: Much of the court's budget was statutorily guaranteed. The judicial staffs, certain fees and other line items were clearly enumerated by statute. There were, however, significant areas of their budgets that were discretionary, e.g., those functions that were delegated to the courts under the reorganization of the Clerk of the Courts Office. It became the role of the Office of the Director to assure that the Courts' budgets were soundly devised and well managed. With the understanding that the courts could speak directly to the board on budget matters, the Office of the Director would make recommendations about the budgets when they related to the court's function and would review and advise on all fiscal items brought before the board. The role of the Office of the Director was to represent the interests of the board in this area by recommending approval or rejection of budgetary requests. Since the District Attorney's Office was discretionary as to the level of funding, the Office of the Director played an active role in the development of its budget. As was the case with the courts, the district attorney was an elected official and could speak directly to the board on budgetary matters. The Office of the Director, therefore, had the responsibility of reviewing all fiscal matters brought before the board and to serve as its adviser by making recommendations for approval or disapproval of budgetary matters.

   d. *Policy:* The courts and the District Attorney had clear responsibility and authority for developing and carrying out their own policies. The role of the Office of the Director was to respond to those policies only if they had an impact on other components of the system.

2. <u>Elected and Appointed State and County Officials</u>
   a. *Personnel:* The two agencies in this category were included in the county's general personal plan. The role of the Office of the Director was to ensure that personnel actions were consistent with the rest of county government, that

personnel administration was conducted in a progressive fashion, and that problems and grievances were resolved. The office played an active role in the personnel policies and administration of these agencies.

b. *Planning:* Initially, the planning of the agencies in this group was only internal. The role of the office of the director was to engage these agencies, particularly the Juvenile Court and Home, in system-wide planning and coordination.

c. *Budget:* Each of the agencies in this category was discretionary as to its level of funding. For that reason, the Office of the Director played an active role in the development of their individual budgets. In addition, the Office of the Director was responsible for presenting all of their fiscal matters to the board with recommendations for approval or disapproval.

d. *Policy:* The Office of the Director played an active role in policy formation and in the implementation of the agencies in this grouping.

3. Appointed County Officials

These agencies, the Sheriff, Corrections and Civil Process constituted the direct line authority organizations of the department. The major goal of the Office of Director was to develop within each agency a strong *management by objective* system of administration.

a. *Personnel:* These agencies operated under the provisions of the county's personnel rules and guidelines. The major objective of the Office of the Director in this area was to build a strong management team in each agency. Further, specific personnel goals and objectives were set in the areas of manpower needs, role identification, management by objective, and participatory management.

b. *Planning:* The major efforts undertaken in this area were two-fold. First, the continuous development of a process to ensure that planning became a part of the day-to-day operation, and that a systems approach was used rather than one which was wholly internal. The second concern was to guarantee that planning became a part of the policy execution process. The Office of the Director worked

to ensure that the planning efforts of the agencies were directed towards addressing policy as well as operational questions. Inherent in this area was an effort to ensure that these agencies were part of the overall coordination of the system.
   c. *Budget:* The role of the Office of the Director was to continually assist in the development of budgets as useful management tools, making sure that they reflected the proper goals and objectives. The Office of the Director had direct budgetary responsibility for decisions in this category.
   d. *Policy:* The role of the Office of the Director was to see that the overall policies of the board and the chairman were reflected in the operations of the agencies in this category. That role included the identification and development of policy issues to present to the board. The agencies themselves, however, were responsible for the execution of operational policies on a day-to-day basis.

4. <u>Public Defender and Legal Aid Services</u>

Since these two offices operated under contract with the county, the Office of the Director was responsible for negotiating, on behalf of the board, those contracts and monitoring services provided to ensure that they were executed as agreed.

JUSTICE COORDINATING COUNCIL

In a further effort to coordinate the county's criminal justice system, the *Multnomah County Criminal Justice Council* was established. This Council was composed of the heads of all the county's justice agencies, including the Police Chiefs of the cities of Portland and Gresham. The Council met once each month to exchange information, address systemic problems and coordinate program activities. In addition, each agency head designated a staff member to serve as staff to the Council. That group met at least twice a month and did the required staff work.

SUMMARY

The Department of Justice Services was a complex and unique agency in county government. The nature of the agencies that made up the department accounted for its complexity. Organizing all of the county's criminal and civil justice components under one umbrella accounted for its uniqueness.

The success of the endeavor was obviously closely related to the cooperation of all agencies involved. The objective was to bring about coordination in what was traditionally an uncoordinated system. The design, as developed and implemented in Multnomah County, was the most systematic, comprehensive and perhaps the most thought-out attempt to create, within limitations, a system out of a non-system for the administration of criminal justice anywhere in the nation.

In 1982 the voters chose to make the sheriff an elected official and the department of Justice Services was abolished, thus bringing closure to a novel organizational structure designed to coordinate the county's criminal justice system.

FEDERAL LAW ENFORCEMENT

Many of the problems confronting American cities have been designated as those that call for a national response. As a result, the Federal government has established agencies designated to leverage a response to those issues. Crime is one of those problems. Over the years, the government created several law enforcement agencies responsible for the enforcement of Federal laws. In other cases, the government has established agencies to conduct research, provide leadership and, in some cases, monetary assistance to local law enforcement agencies.

As of September, 2004 there were approximately 106,000 Federal law enforcement officers in America.[12] They were distributed as follows:

Table 1: Number of Federal Law Enforcement Officers in 2004[13]

Criminal investigations/enforcement	40,408
Police response and patrol	22,278
Inspections	17,280
Corrections/detention	16,530
Court operations	5,158
Security/ protection	4,524
Other	176
Total	106,354

Approximately 63 percent of Federal officers were employed as: (1)

U.S. Customs and Border Protection – 27,705, (2) Federal Bureau of Prisons - 15,214, (3) Federal Bureau of Investigations - 12,242 and (4) U.S. Immigration and Customs Enforcement – 10,399.[14]

The vast majority of Federal officers were assigned to the following departments of the government:

DEPARTMENT OF JUSTICE[15]
- *Federal Bureau of Investigation:* Responsible for the enforcement of Federal criminal laws. It is also responsible for counter terrorism.
- *Drug Enforcement Administration*: Responsible for the enforcement of the Federal drug laws in the United States and abroad.
- *U.S. Marshals:* Responsible for apprehending fugitives, protecting Federal witnesses, protecting the Federal courts and arrest of Federal fugitives.
- *Bureau of Alcohol, Tobacco, Firearms and Explosives:* Responsible for investigating Federal crimes involving firearms, explosives, arson, bombings, and alcohol and tobacco.

DEPARTMENT OF HOMELAND SECURITY[16]
- *U.S. Customs and Border Protection*: Responsible for protecting the nation's borders to prevent terrorist and terrorist weapons from entering the United States.
- *U.S. Immigration and Customs Enforcement*: Responsible for identifying and alleviating vulnerabilities in the nation's economic, transportation and infrastructure security.
- *Transportation Security Administration:* Responsible for protecting the nation's transportation system to ensure freedom of movement of people and commerce.
- *United States Secret Service:* Responsible for protecting the President and other high-level officials and the investigation of counterfeiting and other financial crimes.

STATE LAW ENFORCEMENT

Each state has a police agency with the authority to perform law enforcement functions state-wide. In most states, their primary responsibility is to enforce traffic laws on state highways and Federal interstate expressways.

In addition, they provide security for state capitols, protect governors and provide a variety of support services to smaller law enforcement agencies, for example, crime labs, major investigations, training and coordination of multi-jurisdictional law enforcement operations.

Every state in the nation, except Hawaii, has a state law enforcement agency. In Hawaii, the sheriff's office provides state-wide law enforcement. Most states call their law enforcement agency "State Police." Some states, however, have different titles, such as *highway patrol, state patrol, department of public safety, state bureau of investigation* or *state highway patrol*. As of September 2004, state police agencies in America employed approximately 89,265 full-time persons. [17]

In addition to their traffic enforcement and criminal investigation responsibilities, some state police also provide recruit training and crime lab services to local police agencies, while others provide state-wide communications and computer systems and assist smaller jurisdictions in criminal investigations, including crime scene analysis.

OFFICE OF THE SHERIFF

The office of the sheriff exists in every state of the nation except Alaska, Connecticut, the District of Columbia and Hawaii.[18] Almost all sheriffs provide traditional law enforcement services (96 percent), court related services (97 percent) along with court security (97 percent). Seventy-eight percent operate at least one jail. [19]

The Los Angeles Sheriff's Office, the largest in the nation (8,239 sworn officers), not only performs police services in the unincorporated areas of Los Angeles County; it also provides contract law enforcement services for several incorporated cities in the county. [20]

With few exceptions, the sheriff is an elected official that has the responsibility of providing law enforcement services to the unincorporated areas of the county.

In September of 2004 sheriff's offices in America had approximately 326,531 full-time employees, and of that number 175,000 were sworn officers.[21] Nearly 71 percent of all sheriffs' offices serve a population of less than 50,000. Those agencies employ 20 percent of all officers.

The office of the sheriff occupies both a historical and unique contemporary role in American policing. From a historical perspective, the sheriff represents the last of the many ancient offices: [22]

> It is not possible to state with exactitude the date when the first sheriff was sworn to protect the lives and property of his

constituents or fellow citizens. Some historians date the office, or rather its prototype, to the ancient Roman pro-counsel. Some express a belief that the office may have derived from Saxon, Germany. Others assume that the word sheriff is an Anglicization of the Arabic word *Sherif,* which literally translates as *illustrious* or *noble* and signifies an Arab Chief or Prince who is a descendant of Mohammed through his daughter Fatima.[23]

Although most state constitutions indicate that the sheriff is the chief law enforcement officer with jurisdiction within incorporated areas, the actual police services are generally provided only in the un-incorporated areas of the county.

LOCAL LAW ENFORCEMENT

Local police departments employ the vast majority of the police officers employed in United States. As of September 2007, there were 601,000 full-time employees of local police departments. Of that number, approximately 463,147 were sworn personnel.[24] New York City, with over 36,000 sworn personnel, was the largest police department in America. The five largest police departments in America are as follows:[25]

New York City, New York	35,973
Chicago, Illinois	13,469
Los Angeles, California	9,307
Philadelphia, Pennsylvania	6,853
Houston, Texas	5,360

Almost 50 percent of all local police departments employed fewer than ten officers and 652 of that number employed only one officer.[26] Approximately 73 percent of all local police departments served jurisdictions with fewer than 10,000 residents and employed 14 percent of all officers.[27]

A clear indication that Community Policing has not been institutionalized throughout the nation is the fact that only "about half of local police officers work in a department with a written Community Policing plan."[28]

Actually, "the number of Community Policing officers in local police departments declined by 54 percent between the years 2000 and 2007."[29] Furthermore, four percent of local police departments designated officers to perform Community Policing activities, indicating that the concept had not been adopted as the dominant style for delivering services to the community.[30] It was encouraging, however, that "more than four in five departments serving 50,000 or more residents had problem solving partnerships with citizen groups during 2007." [31]

FUTURE OF THE POLICE ENTERPRISE

Although most police agencies in America claim to have adopted Community Policing, few have fully institutionalized the concept. Yet, Community Policing will continue to evolve in America.

Before long it will become the dominant style for delivering police services in the United States. As police departments gain more experience with the concept and institutionalize it, Community Policing will become what traditional or professional policing became after the reform movement removed the police establishment from the political era.

The transformation will take at least another generation. During this transitional stage, there will be a greater understanding of Community Policing, in addition to the following trends that will influence policing in America.

GEOGRAPHY

Increasingly, policing will be geared towards the unique characteristics of neighborhoods. Police agencies will recognize that the problems, issues and priorities of one neighborhood are not necessarily the same in other neighborhoods. Neighborhoods, therefore, will become the primary focal point of police agencies and all structures will be focused on the neighborhood. This will include assigning officers to a neighborhood on a relatively permanent basis and requiring that they remain there during their tours of duty, except in cases of emergencies. The officers will also be accountable for what happens in their areas of responsibility.

ACCOUNTABILITY

First and foremost, police managers will be held accountable for everything that occurs in their areas of responsibility. Not only will this include crime and solving problems, it will also include holding managers accountable for the performance and conduct of the officers assigned to their command. In order to hold managers accountable, they must be given the authority commensurate with their responsibilities.

FOCUS ON COMMUNITY

The ultimate goal of the police will be to improve the quality of life in the community. They will strive to make the community better places in which to live. This will involve focusing on problem solving and not solely on apprehending offenders and order maintenance. The primary goal will be prevention. Addressing crime will always be a responsibility of the police, but there will be a greater recognition and appreciation of their non-law enforcement responsibilities. The objective will be to use the resources of the police to create safe communities and to improve the quality of life in the neighborhoods.

CUSTOMER SATISFACTION

The ultimate goal of the police will be to satisfy the people they serve. Measures will be taken to determine customer satisfaction. Such measures will focus on the level of service rendered to the public, the actions and attitudes of the officers and the degree to which the police are able to solve neighborhood problems. Similar to what occurs in the private sector, the police will strive to please their customers – the law-abiding community. A variety of techniques will be used to measure customer satisfaction such as surveys, comment cards and mystery shoppers.

PROBLEM SOLVING

Problem solving will become the hallmark of the police in the future. This will require the police to undertake analysis of repeat calls in order to understand the nature of the problems that come to their attention. It will also necessitate that the police not only cultivate meaningful collaboration with the community, but also government agencies and private sector organizations.

STRATEGIC CRIME CONTROL

The police will focus on reducing crime by involving all segments of the community and employing proven technologies such as ComStat and Intelligence-LED Policing. The emerging technologies will not only provide the police with timely intelligence, strong analysis, quick deployment and strong accountability, but also the ability to predict the probability of crime occurring in given locations.

NEW SOPHISTICATION

In addition to developing sophistication in problem solving, the police will also improve their image in the community, especially minority communities. They will accomplish this by having more non-threatening contacts with the public, resolving the issue of racial profiling, understanding the dynamics of race and religion in America and learning techniques to deescalate contacts with the public – including the stopping of cars driven by members of minority groups.

NEW TECHNOLOGIES

The police will take advantage of new technologies and systems such as wireless information systems, global positioning systems (GPS), smart cars, seamless integrated data systems, expanded 311, greater use of ComStat, internet reporting, improved access to crime data, productive crime analysis, facial recognition systems, smart-card access systems and embedded driver's licenses.

POLICING BY INFORMATION

Operating in a post 9/11 environment, the police will continue to focus on homeland security. This will require the police to be able to use race and/or religion in a manner that does not offend members of the public and in a way that does not violate the law or the Constitution of the United States. Wireless data collection will become a standard practice and the police will gain access to all city service data. That data will be used to reinforce a strong commitment to the quality of service delivery.

INTEGRATED GOVERNMENT

There will be a greater recognition that the police are an integral part of the service delivery system of government. Coupled with the focus on strong neighborhoods, there will be integrated team management for each neighborhood. With citizen involvement in all areas of service delivery, service standards will be established for all major services, with support services provided centrally. Funding will be predicated on the successful delivery of services. It will no longer be acceptable to continue to do the same things in the same way with the same results.

COMMUNITY JUSTICE

As it operates today, the criminal justice system is an ineffective model for crime control. There are no meaningful interactions between the various components that have different and often contradicting goals. Each component's policies and procedures are developed in isolation to support their agency's goals. There is a lack of coordination and as a result, the current system is inappropriate for addressing the social issues that may ultimately result in crime.

In order to be effective, the criminal justice system must move beyond reacting to what the police, the gatekeepers, bring into the system. If the crime cycle is to be broken, there must be mechanisms for addressing the deeper problems that result in crime by focusing on the underlying causes.

If America is ever going to control its crime problem there must be a fundamental change in how the system for its control operates, calling for a comprehensive overhaul of the criminal justice system. It must involve all components of the criminal justice system working with all segments of the community. The newly emerging concept of community justice offers a model for achieving that goal.

Community Policing has spawned a movement that goes beyond the police. The concept is now being recognized as applicable to other components of the criminal justice system - *prosecution, courts* and *corrections*. It should be recognized, however, that Community Policing itself has not fully evolved and institutionalized as the dominant style for delivering police services in America, and community justice is even further behind in its evolution.

The *community justice* movement does, however, hold great promise for resolving some of the problems that are inherent in the current system for the administration of criminal justice. The other components of the criminal justice system are learning from the evolving experiences of Community Policing.

"Criminal Justice refers to all variants of crime prevention and justice activities that explicitly include the community in their processes and establish the enhancement of community quality of life as a goal." [32]

Conceptually, it is about improving the quality of life in local communities by involving all elements of the criminal justice system as partners with the community to address the problem of crime that has a negative impact. As a process, Community Justice has the following characteristics: [33]

- Active collaboration of citizens, elected officials, and public and private service agencies in community governance
- A focus on preventing social problems rather than cursing them
- Recognizing and building on community strengths and assets
- Involving community members in defining and resolving problems before they reach a crisis stage
- Repairing harm to victims of crime and their communities
- Holding offenders accountable and improving their competency as productive community members

Quinn has pointed out how *community justice* differed from the traditional model of the criminal justice system's process, and its desired outcomes:

> The process emphasizes full involvement of the key involved parties (victim and offender) and an understanding of the underlying issues and effects of the crime. This addresses the history of conflict that is sometimes evident and relevant, but excluded from official court processes as inadmissible relating to a specific charge. It also allows the victim to get questions answered (such as "why was I selected?"), express outrage and explain the impact of crime, and work out the details of the restitution agreement. [34]

Community justice calls for a new level of cooperation between the various components of the criminal justice system, other agencies of governments, not-for-profit organizations and the private sector. Community justice is about ownership and stewardship. It involves the inclusion of local people in the process. For it to be successful, members of the community must feel that the system is fair, reasonable and actions taken are proportionate to the crimes, with an overarching concern for victims.

COMMUNITY PROSECUTION

The office of the prosecutor is an extremely important, but generally overlooked component of the criminal justice system. *The 1967 Presidential Crime Commission* highlighted the significance of the prosecutor's role when it said:

> The prosecutor's discretion to file charges and prosecute an offender is indicative of his critical position in the law enforcement system.

The prosecutor is particularly able to influence police operations. He impacts the development of legal rules by his arguments in court. He can help to bring about needed reforms by pressing for changes in bail practices, for example, or in procedures for the appointment of counsel. Except for the judge, he is the most influential court official. Yet many prosecutors are part-time officials. They generally are elected or selected on a partisan political basis and serve for relatively short terms. [35]

Community prosecution originated in Portland, Oregon in 1990. It was founded on the Community Policing model that was designed to forge relationships between the police and the community. It started in response to the business community's concern about quality of life crimes that were threatening their businesses. In response to that concern, the district attorney assigned the first *Neighborhood District Attorney* to augment the efforts of the police by providing ongoing legal advice to address problems on the streets.

As stated by the first Neighborhood District Attorney, Wayne Pearson, "It became apparent that Community Policing could be exponentially greater if we had a community prosecutor in place to provide ongoing legal strategy, and to bring together both practical and legal solutions to the street behavior problems."[36]

Community prosecution is defined as "... a long term proactive partnership among the prosecutor's office, law enforcement, the community, public and private organizations, where the authority of the prosecutor's office is used to solve problems, improve public safety and enhance the quality of life of community members."[37]

Conceptually, it involves an expansion of the role of the prosecutor to include crime prevention, crime reduction, partnerships and problem solving. It involves moving beyond the mere prosecution of cases brought to their attention by the police towards working with other government agencies to determine and resolve problems. This involves a closer relationship with other components of the criminal justice system, other agencies of government and the community. It also includes the use of civil remedies such as restraining orders and nuisance abatement laws to solve problems.

Community prosecution, as it has developed to date, can be viewed in seven dimensions:[38]

TARGET PROBLEMS
Focus on crime problems that impact specific geographic areas, for example, quality of life issues, drug problems, gang violence, juvenile crime, truancy, prostitution, housing and environment issues, landlord/tenant issues and failures of the justice system to address the community's needs.

TARGET AREAS
Focus on specific areas within the community that have problems unique to the area; for example, urban/inner city, rural/suburban, business districts or residential areas.

ROLE OF COMMUNITY
The community plays a variety of roles in community prosecution. The roles include those who are recipients of the services of the office of the prosecutor, advisers to the office, participants in problem solving and participants in the implementation of solutions to problems. Other elements of the criminal justice system, ad hoc groups and segments of the community targeted by the office are included.

RESPONSE TO COMMUNITY PROBLEMS
The response to problems of the community may vary. They range from prosecuting cases of interest to the community, receiving non-criminal as well as criminal complaints, undertaking crime prosecution efforts, and facilitating community self-help efforts.

ORGANIZATIONAL ADAPTATION/EMPHASIS
A wide range of models have been experimented with such as field offices staffed by attorneys or non-attorneys, assigning attorneys to neighborhoods, creation of special units or organizing all of the offices around the community prosecution model.

CASE PROCESSING ADAPTATIONS
Cases may be referred to the central office for prosecution or the neighborhood prosecutor may handle the prosecution.

POLICING IN THE 21ST CENTURY | 519

INTER-AGENCY COLLABORATION/PARTNERSHIPS
Agencies and relationships that are not normally pursued by the prosecutor's office are cultivated by the police, city attorney, housing authority, community, other courts, other criminal justice agencies, social service agencies and other regulatory agencies.

Community prosecution benefits from the experience gained by the police under the philosophy of *Community Policing*. It entails the development of a new set of principles and values that are being used to refine the mission of the prosecutor. Although many elements of traditional prosecution are retained, *community prosecution* involves a new mission and outcomes. [39]

Mission: Prevent, reduce and manage crime and quality-of-life offenses. Prosecute felonies and low-level crimes and misdemeanors corresponding to citizen priorities. Create partnerships with the community.

Outcomes: Quantitative measures are used to reflect cases screened, pled, tried, and disposed; in addition to crime prevention/reduction, fear reduction and improved quality-of-life activities.

CASE STUDY: MULTNOMAH COUNTY (PORTLAND, OREGON)
Michael D. Schrunk was elected District Attorney of Multnomah County, Oregon (Portland) in 1981 and was looking forward to prosecuting murderers, rapists and robbers. It did not take him long to realize that his constituents were equally interested in quality of life issues such as speeding, public urination and open drug sales. He soon discovered that in the Lloyd District of Portland, the community had little confidence in the criminal justice process, complicated by the fact that his prosecutors found it difficult to get citizen support for the investigation and prosecution of criminals in the area.

In response to that problem, Shrunk launched the *community prosecution* program in the Lloyd District in 1990. He assigned one of his most talented Assistant District Attorneys to the office. Unlike the Assistant District Attorneys (ADA) at the central office who specialized in cases, the Neighborhood Assistant District Attorney (NADA) was responsible for handling all the cases that originated in the area. In the beginning, the business community paid the Neighborhood ADA's salary.

In a short period of time, after meeting with all of the stakeholders in the area, the NADA obtained the confidence of the community. The hostility vanished and the residents cooperated with the NADA.

The NADA learned that the community wanted action taken against serious crimes, but they also wanted something done about less serious offenses such as crack abuse, street corner drug markets, public prostitution and landlord violations. They wanted assistance for their children who got into trouble or needed assistance in school. In effect, they wanted a legal system that reflected their priorities.

The Portland's experience, because of its success, has been duplicated in many communities throughout the nation.[40]

Community prosecution is still in its early stages of development. It is based upon the principles of Community Policing and crime control is its goal. It is a proactive, problem-solving approach to addressing crime that involves the establishment of partnerships with the community. Similar to community policing, it also has as a major goal the improvement of the quality of life in the community. It complements the work of the police by engaging both public and private agencies in its crime control efforts. [41]

Community Prosecution, in practice, is a proactive approach to the prosecution of offenders that gives the community a greater role in identifying and determining solutions to neighborhood problems. It allows the prosecutor to move beyond the mere focus on convictions of offenders to solving problems of neighborhoods in order to prevent crimes from repeating themselves. It is supportive and complementary of law enforcement's Community Policing efforts and allows community residents to participate in improving the quality of life in the areas where they live.

COMMUNITY COURTS

The courts represent the third component of the criminal justice system. As such, they play an important role in the community justice movement. Community courts had their start in 1993 when the *New York Midtown Community Court* was opened. The Midtown Business Improvement District, having a vested interest in the Times Square area of New York City, spearheaded it. The objective of the court was to have people who were arrested in Times Square processed in the same area. This included booking, arraignment and adjudication. The sanctions were also administered in the Midtown area and included community service, court administered drug treatment programs, job training and placement and anger management treatment.[42]

Community Courts, similar to *Community Policing* and *community prosecution* work to solve neighborhood problems and contribute to building stronger communities that result in improving the quality of neighborhood life. The Midtown Community Court provided a model for community courts that consisted of:[43]

- Locating the court in the community, close to where crimes occurred.
- Repaying the community damaged by low-level crime by requiring offenders to compensate neighborhoods through community service.
- Using the leverage of the courts to sentence offenders to complete social services programs that helped to address problems such as addiction and prostitution.
- Bringing the court and the community closer together by making the courthouse accessible, establishing a community advisory board and publishing a quarterly newsletter.
- Using the court as a gateway to treatment and making social services available to offenders at the courthouse.

Community Courts also advance the Community Policing model by bringing the criminal justice system and community stakeholders together to solve problems that are of concern to the community. Similar to the police, the courts continue to have crime control/reduction as its main objective. But in addition, they focus on finding means of breaking the crime cycle. This is done by collaboration between communities, other components of the criminal justice system, including the public defender.

The courts started most community courts, but some were created because of prosecutors. Most Community Courts serve only one neighborhood. They "... focus on neighborhoods and are designed to respond to the concerns of individual communities. Moreover, community courts are shaped by the particular political, economic and social landscapes in each community."[44]

Based on experiences to date, the following are the major elements that comprise the Community Court movement:[45]
- Assumes a problem-solving role in the life of the community by bringing people together and helping craft solutions to problems faced by the community

- Addresses the impact that chronic offenders have on a community
- Improves the quality of life in the community
- Engages local voices - residents, merchants, community groups - in the administration of justice

Community Courts can best be seen as an important component in the community-based justice movement. Its overall objective is equity in the process. This is pursued by moving beyond the traditional role of the courts, adjudication and sentencing, to one of focusing on the best interests of the community. They involve considering the needs of the offenders, involving the community in the process and focusing on ways of improving the quality of life in neighborhoods. Similar to community policing, community courts also encourage involvement of the community.

CASE STUDY: RED HOOK[46]

The Red Hook Community Court is recognized as a model throughout the nation. Established in the spring of 2000 in an abandoned Catholic school, the Red Hook Community Justice Center is the nation's first multi-jurisdictional community court. Red Hook is a community located in a low-income neighborhood in Brooklyn, New York.

The Court is designed to go beyond the adjudication of cases by addressing the needs of the community, such as education, job training and youth development programs. The goal is to address chronic neighborhood problems such as minor offenses, youth crimes, domestic violence and disputes between landlords and tenants. To accomplish its goals, the court adopted a five-pronged approach: [47]

1. Promoting Accountability:
This is accomplished by ensuring that even minor offenders receive some consequence for their actions.

2. Repairing Conditions of Disorder:
Quality of life issues such as graffiti and broken windows are addressed by using supervised offender work crews and other community service programs. This is done to deter more serious crime.

3. Solving the Underlying Problems:

On-site social services address problems such as drug abuse. The goal is to resolve problems so offenders will not become repeat offenders.

4. <u>Engaging the Community</u>:
Efforts are made to improve public confidence in the justice system by forging links between the court, citizens and community groups.

5. <u>Making Justice Visible</u>:
The Justice Center is located in the community as a means of reducing fear, and improving the public perception of safety.

The community is integral to the success of the Center. It is a partnership in which the community not only identifies problems, but also partners in helping to find solutions. In addition, the Center provides jobs, meeting rooms and expertise in problem solving situations.

"Community engagement is embedded in the DNA of the project."[48] Members of the community play a variety of roles: (1) advisers, (2) evaluators, (3) problem solvers, (4) volunteers, (5) co-producers of justice, (6) service providers, (7) service recipients, and (8) employees. [49]

Red Hook, in the tradition of Community Policing, has been a successful component of the community justice movement.[50] It has proven that the court can reach out and involve the community in a meaningful way and in doing so, improve the quality of life in the community. This is accomplished by addressing the causes that brought the offender to court. Red Hook serves as a model for those who wish to adopt the Community Court concept.

Community Defender Services have emerged much slower than Community Courts. The New York City based Vera Institute established the first Neighborhood Defender Service (NDS) in the Harlem community of New York City in 1990. The services are based in the community and assist people who cannot afford to pay for legal services. The accused are encouraged to contact the service once they are arrested, giving lawyers more time to prepare their cases. The NDS team consists of a lawyer, administrative assistant, community worker and a senior attorney. The team approach enables them to handle more than the assigned case by engaging in mediation and thereby resolving problems that would otherwise be ignored by the court. A holistic approach to individuals and problems is taken. For example, they work to promote safety in the community and provide legal workshops to teach young people how to conduct themselves, especially when they are stopped by the police.[51]

Experience has shown that the *Neighborhood Defense Services* approach has the following advantages over traditional defense services: [52]

- Because the attorney is closer to the community, they are more likely to get witnesses to support the defendant at trial.
- Since many of the crimes are committed occur in the neighborhood were the offenders live, the attorneys are more likely to obtain evidence that could be used if the case goes to trial.
- The defender gets to know the community and as a result can establish relationships with businesses and churches that can provide support to the defendant.
- The defender becomes familiar with the social services agencies that might be able to assist clients deal with problems that caused their initial difficulties.
- The defender takes a more personal interest in the clients by helping them get services such as drug treatment, childcare or family services.

Neighborhood Defense Services has not evolved into the status of a movement, as is the case with Community Policing. Yet it holds great promise as a vital part of the community justice movement that is taking place in America.

COMMUNITY CORRECTIONS

Community Corrections is a term that the final component of the criminal justice system, corrections, has used for several decades. The meaning of Community Corrections does not, however, have the same meaning as it does for the other components of the community justice system.

Historically, Community Corrections referred to a variety of alternatives ordered by the court that did not involve incarceration. It is often used to address the problem of overcrowded prisons. A distinction should be made between *Community Policing, community prosecution, community courts* and *community corrections* because of their differences in philosophy. In fact, the use of the term 'Community Corrections' is better labeled "Community Based Corrections Programs."

Community Corrections, as practiced today "... is a legal status, an alternative to incarceration, a service-delivery mechanism and an organizational entity."[53] The two best-known forms of community corrections are probation and parole, both which date back to the 1800s. It also includes other programs where offenders are allowed to remain in the community instead of being incarcerated, e.g., *work furlough programs, halfway houses, residential centers* and *electronic monitoring*.

Probation is a sentence imposed by the court in lieu of incarceration that requires the convicted offender to remain in the community under the supervision of a probation officer.

The court imposes certain conditions on the offender as a condition of probation. Those conditions could include requirements that the offender remain gainfully employed, live in a certain location, not violate any laws, travel selectively and regularly report to a probation officer.

The goal of probation is to assist the offender in not violating additional laws and teach him how to become a productive citizen. Probation is a function of the court and may be revoked, resulting in the offender being incarcerated.

Parole is the conditional release of an inmate from prison after serving part of a sentence. A parole board or commission makes parole decisions. The parolee must agree to certain restrictions, such as regular meetings with a parole officer, maintaining gainful employment, refraining from the use of drugs and alcohol, and not fleeing the jurisdiction. Parole represents a bridge between incarceration and the offender's return to the community.

The parolee is not free, and if the conditions of parole are not met, the parole board can return him to prison. Parole is similar to probation in that the offenders serve part of their sentences in the community after a period of incarceration.

Community-based corrections gained favor in America during the early 1970s. The idea was to allow offenders the opportunity to become socialized in the community, rather than being incarcerated in an institution that did not represent the totality of the real world.[54]

Community-based corrections were viewed as another form of treatment, yet there was no consensus on the most effective method of addressing crime - confinement or in the community. Many, however, felt that the rehabilitation of the offender could be best achieved in the community, provided that they received the necessary help. It was also viewed as more cost-effective than incarceration.

At the end of 2005, over 4.9 million adult men and women were on parole or probation at the Federal, state or local levels. Of that number, 4,164,500 were on probation and 784,400 were on parole. At the same time, there were 1,525,924 prisoners in Federal and state correctional facilities. Almost one in every 32 adults in America was either in prison, jail, on probation or parole on December 31, 2005.[55] Considering the fact that the vast majority of convicted offenders continue to reside in the community, and those that are incarcerated will eventually be returned to the community, community corrections should be viewed in the same context as Community Policing. To do so, it must highly consider the following: [56]

- Focus on geographic areas rather than general assignments.
- Focus on community involvement rather than professional problem solving.
- Focus on a presence in the community, rather than being bound to the office.
- Focus on individual responsibility rather than diffuse agency responsibility.
- Focus on the community rather than just the offender.

CASE STUDY: PROJECT SAFEWAY[57]

Project Safeway was implemented on November 1, 1991 on the west side of Chicago to serve offenders who resided in that area. To meet the needs of the offenders, the project maintained extended hours and had three goals:
- To strengthen the system of probation's relationship with the community
- To offer "full-time service" models of probation
- To create a substantial and lasting change in the lives of offers through personal, family and neighborhood interventions

The first thing the program did when it was started was establish a local advisory committee that consisted of local residents, representatives of the business community and police department to assist the project staff in identifying the needs of both the community and offenders. It communicated the project goals and objectives to the larger community, addressed issues regarding program development and implementation and recruited community volunteers to work with offenders. In order to achieve its goals, the project implemented the following programs:

Community Contact: The project staff was required to visit community organizations, service providers, businesses, clubs and churches to establish communications and gain support.

Offender Programs: The project provided on-site programs for offenders that involved the community. Examples of such programs were:
1. An orientation program designed to prepare offenders for their probation experiences.
2. The faculty of the local community college provided on-site General Education Development (GED) and other education courses.
3. Treatment alternatives for special clients were provided on-site to perform substance abuse evaluations, refer offenders to treatment agencies, and conduct education classes with those who refused to knowledge that they had drug problems and those who were waiting for substance-abuse treatment.
4. Provided venues for offenders to meet their community service mandates such as neighborhood clean-up programs.
5. Provided readiness skills, and job placement services through community agencies.
6. Collaborated with government agencies and other service providers to address various offender needs such as HIV prevention, parenting skills, and health education.

FIELD SERVICES LINK

The Cook County Adult Probation Department's Field Services units used the program as a base of operation. This included an extensive probation supervision program, and a home confinement program. Field Services officers, who carried radios and firearms, made frequent home visits and established contact with the Chicago Police Department and the State Parole Authority, which supported the program's surveillance and enforcement capabilities.

The program obtained the support and cooperation of several community organizations. It represented a model of how probation agencies can work with the community to assist probationers make the transition from being a convicted offender to becoming a productive member of society.

Project Safeway served as an example of how probation departments can collaborate with the community to support offenders in a community environment in order to change their behavior, reduce recidivism and ultimately improve public safety in the community, which improves quality of life in the neighborhood.

COMMUNITY GOVERNMENT

The principles inherent in the criminal justice model that are being implemented under the rubric of *Community Policing, community prosecution, community courts,* and to a lesser degree *community corrections* are also applicable to local and national governments. The implementation of *Neighborhood Oriented Government* in Houston demonstrated that the concepts inherent in community policing could also work for other cities and their citizens. [58]

CASE STUDY: HOUSTON

Neighborhood Oriented Government (NOG) was a proactive, ongoing partnership among individual citizens, community volunteers, neighborhood associations, civic organizations, businesses, private-sector leaders, schools, elected officials and city employees to provide effective and efficient city services. Citizen participation in NOG was essential to the success of the concept. Citizen participation made community policing successful. It has the same positive impact in the administration of all segments of city government.

NOG had three broad principles: (1) solving problems at the neighborhood level, (2) improving access to city government and (3) delivery of services in a prompt and courteous manner.

PROBLEM SOLVING AT THE NEIGHBORHOOD LEVEL:

A Super Neighborhood Program was created to provide avenues for more effective community input into city government policy-making Eighty-eight super neighborhoods were created to encourage residents of neighboring communities to work together; to identify, plan, and set priorities to address the needs and concerns of their communities.

The boundaries of each Super Neighborhood were developed around major physical features - bayous, freeways, and the like - in order to group together contiguous communities that shared common physical characteristics and infrastructure. *Super Neighborhood Councils* were established to serve as forums where residents and stakeholders addressed issues, identified priority projects for the areas, and developed *Super Neighborhood Action Plans* (SNAP).

In addition to offering residents real solutions to neighborhood problems, the SNAPs served as a valuable tool for the city as it planned and funded its capital improvement projects. Depending on the community's needs, projects could include street repaving, new bike and walking trails, sewers, water main replacement, treatment plant refurbishing, renovation of police and fire stations, tennis courts, renovation of libraries, resurfacing of parking lots and a host of other neighborhood projects. The list was limited only by the needs identified. If a project was needed and the residents wanted it, the city worked it into the capital plans.

Super Neighborhood Councils met on a regular basis. Frequently, two or three Super Neighborhoods joined together. Department directors accompanied the mayor to the meetings so he could provide detailed answers to the questions raised by citizens. Typically, 100 citizens attended an average meeting.

A number of programs were operated under the Super Neighborhood umbrella:

NEIGHBORHOODS TO STANDARDS

This program was designed to bring city services up to the same standards in the city's various neighborhoods so that residents enjoyed the same level of services no matter where they lived. Services provided included street overlays, removal of dangerous buildings and installation of additional street lighting.

CLEAN NEIGHBORHOODS

This initiative relied on the active participation of residents, civic clubs and businesses to remove litter, paint over graffiti, eliminate illegal dumpsites, and clean neighborhoods. The National *Partnership to Prevent Urban Litter*, a coalition between the United States Conference of Mayors and Keep America Beautiful selected the program as a research site and a model for other cities.

OPERATION RENAISSANCE

This neighborhood cleanup program focused on eliminating illegal dumping and heavy trash violation in the city. It started with the city's 'Public Works and Engineering Department' conducting a massive cleaning in selected areas. That was followed by an aggressive police presence to enforce no dumping laws. Another component of the program focused on graffiti abatement.

PARKS TO STANDARDS

This program involved the renovation of city parks. Parks were viewed as essential to neighborhoods and in a very real sense empowered neighborhoods because families quickly realized the inherent value a park brought to the community when they used them.

SCHOOLS TO STANDARDS

This program was designed to upgrade signs, street lighting, drainage and other infrastructure projects around schools to make them safer, aesthetically pleasing and functional.

The concept proved that problem solving at the neighborhood level works. In less than two years, neighborhood councils became extremely active and effective. City departments – notably police, fire and public works - developed a heightened presence throughout the city and citizens developed a sense of responsibility for their communities' destinies.

IMPROVED ACCESS TO CITY GOVERNMENT

Improving access to city government was the second underlying principle of an effective neighborhood based government. Empowering communities so they could actively get involved in the process of bettering their own future demonstrated that government bureaucracy was navigable and could lead to even more involvement. Several initiatives were directed at improving citizens' access to city services and officials:

MAYOR'S TOWN HALL MEETINGS.

These meetings, conducted by the mayor, were held across the city so that citizens could ask questions about city services and facilities, and voice their views about how to improve the quality of life in their neighborhoods. The meetings afforded citizens the opportunity to meet directly with department directors to discuss issues and resolve problems. Town hall meetings were also held for the African community, Asian community, Hispanic community and people with disabilities.

MAYOR'S NIGHT IN

This program gave citizens direct access to city hall. Citizens were periodically invited to visit city hall in the evenings to meet with the mayor, department directors, and members of the city council. At those meetings, the participants asked questions or registered complaints about city services.

MAYOR'S MOBILE CITY HALL

This program was designed to complement the town hall meetings and Mayor's Night In. The mobile city hall was a large van that was parked at locations were large crowds gathered - parks and shopping centers - on weekends. The mayor set up office in the van. The mobile city hall program was well advertised before the date of the event. This program made city resources more accessible to people with limited ability to leave their immediate neighborhoods. Seniors, people with disabilities, and those who simply could not travel downtown took advantage of the program

CITIZENS ASSISTANCE OFFICE (CAO)

This office provided citizens with direct access to the mayor. Each day, the CAO submitted a report to the mayor that documented citizen telephone calls from the prior day. CAO employed specialists to receive phone calls from residents and refer complaints directly to the appropriate city departments. The specialists remained in contact with the citizens until their problems were resolved. Community liaisons in this office worked with more than 600 civic associations throughout the city.

MUNICIPAL SATELLITE COURTS

The city created five new satellite courts to make municipal court services available in neighborhoods. Citizens could use these Neighborhoods Courts to take care of citations for certain traffic, parking and other minor violations rather than going downtown.

MAYOR'S OFFICE OF IMMIGRANT AND REFUGEE AFFAIRS

This office assisted immigrants with accessing and using basic city services such as the city's network of health clinics. The program allowed the city to ensure that the children of immigrants were properly immunized and received other services they needed.

3-1-1 NON-EMERGENCY PHONE SERVICE.

This service allowed citizens to use a single telephone number (311) to access all city departments.

E-GOVERNMENT

The city developed a web site that allowed citizen access to many city online services. Information about all of the above programs, plus more information about individual city departments was available.

DELIVERING CITY SERVICES PROMPTLY AND COURTEOUSLY

This final principle is essential to neighborhood-based government. Access to city services is not enough; citizens must receive those services in a timely and pleasant manner. The city's *Continuous Management Improvement* initiative evaluated each department to determine the time required for obtaining equipment and supplies, accuracy of meter reading and all other measurable processes, including response times to requests made by citizens. The city employed a mystery shopper that constantly tested how the city's services were delivered.

Neighborhood-Oriented Government offered a new way for people to interact with their municipal government and receive services they rightfully deserved. It provided the opportunity for interaction, corporation and participation of all city departments with all segments of the community.

Furthermore, it was the vehicle that allowed all elements of the community to come together and work towards a common goal, improving the quality of life in each city neighborhood. Unlike the implementation of Community Policing in Houston, where I served eight years as Police Chief and institutionalized the concept, Neighborhood Oriented Government faded away after my six years as mayor came to an end.

SUMMARY

The *Community Policing* concept has provided a model for other components of the criminal justice system and city government to emulate by adopting the same principles for their operations.

Succinctly stated, the Community Policing philosophy is based on two basic premises: (1) problem solving is best achieved if the problems are reduced to a manageable size. Organizing and delivering services on a neighborhood, rather than a citywide basis can best accomplish this, and (2) community-based initiatives can only be successful in the long run if they mobilize a broad cross disciplinary, cross professional network of community leaders, professionals, civil servants, academics and local citizens to developed a coherent sense of community within each specific geographic area.

Programs must be designed to identify and solve problems that are of concern to the people who reside in the neighborhoods. The community must be involved in all phases of the problem solving process, from conception to implementation.

Just as the community-based philosophy has proved to be successful in the criminal justice system and, to a limited degree, in municipal government, the philosophy is also applicable as a national urban policy.[59]

History has proven that when large urban areas are dealt with as a whole, the problems become overwhelming, complex and intractable. In the end, success can best be achieved when individuals are provided with a sense that government cares and that they are able to live in a vital, thriving, caring and supportive community in which they can raise children safely, work productively and live healthy lives.

Community Justice, *Community Policing, community prosecution, Community Courts, community corrections*, community schools, community development and community governments are all based on the same basic assumptions. When problems are reduced to a manageable scale, and the community is actively involved in the community building process, communities can be better.

Scale alone is not sufficient for building a sense of community in cities. In addition there must be participation from all segments of the community that come together to form a network that achieves common goals.

The Community Policing model offers great promise for changing America's national policy by encouraging community involvement in initiatives at the neighborhood level, creating community pride and resulting in cost-effective utilization of existing resources. Community Policing also fosters to rebuild communities and forge new connections for an improved quality of life in city neighborhoods throughout America.

NOTES: CHAPTER SIXTEEN

1. The President's Commission on Law Enforcement and Administration of Justice, The Challenge of Crime in a Free Society, Washington DC: United States Government Printing Office, 1967

2. See Chart, Ibid. pp. 8-9

3. Ibid. p. 7

4. National Advisory Commission on Criminal Justice Standards and Goals, A National Strategy to Reduce Crime, Washington D.C: United States Government Printing Office, 1973, p.31

5. Beatty, John, Multnomah County, Oregon Circuit Court Judge, unpublished, undated speech

6. Murphy, Patrick, in Daniel Skoler, Organizing the Non-System, Lexington, MA: Lexington Books, 1977, p. xvii

7. Brown, Lee P., Department of Justice Services, Multnomah County Oregon, unpublished, untitled, undated report

8. Op. Cit., Note 1, p. 15

9. Op. Cit., Note 1, p 7-15

10. Multnomah County, Oregon, Ordinance No. 64, enacted December 21, 1997

11. Multnomah County, Oregon, Board of County Commissioners, Board Order, issued March 24, 1977

12. Reaves, Brian, Federal Law Enforcement Officers, 2004, Bureau of Justice Statistics, Washington, D.C., U.S. Department of Justice, Office of Justice Programs, July 2006, p. 2

13. Ibid. p.2

14. Ibid.

15. Ibid. p.3

16. Ibid. p.2

17. <u>Census of State and Local Law Enforcement Agencies, 2004</u>, Washington, D.C.: U.S. Department of Justice, Office of Justice Programs, Bureau of Justice Statistics, June, 2007, p.6

18. Ibid. p.5

19. Ibid.

20. Op. Cit., Note 17, p. 5

21. Ibid. p. 5

22. Walrod, Truman, <u>The Role of Sheriff Past-Present-Future</u>, Washington, D.C.: National Sheriffs' Association, 1975

23. Ibid.

24. <u>Local Police Departments, 2007</u>, Washington, D.C.: U.S. Department of Justice, Office of Justice Programs, Bureau of Justice Statistics, Law Enforcement Management and Administrative Statistics, December 2010, p. 8

25. Ibid. p. 9

26. Ibid.

27. Ibid.

28. Ibid. p. 26

29. Ibid. p. 28

30. Ibid. p.27

31. Ibid.

32. Karp, David R. and Todd R. Clear, <u>Community Justice: A Conceptual Framework in Boundary Changes in Criminal Justice Organizations</u>; Washington, D.C.: United States Department of Justice, National Institute of Justice, pp. 323-368

33. Karp, David R. and Todd R. Clear, (EDS), <u>What is Community Justice: Cast Studies of Restorative Justice and Community Supervision</u>, Thousand Oaks: Sage Publications, 2002, p.138

34. Quinn, Thomas, "Beyond Community Policing: Community Justice," <u>The Police Chief</u>, Vol. 64, No. 10, October 1997, p.107

35. Op. Cit., Note 1, p. 147

36. "Multnomah County (Portland, Oregon,) <u>Lessons from the Field</u>, Alexandria, Va.: American Prosecution Research Institute, p.53

37. National District Attorneys Association, "National Center for Community Prosecution," http://www.ndaa.org/nccp <u>home.html p.2</u> (10/19/11)

38. Goldkamp, John S., Cheryl Irons-Guynn and Doris Weiland, "<u>Community Prosecution Strategies: Measuring Impact</u>," Washington, D.C.: U.S. Department of Justice, Office of Justice Assistance, Bureau of Justice Programs, November 2002, p. 4

39. Coles, Catherine M. and George Kelling, "Prosecution in the Community: A Study of the Emergent Strategies: A Cross Site Analysis," Program in Criminal Justice Policy and Management of the Malcolm Wiener Center for Social Policy, John F. Kennedy School of Government, Cambridge, Mass.: Harvard University, p.32 and 34

40. Op.Cit., Note 36

41. Op. Cit., Note 37, P.1

42. Clear, Todd R. and Eric Cadora, Community Justice, Belmont, CA.: Thompson Wadsworth Publishers, 2003, pp. 56-57

43. Lee, Eric, Community Courts: An Evolving Model, Washington, D.C.: United States Department of Justice, Office of Justice Programs, Bureau of Justice Assistance, October, 2000, p. 3

44. Ibid. p.1

45. Ibid.

46. Berman, Greg and Aubrey Fox, From the Bench and Trenches: Justice in Red Rock, http://72.14.209.104/search?q=cache:C214ihudMOSJ:www.ncsconline.org/wc/Publications/...

47. Ibid. pp.81-82

48. Ibid. p.82

49. Ibid. pp.83-84

50. Berman, Greg and Aubrey Fox, "From the Margins to the Mainstream: Community Justice at the Crossroads", 22 Justice System Journal 1.

51. Op. Cit., Note 42, p.61

52. Ibid. pp. 61-62

53. Petersilia. Joan, Community Corrections: Probation, Parole and Intermediate Sanctions, New York: Oxford University Press, 1998, p.1

54. Dean-Myrda, Mark C. and Francis T. Cullen, "The Panacea Pendulum: Community as a Response to Crime", Ibid., p.12

56. Nevers, Dan, "Neighborhood Probation: Adopting a 'Beat Cop' Concept in Community Supervision", Op. Cit., Note 3, p.64

57. Leaf, Robin, Arthur Lurigio and Nancy Martin, "Chicago's Project Safeway: Strengthening Probation's Link With the Community", Op. Cit., Note 53, p.168

58. Modified from Brown, Lee P., "Houston's Neighborhood Oriented Government: "Expanding the Concept of Community Policing to Municipal Government Can Make a City "Work" for its Citizens", Focus, Vol. 29, No. 8. September 2001

59. The idea was first advanced by Dr. Gregory Prince, President of

Hampshire College in an unpublished, undated paper entitled "Community Policing: A Model for a New National Urban Policy". The work resulted from a conference on urban initiatives that was sponsored by Hampshire College

Appendix A

IMPLEMENTATION OF COMMUNITY POLICING TASKS: NEW YORK CITY POLICE DEPARTMENT

1. Conduct neighborhood analysis to determine the number of discrete neighborhood areas used in identifying patrol sectors; develop new sectors based on neighborhood boundaries.

2. Identify the procedure to be used in initiating review of the 1970 coterminosity as it impacts precinct boundaries matching current neighborhood boundaries.

3. Develop and test a model for precinct structure in a single precinct; fully staff the precinct (reflecting recommendations in the Resource Allocation and Staffing Plan);[11] fully integrate 911 response units, specialized task forces and other specialized units with the Community Policing initiative.

4. Require each of the remaining seventy-four precinct commanders to implement Community Policing commensurate with existing resources.

5. Match civilianization needs with position requirements throughout the department; determine the exact number of civilians needed when positions are civilianized.

6. Revise and re-issue the Community Policing Officer Program problem analysis model for use by all precinct personnel.

7. Devise new reporting mechanism for officers to report on problem analysis, actions proposed and actions taken.

8. Retrain sergeants in their roles of facilitating of patrol problem solving.

9. From the "corporate perspective" undertake semi-annual analysis of selected crimes, detailing specific crime prevention and interdiction strategies based on the nature of the crime problem being addressed. Develop action plans for detectives, organized crime control, and patrol bureaus to implement these strategies.

10. From the "corporate perspective", undertake semi-annual analysis of narcotic problem, developing specific narcotic interdiction strategies for implementation by all bureaus.

11. Develop a capacity to analyze repeat calls-for-service and provide patrol units with a monthly report on addresses of key call generators; develop a monthly management summary of repeat calls by location.

12. Ensure that there are no duplicative command and supervisory assignments, and that each command officer and supervisor is assigned to an area of responsibility with clear objectives and specific responsibilities.

13. Develop a strategy for all executive staff to serve as a "corporate board" and for all commanders, above the rank of captain, to assume Community Policing responsibilities.

14. Review unit staffing levels to maximize Community Policing assignments.

15. Develop a plan for precinct officers to become more involved in crime prevention and interdiction efforts in their assigned sectors, especially in the areas of drug enforcement and violent crime reduction; create reporting mechanism for precinct sector officers.

16. Initiate a committee on Community Policing implementation.

17. Work with labor unions to find ways to revive peer participation in training and decision-making; build peer input into in-service training.

18. Educate the public to use 911 for emergencies only.

19. Implement civilianization or unit abolition recommendations contained in the Resource Allocations and Staffing Plan.[2]

20. Rework Patrol Allocation Plan to reflect the integrated model of Community Policing and its precinct structure.

21. Initiate recruitment enhancements; reduce lag time between filing and test results; and increase efforts to retain minority candidates.

22. Expand background investigations and re-validate psychological screening.

23. Encourage city personnel departments to use Community Policing criteria and establish professional assessment centers for promotion.

24. Expand department awards to include community service and excellence in problem solving.

25. Develop department-wide training plan, including police academy training of recruits to work in Community Policing and train officers in facilitation skills, and problem solving.

26. Develop new tasks and standard performance based evaluations.

27. Create precinct assignments for specialized units, so they will have a Community Policing responsibility during their uncommitted times.

28. Collaborate with the District Attorneys' offices in the five counties to reduce overtime and time spent off patrol by arresting officers.

29. Work with the media to increase their understanding of Community Policing.

30. Develop strategies for increasing community participation in Community Policing initiatives.

31. Initiate a Committee on Crime Control Strategy.

32. Initiate a Committee on Drug Control Strategy.

33. Initiate a Committee on Community Crime Prevention.

34. Initiate a Committee on Discipline to address the disciplinary process within the department.

35. Initiate a Committee on Information and Technology.

36. Initiate a Committee on Corruption Prevention and Control.

37. Initiate a Committee on Patrol Enhancement.

38. Develop a Department-wide space plan.

39. Develop a strategic plan to achieve the inter-agency coordination required to implement Community Policing.

40. Design and implement enhancement of the Communications Center, including a new 911 Center.

41. Develop a new computer aided dispatch system (CADS).

42. Review call classification schemes and develop the capacity to alter call prioritization.

43. Conduct a survey and analysis of successful officers to identify factors that can be used in recruitment efforts.

44. Develop internal and external marketing plans to get the Community Policing message out in an effective manner.

45. Develop a process to evaluate agency performance.

46. Develop a plan to solicit and apply external resources in support of Community Policing.

47. Prepare analysis of differential police response with recommendations for action.

48. Review conduct of preliminary investigations, exploring whether officers take these investigations as far as they can, especially given the planned changes to 911.

49. Develop a plan for the role of Precinct Community Councils under Community Policing.

50. Analyze and make recommendations on the role of investigations under Community Policing.

51. Examine the role of civil remedies in Community Policing, using the results of the 5th Precinct Project.

52. Conduct a paperwork review in the context of Community Policing, including form's control and implementation of the paperless arrest system.

53. Identify the issues to be resolved in developing a precinct-wide problem solving model.

54. Initiate a task force to assess the effectiveness of the department.

55. Develop crime analysis under Community Policing.

BIBLIOGRAPHY

Aguirre, B.E, Rogelino Saenz and Brian Sinclair James, "Marielites Ten Years Later: The Scar Face Legacy," Social Science Quarterly, Vol. 78, No. 2, June 1997

American Bar Association Project on Standards for Criminal Justice, Standards Relating to the Urban Police Function, Washington, D.C.: American Bar Association, 1972

Anderson, Staley V., "The Ombudsman: Public Defender Against Maladministration," Public Affairs Report, Bulletin of the Institute of American Studies, Berkeley: University of California, Volume 6, April 1965

Bales, John P. and Timothy N. Oettmeir, "Houston's D.A.R.T. Program: A Transition to the Future," Houston Police Department, unpublished, no date

Bankston, Carl L.III, and Danielle Antoinette Hidalgo, "The Waves of War: Immigrants, Refugees, and New Americans from Southeast Asia," in Zhou, Min and J.V. Gatewood (EDS), Contemporary Asian America: A Multidisciplinary Reader, New York: University Press, 2007

Barnes, Jessica S. and Claudette E. Bennett, The Asian Population: 2000, United States, February 2002, Washington, D.C.: Department of Commerce, Economics and Statistics Administration, United States Census Bureau

Barringer, Mark "The Anti-War Movement in the United States," http://www.english.illinois.edu/maps/vietnam/antiwar.html

Bell, Derrick, Race, Racism and America, Boston: Little Brown and Co., 1980

Berman, Greg and Aubrey Fox, "From the Benches and Trenches: Justice in Red Hook," Justice System Journal, Vol. 26, No. 2, 2005

Berman, Greg and Aubrey Fox, "From the Margins to the Mainstream: Community Justice at the Crossroads, Justice System Journal, Vol. 22, No. 2, 2001

Bexelius, Alfred, "The Origin, Nature and Functions of the Civil and Military Ombudsman in Sweden," The Annals of the American Academy of Political and Social Science, Vol. 377, May 1968

Bittner, Egon, The Functions of Police in Modern Society, Washington, D.C.: United States Government Printing Office, 1971

Black Panther Party and Peace and Freedom Movement, "Berkeley Petition for Community Control of the Police: Summary of Berkeley Police Control Amendment," Berkeley: unpublished, 1970.

Bloch, Peter B., and Donald R. Weldman, Managing Criminal Investigations, National Institute of Law Enforcement and Criminal Justice, Washington, D.C.: U.S. Government Printing Office, 1975

Bolz, Frank Jr., Kenneth J. Dudonis and David P. Shultz, The Terrorism Handbook: Tactics, Procedures and Techniques, New York: Elsevier Science New Publishing Company, 1990

Boydsun, John, and Michael E. Sherry, San Diego Community Profile: Final Report, Washington, D.C.: Police Foundation, 1975

Boydstun, John E., San Diego Field Interrogation – Final Report, Washington, D.C.: Police Foundation, 1975

Brown, Lee P. "A Police Department and its Values," The Police Chief, Vol. LI, No. 11, November 1984

Brown, Lee P., An Evaluation of the Houston Police Department's D.A.R.T. Program, Houston Police Department, unpublished, 1984

Brown Lee P. "An Unforeseen Problem Resulting From College Educated Policemen," Police, Vol. 10, No. 3, January-February, 1965

Brown, Lee P., "Beat Profiling," Management Report 9, Houston Police Department, unpublished, no date

Brown, Lee P., "Bond Program," Management Report 23, Houston Police Department, unpublished, no date

Brown, Lee P. Civil Enforcement Initiative, New York City Police Department, unpublished, June 1992

Brown, Lee P., Crime Control Plan: A Citizen/Police Partnership, New York City Police Department, unpublished, 1991

Brown, Lee P., "Community Policing: A Practical Guide for Police Officials," Perspectives on Policing, Washington, D.C.:U.S. Department of Justice, National Institute of Justice and the Program in Criminal Justice Policy and Management, John F. Kennedy School of Government, Cambridge Mass.: Harvard University, September, 1989, No. 12

Brown, Lee P., "Department of Justice Services," Multnomah County Oregon, unpublished, no date

Brown, Lee P., (ED), Developing Neighborhood Oriented Policing, Washington,. DC.: International Association of Chiefs of Police, 1988

Brown, Lee P., Directed Area Responsibility Team, Houston Police Department, unpublished, 1982

Brown, Lee P., "Dynamic Police-Community Relations at Work," The Police Chief, Vol. 35, No. 4, April 1968

Brown, Lee P., "Fear Reduction Project," Management Report 2, Houston Police Department, unpublished, no date

Brown, Lee P., "Houston's Neighborhood Oriented Government: Expanding the Concept of Community Policing to Municipal Government Can Make a City 'Work' For Its Citizens." Focus, Vol. 29, No. 8, September 2001

Brown, Lee P. and Mary Ann Wycoff, "Policing Houston: Reducing Fear and Improving Service," Crime and Delinquency, Vol. 33. No 1, January 1987

Brown, Lee P., "Beat Profiling" Management Report 9, Houston Police Department, unpublished, no date

Brown, Lee P. (ED), Neighborhood Team Policing: The Multnomah County Experience, Portland, Oregon: Multnomah County Sheriff's Office, December 1976

Brown, Lee P., "New York City Police Department Proposal: Development of a Performance Measurement System for Community Policing," A proposal submitted to the National Institute of Justice by the New York City Police Department, June 2, 1992

Brown, Lee P., New York City Council Committee on Public Safety, Public Hearing: "How to Evaluate the Effectiveness of the Police Department's Community Policing Program," New York City, November 14, 1991.

Brown, Lee P, Policing New York City in the 1990s, New York City Police Department, unpublished, January, 1991

Brown, Lee P., The Development of a Police Community Relations Program: An Assessment of the San Jose Project, Master's Thesis, Berkley: University of California, 1964

Brown, Lee P., The Death of Police-Community Relations, Institute for Urban Affairs and Research, Washington, D.C.: Howard University, Occasion Paper, Vol.1, No. 1, 1973

Brown, Lee P, Plan of Action, Houston Police Department, April 1983, unpublished

Brown, Lee P., "Police Activities League," Management Report 14, Houston Police Department, unpublished, no date

Brown, Lee P., Police Department City of New York: Executive Session Training Implications for Community Policing, New York City Police Department, 1992

Brown, Lee P., Problem-Solving Strategies for Community Policing: A Practical Guide, New York City Police Department, 1992

Bureau of Indian Affairs, Indian Law Enforcement History, Washington, D.C.: Department of Interior, Law Enforcement Services, 1975

Carte, Gene E. and Elaine Carte, Police Reform in the United States, The Era of August Vollmer, Berkeley: University of California, 1975

Carvalho, Irene and Dan A, Lewis, "Service Beyond Community: Reactions to Crime and Disorder Among Inner-City Residents," Criminology, Vol. 41, Issue 3, August 2003

Cassidy, William L., Observations on the Investigation of Crime Involving Vietnamese Subjects, Oakland, CA.: Intelligence Studies Foundation Inc., 1984

Chaiken, Jan M., Peter W. Greenwood and Joan A. Petersillia, The Criminal Investigation Process: A Summary Report, Santa Monica, CA.: The Rand Corporation, June 1976

Chin, Laura (ED), Civil Rights Issues of Asians and Pacific Americans: Myths and Realities, A Consultation Sponsored by the United States Commission on Civil Rights, May 8-9, 1979, Washington, D.C.: U.S. National Institute of Education, Department of Health, Education and Welfare, 1980

Christopher, Warren, "Report of the Independent Commission of the Los Angeles Police Department," Los Angeles, California, July 1991

Civil Rights Issues Facing Asian Americans in the 1990s, A Report of the United States Commission on Civil Rights, Washington, D.C.: U.S. Government Printing Office, February 1992

Clear, Todd R. and Eric Cardova, <u>Community Justice</u>, Belmont CA.: Thompson/Wadsworth Publishers, 2003

Cohen, Bernard and Jan Chaiken (1987), <u>Investigators Who Perform Well</u>, U.S. Department of Justice, National Institute of Justice, Washington D.C.: U.S. Government Printing Office, 1987

Coles, Catherine M. and George Kelling, "<u>Prosecution in the Community: A Study of the Emergent Strategies: A Cross Site Analysis,</u> " Program in Criminal Policy and Management of the Malcolm Wiener Center for Social Policy, John F. Kennedy School of Government, Cambridge, Mass.: Harvard University

Commission on Wartime Relocation and Internment of Civilians, <u>Personal Justice Denied</u>, Washington, D.C.: U.S. Government Printing Office, 1983

Commission to Investigate Allegations of Police Corruption and Anti-Corruption Procedures of the Police Department, <u>Commission Report</u>, New York City, New York, 1972

Committee on Science and Technology for Countering Terrorism, Division of Engineering and Physical Sciences, National Research Council," Making the Nation Safer: The Role of Science and Technology in Countering Terrorism," Washington, D.C.: National Academy Press, 2002

Community Relations Service, United States Department of Justice "Police use of Force: Addressing Community Racial Tensions" http: www.usdoj.gov/crs/pubs/pubbullpoliceuseofforcedraftrevision7202.htm

Cordner, Gary W. <u>The Baltimore County Citizen Oriented Police Enforcement COPE Project: Final Evaluation</u>, Final report to the Florence W. Burden Foundation: Crime and Justice Department, College Park, Maryland: University of Maryland, 1986

Covey, Stephen R., <u>Principle Centered Leadership</u>, New York: Free Press, 1992

Crowe, Timothy D., <u>Crime Prevention Through Environmental Design</u>, Boston, Mass.: Butterworth-Heinmann, 1991

Currie, Elliot, *Confronting Crime: An American Challenge*, New York: Pantheon Books, 1988

Dalton, Patricia A., "Homeland Security: Effective Intergovernmental Coordination is Key to Success," Testimony before the Subcommittee on Government Efficiency, Financial Management, and Intergovernmental Relations, Committee on Government Reform, U.S. House of Representatives, August 20, 2002

Daly, Emmet, *Guide to Race Relations for Peace Officers*, Sacramento: State of California: Department of Justice, 1952

Daniel, Roger, *Asian America; Chinese and Japanese in the United States Since 1850*, Seattle: University of Washington Press, 1988

Davis, Robert C., Nicole J. Henderson, Janet Mandelstam, Christopher W. Ortiz and Joel Miller, *Federal Intervention in local Policing: Pittsburgh's Experience with a Consent Decree*, Washington, D.C., U.S. Department of Justice, Office of Community Policing Services, undated

de Lint, Willem, "Intelligence in Policing and Security: Reflections in Scholarship:" *Policing and Society*, Vol. 16, No. 1, March 2006

Demaris, Ovid, *J. Edgar Hoover: As They Knew Him*, New York: Carroll and Graf Publishers, 1975

Department of Justice Study Group, *Report to the Attorney General: Restructuring the Justice Department's Program of Assistance to State and Local Governments for Crime Control and Criminal Justice System Improvement*, Washington, D.C.: U. S. Department of Justice, June 23, 1967

Doherty, Stephen and Bradley G. Hibbard, "Community Policing and Homeland Security," *The Police Chief*, Vol. 23, No. 2, February, 2006

Dostoyevsky, Fyodor, *The House of the Dead*, London: Penguin Books, 1862

Dunham Roger and Geoffrey P. Alpers, *Critical Issues in Law Enforcement*, Prospect Heights, Ill: Waveland Press Inc., 1987

Eck, John E., <u>Managing Case Assignments: The Burglary Investigation Decision Model Replication</u>, Washington, D.C.: Police Executive Research Forum, 1979

Eck, John, <u>Solving Crimes: The Investigation of Burglary and Robbery</u>, Washington, D.C.: Police Executive Research Forum, 1983

Eck, John and William Spelman, <u>Problem-Oriented Policing in Newport News</u>, Washington, D.C: Police Executive Research Forum, 1987

Eck, John and William Spelman, et al, <u>Problem Solving: Problem- Oriented Policing in Newport News, Va. and Washington, D.C.</u>: Washington, D.C.: Police Executive Research Forum, 1987

Edwards, George, <u>The Police on the Urban Frontier – A Guide to Community Understanding</u>, New York: Institute of Human Relations Press, 1968

Endore, S. Guy and Orson Wells, <u>The Sleepy Lagoon Case</u>, Los Angeles CA.: The Committee, 1943

Franklin, John Hope, <u>From Slavery to Freedom</u>, 5th ed., New York: Alfred A. Knopf, 1980

Fridell, Lorie, Robert Lunney, Drew Diamond and Bruce Kudu, <u>Racially Based Policing: A Principled Response</u>, Washington, D.C.: Police Executive Research Forum, 2001

Fyfe, James, "Shots Fired: Examination of New York City Police Department Firearms Discharge," Diss., Albany: State University of New York, 1978

Federal Bureau of Investigation: <u>History of the FBI:</u> http://www.fbi.gov/libref historic/historic/text/htm

Federal Bureau of Investigation, <u>Crime in the United States,</u> Washington, D.C.: United States Department of Justice

Fields, John, <u>Social Capitol</u>, New York: Rouledge, 2003

Fogelson, Robert M., Big City Police, Cambridge, Mass.: Harvard University Press, 1977

Franklin, John Hope, From Slavery to Freedom: A History of American Negroes, New York: Alfred A. Knopf, 1948

Gay, William G, June P. Woodward, H. Talmadge Day, James P. O'Neil and Carl Tacher, Issues in Team Policing: A Review of the Literature, Washington, D.C.: National Sheriff's Association, 1975

Gash, Norman, Peel, London: Longman, 1979

Geller, William A. and Michael S. Scott, Deadly Force, What We Know - A Practitioner's Desk Reference on Police-Involved Shootings, Washington, D.C.: Police Executive Research Forum, 1992

Gentry, Curt, J. Edgar Hoover: The Man and the Secrets, New York: Norton and Company, 1991

Georgakas, Dan, The Broken Hoop, Garden City, New York: Doubleday and Company Inc, 1973

Goldkamp, John S., Cheryl Irons-Guynn and Doris Weiland, "Community Prosecution Strategies: Measuring Impact," Washington, D.C., U.S. Department of Justice, Office of Justice Assistance, Bureau of Justice Programs, November 2002

Fife, James (ED), Readings on Police Use of Deadly Force, Washington, D.C.: Police Foundation, 1982

Goldstein, Herman, "Improving Policing: A Problem-Oriented Approach," Crime and Delinquency, Vol. 25, Issue 2, April 1979

Goldstein, Herman, Policing A Free Society, Cambridge, Mass.: Ballinger Publishing Company, 1977

Goldstein, Herman, Problem Oriented Policing, New York: McGraw Hill, 1990

Gossett, Thomas F., Race: The History of an Idea in America, New York: Schocken Books, 1965

Green, Mark, (ED) Changing America: Blueprints for the New Administration, New York: New Market Press, 1992

Greenberg, Ilene and Robert Wasserman, Managing Criminal Investigations, Washington D.C.: U.S, Department of Justice, National Institute of Law Enforcement and Criminal Justice, 1979

Greenwood, Peter, Jan M. Chaiken, Joan Petersilia and Linda Prusoff, The Criminal Investigation Process, Vol. III: Observation and Analysis, Santa Monica, CA.: The Rand Corporation, 1975

Greenwood, Ilene and Robert Wasserman, Managing Criminal Investigations, Washington, D.C.: U.S. Department of Justice, Law Enforcement Assistance Administration, National Institute of Law Enforcement and Criminal Justice, 1979

Greenwood, Peter W., An Analysis of the Apprehension Activities of the New York City Police Department, New York: New York-Rand Institute, R-529 NYC, September 1970

Grieco, Elizabeth and Rachel C. Cassidy, "Overview of Race and Hispanic Origin, Census 2000 Brief, Washington, D.C.: U.S. Census Bureau, March 2001

"Growth of the United States through Immigration – The Chinese," New York Times, September 3, 1865

Hata, Don Teruo, Jr., and Nadine Ishitani Hata, "Run Out and Ripped Off: A Legacy of Discrimination" Civil Rights Digest, Vol. 9, No.1, Fall, 1976

Harrison, Burr P., "Recent Court Decisions Hamper Effective Law Enforcement," The Police Chief, Vol. XXV, No. 4, April 1958

Hartman, Francis X, "Debating Evolution of American Policing," Perspectives on Policing, Washington, D.C, United States Department of Justice, National Institute of Justice and the Program in Criminal Justice Policy and Management, John F. Kennedy School of Government, Cambridge, Mass.: Harvard University, November 1988, No. 5

Harton, Thomas R. "Qualities of Successful CEO", <u>Hyatt Magazine</u>, Fall, 1987

Hesser, Larry "Leadership Verses Management," unpublished, undated

Higginbotham, A. Leon Jr. <u>In the Matter of Color: Race and the American Legal Process: The Colonial Period</u>, New York: Oxford University Press, 1978

Hoffman, Bruce, <u>Inside Terrorism</u>, New York: Columbia University Press, 1998

Home Office and the Central Office of Information, <u>The Story of our Police: Preserving Law and Order from Earliest Times to the Making of the Modern Police Force</u>, Norwich, England: Soman-Wherry Press Ltd., 1976

Hoover, J. Edgar, <u>A Study of Communism</u>, New York: Holt, Rinehart and Winston, 1962

Hoover, J. Edgar, <u>Masters of Deceit: The Story of the Communist Party in America and How to Fight It</u>, New York: Henry Holt and Company, 1958

Hoover, J. Edgar, <u>Persons in Hiding</u>, New York: Little, Brown, 1938

<u>Houston Chronicle,</u> "Terrorism Pushes FBI into Unknown Territory," August 20, 2006

Houston Police Depart,<u>" Community Service Division: Operational Profile</u>," unpublished paper, 1982

H.R. 3162 , 107th Congress, "Uniting and Strengthening America by Providing Appropriate Tools Required to Intercept and Obstruct Terrorism," (Patriot Act) Washington, D.C.: October 24, 2001

Hudiburg, David L. <u>The Origin of Team Policing</u>, copyright, David L. Hudiburg, 1975

Hurt, Harold L., <u>General Orders</u>, "Department Mission, Values, and

Guiding Principles," Houston Police Department No. 100-06, April 22, 2008

Independent Commission on the Los Angeles Police Department, <u>Report of the Independent Commission on the Los Angeles Police Department</u>, Los Angeles, Calif., 1991

International Association of Chiefs of Police and the United States Conference of Mayors, <u>Police-Community Relations and Practices – A National Survey</u>, Washington D.C., 1967,

International Association of Chiefs of Police, <u>Leadership in Police Organizations</u>, Vol. 1, Area 1-2, New York: McGraw-Hill Custom Publishing, 2004.

International Association of Chiefs of Police, <u>Patrol Staffing and Deployment Study</u>, unpublished, no date

Jenkins, Brian, "On Emergency Terrorism," Emergency Preparedness Project, Center for Policy Research, National Governors' Association, Washington D.C., May, 1979

Johnson, Samuel, <u>Lives of the English Poets</u>, London: Jones and Company, 1825

Johnson, Thomas A., Gordon Misner and Lee P. Brown, <u>The Police and Society: An Environment for Collaboration and Confrontation</u>, Upper Saddle River, New Jersey: Prentice Hall, 1981

<u>Justice Issues: Intelligence-Led Policing</u>, US Department of Justice, Office of Justice Programs, Bureau of Justice Assistance http://www.ojp.u.s.doj.gov/BJA/topics/ilp.html (10.2.11)

Kamisar, Yale, "When the Cops Were Not Handcuffed," <u>The New York Times Magazine</u>, Nov. 7, 1965

Kansas City Police Department, "Directed Patrol: A Concept in Community- Specific, Crime-Specific, and Service-Specific Policing," Kansas City, Missouri, 1974

Karp, David R. and Todd R. Clear, (EDS), <u>What is Community Justice:

Case Studies of Restorative Justice and Community Supervision, Thousand Oaks, CA: Sage Publications, 2002

Kelling, George L. "Neighborhood Cops," *City Journal*: Winter, 1994

Kelling, George L. "Police and Communities: The Quiet Revolution," *Perspectives on Policing*, Washington D.C.: U.S. Department of Justice, National Institute of Justice, and the Program in Criminal Justice Policy and Management, John F. Kennedy School of Government, Cambridge, Mass: Harvard University, June 1988, No. 1

Kelling, George L., Robert Wasserman and Hubert Williams, "Police Accountability," *Perspectives on Policing*, U.S. Department of Justice, Office of Justice Programs, National Institute of Justice and the Program in Criminal Justice Policy and Management, John F. Kennedy School of Government, Cambridge, Mass: Harvard University, November, 1988 No.7

Kelling, George, Tony Pate, Duane Dieckman, Charles E. Brown, *The Kansas City Preventive Patrol Experiment*, Washington D.C.: The Police Foundation, 1974

Kelling, George L., Anthony Pate, Amy Ferrara, Mary Utne and Charles E. Brown, *The Newark Foot Patrol Experiment*, Washington, D.C.: Police Foundation, 1981

Kelling, George and Mark H. Moore, "The Evolving Strategy of Policing," in *Perspectives on Policing*, Washington, D.C., National Institute of Justice, United States Department of Justice and The Program in Criminal Justice Policy and Management, John F. Kennedy School of Government, Cambridge, Mass: Harvard University, November, 1988: No. 4

Kelling, George L. Robert Wasserman and Hubert Williams, "Police Accountability," *Perspectives on Policing*, Washington, D.C., National Institute of Justice, United States Department of Justice and the Program in Criminal Justice Policy and Management, John F. Kennedy School of Government, Cambridge, Mass: Harvard University, November, 1988, No. 7

Kenney, Jay and Robert P. McNamara, <u>Police and Policing: Contemporary Issues,</u> Westport, CT: Prager Publishers, 1999

Kerlikowske, Gill, "Invest in Kids Now, Prevent Crime Later," <u>Subject to Debate</u>, A newsletter of the Police Executive Research Forum, Volume 10, No. 10, October 1996,

Kessler, David A., "The Effects of Community Policing on Complaints Against Officers," <u>Justice Research and Statistics Association</u>, Washington, D. C., unpublished and no date

Kibbe, Pauline R., <u>Latin Americans in Texas</u>, Albuquerque, New Mexico: University of New Mexico Press, 2000

Kluchesky, Joseph T., <u>Police Action on Minority Problems</u>, New York: Freedom House, 1946

Laqueur, Walter,<u> A History of Terrorism</u>, New Brunswick: Transaction Publishers, 2001

Laqueur, Walter, "Terrorism: a Brief History," http://www.laqueur.net/index2.php?r=28id=71

Lewis, Dan A., (Ed), "Reactions to Crime," <u>Sage Criminal Justice System Annuals</u>, Vol. 16, Beverly Hills, CA: Sage Publications, 1981

Lee, Eric, <u>Community Courts: An Evolving Model</u>, United States Department of Justice, Office of Justice Programs, Bureau of Justice Assistance, Washington, D.C., October, 2000

Lehman, Jeffery, Sherelle Phelps and Thompson Gale (EDS) 2005, "Deadly Force," <u>West's Encyclopedia of Law.</u> 2nd Ed. ENotes.com.2006. 7 Jan, 2006 http://Law.enotes.com/wests-law-encyopedia/deadly-force

Lewis, Dan A, (ED), "Reactions to Crime," <u>Criminal Justice System Annuals</u>, Vol. 16, Beverly Hills, Calif.: Sage Publications, 1981

Lewis, Dan A., Wesley G. Skogan, Aaron Podolefsky, Fredric DuBow and Margaret T. Gordon, <u>The Reactions to Crime Project</u>, Washington D.C.: U.S. Department of Justice, National Institute of Justice, May 1982

Lohman, Joseph D. <u>The Police and Minority Groups</u>, Chicago: Chicago Park District Police, 1947

London, Scott, <u>Understanding Change: The Dynamics of Social Transformation,</u> http://www.scottlondon.com/reports/change.html

Los Angeles Police Department, <u>The Los Angeles Police Department's Basic Car Plan</u>, unpublished, April 1, 1972

Manning, Peter K., <u>Police Work: The Social Organization of Policing</u>, Prospect Heights, Ill.: Waveland Press, 1997

Marighella, Carlos, <u>Minimanual of the Guerrilla</u>, June 1969, http://www.usma.edu/dmi/IWmsgs/LoweProfile=InsideOut.pdf

Martin, G. Arthur "Police Interrogation Privileges and Limitations Under Foreign Law." <u>Journal of Criminal Law, Criminology, and Police Science</u>, Vol. 53, No. 1 May, 1961

McEntire, Davis and Robert B. Powers, <u>Guide to Race Relations for Police Officers</u>, Sacramento, CA: Department of Justice, State of California, 1946

McKinnon, Jessie, 2003, <u>The Black Population in the United States: March 2002</u>, Washington, D.C.: U.S. Census Bureau, Current Population Reports, Series P20-541.

Melendy, H. Brett, <u>Asians in America: Filipino, Korean and East Asians</u>, Boston: Twayne Publishers, 1977

Milton, Catherine, <u>Women in Policing</u>, Washington D.C.: Police Foundation, 1972

Mintz, Ellen and Georgette Bennett Sandler, "Instituting a Full-Service Orientation to Policing," <u>The Police Chief</u>, Vol: 41, Issue: 6, June, 1974

Miron, H.J., et. al, <u>Managing Criminal Investigations, A Handbook</u>, U.S. Department of Justice, Law Enforcement Assistance Administration, Washington, D.C.: U.S. Government Printing Office, 1979

Montero, Darrell, "Vietnamese Refugees in America," International Migration Review, 13, winter 1979

Moore, Mark H., Robert C. Trojanowicz and George Kellings, "Crime and Policing," Perspectives on Policing, Washington D.C., U.S. Department of Justice, National Institute of Justice and the Program in Criminal Justice Policy and Management, John F. Kennedy School of Government, Cambridge: Mass, Harvard University, June 1988, No. 2.

Morris, Albert, "The American Society of Criminology: A History: 1941-1974," Criminology, August 1975

Murphy, Patrick and Thomas Plate, Police Commissioner, New York: Simon & Schuster, 1977

Murray, Charles A. and Robert Krug, The National Evaluation of the Pilot Cities Program: Executive Summary, United States Department of Justice, Washington, D.C.: United States Government Printing Office, 1975

Myrdal, Gunnar, American Dilemma: The Negro Problem and Modern Democracy, New York: Harper and Brothers Publishers, 1944

Naisbitt, John, Megatrends, New York: Warner Books, 1982

National Advisory Commission on Civil Disorders, Report of the National Advisory Commission on Civil Disorders, Washington, D.C.: U.S. Government Printing Office, 1968

National Advisory Commission on Criminal Justice Standards and Goals, Police, Washington D.C: U.S. Government Printing Office, 1973

National Association for the Advancement of Colored People, Thirty Years of Lynching in the United States, New York: Arno Press, 1969

National Commission on Law Observance and Enforcement, Washington D.C.: U.S. Government Printing Office, 1931

National Conference of the National Association of Human Rights Workers, Nashville, Tennessee, United States Department Justice, Community Relations Services, Washington D.C.: U. S. Government Printing Office, October 1978

NIJ Quick Response Evaluability of Oasis Projects Final Report, Prepared for the National Institute of Justice, U.S Department of Justice, Washington D.C., by Research Management Associates, Inc., Alexandria VA, August 1986

Nicola Machiavelli, The Prince, Italy: Antonio Blado d' Asola, 1532

Naisbitt, John, Megatrends, New York: Warner Books, 1982,

National Institute on Drug Abuse and National Institute on Alcohol

Abuse and Alcoholism, the Economic Costs of Alcohol and Drug Abuse in the United States 1992, Rockville, Md.: U.S. Department of Health and Human Services, 1998

National Minority Advisory Council on Criminal Justice, The Inequality of Justice: A Report on Crime and the Administration of Justice in the Minority Community, Washington D.C: Law Enforcement Assistance Administration, U.S. Department of Justice, 1982,

National Opinion Research Center, A National Sample Survey Approach to the Study of the Victims of Crime and Attitudes Towards Law Enforcement And Justice, Chicago, Unpublished, 1966,

New Haven Department of Police Services, Directed Deterrent Patrol, New Haven, Conn., 1976

New Westminster Police Service, Sir Robert Peel's Nine Principles of Policing, http: www.newwestpolice.org/peel.html February 1. 2009

Osofsky, Gilbert, (ED) Puttin' on Ole Massa: The Slave Narratives of Henry Bib, William Wells Brown and Solomon Northup, New York: Harper Torch Books, 1969

Oettmeir, T. N. and W. H. Beck, "Developing a Policing Style for Neighborhood Oriented Policing: Executive Session No.1," Houston Police Department, unpublished, 1987

O'Keefe, James and Timothy N. Oettmeir, Neighborhood Oriented Policing – Role Expectations, Concept Paper No. 2, Houston Police Department, 1988, unpublished

Parker, Alfred E., <u>Crime Fighter: August Vollmer</u>, New York: McMillan, 1961

Parker, William, <u>Parker on Police</u>, Springfield, Ill: Charles C. Thomas, 1957

Pate, Anthony M. and Lorie A., Fridwell, <u>Police Use of Force: Official Reports, Citizen Complaints and Legal Consequences</u>, Washington DC: Police Foundation, 1993

Pate, Antony M., Mary Ann Wycoff, Wesley G. Skogan and Lawrence W. Sherman, <u>Reducing Fear in Houston and Newark</u>, Washington D.C.: Police Foundation, 1986

Pate, Tony, Robert A. Bowers, Ron Parks, <u>Three Approaches to Criminal Apprehension in Kansas City: An Evaluation Report</u>, Washington D.C.: Police Foundation, 1978

Patmeotto, Micheal J., <u>Criminal Investigations</u>, 3rd Edition, Lanham, Md.: University Press of America, Inc., 2004

Peak, Kenneth J., <u>Policing America: Methods, Issues, Challenges</u>, Upper Saddle River, New Jersey: Prentice Hall, 1997

Peters, Thomas J. and Robert H. Waterman, Jr., <u>In Search of Excellence: Lessons From America's Best-Run Companies,</u> New York and London: Harper and Row Publishers, Inc., 1982

Peters, Tom "Structure is not Organization," <u>Business Horizons</u>, June, 1980

Peters, Thomas J. and Robert H. Waterman, Jr., <u>In Search of Excellence: Lessons from America's Best-Run Companies</u>, New York: Warner Books, 1982

Petersilia, Joan, <u>Community Corrections: Probation, Parole and Intermediate Sanctions</u>, New York: Oxford University Press, 1998

Pierce, G. S. Spaar and L. Briggs, <u>The Character of Police Work: Implications for Delivery of Police Services</u>, Final Report to the Department of Justice, Washington D.C.: National Institute of Justice, 1988

Pollard, Niklas, "U.N. Report Puts World's Illicit Drug Trade At Estimated $321B," The Boston Globe, June 30,

Powers, Richard G., Secrecy and Power: The Life of J. Edgar Hoover, New York: The Free Press, 1987

President's Commission on Law Enforcement and Administration of Justice, The Challenge of Crime in a Free Society, Washington D.C.: U.S. Government Printing Office, 1967

President's Commission on Law Enforcement and Administration of Justice, Task Force Report: The Police, Washington D.C: U.S. Government Printing Office, 1967

Pringle, Patrick, Henry and Sir John Fielding: The Thief-Catchers, London: Dobson Books Ltd., 1968

Punch, Maurice (Ed), Control in the Police Organizations, Cambridge, Mass: MIT Press, February, 1983

Putnam, Robert, Bowling Alone, The Collapse and Revival of American Community, New York: Simon and Schuster, 2000

Putnam, Robert D., "The Prosperous Community: Social Capitol and Social Life," The American Prospect, No. 13 (spring) 1993

Quinn, Thomas, "Beyond Community Policing: Community Justice," The Police Chief, Vol. 64, Issue: 10, October 1997

Radelet, Louis A. The Police and the Community, New York: McMillan Company, 1973

Ramirez, Robert R. and G. Patricia de la Cruz, The Hispanic Population in the United States: March 2002, Current Population Reports, P250-545, Washington, D.C: U.S. Census Bureau,

Ray, Jeffery C., Crime Prevention Through Environmental Design, Beverly Hills, CA: Sage Publications, 1991

Rees, Dennis M., "Post September 11: Policing in Suburban America," The Police Chief, Vol: 73, Issue 2, February, 2006

Reaves, Brian, <u>Federal Law Enforcement Officers, 2004</u>, Bureau of Justice Statistics, U.S. Department Justice, Office of Justice Programs, July 2006

Reeves, Terrence and Claudette Bennett, 2003, <u>The Asian and Pacific Islander Population in the United States</u>: March 2002, Current Population Reports, P20-540, U.S. Census Bureau, Washington D.C.

Recklies, Dagmar, "The 7-S- Model" http://www.themanager.org/models/7SModel.htm

Reed, Ray "25,000 go to Alabama's Capitol: Wallace Rebuffs Petitioners: White Rights Worker is Slain, <u>New York Times</u>, March 26, 1965

Regents of the University of California, August, Vollmer, Bancroft Library, Berkeley, CA, 2 Vols. http://www.ci.berkeley.ca.us/police/History/history.html (10.05.11)

Reiss, Albert J., Jr., <u>The Police and the Public</u>, New Haven, Conn: Yale University Press, 1971

<u>Report of the National Advisory Commission on Civil Disorder</u>, Washington D.C.: U.S. Government Printing Office, 1968

Rivera, Cesar Iglesias, <u>Memoirs of Bernardo Vega; A Contribution to the History of the Puerto Rican Community in New York City</u>, New York: Monthly Press, 1984

Rodriguez, Clara E., <u>Puerto Ricans: Immigrants and Migrants, A Historical Perspective, American All, A National Education Program, no date,</u> http://www.americansall.comPDFs/02-americanc.all/9.9pdf

Rubin, Joel, "U.S. Judge Ends Federal Oversight of the LAPD", <u>Los Angeles Times</u>, July 18, 2009

Sabol, William L., Heather C. West and Matthew Cooper, <u>Prisoners in 2008,</u> Bureau of Justice Statistics, Washington DC: Department of Justice, December, 2009

Sampson, Robert J., Stephen W. Raudenbush and Felton Earls,

"Neighborhood and Violent Crime: A Multilevel Study of Collective Efficiency," Science, Vol. 277, August 1897

Schlesinger, Arthur M. Sr., The Rise of the City, 1878-1898, A History of American Life in 12 Volumes, Vol. X, Arthur M. Schlesinger, Jr. and Dixon Ryon Fox, (EDS), New York: The McMillan Company, 1934

Sessions, Peter L., The Hispanic Experience of Criminal Justice, Hispanic Research Center, New York: Fordham University, 1979

Sherman, Lawrence W., "Execution Without Trial: Police Homicide and the Constitution," Vanderbilt Law Review, Volume 33, Number 1, 1980

Sherman, Lawrence W., Catherine H. Milton and Thomas V. Kelly, Team Policing: Seven Case Studies, Washington D.C.: Police Foundation, August 1973

Sherman, Lawrence W. and Richard A. Berk, The Minneapolis Domestic Violence Experience, Washington, D. C.: Police Foundation, April, 1984

Sherman, Lawrence W. and The National Advisory Commission on Higher Education for Police Officers, The Quality of Police Education, Washington D.C.: Jossey-Bass, 1978

Silver, Isidore, The Challenge of Crime in a Free Society, New York: Avon Publishers, 1968

Sitton, Claude, "Rioting Negroes Routed by Police in Birmingham, New York Times, May 8, 1963

Skogan, Wesley G., Disorder and Decline: Crime and Spiral Decay in American Neighborhoods, Berkeley, CA: University of California Press, 1991.

Skoler, Daniel, (ED) Organizing the Non-System, Lexington, MA: Lexington Books, 1977

Skogan, Wesley G. "Community Organizations and Crime," Crime and Justice: A Review of Research: An Annual Review, Vol. 10, (1988),

Smith, Bruce, Police Systems in the United States, New York: Harper Brothers Publishers, 1949

"Special Report: The Impact of the Los Angeles Riots on the Korean American Community," Asia Today, April 12, 2009

Spelman, William and John E, Eck, Research In Brief: Problem-Oriented Policing, Washington D.C.: Police Executive Research Forum, 1987

SRI Gallup, New York City Police Department: Community-Oriented Police Officers, Lincoln, Nebraska: Gallup Organization, September 1992

Steinzor, Ruth, "Democracy Dies Behind Closed Doors: The Homeland Security Act and Corporate Accountability," Center for Progressive Regulation, Washington, D.C., March 12, 2003

St. Louis Metropolitan Police Department, History of Police-Community Relations, unpublished, undated

Stone, Christopher, Todd Foglesong and Christine M. Cole, "Policing Los Angeles Under a Consent Decree: The Dynamics of Change at the LAPD," Program in Criminal Justice Policy and Management, John F. Kennedy School of Government, Cambridge, Mass.: Harvard University, May 2009

Svindoff, Michele, Calls for Service: Recent Research on Measuring and Managing Demand, New York, Vera Institute of Justice, unpublished, October 14, 1982

Sykes, Richard E. And Edward E. Brent, Policing: A Social Behaviorist Perspective, New Brunswick, New Jersey: Rutgers University Press, 1983

Taft, Phillip B., Jr., Fighting Fear in Baltimore County COPE Project, Washington D.C.: Police Executive Research Forum, February, 1986

Takaki, Ronald, A History of Asian Americans: Strangers From a Different Shore, New York: Little Brown and Company, 1989

Tannerbaum, Robert and Warren H. Schmidt, "How to Choose a

Leadership Pattern," Harvard Business Review, Cambridge, Mass: Harvard Business Press Books, May-June, 1973

The 9/11 Commission Report: Final Report of the National Commission about Terrorist Attacks on the United States, Washington D.C.: U.S. Government Printing Office, July, 2004

Theoharis, Athan, From the Secret Files of J. Edgar Hoover, Chicago: Ivan R. Dee Publishers, 1992

Thernstrom, Stephan, Ann Orlov and Oscar Handlin, (EDS) The Harvard Encyclopedia of American Ethic Groups, Cambridge, Mass.: The Belknap Press of the Harvard University Press, 1980

Thielepape, Joyce, Positive Interaction Program: Community Involvement in Crime Prevention, Houston Police Department, unpublished brochure, no date

The 9/11 Commission Report, Final Report of the National Commission on Terrorist Attacks Upon the United States, Executive Summary, http://govinfo.library.unt.edu/911/report/911report Exc.pdf

The Commission to Investigate Alleged Police Corruption, The Knapp Commission Report on Police, New York: G. Braziller, 1973

Thompson, Joseph J., "Law Against the Aborigines of the Mississippi Valley, 6 ILL., L.Q. 204, (1924)

Chinn, Thomas, (ED), A History of Chinese in America, San Francisco CA: Chinese Historical Society of America, 1969

Tien, J.M, J.W. Simon and R.C. Larson, An Evaluation Report of an Alternative Approach to Police Patrol, The Wilmington Split Force Experiment, Cambridge, Mass.: Public Systems Evaluation, Inc., 1977

Trojanowiez, Robert C., An Evaluation of the Neighborhood Foot Patrol Program in Flint, Michigan, The National Neighborhood Foot Patrol Center, East Lansing, Michigan: Michigan State University, 1985

Trojanowicz, Robert, "Community Policing Curbs Police Brutality," Footprints: The Community Policing Newsletter, Volume III, Spring/

Summer, National Center for Community Policing, East Lansing, Michigan: Michigan State University, 1991

Tully, Edward J., "Terrorism: The impact on State and Local Law Enforcement," Major Cities Chief's Association Intelligence Commanders Conference Report, unpublished, June 2002

Tumin, Zachary, Community Based Policing: The Houston Experience, Case Study, Program in Criminal Justice Policy and Management, John F. Kennedy School of Government, Cambridge, Mass: Harvard University, unpublished, no date

Uelman, Gerald F., "Varieties of Public Policy: A Study of Policy Regarding the Use of Deadly Force in Los Angeles County," University of Loyola at Los Angeles, Law Review, Number 6, 1973

Federal Bureau of Investigation, Uniform Crime Report: Crime in the United States, 2009, U.S. Washington: U.S. Department of Justice, September, 2009

United States Commission on Civil Rights, Who is Guarding the Guardians? A Report on Police Practices, Washington D.C.: U.S. Government Printing Office, October 1981

United States Census Bureau, American Fact Finder, "United States – ACS Demographic and Housing Estimates: 2007" Washington D.C. factfinder2.census.gov.

United States Census Bureau, Census of State and Local Law Enforcement Agencies, 2004, Washington, D.C., U.S. Department of Justice, Office of Justice Programs, Bureau of Justice Statistics, June, 2007

United States Commission on Civil Rights, Mexican Americans and the Administration of Justice in the Southwest, Washington, D.C.: U.S. Government Printing Office, 1970

United States Civil Rights Commission on Civil Rights, The Tarnished Golden Door: Civil Rights in Immigration, Washington D.C., September 1990

United States Commission on Civil Rights, "Intimidation and Violence: Racial and Religious Bigotry in America," January. 1983

U.S. Department of Justice, "Attorney General's Task Force on Violent Crime," Final Report, Washington D.C., August 17, 1981

U.S. Department of Justice, Boundary Changes in Criminal Justice Organizations, Washington, D.C.: United States Department of Justice, National Institute of Justice, Office of Justice Programs, Vol. 2, 2000

U.S. Department of Justice, Bureau of Justice Statistics, Police Departments in Large Cities, 1990- 2000, Special Report NCJ 177775703, Washington D.C.: U.S. Department of Justice, May 1996

U.S. Department of Justice, Federal Bureau of investigation, Terrorism in the United States, Washington D.C., 1999,

U.S. Department Justice, Office of Justice Programs, Bureau of Justice Statistics, Law Enforcement Management and Administrative Statistics, Local Police Departments, 2007, December 2010

United States v. City of Los Angeles Board of Police Commissioners of the City of Los Angeles, and the Los Angeles Police Department, http://www.lapdonline.org/assets/pdf/final_consent_decree,pdf

United States v. State of New Jersey and Division of State Police of the New Jersey Department of Law and Public Safety, http://www.state.nj.us/oag/jointapp.htm

U.S. Department of State, Foreign Terrorist Organizations http://www.state.gov/s/ct/rls/other/des/123085.htm *(10.12.11)*

U.S. Department of State, State Sponsors of Terrorism, http://www.boogieonline.com/revolution/commerce/taxes/posse. Html

Volkow, Nora D., "Threat the Addict, Cut the Crime Rate," Washington Post, August 19, 2005

Vollmer, August, "Abstract of the 'Wickersham' Police Report," Journal of Criminal Law and Criminology, V. 22, Jan., 1932

Vollmer, August, The Criminal, Berkeley and New York: Foundation Press, 1949

Vollmer, August, The Police and Modern Society, Berkeley: University of California Press, 1936

Walker, Samuel, A Critical History of Police Reform, Lexington, Mass.: D.C. Heat and Company, 1977

Walker, Samuel and Charles M. Katz, Police in America: An Introduction, New York: McGraw-Hill, 2002

Walrod, Truman, The Role of Sheriff Past-Present-Future, Washington, D.C., National Sheriffs' Association, 1975

Wardlaw, Grant, Political Terrorism: Theory, Tactics, and Countermeasures, New York: Cambridge University Press, 1989

Ward, Benjamin, Community Patrol Officer Program: Problem Solving Guide, New York City Police Department, New York, 1988

Waskow, Arthur I., Community Control of the Police: Report of a conference co-sponsored by the Institute for Police Studies and the Center for the Study of Law and Society, Berkeley CA.: University of California, unpublished, no date

Wasserman, Robert, Michael Paul Gardner and Alana S. Cohen, Improving Police Community Relations, Washington D.C.: U.S. Department of Justice, National Institute of Law Enforcement and Criminal Justice, 1973

Watson, Nelson A. (ED), Police and the Changing Community: Selected Readings, Washington, DC: International Association of Chiefs of Police

Weber, Alan M., "Four Hours on the West side, Listening to the Rank and File," Cambridge, Mass.: Harvard Business Review, May/June, 1991

Webster's New Riverside University Dictionary, Boston, Mass: Houghton Mifflin, 1988

Wei, William, The Chinese American Experience: An Introduction http://immigrants.harpweek.com/ChineseAmericans/.1Introduction/BillweiIntro.htm

Weckler, J. E. and Theo E. Hall, The Police and Minority Groups, Chicago: International Association of Chiefs of Police, 1944

Williams, Hubert and Antony M. Pate, "Returning to First Principles: Reducing the Fear of Crime in Newark," Crime and Delinquency, Vol. 33, No. 1. January 1987

Wilson, James Q. and George L. Kelling, "Broken Windows," Atlantic Monthly, March 1982, VOL. 249, No. 3

Wilson, O. W., Police Administration, New York: McGraw Hill Company, 1963

Wilson, O. W. and V.A. Leonard, Police Organization and Management, New York: The Foundation Press, Inc., 1951

Whitehead, Don, The FBI Story: A Report to the People, New York: Random House, 1956

Williams. Herbert and Patrick V. Murphy, "The Evolving Strategy of Police, The Minority View," Perspectives on Policing, , Washington D.C., U.S. Department of Justice, National Institute of Justice and the Program in Criminal Justice Policy and Management, John F. Kennedy School of Government, Cambridge, Mass: Harvard University, January 1990, No. 13,

Wilson, O. W. and V.A. Leonard, Police Organization and Management, Brooklyn, New York: The Foundation Press, Inc., 1951

Wilson, O. W., Police Administration, New York: McGraw–Hill Company, 1963

Wilson, O. W., Police Planning, Springfield, Illinois: Charles. C Thomas, 1957

Wolf, Robert L. and John L. Worrall., Lessons from the Field: Ten

Community Prosecution Leadership Profiles, Alexandria VA: American Prosecutors Research Institute, November, 2004

Young, Robert W. Campo, Historical Backgrounds for Modern Indian Law and Order, Washington D.C, Bureau of Indian Affairs, Department of Interior, Division of Law Enforcement Services, 1969

Zhigham, John, Strangers in the Land: Patterns of American Nativism: 1860-1925, New York: Athenaeum, 1963

Zhou, Min and J.V. Gatewood (EDS), Contemporary Asian America: A Multidisciplinary Reader, New York: New York University Press, 2007

INDEX

A

Abdulmutallab, Omar Farouk, 488–89
Aberdeen, Scotland, team policing in, 131–33
Abu Nidal Organization, 458
Abu Sayyaf Group, 458
abuse. *See* complaints, against police; corruption; excessive force
access control, natural, 130
accountability
    in community policing, 162, 331–32
    community role in, 331–32, 342–46
    complaints and, 335–39
    corruption role, 52
    in criminal justice system, 522
    in deadly force incidents, 355–63
    of departments, 332
    individual, 332–35
    integrity and, 346–55
    management and, 306–7
    of media, 369–74
    need for, 512
    of officers, 374
    ombudsmen and, 339–42
    organizational change and, 267–68
    overview, 329–31, 374
    in police/government relationships, 364–67
    political factors, 330, 363–64
    in racial profiling elimination, 439

accreditation, of law enforcement agencies, 59
achiever life theme, 204
action plans, 272–78
activism, in policing, 207, 219
adaptiveness life theme, 208
adventure, as context for policing, 201–3
Advisory Commission on Civil Disorders, 28
advisory committees, for police/media relations, 370
African Americans
    advisory council role, 47
    deadly force and, 355
    demographics, 265–66
    historical background, 19–20, 411–16
    professional organizations, 57–58, 59, 359
    recruitment of, 200, 210–14
Al Shabaab, 458
Al-aqsa Martyrs Brigade, 458
alcohol abuse treatment programs, 499. *See also* drugs and drug use
Aldawsari, Khalid, 489
alert system, for terrorist activity, 486–87
ALF (Animal Liberation Front), 456
Al-Qaeda-linked organizations, 451, 463–64, 490
American Bar Association Standards Committee, 46

American Dilemma (Myrdal), 414
American Indians, 47
American Leadership Forum, 295–97
American Library Association, 482
analysis. *See also* statistics
  as leadership skill, 308
  in SARA, 140
anarchist groups, 454
Anderson, Stanley, 339–40
Anglo-Saxon era policing, 10–11
Animal Liberation Front (ALF), 456
Ansaar al-Islam, 458
appointed officials, in criminal justice system, 505–7
Al-aqsa Martyrs Brigade, 458
Area Law Enforcement Committees, 120–21
Army of Islam, 466
arrests
  in community policing, 152–53
  false, 98
  as measure of police success, 5, 236–37
  record of, as employment barrier, 121–22, 214
Aryan Nation, 456
Asbat al-Ansar, 459
Ashcroft, John D., 471–72
Asian Americans, 47, 211, 265–66, 423–33
assessment
  crime control role, 399
  departmental direction of, 268–69
  of departments, 177
  as leadership skill, 308, 310
  of racial profiling, 441
  in SARA, 140
AT&T, 274
Atlanta
  police shooting study, 360–61
  Public Safety Commissioner, author as, 304–5, 321
Attorney General's Task Force on Violent Crime, 386–87
attorneys, 90–91, 499, 507, 523–24
audio taping, of incidents, 54
Aum Shinrikyo, 459

Australia, crime rates in, 386
authority. *See* command and control structures; leadership
awareness, in decision-making, 293

B

Baltimore County, Problem Oriented Policing case study, 138–39
banishment, 18
Basic Car Radio Program, 140–41
basic police training, 221–22, 223
Basque Fatherland and Liberty, 459
Be Aware program, 128
beat boundaries, 70, 230, 248
beat profiling, 71–72, 400
Beatty, John, 498
Beck, W.H., 269
Bennett, Georgette, 67
Berkeley, community control model, 343
bias. *See* discrimination
bin Laden, Osama, 451, 489–90
Birmingham, March on, 437
"Black Codes," 413
Black Panther Party, 343
Blackmore, J.R., 119
Blacks. *See* African Americans
blighted neighborhoods, 251–52
Blocks Organizing Neighborhood Defense (BOND), 253
"blue code of silence," 436
BOND (Blocks Organizing Neighborhood Defense), 253
Border and Transportation Directorate, 484
Boston, history of policing in, 21
boundaries
  in change implementation, 276
  for patrol beats, 70, 230, 248
Bow Street Runners, 13–14
Boynton v. Virginia, 415
Bracero program, 418–19
Bradley, Tom, 53, 331
Britain. *See* Great Britain
"Broken Windows" (Kelling and Wilson), 72, 397
Brown, Edmund G., 116
Brown, Lee P.

on leadership, 301–8
profile of, 321–24
racial profiling experiences, 438
Brown v. Topeka Board of Education, 414–15
budgetary considerations, 65, 330, 505, 506, 507
burglary, 77, 127, 232–33
business community, 392, 468–69

C

California. *See also* Los Angeles Police Department; San Jose Police Department
  demographics, 427
  foreign miner tax, 425
  historical background, 417
  training standards, 217
calls-for-service
  management of, 7, 170
  nature of, 170
  proactive vs. reactive response, 158–59, 225–26, 308, 397
  in Problem-Oriented Policing, 137–40
  research regarding, 75–76
  time demands, 230
  in traditional policing, 150–51
Campos, Daniel, 119
Canada
  crime rates, 385–86
  investigation procedures in, 237
CAOs (Chief Administrative Officers), of cities, 365
career advancement, 236
Carmichael, Stockley, 344
Carter, Jimmy, 432
Chaiken, Jan M., 233–35
chain of command. *See* command and control structures
The Challenge of Crime in a Free Society, 113, 497
change
  in criminal justice system, need for, 515
  goals/objectives, 270–72, 274
  impediments to, 269–70, 271

leadership and, 289–90, 297, 298
mindset for, 277–78
1980s conditions for, 281–82
planning steps for, 272–78
understanding, 263–67
"Charlies," 11–12
Cheyenne tribe, law enforcement traditions, 18
Chicago
  demonstrations in, 4, 28, 43
  Project Safeway case study, 526–28
Chicago Police Department, 67, 317
Chief Administrative Officers (CAOs), of cities, 365
Chiefs of Police. *See* Police Chiefs
children and youth. *See also* schools
  criminal offenders, 390
  drug abuse prevention, 391
  programs/services for, 38, 122, 129, 206, 252–53
  social policy and, 45
Chinese Americans, 425–27
Christopher, Warren, 53
Christopher Commission, 53, 331
citizen involvement. *See* community participation
citizen recognition programs, 123
Citizen's Alert Program, 343–44
Citizens Assistance Office, 531
Citizens Oriented Police Emergency (COPE), 138–39
citizenship rights, 413, 420
city government, 364, 366–69, 533–34
The City in Crisis, 55–57
civil disorder
  commissions regarding, 28, 42–43
  contributing factors, 36
  riots, 4, 28, 43, 55–57, 430–31
Civil Enforcement Initiative, 400–402
civil process, 500
Civil Rights era, 35, 414–16
civilian authorities, 364
civilian deployments, 229
Civilian Review Boards, 28, 331, 337–38, 339
civility, 111
Clark, Jim, 437

class structures. *See* socio-economic factors
Clean Neighborhoods program, 529
Clinton, William, 322, 423
coaching role, of supervisors, 223, 226
co-active police response, 225–26
Coast Guard, 485
"Coddling the Criminal" (Nott), 86
code of silence, 436
codes of conduct, 22–23, 195–97
CointelPro, 316
collaboration, in decision-making, 293. *See also* community participation
college-level education
    leadership and, 290
    as requirement for police, 50, 198–99, 200–201
    training considerations, 219
command and control structures. *See also* decentralized authority; organizational structures
    accountability in, 52
    changes in, 179–80, 223–24
    governmental oversight, 65, 364
    in history of policing, 16
    leadership and, 283, 287–88
    participatory management, 134–36, 151–52
    pitfalls of, 166
    seven S concept, 183–87
    values and, 161, 162
command life theme, 207–8
Commission on Civil Rights, Mexican Americans and the Administration of Justice in the Southwest, 420
Commission on Wartime Relocation and Internment of Civilians, 428–29
Commission to Investigate Alleged Police Corruption, 50
communication. *See also* calls-for-service; media and media relations; public relations
    accountability role, 334–35
    in anti-terror efforts, 469–74
    Chief's role in, 305, 365–66
    in decision-making, 292
    with government agencies, 364–65
    in homeland security efforts, 475
    Houston case study, 530–32
    information sources, 476–77
    leadership and, 286, 302
    911 system, 27, 40
    in planning for change, 273–74
    police systems for, 27
    recruitment role, 216
    311 system, 532
    training for, 221
    of vision, 310
    in watch programs, 124
Communist Party of Philippines, 459
community
    accountability to, 331–32
    anti-terrorism role, 469–74
    drug abuse prevention role, 392
    dysfunction in, as factor in crime, 385
    engagement of. *see* community participation
    as focus of policing, 513
    police as part of, 357, 441
    policy and, 407
Community Based Corrections Programs, 524–28
community control, of police department, 342–43
community courts, 520–24
community government, 528–33
community justice, 514–16
Community Organizing Response Team (CORT), 249
community organizing, training for, 222
Community Oriented Policing Services (COPS), 404, 407
community participation. *See also* community policing
    author's experiences, 303–4
    case studies, 123–24
    changes in policing and, 267
    co-active responses, 225–26
    in deadly force policy development, 362, 363
    development of, 275, 523
    education for, 163
    in homeland security, 473–78

Houston case study programs, 248–53
interagency partnerships, 159–61
law enforcement role, 17, 110, 152, 153, 171, 381, 396
neighborhood safety development, 157–58
policy changes and, 273–74
power sharing and, 163
programs for, 127
vs. public relations, 165
in reducing fear of crime, 389
Community Patrol Officers Program, 142
community policing
arguments against, 169–71
benefits of, 168–69
compared to programs/concepts, 1–2, 163–65
crime control/prevention role, 126–30, 155–56, 389, 394–402
vs. criminal investigations, 24–25
departments using, in US, 176, 511–12
development of, 15, 107–10, 165–68, 512–14
evaluation of, 171–72, 254–55
goals/objectives, 18, 151–63, 178
historical background, 496
implementation of. *see* implementation
Kerner Commission on, 43
overview, 6–8, 144, 149–50, 533–34
vs. Police-Community Relations, 110–26, 180–81
problem-solving in, 156
program examples, 140–44
recommendations for, 55–56
terrorism and, 490–91
vs. traditional policing, 150–53
Community Policing Consortium, 60, 403–4
community prosecution, 516–20
community relations program, in St. Louis, 117–18. *See also* public relations
Community Relations Services (CRS), 117, 355–56
community representatives, 141

community support, for police, 172
Community Watch Program, 124
Community-Oriented Programs. *See* Police-Community Relations programs/units
compassion life theme, 206
complaints, against police
accountability role, 334
case studies, 339
procedures for, 124–25, 335–39
Rodney King case, 53, 55–57, 430–31
Comprehensive Crime Control bill, 380
compromise, 287
ComStat (Computer Statistics), 322, 398–401
concept life theme, 205
conduct, principles of, 22–23, 195–97
conferences, 58
confessions, 88–89
conflict, leadership and, 287
Confronting Crime (Elliot), 382, 394
Connor, Eugene, 415, 437
consensus, in decision-making, 292–93
consent decrees, 97–100
consistency, as leadership quality, 299, 311
constables, 11, 15, 20
constitutional rights. *See* democratic principles; rights
Continuity Irish Republican Army, 459
Continuous Management Improvement program, 532
convictions, as performance evaluation tool, 236–37
coordination, in implementation, 179
COPE (Citizens Oriented Police Emergency), 138–39
COPS (Community Oriented Policing Services), 404, 407
Corey, Stephen, 346
corporate crime, 406
corrections, 497–98, 499, 509, 524–28. *See also* criminal justice system
corruption. *See also* excessive force
case studies, 317–18
community policing and, 346
corporate, 406

historical background, 15, 22, 23
initiatives against, 50–53
reforms arising from, 319
tolerance of, 354
CORT (Community Organizing Response Team), 249
costs. *See also* budgetary considerations
of crime control, 380
of drug abuse, 390, 391
counter terrorism, 483–87
counter-intelligence programs, 316
courage life theme, 207
court system. *See also* criminal justice system; Supreme Court
community-based, 520–24
consent decrees, 97–100
municipal, 532
overview, 83–84, 100, 499
rights vs. law enforcement in, 84–87
court-appointed attorneys, 90–91
CPTED (Crime Prevention Through Environmental Design), 129–30
crack cocaine, crime and, 5
Crackdown program, 393
creativity, 268, 273, 285–87, 296–97, 309–10
credibility, in values statements, 192
crime
causes of, 245–47, 382–88, 395
drug trade and, 4–5
fear of, 154–55, 172, 249–51, 254, 388–90
federal policy and, 508–9
overview, 379–81, 407–8
as quality of life issue, 58
signs of, 72, 74–75, 249, 388–90, 397
crime analysis, 159, 222, 238. *See also* productivity measures
crime control. *See also* crime prevention
as evaluation criteria, 171–72, 254
federal government role, 402–7
vs. law enforcement, 380–81
model for, 26–27
police role in, 394–402, 513
crime mapping, 322, 475
crime prevention. *See also* crime control
commission reports on, 37, 38, 163

community policing and, 155–56
defined, 126–27
in history of policing, 16, 22–23
patrols in, 68–69
vs. preventing crime, 129
programs for, 4, 6, 126–30, 142
Crime Prevention Through Environmental Design (CPTED), 129–30
crime rates, 35–36, 37, 84–85, 332–33
Crime Stoppers, 127
The Criminal Investigation Process (Chaiken, Greenwood, and Petersillia), 233–35
criminal investigations. *See* investigations
criminal justice system. *See also* corrections; court system
accountability of, 395
change needed, 515
commission reports on, 37–38, 45–46
in community policing model, 533–34
crime and, 384, 387, 394
educational programs, 49–50
flow chart of, 40, *41*
LEAA and, 65
minorities and, 47–48
Multnomah County case study, 498–508
overview, 497–98
vs. police effectiveness, 165
research needs, 40
critical thinking, 219
CRS (Community Relations Services), 117, 355–56
Cuba, 457
Cuban Americans, 422–23
culture. *See* organizational culture/style
Currie, Elliot, 382, 394
customer satisfaction, as goal of police, 513

D

Dalton, Patricia A., 483
DART (Directed Area Responsibility Team), 142–44, 248–49
data. *See* statistics

deadly force, 48, 95–96, 351, 355–63, 365
decentralized authority. *See also* command and control structures; organizational structures
    effects of, 467
    historical background, 21
    Houston case study, 247–48
    of management, 274
    seven S concept, 182–87
    as social trend, 265
    in Team Policing, 132
Decision Directive 39, 483
decision-making, 132, 286, 292–95, 309, 350, 352
Declaration of Independence, 347
dedication life theme, 204
Defense Against Weapons of Mass Destruction Act, 483
defense attorneys, 499, 507, 523–24
"defense of life" policy, 359
delegation, 300–301, 308–9
Democratic National Convention demonstrations, 4, 28, 43
democratic principles
    crime control role, 396–97
    deadly force and, 356–57
    leadership and, 299
    press freedom, 369
    vs. racial profiling, 438, 440
    South African Police and, 307–8
    terrorism and, 471–72
    in values statements, 190
demonstrations. *See* protests and demonstrations
Department of Homeland Security (DHS), 270–71, 482–87, 509
Department of Justice (DOJ)
    consent decrees, 97–100
    CRS, 117, 355–56
    deadly force policy, 360
    divisions of, 509
    OLEA, 113, 119
deployment, of officers, 227–31
detectives, 7, 15, 159, 231, 236–39. *See also* investigations

detention, unlawful, 89. *See also* corrections
development programs, for managers, 291
DeWitt, John L., 428
DHS. *See* Department of Homeland Security
Dickerson v. United States, 94
DiGeraldo, Benedict, 91–92
Direct Citizen Contact Program, 250–51
Directed Area Responsibility Team (DART), 142–44, 248–49
directed patrols, 69–70
disciplinary actions, 336–37, 344–46
discretion
    racial profiling and, 438, 439–40
    in use of deadly force, 355, 356, 358
discrimination. *See also* race relations; racial profiling
    against African Americans, 19–20, 35, 355, 411–16, 434
    against Asians, 424, 425–26, 428, 429, 430
    avoiding, 349
    commissions/advisory councils on, 47–48, 212
    community relations and, 28
    excessive force and, 54
    against Hispanics, 419–20, 421
    Kerner Commission on, 42–43
    in police hiring, 213–14
    police response/treatment disparities, 111–12
    policies regarding, 54–55
dispatching systems, 40
disposition, in complaint procedures, 336–37, 339
district attorneys, 517
diversity, 275, 300, 308
doctor/sickness analogy, 381
documentation. *See also* communication; statistics
    of deadly force incidents, 360–61
    in investigations, 234
DOJ. *See* Department of Justice
domestic terrorism, 455–57
Domestic Violence Experiment, 75

Dostoevski, Fyodor, 380–81
draft, military, 45
Dred Scott decision, 413
"driving while black," 434. *See also* racial profiling
drugs and drug use
    as factor in crime, 383–84, 390–93
    as recruitment issue, 216–17
    trafficking laws, 426
    treatment programs, 127–28, 390, 393, 406
D-runs, 69–70
due process, 351

E

Earls, Felton, 157–58
Early Warning Group, 469
Earth Liberation Front (ELF), 456
economic factors. *See* socio-economic factors
editorial boards, 370
education. *See also* training
    in change implementation, 276–77
    of city council members, 367–68
    commissions regarding, 48–50
    conferences, 58
    in criminal justice system, 317
    leadership and, 290
    low levels of, as factor in crime, 382–85, 406
    minorities and, 419–20
    police performance and, 39
Edwards, George, 112
"The Effects of Community Policing on Complaints against Officers" (Kessler), 345–46
e-Government, 532
Eisenhower, Dwight D., 309
elected officials, 58, 364–67, 504–5, 510. *See also* politics/political control
ELF (Earth Liberation Front), 456
emergencies. *See also* calls-for-service
    911 call program, 27, 40
    rapid response to, 152–53
Emergency Preparedness and Response Directorate, 484–85
Emmet, Daly, 116

employment opportunities
    arrest record and, 121–22, 214
    crime prevention role, 129, 383, 384–85
England. *See* Great Britain
entrepreneurial imagination. *See* creativity
environment
    in crime prevention, 129–30
    for work, 298–99. *see also* organizational culture/style
equality, ideals of, 349, 352–53, 439–40
equipment, purchase of, 65
Escobedo v. Illinois, 91–92
ethics. *See also* values
    in accountability, 346–55
    in leadership, 300, 311
    as life theme, 208–9
    in values statements, 192
ethnic bias, 54–55. *See also* discrimination
Europe, crime rates in, 385–86. *See also* Great Britain
eviction actions, 402
"The Evolving Strategy of Police" (Williams and Murphy), 412–13
exams, in recruitment, 213–14
excessive force, 53–57, 98, 351
exclusionary rule, 89–90
Executive Order 9066, 428
executive sessions, 82

F

false arrests, 98
family traditions/values
    constitutional rights and, 87, 91
    crime and, 5, 129, 383, 396
    drug abuse prevention role, 391
    police integrity and, 348
    policy and, 407, 426
FARC, 464
farm workers, 418–19
FBI. *See* Federal Bureau of Investigation
fear
    of crime, 154–55, 172, 249–51, 254, 388–90
    in terrorism, 471

Fear Reduction Project, 74–75
Federal Bureau of Investigation (FBI), 23–24, 315–16, 360, 455–56, 467
Federal Bureau of Prisons, 509
federal government
    crime control role, 402–7
    DHS, 270–71, 482–87, 509
    FBI, 23–24, 315–16, 360, 455–56, 467
    funding provided by, 407
    law enforcement oversight, 65
    policies of, 508–9
Feingold, Russell, 481
Field Interrogation Practices, 71
field training, 290–91, 351
Fielding, Henry, 12, 13
Fielding, John, 12–13, 14
Filipino Americans, 429–30
financial considerations, 330
fingerprint identification, 234, 314, 315
firearms, police use of, 48, 356–63. *See also* gun violence
"fleeing felon" standard, 359
fleeing vehicles, 362–63
flexibility
    in decision-making, 293–94
    as leadership quality, 298
    vs. specialization, 180, 181
    values and, 188
Flint, foot patrol experiment in, 77
follow up, crime control role, 399
foot patrols, 2, 72–73, 77
Ford, Gerald, 429
Foreign Terrorist Organizations (FTOs), listed, 457–66
forfeiture actions, 401–2
Freedom Riders, 415
FTOs (Foreign Terrorist Organizations), listed, 457–66
funding sources, 65

G

Gama'a al Islamiyya, 459
gang activities, 432
Garner, Edward, 96
gender bias, 54–55, 73
generalization, vs. specialization, 132
geographical locations. *See* neighborhoods
ghetto communities, 212
Gideon v. Wainwright, 90–91, 92
gifts, 349–50, 353–54
Goldstein, Herman, 76, 137, 138, 231–32, 320, 439–40
goodwill life theme, 206
governmental agencies. *See also* federal government
    access to, 530–32
    city government, 364, 366–69, 533–34
    community-based, 528–33
    crime control role, 394, 402–7
    integration of, 514
    support for police, 172
"grass-eater" officers, 50
gratuities, 349–50, 351, 353–54
Great Britain
    Aberdeen, team policing in, 533–34
    common law in, 356
    history of policing in, 2–3, 10–18
    Intelligence Lead Policing in, 144
    Judge's Rules, 86–87
green cards, 419
Greenwood, Peter, 73, 233–35
"Guide to Race Relations for Peace Officers" (Emmet), 116
"A Guide to Race Relations for Police Officers" (McEntire and Powers), 115–16
gun violence, 4–5, 46, 385–86

H

habeas corpus, writ of, 102
Hall, Theo E., 115
Hamas, 459–60
handbills, 12–13
handguns. *See* firearms, police use of; gun violence
Harakat ul Mujahadin, 460
Harakat ul-Ji-Island/Bangladesh, 460
Harakat-ul Jihad Islami, 465
Harrison, Burr P., 85
Harvard Executive Session, 78
Hassan, Nidal, 488
health care, 403, 405–6, 430

Herman Goldstein Award, 320
hierarchical structures, 183. *See also*
  command and control structures
Hispanic Americans, 47, 48, 210–11,
  265–66, 355, 416–23
Hizballah, 460
home confinement programs, 527
homeland security, 451, 470, 479–87,
  514. *See also* Department of Homeland
  Security
Homeland Security Advisory System
  (HSAS), 486–87
Hoover, J. Edgar, 23–24, 315–16
horse patrols, 14
The House of the Dead (Dostoevski),
  380–81
housing, as factor in crime, 403, 405
Houston
  author as mayor of, 322
  Crackdown program, 393
  Fear Reduction Project, 74–75,
    388–89
  Neighborhood Oriented Government,
    528–33
Houston Police Department
  author's experiences, 305, 321
  beat profiling, 400
  community policing programs, 7–8,
    127–28, 245–53
  DART, 142–44, 248–49
  Fear Reduction Project, 249–51
  performance evaluations, 240–43
  terrorism prevention case study,
    477–78
  training model, 216
  values statements, 188–93
Houstonians on Watch, 128
"How to Choose a Leadership Pattern"
  (Tannenbaum and Schmidt), 294
HSAS (Homeland Security Advisory
  System), 486–87
"hue and cry," 12–13
human rights, 195, 440, 473. *See also*
  democratic principles
Hussein, Saddam, 451
hybrid systems, for handling complaints,
  339

I

IACP. *See* International Association of
  Chiefs of Police
ideological mercenaries, 455
illicit drugs. *See* drugs and drug use
immigrant affairs program, 532
immigration
  homeland security and, 481, 485–86
  race relations and, 418, 421, 422–23,
    426–27, 429, 431
Immigration and Customs Enforcement,
  509
impartiality, 17
implementation
  evaluation of, 254–55
  Houston case study, 245–53
  investigations, 231–39
  overview, 176–80, 255
  performance evaluations, 239–44
  programs vs. process, 180–81
  resource deployment, 227–31
  reward/incentive programs, 244–45
  role changes, 225–27
  sample task list, 539–43
  seven S concept, 181–87
  staffing/recruitment, 198–217
  training, 217–25
  values, 187–97
*Implementing Neighborhood Oriented
  Policing in the Houston Police
  Department* (Oettmeir and Beck), 269
In Search of Excellence (Peters and
  Waterman), 224
incident response, 137, 153
indentured servitude, 412
India, crime rates in, 385
Indian Americans, 432–33
Indian Mujahideen, 466
individual accountability, 332–35
Industrial Revolution, 12
inebriate detoxification program, 499
Information Analysis and Infrastructure
  Protection Directorate, 485
information society, 264
information systems. *See* technology
infrastructure, 468, 474
initiative, as leadership quality, 302–3

inmates, programs for, 38
innovation, 227, 268, 273, 277–78, 309–10
Institute of Defense Analysis, 232
Institutionalization Phase, 168
intake, in complaint procedures, 335–37, 338–39
integrity, 192, 208, 311, 346–55, 439
intelligence activities, 467, 471, 476–77, 478–79
Intelligence-Led Policing, 144
interagency partnerships, 159–61, 276–77, 469–73, 498–508, 514
internal affairs units, 125, 303–4, 317–18, 335–37, 345
International Association of Chiefs of Police (IACP), 57, 59, 112–15, 228–29, 277
international terrorists organizations, listed, 457–66
internment camps, 428
interpersonal skills, 221
interrogation, 71, 88–89, 92, 93
investigations. *See also* detectives
   community policing and, 24–25, 152–53
   of complaints against police, 336, 338
   detective role in, 236–39
   historical background, 21, 231–36
   research studies, 73–74, 76–77
   solvability factors, 232–36
Iran, 457
Iraq, 451
Islamic Group, 459
Islamic Jihad Union, 460
Islamic Movement of Uzbekistan, 460
Islamic Resistance Movement, 459–60

J

Jackson, Maynard, 307, 360–61
Jacobins, 452
jails. *See* corrections; criminal justice system
Jaish-e-Mohammed, 460–61
Japan, 2, 385
Japanese Americans, 427–29
Jaworski, Joseph, 295–97

Jemaah Islamiya, 461
John F. Kennedy School of Government, 7–8
Johnson, Lyndon, 26, 28, 43–44
Johnson, Samuel, 86
Joint Terrorism Task Forces, 469–70, 478–79
Judge's Rules, 86–87
Jundallah, 466
justice, 523
Justice Coordinating Council, 507
Justices of the Peace, 11, 20
Juvenile Justice System, 499–500. *See also* children and youth

K

Kahane Chai, 461
Kamisar, Yale, 86
Kansas City, research studies based in, 68, 69–70
Kata 'ib Hezbollah, 461
Kelley, Clarence, 68
Kelling, George, 36, 72, 397
Kennedy, John F., 202
Kennedy, Robert, 43
Kerner, Otto, 42
Kerner Commission, 42–43, 416
Kessler, David A., 345–46
King, Martin Luther, Jr., 43, 415
King, Rodney, 53, 55–57, 430–31
Kluchesky, Joseph T., 116
Knapp Commission, 50
knowledge, skills and abilities (KSA), 243
Koban System, 2
Kongra-Gel, 461
Korean Americans, 430–31
KSA (knowledge, skills and abilities), 243
Ku Klux Klan, 432
Kurdistan Workers Party, 461

L

Lamb, Robert, 358–59
land grants, 417–18
Landrieu, Mitchell J., 100
LAPD. *See* Los Angeles Police Department
LaRose, Colleen, 488

Lashkar I Jhangvi, 462
Lashkar-e-Tayyiba, 461–62
law enforcement
   vs. community policing, 169–71
   vs. crime control, 380–81
   criminal justice system and, 499
   local responsibility for, 470–73
   Native American traditions for, 18–19
   Peelian Principles of, 17–18
   vs. rights protection, 96–97
   terrorism and, 466–73
   values for, 195–96
Law Enforcement Assistance Administration (LEAA), 28, 46, 64–67, 73–74, 402
Law Enforcement Education Program (LEEP), 49
LEAA. *See* Law Enforcement Assistance Administration
leader-managers, 286, 301–2, 304–8
leadership. *See also* management
   author on, 301–8
   vs. authority, 283
   change and, 267–70
   characteristics of, 295–301
   context of, 282–84
   decision-making and, 292–95
   development of, 289–91
   integrity and, 354
   levels of, 282, 301–8
   life themes reflective of, 205, 207–8
   vs. management, 283, 284–89
   overview, 281–82, 308–11
   planning role, 270–78
   presidential, crime control role, 404–5
   profiles, 313–24
   role determination, 275–76
   in seven S concept, 185–86
   training for, 223–25
   vision and, 291–92
leader-supervisors, 303–4
LEEP (Law Enforcement Education Program), 49
left wing terrorists, 456–57
Legal Aid services, 507
legitimacy, of police, 152

lethal force. *See* deadly force
Lewis, Dan A., 72
Liberation Tigers of Tamil Eelam, 462
Libyan Islamic Fighting Group, 462
Lindley, Curtis, 86
Lindsay, John V., 50
Lives of the English Poets (Johnson), 86
local oversight, 65, 470–73. *See also* city government
Locator Patrol-Perpetrator Oriented Patrol (LOP-POP), 69–70
Lohman, Joseph, 114–15
London, history of policing in, 12–18
London, Scott, 272
LOP-POP (Locator Patrol-Perpetrator Oriented Patrol), 69–70
Los Angeles
   Community Alert Patrols, 344
   riots in, 430–31
Los Angeles Police Department (LAPD)
   Basic Car Radio Program, 140–41
   Commission's reports regarding, 53–57
   consent decree, 97–99
   Parker at, 318–19
Los Macheteros, 456–57
loyalty, corruption and, 51

M

Machiavelli, Nicola, 263
Magnuson Act, 427
Mallory, Andrew, 87–88
management. *See also* leadership
   accountability and, 306–7, 345
   of calls-for-service, 170
   change and, 72, 226–27, 268
   in decentralized authority, 274
   implementation support, 179
   vs. leadership, 283, 284–89
   participatory styles in, 133–36, 151–52
   skills training, 223–25
   as supportive officers, 177
Managing Criminal Investigations (MCI), 74, 235
"man-eater" officers, 50
Mann Act, 23

manufacturing facilities, as emergency response focus, 468–69
Mapp v. Ohio, 89–90
March on Birmingham, 437
Marielitos, 423
marijuana use, as recruitment issue, 217
marketing, of police department, 372
Marxist revolutionary groups, 454
Matheson, Alexander John, 131–32
Mayne, Richard, 15
mayors, 364–67, 531
McConnach, James, 131
McCormack, John, 85
McEntire, Davis, 115–16
McGraw Crime Dog, 129
MCI (Managing Criminal Investigations), 74, 235
McKinsey 7- S Model, 182–87, *182*
measures, of police success. *See* productivity measures
media and media relations, 250, 365, 369–74, 406
medical examinations, 214
Megatrends (Naisbitt), 292
mentors, training for, 223
mercenaries, 455
Metropolitan Police Act of 1829 (London), 15, 16–17
Mexican Americans, 417–20
Mexico, relationship with United States, 417–20
Middle Ages, policing in, 11
migrant workers, 418–19
military draft, 45
military forces, in security details, 472
military structures. *See* paramilitary structures
Minneapolis, Domestic Violence Experiment, 75
minorities. *See also* racial profiling
  in history of policing, 20
  media of, 371
  police-community relations. *see* Police-Community Relations programs/units
  recruitment programs, 50, 199–200, 209–17

representation in law enforcement, 110–11, 210
minority nationalist groups, 454
Mintz, Ellen, 67
Miranda, Ernesto, 93
Miranda v. Arizona, 93–94
misconduct. *See* complaints, against police
mission statements, 193, 215, 295, 333. *See also* vision
Mohammad, Khalid Sheikh, 451
Mollen Commission, 52
morals, 311. *See also* ethics
Moroccan Islamic Combatant Group, 462
motivational systems, 244–45
Mujahedin-e Khalq Organization, 462
multi-level lateral entry, 39
Multnomah County
  author's experiences, 133–36, 304, 502
  community prosecution case study, 519–20
  Department of Justice Services case study, 498–508
  firearms use policy, 359
Municipal Satellite Courts, 532
murder rates, 385–86, 403
Murphy, Patrick V., 51, 67, 319–20, 412–13, 498
Muslim community, 212
Myrdal, Gunnar, 414

N

NADAs (Neighborhood Assistant District Attorneys), 519–20
Naisbitt, John, 292
Napolitano, Janet, 486
narcotics officers, 159. *See also* drugs and drug use
Nassau County, ombudsman in, 340–41
National Advisory Commission on Civil Disorders, 42–43, 112, 200, 209, 212, 416
National Advisory Commission on Criminal Justice Standards and Goals, 45–46, 199–200, 209–10

National Advisory Commission on the Causes and Prevention of Violence, 43–45
National Center on Police and Community Relations, 113, 117
National Commission on Accreditation of Law Enforcement Agencies, 59
National Commission on Higher Education for Police, 48–50
National Commission on Law Observance and Enforcement, 22, 110–11
National Commission on Terrorist Attacks on the United States, 451
National Conference of Christians and Jews (NCCJ), 114, 116
National Crime Prevention Council (NCPC), 129
National Crime Prevention Institute, 126–27
National Criminal Justice Statistics Center, 40
National Institute of Criminal Justice and Law Enforcement, 235–36
National Institute of Justice (NIJ), research studies, 74–75, 78–79
National Institute on Police and Community Relations, 116
National Liberation Army, 462–63
National Minority Advisory Council on Crime and Criminal Justice, 46–48
National Organization of Black Law Enforcement Executives (NOBLE), 57–58, 59, 359
National Sheriffs Association, 57, 59
National Terrorist Advisory System (NTAS), 486–87
nationalist-independence movements, 452–53
Native American law enforcement traditions, 18–19
natural access control, 130
natural surveillance, 130
NCCJ (National Conference of Christians and Jews), 114, 116
NCPC (National Crime Prevention Council), 129

"Neighborhood and Violent Crime" (Sampson, Raudenbush and Felton), 157–58
Neighborhood Assistant District Attorneys (NADAs), 519–20
Neighborhood Defender Service, 523–24
Neighborhood Information Network, 250
Neighborhood Oriented Government, 322, 477–78, 528–33
Neighborhood Oriented Policing. *See* community policing
Neighborhood Storefronts strategy, 250–51
Neighborhood Team Policing, 133–36
neighborhood watch programs, 124, 128
neighborhoods
  beat boundaries in, 70, 230, 248
  blighted, 251–52
  community courts in, 521
  crime rate variability, 386
  district attorneys for, 517
  as focus of service delivery, 162
  influence on policing, 512
  investigation assignments in, 237–38
  media relations considerations, 371
  safety development, 157–58
  service demands in, 153
Neighborhoods to Standards program, 529
neo-fascist right wing organizations, 455
networking, 291, 309
New Haven, directed runs program, 69
New Jersey State Police, consent decree, 99–100
New Orleans Police Department, 100
New People's Army, 459
New York City
  Civilian Complaint Review Board, 339
  history of policing in, 21
  Midtown Community Court, 520–21
New York Police Department (NYPD)
  author's experiences, 306–7, 321–22
  Civil Enforcement Initiative, 400–402
  commissions regarding, 50–53

Community Patrol Officers Program, 142
community policing implementation, 269, 539–43
ComStat, 322, 398–401
excessive force issues, 56–57
Murphy in, 319
officer modeling research, 203–9
Patrol Initiative, 67
performance evaluations, 239–42
training model, 218
value statements, 195
Newark
Fear Reduction Project, 74–75, 388–89
Foot Patrol Experiment, 72–73
Newport News Police Department case study, 139
news media. *See* media and media relations
Nigerian Police Force, 323
night watchman concept, 11
NIJ (National Institute of Justice), research studies, 74–75, 78
911 emergency number program, 27, 40. *See also* calls-for-service; September 11 terrorist attacks
Nixon, Richard, on leadership, 309
NOBLE. *See* National Organization of Black Law Enforcement Executives
non-lethal alternatives, 363
Nott, Charles, 86
NTAS (National Terrorist Advisory System), 486–87
nuisance abatement, 401
NYPD. *See* New York Police Department

O

Oettmeir, T.N., 269
Office of Law Enforcement Assistance (OLEA), 113, 119
officer-leaders, 301–3
officers
accountability, 334, 374
author as, 301–3
changing roles of, 225–26
deployment of, 227–31

initiative of, 169, 277. *see also* decentralized authority
integrity of, 348
investigation role, 237, 239
as ombudsmen, 219
as public servants, 348–49
responsibilities of, 180
selection of. *see* recruitment programs
support systems for, 177–78
OLEA (Office of Law Enforcement Assistance), 113, 119
"The Ombudsman" (Anderson), 339–40
ombudsmen, 219, 339–42
Omnibus Crime Bill, 64–65
Operation Identification, 128
Operation Renaissance, 530
operational research. *See* research studies
oral interviews, 213–14
organizational culture/style. *See also* values
changes in, 179
deadly force policies, 355–63
development of, 167–68
integrity in, 349–51
leadership and, 298–99
in seven S concept, 185–86
values role, 161
organizational structures. *See also* command and control structures; decentralized authority
change and, 182–83, 267–70, 272–78
early precedents, 16
leadership contexts, 282–84
multi-level lateral entry, 39
Multnomah County case study, 134–36, *135*
overview, 3
paramilitary, 16, 151–52, 282–84
Oxford Place project demonstration site, 252

P

"paddy rollers," 20
padlock actions, 401
Palestine Islamic Jihad, 463
Palestine Liberation Front, 463

paramilitary structures, 16, 151–52, 282–84
Parker, William H., 26, 318–19
Parks, Rosa, 415
Parks to Standards program, 530
parole, 498, 525–26
Party of God (Hizballah), 460
pathological groups/individuals, 455
Patriot Act, 480–82. *See also* homeland security
patrol officers. *See* officers
patrols
    beats in, 70, 71–72, 230, 248, 400
    crime prevention role, 68–69, 318
    emergency response focus, 469
    foot patrols, 2, 72–73, 77
    historical background, 14, 20, 25
    horse patrols, 14
    one- vs. two-officer, 71
    permanent assignments, 71–72
    programs/experiments in, 67, 68–70, 72–73, 77, 142, 344
    random, 7, 68–69, 137, 158–59
    slave patrols, 20
Peace Corps, 202
Peace Officers Standards and Training (POST), 217
Pearson, Wayne, 517
Peel, Robert, 2–3, 14–18
Peelian Principles of Law Enforcement, 17–18
peer assessments, 237
penal systems, in England, 14. *See also* corrections
People's Express Airlines, 264
PERF. *See* Police Executive Research Forum
performance evaluations
    accountability role, 333
    case studies, 239–44
    in community policing, 168
    importance of, 219
    overview, 239, 243–44
    tools for, 236–37
perjury, 351
personnel assignments. *See* staffing
Personnel Concerns Program, 334

"Perspectives on the Police," 78
Peters, Thomas J., 224
Petersillia, Joan A., 233–35
PFLP-General Command, 463
Philippines, immigrants from, 429–30
Phoenix Police Department, recruitment materials, 201–2
physical evidence, processing of, 234
Pilot Cities Program, 66–67
PIP (Positive Interaction Program), 251
planning
    accountability role, 333
    for change, 270–78
    for homeland security, 474
    leadership role in, 270–78
    Multnomah County case study, 506–7
Plessy v. Ferguson, 414
police
    criminal justice system role, 511–12
    effectiveness of, 165, 387
    as first responders, 470
    homeland security role, 487
    occupational subcultures in, 436
    public image of, 4
    responsibilities of, 83–84
    support of, as evaluation criteria, 254–55
    visibility of, 159. *see also* patrols
"Police Action on Minority Problems" (Kluchesky), 116
Police Activities League, 252–53
Police Administration (Wilson), 3, 316
The Police and Minority Groups (Lohman), 114–15
The Police and Minority Groups (Weckler and Hall), 115
Police Athletic League, 124
Police Chiefs
    accountability, 332
    disciplinary role, 336–37
    political relationships, 22–23, 54
    professional organizations, 57
    responsibilities of, 197, 200, 305, 365–66
    selection of, 343
    term duration, 306, 330, 364

Police Commission, in Los Angeles, 54
Police Commissioners, 236
Police Community Relations Aide Program, 124
"Police Community Relations Policies and Practices," 112–13
Police Executive Research Forum (PERF)
  about, 57
  research studies, 59, 75–77, 233, 236, 434, 441
Police Foundation, 29–30, 48–50, 58–59, 65–66, 319
Police Planning (Wilson), 316
Police Policy Board, 319
Police Systems in the United States (Smith), 111
Police-Community Relations programs/units. *See also* community policing
  black community as focus of, 118
  vs. community policing, 163, 180–81
  demise of, 126
  development of, 2, 4, 6–8, 110–26
  examples of, 117–26
  vs. public relations, 39, 125
policing. *See also* community policing
  commissions regarding, 43
  evaluation criteria, 171–72. *see also* performance evaluations
  excellence in, 291
  future of, 512–14
  goals of, 513
  historical background, 2–3, 9–30, 110, 412–13
  marketing of, 372
  myths of, 7
  organizational structures, 16
  as profession. *see* professional policing
  programs vs. models of, 180–81
  reform era, 36, 38–40, 45
  research needs, 40
  vs. social work, 170–71
Policing in a Free Society (Goldstein), 320, 439–40
policy
  codes of conduct, 22–23, 195–97
  as factor in crime, 384

Multnomah County case study, 505, 506, 507
  social effects of, 407, 426
  values statements and, 192–93
Political Terrorism (Wardlaw), 453–54
politics/political control
  accountability and, 330, 363–64
  historical background, 16–17, 21–22, 25, 36, 315–16, 329–30
  integrity issues, 351–52
  Police Chiefs and, 22–23
  Wilson and, 317
Popular Front for the Liberation of Palestine, 463
Popular Puerto Rican Army, 456–57
Portland, 517. *See also* Multnomah County
Positive Interaction Program (PIP), 251
Posse Comitatus, 456
POST (Peace Officers Standards and Training), 217
"Post September 11" (Rees), 468
poverty, 47, 385, 405
power
  in leadership, 296
  of police, 329, 355
  sharing of, 163
Powers, Robert, 115–16
prejudice. *See* discrimination
presidential leadership, crime control role, 404–5
President's Commission on Law Enforcement and Administration of Justice
  on criminal justice system, 497
  on need for reform, 500
  overview, 26–28, 36–42
  on personnel, 198, 209
  on police-community relations, 113
  on prosecutors, 516–17
  solvability factors, 232
press freedom, 369
press kits, 372–73
preventative police patrols, 318
preventing crime, 129. *See also* crime prevention
The Prince (Machiavelli), 263

Principle Centered Leadership (Corey), 346
principles, statements of, 194
prisoners, 38, 384. *See also* corrections; probation
privacy issues, 482
private security organizations, 108, 478
proactive, vs. reactive police response, 158–59, 225–26, 308, 397
probation, 525–28
Problem-Oriented Policing, 7, 137–40, 320. *See also* SARA
problem-solving
    accountability and, 334
    community court role, 522–23
    in community policing, 170–71, 513
    in investigations, 238
    in leadership, 296–97
    for negative events follow-up, 307
    at neighborhood level, 528–29
    as organizational objective, 180
    training considerations, 219, 222
problem-solving policing, 76, 78, 125, 156, 160, 164
procedures, informal, 184–85
processes, vs. programs, 180–81
productivity measures, 22, 69–70, 171–72, 254–55, 293, 332–35
professional organizations, 57–59
professional policing. *See also* traditional policing
    commission reports on, 38–39, 43
    conduct in, 22–23, 346
    court decisions and, 87–97
    crime control model and, 29
    development of, 3–4, 24–30
    historical background, 12–14
    overview, 35–36, 61
    professional organizations, 57–59
Program Phase, 166–67
programs vs. processes, 180–81. *See also individual programs*
progressive discipline, 336–37
prohibition, 23
Project Oasis, 251–52
Project Safeway case study, 526–28
promotions, 236

prosecuting attorneys, 499
protests and demonstrations, 4, 26, 28, 43, 44. *See also* riots
psychological examinations, 214
public, contact with, 151. *See also* community participation
public defenders, 499, 507, 523–24
public health threat, violence as, 403
public housing, 403
public perceptions
    media role in, 369–74
    regarding police, 111, 254–55
    regarding safety, 72–73
Public Protector, 340–41
public relations
    accountability and, 334
    case studies, 122–24
    vs. community participation, 165
    vs. community relations programs, 39, 125
    in handling bad news, 307
    vs. marketing, 372
    recruitment and, 215
Public Safety Commissioner, author as, 304–5
public servants, officers as, 348–49
public speaking, training for, 221–22
Puerto Ricans, 420–22
Purdy, E. Wilson, 85

Q

al-Qaeda/al-Qaeda-linked organizations, 451, 463–64, 490
quality of life issues, 58, 249, 519–20, 522
quasi-military structures. *See* paramilitary structures

R

race relations. *See also* discrimination; racial profiling
    advisory council findings, 46–48
    African Americans, 411–16
    Asians, 423–33
    Hispanics, 416–23
    overview, 411, 442

racial profiling. *See also* discrimination; race relations
   effects of, 437
   minority view of, 436–38
   New Jersey consent decree, 99–100
   overview, 433–35
   police view of, 435–36
   September 11 attacks and, 425, 471–72
   solutions for, 438–41
"Racially Based Policing," 434–35
radios
   in patrol vehicles, 27
   in watch programs, 124
Rand Institute experiments/studies, 73–74, 232, 233–35
random patrols, 7, 68–69, 137, 151, 158–59
Rape Prevention program, 128
Raudenbush, Stephen W., 157–58
reactive, vs. proactive police response, 158–59, 225–26, 308, 397
Real IRA, 464
reciprocity, 157
Reconstruction, 413–14
recruitment programs. *See also* staffing
   case studies, 124
   in community policing, 168, 198–99
   context of, 201–3
   educational considerations, 50
   flaws in, 209–14
   follow up in, 216
   materials for, 215–16
   for minorities, 122, 209–17
   program administration, 215
   strategies for, 216
Red Hook Community Court, 522–23
Rees, Dennis, 468
referrals, 216
Refugee Act of 1980, 432
refugee affairs program, 532
Reiss, Albert, Jr., 67
relationship-building, 272–73, 309
religious institutions
   crime prevention/control role, 129, 396
   drug abuse prevention role, 392

recruitment considerations, 212
research studies. *See also individual commissions*
   Harvard Executive Session, 78–79
   LEAA, 64–67, 73–74
   on minority issues, need for, 48
   NIJ, 74–75, 78–79
   overview, 79
   PERF, 59, 75–77, 233, 236, 434, 441
   Police Foundation, 48–50, 67–73
   Rand Institute, 73–74, 232, 233–35
   resistance to findings, 67
   SRI Gallup, 203
   Stanford Research Institute, 232–33
respect, 440. *See also* integrity
response, in SARA, 140
retreat and conceal policies, 362
revitalization projects, 405
Revolutionary Armed Forces of Columbia (FARC), 464
Revolutionary Organization 17 November, 464–65
Revolutionary People's Liberation Party/Front, 465
Revolutionary Struggle, 465
reward programs
   for citizens, 12–13
   for police, 244–45
right wing terrorists, 455, 456
rights. *See also* democratic principles
   constitutional, 87, 91, 412, 413, 439–40
   human rights, 195, 440, 473
   protection of, 83–84, 93–94, 96–97
riots, 4, 28, 43, 55–57, 319, 430–31
risk-taking, 286, 296–97
River Police, in London, 13–14
robbery, 77, 127–28, 238
"Robin Redbreasts," 14
Rogovin, Charles, 66
Roosevelt, Franklin D., 428
Roosevelt, Theodore, 23
"rotten apple" theory, 51
Rowan, Charles, 15
Ruby Ridge FBI standoff, 360

S

Sampson, Robert J., 157–58
San Diego, research studies based in, 70–72
San Francisco, Citizen's Alert Program, 343–44
San Jose Police Department
  leadership case study, 301–3
  Police-Community Relations program, 119–26
SARA (scanning, analysis, response and assessment), 140, 320
Saxbe, William B., 402–7
scanning, in SARA, 140
Schmidt, Warren H., 294
schools. *See also* children and youth
  crime prevention/control role, 5, 129, 395–96
  educational programs in, 124, 391
  as emergency response focus, 468–69
Schools to Standards program, 530
Science and Technology Directorate, 485
Scotland, team policing in, 131–33
Scotland Yard, 15
screening
  of cases, 233, 235
  of personnel, 213, 236
search and seizure practices, 26, 87, 94–95, 98
Secret Service, 470–71, 485
security
  sense of, 155, 156. *see also* fear, of crime
  terrorism and, 470–72
security services, 108, 128
segregation, 352, 413–15
seizure, of property, 401–2. *See also* search and seizure practices
self-confidence, as leadership quality, 298
senior citizens, programs for, 128
September 11 terrorist attacks, 211–12, 266, 425, 450–51
sergeants, 303–4
service, as context for policing, 200–203
service demands, 153. *See also* calls-for-service
seven S concept, 182–87, *182*

Al Shabaab, 458
Shaffer, Paul, 85
Shahzad, Faisal, 489
shared values, in seven S concept, 186–87
sheriffs
  criminal justice system role, 510–11
  history of title, 10–11
  Multnomah County case study, 506–7, 508
  professional organizations, 57
Shining Path, 465
shootings. *See* deadly force; gun violence
shoplifting, 128
Sicarii, 452
signs of crime, 72, 74–75, 249, 388–90, 397
skills
  in KSA, 243
  in seven S concept, 186
  training for, 221–23
slavery, 20, 411–14
Sleepy Lagoon case, 419
Smith, Alfred E., 116
Smith, Bruce, 111
Smith, William H.T., 85
social capital, 157, 274–75
social contract, 396–97
social institutions, crime prevention role, 129. *See also* socio-economic factors
social science research. *See* research studies
social work, vs. policing, 170–71
socio-economic factors, 5, 47, 264–67, 382–88, 405
solvability factors, in investigations, 232–36, 237–38
South African Police, 307–8, 323
special events, security for, 470–71
specialization
  vs. flexibility, 180, 181
  vs. generalization, 132
  as recruitment pitfall, 201–2
spokesperson, Police Chief as, 305, 365–66
sports programs, 124, 252–53
SRI Gallup study, 203
St. Louis Police Department, community relations program, 117–18

staffing. *See also* recruitment programs
   in community policing, 197, 198
   deployment standards, 227–31
   life themes, 203–9
   Multnomah County case study, 504–9
   in seven S concept, 186
Stamp Out Crime Crusade, 123
Standards for Law Enforcement Agencies, 59–60
Stanford Research Institute study, 232–33
state law enforcement
   criminal justice system role, 509–10
   homeland security role, 487
state-sponsored terrorism, 457
statistics, 40, 398–401, 441, 514. *See also* productivity measures
Statute of Winchester, 11
Sticks Everything Under His Belt, 18
"street smart," 206
structure, in seven S concept, 183–84
Stuart era policing, 11–12
style, in seven S concept, 185–86. *See also* organizational culture/style
success, definitions of, 293
Sudan, 457
supervisors. *See also* management
   accountability, 334
   role of, 72, 226, 303–4
   skills training, 223
support systems
   for innovation, 270–71
   for officers, 177–78
Supreme Court
   on citizenship rights, 413
   landmark decisions, 87–97, 414–15
   overview, 83
   police practices, decisions affecting, 26, 357–58
surveillance
   natural, 130
   under Patriot Act, 481–82
Sweden, ombudsman office in, 339–40
Syria, 457
systems, in seven S concept, 184–85

T

Taft, William Howard, 23
Tamil Tigers, 462
Tannenbaum, Robert, 294
team life theme, 205
Team Policing, 6–7, 29, 130–36, 164–65
teamwork, in implementation, 179
technology. *See also* communication; media and media relations
   commission reports on, 39–40
   in decision-making, 293
   future of policing and, 514
   in homeland security efforts, 475–76
   police responsibility and, 27
   social change and, 264–67
Tehrik-e Taliban Pakistan, 465–66
television, 372, 406
Tennessee v. Garner, 95–96, 357–58
territorial reinforcement, 130
terrorism. *See also* homeland security
   attacks, listed, 487–89
   defined, 452–54, 455–56
   domestic, 455–57
   group types, listed, 454–55
   international, 457–66
   law enforcement and, 270–71, 466–73
   overview, 450–51, 455, 487–91
   state-sponsored, 457
Terry v. Ohio, 94–95
Texas, historical background, 417
theft prevention programs, 127
311 non-emergency phone access, 532
time demands
   of calls-for-service, 230
   in community policing, 170
torture, 196
traditional policing. *See also* professional policing
   change and, 263–67, 278
   vs. community policing, 150–53
   described, 137–40
   leadership change and, 290
   management in, 285
   principles of, 108
   random patrols in, 151
   training in, 217

training. *See also* education
  accountability role, 333
  for change, 225
  for community policing, 125, 168
  defined, 218–21
  for emergency response, 469
  in the field, 290–91, 351
  on firearms policies, 363
  for homeland security, 475
  for integrity, 350–51, 352
  for managers, 223–25, 290–91
  overview, 217–20
  professional organizations for, 60
  of recruits, 221–23
  standards for, 39
  for supervisors, 223
transforming leaders, 297
tribal law enforcement, 47
trust, 299–300, 335, 372. *See also* integrity
Tudor era policing, 11–12
tything groups, 10–11

U

"Understanding Change" (London), 272
unemployment, as factor in crime, 383, 384–85
Uniform Crime Reports, 172, 315, 395
United Nations, Code of Conduct, 195–97
United Self-Defense Forces of Columbia, 465
United States
  relationship with Mexico, 417–20
  social change in, 264–67
United States Commission on Civil Rights, 424
United States Conference of Mayors, 112–13
U.S Constitution, 87, 91, 412, 413
U.S Customs and Border Protection, 509
U.S Supreme Court. *See* Supreme Court
University of California, School of Criminology, 317
Urban Institute studies, 73–74
urban violence. *See* civil disorder

V

Vail, Theodore A., 274
values
  accountability role, 333
  case studies, 245–46
  in community policing, 151, 161, 167–68
  in deadly force policies, 363
  in decision-making, 293
  ethical guidance in, 347
  examples of, 189–97
  integrity and, 353
  for law enforcement, 195–96
  in leadership, 296
  overview, 187–89
  personal, 188
  purposes of, 188
  racial profiling and, 440
  in seven S concept, 186–87
  training for, 223
vehicles, firearms policies for, 362–63
Vera Institute, 523–24
Victim Re-contact Program, 249
victimization, 154, 172
victims assistance programs, 74
video taping, of incidents, 54
Vietnam War protests, 26
Vietnamese Americans, 431–32
vigilance life theme, 206–7
violence. *See also* civil disorder; excessive force
  against Blacks, 414
  drug use and, 390
  language of, 56
  prevention programs, 403
  research regarding, 43–45, 386–87
  social effects of, 44
  on television, 406
Virginia, history of policing in, 20
visibility
  as leadership quality, 299
  of police, 159
vision, 274, 291–92, 295–96, 310. *See also* mission statements; values
Vollmer, August, 3, 22, 24–25, 313–15
voting age, 45

W

wanted posters, 12–13
Wardlaw, Grant, 452–53
warning shots, 362
watch system, in Great Britain, 2–3, 11, 15
Waterman, Robert H., 224
Watts
  Community Alert Patrols, 344
  riots in, 319
WCOTC (World Church of the Creator), 456
Weaver, Randy, 360
web sites, for citizen information, 532
Weckler, J.E., 115
Weed and Seed program, 403
White Slave Act, 23
Wickersham, George, 22
Wickersham Commission Report, 22, 110–11
Williams, Herbert, 412–13
Wilmington, research studies based in, 70
Wilson, James Q., 72, 397
Wilson, Orlando Winfield, 3, 24–26, 316–18, 397
wireless data collection, 514
Wolf vs. Colorado, 90
women, in policing, 54–55, 73
work environment, 298–99. *See also* organizational culture/style
work/study programs, 38
World Church of the Creator (WCOTC), 456
writ of habeas corpus, 102
written examinations, 213, 236

Y

youth. *See* children and youth
The Youth in Arabic (Al Shabaab), 458

Z

Zazi, Najibullah, 488

CPSIA information can be obtained at www.ICGtesting.com
Printed in the USA
LVOW06*1922160915

454452LV00010B/117/P